THE ROUTLEDGE HANDB
PHILOSOPHY OF COLOUR

From David Hume's famous puzzle about "the missing shade of blue," to current research into the science of colour, the topic of colour is an incredibly fertile region of study and debate, cutting across philosophy of mind, epistemology, metaphysics, and aesthetics, as well as psychology. Debates about the nature of our experience of colour and the nature of colour itself are central to contemporary discussion and argument in philosophy of mind and psychology, and philosophy of perception.

This outstanding Handbook contains 29 specially commissioned contributions by leading philosophers and examines the most important aspects of philosophy of colour. It is organized into six parts:

- The Importance of Colour to Philosophy
- The Science and Spaces of Colour
- Colour Phenomena
- Colour Ontology
- Colour Experience and Epistemology
- Language, Categories, and Thought.

The Routledge Handbook of Philosophy of Colour is essential reading for students and researchers in philosophy of mind and psychology, epistemology, metaphysics, and aesthetics, as well as for those interested in conceptual issues in the psychology of colour.

Derek H. Brown is Senior Lecturer in the Department of Philosophy at the University of Glasgow, Scotland, where he is also Deputy Director of the Centre for the Study of Perceptual Experience. He is a co-editor of *Analysis and Interpretation in the Exact Sciences: Essays in Honour of William Demopoulos* (with Mélanie Frappier and Robert DiSalle, 2012).

Fiona Macpherson, FRSE, MAE, is Professor of Philosophy at the University of Glasgow, Scotland, where she is also Director of the Centre for the Study of Perceptual Experience. She has published numerous edited collections including *Sensory Substitution and Augmentation* (2018) and *Perceptual Imagination and Perceptual Memory* and *Phenomenal Presence* (2018, both with Fabian Dorsch).

Routledge Handbooks in Philosophy

Routledge Handbooks in Philosophy are state-of-the-art surveys of emerging, newly refreshed, and important fields in philosophy, providing accessible yet thorough assessments of key problems, themes, thinkers, and recent developments in research.

All chapters for each volume are specially commissioned, and written by leading scholars in the field. Carefully edited and organized, *Routledge Handbooks in Philosophy* provide indispensable reference tools for students and researchers seeking a comprehensive overview of new and exciting topics in philosophy. They are also valuable teaching resources as accompaniments to textbooks, anthologies, and research-orientated publications.

Also available:

The Routledge Handbook of Philosophy of Relativism
Edited by Martin Kusch

The Routledge Handbook of Metaphysical Grounding
Edited by Michael J. Raven

The Routledge Handbook of Philosophy of Colour
Edited by Derek H. Brown and Fiona Macpherson

The Routledge Handbook of Collective Responsibility
Edited by Saba Bazargan-Forward and Deborah Tollefsen

The Routledge Handbook of Phenomenology of Emotion
Edited by Thomas Szanto and Hilge Landweer

The Routledge Handbook of Hellenistic Philosophy
Edited by Kelly Arenson

The Routledge Handbook of Trust and Philosophy
Edited by Judith Simon

For more information about this series, please visit: www.routledge.com/Routledge-Handbooks-in-Philosophy/book-series/RHP

THE ROUTLEDGE HANDBOOK OF PHILOSOPHY OF COLOUR

Edited by Derek H. Brown and Fiona Macpherson

Routledge
Taylor & Francis Group

LONDON AND NEW YORK

First published 2021
by Routledge
4 Park Square, Milton Park, Abingdon, Oxon OX14 4RN
605 Third Avenue, New York, NY 10017

First issued in paperback 2023

Routledge is an imprint of the Taylor & Francis Group, an informa business

British Library Cataloguing-in-Publication Data
A catalogue record for this book is available from the British Library

Library of Congress Cataloging-in-Publication Data
Names: Brown, Derek H, editor. | Macpherson, Fiona, editor.
Title: The Routledge handbook of philosophy of colour / edited by Derek H Brown and Fiona Macpherson.
Description: Abingdon, Oxon ; New York, NY : Routledge, 2020. | Series: Routledge handbooks in philosophy | Includes bibliographical references and index. |
Identifiers: LCCN 2019044408 (print) | LCCN 2019044409 (ebook) |
ISBN 9780415743037 (hardback) | ISBN 9781351048521 (ebook)
Subjects: LCSH: Color (Philosophy)
Classification: LCC B105.C455 R68 2020 (print) | LCC B105.C455 (ebook) |
DDC 121/.35–dc23
LC record available at https://lccn.loc.gov/2019044408
LC ebook record available at https://lccn.loc.gov/2019044409

ISBN: 978–1–03–256970–3 (pbk)
ISBN: 978–0–415–74303–7 (hbk)
ISBN: 978–1–351–04852–1 (ebk)

DOI: 10.4324/9781351048521

Typeset in Bembo
by Wearset Ltd, Boldon, Tyne and Wear

Publisher's Note
The publisher has gone to great lengths to ensure the quality of this reprint but points out that some imperfections in the original copies may be apparent.

For David and Jasper Brown

CONTENTS

Contents

Contents

CONTRIBUTORS

Keith Allen is Senior Lecturer in the Department of Philosophy at the University of York. His research interests include colour, perception, and related issues in the history of philosophy. He is the author of *A Naive Realist Theory of Colour* (Oxford University Press, 2016).

Wylie Breckenridge is Lecturer in Philosophy at Charles Sturt University in Australia. He is author of *Visual Experience: A Semantic Approach* (Oxford University Press, 2018).

David Briggs is Lecturer at the National Art School (Sydney) where he teaches several colour-related courses in the Public Programs Department and has conducted an undergraduate elective on colour in the Art History and Theory Department. He is national Vice President and New South Wales Divisional Chair of the Colour Society of Australia and also serves on a committee of the Inter-Society Color Council (ISCC). His work explaining and illustrating colour science for painters appears primarily on his website *The Dimensions of* Colour (www.huevaluechroma.com/, 2007–present). A webinar given as the ISCC International Colour Day 2018 event, and two invited presentations for the ISCC Munsell Centennial Color Symposium in Boston in the same year, are available through the ISCC website (https://iscc.org/).

Robert Briscoe is Professor of Philosophy at Ohio University. Briscoe works primarily in the philosophy and cognitive science of perception with a focus on vision. He has written papers on a wide range of topics, including spatial representation, the relation between action and perception, cognitive penetration, multisensory perception, mental imagery, sensory substitution, depiction, and pictorial experience. Briscoe was a Fulbright-Scotland Visiting Professor at the University of Glasgow during the 2017–18 academic year.

Berit 'Brit' Brogaard is Professor of Philosophy at the University of Miami and Professor II at the University of Oslo. Her areas of research include philosophy of perception, philosophy of emotions, and philosophy of language. She is the author of *Transient Truths* (Oxford University Press, 2012), *On Romantic Love* (Oxford University Press, 2015), *The Superhuman Mind* (Penguin, 2015), and *Seeing & Saying* (Oxford University Press, 2018).

Derek H. Brown is Senior Lecturer in the Centre for the Study of Perceptual Experience and Department of Philosophy at the University of Glasgow. He works in philosophy of mind and perception, with particular interests in philosophy of colour, perceptual constancies, 'indirect' approaches to perception, imagination, projection in perception, and perceptual demonstratives. He is co-editor of *Analysis and Interpretation in the Exact Sciences: Essays in Honour of William Demopoulos* (with Mélanie Frappier and Robert DiSalle, Springer, 2012). He has held visiting appointments in philosophy at the University of Pittsburgh, the University of Glasgow, and the University of Cambridge.

Alex Byrne is Professor of Philosophy at the Massachusetts Institute of Technology, and Head of the Department of Linguistics and Philosophy. His main research interests are in philosophy of mind, metaphysics, and epistemology. He has written many papers on colour with David Hilbert (University of Illinois at Chicago), and is the author of *Transparency and Self-Knowledge* (Oxford University Press, 2018).

John Campbell is Willis S. and Marion Slusser Professor of Philosophy at the University of California, Berkeley. His main interests are in theory of meaning, metaphysics, and philosophy of psychology. He is currently working on the question whether consciousness, and in particular sensory awareness, plays any key role in our knowledge of our surroundings. He is also working more generally on causation in psychology. He is the author of *Past, Space and Self* (MIT Press, 1994) and *Reference and Consciousness* (Oxford University Press, 2002).

Mazviita Chirimuuta is Associate Professor of History and Philosophy of Science at the University of Pittsburgh. She received her PhD in visual neuroscience from the University of Cambridge in 2004, and held postdoctoral fellowships in philosophy at Monash University (2005–8) and Washington University St. Louis (2008–9). Her principal area of research is in the philosophy of neuroscience and perceptual psychology. Her book *Outside Color: Perceptual Science and the Puzzle of Color in Philosophy* was published by MIT Press in 2015. She is currently working on a new project on abstraction in neuroscience under the working title *How to Simplify the Brain*.

Jonathan Cohen is Professor of Philosophy and faculty member of the Interdisciplinary Cognitive Science Program at the University of California, San Diego. Before coming to UC San Diego, he was a Killam Postdoctoral Fellow in philosophy at the University of British Columbia. He earned his PhD in philosophy at Rutgers University. He has published extensively in philosophy of perception (particularly on colour and on informational interactions within and between perceptual modalities) and philosophy of language (especially on issues about context sensitivity and the semantics/pragmatics interface). He is the author of *The Red and the Real: An Essay on Color Ontology* (Oxford University Press, 2009) and co-editor of *Contemporary Debates in the Philosophy of Mind* (with Brian McLaughlin, Wiley-Blackwell, 2007) and *Color Ontology and Color Science* (with Mohan Matthen, MIT Press, 2010).

Don Dedrick is Associate Professor of Philosophy, cross appointed to Psychology, at the University of Guelph, Ontario, Canada. He is the author of *Naming the Rainbow: Colour Language, Colour Science and Culture* (Kluwer, 1998) as well as many articles and book chapters related to the topics of colour classification and colour ontology. He has particular interest in cross-cultural claims about colour, and in the relationship between culture and cognition, in general. He was an editor for the collections *The Anthropology of Colour* (with Robert E. MacLaury and Galina V. Paramei, John Benjamins Press, 2007) and *Computation, Cognition and Pylyshyn* (with Lana Trick, MIT Press, 2009).

Joshua Gert is the Leslie and Naomi Legum Professor of Philosophy at The College of William and Mary. His primary research interests are colour, philosophy of perception, and neo-pragmatism, as well as practical rationality and normative reasons. He is the author of *Brute Rationality: Normativity and Human Action* (Cambridge University Press, 2004) and *Normative Bedrock: Response-Dependence, Rationality and Reasons* (Oxford University Press, 2012), both of which develop a particular account of rational action and normative practical reasons. He is also the author of *Primitive Colors* (Oxford University Press 2017), which uses neo-pragmatist techniques to defend a common-sense version of colour primitivism.

Frederik Gierlinger is an external lecturer at the University of Vienna, the Freie Universität Berlin, and the University of Münster. His main area of research is Ludwig Wittgenstein. He has written on various topics in the philosophy of colour and published a number of texts on metaphysical and epistemological questions concerning necessity and possibility. He is currently developing ways to engage children at elementary school level in philosophical thinking.

David R. Hilbert is Professor of Philosophy and Chair of the Philosophy Department at the University of Illinois at Chicago. He primarily works on issues in philosophy of perception and philosophy of cognitive science. Many of his publications focus on issues concerning colour and colour vision. He also has an interest in history of early modern philosophy, especially Berkeley's economic and social thought.

Mark Eli Kalderon is Professor of Philosophy at University College London. He is a former editor of the *Proceedings of the Aristotelian Society* and former Assistant Editor for *Mind*. He has published in a variety of areas, but his current work focuses on philosophy of perception and its history. His books include *Moral Fictionalism* (Oxford University Press, 2005), *Form without Matter: Empedocles and Aristotle on Color Perception* (Oxford University Press, 2015), and *Sympathy in Perception* (Cambridge University Press, 2018), and he edited the anthology, *Fictionalism in Metaphysics* (Oxford University Press, 2005).

John Kulvicki is in the Philosophy Department at Dartmouth College. He works mainly on understanding non-linguistic representation, and its role in the arts and perception. He is the author of numerous articles and *On Images: Their Structure and Content* (Oxford University Press, 2006), *Images* (Routledge, New Problems of Philosophy Series, 2014), and the forthcoming *Modeling the Meanings of Pictures: Depiction and the Philosophy of Language* (Oxford University Press).

Fiona Macpherson is Professor of Philosophy at the University of Glasgow, where she is also Director of the Centre for the Study of Perceptual Experience. She is a Fellow of the Royal Society of Edinburgh and a Member of Academia Europaea. She sits on the Arts and Humanities Research Council and is a trustee of the Kennedy Memorial Trust. She is President of the British Philosophical Association. Her work concerns the nature of consciousness, perception, introspection, imagination, and the metaphysics of mind. She has written extensively on the nature of the senses, cognitive penetration, and illusion and hallucination. She has published numerous edited collections: *Disjunctivism* (with Adrian Haddock, Oxford University Press, 2008), *The Admissible Contents of Experience* (with Katherine Hawley, Wiley-Blackwell, 2011), *The Senses* (Oxford University Press, 2011), *Hallucination* (with Dimitris Platchias, MIT Press, 2013), *Sensory Substitution and Augmentation* (Oxford University Press, 2018), *Perceptual Imagination and Perceptual Memory* (with Fabian Dorsch, Oxford University Press, 2018), and *Phenomenal Presence* (with Fabian Dorsch, Oxford University Press, 2018).

Mohan Matthen is Professor of Philosophy and Canada Research Chair in Philosophy of Perception at the University of Toronto. He is Fellow of the Royal Society of Canada. He has worked on many topics in philosophy of perception, including the nature of colour, sound, and touch. He edited the *Oxford Handbook of the Philosophy of Perception* (Oxford University Press, 2015) and is the author of *Seeing, Doing, and Knowing: A Philosophical Theory of Sense Perception* (Oxford University Press, 2005). He is currently working on a monograph entitled *Sensing Space* and on a new account of the role of pleasure in the appreciation of art.

Barry Maund is Senior Research Fellow in Philosophy at the University of Western Australia. He is the author of two books: *Colours: Their Nature and Representation* (Cambridge University Press, 2009) and *Perception* (Acumen, 2013). As well, he is the author of the entry on colour in the *Stanford Encyclopaedia of Philosophy*, and of numerous papers in the Philosophy of Colour, Philosophy of Perception, and in History and Philosophy of Science.

Brian P. McLaughlin is Distinguished Professor of Philosophy and Cognitive Science at Rutgers University, and Director of the Rutgers Cognitive Science Center. He has published numerous papers in a wide range of fields, including philosophy of mind, philosophy of psychology, metaphysics, epistemology, and philosophical logic. He has a forthcoming book with Oxford University Press, co-authored with Vann McGee, entitled *Terrestrial Logic: Formal Semantics Brought Down to Earth*.

Adam Pautz is Professor of Philosophy at Brown University. His work concerns consciousness, intentionality, colour, and the mind-body problem. He has recently edited (with Daniel Stoljar) *Blockheads! Essays on New Block's Philosophy of Mind and Consciousness* (MIT Press, 2019). His book *Perception* is forthcoming with Routledge.

Duncan Pritchard is UC Distinguished Professor of Philosophy at the University of California, Irvine, and Professor of Philosophy at the University of Edinburgh. His monographs include *Epistemic Luck* (Oxford University Press, 2005), *The Nature and Value of Knowledge* (co-authored, Oxford University Press, 2010), *Epistemological Disjunctivism* (Oxford University Press, 2012), and *Epistemic Angst: Radical Skepticism and the Groundlessness of Our Believing* (Princeton University Press, 2015).

Diana Raffman is Professor and Chair of Philosophy at University of Toronto, Mississauga. She is author of numerous articles and two books, *Language, Music, and Mind* (MIT/Bradford Books, 1993) and *Unruly Words: A Study of Vague Language* (Oxford University Press, 2014). She is also editor of *Modality, Morality, and Belief: Essays in Honor of Ruth Barcan Marcus* (with Walter Sinnott-Armstrong and Nicholas Asher, Cambridge University Press, 1994).

Christopher Ranalli is a philosopher at the Vrije Universiteit Amsterdam. He works on topics in epistemology of perception, social epistemology, and epistemic value.

Howard Robinson is Distinguished Visiting Professor at Central European University, Budapest and Vienna; Recurrent Visiting Professor, Rutgers University; Senior Fellow, Rutgers Center for Philosophy of Religion; Research Fellow, Blackfriars Hall, Oxford; and Recurrent Visiting Scholar, Fordham University. He has written mainly on the philosophy of mind and the philosophy of perception, with some work on the history of philosophy and the philosophy of religion. His most recent book is *From the Knowledge Argument to Mental Substance: Resurrecting the Mind* (Cambridge University Press, 2016).

Peter W. Ross is Professor in the Philosophy Department, and Director of the Science, Technology, and Society program, at California State Polytechnic University, Pomona. He has written numerous papers on, among other topics, the nature of colour and perceptual states, the primary/secondary quality distinction, and the distinction among the senses.

Dustin Stokes is Associate Professor in Philosophy at the University of Utah, and is interested in perception, cognition, imagination, art, and creativity. He has published numerous essays on these topics. He edited *Perception and Its Modalities* (with Stephen Biggs and Mohan Matthen, Oxford University Press, 2014).

Michael Watkins is Professor of Philosophy at Auburn University and Adjunct Professor at Dalhousie University. He has published on the metaphysics of colours, perception, aesthetics, and ethics.

Jonathan Westphal is Professor Emeritus in Philosophy of Hampshire College, Amherst, Massachusetts and a Permanent Member of the Senior Common Room at University College, Oxford. He has over one hundred publications including *Colour: Some Philosophical Problems from Wittgenstein* (Basil Blackwell, 1987), *Colour: A Philosophical Introduction* (Blackwell, 1991, 2nd ed.), *Philosophical Propositions: An Introduction to Philosophy* (Routledge, 1998), and *The Mind-Body Problem* (MIT Press, 2016).

Wayne Wright is Professor of Philosophy at Long Beach State University. His research is primarily focused on foundational issues for the scientific study of vision, especially colour vision.

PREFACE AND ACKNOWLEDGEMENTS

This volume was first envisaged during Derek Brown's visit to the Centre for the Study of Perceptual Experience at the University of Glasgow to work with Fiona Macpherson. We are grateful to the Royal Society of Edinburgh for the grant that facilitated this visit in Autumn 2012.

We would like to thank enormously all of the contributors for their essays, and for their quite considerable patience while we produced this volume containing them. And we would like to thank Tony Bruce and Adam Johnson at Routledge for their help, support, and encouragement during the time that it took to gather the material required for this volume.

The Routledge Handbook Series has produced such wonderful volumes that we feel that we have big boots to fill. But we hope that with the help of our exceedingly knowledgeable and erudite contributors we have done justice to the subject of colour which has inspired a great deal of our own work in philosophy. And we hope that some of our love and enthusiasm for the topic is manifest in the pages of this volume.

Finally, we would like to thank each other for the encouragement, cajoling, and patience during busy schedules that we have shown to each other. Editing this book happily coincided with Derek taking up a position at the Centre for the Study of Perceptual Experience and moving to the city of Glasgow. We like to think that colour both made, marks, and sustains our great friendship in many ways.

The editing of this book also occurred during some momentous personal events: the birth of Derek's son Jasper, and the death of his father, David, and we dedicate this book to both of them.

Fiona and Derek
August 2019, Glasgow

INTRODUCTION TO THE PHILOSOPHY OF COLOUR

Derek H. Brown and Fiona Macpherson

Why colour?

Why has the examination of many different aspects of colour been a prominent feature in philosophy, to such an extent that the topic is worthy of a handbook? Here are two related answers. First, colours are exceedingly familiar, seemingly simple features that become enigmatic under scrutiny, and they are difficult to capture in any familiar-sounding, unsophisticated theory. Second, through colour one can confront various problems that span the breadth of philosophy, including problems pertaining to perception, the mind-body relation, the nature of science, scepticism, vagueness, meta-ethics, and aesthetics. Let us elaborate.

Colour is, unsurprisingly, central to work in vision and, for better or worse, vision often dominates philosophy of perception. In this way, colour informs our understanding of the nature of perceptual states, the appearance-reality division, and of perceptual phenomenal character (that is, "what it is like" to have perceptual states; see Nagel, 1974). The study of colour has taught us about numerous surprising phenomena, including various kinds of illusions and hallucinations (roughly, cases in which experience fails to accurately represent the way the world is—or isn't connected to it in the right way, in the case of veridical illusion or hallucination), the potential for perceptual constancies and variations to coexist (roughly, the potential for there to be cases in which we experience a colour to be the same under different illuminations, yet also to somehow look different), and particular associations between perception, cognition, and language. It exemplifies the rich relationship between empirical and philosophical research.

But colour's reach is much broader than this. Through spectrum inversion scenarios,[1] "Purple Haze",[2] and of course a certain Mary,[3] colour has anchored debates about physicalism, functionalism, and the explanatory gap. Colour is an ever-ready case study for perceptual variation. The same surfaces can look differently to a person in different conditions, and can look differently to different persons in the same conditions, thus helping fuel sceptical challenges and our accounts of the nature of knowledge. Colour is a stock example of vagueness, which continues to puzzle philosophical logicians. Models for balancing the perspectival nature of colour and the reality of colour have been analogized for use in meta-ethics. Studies suggest that in some respects colours are *out there* in the objective world yet in other respects inherently *perceiver-dependent*, in effect sitting at the intersection of perceiver and environment. This makes colour ontology—attempts to say what and where colours are—highly complicated. This list could continue.

Colour is thus a sparkling lens through which to philosophize. That is "Why colour?"—or at least a quick and dirty answer. A less quick but manageable answer is the rest of this volume. A long, rather unmanageable one, is the now thousands of works published on the topic in philosophy, and many thousands more found outside philosophy. Our focus in this volume is on the philosophical work, aimed at students and professionals inside and outside philosophy who want a picture of where we are at in that philosophical work. (Although we do include two papers that summarize the contemporary science of colour and empirical work on colour spaces.) However, before saying where philosophy of colour is at the moment, it is worth quickly remarking on how we got here.

Philosophers of colour frequently thank Larry Hardin for writing *Color for Philosophers* (1988). We wish to do so again. The work demonstrates, in beautiful detail, numerous ways in which empirical research can and should be brought to bear on basic questions about the nature and epistemology of colour. It stands today as a fine example of how to do empirically informed philosophy of mind, and it was central to what sparked the current interest in philosophy of colour. Although Hardin was unable to contribute to this volume directly, there is little doubt that his influence can be felt throughout.

There was also a broader group of philosophers who made a commitment to philosophy of colour in the last decades of the 20th century—and to great effect. Many of us became aware of this broader movement through Alex Byrne and David Hilbert's two-volume set *Readings on Color* (1997, MIT). The science volume was a fantastic way for philosophers to introduce themselves to what scientists in the field were doing. The philosophy volume made it plain to all how much first-rate philosophy was being done on the topic. The numerous unresolved challenges and disparate approaches on offer showed many of us that a viable subfield in philosophy had been launched.

Since that time, several thousand philosophical works have been published on colour (as a quick search on PhilPapers reveals). And there is no sign of the field cooling off: several recent collections (for example, Cohen & Matthen 2010; Silva 2017) and monographs (for example, Chirimuuta 2015; Allen 2016; Gert 2017) are sure to stimulate research in the foreseeable future.

Unfortunately, the field of philosophy of colour is now extensive enough to be challenging to newcomers and to established philosophers interested in incorporating colour into their work. The field is even more difficult to penetrate for non-philosophers. We would benefit from a map of the terrain organized around issues of current interest. This Handbook aims to provide one such map. It is not a complete map. But we hope its scope locates the main countries of the field, and its details trace some of the interconnected networks within and between them.

The initial section—*The Importance of Colour to Philosophy*—surveys some broad areas in philosophy to which colour has direct application. This serves as a primer for why many philosophers are interested in colour, and why many more philosophers and non-philosophers should be too. The *Interlude* that follows contains summaries of the science and spaces of colour. These chapters swiftly bring readers to a practical baseline of knowledge on these topics, so that readers can delve into the many chapters that reference or discuss their topics. *Colour Phenomena* examines a suite of issues about colour that have been puzzling philosophers in recent years (and in many cases for much longer). The fundamental question 'Where are colours and what is their nature?' is the topic of *Colour Ontology*, introducing readers to a wide array of proposals defended in contemporary research. *Colour Experience and Epistemology* follows colour through the main, current models for perceptual experience and the challenges that notions like 'looks' generate in perception. Finally, *Language, Categories, and Thought* confronts readers with issues at the intersection of these three domains.

Overview of the sections

§1 The importance of colour to philosophy

This section offers a broad sample of the many topics in philosophy that can be profitably studied through colour. Why does colour have such wide philosophical applicability? One way to address the question is to highlight aspects of colour that make it suitable for such applications. These include (but are not limited to) colour's phenomenal character, the persistence of colour variation, and the internal features of colours (that is, their apparent similarities and differences to each other). These aspects of colour have, perhaps unsurprisingly, given rise to a rather sophisticated space of options regarding the nature of colour and regarding the relation between colour and colour experience. We won't work through too many of the details here, but a few remarks on these issues will help readers conceptualize some of the many roles colour occupies through the chapters in this opening (and subsequent) sections.

One important aspect of colour is that it is both susceptible to empirical study, and remains a vivid example of the seeming gap between the world as it is experienced (with its blues and greens, reds and yellows) and the frequently held conception of a colourless physical world of spectral power distributions, light reflectance profiles, and neural pathways. We can think of this as part of the challenge of incorporating phenomenal character, or what we acquire via experience, into our understanding of the physical world. The challenge is non-trivial. We posit colours because we experience them, and we experience them to be in the world around us. Yet physics, chemistry, and neuroscience don't seem to need colours. The problem could be one of fitting *colours* into the physical world, or it could be one of fitting colour *experience* into the physical world, or both. To take but two examples, this issue has immediate impact on philosophy of mind and philosophy of science.

McLaughlin (Chapter 1) argues that both colour and colour experience create problems for physicalism, although only the latter directly impinges the mind-body problem. Part of the challenge colour poses is connected to its status as a secondary quality, which yields difficult questions about the relationship between colours and colour experience. Should we explain colour in terms of colour experience or colour experience in terms of colour? Various options are available; all bring distinct challenges.

From the perspective of philosophy of science, Chirimuuta (Chapter 3) frames the problem of fitting colour and colour experience into the physical world as an important example of the tension between the manifest and scientific image (Sellars 1956). Chirimuuta first considers the possibility that the purported "gap" between the manifest and scientific image is mostly a 20th-century phenomenon. It has earlier roots, to be sure. But there is reason to believe that our routine attribution of this "gap" to earlier thought is inaccurate, something we have foisted on it in retrospect. Interestingly, work on the manifest and scientific image in contemporary philosophy of science continues to receive inspiration from the case of colour. Chirimuuta discusses two cases. In Wilson's (2006) deflationary approach, the many nuances of colour in our speech and actions are used to help deflate or significantly disintegrate the distinction between the objective and the subjective. Giere's (2006) perspectivism, a proposed middle ground in the debate between scientific realism and instrumentalism, is built on the idea that colours can be both real and perspectival (specifiable only relative to a perceiver). For him, scientific assertions are analogous, they are assertions about how the world is from this theory, or using this instrument. There is no unique, unified description of the world that is the "real" one.

Colour's usefulness in philosophy is also due to colour being an enduring example of perceptual variation: the experienced colour of a jacket can change depending on lighting conditions, one's previous retinal state, and the absorption curves of different perceivers' cones, among other things. And the jacket can arguably remain intrinsically unchanged throughout. This ancient observation applies to many features outside colour, and has been reinforced through centuries of intellectual developments. In the case of colour, it is now underpinned by a wealth of solid empirical data, yielding numerous philosophical applications throughout this Handbook.

One philosophical application of perceptual variation occurs in Pritchard and Ranalli's chapter on scepticism in epistemology (Chapter 2). If, strictly speaking, we experience something variable in colour vision, and the objective world we purportedly inhabit isn't quite so variable, then arguably the world as it appears to us is different from the world as it is independently of us. Finding a way to accommodate variations in appearances with the acquisition of knowledge of an objective world is a central goal in epistemology, and Pritchard and Ranalli illustrate how colour is a profitable means of working through these struggles.

Another striking feature of colours is their robust categories (for example, the collection of all the blues, or of all the purples) and the undeniable respect in which they bleed into one another. This makes colour a staple case in studies of vagueness, the topic of Raffman's contribution (Chapter 4). The blues merge into the purples, with no discernible point marking the boundary between them. Is the boundary there but inaccessible, leaving us in an epistemically impoverished state? Or is the boundary simply vague, leaving our statements about it susceptible to a host of different semantic analyses? Colour is particularly interesting here because it has been used to test whether or not the rough location of boundaries between its categories are stable when approached from different perspectives. For example, is the location of the boundary between blue and purple the same when approaching the blues from the purples, as opposed to when approaching the purples from the blues? Raffman presents recent research suggesting that the boundary is direction sensitive.

In studying the logic of colour concepts, Gierlinger and Westphal (Chapter 5) examine the structure of colour propositions and inferences involving them in an effort to define colours (if possible) and, more modestly, to develop accounts of important colour phenomena. Such phenomena include, for example, colour opponencies (for example, red versus green and blue versus yellow), and colour incompatibilities more broadly, topics that re-emerge elsewhere in this Handbook (see below for guidance). Red and green are standardly taken to be incompatible in one or more senses. One can ask whether this incompatibility applies to the colours of things (for example, no thing can be both red and green all over at a time), to experience (for example, no perceiver can experience a reddish-green colour), or to colours themselves (for example, there is no reddish-green colour). When propositions containing these sorts of incompatibilities are regarded as true, what is the strength and nature of their truth and of the knowledge we might have of it? For example, are these propositions analytic, are they necessary, is our knowledge of them a priori? Further, if one isolates an incompatibility or set of incompatibilities that is unique to a colour, then one might use that to define the colour.

It is obvious that colour is significant to aesthetics—painters and dye producers, for example, have been at the leading edge of colour knowledge throughout our history. Yet it is daunting to try and summarize this significance. A good starting point is to focus on the importance of depiction to works of art, as Kulvicki does (Chapter 6). Depiction is roughly representation via 'picturing'. On one influential account, depiction essentially involves some form of resemblance between the depiction and what it depicts. For better or worse, philosophers of perception have often appealed to the painterly attitude in their discussion of art. In brief, the idea is that to produce a realistic painting—the staple form of depiction—the painter often looks at a three-dimensional scene as a two-dimensional artefact to be copied onto her canvas. Setting aside how accurate this is of artistic practice, the idea is straightforward enough for geometric properties: the shapes of objects in the scene are "collapsed" into their outlines, and the sizes of those outlines are the sizes projected to an image at the canvas surface. What is the analogue for colour? A first thought is that one only need look at the colours of surfaces in the scene, and then find paints that match them to depict them. A moment's reflection reveals, however, that the colours experienced in a scene are typically impacted not only by surfaces but also by illuminants, shadows, the medium through which one looks, and so on. An accurate two-dimensional depiction of this "collapses" these many elements into one colour at each point on the canvas. How can this be achieved? Is something lost in the process? And what might this teach us about colour vision? These are some of the issues brought forth by this inquiry.

At least some readers will see Gert's Chapter 7 and wonder: what is the color/value analogy and why should I be interested in it? The aforementioned features of colour are part of the reason why there are numerous rich colour ontologies (accounts of the underlying nature of colour) and why understanding them and their relations is now rather complicated (see below and esp. §IV). As Gert illustrates, several of these colour ontologies have analogues in the space of value ontologies (accounts of the underlying nature of value). For example, there are theses asserting the reality or objectivity of colour/value, the relativity of colour/value, the fundamentally subjective or expressive character of colour/value, the error-ladenness of our claims about colour/value, and so on. On top of this, questions about how to fit colour into the physical world have interesting parallels with analogous questions about values. Work on the colour/value analogy stems from the intuitively plausible idea that the nature of colour can afford insight into the nature of value. The analogies aren't perfect, and whether or not these differences dilute the usefulness of the analogy is part of the interest in the topic. In the context of this Handbook, this chapter is not merely an invitation for people interested in colour to consider whether views about colour may have valuable lessons for normative theory. It is also an invitation to consider the reverse.

§2 Interlude: the science and spaces of colour

There is now little question that informed philosophical contributions to colour theory often require basic technical knowledge concerning the science and spaces of colour, and in specific cases requires more than basic knowledge. Our goal has been to find a way to integrate technical colour knowledge into this Handbook that isn't off-putting to newcomers, but doesn't pretend that these details can generally be glossed over. Central to our strategy is this section, a basic course in the science and spaces of colour. They are suitable as introductions for new readers, and as reliable points of reference for all readers. Within this Handbook, these chapters allow authors of other chapters to presuppose this basic knowledge and, as is often needed, jump into particulars that are germane to their topic.

Byrne and Hilbert's chapter on colour science (Chapter 8) provides an overview of the relevant topics in optics, physiology, psychophysics, the visual cortex, visual defects, and animal vision. From the perspective of optics, understanding colour vision requires consideration of numerous factors, including properties of light (especially wavelength), light reflectance properties of surfaces, and light transmission properties of media through which light travels. The light that enters the eye—the colour signal—is a function of these kinds of properties and generates an image on the back of the retina. At this point, physiology becomes crucial. In humans, colour vision utilizes the three different wavelength sensitive cone receptors (see below for exceptions), which send signals to retinal ganglion cells, which in turn send signals to the visual cortex, where a significant amount of colour processing occurs.

Scientists also approach the topic of colour from the perspective of psychophysics, the study of how subjects respond to coloured stimuli. This has led to various insights into types and variations in colour appearances and colour spaces, and notably to the opponent-processing theory of colour vision (though the status of the opponent-process theory is less secure today than it was in preceding decades).

In addition, colour scientists have deepened our understanding of colour through studying defects in colour vision. Many defects arise from abnormalities in cone receptors (yielding different kinds of what is commonly called "colour blindness", a matter discussed below and in some of the chapters in in this volume, especially Chapters 8 and 11). There are also defects due to abnormalities in the visual cortex, notably cerebral achromatopsia and colour agnosia. Very roughly, cerebral achromatopsia occurs when subjects exhibit few or no abilities to visually distinguish chromatic colours, while retaining a comparably sophisticated ability to distinguish visual form (that is, shapes and locations) by detecting differences in luminance. Very roughly, colour agnosia occurs when subjects exhibit sophisticated or even normal abilities to visually distinguish colours and to talk about colours in the abstract (for example, to recall that bananas are yellow), yet limited ability to talk about the colours they see. At present cerebral achromatopsia and colour agnosia are only partially understood phenomena. They are of interest for example for their capacity to provide insight into previously undocumented dissociations between colour and form perception (in the case of cerebral achromatopsia), and colour perception and colour language (in the case of colour agnosia). Finally, colour scientists have made remarkable progress in understanding colour vision by studying non-human animals (more on this below). These are, in broad outline, the topics discussed in Byrne and Hilbert's colour science chapter.

Briggs' chapter on colour spaces (Chapter 9) provides an overview of what colour spaces are, the main contemporary models of colour space, and the history of the topic. Colour spaces are representations of colours in some geometric space, where the dimensions of that space are defined in terms of colour-relevant attributes. There are numerous ways to do this (for example, Kuehni and Schwarz (2008) is a recent historical survey that identifies over 170 colour spaces). An important division within colour spaces is that between what one might call "perceptual" and "psychophysical" models. Whereas perceptual models are squarely focused on appearance or perceived colour, psychophysical models map classes of spectral distributions or reflectances that match in appearance under assumptions including a "standard" human observer. We will give a brief example of each.

Perceived colour can be described in terms of the attributes of hue, brightness (or lightness), and colourfulness (or saturation or chroma). Following Hering, it is now common to posit four unique or fundamental hues (blue, green, yellow, and red) for humans. Lightness is perceived position on a scale from black to white (for example, robin egg blue is a light colour, and navy blue a much darker one). Within these constraints it is easy to conceptualize many colour similarity relations (for example, yellows are more similar to oranges than to blues), and identify the fundamental colour opponencies (that is, blue-yellow, red-green, and black-white). In addition, colours possess robust categories (for example, the collection of all the blues, the collection of all the greens) that bleed into one another. Collectively, these features build up a rich and important example of a perceptual model of colour space.

By contrast, a psychophysical model maps colour specifications in terms of tristimulus values (such as CIE XYZ) or psychophysical measures such as dominant wavelength, purity, and luminance. Such a model has wavelength (or light reflectance) as a basic dimension. Since we know that the perceived or appearance colour induced by a stimulus can vary depending on a host of contextual factors, psychophysical models generally make operational assumptions to mitigate

6

these effects. For example, the perceived colour of an object can vary across illumination conditions. Thus, a psychophysical model that maps colours to surface reflectances might presume a "standard illuminant" so as to capture a mapping between perceived colour and stimulus that holds *if* those stimuli are perceived under a standard illuminant, even if the mapping is distorted when different illuminants are in play. Another important operational assumption might be that of a "standard observer".

Colour spaces are of interest to philosophers for several reasons. Perceptual models aim to systematize the characteristics of colours themselves, and thus contribute to our understanding of the *explanandum* in theories of colour (for example, Chapter 10 delves more deeply into the hue facet of perceptual models). Psychophysical models illustrate various ways of mapping colour to stimuli, but require important assumptions to mitigate the variations between stimuli and perceived colour that occur in "real" scenarios. The significance of this variation between stimuli and perceived colour is a matter of great debate in philosophy of colour. Very roughly, one might view the presumption of a "standard illuminant" as helping us identify good epistemic conditions for perceiving colour, or one might view it as a means of ignoring crucial facts about the nature of colour. Psychophysical models are thus able to clarify what kinds of assumptions are needed to enhance the mappings between perceived colour and stimuli, providing an important empirical touchstone for these philosophical debates. The history of colour spaces naturally illuminates the development of our thinking about colour, including ways that this thinking is influenced by, and influences, factors of significance to the individual or time period. Thus, one might view the centrality of colour-wavelength mappings to Newton's colour space as not only illuminating on its own, but as also reflecting his well-known preoccupation with the nature of light. The insights contained in Newton's colour space are remarkable, but also important is its arguably limited use when considering the colours associated with surfaces as opposed to lights. Finally, one might argue that the mere proliferation of colour spaces contains an important lesson about colour. There are comparatively few perceptual or psychophysical spaces for other domains such as shape, sound, odours, and so on. Our understanding of colour is thus systematizable, but there are glaring constraints on how "unified" the resulting understanding is, making colour an intriguing topic of study. There is thus much of philosophical interest in the study of colour spaces, and Briggs' chapter provides the requisite background for thinking about these issues.

§3 Colour phenomena

Colour phenomena are what theories of colour perception and colour ontology must account for—they are the explananda for colour theory. There are far more colour phenomena than are treated in this section, but each of the eight phenomena that appear here have received focused philosophical attention in recent years. Although all are relevant to questions in colour perception or colour ontology, the focus of each chapter is not on a particular view about these matters but instead on the phenomenon at issue. Collectively, these chapters illustrate the diversity of phenomena to be explained in a philosophy of colour, and implicitly how challenging it is to build a theory that does justice to them all. It is worth saying a few words about each.

As mentioned above, it is common to recognize four basic hues in human colour vision: blue, green, red, and yellow. Matthen's topic is *unique* or *pure* hues (Chapter 10), instances of basic hues that contain no trace of other hues. For example, a blue that has no reddishness and no greenishness but only bluishness. Sticking with the example, unique blue is a collection of blues, as such blues can vary in lightness and saturation without inheriting any other hues. Unique colours are first and foremost identified through perceptual experiences; the nature of stimuli that give rise to these experiences can be subsequently studied. The phenomenon is of interest to philosophers of perception for at least two reasons. Unique hues are examples of unitary or pure perceptual qualities, identifiable through perceptual experience. They thus provide insight into the basic machinery of the (human) colour domain, a foundation from which other colours can be built. Second, we now have good empirical evidence for there being considerable variation in what stimuli induce experiences of a given unique hue across normal human trichromats. (Trichromats have three types of cones cells in the eye that are responsive to different wavelengths—in humans, short, medium, and long wavelengths.) For example, a stimulus that induces an experience of unique green in one perceiver might induce an experience of a strongly bluish-green in another perceiver. Variation in unique hue perception is thus an example of perceptual variation across normal perceivers that sits at the foundations of colour theory.

Recall that using basic hues (blue, green, red, yellow), saturation, lightness, and colour categories we can build a perceptual space for human colours. Are there colours or experiences of colours that are outside this space—are there *novel colours*? The question can be asked of human colour perception and of non-human perception. In the human case a central issue is whether or not a human can perceive a colour that is not localizable within the human colour space or somehow at odds with that space. Macpherson (Chapter 11) discusses reasons to believe in novel colours, including a fascinating case study, namely experiments that purport to induce experiences of reddish-green and bluish-yellow colours in humans. Since in our standard model red and green are colour opposites, experiences of reddish-green colours are by default impossible. Thus, these experiments create a dilemma: either the experiences are somehow misdescribed or the red-green opponency in the standard model is not an in-principle opponency.

Within humans, questions about novel colours also arise from the existence of 'colour blind' humans, which Macpherson also discusses. "Colour blind" is a term generally designating any human dichromat, monocromat, or anomalous trichromat. Red-green colour blind people don't fail to experience colours when looking at red or green things. Instead, roughly speaking, they experience the same colour when looking at red or green things—whatever that colour is. On the traditional picture, when looking at red or green things (things in the "confusion zones"), colour blind people experience one familiar colour (for example, brown or green). But, according to another more recent theory, they experience a colour that is novel to the rest of us. Either way, many people have concluded that since trichromacy is the statistical norm, on this picture the reds and greens that trichromats experience are the actual or real colours of the things at issue, and the colours experienced by the colour blind are abnormal and hence erroneous colours.

Reflection on this picture might prompt one to wonder why the colour a dichromat sees when looking at an apple is the wrong colour—what's wrong with it? Suppose it is true that such people don't see starkly different colours when looking at Granny Smith versus Red Delicious apples. In this way their discriminatory capacities are less powerful than those of trichromats. But still, why does that make the colour they see a wrong one, as opposed to simply a different one from those with normal colour vision?

Inspired by the thought that the colour blind's experience of colour is not incorrect, some people have fundamentally rethought the nature of veridicality in colour perception and, in some instances, the nature of colour blindness itself. For example, there is evidence that dichromats can and do see different colours when looking at various objects in their confusion zones. It is just that they need some time to inspect or explore these objects' colours, to look at them from different angles, against different backgrounds, and so on. Their deficiency thus might not be the principled one that they can't see reds and greens (to stick with our example), but instead the more limited one that it is harder for them to see these colours. If so, there are still difficult questions about what colours such persons experience when a red object and a green object look to have the same colour. But if they can distinguish between reds and greens given the opportunity, then they may be in a better position than we previously thought to tell us about any experience of novel colours that they have.

Synaesthesia, Brogaard's topic (Chapter 12), occurs when people have an extra experience, or element of experience, in response to a certain stimulus. Sometimes synaesthesia is loosely described as consisting of cases of hearing colours or tasting shapes, etc. These cases involve, for example, people experiencing sounds of a certain pitch when they experience different colours, or feeling shapes when they experience different tastes. A person who has synaesthesia can communicate that they have this extra experience in their mental life—often called a *concurrent*—although disagreement remains about the exact nature of that experience, for example, whether the concurrent is somehow attributed to the inducing stimulus or not. An interesting philosophical aspect of synaesthesia is that it involves aspects of perceptual experience being produced in unexpected ways, and it has been intensely studied in recent years.

Interestingly, it turns out that the most common type of synaesthesia isn't cross-modal. It is instead intramodal: experiencing visually perceived graphemes (for example, letters, numbers) as having certain colours—irrespective of the colour of the ink that they are printed in. There are interesting questions about different forms of synaesthesia. In some cases, the concurrent is experienced as being in the world in front of subjects. In other cases it is experienced imaginatively, as being in the "mind's eye". Some concurrents seem to be experienced in response only to perceptual stimuli and their basic perceptual features, while some concurrents are experienced in response to the concept of the relevant inducer, and might be brought on by thought of that inducer as well as perception of it. In the last few years, synaesthesia has grown from an elusive, barely understood phenomenon, to a multi-faceted one that has been discovered to be present in a significant portion of the population.

Philosophers are interested in synaesthesia for several reasons. The triggering of colour experience by non-traditional stimuli is often classified as a form of colour illusion, and the extent and nature of colours illusions is always a crucial topic to philosophy of perception. Beyond this, synaesthesia provides insight into various stable, unexpected pathways for triggering perceptual experience, and, as such, there has been discussion of whether synaesthesia provides a challenge for functionalist or representationalist theories of perceptual experience.

Synaesthesia brings our attention to unexpected associations between experiences of colour and other perceptual qualities. Colour blindness highlights the potential for colour experiences that cannot be communicated between humans with disparate colour visual systems. Spectrum inversion is an extreme case involving both unexpected experiential associations and potentially incommunicable experiences. It is Ross's topic (Chapter 13). Locke wondered whether the colour idea or sensation produced in me by a marigold might be the same as the one produced in you by a violet, noting that we could arguably never detect this difference. In theory, one could take any quality, such as pitches of sounds or degrees of sourness, and imagine some kind of inversion scenario about it, but it is standard to use colour as the focal case. If Locke is right, spectrum inversion would involve an otherwise unexpected swapping, across inverted perceivers, of associations between colour experiences and objects. This would arguably generate a seemingly impenetrable communication barrier between them, guaranteeing the privacy of an individual's colour experience.

Independently of Wittgenstein's invective against private languages, spectrum inversion has variously impacted contemporary philosophy. It poses a challenge for functionalist theories of mind, if two similarly functioning perceivers might nonetheless have inverted colour experiences. It highlights the tenuous relationship between colour experience and the meanings of colour terms, and makes us question the representational character of said experience. In addition, there are now important arguments in favour of the empirical possibility and indeed probability of spectrum inversion within a small portion of humanity (Nida-Rümelin, 1996)—although such cases have raised vital questions about whether such an inversion could indeed go undetected. For some, the theoretical possibility of spectrum inversion is enough to pose the above philosophical problems, but for those who want a non-zero, or better non-trivial, empirical probability that it obtains, these latter arguments are of great interest.

Although *interspecies* studies in colour vision don't provide evidence for an extreme circumstance like spectrum inversion, Allen demonstrates (Chapter 14) that they do provide evidence for robust variations in the nature of colour visual systems and of uses of colour vision. Among other things, this has helped us to formulate a less humancentric conception of colour, forcing us to: more broadly conceive of what the *functions* of colour vision are for different organisms; recognize substantive differences in colour *perceptions* across species; wonder whether or not various non-human animals have categorically different colour *experiences* from our own; and revisit how we think of colour illusion. Further, by virtue of these items making colour appear highly species specific, they challenge non-relativized, objectivist views about colour.

The above phenomena belong to a long list of phenomena that inform questions about the nature and scope of error or "bad cases" in colour perception. Perceptual error has always been central to philosophy of perception, especially to our understanding of the nature of perceptual experience and to perceptual epistemology. We typically distinguish illusion from hallucination, taking the former to involve misperceiving something before you and the latter to involve experiencing something that (in some sense) is not there at all. Visit *The Illusions Index* (www.illusionsindex.org) to experience numerous relevant examples. Two important philosophical issues concern the *scope* of perceptual error (that is, which perceptions count as erroneous and which do not), and the *nature* of perceptual error (that is, how should we understand the nature of the experiences one undergoes during colour illusions and hallucinations). The nature of error in colour perception is discussed throughout this volume, though most directly in §V. Watkins' contribution (Chapter 15) is largely focused on the scope of colour illusion.

The scope of colour illusion is of particular interest because it has proven so difficult to identify an agreed conception of what colours are, and such an agreed conception would otherwise be used to identify when illusion occurs. By comparison, we have an agreed conception of what shapes are and what the shapes of things in our world are. With this in hand we can examine shape perceptions, and when these deviate from perceived shapes we have a solid basis from which to infer that perceptual illusion occurs. But in the case of colour there is no agreement on what colours are (see §IV), and thus we must find another way to motivate judgements about when colour illusion occurs.

One traditional means of identifying colour illusions is by appeal to colour variation. Due to perceptual variation, the colour some object O (or some suitably uniform part of O) appears to have varies as a host of perceptual factors change. On the traditional view O can't have all these colours in itself. On that view, due to the aforementioned colour incompatibilities, O can have at most one colour in itself (that is, if O is green all over at some time then it isn't also any other colour at that time). It follows that either O doesn't have colour in itself, or all but one of O's apparent colours are illusory.

Traditionally, advocates of the subjectivity or mind-dependence of colour opt for the first disjunct, and advocates of the objectivity or mind-independence of colour opt for the second. One difficulty for objectivists is that colour variation is now recognized as being very pervasive. It is found for example within any reasonable construal of normal or ideal perceptual conditions.

This makes it difficult to identify *which* apparent colour is O's colour, and more deeply undermines the credibility of the commitment to O having a unique colour in itself. In recent years, objectivists have developed various lines of response. One is to question the extent of *colour incompatibility*: why did we think that O (or the relevant uniform part of O) can only have one colour in itself? Perhaps O can have one human colour and at the same time have a different pigeon colour. Another is to question the idea that a given colour can only correctly manifest or display one colour appearance. Perhaps blue things can sometimes look green, without error being present—blue can simply appear green in some contexts. These and other strategies are developed in various chapters in this Handbook. The aim of Watkins' chapter is not so much to defend colour objectivism as it is to demonstrate the various means objectivists have available to them to minimize the ascription of colour illusion in the face of colour variation. Watkins' more general goal is to dissuade us from thinking that we can or should aim to settle which colour perceptions are illusory first, and proceed to reach conclusions about colour ontology from there.

In the final chapter in this section, Brown's (Chapter 16) focus is not on colour variation but colour constancy. Very roughly, colour constancy is the tendency of a colour visual system to register a stable colour in a surface across variations in illumination conditions that surface is under. This is important in part because it can serve as a counter to colour variation: certainly illumination conditions change and, to some extent, colour perception changes with it, but there is an underlying sameness in colour perception that remains throughout. Although the details matter (and they are complicated), in this rough way, colour constancy can counterbalance some of the pressures variation places on objectivist theories of colour, and interplay with the above-mentioned connections between variation and illusion.

There are related reasons for interest in colour constancy. The phenomenon is found in many non-human species, making it a central facet of colour vision. Its existence implies that colour vision isn't only concerned with analysing incoming light, but is also concerned with isolating aspects of one's environment that remain constant across light changes. This helps one shift from thinking of colour vision as focused on the proximal signal to a system that also has interest in distal things—in the surface qualities of objects and therefore in those objects themselves. Because of this one might think that colour constancy helps explain *why* we see colours on rocks and trees (and not as aspects of the light arrays striking our eyes), and why we experience colours as illumination-independent properties (if in fact we do).

Finally, difficult questions about the nature of colour perception, experience, and judgement arise when trying to "fit" colour constancy with colour variation. Consider a simplified example. When, by hypothesis, we experience a wall as differently illuminated and stably coloured, does the experienced illumination variation constitute a difference in experienced colour? In at least some respects it seems that it does: the wall looks darker in colour in the shadowed part and lighter in colour in the unshadowed part. But then in what way is the wall experienced as stably coloured—how can something look to be both the same colour and differently coloured? Perhaps some aspects of the case are reflections of colour *experience*, and others are reflections of *judgements* made about that experience. Alternatively, perhaps we can construct a more sophisticated account of colour experience that resolves the tension between the overlapping apparent colour difference and sameness.

Colour constancy has thus emerged as a fruitful phenomenon: for defending the objectivity of colour against pressures from colour variation; for helping us conceive of colour perception as targeting distal things in our environment, as opposed to light arrays striking our retinas; and for providing us with a difficult and basic case study situated at the intersection of colour experience and judgement.

§4 Colour ontology

What are colours exactly, and where precisely are they? These are arguably the guiding questions for colour ontologists. They are daunting ones, as should be apparent given our discussion thus far about the numerous ways colour is used in philosophy, the rich knowledge we are acquiring about the science and spaces of colour, and the variety of colour phenomena that need explanation. Our aim in organizing this section was to identify a cluster of colour ontologies that accurately represent those ontologies that people hold and discuss in contemporary philosophy. We will present them by locating each within a broader landscape of colour ontologies. Unfortunately, some locations in this landscape do not have dedicated chapters in this volume—we had to be selective—but we provide references to sources for these which the interested reader can pursue. To keep this introduction manageable, our remarks aim to differentiate various colour ontologies but *not* to motivate them. Readers can learn about those motivations by consulting the relevant chapters.

As just stated, the overarching tasks of colour ontology are to determine what kinds of properties colours are and where we can find them in our world (if anywhere). These tasks should be clearly differentiated from the related ones of determining what causes colour experiences and determining what causes some object to have a given colour, although determining these things may be helpful in carrying out the overarching task. The issue is also not to determine what makes some experience a colour experience or what makes a perception one of colour. In colour ontology, the focus is on colours themselves. That said, adopting an account of colour experience, colour perception, the causal antecedents of colour, and of course of colour illusion and hallucination, can impact one's colour ontology—and vice versa.

There are numerous ways to parse the space of colour ontology. Our parsing centres on two broad and orthogonal dimensions, the subjectivist-objectivist dimension and the reductionist-non-reductionist dimension. The former concerns the extent to which colours are dependent on perceivers (and thus subjective) or independent of perceivers (and thus objective). The latter roughly concerns the extent to which colours are physically reducible or have non-physical aspects (and are therefore non-reductive).

Regarding the *subjectivist-objectivist* dimension, the broad options are that colours are entirely independent of perceivers (objectivism), that colours are only dependent on perceivers (mentalism), and that they are dependent on both perceivers and the world outside of them (relationalism).

What would it mean for colours to be *objective* (Chapters 17 and 18)? With respect to the debate in colour ontology, what is meant is that the nature of colour does not require appeal to perceivers at all. Thus, bananas are yellow and the nature of that yellowness does not depend on any facts about any perceivers. One version of this theory, defended by Byrne and Hilbert (Chapter 17), draws on contemporary colour science and identifies a particular shade of yellowness with a class or disjunction of surface spectral reflectances (SSRs). Call that class C_1. The SSR of a surface is the percentage of light that it reflects of each wavelength of light. We know that objects that look to normal human perceivers in normal conditions to have the same shade of colour can have various different SSRs. The disjunction of those SSRs, C_1, causes experiences of that particular shade of yellow in normal perceivers in our world (as opposed to other possible worlds where it may not), and that shade may bear other interesting relations to the perception of yellow. Furthermore, it may be that it is only via experiences of yellow (in this world) that we are able to identify C_1 as the property yellow. Nonetheless, what objectivists insist on is that C_1's nature, that is the nature of that shade of yellow, does not depend on any of these relations (for objectivists, contingent relations) to perceptual states—C_1 is a wholly objective property. It can be specified in wholly objective terms—in terms of SSRs—without mention of the nature of its effects on perceivers.

In contrast to the notion of objectivity just outlined, there is an alternative notion of what it is for colours to be objective that one might have taken to be plausible: colours are objective if and only if they are properties of things that persist independently of perceivers. What is crucial for objectivity on this view is that bananas could have been yellow before perceivers were around and could maintain their yellowness were perceivers to disappear. This is a weaker account of objectivity, for it is consistent with the nature of yellowness requiring appeal to perceptual states. For example, yellowness might be defined as the power to induce perceptions of yellow in perceivers, regardless of whether or not colour perceivers are around to help bananas exercise that power. Even though this kind of Lockean ontology satisfies one intuitive notion of 'objective', in colour ontology discussions it is typically regarded as a perceiver-dependent or subjectivist one. In fact it is considered a form of *colour relationalism*. This is because what it is for something to be a colour is defined in terms of its relation to perceivers of a certain sort (in terms of its power to affect them)—albeit a sort of perceiver that may not exist at a given time or place.

There is another feature of colour relationalism that is worth considerable attention. Colour relationalists maintain that colours minimally depend on both perceivers and the perceived. A classic example is the Lockean dispositionalist just mentioned, for whom yellow is a power to produce experiences of yellow in perceivers. However, in most contemporary literature colour relationalists typically maintain that the colour of a thing, say our banana, is a complex relational property with relata that include not only particular perceivers and the banana, but also the lighting conditions, neighbouring colours, and perhaps other features of the environment. Such a view is the topic of Cohen's contribution (Chapter 19). According to it, colour depends not only on perceiver and perceived, but also on perceptual conditions. When speaking precisely, these contemporary relationalists won't say that a banana has a colour *simpliciter*, but instead that a given banana has some colour for some perceiver in some viewing condition, where various facets of the perceiver and viewing condition need specification to fully explicate the relevant colour. Despite this difference between the views, both Lockean and contemporary relationalist views assert that colours are relational as opposed to intrinsic properties. And, crucially, the kind of relational property colours are is the kind that depend on the nature of perceptual states. The nature of colour for relationalists therefore depends both on environmental and perceptual factors.

We previously saw that there are two notions of "objective", and that the stronger, rather than weaker, one was what was that employed by those holding colour objectivism. The situation is similar with respect to "relational". Relationalists about colour hold that colour is a relational property that makes reference to both perceivers and the colour-relevant facets of their environment. However, there is a much looser sense of "relational" which might be applied to colours, according to which colours are relational as opposed to intrinsic properties *simpliciter*. That is, their nature involves specification of some form of relation—but it needn't be a relation between perceivers and their environment. This is a different idea and isn't typically what is meant by "colour relationalism". One example of such a view would be the identification of colours with SSRs, for SSRs are relational properties. They are properties specifying the ways in which a given surface reflects different wavelengths of light. The relation in question is one that relates parts of the environment to each other: lightwaves to surfaces. One who identifies colours with classes of SSRs is a colour relationalist in this looser sense, but is definitely *not* a colour relationalist in the first sense. Similarly, one might identify colours with colour sensations or colour qualia. Qualia are private mental items posited to explain the seemingly subjective character of consciousness. Qualia are typically conceived of as mind-dependent features. Thus, someone who believes that colours are a kind of qualia would arguably hold that colours are mind-dependent. One would thereby be a colour relationalist in the looser sense, but again wouldn't be in the first more relevant sense. The relation employed here does not involve the environment of the perceiver. We stick to current convention and by "colour relationalism" mean the view that colours are properties whose nature depends on both environmental and perceptual factors.

In contrast to both colour objectivism and relationalism, the colour *mentalist* takes colours to be properties whose nature depends only on perceptual states, narrowly construed to include only states whose nature can be specified by saying what is going on within the head or within mental states. Colour mentalism is the focus of Robinson's contribution (Chapter 21). Mentalists might take colours to be features of neural states or to be a subset of mental qualia, and it is reasonable to regard those who take colours to be properties of sense-data to be mentalists in this sense (sense-data are mind-dependent perceptual objects discussed below and in detail in Chapter 24). Mentalists agree with their rivals that environmental factors like SSRs and relations between surfaces, illumination conditions and the like, are critical to understanding when a perceiver will likely enter into a given perceptual colour state. These environmental factors are thus also critical to understanding when a given colour will likely be instantiated in a world. However, these environmental factors are not regarded as part of the nature of colour, but only as part of what typically causes colours to be instantiated (in the minds or brains of perceivers). With this rough understanding of the subjectivist-objectivist dimension of colour ontologies, we proceed to the reductionist-non-reductionist one.

As the subjective-objective and reductionist-non-reductionist dimensions are orthogonal, each of objectivism, relationalism, and mentalism can be developed in a *reductionist* or *non-reductionist* manner. The issue, as it manifests itself in colour studies, concerns the extent to which colour properties are physical. (In different domains within philosophy, what counts as a successful reduction differs. For example, in moral philosophy reduction of goodness or badness to mental states, counts as a success. In aesthetics, reduction of beauty to colour and form would be a success. In philosophy of mind, reduction to physical states is what counts.)

Let us start with reductivism. One influential form of colour objectivism, which we have encountered already, is a reductionist view. It is the reductionist view that identifies surface colours with classes of SSRs and colours more broadly with ways that things manipulate or produce light (Chapter 17). Contrasting with this, though not a popular view, mentalism in a reductive form identifies colours with properties of neural states. Different again is a relationalist reductionist view. In order for a relationalist to be a reductionist they must hold that all of the relata that make up a colour relation are physical. To take a simple example, if blue is the power to produce experiences of blue in perceivers, then both the power and the experience must be physical.

While physicalism is a dominant force in contemporary analytic philosophy, we mentioned at the outset that colour has been a persistent source for resistance by the non-physicalist. Sometimes the resistance stems more directly from considerations about the ability to naturalize colour experience qua experience, rather than from considerations about colour ontology, but not always. There are a variety of non-reductive ontologies. *Colour primitivism* is the thesis, defended by Gert (Chapter 18), that colours are wholly objective properties that are *sui generis*. According to primitivists, colours bear important relations to physical properties like SSRs, perhaps in some sense supervening on them. But colours themselves are not identifiable with anything like SSRs. Instead they are non-physical, objective properties of things in our environment. Here are two straightforward examples of non-reductivist views that are forms of mentalism (Robinson's topic in Chapter 21). Those who take colours to be properties of sense-data are non-reductionist colour mentalists, at least to the extent that sense-data are taken to be non-physical and mind-dependent (as they usually are). Similarly, people who identify colours with colour qualia will be non-reductionists, to the extent that they take qualia to be non-physical properties (as they often are). Finally, a straightforward example of a relationalist position that is non-reductionist is the view that that colours are powers to produce colour experiences in perceivers, and that colour experiences are non-physical states.

In addition to chapters on the preceding views, the other two ontology chapters in this volume are titled "Eliminativism" and "Monism and Pluralism". Both headings are potentially ambiguous so it is worth stating how they should be understood in this volume. On one reading—that which is the focus of Wright's contribution (Chapter 22)—colour eliminativism asserts that nothing in one's *surrounding environment* has colour. Bananas aren't yellow or any other colour, nor are trees green, postboxes red, or blueberries blue. Such a view doesn't entail colour mentalism, as it is strictly the negative thesis that nothing in one's surrounding environment is coloured. However, it is consistent with mentalism, since one's mental states (again narrowly construed) do not extend into one's surrounding environment.

A stronger reading of 'eliminativism' asserts that *nothing in our world* has colour, not bananas and blueberries, but also not sense-data, neural states, or mental states. On this view, colours are not the kind of property one finds instances of in our world at all. Advocates of this stronger form of eliminativism are obliged to give some kind of positive story to explain our various colour commitments. One proposal might be that colours are useful fictions (Gatzia, 2010), and another that colours are properties found in some other more perfect world such as Eden (Chalmers, 2006)—though in theory these proposals could be consistent with one another. Either way, nothing in *our* world has colour. There is unfortunately no chapter in this volume dedicated to this stronger eliminativism.

The colour pluralist believes that there are multiple colours, in some more interesting way than that there are blues and greens. However, there are different ways in which this might be the case. One could for example believe that there is a sense in which colours are mental properties and a sense in which they are objective properties, yet see no credible means of collapsing colour ontology into one or the other. So why not accept both? This idea has been defended by some authors (Maund 1981; Brown 2006), and while it could be described as a kind of colour pluralism, it is more usefully referred to as the *dual-referent view* or the *colour ambiguity* view. There is unfortunately also no chapter dedicated to this idea. The phrase "colour pluralism" is typically reserved for a different and, in a way, more radical idea.

The more radical idea is that the same part of the same object simultaneously has multiple colours. A ripe banana may be yellow all over but it is also other colours all over at the same time. This is the colour pluralism Kalderon discusses (Chapter 20). It is *prima facie* in tension with colour incompatibilities, like the purported truism that nothing can be black and white and red all over. Under scrutiny, which incompatibilities a given colour pluralism excludes depends on which colours that pluralism allows to be co-instantiated. Unrestricted pluralism recognizes no genuine colour incompatibilities (for example, everything can have every colour). More restricted pluralisms might recognize incompatibilities between say the colours that humans experience (for example, something can't be red and purple all over), but no such incompatibilities between the colours that humans experience and those that pigeons experience, presuming that those are different (for example, something can be "human orange" all over and have some other "pigeon colour" all over as well).

One form of colour pluralism stems from colour relationalism. A given object can, in theory, enter into multiple colour relations with perceivers in different perceptual conditions. Since the relationalist holds that these relations *are* colours, if we assume that there is no principled means of singling out one of these scenarios as uniquely correct, a given object will have multiple colours. Via this reasoning, contemporary relationalists tend towards being unrestricted colour pluralists. By contrast, traditional Lockean dispositionalists typically do not have this commitment. For them, the perceptual relation that obtains in "normal" conditions is often presumed unique and uniquely correct—although this is an optional feature of their view.

There can also be pluralist versions of objectivism about colour. Recall that according to objectivism colours are not perceiver-dependent, but instead classes of SSRs or *sui generis* objective properties, or somesuch. Either way, different colours can be possessed by a surface at a given time. How is this explained? If colours are classes of SSRs, then the explanation proceeds by pointing out that a given SSR can be a member of various colour classes. Thus, a surface with a given SSR can have many different colours. If colours are *sui generis* properties, then the explanation stems from the account what these *sui generis* properties are like. One can certainly develop an account according to which a surface can have multiple such properties.

§5 *Colour experience and epistemology*

Recall that part of the philosophical challenge of colour stems from its status as a secondary quality, which in part means that it is difficult to formulate accounts of colour independently of accounts of colour experience, and vice versa. Because of this, experience has an elevated role in colour theory, compared for example, to its role in shape theory. The aims of this section are to introduce readers to how colour relates to three dominant approaches to perceptual experience, and to provide readers with a very brief introduction to "looks" statements involving colour terms.

We begin with a brief outline of the three accounts of perceptual experience and subsequently apply them to colour. The accounts are representationalism, naïve or direct realism, and indirect realism (for example, sense-datum theory). There are numerous ways of developing these accounts, and some controversies over how to characterize them. We nonetheless hope that the following sketch, which leaves out many subtleties, is informative.

Pautz (Chapter 23) discusses the currently dominant representational approach to perceptual experience. Its central tenet is that perceptual experiences are inherently representational states, which is to say that they express "contents" which may, to varying extents, be satisfied by (or be accurate of) the relevant part of world before the subject. For example, a common experience might be one that represents that there is a blue square in front of me. The content of that experience is that there is a blue square in front of me. This content would be accurate if there was indeed a blue square in front of me and would be inaccurate if there was not. Because perceptual contents can diverge from the world before the subject, the two are distinct kinds of things, and in many cases it is helpful to think of contents as abstract entities (for example, propositions). Within this framework, the relationship between the phenomenal character of perceptual experience and perceptual content is a contentious issue: phenomenal character might be determined by perceptual content, or vice versa, or both; phenomenal character might outstrip perceptual content, or vice versa, or both; phenomenal character might be identical to perceptual content; and so on. We won't discuss the nuances of these debates, but it is fair to say that the representational approach is committed to *explaining* phenomenal character in terms of perceptual contents, in some substantive sense of 'explain'. In Pautz's stronger formulation, "experiencing is *nothing but* representing" (p. 366).

Representational approaches can be contrasted with acquaintance approaches. The latter assert that perceptual experience constitutively involves those things that a subject experiences, for example objects, properties (or property instances), relations, or, most commonly, some combination thereof. Crucially, since the perceptual experience constitutively involves the relevant entity, there is no opportunity for the experience to be variously accurate of, or satisfied by, that entity. That is, experiential states conceived in this way make no appeal to truth-conditions or accuracy-conditions in the way that contents do, and thus they are not representational.

The two acquaintance-based chapters in this Handbook differ on what they take perceivers to be acquainted with. According to naïve or direct realism, the topic of Campbell's contribution (Chapter 25), in perception, subjects are acquainted with the objective reality before them. Thus, perceptual experience constitutively involves objective or mind-independent entities in our world. To have a perceptual experience is to be *open to* the world before you. By contrast, the indirect realist views discussed by Maund (Chapter 24) hold that in perception subjects are acquainted with mind-dependent entities like sense-data. Thus, perceptual experience constitutively involves sense-data. Experiences of these mind-dependent entities are typically taken to generate the possibility of indirect perceptions of the objective world. Before introducing more machinery, it is worth making three clarifications.

First, it is fairly straightforward that whereas direct realism is constructed to secure direct perception of the objective world, indirect realism is constructed to secure at most indirect perception of the objective world. One might ask: should the representational approach be understood as a model that permits direct perception of the objective world, or as a model that permits only indirect perception of the objective world? This is a contentious issue, in part, but not only because there are controversies surrounding what counts as direct or indirect perception. It is nonetheless fair to say that representationalists have sought to avoid asserting that we can only indirectly perceive the objective world. This may be because representationalism permits direct perception of the objective world, or because it is a theory in which the question of how directly we can perceive the world doesn't apply in any straightforward sense. Detractors roughly argue that, because contents are essential to the representationalist account of perceptual experience, and by their nature contents are distinct from the objective world, perceptions of the objective world are in some sense "mediated" by contents. We won't wade into these waters more deeply than this.

Second, is the indirect realist approach a representationalist view? While it is true that on this view perceivers are acquainted with mind-dependent entities like sense-data, this question can nonetheless arise in a number of ways. Might perceivers also perceptually represent sense-data? Might sense-data represent the objective world? Perhaps most crucially, aren't the indirect perceptions perceivers have of the objective world representational states (perceivers certainly aren't acquainted with the objective world on this account)? It is a well-known historical fact that indirect realist views were originally called "representative realist" views, a matter that caused confusion when what we're calling "representationalism" came to the fore. Our own view is that this is a complicated question (see for example Maund's chapter in this volume and Macpherson 2014), and that on many, though not all, formulations of indirect realism perceptual representation is utilized in some way or other. Let us move on.

Third, there is much value to hybrid views proposing that perceptual experience involves both acquaintance with *and* representation of the objective world. However, since there is no consensus on the landscape for such views (two sources are Brown 2012 and Schellenberg 2014) there is no chapter in this Handbook dedicated to the topic.

Given the complications inherent in representationalism and indirect realism, and the simplicity of the naïve realist thesis that perceptual experience is constituted by being acquainted with the objective reality before the subject, why not be a naïve realist? Matters are not this straightforward because we have yet to focus on how these accounts deal with perceptual illusions and hallucinations, otherwise known as the "bad" cases in perception. Indeed representationalism and indirect realism were developed in part with an eye to giving a compelling account of (a) what is happening in bad cases and (b) why there seem to be similarities between the bad and good (veridical perceptual) cases. Regarding (a), there are numerous kinds of perceptual illusions and hallucinations that need explanation, something that can be safely inferred from our discussion to this point. Regarding (b), in theory a hallucination of a blue ball can be subjectively indistinguishable from a perception of a blue ball, and illusions in which one experiences a blue ball to be purple can be indistinguishable from experiences of a purple ball as purple. Here is an over-simplified guide of how to incorporate these issues into our three accounts of perceptual experience.

According to representationalism, perceptual experience is explained in terms of perceptual contents. Thus, perceptual illusions and hallucinations are states whose contents are to some degree or other not satisfied by the world before the subject—or it is simply luck that they are. Similarities between good and bad perceptual cases are explained in terms of similarities in perceptual contents. Suppose one is having an experience as of a blue ball. This means that one is perceptually expressing a content such as <there is blue ball>. If the state is hallucinatory then that content is either not satisfied by the world before the subject—or it is merely luck that it is (to allow for the possibility of veridical hallucination). If the state is illusory then at least part of the content is not satisfied by the world before the subject (for example, a purple ball is before the subject)—or it is merely luck that it is so satisfied (to allow for the possibility of veridical illusions). If the state is a case of veridical perception (a good case) then the whole content is satisfied by the world before the subject, and that content is connected up to the world in the right way to rule out luck playing a role in the content being satisfied. In our example, there is a blue ball before the subject and the blue ball is connected to the content in the right way.

The indirect realist model is similar, except perceptual experiences are explained in terms of sense-data instead of perceptual contents. Thus, perceptual illusions and hallucinations involve being acquainted with sense-data whose features to some degree or other do not "match" the objective world before the subject—or are not connected up to it in the right way. Subjective similarities between good and bad perceptual cases are explained in terms of similarities between the sense-data experienced in these cases. Suppose again that one is having an experience as of a blue ball. It follows that one is acquainted with a blue, round sense-datum. If the state is hallucinatory, then the world before the subject contains no blue ball—or it is merely luck that it is (to allow for the possibility of veridical hallucination). If the state is illusory, then there is a partial match between the sense-data and the world (for example, a purple ball is before the subject)—or it is merely luck that it is so satisfied (to allow for the possibility of veridical illusions). If the state is purely veridical (a good case), then there is a "complete match" between the sense-data and the world before the subject, and the sense-data are connected up to the world in the right way to rule out luck playing a role in the content being satisfied. In our example, there is a blue ball before the subject, and one's round, blue sense-datum is appropriately related to the world.

The naïve realist picture is very different. Perceptual experiences are constituted by acquaintance with the objective reality before the subject. Since bad cases (perceptual illusions and hallucinations) involve failures to pick up on the objective reality before the subject, the naïve realist regards these as fundamentally different kinds of cases from good cases. This is why naïve realism is also called "disjunctivism": one is either in a good case or a bad case, and these are very different kinds of states, despite there being subjective similarities between them. Disjunctivists disagree about how to characterize bad cases, and about how to characterize the subjective similarities between good and bad cases. However, they are often engaged in a collective effort to minimize the number of bad cases, for example arguing that some purported cases of hallucinations are cognitive instead of perceptual, and that some purported cases of illusion involve not perceptual error but awareness of things like objective appearance properties. These important details, however, can be set aside.

What does all of this have to do with colour? As should be plain to this point, colour is a fantastic case study for theories of perceptual experience. Colour is a vivid, familiar phenomenon. It has been studied intensely, yielding a rich stock of explananda. And colour experience plays a substantive role in debates about colour ontology, in part owing to the difficulties many have had with defending colour objectivism. In theory, there are numerous colour ontologies that one could attach to each theory of experience. In practice, there are natural or familiar pairings that are emphasized by each author. With that in mind, here is a brief remark on what readers can find in each chapter in this section.

After outlining representationalism, Pautz (Chapter 23) considers and assesses various colour ontologies that could be expressed within representationalism. These notably include relationalist (what he calls "response-dependent"), objectivist (what he calls "response-independent"), and eliminativist (what he calls "irrealist") ontologies. Maund (Chapter 24) discusses various motives for indirect realism, numerous ways of developing the view, and focuses on applying indirect realism to two colour ontologies: mentalism and relationalism. Campbell (Chapter 25) matches naïve realism with primitive objectivism about colour—this arguably being the most natural ontology for naïve realists. From this perspective he discusses various perceptual phenomena, including the transparency of experience, perceptual colour space, imagination *de re*, Mary the colour scientist, and spectrum inversion.

The final chapter in this section, Breckenridge's contribution (Chapter 26), concerns the perplexing topic of the looks of colours. It is straightforward that the difference between "I see x to be y" and "x looks y" has been important to philosophy of perception. There is a difference between seeing something to be blue and something looking blue. Indeed this difference is often associated with the riddles surrounding colour variation. It is also well known that it is difficult to interpret "x looks y". What precisely does one mean when one says that something looks blue? On one influential analysis, there are comparative, epistemic and phenomenal uses of "looks" statements. On comparative uses, to say that "x looks y" is to say that x looks as ys do (for example, that thing looks as cellphones look, or that thing looks as blue things do). On epistemic uses, "x looks y" means roughly that one is acquiring evidence (or justification), by looking, that something is some way (for example, it looks like that thing is a cellphone, or is a blue thing). On phenomenal uses, "x looks y" means roughly that x is presenting a y appearance (for example, that thing is presenting a cellphone appearance, or a blue appearance). These different senses of "x looks y" are fairly clear, but there are other analyses available, most of which distinguish between two or more senses of "x looks y". Breckenridge discusses the many analyses that have been offered, and proposes a theory according to which all uses of "x looks y" can be reduced to a single, new sense of "looks" introduced in the chapter. Readers are invited to read Breckenridge's chapter for detail.

§6 Language, categories, and thought

This section considers select topics about the vast number of relations between colour on one hand, and language, categorization, and thought on the other. There is one essay each on colour language, colour categorization, and cognitive penetration. Here is a brief summary.

Much work has been done outside of philosophy—in anthropology, literature, history, and psychology—on the cultural variations of colour language. One question is whether there are such variations or not. Another is whether either of the answers that could be given to the question could or should be explained by the physiology of colour vision, colour experience, culture, thought, language alone, all of these, some of these, or none.

This is the topic that Dedrick (Chapter 27) turns his attention to. Given that the different shades of colour form a visual continuum, and given that we divide that continuum into different sets of colours—colours like red and orange ("colour2s" as Dedrick labels them), as opposed to very specific shades of colour ("colour1s"), like the very different particular shades of red that there are—Dedrick asks, "where do the divisions originate? [And w]hat is the basis for our classifications?" (p. 437 of his chapter). Colour1s can be ordered in a natural way using judgements of similarity and difference to yield a colour space. But are colour2 divisions in any way natural? Dedrick explains that Quine thinks not: they are arbitrary and depend on language and culture. But this has proven to be a very contentious answer that has been greatly disputed over the last 50 years or so. Dedrick lays out the arguments for and against the naturalness of the divisions of colour2s. Some of this debate turns on the question of whether language and words on the one hand, or ideas and concepts on the other, of colour2s (presumably based on common perceptual saliences) are more basic. And some of the debate turns on the highly related question of to what extent the divisions of, or names for, colour2s vary across cultures. The greater the lack of variation across cultures, the more reason there is to think that the divisions of colours2 are not arbitrary.

The state of the debate now seems to suggest that there is a subtle interplay between colour language, colour concepts, human culture, and colour vision on our subsequent perceptual experience and/or perceptual judgements involving colour categories. This debate is further examined by Briscoe (Chapter 28), who focuses on the several decades of psychological research on the exact nature of colour categorical perception. He discusses in detail the notions of perceptual salience and linguistic relevance, and what work they might do to explain human categorization behaviour. And, finally, he examines whether colour perception is indeed categorical.

Lastly, the question of whether beliefs and desires can have an effect on the nature of colour perception and/or experience is covered in an essay on cognitive penetration—a re-emerging topic in philosophy of perception and in cognitive psychology in which colour plays a central role. Stokes (Chapter 29), explains why this debate is so important. It concerns the functional and modular organization of the mind, the role of experience in justifying beliefs, and the nature of perceptual experience. As Stokes emphasizes, debates about cognitive penetration sometimes concern what exactly the nature of the phenomenon is that is called "cognitive penetration", and that debate often alerts us to which features of the mind are most interesting or important to us.

Omissions

Despite the length of this volume, and for all of the ground that it covers, we were not able to include essays on all of the topics that might have proved interesting or useful. As previously stated, we have not included a separate chapter on colour blindness, however, several of the other chapters discuss it and Chapters 8 and 11 cover it in some detail. We have no essays that cover colour in philosophical history, before the 20th century. We have no chapter that covers traditional colour dispositionalism in the same sort of detail as some of the other topics in colour ontology, although we hope that this introduction, and the other essays in the ontology section, given the reader enough of an introduction to that topic. Sadly, we have no essay on the development of colour vision. This is quite a neglected topic in philosophy and psychology, and that in part speaks to our inability to cover it. No doubt there are other areas of research on colour that will not have received as much attention as their importance deserves. However, we hope that this volume will sufficiently inspire the philosophical study of colour, and motivate people to further explore this rich and exciting area of study.

Notes

1 Spectrum inversion scenarios (Chapter 13) are ones that philosophers imagine in which someone experiences colours on the opposite side of the colour wheel to another person when looking at the same objects.
2 "Purple Haze" is representative of conscious experiences of colour that Joe Levine (2001) thinks cannot be given an explanation.
3 Mary is philosopher Frank Jackson's (1982) imagined neuroscientist who knows all the physical facts but, as she has experienced only black and white, allegedly does not know all the facts about colour.

References

Allen, K. 2016. *A Naïve Realist Theory of Colour.* Oxford University Press: Oxford, UK.
Brown, D. H. 2006. On the Dual Referent Approach to Colour Theory. *Philosophical Quarterly 56*: 96–113.
Brown, D. H. 2012. Losing Grip on the World: From Illusion to Sense-Data. In A. Raftopoulos & P. Machamer, eds., *Perception, Realism and the Problem of Reference,* pp. 68–95. Cambridge: Cambridge University Press.
Byrne, A., & D. Hilbert, eds. 1997a. *Readings in Color, vol. 1: The Philosophy of Color.* MIT Press: Cambridge, Mass.
Byrne, A., & D. Hilbert, eds. 1997b. *Readings in Color, vol. 2: The Science of Color.* MIT Press: Cambridge, Mass.
Chalmers, D. 2006. Perception and the Fall from Eden. In T. Gendler & J. Hawthorne, eds., *Perceptual Experience,* pp. 49–125. Oxford University Press: Oxford, UK.
Chirimuuta, M. 2015. *Outside Color: Perceptual Science and the Puzzle of Color in Philosophy.* MIT Press: Cambridge, Mass.
Cohen, J., & M. Matthen, eds. 2010. *Color Ontology and Color Science.* MIT Press: Cambridge, Mass.
Gatzia, D. 2010. Colour Fictionalism. *Rivista Di Estetica 1*(43): 109–23.
Gert, J. 2017. *Primitive Colors.* Oxford University Press: Oxford, UK.
Giere, R. 2006. *Scientific Perspectivism.* University of Chicago Press: Chicago, USA.
Hardin, C. L. 1988. *Color for Philosophers, expanded edition.* Hackett: Indianapolis, ID.
Jackson, F. 1982. Epiphenomenal Qualia. *Philosophical Quarterly 32*: 127–36.
Kuehni, R., & A. Schwarz. 2008. *Color Ordered: A Survey of Color Order Systems from Antiquity to the Present.* Oxford University Press: Oxford, UK.
Levine, J. 2001. *Purple Haze: The Puzzle of Consciousness.* Oxford University Press: Oxford, UK.
Macpherson, F. 2014. Is the Sense-Data Theory a Representationalist Theory? *Ratio 27*(4): 369–92.
Maund, B. 1981. Colour—A Case for Conceptual Fission. *Australasian Journal of Philosophy 59*(3): 308–22.
Nagel, T. 1974. What Is it Like to Be a Bat? *The Philosophical Review 83*(4): 435–50.
Nida-Rümelin, M. 1996. Pseudonormal Vision: An Actual Case of Qualia Inversion? *Philosophical Studies 82*(2): 145–57.
Schellenberg, S. 2014. The Relational and Representational Character of Perceptual Experience. In B. Brogaard, ed. *Does Perception Have Content?*, pp. 199–219. Oxford University Press: New York, NY.
Sellars, W. 1956. Empiricism and the Philosophy of Mind. In H. Feigl & M. Scriven, eds., *Minnesota Studies in the Philosophy of Science, vol. I,* pp. 253–329. University of Minnesota Press: Minneapolis, MN.
Silva, M. ed. 2017. *How Colors Matter to Philosophy.* Cham: Springer.
Wilson, M. 2006. *Wandering Significance: An Essay on Conceptual Behavior.* Oxford University Press: Oxford, UK.

PART I

The importance of colour to philosophy

1

COLOUR, COLOUR EXPERIENCE, AND THE MIND-BODY PROBLEM

Brian P. McLaughlin

Experiences of colour are relevant to the mind-body problem, because they are mental states or events. The solution to the mind-body problem turns, in part, on the ontological status of, for instance, experiences of red. Whether the solution turns in part on the ontological status of redness is another matter. Colour experiences are relevant to the mind-body problem, but whether colours are is a controversial issue.

My aim is to explore the relationship between colour and the mind-body problem. By colour, I mean chromatic colour, colour with hue (unique or binary), and achromatic colour (white, black, and shades of grey). I won't take sides either on competing theories of colour or on proposed solutions to the mind-body problem. My concern is just to make explicit the fundamental issues that bear on whether, and, if so how, colour is related to that perennial problem. I'll be engaged in a kind of metaphysical cartography, but will refrain from recommending a location on the map.

Physicalism figures prominently in contemporary discussions of the mind-body problem, either as a doctrine to be defended, or rejected, or as the lesser or greater partner in a comparison with some or other alternative view. I'll begin by stating a necessary condition for physicalism, distinguishing some notions of physicality, and pointing out that it is straightforward that colour is relevant to whether physicalism is true. I'll then turn to the difficult issue of whether the ontological status of colours is tied to the mind-body problem.

I won't attempt to decide the matter. I'll argue only that whether the ontological status of colours is tied to the mind-body problem depends on how colours are related to experiences of colours, an unresolved issue that I won't attempt to resolve.

1 Colour and physicalism

Colour is sometimes invoked in critical discussions of physicalism. For example, Frank Jackson's (1982) version of the knowledge argument against physicalism invokes colours. But his knowledge argument is, in the first instance, about colour experience. We have a colour experience whenever something looks some or other colour to us. Jackson focuses on the experience of something's looking red. Bertrand Russell no doubt had in mind, more generally, visual experience when he argued: "It is obvious that a man who can see knows things which a blind man cannot know; but a blind man can know the whole of physics. Thus the knowledge which other men have and he has not is not a part of physics" (1927: 389). One of the things the sighted know that the (congenitally, completely) blind don't is what it is like to have visual experiences, that is, what it is like for something to look some way. C.D. Broad (1925) invoked the odours of chemicals in his version of the knowledge argument, but his primary focus was on olfactory experience.

Sense experiences are subjective experiences: it is like something for the subject having or undergoing them to have or undergo them. This what-it-is-like for the subject aspect of a subjective experience is its phenomenal character. You could construct a knowledge argument for what it is like to feel the jagged shape of a piece of metal, or for what it is like to feel sand run through your fingers. Tactual experiences of the jagged shape of a piece of metal, and of sand running through your fingers, pose a formidable problem for physicalism. Pieces of metal with jagged shapes, and events such as sand running through fingers arguably don't. Thus, in these cases, even though the subjective experiences in question pose a formidable problem for physicalism, what they are experiences of arguably doesn't.

Colour experiences are subjective experiences, and subjective experiences pose a formidable problem for physicalism. Indeed, of all mental phenomena, they may pose the most formidable problem for that doctrine. Physicalists must tell us how they can accommodate them. If, instead, they deny there are subjective experiences, then they deny our subjectivity.

Colour experiences pose a difficulty for physicalism. Do colours?

Nowadays philosophers who count themselves as physicalists typically aren't nominalists. They typically hold that there are properties, and that instances of certain kinds of properties have causes and effect. I'll take it as given that there are properties, and that instances of certain kinds of properties have causes and effects. If physicalism requires that every instantiated property be a physical property, then whether physicalism is true depends on whether anything has colour properties, and if anything does, whether they are physical properties.

Physicalists, however, typically don't hold that all properties are physical properties. If there are properties, then it seems that they have properties. Given that causes and effects are property instances, among the properties a property can have is the property of being such that instances of it occupy a certain conditional causal role, a certain conditional role as cause and/or effect. Such causal role properties of properties are called 'functional properties'. Physicalists typically maintain that there are functional properties.[1] The properties that have functional properties, realize them. Realization, in this sense, is just a property's having a causal role property. The property with the causal role property realizes the functional property. Physicalists who countenance functional properties readily acknowledge that it is possible for such properties to be possessed by properties that are not physical. Such physicalists maintain that it isn't necessary for the truth of physicalism that it is only possible for functional properties to be realized by physical properties. They maintain that physicalism requires only that in our world and worlds relevantly like our world (of this, more later), functional properties are ultimately realized by physical properties.

What is it, though, for a property to be a physical property? There is a dispute about that. (The literature is large, but see, for example, Crane and Mellor (1990) and Montero (2009).) If, for instance, a property is a physical property if it can be possessed by a physical object, then colours are physical properties provided that a physical object can have them. Thus, for instance, if a rock can be brown, then brownness is a physical property in the sense in question. Physicalists, however, typically don't invoke this notion of a physical property. They take it as a substantive issue whether mental properties are physical properties even if beings with mentality are complex physical objects. Even if Cartesian substance dualism is false, it remains whether Cartesian property dualism is true.

It is nowadays fairly common for physicalists to tie the idea of physicality to physics. It wouldn't do, however, for the purposes of characterizing physicalism to say that something is physical just in case it is posited by current physics. Physicalists want to allow for new discoveries. Moreover, there is good reason to think that not all of current physics is true. (Reconciling quantum mechanics and general relativity, for example, may require a scientific revolution.) It also won't do to say that something is physical just in case it is posited by the physics that is in fact true of our world, whatever that physics is. It is an *a posteriori* issue whether Cartesian physics is true of our world, a physics according to which immaterial minds can influence the movements of atoms in the brain. If physicists can be trusted, Cartesian physics is patently false. But we don't know *a priori* that Cartesian physics is false.

Perhaps the current leading strategy for physicalists who appeal to physics is to take the physical to be whatever is posited by current physics or some recognizable descendant of current physics.[2] Although the notion of a recognizable descendant is quite vague, it has substantial content. On this notion of the physical, if the physics that is true of our world (a physics that is now written only in a book in Plato's Heaven) is not at least a recognizable descendant of current physics, then physicalism is false. This notion of physicality thus ties the fate of physicalism to the assumption that current physics is at least basically on the right track to the physics that is true of our world.

Some physicalists characterize physicality just by appeal to microphysics, but some appeal as well to macrophysics. All physicalists, however, exclude a certain area of psychophysics as part of physics properly so-called, namely, the psycho-part, the part that invokes sensations and the like. By "physics", let's mean both microphysics and macrophysics. (I'll side-step the issue of whether microphysics completely determines macrophysics, an issue orthogonal to my main concerns here.) The idea, then, is that a property is a physical property just in case it is posited by current (micro or macro) physics or some recognizable descendant of current physics. For now, let's use 'physical property' to mean such a property. (Later, I'll invoke some broader notions of a physical property.)

Current physics doesn't posit colours, at least *as such*. It contains no talk of red, green, grey, or the like.[3] Macrophysics posits light dispositions that surfaces can possess such as reflectances, spectral reflectances, and triples of integrated reflectances. But in so doing, it doesn't, thereby, posit colours *as such*, even if surface colours should turn out to be reflectance properties of some sort (a controversial matter). Nor would any physics that is a recognizable descendant of current physics posit colours as such. If the physics that is, in fact, true of our world will posit colour as such, then it won't be a recognizable descendent of current physics.

It is certainly not *a priori* that colours are physical properties. Nor is it *a priori* that colours are causal role properties of physical properties. There is, however, nothing distinctive about colour properties in that regard. Virtually all the properties that folks ordinarily talk about, and, even to put it conservatively, most of the properties cited in the special sciences, including chemistry and biology, are such that it is not *a priori* that they are physical properties or causal role properties of physical properties.

There is a problem of the one and the many for science. Why do we have many sciences rather than just one science? The initial answer is that we have many sciences rather than one, because we find it necessary for explanatory and predictive purposes to posit properties and kinds at various levels of complexity and organization, properties and kinds that figure in proprietary laws. For the most part, the properties and kinds in question are not posited as such by current physics, would not be posited as such by any recognizable descendent of current physics, and are not such that it is *a priori* that they are functional properties and kinds that are realized by such properties and kinds.

Physicalists acknowledge that. But what, then, exactly, is the doctrine of physicalism? There is no consensus about that. It is nowadays fairly widely held, however, that any doctrine deserving of the name "physicalism" should entail the following global supervenience thesis:

> Any minimal physical duplicate of our world is a duplicate *simpliciter* of our world.
>
> *(Jackson 1998: 12)*

That is to say, it is fairly widely held that physicalism is true *only if* that supervenience thesis is true.[4] I'll assume that the supervenience thesis indeed states a necessary condition for physicalism: physicalism is true only if the supervenience thesis is true.

A duplicate *simpliciter* of our world is a possible world that is exactly like our world in every respect, and so an exact duplicate of our world. A world is a physical duplicate of our world just in case it is exactly like our world in every physical respect: with respect to the world-wide pattern of distribution of kinds of physical objects and physical properties, with respect to what physical laws hold, and so on. Call all and only the worlds that are physical duplicates of our world "P-worlds". Then, following David Chalmers and Frank Jackson, let us say that "a minimal P-world is a P-world that outstrips no other P-world" (2001: 317). Here is what it is for a world to outstrip another world: "a world W1 outstrips a world W2 if W1 contains a qualitative duplicate of W2 as a proper part and the reverse is not the case" (2001: 317). A world is a minimal physical duplicate of our world just in case it is a minimal P-world.

The supervenience thesis is valuable for assessing physicalism because it is open for a single kind of case to show that the supervenience thesis is false, and thus that physicalism is false. If there is even a single respect in which some minimal physical duplicate of our world fails to be a duplicate *simpliciter* of our world, then physicalism is false. If, for instance, there is a minimal physical duplicate of our world that differs from our world in any way whatsoever with respect to its world-wide pattern of distribution of colour properties, then physicalism is false.[5] It is an *a posteriori* issue whether a minimal physical duplicate of our world would have the same world-wide pattern of distribution of colour properties as our world. Thus, to repeat: colours pose an issue for physicalism. But, to repeat again, there is nothing distinctive about colour in that respect.

It is useful to see that the supervenience thesis is equivalent to a certain claim about our world, namely that our world is a minimal physical duplicate of itself. To see this, note, first, that if our world is a minimal physical duplicate of itself, then any minimal physical duplicate of our world is a duplicate *simpliciter* of our world. To see why, suppose that there is a minimal physical duplicate of our world that is not a duplicate *simpliciter* of our world. Then, our world outstrips that world. It follows that our world is not a minimal P-world, and so not a minimal physical duplicate of itself. Given contraposition for entailment,[6] if our world is a minimal physical duplicate of itself, then any minimal physical duplicate of our world is a duplicate *simpliciter* of our world. To see the implication in the other direction, suppose that any minimal physical duplicate of our world is a duplicate *simpliciter* of our world. Then, our world is a minimal physical duplicate of itself. To see why, suppose that our world is not a minimal physical duplicate of itself. Then, it outstrips some P-world, namely the P-world that is a qualitative duplicate of a proper part of our world. That world is a minimal P-world, yet not a duplicate *simpliciter* of our world. Thus, if any minimal physical duplicate of our world is a duplicate *simpliciter* of our world, then our world is a minimal physical duplicate of itself. The claim that our world is a minimal physical duplicate of itself is thus equivalent to the supervenience thesis.

Our world is, trivially, a physical duplicate of itself: it is exactly like itself in every respect, and so in every physical respect. What is controversial, indeed, deeply controversial, is whether our world is a minimal physical duplicate of itself. That is required for physicalism to be true, which is one reason why physicalism is deeply controversial.

As I noted, physicalists acknowledge that there are contingent properties that are not physical properties. But what kinds of non-physical properties can physicalism countenance? I mentioned that it is assumed that it can countenance certain functional properties, since the physical properties instantiated in our world will have causal role properties. But the initial general answer to the question is: physicalism can countenance whatever contingent properties are such that the way the world is with respect to them is compatible with physicalism. That answer, however, is unhelpful since I haven't stated both necessary and sufficient conditions for physicalism. I won't attempt to state such conditions here. So I won't attempt to provide a general informative answer to the question. I have, however, stated a necessary condition for physicalism, and that yields a partial answer to the question. That will do for present purposes.

Let's call a contingent property that physicalism can countenance "a physically kosher property" ("physical$_k$ property" for short). The following is a necessary condition for being a physical$_k$ property:

> A contingent property is a physical$_k$ property only if it is such that the way that our world is with respect to it is compatible with our world being a minimal physical duplicate of itself.

Given this condition, it is possible to show that physicalism cannot countenance a certain would-be property by showing that the way our world is with respect to it is incompatible with our world being a minimal physical duplicate of itself.

Appeal to this necessary condition for being a contingent physical$_k$ property suffices to show that colour properties pose an issue for physicalism. The same, though, is true of most special science properties, including various chemical properties, given the notion of a physical property that we have been employing, namely being a property posited by current physics or a recognizable descendent of current physics. Given that notion of a physical property, it is an *a posteriori* issue whether any minimal physical duplicate of our world would be a chemical duplicate of our world. Colours, though, would pose a problem for physicalism even if we broadened the notion of physicality as follows: a property is a physical property just in case it is posited by current physics or chemistry or a recognizable descendent of one of them. Current chemistry doesn't posit colours as such, and no recognizable descendent of current chemistry would posit colours as such. This is so even if surface colours, say, turn out to be identical with certain molecular properties that are posited as such by chemistry, since surface colours won't be posited as such by chemistry. Even given this more liberal notion of physicality, then, colours pose an issue for physicalism. Indeed, even if we appeal to the yet more liberal notion of a physical property as a property posited by current physics, or current chemistry, or current neuroscience, or some recognizable descendent of one of them, it is still a controversial matter whether colours are physical properties. Moreover, even given this broader notion of a physical property, it is still controversial whether a minimal physical duplicate of our world would be exactly like our world with respect to the distribution of colour properties, and so whether the correspondingly more liberal notion of physicalism is true.[7]

Just in order to avoid the eye-sore "physical$_k$ property", I'll now extend the elastic notion of a physical property to physical$_k$ properties, counting them as physical properties, too. I'll take the notion a physical property in the characterization of a world's being a minimal physical duplicate of our world, however, to be any property posited by the physics, or by the chemistry, and or by the neuroscience true of our world, provided that each is, respectively, a recognizable descendant of current physics, chemistry, and neuroscience. Call that notion of a physical property, "a physical $_{\text{chemical or neuroscientific property}}$". Thus, the notion of a minimal physical duplicate of our world is to be understood in terms of the notion of a physical $_{\text{chemical or neuroscientific property}}$, but I'll now use "physical property" in a very broad sense to mean a physical$_k$ property. Given this expanded notion of a physical property, we now have only a necessary condition for a property's being a physical property (despite having a necessary and sufficient condition for being a physical $_{\text{chemical or neuroscientific}}$ property), since we have only a necessary condition for physicalism. But it will suffice to do the required work in what follows.

Not only colour experiences, then, but colours themselves pose an issue for physicalism. That is straightforward. Physicalists must justify the claim any minimal physical duplicate of our world would have exactly the same pattern of distribution of colour properties as our world.

2 Colour and mentality

It is trivial that the ontological status of colours bears on whether physicalism is true. The question of whether, and if so how, the ontological status of colours is tied to the mind-body problem is by no means straightforward.

Colours are properties, and I take it that whether the ontological status of colours is tied to the mind-body problem turns on how colours are related to mental properties. A central part of the mind-body problem is whether mental properties are physical properties. I cannot canvass here the many and varied would-be solutions to the mind-body problem. In addressing the issue of whether the ontological status of colours is tied to the mind-body problem, I'll focus just on whether the issue of whether colour properties are physical properties is linked to the issue of whether certain mental properties are physical properties. It will have to suffice for me to claim that the reasons for and against such linkage will be relevant to any would-be solution to the mind-body problem, even one that entails the falsity of both dualism and physicalism.

Of course, if colours are mental properties, then it is trivial that the ontological status of colours is tied to the mind-body problem. Galileo maintained that colours "reside in consciousness", so that "if the living creature were removed", they "would be wiped out and annulated" (1623). On this view, although entities in the physically constituted scenes before our eyes look coloured to us, they are not actually coloured. Our visual consciousness merely projects colours onto them. Let's assume that the residents of consciousness are mental. Then, if Galileo is right, colours are mental, and so are trivially part of the mind-body problem.

We experience colours whenever something looks some way to us. In 'The Refutation of Idealism', G.E. Moore (1903) reminded us that although experiences are mental, what an experience is an experience of is not, thereby, mental. An experience of a piece of metal is mental, but the piece of metal isn't, thereby, mental. Although the ontological status of metal is relevant to physicalism, it is arguably irrelevant to the mind-body problem. The fact that we have experiences of colour is itself no reason at all to think that colours are mental properties. Colours, however, may be related to experiences of them in a way that pieces of metal aren't related to experiences of them.

Newton, who unweaved the rainbow, told us: "the [light] rays, to speak properly, are not coloured. In them there is nothing else than a certain power or disposition to stir up a sensation of this or that colour" (1704/1998: 125). Powers to stir up sensations of colour are not themselves mental properties. If, however, colours just are such powers, then colours are tied to those sensations in a way that makes the ontological status of colours depend on the ontological status of sensations of colour. If colours are such powers, then colours will fail to be physical properties if sensations of colour fail to be physical. So, on this view, the ontological status of colours is tied to the mind-body problem.

Although a number of contemporary theories of colour are variants on Newton's idea, this sort of view of colour is by no means the only one in the contemporary literature. Some theorists hold that colours can be found among light-dispositions such as spectral reflectances, or among other kinds of light-dispositions. Such light-dispositions are physical, so this is a kind of physicalist view of colours. As we'll see in due course, even if such a view is correct, the ontological status of colours may nevertheless fail to be linked to the mind-body problem.

I maintain that whether the ontological status of colours is tied to the mind-body problem depends on how colours are related to colour experiences. Whether the ontological status of colours is relevant to the mind-body problem doesn't, however, just turn on whether colours are non-contingently related to colour experiences. To see that, suppose that the causal theory of properties is true, and that a certain property has as one of its forward-looking causal features that it would produce a colour experience in certain conditions (Shoemaker 1980).[8] On the causal theory of properties, that forward-looking causal feature will be an essential property of the property in question, and so there will be a non-contingent relation between that property and the property of being an experience of colour. But whether the property with that forward-looking causal feature is a physical property could be independent of whether being an experience of colour is a physical property; and whether being an experience of colour is a physical property could be independent of whether the property in question is a physical property. So colours could be non-contingently related to colour experience, and yet the ontological status of colours be independent of the mind-body problem.

In due course, I'll formulate the issue of whether the ontological status of colours is tied to the mind-body problem in part by appeal to a certain "Euthyphro question". But let's first turn to Euthyphro questions themselves, and then to ways of type individuating experiences.

3 Euthyphro questions

Euthyphro questions are so-called because they resemble a question Socrates asked Euthyphro, namely (changing the wording a bit) whether something is right because the Gods command it, or whether the Gods command something because it is right (Plato 1914).[9] The "because" here isn't that of causal explanation. The questions can be reformulated using "in virtue of" rather than "because". "In virtue of" implies "because of", but "in virtue of" is typically used to express a non-causal explanatory relation (McLaughlin 1989/2008). It is typically so used, but not always so used. "The team won in virtue of its superior speed" expresses a kind of causal explanation. But I'll be concerned only with the non-causal use. The kind of explanatory relation in question is, arguably, more akin to Aristotle's notion of formal causation than his notion of efficient causation. In any case, the relevant notion of one thing being the case in virtue of another thing's being the case should be clear enough for present purposes. My unit set exists in virtue of my existing (Fine 2001). I'm touching my laptop in virtue of touching the keys of my laptop (see, e.g., Jackson 1977). And, I live in New Jersey in virtue of living in Warren County.

Three points should be noted. First, "in virtue of" doesn't mean "only in virtue of" (McLaughlin 1989/2008). Although I touch my laptop in virtue of touching the keys of my laptop, I don't touch my laptop only in virtue of touching the keys of my laptop. The keys must be appropriately attached to my laptop. Second, the in-virtue-of relation is asymmetric. It is a kind of explanatory relation, and explanation is asymmetric. If A explains B, then B cannot explain A (in the same sense of "explain"). Third, since the in-virtue-of relation is an explanatory relation, it holds between facts only under descriptions or conceptualization of the facts. A fact explains another only under descriptions or conceptualizations of each of them. The context "___ in virtue of ..." is hyper-intensional: necessarily co-extensive terms aren't substitutable *salva veritate*. To avoid tedious prolixity, I won't explicitly appeal to descriptions or conceptualizations in what follows. I'll take it to be understood that such relativization is required. In the cases I'll discuss, it should be clear what the relevant kinds of descriptions or conceptualizations are. Earlier I used "as such" to indicate relativization to a description, or term, or concept. I'll continue to so use it.

Consider this Euthyphro question: Is an act illegal in a country in virtue of the laws of the country forbidding it, or do the laws of a country forbid it in virtue of its being illegal in the country. This one is easy. An act is illegal in a country in virtue of the laws of the country forbidding it.

Water is a kind of stuff. We have subjective experiences of water whenever some body of water looks (feels, etc.) some way to us. Consider this Euthyphro question: Is a kind of stuff water in virtue of a relation it bears to experiences of water, or is an experience an experience of water in virtue of the relation it bears to the kind water? I would answer: An experience is an experience of water in virtue of a relation it bears to the kind water.

Experiences of water played an epistemic role in helping us to locate water among physical stuff. But the ontological status of water isn't tied to the mind-body problem. We've determined that water is H_2O. That is compatible with all extant theories of mind. ("All" means all, and so includes idealism. Idealists readily acknowledge that water is H_2O.) Given that water is H_2O, the inhabitants of Hilary Putnam's (1975) Twin Earth don't have water experiences. They don't have water experiences, even though they have experiences with the same phenomenal characters—the same what-it's-like for the subject aspects—as the various experiences we have of water. They don't have water experiences, because they don't have experiences induced by the presence of water.

It is both the case that whether water is physical is independent of whether water experiences are physical, and also the case that whether water experiences are physical is independent of whether water is physical. It is, no doubt, obvious that even though water is physical, it is another issue whether experiences of water are physical. The converse claim is not obvious, but it's true, too. Had water turned out not to be physical, it wouldn't have followed that experiences of water aren't physical. To see why, consider a possible scenario involving a kind of stuff different from water. Suppose that there is somewhere in the vast universe a kind of stuff entirely unanticipated by contemporary physics, chemistry, and biology, a kind of stuff so different from the posits of such theories that no theory that is a recognizable descendent of any of them will posit it. We can imagine that the stuff is as different from their posits as superconductivity is from the posits of the ancient air, earth, fire, and water theory. The stuff thus wouldn't be physical. Suppose further, then, that some future astronaut encounters some of the stuff, and it looks some way to her.[10] It is compatible with this scenario that visual experiences are physical (because some or other physicalist theory of visual experiences is true), even though the stuff in question isn't physical. Thus, it could turn out that visual experiences of the stuff are physical, even though the stuff itself isn't physical. Where X is a kind of stuff, whether experiences of X are physical and whether X is physical are independent issues.

Colour isn't, of course, a kind of stuff. Colours are properties. So, let's turn to properties.

Consider the Euthyphro question for the experience of embarrassment and the property of being embarrassing. A situation, for instance, can be embarrassing, and so have the property of being embarrassing. We can all describe types of situations that we take to be embarrassing situations. We experience embarrassment, in the relevant sense, by feeling embarrassed.[11] The

(EG3) A property is redness for a P in V in virtue of being the most determinable property that disposes its bearers to look red to a P in V.[19]

Looks-red states or events are to be here understood as visual experiences of red, typed by their phenomenal characters. An instance of (EG1) is: a property is redness for a normal visual perceiver in normal viewing circumstances in virtue of being the disposition to look red to a normal visual perceiver in normal viewing circumstances.[20] In recent decades, a number of experience-grounded theorists of colour have maintained that kinds of perceivers and kinds of viewing circumstances must be individuated far more finely (Jackson and Pargetter 1987; McLaughlin 2000, 2003; and Cohen 2004, 2009), because of "standard variation" (McLaughlin 2003): what colour something looks can vary for normal perceivers in normal viewing circumstances.[21]

On a role-functionalist theory of dispositions, dispositions are states of being in some state or other that occupies a certain causal role (McLaughlin 1994). For example, on a role-functionalist view of dispositions, water-solubility is the property of having some property or other that disposes its bearers to dissolve when immersed in water. If a role-functionalist view of dispositions is assumed, then (EG1) and (EG2) are equivalent on a fairly uncontroversial assumption, namely that something has a role-functionalist disposition in virtue of having a property that has the property of having a certain appropriate causal role. Given that view of dispositions, on (EG1) and (EG2), whether redness is a physical property will depend on whether being an experience of red is a physical property. If the experience of red is not physical, then redness is not physical (even if the property that has the relevant causal role property is physical). On these theories, which generalize, the ontological status of colours is tied to the mind-body problem.

(EG3) is a filler-functionalist experience-grounded theory of colour: colours are the properties, if any, that fill the (relativized) colour roles. Unlike (EG1) and (EG2), (EG3) is not a relationalist theory of colour (Cohen 2009), since it doesn't entail that colours are relations to experiences. But like (EG1) and (EG2), (EG3) is a relativist theory of colour. (EG3) is compatible with colour physicalism (for relativized colours), because it could turn out to be the case that there is a physical property that is the most determinable property that disposes its bearers to look red to a P in V. But it doesn't entail that the most determinable property that disposes its bearers to look red to a P in V is a physical property. The filler-functionalist experience-grounded theory of colour is logically compatible with the property in question being a non-physical property.[22] On the filler-functionalist theory of colour, the ontological status of colours is independent of the mind-body problem. Colours can be physical, and colour experiences non-physical; and colour experiences can be physical, yet colours be physical. For instance, redness for a P in V might be a physical property, yet experiences of red not be physical. Moreover, experiences of red might be physical yet redness for a P in a V-circumstance not be.

One cannot hold both an experience-grounded theory of colour and a colour-grounded theory of colour experiences, on pain of inconsistency. The distinction between theorists who hold a colour-grounded theory of colour experience and theorists who hold an experience-grounded theory of colour cuts across some familiar distinctions.

Some proponents of colour-grounded theories of colour experience hold that colours are physical (see, e.g., Campbell 1994; Dretske 1995; and Tye 2000). But some hold that colours are mental (see, e.g., Jackson 1977; Chalmers 2006; and Pautz 2006). And, some hold that colours are neutral properties, and so neither mental nor physical (see, e.g., Broad 1925). Proponents of colour-grounded theories of colour experiences can thus be physicalists or non-physicalists about the experience of red. But their stand on whether the experience is physical depends, in part, on their stand on whether redness is physical. It is open to proponents of experience-grounded theories of colour, whether they are role-functionalists or filler-functionalists, to be physicalists about colour or instead to be non-physicalists about colour. On the role-functionalist experience-grounded theory of colour, however, colours will be physical only if colour experiences are physical, while on the filler-functionalist experience-grounded theory of colour, as I noted, whether colours are physical is independent of whether colour experiences are physical. The distinction between colour-grounded theorists of colour experience and experience-grounded theorists of colour thus cuts across the distinction between physicalists and non-physicalist about colour, and between the distinction between physicalists and non-physicalists about colour experience.

It is also the case that some proponents of colour-grounded theories of colour experience are colour realists in that they maintain that some physical things are actually coloured in the way in which they look coloured (Campbell 1994; Dretske 1995; and Tye 2000), while some are colour irrealists in the sense that they hold that nothing is coloured in the way that it looks coloured (Chalmers 2006; Pautz 2006, forthcoming). It is open to proponents of experience-grounded theorist of colour, whether they are role-functionalists or filler-functionalists, to be colour realists or to be colour irrealists (where colour irrealism is understood as the view that nothing is in fact coloured). The filler-functionalist experience-grounded theory of colour is compatible with colour irrealism, since it could prove to be the case that no matter how specific the kind of perceiver and the kind of viewing circumstance, there is no most determinable property that disposes its bearers to look red to that kind of perceiver in that kind of viewing circumstance. If that is so, then there is no such property as redness for a P in V, even if there are things disposed to produce experiences of red in a P in V. The role-functionalist experience-grounded theory of colour is compatible with colour irrealism, understood as the view that nothing is in fact coloured, because it is logically possible that nothing in fact has the disposition to look coloured to perceivers in any kind of viewing circumstance. Thus, the distinction between colour-grounded theorists of colour experience and experience-grounded theorists of colour cuts across the distinction between colour realists and colour irrealists.

As I noted above, on the role-functionalist experience-grounded theory of colour, the ontological status of colours is tied to the mind-body problem. If experiences of colour are not physical, then colours are not physical. In contrast, the filler-functionalist experience-grounded theory of colour doesn't entail that the ontological status of colours is linked to the mind-body problem. On the filler-functionalist experience-grounded theory of colour, whether colours are physical is entirely independent of whether experiences of colour are physical.

7 Conclusion

In summary, although it is trivial that the ontological status of colours is relevant to whether physicalism is true, it is by no means trivial whether the ontological status of colours is relevant to the mind-body problem. There is a distinction between colour-grounded theories of colour experience and experience-grounded theories of colour. No one can hold both kinds of theories, on pain of inconsistency. If neither a colour-grounded theory of colour experience nor an experience-grounded (nor any mental-grounded) theory of colour is correct, then the ontological status of colours is independent of the mind-body problem. If, however, a colour-grounded theory of colour experience is correct, then the ontological status of colour is tied to the mind-body problem. Moreover, if a role-functionalist experience-grounded theory of colour is correct, then the ontological status of colours is tied to the mind-body problem. But if a filler-functionalist experience-grounded theory of colour is correct, then the ontological status of colours is independent of the mind-body problem.

Whether the ontological status of colour is tied to the mind-body problem remains unsettled since these matters remain unsettled. My aim has not been to determine whether it is so tied, but rather just to pinpoint what the issue turns on. It turns on how colours are related to colour experiences.[23]

Notes

1 Some philosophers maintain that there are no functional properties, only functional concepts (see Kim 1998; and Shoemaker 2007). Let it suffice to note that I'm using "properties" in an abundant sense rather than a sparse sense (Lewis 1986). As I'm using "properties", properties are just ways things might be. If there are properties, there are ways they might be, and so second-order properties. Functional properties are kinds of second-order properties.
2 I take the useful phrase "recognizable descendant" from Jackson 2007.
3 "Colour" is used in physics in discussing quarks, but it should go without saying that it is a different use of "colour" than one that concerns us.
4 One reason that the truth of this (global) supervenience thesis is not a sufficient condition for physicalism is that it is compatible with the existence of a necessary God (Jackson 1998) and physicalism isn't. There are other reasons why the truth of the supervenience thesis is not a sufficient condition for physicalism, reasons that appeal only to contingent properties, properties that something can have and can fail to have (Hawthorne 2002). I won't discuss them since it isn't my concern here to define physicalism.
5 Jackson (1998) has explicitly addressed the issue of whether physicalism, understood as above, can accommodate colours.
6 It holds in classical logic, and in many, though by no means all, non-classical logics.
7 See Byrne 2006, an insightful and delightful paper, for a discussion of problems colours pose for physicalism.
8 According to the causal theory of properties, no two properties can have exactly the same forward-looking and backward-looking causal features (Shoemaker 1980, 2006). The theory is not intended to apply to causal features themselves, which count as properties in our abundant sense, specifically as functional properties.
9 Crispin Wright (1994) has called attention to the importance of Euthyphro questions in metaphysics, including the metaphysics of colour.
10 In assuming this, we needn't assume that it reflects or emits light. It might take some other causal path to activity in the optic nerve of the astronaut, and, thereafter, the usual consequences ensue resulting in the astronaut having a visual experience of the stuff.
11 This is a determinable feeling that has different determinates. There are many ways of feeling embarrassed.
12 Heat isn't mean kinetic energy. Temperature isn't mean kinetic energy either. There is negative temperature, but there is no such thing as negative mean kinetic energy. Heat, or temperature, in an ideal gas is mean kinetic energy. That doesn't entail that heat = mean kinetic energy. Temperature is, arguably, a causal role property, and mean kinetic energy is the property that plays or occupies the role in an ideal gas. But I won't fuss about such matters. Kripke's distinction is clear enough.
13 The experience of red is a highly determinable type of experience, one that has many determinates. The experience of maroon, for instance, is a determinate of the experience of red. But I'll take it that the highly determinable type of experience has a distinctive (yet highly determinable) type of phenomenal character.
14 Hereafter, I'll often leave this qualification unvoiced.
15 Hilbert's position in Hilbert 1987 is complicated in that he also held that there are anthropocentric colours, and that they are triples of integrated reflectances. If there, he took take triples of integrated reflectances to be anthropocentric colours in virtue of their being the properties that things look when they look coloured to a normal human perceiver in normal viewing circumstances, then he held there an experience-based theory of anthropocentric colours. I'll leave that exegetical question open.
16 Versions of this kind of view can be found, I maintain, in, for example, Broad 1925; Jackson 1977; Campbell 1994; Dretske 1995; Tye 2000; Chalmers 2006; and Pautz 2006, forthcoming.
17 See, for example, Mark Johnston 1992.
18 See Cohen 2004, 2009.

19 See McLaughlin 2003.
20 See, for example, McGinn 1983; and Wright 1994.
21 See also, in this connection, Cohen, Hardin, and McLaughlin 2006; and Cohen, Hardin, and McLaughlin 2007.
22 Cohen 2009 mistakenly claims that the filler-functionalist theory of colour in McLaughlin 2003 is a physicalist theory of colour. Given global theoretical considerations, I maintain that if there are properties that fill the colour roles, they are physical properties. I'd be an eliminativist about colours if no such physical properties could be found. But that position isn't dictated by my theory of colour. That filler-functionalist theory is perfectly compatible with the falsity of physicalism.
23 Thanks are due to Janet Levin for comments on an earlier version of this chapter.

References

Broad, C.D. (1925), *The Mind and Its Place in Nature* (London: Kegan Paul, Trench, Trubner & Co., Ltd).

Byrne, A. (2006), 'Color and the Mind-Body Problem', *dialectica* 60, 3: 223–44.

Byrne, A., and Hilbert, D. (1997), 'Colors and Reflectances', in A. Byrne and D.R. Hilbert (eds.), *Readings on Color, Volume 1: The Philosophy of Color* (Cambridge, Mass.: MIT Press).

Campbell, J. (1994), 'A Simple View of Color', in J. Haldane and C. Wright (eds.), *Reality, Representation, and Projection* (Oxford: Clarendon Press), 257–69.

Chalmers, D. (2006), 'Perception and the Fall From Eden', in T.S. Gendler and J. Hawthorne (eds.), *Perceptual Experience* (New York: Oxford University Press).

Chalmers, D., and Jackson, F. (2001), 'Conceptual Analysis and Reductive Explanation', *Philosophical Review* 110: 315–60.

Cohen, J. (2004), 'Color Properties and Color Ascriptions: A Relational Manifesto', *The Philosophical Review*, 133, 4: 451–506.

Cohen, J. (2009), *The Red & The Real* (Oxford: Oxford University Press).

Cohen, J., Hardin, L., and McLaughlin, B.P. (2006), 'True Colors', *Analysis*, 66: 355–40.

Cohen, J., Hardin, L., and McLaughlin, B.P. (2007), 'The Truth About the "The Truth About True Blue"', *Analysis* 67: 294: 162–6.

Crane, T., and Mellor, D.H. (1990), 'There Is No Question of Physicalism', *Mind*, 99, 394: 185–206.

Dretske, F. (1995), *Naturalizing the Mind* (Cambridge, Mass.: MIT Press).

Fine, K. (2001), 'The Question of Realism', *Philosophers' Imprint*, 1: 1–30.

Galileo, G. (1623/1957), 'The Assayer', in S. Drake (Trans.) *Discoveries and Opinions of Galileo* (New York: Random House).

Hawthorne, J. (2002), 'Blocking Definitions of Physicalism', *Philosophical Studies*, 110, 2: 103–13.

Hilbert, D. (1987), *Color and Color Perception: A Study in Anthropocentric Realism* (Stanford: CSLI).

Jackson, F. (1977), *Perception: A Representative Theory* (New York: Cambridge University Press).

Jackson, F. (1982), 'Epiphenomenal Qualia', *The Philosophical Quarterly*, 32: 127–36.

Jackson, F. (1998), *Metaphysics to Ethics: A Defense of Conceptual Analysis* (Oxford: Oxford University Press).

Jackson, F. (2007), 'A Priori Physicalism', in B.P. McLaughlin and J. Cohen (eds.), *Contemporary Debates in Philosophy of Mind* (Oxford: Blackwell).

Jackson, F., and Pargetter, R. (1987), 'An Objectivist's Guide to Subjectivism About Color', *Revue Internationale de Philosophie*, 160: 127–41.

Johnston, M. (1992), 'How to Speak of the Colors,' *Philosophical Studies*, 68: 221–63.

Kim, J. (1998), *Mind in a Physical World: An Essay on the Mind-Body Problem and Mental Causation* (Cambridge, Mass.: MIT Press).

Kripke, S. (1980), *Naming and Necessity* (Cambridge, Mass.: Harvard University Press).

Lewis, D.K. (1986), *The Plurality of Worlds* (Oxford: Basil Blackwell).

McGinn, C. (1983), *The Subjective View: Secondary Qualities and Indexical Thoughts* (Oxford: Oxford University Press).

McLaughlin, B.P. (1989/2008), 'Type Epiphenomenalism, Type Dualism, and the Causal Priority of the Physical', reprinted in W. Lycan and J. Prince (eds.), *Mind and Cognition: A Reader* (Oxford: Wiley-Blackwell).

McLaughlin, B.P. (1994), 'Dispositions', in J. Kim and E. Sosa (eds.), *A Companion to Metaphysics* (Oxford: Basil Blackwell), pp. 120–3.

McLaughlin, B.P. (2000), 'Colors and Color Spaces', in R. Cubb-Stevens (ed.), *Proceedings of the Twentieth World Congress of Philosophy*, Volume 5 (Philosophy Documentation Center).

McLaughlin, B.P. (2003), 'Color, Consciousness, and Color Consciousness', in Q. Smith and A. Jokic (eds.), *Consciousness: New Essays* (Oxford: Oxford University Press).

Montero, B. (2009), 'What Is Physical?', in B.P. McLaughlin, A. Beckermann, and S. Walter (eds.), *The Oxford Handbook of the Philosophy of Mind* (Oxford: Oxford University Press).

Moore, G.E. (1903), 'The Refutation of Idealism', *Mind* 12: 433–53.

Nagel, T. (1974), 'What Is it Like to Be a Bat?', *Philosophical Review* LXXXIII, 4: 435–50.

Newton, I. (1704/1998), *Opticks: or, a treatise of the reflexions, refractions and colours of light*. N. Humez (ed.), (Palo Alto, Cal.: Ocavo).

Pautz, A. (2006), 'Can the Physicalist Explain Colour Structure in Terms of Colour Experience?,' *Australasian Journal of Philosophy* 84, 4: 535–64.

Pautz, A. (forthcoming), 'Color Eliminativism' www.i-m.mx/apautz/adampautz/.

Peacocke, C. (1984), 'Colour Concepts and Colour Experience', *Synthese* 58: 365–82.

Plato (1914), *Euthyphro* (Barnes and Noble).

Putnam, H. (1975), 'The Meaning of "Meaning"', *Minnesota Studies in the Philosophy of Science*, 7: 131–93.

Russell, B. (1927), *The Analysis of Matter* (London: Kegan and Paul).

Shoemaker, S. (1980), 'Causality and Properties', in P. Van Inwagen (ed.), *Time and Cause* (Dordrecht: D. Reidel), pp. 109–35.

Shoemaker, S. (2007), *Physical Realization* (Oxford: Oxford University Press).

Sprigge, T.S.L. (1971), 'Final Causes', *Proceedings of the Aristotelian Society*, 45: 166–8 (Oxford: Oxford University Press).

Tye, M. (1989), *The Metaphysics of Mind* (Cambridge, England: Cambridge University Press).

Tye, M. (2000), *Consciousness, Color, and Content* (Cambridge, Mass.: MIT Press).

Wright, C. (1994), *Truth and Objectivity* (Cambridge, Mass.: Harvard University Press).

2

COLOUR, SCEPTICISM, AND EPISTEMOLOGY

Duncan Pritchard and Christopher Ranalli

1 Introduction

Colours provide a paradigm example of how one can introduce sceptical challenges to our ordinary beliefs about the world. These sceptical challenges come in at least three forms: the *Pyrrhonian challenge*, the *traditional problem of the external world*, and the *problem of acquaintance*. The task of this chapter is to examine each of these challenges in turn.

2 Colour and the Pyrrhonian challenge

The Pyrrhonian sceptical challenge that is posed by colours can be expressed as both a first-order epistemological challenge and also as a higher-order epistemological challenge. This section will examine both forms of the Pyrrhonian challenge. Note that in saying that the challenge is 'epistemological', we are drawing attention to the fact that the problem concerns not the truth-value of the claim that there are things in the world that are coloured, but instead our epistemic support for that claim.

Suppose that you are looking at a ripe lemon. One question you might ask is this: although the lemon looks yellow, is the lemon *really* yellow? It is appropriate because we are familiar with a thing looking one way while in fact being another way. When we ask whether the lemon really is yellow (whether the object really is coloured), we are asking more than whether that's how it appears to us, but whether that's how it is anyway, independent of its appearance.[1] Sextus Empiricus expresses this point as follows:

> When we question whether the underlying object is such as it appears, we grant the fact that it appears, and our doubt does not concern the appearance itself, but the account given of the appearance.
>
> *(PH I: 19–20)*

So, the question does not concern whether we are right about how the lemon looks: that it looks yellow. The question is whether the lemon *is* yellow. Crucially, for our discussion, the question is more specifically: do we have epistemic support which favours the lemon really being yellow versus any alternative explanation?

Colour provides a useful example of the following sceptical 'modes' employed by Pyrrhonian sceptics:

> M1. Members of the same species, including the same subject that is a member of the target species, can have different colour experiences of the same object.

> M2. Members of different species can have different colour experiences of the same object.[2]

The first challenge is that members of the same species can have conflicting colours experiences of the same object. For example, two people might be looking at the same apple, and one will have an experience as of the apple being red, while the other will have an experience as of the apple being grey (e.g., due to colour blindness). The second challenge reminds us that different species might have colour experiences which conflict from our own. So, while human beings might perceive a number of objects as having such-and-such colour, different non-human animals might perceive the same objects as having a different colour.

The template-Pyrrhonian challenge for colour can be put as follows, where '*o*' is the target object, and '*S*' and '*S**' pick out distinct subjects:

1   *o* looks colour C to *S*
2   It's not the case that *o* looks colour C to *S**

The Pyrrhonist then derives the following epistemological claim from this case of conflicting colour experiences:

> (C1)   Our epistemic support does not favour *o* being C versus its not being C (and *vice versa*).

Finally, the Pyrrhonist infers that:

> (C2)   We should neither affirm that *o* is C nor that it's not the case that *o* is C.

The conclusion of the argument is thus a basis for suspending judgement about colours, in keeping with the ultimate aim of all Pyrrhonian sceptical challenges. That is, the Pyrrhonian goal is to counter what they regard as dogmatism in our judgements by offering a countervailing argument (*isosthenia*) which would engender a neutral attitude (*epoche*) and eventually lead to a tranquil and untroubled state of mind (*ataraxia*).

One might wonder what underlies the inference from the case of conflicting colour experiences to the epistemological claim that our epistemic support fails to favour the object *o* being colour C versus its failing to be C. One thought is that the Pyrrhonist is drawing our attention to the compelling idea that the epistemic support that *S* has in favour of *o* being C and the epistemic support that *S** has in favour of *o* not being C is the same (i.e. it is the same strength of epistemic support), and therefore provides at least as much epistemic support for their target beliefs. The idea that this epistemic phenomenon demands a suspension of judgement effectively appeals to what is known in the epistemological literature as an *underdetermination principle*. Here is a plausible rendering of the principle in play here, which we will call *Pyrrhonian Underdetermination*:

Pyrrhonian Underdetermination
If S knows that *p* and *q* describe incompatible scenarios, and yet *S* lacks an epistemic basis which favours *p* over *q*, then *S* should suspend judgement that *p*.

Underdetermination principles are widely endorsed in epistemology, though they are usually formulated in terms of how one cannot have rationally grounded belief in the target proposition, rather than in terms of the suspension of judgement.[3] Even so, this Pyrrhonist version of the principle is no less plausible than its contemporary counterparts. Consider the simple case of a proposition and its negation. If one recognizes that one has no epistemic basis which favours *p* over not-*p*—i.e. no more reason to think that *p* is true than to think that not-*p* is true—then surely it follows that one should suspend judgement that *p*. What goes for the case of contradictions, where the incompatibility is manifest, obviously also applies more generally to propositions that are known to be incompatible. It follows that if the Pyrrhonist is right that in the domain of colour we lack an epistemic basis to prefer our colour judgements over known to be incompatible alternatives, then we ought to suspend those judgements.

We should note that the Pyrrhonian conclusion is *prima facie* at odds with our ordinary epistemic practices in the following sense: the Pyrrhonist recommends that we revise our epistemic practices to fit with the Pyrrhonist's conclusion (e.g. suspending judgement). So, one might think that we are prone to disagree on occasions about whether an object is a certain colour or not. For example, I might judge, in otherwise normal conditions, that the apple in front of me is red, while a person I trust, in otherwise normal conditions, judges that the apple is not red. In such a case, we might just disagree, maintaining that our respective (though conflicting) colour experiences provide us with epistemic support for our respective (though conflicting) judgements, that one of us is correct, while the other is not. The problem here, however, is that we presumably don't want to say that the apple is both red and not red. And we don't want to say that the apple is not red because it's not any colour at all. So, the problem that our (imagined) disagreement suggests is that, in order to avoid dogmatism—a dogmatic presumption that our judgement is true and the conflicting judgement is false because it is *our* judgement—we ought instead to suspend judgement.[4]

A related, though distinct, Pyrrhonian challenge can arise at a higher-order level from our reflection on colours and disagreement. On the one hand, post-Newtonian science suggests that particles are not coloured, so that it's hard to see how a composition of particles is coloured. In short, colours do not form part of the scientific world picture.[5] On the other hand, our visual experiences and ordinary beliefs about physical objects suggest that objects are coloured. When I look at a red apple, for example, I take it that the apple is red—that this is no mere illusion that I'm suffering—such that legitimate disagreement can occur between others and me.

So, there is a tension between the scientific picture, which suggests that physical objects aren't coloured, and the picture suggested by ordinary visual experience, that physical objects are coloured. Notice here that there seems to be a disagreement between the two pictures, and the Pyrrhonist will recommend that we suspend judgement because of the conflict between the two pictures.

3 Colour and the traditional problem of the external world

In his *Principles of Human Knowledge*, George Berkeley famously challenges the *indirect realist theory of perception*, according to which we perceive ordinary macro-physical objects in virtue of perceiving mind-dependent 'ideas' of them. 'Ideas' are mind-dependent entities, which are taken to have representational properties. The indirect realist maintains that we *indirectly* perceive ordinary physical objects by *directly* perceiving 'ideas' which represent them.

Contemporary vision science seems to be sympathetic to the view that colour properties are not properties of external physical objects, but rather internal psychological properties:

> There may be *light* of different wavelengths independent of an observer, but there is no *colour* independent of an observer, because colour is a psychological phenomenon that arises only within an observer.
>
> *(Palmer 1999, 97)*

Berkeley would agree. And not only does Berkeley think that colours are mind-dependent psychological properties, but he also claims that other alleged external physical properties, such as shape and weight, are mind-dependent psychological properties:

> For can there be a more delicate and precise strain of abstraction than to distinguish the existence of perceptible things from their being perceived, so as to conceive them existing unperceived? Light and colours, heat and cold, extension and shapes, in a word the things we see and feel—what are they but so many sensations, notions, ideas, or sense impressions? And can any of these be separated, even in thought, from perception? ... Therefore, because I can't possibly see or feel a thing without having an actual sensation of it, I also can't possibly conceive of a perceptible thing distinct from the sensation or perception of it.
>
> *(Berkeley 2017[1710], 12)*

Berkeley's criticism begins with the thought that since we cannot conceive of *colour* as independent of our various *perceptions of colour*, we thereby cannot conceive of colour as existing *unperceived*. Berkeley then argues that what goes for colour goes for other properties as well, such as extension and weight, what we would otherwise consider paradigm examples of mind-independent properties. This is the first step of the traditional problem of the external world, that what we directly perceive are only *mind-dependent* properties. The second step is to counter the indirect realist's thesis that our mind-dependent ideas, such as our idea of colour, for example, can *represent* the mind-independent colour properties. Against this suggestion, Berkeley maintains that our mind-dependent ideas cannot represent mind-independent properties: "[T]he only thing an idea can resemble is another idea; a colour or shape can't be like anything but another colour or shape. Attend a little to your own thoughts and you will find that you can't conceive of any likeness except between your ideas" (Berkeley 2017[1710], 12). So Berkeley is arguing that we cannot conceive of our ideas of colour representing mind-independent properties, concluding that we can only conceive of our ideas of colour resembling other ideas of colour, among other mind-dependent properties. This second step forces the indirect realist into a 'veil of perception' conception of our relation to the world.[6] For how could we know anything at all about mind-independent things if we only directly perceive our own mind-dependent ideas? Berkeley's argument is that it doesn't help to reply that our mind-dependent ideas represent mind-independent things, since reflection reveals that we cannot even conceive of this possibility.[7] The conclusion, then, is that if there are mind-independent things, we don't know anything about them. All we are in a position to know about are our mind-dependent ideas.

There are at least four reactions to this argument. The first is the *sceptical realist* response, that although there are mind-independent things, we cannot know anything about them. Applied to colour, the view is that although there are mind-independent colour properties, we cannot know anything about them. The second is the *Berkeleyean idealist* response, which says that all that exists are mind-dependent things, and thus our knowledge doesn't extend to anything more than mind-dependent things. Applied to colour, the Berkeleyan idealist maintains that there are no unperceived colour properties. The other two responses are less revisionary than the first two. The *indirect realist* might maintain that it doesn't follow from the fact that we only directly perceive mind-dependent ideas that we cannot know anything about mind-independent things. The indirect realist here will reject Berkeley's *Likeness Principle*, that *only* mind-dependent ideas can represent mind-dependent ideas.[8] Applied to colour, indirect realists have typically maintained that colour is a mind-dependent, psychological property, one that is caused by an agent's relation to some mind-independent physical property, such as the reflectance property of a surface. What they then dispute is the claim that what's true of colour properties is true of other types of properties. Finally, the *naïve realist* will insist that we can directly perceive mind-independent things, as opposed to merely mind-dependent ideas. This is consistent with allowing that colour is a mind-dependent psychological property, of course, and to this extent there may not be a practical difference between naïve realism and indirect realism when it comes to our perception of colours. Where the two views come apart is rather on whether in general we only directly perceive mind-dependent ideas. In order to explore the prospects of naïve realism and indirect realism further, it will be useful to examine our third sceptical challenge arising from the nature of colour, which is the problem of acquaintance.

4 Colour and the problem of acquaintance

The traditional problem of the external world can arise from the split between the primary qualities of objects and the secondary qualities of objects. Recall that the idea is that a property like *being the colour red* is too differential in subjects' experiences to be among the primary qualities. The epistemological problem that arises from this is that if visual experience can so easily lead us to think that the redness of an object is a mind-independent property (a property that some objects have anyway, independently of our perception of them), then we might wonder whether all of the properties we ascribe to objects, on the basis of sensory experience, are like colour, in being mind-dependent. This would lead us to abandon a commonsense commitment to naïve realism, and thereby endorse (at most) indirect realism. The crux of the epistemological worry here is how we can know that colour is merely a special case of our visual experience misleading us, rather than a vivid instance of our ordinary epistemological predicament.

A related epistemological worry arises from the thought that our knowledge of the world is not simply propositional knowledge, or what Bertrand Russell (1912) called our "knowledge of truths", but also *acquaintance knowledge*, our knowledge of things rather than facts about those things. For example, we know many true propositions about the colour red, but many of us also seem to know what the colour red is visually like. That is, in addition to knowing many true propositions about redness, we also know what redness is. And this latter knowledge doesn't seem to be something that could be transmitted to someone by surveying all the true propositions about red. To foster intuitions, suppose that, although I've never seen anything that is red, I come upon a grand list of all the true propositions about the colour red. I grasp all of these propositions, and you thereby have complete propositional knowledge of red. But surely you are lacking some knowledge of red, so the thought goes, because you have never seen anything red. The knowledge that you are lacking, then, cannot be knowledge of a proposition (if it were, then the list wouldn't be complete after all!) and is thereby some other type of knowledge.[9]

With the *prima facie* distinction between perceptual propositional knowledge and acquaintance knowledge in hand, consider the brain-in-a-vat (BIV) thought-experiment, in which you are a disembodied brain, living in a vat of fluid, where you are hooked up to a complex computer system, stimulating your brain so as to cause all of your sensory experiences. Naturally, the

BIV doesn't know anything about the outside world, since it's stuck inside its own personal sensorium, ignorant of what lies beyond the confines of that sensorium. Indeed, it's ignorant that it is a BIV, since it appears to itself to be a fully embodied human being. Moreover, the BIV isn't acquainted with the objects and properties in the world. Instead, it suffers systematic hallucinations. So, not only does the BIV lack propositional knowledge of the world, it also lacks acquaintance knowledge of the world. Compare that case—call it 'the bad case'—with our presumed case, 'the good case'. In our presumed case, we perceive the world around us. Intuitively, we're acquainted with the colours of objects in the world, and not suffering systematic hallucinations as of being acquainted with them. We're not stuck in our own personal sensoriums, ignorant of anything independent of that sensorium.

However, as Mark Johnston (1996) argues, as far as acquaintance knowledge of the world goes, it's hard to see how agents in the good case are any better off than the agents in the bad case with respect to acquaintance knowledge of the world:

> The case of the brain in the vat shows that our experience does not discriminate between many different kinds of external features so long as their effects on our sensibility are isomorphic in certain ways. Therefore, despite the seductive offer that perception makes, we cannot take our perceptual experiences to reveal the natures of external things. For no perceptual experience could at the same time reveal two things so intrinsically unalike as life in Boise and the inner workings of the vat computer. Conclusion: perceptual experience does not reveal the nature of its causes. In other words, it does not acquaint us with the external features causally responsible for our experience but only with their effects in us.
>
> *(Johnston 1996, 188)*

So, according to Johnston:

> Perceptual experience in no way acquaints the brain … with the nature of the external causes of that experience. In this respect, perceptual experience is unsatisfyingly like Morse code reception; both involve interpretable effects at the end of an information-bearing process or signal. But the intrinsic natures of the originators of the signal are not manifest in the signal. This is a depressing comparison. Perception represents itself as (or is at least spontaneously taken by its possessors as) a mode of access to the perceptible natures of things; a mode of acquaintance with their perceptible properties.
>
> *(Johnston 1996, 188)*

The sceptical predicament Johnston is pointing to here is that even if we have perceptual propositional knowledge of the colour of the tomato in front of us, without acquaintance knowledge of the colour of the tomato we will be lacking a kind of knowledge of the colour that is valuable to possess.[10] To illicit intuitions, consider the following suggestion from Johnston:

> Once my eyes were covered with bandages for five days. Part of what I longed for in longing to see again was not simply more information by which to negotiate my environment, nor simply more visual sensations. I longed for the cognitive contact with external features which vision seems to provide. It is depressing to conclude that what I longed for—acquaintance with visible properties—can never be had, even with the bandages off.
>
> *(Johnston 1996, 189)*

We noted that colours seem to be mind-independent properties of objects. Now if colours turn out to be mind-dependent properties, then a rich variety of our knowledge turns out to be very different than we pre-theoretically thought. For it seems to us that our knowledge that the tomato before us is red, say, is knowledge *of the tomato*, and how it would be independently of being perceived. A related worry arises with acquaintance knowledge. Even if colours are mind-independent properties, the worry here is that we cannot come to know what the colours of things are like *for ourselves*. Instead, we can only acquire a "schematic and bloodless knowledge of the colours of things because it includes no acquaintance with properties and hence no acquaintance with the natures of things and hence no real acquaintance with things" (Johnston 1996, 190).

Johnston's argument can be summarized along the following lines:

(1) The sensory experience in the good case has the same nature as the sensory experience in the bad case.
(2) The sensory experience in the bad case does not acquaint the agent with colour properties in the world.

Therefore,

(C1) The sensory experience in the good case does not acquaint the agent with the colour properties in the world.

Therefore,

(C2) The sensory experience in the good case does not put us in a position to acquire acquaintance knowledge of the colour properties in the world.

How might one respond to this argument? A certain kind of naïve realism about the nature of sensory experience, known as *disjunctivism*, would reject the first premise.[11] This premise expresses what Michael Martin (2004) calls the *common kind assumption*: the thesis that the nature of our sensory experiences in the good case and the bad case are the same.[12] The common kind assumption motivates the thought that if the nature of the experience in the bad case does not put the agent in a position to acquire acquaintance knowledge of the colours of things, then how could the nature of the experience in the good case being the same put the agent in a position to acquire acquaintance knowledge? According to disjunctivism, however, there is no sound philosophical basis for the common kind assumption. That the good case and the bad case share the negative epistemological property of being in some sense indistinguishable does not suffice to ensure that there is a common metaphysical core to the perceptual experiences in both cases (i.e. that they are essentially the same perceptual experiences). In particular, it is open to one to argue that the very nature of one's perceptual experiences in the good case is very different from how it is the bad case, to the extent that one has a direct acquaintance with a coloured object in the good case (the kind of direct acquaintance with a coloured object that is manifestly lacking in the bad case).

If one is not persuaded by the philosophical heroism of disjunctivism, then one might instead respond to the argument by seeking to undermine the move from premise (1) and (2) to the sub-conclusion (C1). On this view, if the colour experience in the good case has the colour itself as a non-deviant cause, then the colour experience can acquaint the agent with the colour. According to this proposal, then, from the fact that the colour experience in the bad case does not acquaint the agent with the real colour of the object, so that she suffers a mere hallucination as of being acquainted with that colour, it does not follow that, in the good case, the colour experience does not acquaint her with the real colour of the object.

However, the proponent of this line of response runs into the following objection:

> Barring a pre-established harmony no such causal process will preserve and transmit information so as to secure a nature-revealing match between how some feature of the cause, say the greyness of my dog's coat, is and the way I am caused to represent that feature as being. To see involves having the natures of visible properties revealed by a causal process, but this is just what no causal process actually does.
>
> *(Johnston 1996, 191)*

The objection is that causation between the colour experience and the mind-independent colour of the object is not sufficient for visual acquaintance with the colour. The argument for this view is that one's visual representation of the colour might have the mind-independent colour as its cause, rendering the colour experience veridical, but being a veridical representation of the colour isn't sufficient for being acquainted with the colour. The reason is that the nature of the visual experience in both the good case and the bad case is fixed by one's internal mental states. *Ipso facto*, if it's fixed by one's internal mental states, then it's not fixed by the properties in the world.

5 Concluding remarks

In the last section we saw how Johnston replies to a broadly causal response to the problem that he poses. If one is persuaded by Johnston's argument in this regard, then that puts the ball back into the court of disjunctivism, which is the other response to this difficulty that we encountered. Disjunctivism is a radical proposal, and we want to close by noting that if this proposal can be made sensible, then it may be able to offer a unified response to all three of the sceptical challenges raised by colour that we have looked at.

We have just seen how disjunctivism applies to the problem of acquaintance, and we noted in §3 how naïve realism (of which disjunctivism is one variety) can be one way of responding to the traditional sceptical problem regarding the external world, so that leaves the Pyrrhonian challenge. Recall that this proceeded by appeal to an underdetermination principle which essentially demanded that if one lacks an epistemic basis which favours scenario *p* over a (known to be incompatible) scenario *q*, then one should suspend judgement that *p*. If one further grants that the kinds of error-scenarios described by the Pyrrhonians motivate the thought that our epistemic support doesn't favour the scenario that an object has the colour that we take it to be as opposed to not having that colour, then it follows that we should suspend all our judgements about colour.

It is precisely this last move that the disjunctivist will object to. In particular, she will argue that it is not the underdetermination principle that is in play which is the joker in the pack here, but rather the idea that the epistemic support one has for one's colour judgements is underdetermined in this fashion. According to disjunctivism, after all, what one has direct access to in the good case is very different from what one has direct access to in the bad case. Disjunctivism may thus potentially offer a route out of this problem too. That said, as we have indicated above, such a proposal is itself highly controversial, so this is far from being a cost-free solution to the sceptical difficulties that we have explored here.

Notes

1 See Williams (1978) for a classic discussion of this point, in the context of Cartesian radical scepticism.

2 For a defense of M2, see Allen in this volume.

3 For some of the main contemporary discussions of underdetermination-style principles and their role in radical sceptical arguments, see Yalçin (1992), Brueckner (1994), Cohen (1998), Byrne (2004), Vogel (2004), and Pritchard (2005a, part one; 2005b). For a recent overview of some of the main issues with regard to underdetermination-style principles, particularly with regard to their role in radical sceptical arguments, see Pritchard (2015).

4 Of course, one could maintain that this consequence is not so bad, because perhaps *o* is both C and not C. Thus, an *epistemic relativist* might maintain that S and S★ are both correct: *o* is C and it's not the case that *o* is C. The epistemic relativist will explain how this is possible along the following lines: relative to S's epistemic support E, it's true that E provides sufficient epistemic support for *o*'s being C, while relative to S★'s epistemic support E★, it's true that E★ provides sufficient epistemic support for *o*'s not being C. For more on epistemic relativism, and a critique of the view, see Pritchard (2009; 2010).

5 There are two related views here. The first view is that, while certain macro-physical objects appear to be coloured, their micro-physical parts do not appear to be coloured. And this raises the question of whether the macro-physical object, which is composed of non-coloured micro-physical parts, is really coloured after all. Note, however, that Hilbert (1987) and Kalderon (2011) have argued that this worry trades on a failure of decomposition. The second view is that it's not clear that the physical sciences require the existence of objective colour properties, so that objective colour properties are superfluous for a completed physical science. See Byrne and Hilbert (2003) for an argument against this view. These two views motivate an intuitive tension between the physical, scientific world-picture and what Sellars (1963) called our "manifest image" of the world—our refined, though still pre-theoretical picture of the world.

6 See Bennett (1971) for the criticism that Locke's indirect realism leads to a 'veil of perception' problem.

7 A related response from Hume is specifically epistemological. Rather than it being impossible to *conceive* of mind-dependent ideas representing mind-independent properties, Hume's suggestion is that we need to *have justification to believe* that the following general principle is true: if S has an idea as of *p*, then it is likely that *p*. Hume, however, thinks that this principle cannot be justified without circularity.

8 For work on Berkeley's Likeness Principle, see Dicker (2011, ch. 7).

9 For a famous contemporary discussion of this issue, in the context of the viability or otherwise of physicalism, see Jackson (1982). For a discussion of the difference between acquaintance and propositional knowledge, see Campbell (2011).

10 In particular, Johnston tells us that: "[t]he originally unbelievable conclusion now follows: we cannot see colour, because our visual experiences as of the colours of things do not reveal to us what the colours of the external causes of our experience are like" (Johnston 1996, 191).

11 For some key defences of disjunctivism, see Hinton (1967a; 1967b; 1973), Snowdon (1980–1; 1990–1), and Martin (1997; 1998; 2002; 2003; 2004; 2006). Note that this disjunctivism is very different from the specifically *epistemological disjunctivism* that has most prominently been defended by McDowell (e.g. 1995), and recently further developed by Pritchard (2012). For more on both types of disjunctivism, and how they both relate to epistemological scepticism, see Pritchard and Ranalli (forthcoming).

12 Martin characterizes the common kind assumption as follows: "The Common Kind Assumption: whatever kind of mental event occurs when one is veridically perceiving some scene, such as the street scene outside my window, that kind of event can occur whether or not one is perceiving" (Martin 2004, 40).

References

Bennett, J. (1971). *Locke, Berkeley, Hume: Central Themes*, Oxford, Oxford University Press.

Berkeley, G. (2017 [1710]). *The Principles of Human Knowledge*, J. Bennett, ed. www.earlymoderntexts.com.

Brueckner, A. (1994). 'The Structure of the Skeptical Argument', *Philosophy and Phenomenological Research* 54, 827–35.

Byrne, A. (2004). 'How Hard Are the Sceptical Paradoxes?', *Noûs* 38, 299–325.

Byrne, A., and Hilbert, D. R. (2003). 'Color Realism and Color Science', *Behavioral and Brain Sciences* 26 (1), 3–21.

Campbell, J. (2011). 'Consciousness and Reference'. In B. McLaughlin, A. Beckermann, and Sven Walter (eds.), *The Oxford Handbook of Philosophy of Mind*, Oxford: Oxford University Press.

Cohen, S. (1998). 'Two Kinds of Sceptical Argument', *Philosophy and Phenomenological Research* 58, 143–59.

Dicker, G. (2011). *Berkeley's Idealism: A Critical Examination*, Oxford: Oxford University Press.

Hilbert, D. R. (1987). *Color and Color Perception: A Study in Anthropocentric Realism*, Stanford, CA: CSLI Press.

Hinton, J. M. (1967a). 'Visual Experiences', *Mind* 76, 217–27.

Hinton, J. M. (1967b). 'Experiences', *Philosophical Quarterly* 17, 1–13.

Hinton, J. M. (1973). *Experiences: An Inquiry into Some Ambiguities*, Oxford: Clarendon Press.

Jackson, F. (1982). 'Epiphenomenal Qualia', *Philosophical Quarterly* 32, 127–36.

Johnston, M. (1996). 'Is the External World Invisible?', *Philosophical Issues* 7, 185–98.

Kalderon, M. E. (2011). 'Color Illusion', *Noûs* 45 (4), 751–75.

Martin, M. G. F. (1997). 'The Reality of Appearances'. In M. Sainsbury (ed.), *Thought and Ontology*, 77–96, Milan: Franco Angeli.

Martin, M. G. F. (1998). 'Setting Things Before the Mind'. In A. O'Hear (ed.), *Contemporary Issues in the Philosophy of Mind*, 157–79, Cambridge: Cambridge University Press.

Martin, M. G. F. (2002). 'The Transparency of Experience', *Mind and Language* 17, 376–425.

Martin, M. G. F. (2003). 'Particular Thoughts and Singular Thought'. In A. O'Hear (ed.), *Thought and Language*, 173–214, Cambridge: Cambridge University Press.

Martin, M. G. F. (2004). 'The Limits of Self-Awareness', *Philosophical Studies* 120, 37–89.

Martin, M. G. F. (2006). 'On Being Alienated'. In T. S. Gendler and J. Hawthorne (eds.), *Perceptual Experience*, 354–410, Oxford: Oxford University Press.

McDowell, J. (1995). 'Knowledge and the Internal', *Philosophy and Phenomenological Research* 55, 877–93.

Palmer, S. E. (1999). *Vision Science: Photons to Phenomenology*, Cambridge, MA: MIT Press.

Pritchard, D. H. (2005a). *Epistemic Luck*, Oxford: Oxford University Press.

Pritchard, D. H. (2005b). 'The Structure of Sceptical Arguments', *Philosophical Quarterly* 55, 37–52.

Pritchard, D. H. (2009). 'Defusing Epistemic Relativism', *Synthese* 166, 397–412.

Pritchard, D. H. (2010). 'Epistemic Relativism, Epistemic Incommensurability and Wittgensteinian Epistemology'. In S. Hales (ed.), *The Blackwell Companion to Relativism*, 266–85, Oxford: Blackwell.

Pritchard, D. H. (2012). *Epistemological Disjunctivism*, Oxford: Oxford University Press.

Pritchard, D. H. (2015). *Epistemic Angst: Radical Skepticism and the Groundlessness of Our Believing*, Princeton, NJ: Princeton University Press.

Pritchard, D. H., and Ranalli, C. (forthcoming). 'Skepticism and Disjunctivism'. In D. Machuca and B. Reed (eds.), *Skepticism: From Antiquity to the Present*, London: Continuum.

Russell, B. (1912). *The Problems of Philosophy*, London: Williams and Norgate.

Sellars, W. S. (1963). 'Philosophy and the Scientific Image of Man'. In R. Colodny (ed.), *Science, Perception, and Reality*, 35–78, New York: Humanities Press/Ridgeview.

Sextus Empiricus, *Outlines of Pyrrhonism* (*Pyrrhoniae Hypotyposes*, [PH]).

Snowdon, P. (1980–1). 'Perception, Vision and Causation', *Proceedings of the Aristotelian Society* (new series) 81, 175–92.

Snowdon, P. (1990–1). 'The Objects of Perceptual Experience', *Proceedings of the Aristotelian Society* (suppl. vol.) 64, 121–50.

Vogel, J. (2004). 'Skeptical Arguments', *Philosophical Issues* 14, 426–55.

Williams, B. (1978). *Descartes: The Project of Pure Inquiry*, Sussex: Harvester Press.

Yalçin, Ü. (1992). 'Sceptical Arguments from Underdetermination', *Philosophical Studies* 68, 1–34.

3

PHILOSOPHY OF SCIENCE

Mazviita Chirimuuta

1 Introduction

Why should philosophers of science be interested in colour? Why should philosophers of mind holding a specialist interest in colour concern themselves with the philosophy of science? This chapter aims to answer these questions by outlining the connections between problems in colour ontology and views concerning the metaphysics and epistemology of science. The problem of colour is often taken as a stand-in for the problem of the secondary qualities more generally, and a common view is that this distinction cannot be understood without examining the way that the study of nature came to be conceived, in its modern form, during the so-called scientific revolution of the seventeenth century.[1] The problem of colour ontology has been diagnosed as a by-product of the modern scientific worldview and for this reason the history and philosophy of science are highly relevant to the philosophy of colour.

1.1 The two images

One twentieth-century philosopher much concerned to develop an integrated approach to both sensory and scientific representation was Wilfrid Sellars. It is worth delineating some major themes from his writing on colour as a prelude to the core topics of this chapter. In his much discussed essay, 'Philosophy and the Scientific Image of Man', Sellars (1963) introduces the famous metaphor of the two images. The "manifest image" is the refined, common-sense account of ordinary objects, and also persons—their thoughts, feelings, and perceptions—that has guided most philosophizing in the Western tradition. One dominant feature of the manifest image is that sensations and perceptions are taken at face value. The pink appearance of a flamingo, seen in conditions in which no illusion or trickery are suspected, is explained by the fact that it is pink. The "scientific image", which has begun more recently to loom on philosophical horizons, tends to view everything through a reductive lens, e.g. as "a swirl of physical particles, forces, and fields" (p. 20). Since colours have no role to play in reductive or mechanistic explanation, the question arises as to how their very real presence in the manifest image can be reconciled with their absence from the scientific image. The challenge to philosophy is to fuse these conflicting images into a "stereoscopic view".

Sellars argues that sensations, such as those of colour, present a particular difficulty for attempts to fuse the images by way of identification. The "homogeneity" of colour does not readily square with the particulate view of reality offered by the biological and physical sciences.

> The trouble is, rather, that the feature which we referred to as 'ultimate homogeneity', and which characterizes the perceptible qualities of things, e.g. their colour, seems to be essentially lacking in the domain of the definable states of nerves and their interactions.
>
> Nor do we wish to say that the ultimate homogeneity of the sensation of a red rectangle is a matter of each physical particle in the appropriate region of the cortex having a colour; for whatever other difficulties such a view would involve, it doesn't make sense to say of the particles of physical theory that they are coloured.
>
> *(Sellars, 1963, 35)*

In essence, the contemporary debate over colour realism is a series of attempts to address the challenge of the two images. Physicalists hold, pace Sellars, that colours can be identified with certain properties figuring in physical explanation, such as spectral surface reflectance. Eliminativists concur with Sellars in emphasizing the mismatch between the colours, as they are grasped in the manifest image, and any physical reduction targets; but unlike Sellars they are nonplussed about the idea of just dropping the manifest image in favour of the scientific one, and eliminating colours from a revised ontology. The hallmark of primitivist theories is their insistence on taking the manifest image at face value. Reconciliation of the images will happen, we are promised, through some clever theory of supervenience or non-reductive physicalism.[2]

One feature of Sellars' discussion is that he makes quite explicit a framing assumption that is often ignored by contemporary philosophers of colour. As he notes, "we are rejecting the view that the scientific image is a mere 'symbolic tool' for finding our way around in the manifest image" (Sellars, 1963, 36). In other words, the clash of the image occurs when scientific enquiry is interpreted as providing a representation of nature that is more true to reality than the picture given to us by sensory experience and common sense alone. This is to assume some version of ontological scientific realism—the belief that the entities posited by physics are the ones actually inhabiting our universe, and thus that the scientific image is a veridical one. This claim is by no means uncontroversial within the philosophy of science. For one thing, most realists within the philosophy of science endorse the weaker claim, that scientific theories aim at truth to nature, while their rivals urge that scientific theories are instruments for predicting phenomena and manipulating matter.[3] As Sellars also suggests, taking up an instrumentalist position in philosophy of science is itself one way to neutralize the problem of the clash of images. This is an option which has not so far been pursued within the recent colour debate.

1.2 Overview

In this chapter I will examine a series of topics which highlight the benefits of addressing the problem of colour from the vantage of philosophy of science, and vice versa. The task of Section 2 will be to examine the links between the history of science and the problem of colour and the secondary qualities more generally. I present criticisms of the standard narrative which dates the origin of the problem of colour to sometime in the seventeenth century. In Section 3 I will discuss Mark Wilson's critical re-evaluation of the primary-secondary distinction, which is itself informed by a complex view of scientific concepts and the way that they attach themselves to natural phenomena.

Section 4 moves towards the epistemology of science, and Ron Giere's influential theory of scientific perspectivism. In his presentation of perspectivism, Giere presents colour vision as the guiding metaphor for how different scientific models and theories offer us a patchwork set of varied views on the world. Finally, in Section 5 we consider the position of colour ontology, as currently practised, within the broader currents of naturalized metaphysics.

2 Philosophy of colour and the history of science

A widely held view is that we should take the philosophical problem of colour seriously because it gets to the heart of the metaphysical commitments of modern science as it emerged in the seventeenth century. Alfred North Whitehead was one philosopher who framed the problem in this way:

> But whatever theory [of light] you choose [i.e. wave or corpuscular], there is no light or colour as a fact in external nature. There is merely motion of material. Again, when the light enters your eyes and falls on the retina, there is merely motion of material. Then your nerves are affected and your brain is affected, and again this is merely motion of material.
>
> (Whitehead, 1938, 69)

Whitehead continues:

> But the mind in apprehending also experiences sensations which, properly speaking, are qualities of the mind alone. These sensations are projected by the mind so as to clothe appropriate bodies in external qualities which in reality do not belong to them, qualities which in fact are purely the offspring of the mind. Thus nature gets credit which should in truth be reserved for ourselves: the rose for its scent; the nightingale for his song; and the sun for his radiance. The poets are entirely mistaken. They should address their lyrics to themselves, and should turn them into odes of self-congratulation on the excellency of the human mind. Nature is a dull affair, soundless, scentless, colourless; merely the hurrying of material, endlessly, meaninglessly. However you disguise it, this is the practical outcome of the characteristic scientific philosophy which closed the seventeenth century.
>
> (Whitehead, 1938, 70)[4]

In this familiar narrative, the rise of the mechanical view of nature (of which Descartes' natural philosophy is exemplary) rested on the distinction between primary and secondary qualities. The primary qualities are properties of bodies which can be measured and quantified, and which feature in mechanical explanations of phenomena such as chemical reactions, the collisions of bodies, and the propagation of light. These are shape, motions, mass, and texture. In contrast, the secondary qualities are tactile sensations (heat, coolness, abrasion), tastes, sounds, smells, and colours. Useless to mechanical explanation and to the mathematization of our world picture, they are stripped from the external world of physics and given a new 'location' in the mind.

It is telling that Sellars characterizes these views as "familiar fact" because this is not the account which we find in the seventeenth-century authors themselves. Yet it was a standard reconstruction of their views amongst early twentieth-century historians of natural philosophy. Along with Whitehead's *Science and the Modern World*, other key texts here are E. A. Burtt's *The*

Metaphysical Foundations of Modern Science (first published in 1924), Edmund Husserl's *Crisis of European Sciences* (written 1934–7).[5]

Lorraine Daston (2017) observes a shared elegiac theme in all of these works: a sense of loss for the innocence of the pre-modern, pre-scientific worldview. The idea is that back in the Middle Ages there was no reason to disavow any naïve belief in the reality of the appearances generated by our senses. The alignment between sensory experience and beliefs about reality made the pre-modern world hospitable just as the modern, scientific world is cold, colourless, and alienating. The primary and secondary quality distinction is not like any usual philosophical refinement—between universals and particulars, induction and deduction—it is a tearing of the very fabric of perceived reality. For instance Burtt (2003, 18) writes that, "[In the Middle Ages] the entire world of nature was held not only to exist for man's sake, but to be likewise immediately present and fully intelligible to his mind." In the following passage from David Chalmers, this theme has a mythological status. Burtt's Middle Ages becomes a pre-lapsarian paradise:

> In the Garden of Eden, we had unmediated contact with the world. We were directly acquainted with objects in the world and with their properties. ... When an apple in Eden looked red to us, the apple was gloriously, perfectly and primitively red. There was no need for a long causal chain from the microphysics of the surface through the air and brain to a contingently connected visual experience. Rather, the perfect redness of the apple was simply revealed to us. ... Eden was a world of perfect color. But then there was the Fall.
>
> *(Chalmers, 2006, 49)*

As Chalmers tells us, we ate first from the "Tree of Illusion", and then from the "Tree of Science".

Compelling as this narrative has been to many twentieth and twenty-first-century historians and philosophers, it must now be scrutinized. Lorraine Daston (1991) argues that the epistemological anxieties which we associate with the primary/secondary quality distinction were simply not there in the Early Modern texts.[6] A popular mis-reading of secondary qualities in these texts is as purely mental. This is Bishop Berkeley's interpretation, but he does this in order to argue for a generalized idealism. Two seventeenth-century writers who popularized the primary/secondary distinction, John Locke (1632–1704) and Robert Boyle (1627–91), present it in the context of matter theory, not theory of mind. The idea is that the 'corpuscles' (atoms) which they believe make up all matter have the primary qualities and they come in special arrangements, 'textures'. These primary qualities give matter the power or disposition to affect our sensory organs in special ways.[7]

At that time—but not now—it remained an open scientific possibility that there would be just one particular arrangement of primary, physical qualities that could be associated with each specific shade of colour, such that our experience of orange, say, just presents a corresponding objective physical property to us. An interesting case in point occurs in Boyle's *Experiments and Considerations Touching Colours* of 1664. An anecdote is reported about a blind man from the low countries who is able to distinguish the colour of ribbons by using his sense of touch. Boyle entertains it as an open possibility that the particular textures associated with black, white, yellow, etc., might be discernible by this individual because his tactile sensitivity is more acute than in the sighted.

Even René Descartes (1596–1650), who in his *Meditations on First Philosophy* speaks quite negatively about the senses as confused and potentially deceptive does tell us that there is a firm physical basis for colour experience. Colour sensations are caused by particular motions of the particles constituting light beams, which have a determinate effect on the motions of the optic nerve fibres. In his *Optics* of 1637 Descartes tells us that:

> regarding light and colour … we must suppose our soul to be of such a nature that what makes it have the sensation of light is the force of the movements taking place in the regions of the brain where the optic nerve-fibres originate, and what makes it have the sensations of colour is the manner of these movements.
>
> *(Descartes, 1985, 167)*

However, he points out, "there need be no resemblance between the ideas which the soul conceives and the movements [of the nerves] which cause these ideas" (Descartes, 1985, 167).

In *An Essay Concerning Human Understanding* (first published in 1689/90), Locke points out that it is incomprehensible to us how particular kinds of primary qualities can bear any relation to the sensory ideas that they cause in us.

> We are so far from knowing what figure, size or motion of parts produce a yellow colour, a sweet taste or a sharp sound, that we can by no means conceive how any size, figure or motion of any particles, can possibly produce in us the idea of any colour, taste or sound whatsoever: there is no conceivable connexion between one and the other.
>
> *(Locke, 1993, IV.iii.13)*

Locke puts this down to "the arbitrary will and good pleasure of the Wise Architect". This passage is quoted by Stroud (2000, 88–9) in order to highlight the lack of a "satisfying natural explanation" of sensory experience. However, this presupposes an opposition of naturalistic and theistic science which is itself only constructed in the nineteenth century (Stanley, 2015). So when Locke invokes God in the context of offering a mechanical explanation of sensory experience, we should not interpret Locke as pointing out an 'explanatory gap' here. We cannot assume that the shift from mechanical to theistic explanation stuck out for Locke in the way that it does for us now.

What we can say is that the innovators in the mechanics and optics of the seventeenth century did sometimes make declarations which prompt questions about the reality of colour. Descartes was one such thinker. Galileo and Newton were others. This passage from Galileo's *The Assayer* of 1623 is quoted by various contemporary philosophers writing on colour:

> Hence I think that these tastes, odours, colours, etc., on the side of the object in which they seem to exist, are nothing else than mere names, but hold their residence solely in the sensitive body; so that if the animal were removed, every such quality would be abolished and annihilated. Nevertheless, as soon as we have imposed names on them, particular and different from those of the other primary and real accidents, we induce ourselves to believe that they also exist just as truly and really as the latter.
>
> *[trans. in Burtt (2003, 85)]*[8]

However, just because we find that these passages reflect our own anxiety about the reality of colour it does not mean that these worries were felt, centuries ago, in the same way. Elsewhere (Chirimuuta, forthcoming) I have argued that the problem of colour took on more of its current form during the nineteenth century, when research was being directed at producing physicalistic explanations for mental capacities—not only perceiving and sensing, but also thinking and acting. For example, the pioneering neurophysiologist Emil du Bois-Reymond was one of the proponents of a fully physicalistic science of the brain and nervous system. In 1872 he lectured on the "limits of our knowledge of nature", spelling out the problem of the impossibility of a scientific understanding of conscious experience, including the sensible qualities of colour and scent (du Bois-Reymond. 1874). The removal of colour from the proper objects of science is one pathway towards the infamous 'explanatory gap'. If qualitative colour cannot be located either in the external physical world, or in the brains of perceivers, then it is left over as a metaphysical mystery.

3 The primary-secondary distinction: Wilson's deflationary approach

Mark Wilson's *Wandering Significance* is a recent work in the philosophy of science which deals extensively with the concept(s) of colour, and how they fit into scientific representations. Indeed, early on in the work, the question of the objectivity or subjectivity of colour and sound—the two most introspectively salient secondary qualities—is presented at length in order to motivate subsequent enquiry into the "conceptual behaviour" associated with a number of terms such as 'force', 'hardness', and 'red'.

Wilson (2006, 75–6) first entertains, and then rejects, the thesis of those such as Sellars who take science to provide a way of describing nature which is fundamentally different from a common sense and sensory one. On his account, concerns about the elimination of colour from the scientific worldview have their roots in "a false dichotomy between objective and subjective traits" (Wilson, 2006, 389)—in other words, in the assumptions that science deals only with a limited class of primary qualities, our concepts of which neatly correspond to mind-independent physical properties; and that science has no place for the secondary qualities, ones which appear to be in some sense response or mind-dependent.

In order to shake us out of our convictions about the sharpness and importance of the objective-subjective and primary-secondary distinctions, Wilson (2006, 6.ix) dwells at length on the puzzles surrounding the seemingly innocuous concept of 'hardness'. Thomas Reid asserted that hardness was a straightforward primary quality, corresponding to the cohesion of the invisible parts of a body. Descartes, on the other hand, conceived of hardness as a response-dependent, secondary property, the disposition of a body to resist any pressure we exert on it, which we in turn associate with a specific sensation of hardness. Wilson's aim is to convince us that there is something wrong with both views. His central claim is that there is no one concept of 'hardness' that orchestrates all of our various uses of the term. For instance, no one test of hardness (scratching, tapping, applying pressure) is appropriate for all the materials whose hardness we might want to assess, and no one physical characteristic, such as cohesion or rigidity of microstructure, accounts for the hardness displayed by very different kinds of substances. Hardness can display a "multi-valuedness"—different tests of hardness can yield conflicting results as to the relative hardnesses of substances, and we would not have grounds to claim that either one of them is the true indicator. The upshot is that "hardness proves to be neither a simple physical quantity nor a constant sensation, but an informational package with characteristics sui generis of its own" (Wilson, 2006, 351).

The next point is that colour and hardness are on precisely the same footing:

> [T]he predicate 'red' is swayed by a swarm of multiple directivities and doesn't reflect any core unity at all. As with 'hardness', 'red' (most of the time) conveys substantive physical information about its objects (roses, fire trucks, neon lights, etc.), but the nature of this information differs widely from target system to target

system. The word's behavioral oddities stem from the same basic circumstances as engender those of 'hardness': we lack the tools to settle a predicate of comparable utility on anything other than an uneven platform patched together through natural continuation. The mild inconveniences so occasioned do not greatly compromise the local objectivity of the physical information conveyed, but they do require us to take ... precautions in working with claims about 'redness' especially over a wider scale.

(Wilson, 2006, 393)

Again, Wilson argues, our philosophical troubles stem from the assumption that there must be one governing concept of 'redness' which accounts for all of our dealings with this term, one which has its source in a canonical sensation of redness. Instead, we have various ways of ascertaining the colours of objects, employing different and more or less exacting lighting and viewing conditions. Most of these assessments provide useful information about the physical nature of the object, and for different practical purposes some methods of colour measuring are more apt than others. For example, technologies of colour reproduction such as the manufacture of paints and dyes, require exact matching of pigments from one occasion to the next, so decontextualized viewing through reduction tubes is particularly useful. Those concerned with colour design must take into account surround contrast effects, so colours need to be seen in their intended context (Wilson, 2006, 456).

As with the case of hardness, the employment of different tests in different circumstances results in colour being a "multi-valued" property.[9] Philosophers have devoted much attention to perceptual variations involving colour—the fact that the apparent colour of an object can vary dramatically with lighting and surrounding conditions (e.g. Kalderon (2007), Cohen (2009)). According to Wilson, this is just a consequence of the patchwork nature of our colour concepts, the fact that what counts as 'being brown' is defined only locally, that is, according to what viewing procedures are suitable for those kinds of occasions, and not in some universal, Platonic manner. He warns us against drawing any strong philosophical conclusions from perceptual variation:

> [O]ne finds occasional squabbles about whether 'brown is really a dark orange' in the color literature. But the fact that color talk commonly becomes multi-valued in this manner does not show that the data locally is not fully 'objective', according to any reasonable construal of the term.
>
> *(Wilson, 2006, 456)*

So the bottom line of Wilson's discussion is that redness is as objective a property as others, such as hardness, whose place within the scientific image is uncontested.[10]

> 'So does being red represent an objective property or not?' The first observation we should make in this regard is that the predicate 'is red' spreads itself over a rather complicated atlas of naturally connected sheets and locally corresponds to quite different forms of evaluations, to the degree that its target objects are not even of the same type ... But ... it manages to encode physical information quite nicely, albeit in a shifty and multi-valued way. True, the ways in which its parcels of usage piece together very much have the signature of human capacity written all over them, but that fact alone doesn't mean that the data entered upon those sheets has become thereby corrupted.
>
> *(Wilson, 2006, 467)*

Thus we must note that Wilson's notion of objectivity is very different from the one which colour realists typically aspire to. The metaphor of the atlas here is telling. Wilson often compares the locally defined use of a concept to a map, and the collection of concepts bound together under one word, such as 'force', as an atlas. Maps are not regions of the Earth, but representations humans have devised in order to find their way around. As Wilson (2006, 6.ii) discusses at length, any projection of three-dimensional geography onto a 2D surface involves distortion, and our practical intentions determine which distortions will be tolerated and where we must place a premium on more veridical projections. When I use my chromatic vision in order to assess the weather conditions that are indicated by the changing spectrum of the light I am tolerant of the colour inconstancy of material surfaces in a way that is completely at odds with the requirements for constancy placed when, for example, I try to find the best viewing conditions to look at fabric samples for new blinds. The different uses of colour, both in my perceptual experience and linguistic communications, are different processes for finding out about my surroundings but they are both, in some sense acknowledged by Wilson, human-centred devices. In contrast, most colour realists have wanted colours to be simply part of fabric of the perceiver-independent world.

In short, Wilson employs his sophisticated account of scientific concepts in order to demonstrate the shakiness of the primary-secondary distinction. Once we drop any simplistic and naïve picture about how seemingly unproblematic scientific concepts attach themselves to natural phenomena, then the idea that colour causes special worries should disappear. But before moving on it is worth considering a disanalogy between colours and properties like hardness. While Wilson (2006, 396) is justifiably critical of the notion that there is one revelatory kind of perceptual experience which grounds our original grasping and subsequent use of a word like 'red', it does seem fair to say that conscious sensory experience plays a role in chromatic conceptual behaviour which is not paralleled in the domain of hardness, friction, etc. One way to parse Sellars' problem of the two images is as averting to the problem of consciousness itself: how could the homogeneous expanse of pinkness, of which I'm consciously aware, be accounted for by the reductive and mechanistic explanations offered by the scientific image? We might settle for a definition of hardness which only ever employs terms such as scratchability and resistance to external pressure, never invoking the feeling of indentation of an object on the skin; but an analogous definition of colour would seem to be missing something central. The challenge for Wilson would be to show that familiar worries about the development of abstraction in science (the so-called mathematization of the world picture) casting out all sensible qualities, are entirely unfounded. While Wilson (2006, 14) assures us that science is continuous with common sense thought, it remains to be seen if all the critical features of the manifest, sensory world can so easily be accommodated by science.

4 Colour vision and scientific perspectivism

In this section we examine the use of colour theory in Ronald Giere's contribution to the debate over scientific realism. Giere's scientific perspectivism asserts that "the strongest claims a scientist can legitimately make are of a qualified, conditional form: According to this highly confirmed theory (or reliable instrument), the world seems to be roughly such and such" (Giere, 2006a, 5–6). The view is intended as a via media between extreme versions of "objectivist" scientific realism (the thesis that theories can in principle provide "a complete and literally correct picture of the world itself" (Giere, 2006a, 6)) and constructivist anti-realism ("scientific claims about any reality beyond that of ordinary experience are merely social conventions" (Giere, 2006b, 26)). Giere employs colour vision as an analogue for scientific perspectivism: "Colors are real enough, but … their reality is perspectival. And it is perspectival realism that provides us with a genuine alternative to both objectivist realism and social constructivism" (Giere, 2006a, 14).

So what does Giere mean by "perspectival realism", and how does the notion apply both to vision and to science? I will first present the core idea and then ask whether the visual comparison does the required work in distinguishing perspectivism from standard versions of scientific realism and anti-realism.

In saying that colours have perspectival reality, the idea is that we cannot make any claims about what colour any object has without first specifying the perspective (the kind of chromatic visual system) from which the colour judgement is made. As such, perspectivism is a variant of relationism.[11] For example, Giere (2006a, 33) writes that, "[t]here is no color that the rug is 'really', that is, objectively. There is only the color of the rug as seen by a dichromat and the color a seen by a trichromat." It follows that different perspectives are compatible: there cannot be genuine disagreement between divergent claims about the world when they are made from independent perspectives. Genuine disagreement is only possible from within one single perspective.[12] This feature of perspectival realism distinguishes it from objectivist realism. According to the latter view, there ought to be a perspective-independent fact of the matter about which colour judgement is the correct one.

Giere (2006a, 33–4) argues that the possibility of genuine disagreement and inter-subjective agreement from within a perspective prevents the encroachment of an "undesirable relativity". Perspectivism is not an 'anything goes', overly permissive theory because enough individuals happen to share a single perspective (e.g. a majority of humans are normal trichromats) such that their judgements are highly constrained.

Giere's central idea is that scientific theories, models, and observations are perspectival in the same way that colour experiences, judgements, and descriptions are. For example, the theories of classical and relativistic mechanics provide different perspectives on the motion of a body through space; the imaging techniques of PET and MRI offer neuroscientists contrasting perspectives on the brain, each suited to different empirical challenges. One disanalogy between the scientific and chromatic perspectives is that colour visual systems are fixed by genetic endowment and development. A dichromat cannot elect to take up the trichromatic view, and vice versa. On the other hand, scientists are typically trained to use a range of theoretical, observational, and modelling perspectives, and gain facility in selecting the most useful model to attack the problem in hand.[13]

Despite Giere's insistence on the distinctness of perspectivism, both scientific realists and anti-realists have argued that perspectivism collapses into one or other of the more traditional views. Before presenting these arguments, we should first note that the analogy between chromatic and scientific perspectives can be unpacked in three distinct ways:

1   **Partiality.** Just as no one individual or species is sensitive to all of the potentially visible wavelengths of electromagnetic radiation (Giere, 2006a, 35), no one theory or model (of a particular phenomenon) captures all of the potentially knowable details.
2   **Interestedness.** Just as the colour visual system of any particular species has been shaped during evolution by the needs and interests of that species (Giere, 2006a, 29), the theories and models of science are shaped by the needs and goals of the scientific community and wider society.
3   **Interaction.** Just as colour phenomena are the result of an interaction between a perceiver and an external environment (Giere, 2006a, 31–2), science is the result of an interaction between human minds and activity on the one hand, and the natural world on the other.

As the citations indicate, Giere himself invokes all three of these senses of perspective at different points in the text. His critics, however, tend to focus in on just one or two of these points of comparison. For example, in his discussion of perspectivism, Chakravartty (2010) emphasizes (1) partiality, invoking the spatial metaphor of different, restricted points of view. He writes that,

> The idea of multiple perspectives does not by itself rule out the possibility that, quite independently of any given perspective on something, there are non-perspectival facts of the matter about it; neither does it rule out, by itself, the possibility that one might come to know what those facts are …
>
> Perspectivism becomes a philosophically controversial thesis, however, when one adds to the notion of perspective the notion that perspectival facts are all that can be known.
>
> *(Chakravartty, 2010, 406)*

Accordingly, he next considers an argument for a philosophically controversial perspectivism which rests on the "partiality of detection", concluding that the restricted range of the sensitivity of scientific instruments cuts no ice against the realist idea that there are knowable, perspective independent facts. Ultimately, (Chakravartty, 2010, 406) holds that, "even though there are thoroughly reasonable senses in which scientific models … are perspectival, this does not entail that we do not or cannot learn nonperspectival facts relating to the things these models model".[14]

On the other hand, Morrison (2011, 350) has recently argued that "perspectivism is simply a re-branded version of instrumentalism". Instrumentalism is the anti-realist view that scientific theories and models are useful devices for predicting future occurrences of regular phenomena, but they should not be interpreted as providing knowledge of any deeper reality behind the appearances. Morrison's argument rests on a case study of the current state of nuclear physics. Physicists employ over 30 models of the atomic nucleus and each is predictively powerful in some more or less restricted domain of application. Yet different models make radically different assumptions about the nature of the nucleus. Morrison urges that these different models should not all be considered as different, compatible perspectives on the nucleus because

> none of these 'perspectives' can be claimed to 'represent' the nucleus in even a quasi-realistic way since they all contradict each other on fundamental assumptions about dynamics and structure. … [I]t becomes difficult to see how to interpret any of these models realistically since each is successful in accounting only for particular kinds of experimental evidence and provides very little in the way of theoretical understanding.
>
> *(Morrison, 2011, 350)*

In her assimilation of perspectivism to anti-realism, Morrison focuses on (2), the practical reasons for constructing different perspectives—the predictive power of the various models of the nucleus. Thus she does not explore the possible forms that representation of the nucleus might take for the different models. Morrison takes mutual inconsistency between models to rule out the interpretation of any of them as representing the nucleus.

To summarize, if we consider perspectivism along the lines of (1), the account is hospitable to a robust scientific realism. That is to say, each theory may capture a mere fragment of reality but is a true representation of that bit of reality nonetheless. On the other hand (2) is friendly to instrumentalist versions of anti-realism. If one emphasizes the interestedness of scientific investigation, it is tempting to take scientific theories to be essentially tools that are built in the service of particular practical ends. (3) puts the world beyond the investigator back in the picture, by asserting that scientific theories come about through sustained interactions with nature. This suggests that there is more to scientific theorizing than a bare-bones instrumentalism would concede.

The interesting question is whether scientific perspectivism can simultaneously hold on to the different insights of (1), (2), and (3). This would best enable the theory to retain an identity distinct from both realism and anti-realism, while sharing some of the virtues of each. Elsewhere I argue that the most promising route for the perspectivist here is to drop the visual metaphor in favour of a haptic one (Chirimuuta, 2016). Because the sense of touch requires bodily contact and purposeful exploration on the part of the perceiver, it is obvious that with touch one apprehends an extra-dermal reality in virtue of and not in spite of its interactive and interested nature. By analogy, perspectivists should investigate the thesis that scientific representations inform us about the natural world in virtue of their interactive and interested qualities. The real break from traditional realism comes when one ceases to conceive of knowledge acquisition as the process of aligning inner representations to external state of affairs, a process which—on the traditional view—should ideally be uncontaminated by pragmatic concerns. But alongside the traditional realist, the perspectivist can hold that science in some sense yields knowledge of nature beyond the observable regularities.

5 Philosophy of colour as naturalized meta-physics

So far in this chapter I have only discussed colour in relation to general philosophy of science. I will now take up the issue of the relationship between philosophy and the particular sciences of colour, and consider the prospects for a naturalized ontology of colour akin to naturalistic theories in the metaphysics of substance, time, etc. That is, I will ask to what extent philosophers who promote particular theories of colour can be said to be unpacking the ontological commitments of contemporary colour science.

5.1 A spectrum of views

The first thing to note is that there are various disciplines of colour science and that researchers who observe very different corners of the world, studying very different kinds of things, are all considered to be specialists in colour. Branches of colour science include:[15]

- Colorimetry and appearance modelling (Fairchild, 2013; Wyszecki and Stiles, 2000)
- Psychophysics (Hurvich, 1981; Kaiser and Boynton, 1996; Gegenfurtner et al., 2001)
- Computational modelling of constancy or discrimination (Gegenfurtner et al., 2001)
- Neurophysiology (Gegenfurtner et al., 2001)
- Genetics (Gegenfurtner et al., 2001)
- Optics (Wyszecki and Stiles, 2000)
- Chemistry of coloured materials (Nassau, 2001)
- Physics of coloured materials (Nassau, 2001)

Note that no one discipline is held up as the 'core', the sine qua non of colour science, and there is a striking absence of antagonism between advocates of these very different approaches to colour. Curiously, scientists do not spend time worrying about how properly to locate colour, and quarrelling with those who locate it differently. It seems to be tacitly accepted that genuine colour science involves the ecumenical study of the various parts of nature that are all relevant to colour. But amongst this methodological diversity, is there any shared ontological commitment amongst colour scientists?

In a *Journal of Philosophy* article Hardin (2003, 191) writes that, "it is a curious sociological fact that many philosophers, but very few visual scientists, are color realists". If we understand colour realism as the view that colours are perceiver independent properties that are instantiated on the surfaces of things, whether or not anybody is there to look, then the realist must hold that colour is in no way a by-product of neural activity. Thus in agreement with Hardin's own anti-realism, some vision scientists have variously claimed that colour is identifiable with states of the brain, or that it is created or constructed by the brain. For example, Kuehni (1997, 26) writes that, "At this point in time our ideas concerning the nature of color are still largely speculative. For now, the most convincing account, in conflict with few if any facts, is that color is identical to a particular brain state."[16] However, in making his sociological claim, Hardin is ignoring the numerous scientists working in the field of computational colour constancy who do express views akin to (but not identical to) physicalist varieties of realism. Maloney (2003, 285–6) reviews his colour constancy research and introduces the notion of "intrinsic colour". He defines this as the "objective correlate of the perceived colour of a surface" which, he adds, could be measured by some computation of the surface's reflectance. Like the colour physicalists Hilbert (1987, 65) and Tye (2000, 147–8), Maloney interprets the phenomenon of constancy as our perception of a stable colour property existing independently of us. In order to study how humans achieve colour constancy, it is fairly intuitive to frame the problem in a realist way: to say that colour constancy is about the recovery of a hypothetical objective property. This leads researchers to posit primary-like qualities—"intrinsic colours"—and then develop models of how these might be recovered. Yet as I have discussed elsewhere, this is not the only theoretical approach to constancy (Chirimuuta, 2008). So colour physicalism is not a compulsory commitment of colour constancy research, even though it does harmonize with some colour constancy models.[17]

Furthermore, the idea that colour is (at least in part) created or constructed by the brain is compatible with the group of theories known as colour relationism. The core relationist thesis is that colours are "constituted in terms of a relation between (inter alia) objects and subjects" (Cohen, 2009, 8), and one way to cash out this perceiver-dependence is in the idea that the brain has a role in 'constructing' colour by partly governing how chromatic properties are perceptually manifest.[18]

Thus, as Giere (2006a, 32) observes, one of the textbook passages which is frequently quoted as an example of anti-realism is as much an expression of relationism: "There may be light of different wavelengths independent of an observer, but there is no color independent of an observer" (Palmer, 1999, 97). Palmer's primary point here is that we cannot identify colour with a perceiver-independent physical property. This is, of course, in keeping with the relationist thesis that colour must be understood in terms of the relationship between perceivers (human or non-human) and objects. An anti-realist theory like Hardin's only follows if one assumes that perceiver-dependence is incompatible with the reality of colour.

In short, we have seen that vision science presents no unified account of its ontological commitments. This supports Wilson's claim that the various practical demands of different scientific sub-disciplines each push for a conception of colour that best suits the tasks in hand (Wilson, 2006, 456–7). If this picture is broadly correct, and if our only methodology is this rather direct reading off of theoretical commitments from the scientific literature, then the result will at best be a set of naturalized ontologies of colour. It would be disingenuous for a metaphysician of colour to present herself merely as an under-labourer excavating the conceptual foundations of contemporary colour science.

However, as I have argued, there are prospects for more synthetic approaches to the naturalistic metaphysics of colour (Chirimuuta, 2015, chapters 5–6). One pathway is to look for theoretical tensions within colour science, such as the need to account for the Janus-faced nature of colour—the way scientists must integrate physical and psychological causes of colour perception—and examine which ontology is most useful in this respect. Another avenue is to examine the very general theoretical framework of perceptual science—notions of perceptual representation, function, and success—and see how the old philosophical debates about primary and secondary qualities appear when cast in those terms.

5.2 Empirical science as a 'raw material' for philosophy

Given the difficulties facing any attempt to develop a naturalistic philosophy of colour simply by reading off the ontological commitments of colour science, it is no surprise that philosophers have been pursuing alternative approaches. One productive strategy has been to mine specialized seams of experimental science which are rich in philosophical interest and relatively unexploited. In such cases we can think of empirical research as a raw material for philosophical enquiry—a source of constraints on proposed theories and counter-examples to commonly held intuitions. In addition, work in naturalistic philosophy of colour is sometimes said to originate more directly from current scientific knowledge and to be guided more closely by the demands of science. Another avenue is for philosophers to conduct experimental work in tandem with non-empirical theorizing. I will give examples of each strategy, noting that there are many more cases to be found in the published literature.

The science of colour constancy has long figured in philosophical debates,[19] with many holding that consistency with constancy phenomena, and with their scientific explanation, is a non-negotiable requirement on any metaphysical theory of colour. In contrast, the phenomenology and psychology of transparency and perceptual scission—the experience of coloured surfaces and volumes as layered one on top of another—has been relatively neglected by philosophers. An exception is recent work by Derek Brown, who presents an account of colour layering as a means to reassess the dispute over the extent to which the supposed experiences of constancy are actually characterized by chromatic variability (Brown, 2014), and to evaluate the force of the variability argument for colour relationism (Brown, 2015). Here, experimental psychology serves as an inspiration for alternative accounts of constancy and variability experiences, and as prompt to examine different kinds of phenomena which go beyond the stock examples.

The fact that a significant proportion of the male population has a dichromatic, rather than trichromatic visual system is often mentioned in passing as one amongst many types of perceptual variability. Broackes (2010) dwells at length on the complex phenomenology associated with dichromacy and anomalous trichromacy, in order to address the question "what do the colour-blind see?". Presenting his own analysis of surface-light interactions, and proposals for new psychophysical experiments, Broackes challenges the dominant scientific explanations of colour-blindness. Synaesthesia is another fairly common source of atypical colour experience. Brogaard's research on the topic has combined experimental investigation (e.g. fMRI, Brogaard *et al.*, 2013) and modelling (Brogaard *et al.*, 2014), while Brogaard (2015) discusses some implications for colour ontology.[20]

Johnson and Wright (2006, 140) make explicit their methodological requirement that a theory of colour should be shaped directly by scientific concerns. They write that "a metaphysical theory of color that is designed to be of use in the sciences should be driven largely (or perhaps entirely) by considerations of what the various sciences need in order to proceed appropriately". They offer a Quinean indispensibility argument for colour realism, noting that colours have an essential role to play in explanations in the special sciences (as opposed to fundamental physics). They also point out that standard arguments against colour realism, ones which focus on the mismatch between physical descriptions of the world and manifest colour appearances, tacitly assume that it should be possible to reduce the causes of particular colour experiences to physical kinds (p. 151). While Johnson and Wright consider just the fact that colours are multiply-realized from the perspective of physics (and the attendant worries for physicalist colour ontologies), it is worth considering if their proposal also undercuts the Sellarsian claims for the incompatibility of the scientific and manifest images. It seems so, to the extent that Sellars (1963) demands a smooth reducibility of theories and kinds in psychology to neurophysiology, and thence to chemistry and ultimately physics. Sellars does not seem to consider that special science kinds may have novel properties, like homogeneity, which do not feature at more fundamental levels; or at least, as Davies (2014) argues, that there may be epistemic barriers to our understanding how such novel properties arise from the fundamental physical structure of the world.

6 Conclusion

A theme of this chapter has been that the philosophy of colour, viewed through the lens of philosophy of science, must resign itself to a quite radical pluralism of concepts, theories, and methodologies. The payoff of pluralism is that it promises to resolve the clash between Sellars' two images. On Wilson's account there is nothing especially problematic about fitting the concept of red into the scientific image, so long as we appreciate that the concept behaves differently depending on the uses to which it will be put. Giere's perspectivism entails that there is no one unified scientific picture of the world, and this makes it unproblematic to accommodate special science properties and kinds which cannot be reduced to fundamental physics.

As I have hoped to show in this chapter, there is much to be gained from marrying the philosophies of science and colour. One may rightly worry, though, that union will turn out to be a rocky one. What if the ties between the philosophy of colour and other branches of philosophy—ones concerned with the analysis of everyday language, and the nature of mental representation—place conflicting demands on theorizing about colour, such that no (fairly) unified account can be expected to satisfy the requirements of semantics, psycho-semantics, and science, all at once? In the end, a restrained methodological pluralism seems reasonable. It is worth heeding Wilson's lesson that we have various concepts of colour, which serve different masters; that does not mean that the philosophy of colour need become entirely fragmented. There is scope for a productive interplay between naturalistic approaches to colour and the traditions more based in the philosophy of mind and language, so long as the different theoretical aims of these projects do not become muddled.[21]

Notes

1 'So-called' because most historians now dispute the idea that the innovations of the seventeenth century can be considered revolutionary in the sense of a complete overturning of previous modes of investigation. Westman (2011), for example, prefers the term "early modern scientific movement".
2 See in this volume Byrne and Hilbert (Chapter 8) on physicalism; Gert (Chapter 18) on primitivism; and Wright (Chapter 22) on eliminativism.
3 E.g. Stanford (2006). See Chakravartty (2013) for a recent overview, and van Fraassen (1980) for an influential alternative to scientific realism.
4 Similarly Sellars writes:

It is familiar fact that those features of the manifest world which play no role in mechanical explanation were relegated by Descartes and other interpreters of the new physics to the minds of the perceiver. Colour, for example, was said to exist only in sensation; its *esse* to be *percipi*. It was argued, in effect, that what scientifically motivated reflection recognizes to be states of the perceiver are conceptualized in ordinary experience as traits of independent physical things, indeed that these supposed independent coloured things are actually conceptual constructions which ape the mechanical systems of the real world.

(Sellars, 1963, 29)

5 Hilary Putnam refers to Husserl in his diagnosis of the philosophical problem of colour. A central role is played by Galileo and his development of techniques of mathematical abstraction. Our metaphysical quandary, Putnam (1987, 29) writes, stems from "Objectivism"—"the great 17th century project of trying to turn physics into metaphysics".

6 In particular, Daston takes issue with Burtt's conflation of mathematized and mechanical natural philosophy. See Baker *et al.* (2015) and Meli (2011) for recent work on the epistemological status of colour in early modern natural philosophy.

7 Note also that the notion the term 'disposition' was used ambiguously in the seventeenth century to refer either to a tendency of an object to modify light or to a power to produce a certain sensory experience (Adams, 2016, 96 fn24).

8 See Boghossian and Velleman (1989, 81), Thompson (1995, 19), Hilbert (1987, 3), and Giere (2006a, 23). For a recent, historically sensitive reading of Galileo see Buyse (2015).

9 The "multi-valuedness" idea entails a more radical pluralism than the conceptual dualism of Maund (1981) or Brown (2006). It would be interesting, though beyond the scope of this chapter, to compare these different views.

10 Another helpful point of comparison is between colour and friction. Wilson (2006, 11) brings our attention to the disjunctive character of friction, while the reality of colour has often been called into question because the mapping between our concepts/experiences of colour and their physical causes is highly disjunctive (Jackson, 1998).

11 See in this volume Cohen, Chapter 19.

12 Cf. Kalderon (2007); Kalderon, Chapter 20 this volume.

13 For this reason, Giere's notion of a scientific perspective has a narrower scope than the Kuhnian paradigm. A paradigm is a general worldview which is pretty much fixed by scientific training (Giere, 2006a, 82–3).

14 Chakravartty does also consider a more robust version of perspectivism which emphasizes interaction ("conditioning"), presenting an argument against any drawing of non-realist conclusions. In the interest of brevity I omit discussion here.

15 References in brackets are to key textbooks.

16 Cf. Sekuler and Blake (1985, 181) and Goldstein (1989, 140).

17 But see Hurlbert (2013), a vision scientist who has recently argued that colour constancy research is not compatible with reflectance realism.

18 This is the "interactionist" version of relationism that Giere (2006a) advocates, not the more familiar dispositionalist one. The interactionist view could also accommodate Wilson's conceptual pluralism if we include cognitive, information-gathering processes into the notion of interaction.

19 See in this volume Brown, Chapter 16, and references therein.

20 See also in this volume Brogaard, Chapter 12.

21 I would like to thank Derek Brown, Ron Giere, and Mark Wilson for helpful comments and interesting discussion while I was writing this chapter. I am also indebted to Zed Adams and Tawrin Baker for numerous helpful comments on the historical material.

References

Adams, Z. (2016). On the *Genealogy of Color*. New York: Routledge.

Baker, T., S. Dupré, and S. Kusukawa (Eds.) (2015). *Early Modern Color Worlds*. Leiden: Brill.

Boghossian, P. and J. D. Velleman (1989). Colour as a secondary quality. *Mind 98*, 81–103.

Broackes, J. (2010). What do the color-blind see? In J. Cohen and M. Matthen (Eds.), *Color Ontology and Color Science*, Chapter 12, pp. 291–405. Cambridge, MA: MIT Press.

Brogaard, B. (2015). The self-locating property theory of color. *Minds and Machines 25*(2), 133–47.

Brogaard, B., K. Marlow, and K. Rice (2014). The long-term potentiation model for grapheme-color binding in synesthesia. In D. Bennett and C. Hill (Eds.), *Sensory Integration and the Unity of Consciousness*. Cambridge, MA: MIT Press.

Brogaard, B., S. Vanni, and J. Silvanto (2013). Seeing mathematics: Perceptual experience and brain activity in acquired synesthesia. *Neurocase 19*(6), 566–75.

Brown, D. (2006). On the dual referent approach to colour theory. *The Philosophical Quarterly 56*(222), 96–113.

Brown, D. (2014). Colour layering and colour constancy. *Philosopher's Imprint 14*(15), 1–31.

Brown, D. (2015). Colour layering and colour relationalism. *Minds and Machines 25*(2), 177–91.

Burtt, E. A. (1932/2003). *The Metaphysical Foundations of Modern Science*. Mineola, NY: Dover Publications.

Buyse, F. (2015). The distinction between primary properties and secondary qualities in Galileo Galilei's natural philosophy. *Cahiers du Séminaire québécois en philosophie moderne/Working Papers of the Quebec Seminar in Early Modern Philosophy 1*, 20–43.

Chakravartty, A. (2010). Perspectivism, inconsistent models, and contrastive explanation. *Studies in History and Philosophy of Science 41*, 405–12.

Chakravartty, A. (2013). Scientific realism. In E. N. Zalta (Ed.), *The Stanford Encyclopedia of Philosophy* (Summer 2013 ed.). http://plato.stanford.edu/archives/sum2013/entries/scientific-realism/.

Chalmers, D. (2006). Perception and the Fall from Eden. In T. Gendler and J. Hawthorne (Eds.), *Perceptual Experience*. Oxford: Oxford University Press.

Chirimuuta, M. (2008). Reflectance realism and colour constancy: What would count as scientific evidence for Hilbert's ontology of colour? *Australasian Journal of Philosophy 86*(4), 563–82.

Chirimuuta, M. (2015). *Outside Color: Perceptual Science and the Puzzle of Color in Philosophy*. Cambridge, MA: MIT Press.

Chirimuuta, M. (2016). Vision, perspectivism, and haptic realism. *Philosophy of Science 83*, 746–56.

Chirimuuta, M. (forthcoming). Colour in the scientific image. *The Dibner Lecture on the History of Science and Technology*.

Cohen, J. (2009). *The Red and the Real*. Oxford: Oxford University Press.

Daston, L. (1991). History of science in an elegiac mode: E. A. Burtt's *Metaphysical Foundations of Modern Physical Science* revisited. *Isis 82*(3), 522–31.

Daston, L. (2017). The history of science and the history of knowledge. *Know 1*(1), 131–54.

Davies, W. (2014). The inscrutability of colour similarity. *Philosophical Studies 171*, 289–311.

du Bois-Reymond, E. (1874). The limits of our knowledge of nature. Translated by J. Fitzgerald. *Popular Science Monthly 5*, 17–32.

Descartes, R. (1985). J. Cottingham, R. Stoothoff, and D. Murdoch (Eds.), *The Philosophical Writings of Descartes*. Cambridge: Cambridge University Press.

Fairchild, M. D. (2013). *Color Appearance Models* (3rd ed.). New York: Wiley.

Gegenfurtner, K. R., L. T. Sharpe, and B. B. Boycott (2001). *Color Vision: From Genes to Perception*. Cambridge: Cambridge University Press.

Giere, R. (2006a). *Scientific Perspectivism*. Chicago: University of Chicago Press.

Giere, R. (2006b). Perspectival pluralism. In S. H. Kellert, H. E. Longino, and C. K. Waters (Eds.), *Minnesota Studies in the Philosophy of Science, Vol. XIX Scientific Pluralism*. Minneapolis, MN: University of Minnesota Press.

Goldstein, E. B. (1989). *Sensation and Perception*. Belmont, CA: Wadsworth.

Hardin, C. (2003). A spectral reflectance doth not a color make. *The Journal of Philosophy 100*, 191–202.

Hilbert, D. (1987). *Color and Color Perception: A Study in Anthropocentric Realism*. Stanford: Stanford University CSLI.

Hurlbert, A. C. (2013). The perceptual quality of colour. In L. Albertazzi (Ed.), *A Handbook of Experimental Phenomenology: Visual Perception of Shape, Space and Appearance*. Somerset, NJ: Wiley.

Hurvich, L. (1981). *Color Vision*. Sunderland, MA: Sinauer Associates Inc.

Jackson, F. (1998). *From Metaphysics to Ethics*. Oxford: Clarendon Press.

Johnson, K. and W. Wright (2006). Colors as properties of the special sciences. *Erkenntnis 64*, 139–68.

Kaiser, P. K. and R. M. Boynton (1996). *Human Color Vision*. Washington, DC: Optical Society of America.

Kalderon, M. (2007). Color pluralism. *Philosophical Review 116*(4), 563–601.

Kuehni, R. G. (1997). *Color: An Introduction to Practice and Principles*. New York: John Wiley and Sons.

Locke, J. (1689/90/1993). *An Essay Concerning Human Understanding*. London: Everyman Library.

Maloney, L. (2003). Surface colour perception and environmental constraints. In R. Mausfeld and D. Heyer (Eds.), *Color Perception: Mind and the Physical World*, pp. 285–6. Oxford: Oxford University Press.

Maund, J. B. (1981). Colour: A case for conceptual fission. *Australasian Journal of Philosophy 59*(3), 308–22.

Meli, D. (2011). The color of blood: Between sensory experience and epistemic significance. In L. Daston and E. Luncbek (Eds.), *Histories of Scientific Observation*. Chicago: Chicago University Press.

Morrison, M. (2011). One phenomenon, many models: Inconsistency and complementarity. *Studies in History and Philosophy of Science 42*, 342–51.

Nassau, K. (2001). *The Physics and Chemistry of Color: The Fifteen Causes of Color* (2nd ed.). New York: Wiley.

Palmer, S. E. (1999). *Vision Science: Photons to Phenomenology*. Cambridge, MA: MIT Press.

Putnam, H. (1987). *The Many Faces of Realism*. LaSalle, IL: Open Court.

Sekuler, R. and R. Blake (1985). *Perception*. New York: A. A. Knopf.

Sellars, W. (1963). Philosophy and the scientific image of man. In *Science, Perception and Reality*. New York: The Humanities Press.

Stanford, P. K. (2006). *Exceeding Our Grasp*. Oxford: Oxford University Press.

Stanley, M. (2015). *Huxley's Church and Maxwell's Demon*. Chicago: Chicago University Press.

Stroud, B. (2000). *The Quest for Reality: Subjectivism and the Metaphysics of Color*. Oxford: Oxford University Press.

Thompson, E. (1995). *Colour Vision*. London: Routledge.

Tye, M. (2000). *Consciousness, Color, and Content*. Cambridge, MA: MIT Press.

van Fraassen, B. C. (1980). *The Scientific Image*. Oxford: Oxford University Press.

Westman, R. S. (2011). *The Copernican Question*. Berkeley: University of California Press.

Whitehead, A. N. (1938). *Science and the Modern World*. Harmondsworth: Penguin.

Wilson, M. (2006). *Wandering Significance: An Essay on Conceptual Behaviour*. Oxford: Oxford University Press.

Wyszecki, G. and W. S. Stiles (2000). *Color Science: Concepts and Methods, Quantitative Data and Formulae* (2nd ed.). Wiley Interscience.

4

TRUTH, VAGUENESS, AND SEMANTICS

Diana Raffman

Colour predicates like 'red' and 'orange' are paradigm cases of linguistic vagueness: they have unclear boundaries of application. There is no clear line between the things to which they apply and the things to which they don't: for example, there is no clear line between red and orange, or between red and violet, or between red and pink. In contrast, objects that reflect light of (e.g.) 450 nanometers are clearly divided from objects of any other reflectance. Vagueness is often defined in terms of two phenomena: (i) *soriticality*, the property of generating the notorious sorites paradox, about which I will say more shortly; and (ii) possession of *borderline cases*, viz. cases where it is supposed to be unclear whether the word applies. A patch whose hue is midway between red and orange may be a borderline case for 'red' (and for 'orange'): the hue of the patch is neither definitely (clearly) red nor definitely not-red.[1] Not surprisingly, a variety of non-classical logics and/or semantics, and multiple species of truth, have been introduced to accommodate the possibility of borderline cases.

At a minimum, an adequate theory of vagueness must provide analyses of vagueness and of borderline cases, and also resolve the sorites paradox. In what follows we will examine and evaluate the principal theories of vagueness that have so far been developed. I should make clear from the start that as far as their vagueness is concerned, colour predicates are not special; they pose no greater or lesser challenge to an adequate theory of vagueness than any other vague terms, observational or otherwise. But they provide a particularly illuminating case of vagueness, and as a result, have been discussed extensively in the philosophical literature.

Before turning to the theories, let me briefly review the sorites paradox. Solving it will be one of their principal objectives.

I The sorites paradox

Vagueness is philosophically important for many reasons, but perhaps most of all because it seems to be both an essential, and yet an incoherent, feature of colour words. Vagueness is essential because without it, these words would be useless in ordinary speech. How could we apply 'red' if determining whether something is red depended on, say, measuring its reflectance? On the other hand, the use of colour words appears to lead to incoherence. That is because they seem to be *tolerant*: they seem to tolerate incremental differences in the dimensions that decide their application (Wright, e.g., 1976/1997). If two objects differ incrementally in hue, if one is red then so is the other; either both are red or neither is.

To see how tolerance breeds incoherence, consider a series of 30 coloured patches proceeding from a central red to a central orange, so ordered that each patch differs only incrementally from the next in hue.[2] Given such a series, it seems we can generate the following argument:

1   Patch #1 is red.
2   For any number *n*, if patch #*n* is red, then patch #(*n* + 1) is red. (tolerance)
3   Therefore patch #30 is red.

Apparently true premises and apparently valid reasoning lead to an absurd conclusion: patch #30 both is, and is not, red. This argument is an instance of the *sorites paradox*, a famous puzzle that philosophers, linguists, and others have been trying to solve since it was first formulated in the fourth century BCE.

How are we to make sense of this perplexing state of affairs? Is there something wrong with the argument (1)–(3), or are colour words really incoherent? Because we use colour words successfully and do not normally land in absurdities like the one above, and because the vagueness of these words appears essential to ordinary linguistic communication, most theorists of vagueness suppose that the paradox is solvable, i.e. that something goes wrong in the paradoxical argument and we can figure out what that is. Many diagnoses have been proposed. In the next section I will briefly review the main contenders.

II Theories of vagueness

In the broadest terms, we can distinguish two families of approaches to vagueness: those according to which vagueness is an epistemic property of a term, and those according to which it is a semantic property (see note 9, though). Let us consider the two approaches in turn.

Epistemic theories

According to epistemicism, the major premise of the sorites argument is false because there is after all a sharp (though unstable) boundary between red and not-red; it's just that we cannot know where the boundary lies.[3] Being a borderline case consists in being neither knowably red nor knowably not-red. On one prominent version of this approach (Williamson 1994), we can't know where the boundary lies because its location is a function—also unknowable, or at least unknown—of our competent applications of 'red' over the entire history of its use; and of course that entire history too is unknowable. (The sharp boundary is unstable insofar as the use of a vague word may change over time.) In other words, 'red' has unknowable sharp boundaries that are fixed by an unknown function of the unknowable history of its competent use. Our use of the predicate is successful, says the epistemicist, because competence does not require knowledge of the boundary's location: competent speakers are permitted to make (what are strictly speaking) errors in their classifications of borderline cases. A contextualist variant of epistemicism holds that 'red' has unknowable sharp boundaries whose locations shift with speakers' interests (Graff 2000). On this view the major premise of the paradox is false but it seems true because the sharp boundaries of 'red' shift in such a way that they are never located where we are currently looking or judging. A claimed virtue of epistemic theories is their retention of bivalence as well as excluded middle: any object either is red or is not, and the sentence '*x* is red' either is true or is false, though we cannot always know which.

While epistemicism is in some ways the simplest theory of vagueness (simplicity being a theoretical virtue), it faces its share of difficulties. For example, the very idea that vague words have sharp but unknowable boundaries is counterintuitive; and the view appears to multiply mysteries. Also, a central argument for epistemicism has been that it alone can retain bivalence, but as we shall see, a recent semantic theory of vagueness, the so-called multiple range theory, also appears to preserve bivalence.

Semantic theories

(i) **Multi-valued** approaches, including three-valued and degree theories, understand the blurred boundaries of vague words in terms of the assignment of one or more truth-values intermediate between true and false. According to *three-valued* theories, the sentence 'x is red' is true of hues that are definitely red, false of hues that are definitely not-red, and *indefinite* of hues that are borderline red, viz. neither definitely red nor definitely not-red. *Degree theories*, which recognize infinitely many truth-values, hold that a borderline red hue satisfies 'red' to some degree intermediate between 0 and 1—say, 0.4 or 0.5.

Multi-valued approaches offer a variety of solutions to the sorites paradox. For example, one three-valued account defines the conditional in such a way that the major premise is indefinite because its instances are indefinite whenever the two hues at issue are borderline cases (Tye 1994, e.g.). On this view the paradoxical argument is valid but unsound. One degree theory has it that since each successive hue in the series satisfies 'red' to a slightly lesser degree, the major premise or each conditional premise is slightly less than true; but the argument is invalid because its conclusion, which is wholly false, is less true than its least true premise. Here *modus ponens* is less than fully valid (e.g., Machina 1976/1997). Another degree theory claims that the argument is valid because the *unverity* of the conclusion is no greater than the sum of the unverities of its premises (essentially, the conclusion is no more false than all of its premises combined) (Edgington 1997).[4]

Like epistemicism, multi-valued approaches face some obstacles. For instance, the non-standard conceptions of validity employed by multi-valued theories, and indeed the very idea that truth comes in degrees, may seem unintuitive and/or ad hoc. The three-valued approach described above yields no tautologies. Also, a degree theory seems unmotivated in the case of a non-gradable vague word like 'medium'.[5] Moreover, it is hard to see how a specific degree of truth could be assigned to a sentence containing a vague term in a non-arbitrary way. Degree theorists have responded to the latter criticism by casting degrees of truth as mere idealizations, rather than representations, of the values of sentences containing vague terms. But then it is unclear what the degree theory can tell us about vagueness as a real ("non-ideal") feature of ordinary speech.

According to **supervaluationism** (e.g. Fine 1975; Keefe 2000), a sentence containing 'red' is true (false) just in case it is true (false) on every admissible way of making 'red' precise. More exactly: 'x is red' is true *simpliciter* or *super-true* (=definitely true) just in case it is true on every complete admissible precisification of 'red'. Super-truth is supposed to be ordinary truth. Roughly, a precisification is a way of making a term's application precise or 'sharp' by classifying any unclear cases either as red or as not-red; and an admissible precisification is one that also satisfies certain intuitive constraints. For instance, any admissible precisification of 'red' will classify (the hue of) a typical ruby as red, and if it classifies a given hue as red, it will also classify any redder hue as red. On this view, the major premise of the sorites paradox is false (*simpliciter*, definitely): every complete admissible precisification of 'red' establishes a sharp boundary between the extensions of 'red' and 'not-red'; hence the major premise is false on every such precisification.

On the supervaluationist view, being borderline consists in belonging to the extension of 'red' on some but not all of its admissible precisifications: x is a borderline case for 'red' just in case 'x is red' is neither definitely (=super) true nor definitely (=super) false. Although its semantics for vague words is gappy, supervaluationism is meant to preserve excluded middle: on each complete admissible precisification, every hue either is red or is not-red; hence the sentence 'x is red or x is not-red' is definitely true, even where x is a borderline case. Thus the theory is not truth-functional: a disjunction can be definitely true even though neither of its disjuncts is.

Among theories of vagueness, supervaluationism enjoys perhaps the greatest following, but it too encounters difficulties. For example, in preserving excluded middle, the supervaluationist must say that a disjunction can be definitely true even if neither disjunct is definitely true; and it turns out that, when applied to sentences containing the 'definitely' operator, a number of classical inference rules including contraposition, conditional proof, and *reductio ad absurdum* no longer hold. Also, ordinary speech does not appear to contain anything analogous to the distinction between truth$_T$ (truth relative to a precisification) and super-truth, so the claim that super-truth is ordinary truth may seem ad hoc.

A recently developed relative of supervaluationism, Nicholas Smith's theory *plurivaluationism* (2008) is motivated in part by a desire to avoid the supervaluationist's counterintuitive interpretation of disjunction. The plurivaluationist assigns multiple precise classical extensions ("acceptable interpretations") to each vague predicate and eschews the semantic notion of super-truth. However, he replaces super-truth with what he calls "just a level of talk" governed by the instruction 'Say that a sentence is simply true if it is true on every acceptable interpretation' (Smith 2008, 109–10). Smith writes:

> The plurivaluationist will tell us that 'This leaf is red' and 'This leaf is not-red' can be said neither to be simply true nor [to be] simply false, while 'This leaf is red or not-red' can be said to be simply true. … [W]e have no violation of truth-functionality [because] [t]here is no level of semantic fact at which … a disjunction is assigned the value True, while neither of its disjuncts is. For the only *semantic* facts are the facts about what is happening in each acceptable interpretation—and these are entirely classical (hence truth-functional). What we have is just a *level of talk* laid on top of these semantic facts. The talk *sounds* non-truth-functional, but it is in fact epiphenomenal … [I]t does not literally describe a non-truth-functional semantic reality.
>
> *(2008, 110)*

While *simple truth* may be importantly different from super-truth, still the plurivaluationist holds onto the idea that properties defined across multiple valuations play a significant role in the verbal behaviour, the communication, of competent speakers.[6]

(iii) The **contextualist** approach to vagueness, originating largely in Kamp 1981, has as its fundamental idea that vagueness is a form of context-sensitivity.[7] One contextualist approach holds that a vague term like 'red' is sensitive to contexts defined in part by the shifting verbal dispositions of competent speakers (e.g. Raffman 1994, 1996), while another has it that vague words behave relevantly like indexicals (e.g. Soames 1999, chapter 7). The most fully developed contextualist theory (Shapiro 2007) provides an account of the sensitivity of vague expressions to conversational contexts. On this dynamical approach, competent speakers have discretion to apply or withhold a vague predicate in borderline cases, depending upon their conversational goals; here, borderline cases are items with respect to which competent speakers can "go either way" (Shapiro 2007, 10), i.e. they can be classified either as red or as not-red. When a speaker chooses to apply a vague term to a borderline case, and his interlocutors acquiesce in his usage, a new conversational context or "score" is established and the extension of the term is adjusted to include the case in question. In both "individual" and "conversational" versions of contextualism, the sorites paradox dissolves essentially because there is no single context relative to which every instance of the major premise is true.[8]

Contextualist theories have been criticized for employing an ad hoc and unintuitive notion of a context, for applying only to a subset of vague words,[9] and for being improperly (or 'merely') psychologistic, among other things. Also, standard contextualist diagnoses of the sorites paradox as a fallacy of equivocation over contexts may overgeneralize, wrongly calling into question much of our ordinary non-soritical reasoning as well (Akerman 2012).

(iv) The *multiple range theory* ('multi-range', for short) is a semantic account of vagueness that preserves bivalence.[10] It is said to be grounded in the character of our ordinary use of vague words. In particular, it is guided by the fact that (e.g.) 'red' and 'orange' admit of multiple equally competent, arbitrarily different ways of being applied. In applying these words to the hues in the red/orange series of 30 patches, for example, competent users stop at different places, and the same competent user will stop at different places on different runs, even relative to a single context.[11] The differences among these stopping places are arbitrary in the sense that there can be no reason for stopping at any *particular* place. By the same token, diverging speakers do not regard each other as mistaken, and individual speakers do not think they are correcting themselves each time they stop at a different place. Various stopping places are (equally) competent.

The multi-range theorist hypothesizes that this variability in the competent application of a vague term provides evidence of the term's semantic structure. Specifically, the multiple competent ways of applying a vague predicate (relative to a given context) are reflected in its semantics in the form of multiple *ranges of application*. A 'range of application' is simply a set of types, or properties if you like, to whose instantiations or tokens the predicate can competently be applied.[12] For example, a range of application of 'tall' is a set of tall heights, and a range of application of 'red' is a set of reds (red hues, shades of red). One range of application for 'red' might be the hues of patches #1–#15; another might be the set of hues of #1–#16; still another #1–#19; and so forth. Relative to a given context, 'red' has multiple ranges of application at each world—as many as there are competent ways to apply the predicate relative to that context. Speaking loosely, we could say that a range of application just is a competent way of applying a vague word. It signifies that a competent speaker could apply the term to all and only the items in question, e.g. could apply 'red' to patches #1–#15, and then stop; #15 is a permissible stopping place.

Note that, strictly speaking, a range of application is not a set of *objects* ("items"), such as a set of tall buildings, or red objects, or old people. Rather it is a set of types or properties, e.g. a set of heights, or hues, or ages. In other words, a range is a set of types whose instantiations are the tall buildings, the red objects, the old people. The multi-range theorist uses the term *V-extensions of 'Φ'* to refer to the sets of objects (tall buildings, red objects) that instantiate the ranges of application of a vague predicate. At any given world, 'red' will have multiple V-extensions relative to each context—one V-extension picked out by each of its ranges.

The existence of ranges of application of 'red' should be acknowledged by anyone (even the epistemicist!) who thinks that competent speakers are permitted to stop applying 'red' at different places in a sorites series; ranges just are permissible ways of applying 'red'. In particular, *the fact that a range of application has a last member does not indicate the presence of a sharp boundary; it signifies only that the item or property in question is a permissible stopping place.* Although the significance of this distinction, between sharp boundaries and permissible stopping places, typically goes unnoticed, any theorist of vagueness who thinks that vague words can be applied *at all* will agree (1) that competent speakers must stop applying the predicate at some point before the end of a sorites series, and (2) that this requirement does not reflect the presence of sharp boundaries.[13] Similarly, the term 'V-extension' is just a fancy name for the innocent notion of a set of (all and only) objects that have the values or properties in a given range.

According to the multi-range semantics, 'red' applies to (i.e. is true of) a given case (item) *relative to one or more of its ranges of* application: the sentence '*x* is red' is true relative to each range of 'red' that contains the hue instantiated by *x*. Thus there is no such thing as being red (orange, borderline red) *simpliciter*. In general, truth is relativized to a (context and) range of application.[14] The sorites paradox dissolves because the major premise is never true: every range of 'red' contains a last hue (a.k.a. a permissible stopping point), so the premise is false relative to any range of application of 'red' at any world. In other words, the major premise is necessarily false (further proof that the argument is valid). So the argument is valid but unsound. In any range of application of 'red', there is a last red hue—where *the last red hue* is simply *a permissible (but arbitrary) stopping place* in a sorites series for 'red'. Again, there are no sharp boundaries, only permissible stopping places, on the multi-range approach. No particular stopping place is mandatory, but stopping *somewhere* is. On reflection, we should not be surprised that the major premise of the paradox is necessarily false, for it is not a contingent feature of 'red', or any other vague predicate, that its application stops before the end of a sorites series.

On the multi-range view, part of the reason we find the major premise of the sorites paradox appealing is that we confuse two claims:

a   The increments between adjacent items in a sorites series are sufficiently small as to leave the application of the predicate unaffected; in other words, if an item in the series satisfies the predicate, so do its immediate neighbours.

b   The increments between adjacent items in a sorites series are sufficiently small as to make any differential application of the predicate as between them, i.e. any application of 'Φ' to one but not to the other, *arbitrary*.[15]

Claim (a) is required to generate a paradox, but only the weaker claim (b) is true. The major premise seems true because we mistake (b) for (a).

As a first approximation, then, on the multi-range view, vagueness consists in possession of multiple ranges of application, i.e. multiple equally competent, arbitrarily different ways of being applied. I say 'as a first approximation' because a further condition must be met: the predicate 'range of application of "red"' too must have multiple ranges, lest there be a sharp boundary between the ways of applying 'red' that are, and those that are not, permissible. Similarly for 'range of application of "range of application of 'red'"', and so on *ad indefinitum*. Hence 'red' is vague just in case 'red', and also 'range of application of "red"' and its indefinitely many iterations, have multiple ranges of application.

This analysis of vagueness appears to assign to 'red' an indefinite hierarchy of orders of vagueness. But consider: a sorites series for 'red' is a series of hues; a sorites series for 'range of application of "red"' is a series of series (candidate ranges); a sorites series for 'range of application of "range of application of 'red'"' is a series of sets of series; and so on. In classifying the members of the series for 'red', one is judging of each hue whether it is red, borderline, or orange. In the series for 'range of application of "red"', one is judging of each series whether it is a permissible way of applying 'red'. In the third series, for 'range of application of "range of application of 'red'"', one is judging, of each set of series, whether each of its members is a permissible way of applying 'range of application of "red"'. Were there a fourth series, one would be judging, of each set of sets of series, whether every series in every set is a permissible way of applying 'red'. And so on. Evidently, after the second order, we are always judging the same thing—viz. whether a certain series is a permissible way of applying 'red'. This picture suggests that there is no *hierarchy* of orders of vagueness; instead, there is the first-order vagueness of 'red', and the second order vagueness of 'range of application of "red"'; and that is the end of it. One might say that, excepting the second order, higher-order vagueness is redundant rather than hierarchical.

Our ability to communicate using vague words may seem mysterious, given the inter- and intra-subjective divergence and variation in their use. Keep in mind, however, that the variability is confined to cases located in what I have called the 'transitional' region between categories. Communication would be threatened if our classifications of *central* cases were similarly variable; but I don't think they are. Also, communication would be threatened if we failed to recognize that the instability of the transitional cases is arbitrary. Because it is arbitrary, it is, from the viewpoint of semantics, just so much noise—blur, if you like. (Since vague predicates are meant to be applicable on the basis of casual consideration, as Wright observes, the noise is essential.) When speaking to one another, we can simply ignore these noisy variations in application, and communication proceeds unimpeded. Indeed, this arbitrariness goes hand in hand with the fact that divergence and variation of our classifications in the transitional region of a sorites series do not prompt—or, more importantly, permit—charges of error.

Borderline cases

I have not yet said how borderline cases are defined on the multi-range theory.[16] I explained earlier that the multi-range theory was a semantic (non-epistemic) theory that preserves bivalence. In its analysis of borderline cases we see how the theory is able to preserve bivalence.

Recall that on the standard analysis, borderline cases for 'red' are *neither clearly red nor clearly not-red*. But now consider these (typical) passages characterizing borderline cases:

> [The] concept of a borderline case is the concept of a case that is neither definitely in nor definitely out.
>
> *(Tye 1994, 18)*

> [Some theorists] represent the sense of a predicate like 'green' or 'child' by its effecting a division of categorially appropriate objects into three sets. This is supposed to do justice to the actuality or possibility of borderline cases: surfaces intermediate between blue and green, people intermediate between childhood and adulthood.
>
> *(Sainsbury 1990/1997, 264)*

> [T]he vagueness of a vague predicate is ineradicable. Thus 'hill' is a vague predicate, in that there is no definite line between hills and mountains. But we could not eliminate this vagueness by introducing a new predicate, say 'eminence', to apply to those things which are neither definitely hills nor definitely mountains, since there would still remain things which were neither definitely hills nor definitely eminences, and so ad infinitum.
>
> *(Dummett 1978, 182)*

Characterizations like these are ubiquitous in the literature. Notice that they define borderline cases in terms of an opposition not between contradictories like 'in' and 'not in', 'blue' and 'not blue', 'child' and 'not a child', but rather between *incompatible* predicates like 'in' and 'out', 'blue' and 'green', 'child' and 'adult'. Inspired by passages like these, the multi-range theorist proposes that borderline cases are plausibly defined in terms of incompatible predicates rather than contradictories as the standard analysis has it. The multi-range theorist defines a relation of *proximate incompatibility*[17] and expresses the incompatibilist analysis of borderline cases this way:

i   For any proximate incompatible predicates 'Φ' and '$\Phi\star$', x is a $\Phi[\Phi\star]$ borderline case if and only if x belongs to a $\Phi/\Phi\star$ ordering but is neither Φ nor $\Phi\star$.

ii For any predicate 'Φ', x is a borderline case for 'Φ' if and only if there is some proximate incompatible predicate '$\Phi\star$' such that x is a $\Phi[\Phi\star]$ borderline case.

When borderline cases are defined in terms of an opposition between incompatibles, the definiteness operator is otiose insofar as it had been introduced to avoid flat-out contradiction. The incompatibilist analysis allows us to apply a bivalent classical logic to borderline sentences: if x is a borderline case for 'red', the sentence 'x is not-red' is true and the sentence 'x is red' is false. In a red/orange series that defines borderline cases for 'red', the not-red items include the borderline cases as well as the orange ones. A crucial difference between the multi-range approach and other theories of vagueness is that on the former view, a predicate like 'not-red', which has no incompatibles as far as I can see, has no borderline cases. Yet 'not-red' is vague: it has blurred boundaries of application. Consequently vagueness cannot be defined in terms of the possession of borderline cases. Not all vague words have borderline cases.

The incompatibilist analysis enjoys a number of advantages over the standard view. Among other things, no definiteness operator is needed, so the incompatibilist is free of the severe complications and implausibilities attending that device. Also, since the vague predicate 'not-red' has no borderline cases, there can be no higher-order borderline cases; see Raffman 2014, chapter 2, for details.

Despite the advantages of the multi-range theory, many philosophers find its extremely fine-grained form of relativism about truth—relativization to a range of application—hard to swallow. Also, the view has been criticized for, among other things, failing to recognize the significance, on its own terms, of sentences that are true (false) relative to all ranges of application of 'red'. And the incompatibilist analysis of borderline cases has been thought inadequate to express borderline status for a vague predicate like 'heap'. Here the charge is that one's classification of (e.g.) a collection of sand grains as not-a-heap does not seem to involve appeal to any incompatible category.

III Is 'true' vague?

Many philosophers have thought that 'true' is vague (e.g. Sorensen 1988; McGee 1990; Horgan 1994). Consider for instance the series of sentences of the form

The sentence 'patch #n is red' is true

ascribed to the hues in our red/orange series. You might reasonably suppose that 'true' has multiple ranges of application that ride piggyback on the multiple ranges of application of 'red'. Intuitively, we may think that our competent application of the two expressions varies in tandem. Fine writes:

The vagueness of 'true' waxes and wanes, as it were, with the vagueness of the given sentence; so that if *a* denotes a borderline case of *F* then *Fa* is a borderline case of 'true'.

(1975, 149)[18]

On the other hand, doesn't it seem far-fetched that the vagueness of 'true' (or any other expression) should wax and wane? *A fortiori* that it should wax and wane with the vagueness of a distinct predicate? Compare:

The sentence '*n* is a prime number' is true.

Here 'true' seems precise—and not because we have arbitrarily precisified any of the terms involved. In the terms of the multi-range theory, 'true' does not impress us here as having multiple ranges of application, as permitting arbitrary variation and divergence in its application. It seems to have only a single permissible way of being applied, corresponding to the single, sharply bounded set of prime numbers.

The point is that 'true' seems to behave like a vague predicate (or operator) when applied to a sentence containing a vague predicate such as 'red', but like a precise predicate (or operator) when applied to a sentence containing a precise predicate like 'prime number'. This suggests that the apparent vagueness and precision of 'true' just are the vagueness of 'red' and the precision of 'prime number'. Thus the right thing to say, I think, is that 'true' itself is neither vague nor precise; it merely behaves *as if* it were vague or precise depending upon the vagueness or precision of the predicates to which it is applied. The distinction between vagueness and precision is often seen as exhaustive, but I know of no good reason why. As a matter of fact, Russell says that 'vague' and 'precise' are contraries, in the sense of opposites: "We are able to conceive precision; indeed, if we could not do so, we could not conceive vagueness, which is merely the contrary of precision" (1923/1999, 65).

Since vagueness is often affiliated with gradability, it may be worth pointing out that 'true' is also not gradable: *pace* degree theorists, it is not the case that one sentence can be truer or less true than another. Closer to or farther from being true, maybe, or more or less similar to a true sentence, but not more or less true. (Saying that one sentence is truer than another may be rather like saying that one action is more perfect or more mandatory than another.) Nor can a sentence be so true, very true, or insufficiently true, except in some epistemic or else merely figurative or elliptical sense. If we say that a sentence '*x* is red' is so true or very true or insufficiently true, we probably mean that *x* is so red or very red or insufficiently red.[19]

IV Why does the major premise seem true?

Most theories of vagueness solve the sorites paradox by rejecting the major premise, taking it to be either untrue (e.g. indeterminate) or false. If the premise is at best untrue, what is the source of its intuitive appeal? Various answers have been proposed. For example: though there is a sharp boundary, we cannot know where it is (e.g. Williamson 1994); though there is a sharp boundary, it is never located where we are looking (Kamp 1981; Graff 2000); no single location in a sorites series is the boundary in every admissible precisification (e.g. Fine 1975); when we go to evaluate the major premise, we naturally visualize item #*n* as a central case of (e.g.) red, thereby guaranteeing on independent grounds that #(*n* + 1) is red (Scharp 2015); and of course there is the widespread intuition that, at least in a certain broad range of cases, likes should be treated alike.[20]

Rejection of the major premise leaves open two possible conclusions about the supposed tolerance of colour terms: either those terms are not tolerant after all, or the major premise, as it stands, does not correctly express their tolerance. Supervaluationism and epistemicism, among others, appear to draw the first conclusion. The multi-range theory defends the second. What might tolerance be, if it is not properly expressed by the major premise of the paradox?

An experimental result may shed light here. Lindsey, Brown, and Raffman had subjects classify the coloured patches in a sorites series presented in successive pairs, i.e. the pair #1/#2, followed by #2/#3, then #3/#4, and so on (reported in Raffman 2014, chapter 5). The task on each trial was twofold: first, to make a same/different judgement of the two items in a given pair, and second, to classify each member of the presented pair (individually) as red or as orange or as "other".[21] The stimuli had been so constructed that the members of each pair were always judged to look the same. Lindsey *et al.* found that subjects always placed members of a pair in the same category; in terms of the paradox, they made every conditional premise true. Since they shifted from 'red' to 'other' or 'orange' somewhere in the series of pairs, at least one patch belonged to different categories in its two different presentations. For example, if the subject classified the #15/#16 pair as red and the #16/#17 pair as orange, patch #16 must have shifted its classification from red to orange, from one pairing to the next.

In light of this result, the multi-range theorist proposes that colour terms are tolerant, and that their tolerance can be expressed by the following principle:

Tol For any items x and y *considered pairwise*: if x and y look the same and x is classified as red, then y should be classified as red.

The discovery that one and the same item (e.g. patch #16) belongs to different categories in its two presentations may help to explain why the major premise seems true. Also, consider that when we go to evaluate the major premise, we have no alternative but to consider (think about, imagine, mentally represent) two items together. The premise just expresses a comparison between two items; and as far as I can see, we cannot *compare* two items solely by thinking about each item independently of the other. This fact, if it is indeed a fact, suggests that the pairwise formulation of the major premise best expresses what speakers who assent to it have in mind.

Notes

1 I insert the hyphen in 'not-red' only in order to avoid scope ambiguities. 'Not-red' means whatever 'not red' means.
2 Neighbouring patches are either indiscriminable or just noticeably different.
3 Sorensen 1988; Williamson 1994; Graff 2000, among others. Williamson allows that God may know the locations of the sharp boundaries of a vague word (1994, 212).
4 Halldén (1949), Körner (1966), and Cook (2002) are some others who have defended multi-valued approaches to vagueness.
5 Suppose that the height of the flame on a gas stovetop is controlled by turning a continuously adjustable knob; and suppose that three settings are marked around the knob—'low', 'medium', 'high'. Presumably the boundaries between the low flames and the medium, and between the medium flames and the high, are unclear in the way that indicates vagueness; the predicates 'low', 'medium', and 'high' are vague. 'High' and 'low' are also gradable: for any two non-identical flames, one is higher and the other lower, and a flame can be so high that it burns the sauce or too low to melt the butter. 'Medium', on the other hand, doesn't seem gradable: we would not say, of two flames, that one is *more or less medium* than the other. Closer to or farther from being medium, perhaps, but not more or less medium. Talk of a very medium or insufficiently medium or too medium flame doesn't sound good either, unless you mean that the flame is very or insufficiently or too *close* to medium.

6 The desire to accommodate vagueness has often motivated a distinction between two (or more) species of truth. Just for example, in addition to the supervaluationist's truth relative to a precisification and super-truth, and the plurivaluationist's truth and simple truth, a distinction between truth and "pluth" (pleonastic truth) is introduced by McGee and McLaughlin (1995). And of course the distinction between truth and definite truth is widespread.

7 See also Pinkal 1983, 1995, Horgan 1994, and Manor 1995. Akerman 2012 provides helpful discussion.

8 As you might expect, the families of theories sketched above have spawned all sorts of hybrids. For instance, Kamp 1981 combines supervaluational and degree-theoretic elements, and Graff 2000 puts contextualism together with epistemicism. Perhaps we should also distinguish a small family of pragmatic approaches to vagueness and the sorites; see e.g. Lewis 1979, Burns 1991, and Van Kerkhove 2003. Burns follows Lewis in defending a pragmatic theory that is supposed to be classical.

9 Specifically, scalar adjectives; see for example Jason Stanley's discussion of Graff's view (2005, 170).

10 The assumption has been that only an epistemic theory can preserve bivalence. Just for example, Williamson writes that "Most work on vagueness has taken it for granted that [epistemicism is] absurd. It therefore rejects the ... supposition that an utterance of 'TW is thin' [where TW is a borderline case] is either true or false" (1994, 185). And Hyde and Raffman note that "the indeterminacy surrounding the application of soritical terms is generally considered to be a semantic phenomenon. ... If seen in this way, classical semantics appears in need of revision, and with it classical logic" (2017, §3.2). Unger (1979) retains a classical logic and semantics for vague words, but at the cost of claiming that they are referentially vacuous. See also Wheeler 1979.

11 See Raffman 2014, 172–5, for experimental evidence supporting this claim.

12 The term 'set' is used here in its ordinary, non-technical sense, as when we talk of a set of dishes or golf clubs.

13 Epistemicists think that a sorites series contains both permissible stopping places and sharp boundaries— not that the former indicate the presence of the latter.

14 Such a relativization of truth may seem extreme, but the multi-range theorist argues (1) that it provides the most straightforward and intuitive way to capture the equal permissibility of the multiple divergent stopping places in a sorites series (multiple divergent ways of applying a vague term); and (2) that the extent to which the term 'true' is relativized in ordinary speech is typically underestimated. See Raffman 2014 for discussion.

15 Of course, applying 'red' to the first patch in the series but not to the second would be incorrect, in addition to arbitrary.

16 This may seem surprising inasmuch as virtually all theories of vagueness define the phenomenon in terms of soriticality or possession of borderlines or, very often, both. However, on the multi-range view, there is no essential connection between soriticality, borderlines, and vagueness; see Raffman 2014, 18–19, 42–3, 130–3 for discussion.

17 Roughly, incompatible predicates Φ and $\Phi\star$ are proximate just in case their extensions partially overlap, so that some items can competently be classified both as Φ and as $\Phi\star$ (relative to the same context).

18 Actually Fine uses the expression 'true$_T$' in this passage, not 'true' *simpliciter*, because he distinguishes between truth in a precisification (truth$_T$) and truth in all (admissible) precisifications (super-truth). On the multi-range theory, there is no analogue to super-truth. Ordinary truth, viz. truth relative to a range of application, is understood in a way that is closer to Fine's truth$_T$; so I don't think it is misleading to cite him as I do here.

19 Given bivalence, 'true' ('false') has no incompatibles; its contradictory 'false' ('true') is its only competitor. Hence on the incompatibilist analysis of borderlines, neither 'true' nor 'false' has borderline cases.

20 See Wright 1976/1997 for further reasons why the premise seems true.

21 'Other' was represented by a question mark in the original experiment. Subjects were instructed to respond with 'other' when "for any reason whatsoever, they were not fully satisfied either with 'red' or with 'orange'". (The experiment used 'blue' and 'green'.)

References

Akerman, J., 2012. 'Contextualist Theories of Vagueness'. *Philosophy Compass* 7: 470–80.

Burns, L., 1991. *Vagueness: An Investigation into Natural Languages and the Sorites Paradox*. Dordrecht: Kluwer.

Cook, R., 2002. 'Vagueness and Mathematical Precision'. *Mind* 111: 227–47.

Dummett, M., 1978. *Truth and Other Enigmas*. Cambridge, MA: Harvard University Press.

Edgington, D., 1997. 'Vagueness by Degrees'. In R. Keefe and P. Smith (eds.), *Vagueness: A Reader*, pp. 294–316. Cambridge, MA: MIT Press.

Fine, K., 1975. 'Vagueness, Truth, and Logic'. *Synthèse* 30: 301–24.

Graff, D., 2000. 'Shifting Sands: An Interest-Relative Theory of Vagueness'. *Philosophical Topics* 28, 1: 45–81.

Halldén, S., 1949. *The Logic of Nonsense*. Uppsala: Uppsala Universitets Årsskrift.

Horgan, T., 1994. 'Robust Vagueness and the Forced-March Sorites Paradox'. *Philosophical Perspectives* 8: 159–88.

Hyde, D. and Raffman, D. 2017. 'Sorites Paradox', *The Stanford Encyclopedia of Philosophy* (Winter 2014), E. N. Zalta (ed.), URL=http://plato.stanford.edu/archives/win2014/entries/sorites-paradox/.

Kamp, H., 1981. 'The Paradox of the Heap'. In U. Mönnich (ed.), *Aspects of Philosophical Logic*, pp. 225–77. Dordrecht: Reidel.

Keefe, R., 2000. *Theories of Vagueness*. Cambridge: Cambridge University Press.

Körner, S., 1966. *Experience and Theory*. London: Routledge & Kegan Paul.

Lewis, D., 1979. 'Scorekeeping in a Language Game'. *Journal of Philosophical Logic* 8: 339–59.

Machina, K., 1976. 'Truth, Belief, and Vagueness'. *Journal of Philosophical Logic* 5: 47–78. Reprinted in R. Keefe and P. Smith (eds.), 1997, *Vagueness: A Reader*, pp. 174–203. Cambridge, MA: MIT Press.

Manor, R., 1995. 'Pragmatic Considerations in Semantic Analyses'. *Pragmatics and Cognition* 3, 2: 225–45.

McGee, V., 1990. *Truth, Vagueness, and Paradox*. Indianapolis: Hackett.

McGee, V., and McLaughlin, B., 1995. 'Distinctions Without a Difference'. *Southern Journal of Philosophy* 33 [Spindel Conference supplement], 203–51.

Pinkal, M., 1983. 'On the Limits of Lexical Meaning'. In R. Bauerle, C. Schwarze, and A. von Stechow (eds.), *Meaning, Use and Interpretation*. Berlin: de Gruyter.

Pinkal, M., 1995. *Logic and Lexicon*. Dordrecht: Kluwer Academic Publishers.

Raffman, D., 1994. 'Vagueness without Paradox'. *The Philosophical Review* 103, 1: 41–74.

Raffman, D., 1996. 'Vagueness and Context Relativity'. *Philosophical Studies* 81: 175–92.

Raffman, D., 2014. *Unruly Words: A Study of Vague Language*. Oxford: Oxford University Press.

Russell, B, 1923. 'Vagueness'. *Australasian Journal of Philosophy and Psychology* 1, 84–92. Reprinted in R. Keefe and P. Smith (eds.), 1997, *Vagueness: A Reader*, pp. 61–8. Cambridge, MA: MIT Press.

Sainsbury, M., 1990. 'Concepts without Boundaries'. Inaugural Lecture, King's College London. Reprinted in R. Keefe and P. Smith (eds.), 1997, *Vagueness: A Reader*, pp. 251–64. Cambridge, MA: MIT Press.

Scharp, K., 2015. 'Tolerance and the Multi-Range View of Vagueness'. *Philosophy and Phenomenological Research*, v.XC, n.2.

Shapiro, S., 2007. *Vagueness in Context*. Oxford: Oxford University Press.

Smith, N., 2008. *Vagueness and Degrees of Truth*. Oxford: Oxford University Press.

Soames, S., 1999. *Understanding Truth*. Oxford University Press.

Sorensen, R., 1988. *Blindspots*. Oxford: Oxford University Press.

Stanley, J. 2005. *Knowledge and Practical Interests*. Oxford: Oxford University Press.

Tye, M., 1994. 'Sorites Paradoxes and the Semantics of Vagueness'. *Philosophical Perspectives* 8: 189–206.

Unger, P., 1979. 'There Are No Ordinary Things'. *Synthèse* 41: 117–54.

Van Kerkhove, B., 2003. 'Vagueness Unlimited: In Defence of a Pragmatical Approach to Sorites Paradoxes'. *Logic and Logical Philosophy* 11: 251–76.

Wheeler, S. C., 1979. 'On That Which Is Not'. *Synthèse*, 41: 155–94.

Williamson, T., 1994. *Vagueness*. London: Routledge.

Wright, C., 1976. 'Language Mastery and the Sorites Paradox'. In G. Evans and J. McDowell (eds.), *Truth and Meaning*, pp. 223–47. Oxford: Clarendon Press. Reprinted in R. Keefe and P. Smith (eds.), 1997, *Vagueness: A Reader*, pp. 151–73. Cambridge, MA: MIT Press.

5

THE LOGIC OF COLOUR CONCEPTS

Frederik Gierlinger and Jonathan Westphal

During the middle part of the twentieth century, in the 1950s and 1960s, though to a lesser extent also earlier, there was a significant debate in philosophy about a problem that came to be known as the problem of the 'incompatibility of colours'. A standard formulation of the key question in this discussion was this: 'Why is it that nothing can be red (all over) and green (all over) at the same time?' We will call this the α-formulation.

There is also a narrower formulation (the β-formulation) that seems *too* narrow: 'Why is it that a point in the visual field cannot be red (all over) and green (all over) at the same time?' We say that this second formulation is *too* narrow because it only applies to a certain class of psychological objects, points in the visual field. Even if it is answered successfully, it will leave part of the first and wider question unanswered. We might want to know 'Why is it that the side of a bus, say a red bus with a green car reflected by its gloss surface, is not red (all over) and green (all over) at the same time?' for example, and we would receive no answer in the β-formulation.

A third variant of the question (the γ-formulation) is found in Wittgenstein's last work, the *Remarks on Colour*. The γ-formulation is due to the painter Phillipp Otto Runge:[1] 'Why can there be no such colour as a reddish-green?' The α-formulation is about physical objects, and makes essential references to space and time. The β-formulation also refers to space and time, but it concerns psychological objects, whose behaviour might be expected to obey psychological laws. The γ-formulation concerns what might be thought to be abstract objects, though if they are, they are abstract objects that we can see and that are paradigmatically the proper objects of vision: colours. The γ-formulation might however be thought to be abstract simply just because it contains no reference to space ('all over') and time ('at the same time'), though here there is an assumption that what lies outside space and time cannot be concrete.

It is significant that the answers to the questions in all three formulations are *modal*. The questions ask why such and such (something red all over and green all over at the same time, a point in the visual field that is red all over and green all over at the same time, or a reddish green) *cannot* exist.

The discussion of the question expressed in the α-formulation more or less coincides with a period in philosophy in which there was a widespread use of the phrase, 'the logic of …', partly due to the influence of the later Wittgenstein, as in "the logic of belief statements" or "the logic of statements about time", or "the logic of colour words", and the implied practice of philosophy as conceptual analysis, or the logical analysis of either concept words, or sentences, or both. Today it is fair to say, we think, that philosophy has changed. Analysis of this sort has been replaced by arguments between proponents of different philosophical theories. 'Isms' are back. They are not automatically suspect. In this way we are back to the nineteenth century, though on a higher dialectical plane.

Whether one thinks there really is something called 'the logic of colour concepts' or 'the logic of colour' will depend on what one makes of the earlier tendency in philosophy according to which philosophy is analysis. Analysing colour terms or propositions about colours, do we find a logic or calculus of colour? We ourselves are with R. B. Braithwaite: 'No calculus without calculation.' Can we infer from '*a* is coloured red all over at time *t*' that '*a* is *not* coloured green all over at time *t*?' If we can, we seem to have a piece of logic, a fragment of a calculus. One might be made suspicious, although less so about the γ-formulation than the others, by the fact that the putative 'logic' is so short on calculations; '*a* is coloured red all over at time *t*' implies '*a* is *not* coloured green all over at time *t*' and its analogues with the other colour terms is apparently the only one. 'Object O is red all over at *t*' and 'O is green all over at *t*', however, are contraries, not contradictories, since most objects are neither.

There is also a deeper problem. By what *logical* principle is the inference made? What other principles belong to this logic, what are its rules of argument and replacement, its semantics, and so on, and how does it relate to propositional and predicate logic?

Wittgenstein had in the *Tractatus* claimed that the α-formulation incompatibility of colours was a purely logical affair. His reason for making this claim had been his conviction that *all* necessity is logical necessity, so that if the incompatibility of colours is necessary, then it is logical. In that case, since 'red' and 'green' are not contradictory but contrary (the contradictories are 'red' and 'non-red' or 'not red', with obversion), the analysis of 'red' and 'green' must be such as to exhibit the required contradiction. Incapable of giving such an analysis, however, Wittgenstein subsequently concluded that colour terms could not be analysed, and so 'red' and 'green', he thought, are not after all contradictory. What then was to prevent the application of 'red' and 'green' to a single object at the same time? The answer was 'the logic of colour'.

Why was it to be called 'logic' or 'the logic of colour concepts'? The answer is simply it that does the job that *should* have been performed, after a suitable analysis, by a contradiction, had there been a contradictory relationship between 'red' and 'green'. There is in fact no contradiction, but the impossibility remains. So we need 'a logic of colour' or 'a logic of colour concepts'. *Something* is causing the impossibility, and since according to the *Tractatus* 'the only impossibility is logical impossibility', that something must be logic, though of a novel sort: the logic of the concept of a colour.

The question in the α-formulation was also one of considerable interest and importance, though for slightly different reasons, to analytical philosophers working in the wake of logical positivism. Logical positivism had divided propositions in their entirety into two mutually excluding groups. The formal ones were said to be analytic, and the empirical ones were said to be synthetic. It seemed as though there was no place for incompatibilities of colours in this dichotomy. Propositions asserting the incompatibilities seem to be both analytic, as they express necessities and are known *a priori*, and synthetic, as they give substantial information about the world and can only be known *a posteriori*.

On the one hand it seems, if someone knows the meaning of the words 'red' and 'green' he or she is in as good a position to assert that nothing can be red (all over) and green (all over) at the same time, as anyone could ever be. Therefore, propositions about colours seem to belong to the same case as propositions belonging to logic and geometry and the other indisputably *a priori* disciplines, and so to be available even to those without colour vision. They are analytic.

On the other hand, it seems that the nature or definitions of the colours can only be discovered empirically or *a posteriori*, by means of colour vision, and that they are a part of the empirically known world. Someone without colour vision would not, it seems, be in a position to offer full assent to 'Nothing can be red (all over) and green (all over) at the same time.' Propositions about colours are more than merely formal. They are empirical and synthetic.

The challenge of the modal propositions was to produce an answer to the question of the basis of their truth that provided both for their apparently simultaneously analytic and synthetic character. Put like this, of course, the challenge is impossible to meet, as 'analytic' and 'synthetic' are flatly contradictory. For a proposition is analytic, in the best available formulation, if it follows from a definition or definitions using logic alone; it is synthetic if it does not.

What was to be done with this contradiction or paradox? A number of approaches suggested themselves, but in the end we think it is fair to say that the discussion gradually petered out, in the way that philosophical discussions sometimes do, without a conclusion to which all could give assent. Or perhaps one should say that philosophical discussions seem to peter out in this way when they have not been worked through by historians of philosophy with a good sense of the philosophical commitments and of the beliefs of the participants in the original discussion. With the history of philosophy, it is often possible to see what the *diminuendo* discussions really meant.

We shall not pursue the question, surely an interesting one, as to why it is colours and not sounds and smells or the proper objects of any of the other sensory modalities that found themselves selected as the foundation of the discussion of incompatibility. It is worth noting, as Justin Broackes has pointed out, that there are incompatibilities of entities other than qualities and properties, for example substances. 'Why can nothing be silver (all through) and gold (all through) at the same time?' is an example.

The idea of a logic of colour concepts, and the use of the phrase 'the logic of colour concepts', came into philosophy as a result of the failure of Wittgenstein's view of the analysis of propositions about colour in the α-formulation in the *Tractatus*, and of a parallel difficulty within logical positivism. For Wittgenstein the difficulty was that the modal propositions are *not* contradictory as they stand. 'My book is red' and 'My book is green' are no more contradictory than 'My book is red' and 'My book is fat.'

The claim of logical positivism was that propositions are either empirical and synthetic, or *a priori* and formal or analytic. Every proposition is either analytic or synthetic. The modal propositions seemed to be neither. Since they threatened the theory of meaning at the centre of logical positivism, it became vital to understand them in a way that was consistent with the sharp distinction between the analytic and the synthetic.

There were not many options, since, it seemed, the α-formulated modal proposition is clearly *not* synthetic. As D. F. Pears put it, "For anyone who contradicted it would betray, without any possibility of an alternative plea, that he did not know the meanings of its words."[2] So the α-formulated modal propositions had to be analytic.

> Thus if I say, 'Nothing can be coloured in different ways at the same time with respect to the same part of itself', I am not saying anything about the properties of any actual thing; but I am not talking nonsense. I am expressing an analytic proposition, which records our determination to call a colour expanse which differs in quality from a neighbouring colour expanse a different part of a given thing. In other words, I am simply calling attention to the implications of a certain linguistic usage.[3]

There might still seem to be a worry that there is more to the necessity of the modal propositions than analyticity in this sense. Suppose we were to decide that brown surfaces were also to be called 'red and green' at the same time, and that this usage was adopted by all speakers of English. It would then be analytically false that nothing can be red and green all over at the same time. *But then the meaning of the colour words would have* changed, intensionally and extensionally. And yet it is more than a verbal definition or rule that is responsible for the impossibility recorded in the α-formulations, one might think; "the suggested verbal rule seems to make no difference since, without it, the sentence already seems necessarily true".[4] It remains a *fact* that brown in our sense is not red, though some browns are reddish, nor is it green, though some browns are greenish.

Frederick Ferré offered a solution, in 1961, that can be taken as representative of the view that modal propositions in the α-formulations are synthetic *a priori* propositions.[5] It purports to be a Wittgensteinian one, but if so it is also a confused one. In 1963, Ronald Arbini, replying to Ferré, pointed out that the modal propositions are not actually propositions *about* facts of nature, nor are they propositions *about* our linguistic practices.[6] Ferré had argued that the modal propositions are *both* necessary and contingent "in different respects", and that those who cannot see this have "failed to appreciate certain implications of Wittgenstein's teaching concerning language-games". The "teaching" upon which Ferré relies is that language-games and forms of life are themselves contingent and arbitrary things. Once these games are established, however, what is described with and in them can assume the form of a necessity. Incompatibilities of colour, according to Ferré, derive from "rules of language", but nature, presumably containing colours, gives these rules their "point".

It is doubtful whether this account is fully coherent. With it the incompatibilities are creatures of language, and there seems no obvious relevance to the reference to the 'point' of the games. One *cannot* get more than four points in a game of tennis, and that is an arbitrary rule. But it is also analytic as it is a definition of 'game' in tennis. 'The point' of the game of tennis does not make it contingent. It is irrelevant that the existence of the game is itself in some sense arbitrary or contingent. As Leibniz pointed out, all eternal truths are anyway hypothetical. *If* you play something that in tennis is called 'a game', then you cannot get more than four points.

One of the well-known mistakes twisted into the whole subject must be mentioned at this point. Philosophers working at 'the logic of colour concepts', especially the logical positivists, did not distinguish the distinctions between the *a priori* and the empirical, the necessary and the contingent, and the analytic and the synthetic, in a proper or principled manner. Today we are well aware, especially following the work of Kripke, how different from one another the distinctions are, and that the first of the distinctions concerns concepts and knowledge, the second concerns truth, and the third propositions or judgements. To those like Kant who believe in the synthetic *a priori* one can ask, 'Synthetic a priori *what*'? Kant's answer is that it is the *judgement* that is synthetic and known *a priori* to be true, without any awareness about the fact that this answer muddles up epistemology and philosophy of language and psychology in the worst possible way—as we now know. Is the judgement the *act* of judging, a mental act, or is the *content* of the judgement, a proposition, that which is judged to be the case? The discussion of the logic of colour concepts mainly took place in the aftermath of the work of Wittgenstein and logical positivism, before it had been appreciated how very different the three distinctions are. For logical positivism the *a priori* was the same thing as the analytic and the necessary.[7]

Ferré himself *seems* to imply that the modal propositions are synthetic *a priori*: we have "a necessity of language" that is part of "a form of life".[8] But then[9] he declares that the language-game itself is contingent, in some unstated but profound sense, whereas the place of the proposition in the language-game is necessary. This seems sheer equivocation. Ferré cannot be claiming that the modal proposition itself is both contingent and necessary. That *would* be a contradiction! Clearly there is a mix-up here of the synthetic with the contingent and the necessary with the *a priori*.

Suppose that in 1930 we were prepared to say that 'Every husband is a man' is analytic; it follows from a definition plus some logic. The situation that Ferré might wish to envisage is one that has become real at the time at which we write, in 2020. Today a partner in a same-sex marriage might refer to her female partner as 'my husband'. Suppose that this practice were to become even more widespread than it is. Shouldn't we then say that the proposition said to be analytic in 1930 is (i) synthetic, and (ii) *a priori* and perhaps (iii) false? It is *a priori* because we can know it from the meanings of the terms 'husband' and 'man', and it is synthetic because it relies on the existence of a social practice that gives us information about the practice. The information has to do with the activities of registry office officials, the existence of the marriage laws, and other social and legal practices.

One tell-tale difficulty with Ferré's view is that it makes *all* candidates for analytic truths turn out to be synthetic *a priori*,[10] even, with a bit of Platonism on board, mathematical ones. It is not hard to see why this utterly unacceptable conclusion follows. For, as Arbini points out, there is a difference between a proposition being synthetic, on the one hand, and it depending on some fact of nature that is contingent, such as a linguistic practice, whose existence will be described in an existential proposition that is synthetic.[11] Or, as Arbini also puts the point, from the dependence of the truth of a proposition *p* on the contingent existence of some set of practices, part of the 'facts of nature', it does not follow that *p* is not analytic. If in 1930 it is true that all husbands are male, what makes that true is the meaning of the English word 'husband' at that time, in spite of the fact that it would not have that meaning but for the existence of traditional marriage arrangements. Still, the meanings of words change, especially where mutable things like social arrangements are concerned. Even the English word 'right' has changed its meaning, though of course it does *not* follow that what is right has changed.

It is interesting that at this point the γ-formulation intrudes into the α-formulation. Thus Pears, for example, writes that one might not feel the α-formulated problem

> so strongly if the colours were red and orange: since the same person might well call the same thing in the same light at one time red and another orange (provided that he did not know that it was the same thing in the same light, and so that he was being inconsistent). But with complementary colours, like red and green, this possibility is remote.[12]

Red and green are not perfectly complementary in a physical sense. It is after all red and cyan that are the complementaries in additive mixing. So here there is an empirical element at play, unless Pears has in mind the psychological sense of "complementary" in which the unique or unitary hues are complementary. But despite Wittgenstein's best efforts in his middle period, the basis of the construction of the colour octahedron is too unclear to allow for a logic of colour concepts in any clear sense.

Yet there is an almost terrifyingly effective argument from Wittgenstein against the claim that the modal α-propositions are synthetic *a priori*. Admittedly it comes from the mouth of the middle Wittgenstein, but it is hard to resist the feeling that it would have commended itself to him at any period.

> Now suppose the statement 'An object cannot be both red and green' were a synthetic judgement and the word 'cannot' meant logical impossibility. Since a proposition is the negation of its negation, there must also exist the proposition 'An object can be red and green.' This proposition would also be synthetic. As a synthetic proposition it has sense, and this means that the state of things represented by it *can obtain*. If 'cannot'

means *logical* impossibility, we therefore reach the consequence that the impossible *is* possible.[13]

At the end of the day, we are left with ordinary logic and definitions or analyses, where Wittgenstein had begun in the *Tractatus*. With these alone we should be able to derive the modal propositions, if this approach is anything like correct. Wittgenstein himself was unable to produce the analyses. But in 'Some Remarks on Logical Form' he was able to produce *a priori* arguments as to why it could not succeed,[14] and so he concluded that there was something beyond logic that was responsible for the modal propositions. This logico-linguistic something, the language-game, which he explored in *Remarks on Colour*, consisted of a mathematics or geometry or logic of colour that combined content and a modal element, but the results are inconclusive or unclear.[15]

Yet the original argument in 'Some Remarks on Logical Form' against the view that colour logic is just logic applied to propositions about colours seems weak.

> For let us call the unit of, say, brightness b and let $E(b)$ be the statement that the entity E possesses this brightness, then the proposition $E(2b)$, which says that E has two degrees of brightness, should be analyzable into the logical product $E(b)$ & $E(b)$, but this is equal to $E(b)$.

Here we have a straightforward confusion about the meaning of 'and' or '&' or "the logical product". Why should $E(2b)$ be analysable as $E(b)$ & $E(b)$? Wittgenstein appears to have forgotten and to need reminding that '$2b$' or 'two degrees of b' does not mean the same as 'b & b', but rather 'b (a quantity) + b (a quantity)'. He cannot have thought that he did not have '+' available to him, as he himself, at *Tractatus* 6.02, had used it in the definition of '$\Omega'\Omega''x$', and '+' is no more the meaning of 'and', than is 'equal to' the meaning of 'is equivalent to'. Yet his comment "this is *equal to* [our emphasis] $E(b)$" really does suggest that Wittgenstein was confused on the point. He could have retained the general doctrine of atomic propositions in the *Tractatus* simply by avoiding the confusion of '&' and '+', and using the latter in his analysis of statements of degree, using his own analysis of mathematics with the Ω operator.

Nevertheless, in 1929 Wittgenstein concluded that we cannot analyse terms for brightness or colour, and so they have no definitions, or their definitions "have not yet been achieved".[16] Hence propositions asserting the incompatibilities of colours are not analytic—because colours cannot be defined—and these propositions are not part of logic, though they are known *a priori*.

In 1956, in one of his first published papers, Putnam describes this as a "charming argument". But he replied to it, and produced a much-discussed account of the basis of colour incompatibility, or of what there is of *logic* in the α-formulation.[17] His conclusion is that, 'Nothing is red (all over) and green (all over) at the same time' is analytic, in the harmless sense of "... is analytic" in which it means "...'s truth depends on definitions plus logic". x and y are exactly the same colour if they are indistinguishable in colour, and if they differ in colour then they are not exactly the same colour. So if $x = y$ and one thing is both red and green, it is distinguishable from itself. Putnam defines 'Col(F)' ('F is a colour') as being true for two things x and y if and only if x and y are exactly the same colour, i.e. the same determinate shade, and 'exactly the same shade' as 'indistinguishable' (in colour!), and he has no trouble deriving 'Nothing is red (all over) and green (all over) at the same time.'

An obvious difficulty is that Putnam's proposal is entirely extensional. Because of this, as Pap pointed out, "it might happen that the predicates 'blue' and 'round', for example, had the same extension" which according to Putnam's proposal "would justify the conclusion that roundness is a color".[18] A further and closely related feature of Putnam's account that might be considered problematic is that in a universe in which everything is a determinate red, say, we would have to conclude that blue is not a colour since nothing blue exists. More generally, one might also worry that we have to know what we have in mind when we take our red and say, '*This* is red.' If we are inclined to heed the words of the later Wittgenstein, we will wonder how we know or how it comes to be that we have not inadvertently named the *thing* that has the colour, or some property of the thing other than a colour property.

One thing is certain. Putnam's account of 'Col' is limited. It generates a one-dimensional colour space, and we have the interesting claim that a colour is a point in colour space having only the dimension of hue. Yet one sense of 'colour' is the sense in which some circumscribed region of the space is called 'a colour', such as the red part, which consists of many points, or the green part, also consisting of many points. Green and blue are different colours, and they are distinguishable, but there is a case for saying that something can be blue and green at the same time, as it can be bluish-green.[19] Putnam himself acknowledges this, and he does not venture into the problems raised by the γ-formulation.

> It should be observed that these postulates define the logical structure of the colour continuum, but not the actual location of the cutting points (or which end is red) … but the rules do not determine *which* shades he would mean.

And in mitigation Putnam writes,

> The relation to natural language should be clear; the rules of natural language also determine that all the shades between red and yellow shall be classified as orange; but they do not determine such a thing as the place where orange stops and yellow begins.[20,21]

Nevertheless, there is room for us to try to understand the phenomenological structure of colour space better, so that we can arrive at definitions that have as consequences all the propositions that Runge's γ-formulation opens up. We would then be left with logic plus the nature of colour and of the colours: a most satisfactory result.

In 1987, building on his own earlier work,[22] Jonathan Westphal offered an analysis of the 'logical' propositions about colour, including incompatibilities of colour, in line with Putnam's results, that also gave answers to Wittgenstein's puzzling questions about the logic of colour concepts, especially in the γ-formulation.[23] Relying on the Kripke-Putnam model for natural-kind terms, and assuming it to be valid for colour terms, Westphal provided definitions for a number of colours. These definitions employ descriptions of the phenomenal, qualitative character of the defined colour and make it explicit that different colours stand in different relations to brightness, darkness, depth, opacity, illumination, etc. This non-reductive approach to the nature of colours allows Westphal to represent claims about the incompatibility of colours as straight logical contradictions of the form 'p and non-p', thereby explaining their impossibility and showing that these propositions are analytic). There is according to this line of thought no special logic of colour. There is logic, and there is logic applied to the special propositions about colour, which are indeed, as Wittgenstein saw in his *Remarks on Colour*, very special indeed, and much more complicated than we might suppose if we were to think that the essence of colour is given by ostensive definitions.[24]

However, as Justin Broackes[25] has pointed out, there is a worrisome feature to Westphal's account: insofar as Westphal's definitions are intended to be real definitions (and are in this sense supposed to give the reference of a colour-term, rather than its sense) it is unclear why we consider propositions about the incompatibility of colours to be necessary, whether or not we are acquainted with real definitions of the involved colours. That is to say, we seem to *recognize* the necessity of incompatibility statements on grounds that are different from the way in which Westphal *explains* this necessity. Then again, it is unclear what the grounds *are*, on which we recognize the necessity of incompatibility statements; and it may be that our knowledge of the necessities, such as it is, is explained by the necessities themselves, and our general ability to know necessary things. Perhaps all we have is a strong feeling of necessity when it comes to propositions about colours, and then subsequently determine, by analysis, that the feeling is very well justified.

Furthermore, should Westphal's approach be wrong, we will apparently have to put up with language-games as a bedrock of colour logic. This in turn seems to imply the unsatisfactory conclusion that the asymmetries in the colours are relative to the culture we happen to inhabit. To be fair, Wittgenstein himself makes it clear that he does not believe the asymmetries in the colours to be grounded in linguistic conventions alone. If he is right, we are not even in a position to *conceive* of fundamentally different language-games with our concepts, let alone adopt new ones at our leisure. "There is, after all, no *commonly* accepted criterion for what is a colour, unless it is one of our colours."[26] But insofar as Wittgenstein's use of the term 'grammar' oscillates unhappily between general facts of nature and linguistic norms, the difficulty becomes this: If the logic of colours does not rest on linguistic convention and if it does not have its basis in the factual nature of colours either, what *are* we to say about it? An understanding of the basis of the phenomenological structure of colour space is clearly one of the first steps.

Notes

1 In Runge's Letter to Goethe of 3 July 1806, part of which Goethe included at the end of the *Farbenlehre*. The complete text can be found in Albus, A., *Art of Arts*, (New York: Knopf, 2001), pp. 80 ff.

2 Pears, D. F., 'Incompatibilities of Colours', in *Logic and Language (Second Series)*, ed. Flew, A., (Oxford: Blackwell, 1953), Anchor edition (New York: Doubleday, 1965), p. 334.

3 Ayer, A. J., *Language, Truth and Logic*, 2nd ed., (London: Gollancz, 1946), p. 106.

4 Pears, D. F., 'Incompatibilities of Colours', p. 333.

5 Ferré, F., 'Colour Incompatibility and Language-Games', *Mind* 70 (1961), pp. 90–4.

6 Arbini, R., 'Frederick Ferré on Colour Incompatibility', *Mind* 72 (1963), p. 587.

7 See for example Ayer, A. J., *Language, Truth and Logic*, p. 84.

8 Ferré, F., 'Colour Incompatibility and Language-Games', p. 93.

9 Same, p. 94.

10 Arbini, R., 'Frederick Ferré on Colour Incompatibility', p. 590.

11 Same.

12 Pears, D. F., 'Incompatibilities of Colours', p. 339.

13 Wittgenstein, L., *Ludwig Wittgenstein and the Vienna Circle*, Conversations Recorded by Friedrich Waismann (Oxford: Blackwell, 1979), pp. 67–8.

14 Wittgenstein, L., 'Some Remarks on Logical Form', *Proceedings of the Aristotelian Society* (1929), Suppl. Vol. 9, pp. 161–71, reprinted in Wittgenstein, L., *Philosophical Investigations 1912–1951*, ed. Klagge, J. C. and Nordman, A. (Indianapolis & Cambridge: Hackett, 1993), pp. 29–35.

15 For an extensive discussion of *Remarks on Colour* see *Wittgenstein on Colour*, ed. Gierlinger, F. and Riegelnik, S., (Berlin/Boston: De Gruyter, 2014).

16 Wittgenstein, L., 'Some Remarks on Logical Form', p. 35.

17 Putnam, H., 'Reds, Greens, and Logical Analysis', *Philosophical Review* 65 (1956), p. 206.

18 Pap, A., 'Once More: Colors and the Synthetic A Priori', *Philosophical Review* 66 (1957), p. 94.

19 See also the chapters on colour categories (by Briscoe) and language (by Dedrick) in the present volume.

20 Putnam, H., 'Reds, Greens, and Logical Analysis', pp. 216–17.

21 See also the chapter on vagueness (by Raffman) in the present volume.

22 For example Westphal, J., 'White', *Mind* 95 (1986), pp. 310–28.

23 Westphal, J., *Colour: A Philosophical Introduction*, (Oxford: Blackwell, Aristotelian Society Monograph Sequence, 1st ed. 1987, 2nd ed. 1991).

24 Wittgenstein, L., *Remarks on Colour*, III 106.

25 Broackes, J., 'Critical Notice of J. Westphal's *Colour: A Philosophical Introduction*', *Philosophical Quarterly* 43 (1993), pp. 233–8.

26 Wittgenstein, L., *Remarks on Colour*, I 14.

Bibliography

Albus, A., *Art of Arts*, (New York: Knopf, 2001).

Arbini, R., 'Frederick Ferré on Colour Incompatibility', *Mind* 72 (1963), pp. 586–90.

Austin, J., 'Wittgenstein's Solutions to the Color Exclusion Problem', *Philosophy and Phenomenological Research* 41 (1980), pp. 142–9.

Ayer, A. J., *Language Truth and Logic*, 2nd ed., (London: Gollancz, 1946).

Beard, R. W., 'Analyticity, Informativeness, and the Incompatibility of Colors', *Logique et Analyse* 10 (1967), pp. 211–17.

Benardete, J. A., 'The Analytic *A Posteriori* and the Foundations of Metaphysics', *Journal of Philosophy* 55 (1958), pp. 503–14.

Brenner, W., 'Wittgenstein's Color Grammar', *Southern Journal of Philosophy* 20 (1982), pp. 289–98.

Brenner, W., '"Brownish-Yellow" and "Reddish-Green"', *Philosophical Investigations* 10 (1987), pp. 200–11.

Broackes, J., 'Critical Notice of J. Westphal's *Colour: A Philosophical Introduction*', *Philosophical Quarterly* 43 (1993), pp. 233–8.

Buckner, D. K., 'Transparently False: Reply to Hardin', *Analysis* 46 (1986), pp. 86–7.

Deshpande, D. Y. 'An Alleged Case of Factual A Priori', *Indian Philosophical Quarterly* 9 (1982), pp. 107–12.

Dolby, R. G. A., 'Philosophy and the Incompatibility of Colours', *Analysis* 34, (1973), pp. 8–16.

Erickson, G. W., 'Wittgenstein's *Remarks on Colour*', *Dialogos* 57 (1991), pp. 113–36.

Ferré, F., 'Colour Incompatibility and Language-Games', *Mind* 70 (1961), pp. 90–4.

Gierlinger, F. and Riegelnik, S., eds., *Wittgenstein on Colour*, (Berlin/Boston: De Gruyter, 2014).

Gilbert, P., 'Westphal and Wittgenstein on White', *Mind* 76 (1987), 399–4 pp. 423–6.

Hacker, P. M. S., *Appearance and Reality*, (Oxford: Blackwell, 1987).

Hardin, C. L., 'Review of J. Westphal's *Colour: Some Philosophical Problems from Wittgenstein*', *Mind* 98 (1989), pp. 146–9.

Harrison, B., 'On Describing Colours', *Inquiry* 10 (1967), pp. 38–52.

Harrison, B., *Form and Content*, (Oxford: Blackwell, 1973).

Harvey, J., 'Challenging the Obvious: The Logic of Colour Concepts', *Philosophia* 21 (1992), pp. 277–94.

Jacquette, D., 'Wittgenstein and the Color Incompatibility Problem', *History of Philosophy Quarterly* 7 (1990), pp. 353–65.

Kenner, L., 'The Triviality of the Red-Green Problem', *Analysis* 25 (1965), pp. 147–53.

Krishna, D., 'Colour Incompatibility and Language-Games', *Indian Journal of Philosophy* 3 (1961/2), pp. 55–60.

McGinn, M., 'Westphal on the Physical Basis of Colour Incompatibility', *Analysis* 51 (1991), pp. 218–22.

O'Hair, S. G., 'Putnam on Reds and Greens', *Philosophical Review* 78 (1969), pp. 504–6.

Pap, A., 'Once More: Colors and the Synthetic A Priori', *Philosophical Review* 66 (1957), pp. 94–9.

Pautz, A., 'Can the Physicalist Explain Colour Structure in Terms of Colour Experience?' *Australasian Journal of Philosophy* 84 (2006), pp. 535–64.

Pears, D. F. 'Incompatibilities of Colours', in *Logic and Language (second series)*, ed. Flew, A., (Oxford: Blackwell, 1953), pp. 330–41.

Putnam, H., 'Reds, Greens, and Logical Analysis', *Philosophical Review* 65 (1956), pp. 206–17.

Putnam, H., 'Red and Green All Over Again: A Rejoinder to Arthur Pap', *Philosophical Review* 66 (1957), pp. 100–3.

Radford, C., 'The Insolubility of the Red-Green Problem', *Analysis* 23, (1963), pp. 68–71.

Radford, C., 'Reply to Mr. Kenner's "The Triviality of the Red-Green Problem"', *Analysis* 25, (1965), pp. 207–8.

Radford, C., 'Incompatibilities of Colours', *Philosophical Quarterly* 15 (1965), pp. 207–19.

Remnant, P., 'Red and Green All Over Again', *Analysis* 21 (1961), pp. 93–5.

Sanford, D., 'Red, Green and Absolute Determinacy: A Reply to C. Radford's "Incompatibilities of Colours"', *Philosophical Quarterly* 16 (1966), pp. 356–8.

Sievert, D., 'Another Look at Wittgenstein on Color Exclusion', *Synthese* 78, pp. 291–318.

Sloman, A., 'Colour Incompatibilities and Analyticity', *Analysis* 24 (1964), pp. 104–19.

Smart, J. J. C., 'Incompatible Colors', *Philosophical Studies* 10, (1959), pp. 39–41.

Srzednicki, D. J., 'Incompatibility Statements', *Australasian Journal of Philosophy* 40, (1962), pp. 178–86.

Westphal, J., *Colour: A Philosophical Introduction*, (Oxford: Blackwell, Aristotelian Society Monograph Sequence, 1st ed. 1987, 2nd ed. 1991).

Westphal, J., 'White', *Mind* 95 (1986), pp. 310–28.

Wittgenstein, L., 'Some Remarks on Logical Form', *Proceedings of the Aristotelian Society* (1929), Suppl. Vol. 9, pp. 161–71, reprinted in Wittgenstein, L., *Philosophical Investigations* 1912–1951, ed. Klagge, J. C. and Nordman, A. (Indianapolis & Cambridge: Hackett, 1993).

Wittgenstein, L., *Remarks on Colour*, ed. Anscombe, G. E. M., trans. Schättle, L. M. (Oxford: Blackwell, 1977).

Wittgenstein, L., *Ludwig Wittgenstein and the Vienna Circle*, Conversations Recorded by Friedrich Waismann, ed. McGuinness, B. trans. Schulte, J. and McGuinness, B. (Oxford: Blackwell, 1979).

6

COLOUR AND THE ARTS

Chromatic perspectives

John Kulvicki

> The painter hath occasion for an abstraction, with regard to visible objects, some-
> what similar to that which we here require: and this is indeed the most difficult part
> of his art.
>
> —*Thomas Reid, Inquiry into the Human Mind, 6.3*

Pictures represent scenes from points of view. Perspective, traditionally conceived, relates spatial features of pictures to spatial features of depicted scenes. Pictures are perceptual surrogates for the scenes they depict in part because both manifest similar two-dimensional spatial patterns. But pictures can also be effective chromatic surrogates, and very little has been said about chromatic perspective.

Chromatic surrogacy can be explained by appeal to awareness of perspectival chromatic qualities, or *colluminations*. Both Thomas Reid (1801) and Hermann von Helmholtz (1867) had related notions in mind, but this idea has not made its way into contemporary discussions of colour and colour experience. Because facts about the depiction of colour are important for understanding collumination, this chapter also shows how issues in the philosophy of art inform the philosophy of perception.

Spatial perspective has received more attention, and is a little easier to understand, than its chromatic counterpart. Section one unpacks the spatial and chromatic surrogacy claims. Section two then explains spatial surrogacy, and this serves as a model for the explanation of chromatic surrogacy in section three. Section four explains and contextualizes colluminations, and section five then shows how they contribute to recent work on colour constancy. Relatively little has been written about colour in depiction, and even less on how the depiction of coloured things might inform philosophy of colour. Much work, however, is relevant to the issues discussed here, so throughout the goal is to provide both an historical and contemporary context that might lead to future efforts.

1 Spatial and chromatic surrogacy

Consider the following two claims, which are relevant to understanding pictures and picture perception. First:

John Kulvicki

Spatial surrogacy

Some visible, flat patterns present much the same spatial patterns to the eyes as complex, three-dimensional scenes do.

Spatial surrogacy is a staple in debates about pictorial representation, and has been prominent in discussions of pictures since the Renaissance (Alberti 1991, 40–9; Leonardo in Kemp 1989, 52–60). Spatial surrogacy compares the perception of two three-dimensional scenes, one of which involves a patterned flat surface.[1] The pattern is *spatial* in the sense that it is independent of colour and other visible features. The same spatial layout can be presented in many different colours, for example. Those who want to understand depiction typically focus on spatial features of pictures and the way they collaborate to represent spatial features of scenes. The next section will offer an explanation of spatial surrogacy, but for now the phenomenon is all that matters.

The second claim focuses on surface colour, illumination, and (semi)transparent media. It's best to work up to the main claim in steps. To start, consider:

Some uniformly illuminated scenes present much the same chromatic patterns to the eyes as irregularly illuminated scenes with different surface colours do.

Claims like this have been much less prominent in discussion of depiction, despite having an important pedigree. Ernst Gombrich, probably in light of Helmholtz (Maynard 2005, 97 n14), focused on this topic in Part 1 of *Art and Illusion* (1960), which in turn started a philosophical renaissance of work on depiction.[2]

Though the chromatic claim does not explicitly mention flat surfaces, they are relevant because few other scenes can be uniformly illuminated. More complex spatial layouts are full of cast and attached shadows, and it is quite impractical, if not impossible, to deploy multiple light sources in such contexts so that every visible surface is illuminated in exactly the same manner.

What kind of pattern is preserved in these cases? Yes, it is in space, but it is neither a surface colour pattern nor an illumination pattern nor a purely spatial pattern. Colour and illumination matter, but it will prove a subtle affair to explicate just what kind of pattern is involved in such cases. One way to see this is to note that 'surface colour' and 'illumination' can be exchanged in the above claim without loss of plausibility.

Some uniformly illuminated (surface-coloured) scenes present much the same patterns to the eyes as irregularly illuminated (surface-coloured) but differently surface-coloured (illuminated) scenes do.

Painted canvasses seen under uniform illumination are exemplary instances of the first version of this claim, while projection screens, painted with patterns of light, are exemplars of the second.

One final complication: medium matters. A canvas seen in white light and in a clear atmosphere can be a great substitute for a scene in which coloured transparencies or haze intervene between a perceiver and the scene she sees. A uniformly mediated scene is one without chromatic transparencies or haze. With that in mind, the most general claim we can make, inspired by experiences with paintings and other pictures, is:

Chromatic surrogacy

Some uniformly illuminated and mediated (surface-coloured) scenes present much the same patterns to the eyes as irregularly illuminated and mediated (surface-coloured) but differently surface-coloured (illuminated and mediated) scenes do.

To be fully general, patterns that share neither illumination, medium, nor surface colours can nevertheless, somehow, be chromatically similar, and perceived as such. Chromatic surrogacy focuses more narrowly than the fully general claim just because the practice of painting provides a raft of examples fitting that pattern. The typical viewing conditions for a painting are those in which the surface is uniformly illuminated and it is not seen through haze or coloured transparencies. Unpacking this point will be the main challenge in what follows. Section two explains spatial surrogacy, and the sections following it use that explanation as a model for understanding chromatic surrogacy.

2 Seeing space pictorially

The features relevant to pictures representing what they do span two spatial dimensions, and these flat arrays are good surrogates for other more complicated 3d scenes. This shows that many cues for depth depend on patterns in two, not three, dimensions. Cues for occlusion, for example, involve boundaries in luminance and colour that a flat pattern can replicate. That a texture decreases in angular scale across a surface suggests that the surface recedes from the viewer. That colours get washed out in a region of a scene suggests recession as well. Flat patterns can thus replicate a suite of 2d cues that give the impression of things in depth.

Pictures do not work perfectly as surrogates, of course. Move around, left to right, and the experience of a scene changes, even viewed only with one eye. Some things seen are now hidden and others occluded come into view. Pictures cannot replicate such parallax effects because they are typically flat. And even when pictures are not flat, their parallax effects are different from those that would characterize the depicted scene. Andrea Pozzo's ceiling at St Ignazio in Rome (Pirenne 1970) depicts heaven from one vantage point but skewed dystopias from others.

Perceptual access to a 3d scene depends partly on 2d cues. In addition, perceivers have access to those 2d patterns from their points of view. The plate looks round and at an oblique angle, from here, but in another sense it looks elliptical. The ellipse, seen head on, shares a quality with the circle seen obliquely, but it's not an ordinary shape or orientation they share, even though 'ellipse' is the only word that seems to capture both. Typical visual experiences of bodies in space thus include awareness of an object's intrinsic shape, its orientation with respect to the viewer, and what has been called its pattern of extrinsic rays (Alberti 1991, 48), visible figure (Reid 1801, Ch 6), square shape (Armstrong 1961, 12–13), p-shape (Noë 2004, 83), occlusion shape (Hyman 2006, 75ff), or outline shape (Hopkins 1998, Ch. 3). Five points about visible figure are relevant for the discussion of colour to follow.[3]

First, it is a 2d spatial property of objects, in relation to points external to them (see Hopkins 1998, Ch. 3 §3). From different points in space, the dinner plate has different visible figures. These are perfectly objective spatial qualities, even if they are relative to points external to the object in question.

Second, visible figures of things are only perceptually available when one occupies the point from which an object has that visible figure (Kulvicki 2006, 201). This is why Reid's terminology is particularly apt. The plate's visible figure from point p is absent from experiences of the plate unless one sees it from p. Related to this is the fact that though visible figure is a perfectly objective, relational shape property, we never have perceptual access to the point from which things have the visible figures we perceive. We always occupy that point, and so might be apt to mistake a visible figure, which is relational, for an intrinsic shape property (Kulvicki 2006, 201–2; Schellenberg 2008, 68; cf. Shoemaker 1994).

Third, visible figure's accessibility from points of view is an artifact of how we process information about 3d scenes with 2d patterns on the retinas. Reliance on 2d cues for the perception of things in depth is due partly to the fact that the retinas are 2d arrays. It is an interesting, though it seems contingent, fact that we have perceptual access to aspects of those 2d patterns, since one could conceive of a perceptual system that represents intrinsic shape and orientation, from here, without also representing visible figure. In this sense, visible figures are available artefacts of our visual perspectives.

Fourth, visible figure does not constitute an independent dimension along which experiences can vary. As an objective matter, fixing the intrinsic shape and orientation also fixes the visible figure. And as the third point suggests, perceptual access to intrinsic shape and orientation depends in part on the representation of 2d cues for depth. They are made perceptually available and not represented independently of these other features, so one should expect that awareness of one is not independent of awareness of the others. Experience bears this out. Try to imagine the visible figure of a cube, seen from here, varying independently of the cube's perceived intrinsic shape and orientation. Visible figure only detaches from intrinsic shape and orientation in the sense that some experiences seem only to involve visible figures. When things are seen from quite a large distance, or in circumstances that prevent parsing the scene into surfaces and orientations, visible figure is all that's available. Visible figure is, to follow Reid, an abstraction from intrinsic shape and orientation that is present in visual experience.

Fifth, from early modern philosophy through the sense datum theorists of the twentieth century, visible figures were the candidates for the spatial features with which perceivers are acquainted. In that sense, they were regarded as more perceptually and hence epistemologically fundamental than intrinsic shapes and orientations. When seeing a coin obliquely G.E. Moore claimed that "the visual sensibles which I directly apprehend in looking at them are visibly elliptical" (1922, 186, see also 243–7). Visible figures were candidates for perceptual acquaintance, and thus the basis of judgements to the effect that there are round coins, at oblique angles, out there. This fifth point relates to the first four. In fact, they might form part of the explanation for the fifth's plausibility, but it would take us beyond the scope of this chapter to unpack that in detail. Gilbert Harman (1990), following David Armstrong (1961, Ch. 1), stressed how perceptual access to such features is important for understanding puzzles of perceptual consciousness, even if one is not tempted by the sense datum theory.[4]

Section one suggests that pictures are good perceptual surrogates for scenes. Specifically, they are good perceptual surrogates for their spatial features. Awareness of visible figures helps explain spatial surrogacy. Many cues for depth are 2d, and flat canvases can replicate such cues. In addition, we are perceptually aware of the visible figures related to perceiving 3d shapes and orientations. Ecologically, it's rare for distinct spatial patterns to be indistinguishable with respect to monocular depth cues, which might go some way to explaining why perceivers rely so heavily on them. Artifice can exploit this fact about perception, however, with the result being a rich tradition of picture making. As the next section shows, depictive practices reveal an important chromatic analogue to visible figure.

3 Chromatic pictorial seeing

Spatial surrogacy leans on a collapse of spatial dimensions: a 2d pattern pairs with many 3d shapes and orientations. Those 2d patterns feature in our experiences as visible figures. It turns out that cues for colour, illuminants, and media (1) collapse the distinctions between them and (2) figure in visual awareness of scenes. Chromatic surrogacy is enabled by a perspective-dependent, perceptual collapse of non-spatial dimensions.

Consider atmospheric perspective. One way to express what happens in such cases is that as things get farther away, their colours seem more and more washed out, or unsaturated. The colours of objects do not seem to change as they move away, however. What changes is that the objects move away and the intervening air affects the perception of their colours. So, the objects don't seem washed out so much as they seem far away, through haze. Similarly, it's tempting to say that a red piece of glass makes the objects behind it look red, but it is more apt to say that the coloured transparency is perceived, and affects the perception of other things' colours. Objects in shadow don't seem to have darker colours than things in bright light so much as they seem illuminated weakly. At sunset, white buildings don't seem orange. They seem white and illuminated with orange light. Considerations like these are staples in discussions of colour constancy and colour experience more generally.

In pictures of coloured things, however, the inapt expressions acquire a strange appropriateness. A painting that captures atmospheric perspective uses relatively unsaturated colours where it represents faraway parts of a scene. Imagining a tree at some distance, Leonardo advised painters to proceed as follows:

> Then in front of the first tree, with a well-steadied piece of glass and a correspondingly fixed eyepoint, draw a tree on the said glass over that of the real one. Then move the glass far enough to one side so that the real one is aligned close to the side of the one you have drawn. Then colour your drawing in such a way that, with respect to colour and form, it is so like the real one that both, if you close one eye, might seem to be painted on the aforementioned glass at one and the same distance.
>
> *(Kemp 1989, 78)*

It's important to do this out in the open, and match the appearance of a painting seen up close with a tree seen through haze. Merely copying the colours of the tree onto the surface will not give the chromatic match the painter seeks, unless that painting is also viewed through haze.[5] Helmholtz nicely captures this claim in an essay on painting:

> Perfected artistic painting comes about when it is no longer the colors of objects, but the work of light upon the eyes that is successfully imitated. Only by interpreting the goal of pictorial representation in this manner is it possible to understand the deviations from nature that artists have allowed in their choices of colors and ranges of brightness.
>
> *(1903 v.2, 114)*[6]

Reddish paint depicts transparent glass, and the objects behind it. Darker shades represent things in shadow, and orange depicts a white house at dusk. The house is depicted as being white, and the depicted object appears to be in shadow, not multi-coloured, of course. But the picture parts representing the white house are orange, and those representing the shadowed part of an object are dark.

Chromatic perception depends in significant measure on the composition and intensity of light reaching the eye (Hardin 1988, 63). Objects absorb and reflect light in differing proportions across the visible spectrum, and two objects that do so differently will tend to look different in surface colour. But the light reaching the eye depends on more than how perceived surfaces reflect and absorb light. It depends on the spectral characteristics, intensity, and direction of the illuminant. Visible aspects of a scene change as light sources move, because their positions determine cast and attached shadows. Likewise, spectral changes of light sources are noticeable, as in the progress from noon to dusk. The light reaching the eye also depends on the media between a perceiver and the objects she sees. Hazy days and tinted glass are selective filters. So, the light reaching the eye is determined by features of surfaces, illumination, and medium. This much has been clear since pseudo-Aristotle's *De Coloribus*:

> all colours are a mixture of three things, the light, the medium through which the light is seen, such as water and air, and thirdly, the colours forming the ground from which the light happens to be reflected.
>
> *(1936, §3, 19)*

The overall chromatic experience we have is not only largely *determined* by these three things. Subjects have perceptual *access* to them. Oddly lit things, or those seen through a glass darkly, on a hazy day, partly in shadow, illuminated from the left, and so on, are often seen to be that way.

Painted images are typically meant to be viewed under good light: not dappled or coloured, too dim or too bright. They are not normally viewed through coloured transparencies, smoke, or at such a distance as to make atmospheric effects apparent. Because they are typically flat, pictures under good light are seen uniformly illuminated. Such uniformly illuminated patterns are good perceptual surrogates for scenes of varying surface colour, illumination, and medium. Projected images precisely reverse the situation in painting. At a movie, a uniformly reflecting surface and complex illumination patterns substitute for a uniformly illuminating light and a varied reflecting surface.

The lesson of chromatic surrogacy is that many irregularly illuminated scenes can be paired with uniformly illuminated ones—pictures seen in good light—in such a way that the two manifest the same perceptible pattern. By hypothesis, such pictures are not seen as being illuminated or coloured in the same way as the scenes they depict. The picture is orange, seen in good light, while the house is white, seen in orange light, and no one is fooled about this. Their commonalities are in neither surface colour nor illumination, but an abstraction from both, of which we are also perceptually aware.

The circle seen obliquely seems to share neither an intrinsic shape nor an orientation with the ellipse seen head-on, but they nevertheless share a visible figure, for which we do not have a special name: 'ellipse' must do. Chromatically, the picture and the scene share neither surface colours nor illuminations, but *colluminations*, features for which we have no terms but ordinary colour words. Pseudo-Aristotle's use of 'colour' twice in the above quote is telling. The first occurrence picks out collumination, I suggest, while the second identifies surface colour.[7] Colluminations are, in brief, the visible figures of chromatic experience.

Some notion of collumination is implicit in scientific and philosophical work on colour. Reid and Helmholtz both seem to have made the notion explicit, but it does not play much of a role in the contemporary literature. The next section unpacks the concept of collumination, and section five then goes on to show how it figures in contemporary debates about colour constancy.

4 Collumination and chromatic perspective

The end of section two lists five features of visible figures that collectively show how they are perspectival in nature. They are 2d, only available from a point of view, and available because of how the visual system processes information. In addition, they are not independent dimensions of visual experience so much as salient abstractions from them, and they were considered candidates for the spatial features with which perceivers are acquainted. These features have analogues in collumination that help with understanding chromatic perspective.

It pays to save a discussion of the dimensionality of colluminations until the end. As for the second and third features of visible figures, colluminations, too, are visually accessible, but only from a certain chromatic point of view. That might seem trite, since no chromatic qualities are perceptually available from any but a visual point of view. But the point is subtler than that. The visual system must respond to the surface colours, illuminations, and media, using a signal that in some sense conflates all of those things. Light reaching the eye is the source of all information about surface colour, illumination, and intervening media (Hardin 1988, 63; Teller 2003, 48). The perspective involved here, then, is not that of a perceiver located so-and-so in space, using 2d retinas to process a 3d scene, so much as one receiving a complex signal which must be parsed into features of surfaces, illuminants, and media.

The fourth point is that just as an orientation and an intrinsic shape determine a visible figure, a surface colour, illuminant, and medium determine a collumination. Different orientations and intrinsic shapes can determine the same visible figure, just as different surface colours and illuminations can determine the same collumination. While both of these perspectival qualities figure in visual experience, neither constitutes a separate dimension along which experiences can vary.[8] Notice that collumination's dependence on the light reaching the eye does not entail that it is a feature of that light, any more than visible figures need to be shapes of light patterns. Visible figures, section two suggests, are abstractions over intrinsic shapes and orientations. In the same way, colluminations are abstractions over surface colours, and chromatic features of illuminants and media.

Both Hermann von Helmholtz and Thomas Reid endorsed claims about chromatic experience that fit very well with this fourth point about collumination. For Helmholtz,

> the qualities of visual sensations are only signs for certain qualitative differences, partly of light, partly of illuminated bodies, but without a precisely corresponding objective significance. ... Thus, we can say at most that under otherwise identical circumstances they occur in the same manner for the same objects.
>
> *(Helmholtz 1903 v.1, 327)*

Vision provides access to both surface colour and illumination, but it does so only via signs for features that are neither. They have no "precisely corresponding objective significance" though they partake of both illumination and surfaces, presumably because rather different combinations of light and surface can be alike in the sensations they produce. Such combinations suffice to determine a collumination, in that the same one occurs whenever we have the same object seen in the same circumstances, that is, under the same illumination in a similar medium.

Reid is so similar that one thinks Helmholtz must have read him. He suggests that we experience "colour appearances" but refuses to identify them with surface colours. In fact, "They have no name in language" but "we are conscious of them when they pass through the mind" (1801, 6.3). We have names for surface colours, of course, but these have a clear "objective significance", to borrow Helmholtz's phrase. Artists "know how to make the objects appear to be of the same colour, by making their pictures really of different colours, according to their distances or shades" (1801, 6.3). The painter effects a colluminous match, not a surface colour match, between the scene she depicts and the painting as it's meant to be viewed. Doing this is the hardest part of her art, as the epigraph suggests. In Helmholtz's terms, the artist imitates not surface colours but "the work of light upon the eyes" (1903 v.2, 114).[9]

The history of this idea brings us to the fifth point. Visible figures were the qualities theorists attributed to sensations or sense data, and the same is true, I suggest, for colluminations. Some of this is already clear from Helmholtz and Reid. For Reid, apparent colours pass through *mind*, often unnoticed as such. And for Helmholtz, too, they are aspects of sensations that serve as signs for worldly features including surface colour and illumination.

Berkeley seems to have collumination in mind when he cautions against thinking of vision as acquainting us with *planar* figures. We are not acquainted with flat planes in space, so much as 2d arrays, and thus we are not acquainted with *surface* colours, either. "What we strictly see are not solids, nor yet planes variously coloured; they are only diversity of colours" (2009 [1732] §158).[10] The suggestion is that Berkeley first talks of surface colours, then talks of colluminations: chromatic features identifiable with neither surface colour nor illumination.

For Berkeley, surface colour is at least one inference away from acquaintance with colour ideas. For his successors Reid and Helmholtz, the relation between sensation and ordinary qualities of objects was not full-blooded inference, even though contact was mediated. And as noted, Armstrong (1961) and Anscombe (1965) clear a path for understanding these perspectival qualities without attributing them to intermediaries like sense data.[11]

Wittgenstein adopts a sceptical attitude to this early modern line of thought in his *Remarks on Colour*. He wonders whether there is a purer or more fundamental concept of colour than that which applies to surfaces. Impurity becomes a concern when he considers how he might depict a white surface partly in shadow.

> This paper is lighter in some places than in others; but can I say that it is white only in certain places and gray in others??—Certainly, if I painted it, I would mix a gray for the darker places.
> A surface color is a quality of a surface. One might (therefore) be tempted not to call it a pure color concept. But then what would a pure one be?!
>
> *(1977, §56)*

He tries, and thinks he fails, to isolate pure colour experience by considering cases that abstract from the surface-illumination-medium distinction.

> There seems to be a more fundamental color concept than that of the surface color. It seems that one could present it either by means of small colored elements in the field of vision, or by means of luminous points rather like stars.
>
> *(1977, §58)*

Such circumstances relate closely to aperture viewing, in which small patches are seen surrounded by dark screens. This spatial trick abstracts from the surface-illuminant-medium distinctions evident in most chromatic experience. In such cases, viewers have chromatic experiences untethered to the world colours typically inhabit.[12]

Wittgenstein rejects this suggestion as a path to purity because it also abstracts from many important aspects of colour experience that result from simultaneous contrast. Nothing looks brown in aperture mode, because things only look brown when they are darker than their surrounds. Absent more investigation it would be hasty to conclude that aperture viewing captures the full range of colluminous variation. In fact, "In everyday life we are virtually surrounded by impure colors. All the more remarkable that we have formed a concept of *pure* colors" (1977, §59).

Wittgenstein inherits this scepticism about the modern impulse to find pure chromatic experience from pre-modern forebears. Leonardo, for example, claims that "No body is ever shown wholly in its natural colour" (Kemp 1989, 74). And Martin Kemp (1989, 284) suggests that Leonardo follows *De Coloribus*. For example,

> We do not see any of the colours as they really are, but all are mixed with others; or, if not mixed with any other colour they are mixed with rays of light and with shadows, so they appear different and not as they are. Consequently things appear different according to whether they are seen in shadow or in sunlight, in a hard or a soft light, and according to the angle at which they are seen and in accordance with other differences as well.
>
> *(pseudo-Aristotle 1936 §3, 17)*

Wittgenstein's point seems to be that it is remarkable to find a notion of pure colour in light of the fact that no experiences genuinely present things that way. Trying to see surface colour or even chromatic aspects of illuminants absent collumination is like trying to see a square, from here, without also seeing its visible figure. We have an understanding of squares that transcends their visible figures from any particular point of view, but all experiences of squares are impure in this respect. The same holds true for surface colour and the chromatic aspects of illuminants and volumes. We understand them in a way that transcends colluminous variation, but can never experience them, as it were, from nowhere.

That doesn't mean philosophers haven't tried. Most attempts to understand colour focus on rather simplified scenarios, in which only one of the trio of surfaces, illuminants, and media are chromatically interesting. Broad-spectrum, reasonably bright illuminants—white lights—are ideal for revealing aspects of surface colour in that one achieves the greatest variation in visual appearances of surfaces under such circumstances. Similarly, surfaces that reflect well and diffusely across the visible spectrum—white surfaces—reveal the most detail about the lights that illuminate them. And by making both the source and nearby opaque bodies white one creates ideal circumstances for noticing the detailed colours of transparencies and haze.[13] In these cases, colluminations are least salient because only one aspect that contributes to chromatic experience is interesting. The analogous spatial case seems to be that of plane figures seen head-on. In such cases, visible figure coincides with intrinsic shape in a manner that minimizes the threefold aspects—intrinsic shape, orientation, visible figure—of such experiences. The circle, seen head on, has, as it were, a circular visible figure. Such cases are obviously poor exemplars of shape perception generally, just as the chromatic cases just outlined simplify in a problematic fashion. The next section shows how collumination helps with understanding complex cases involving colour constancy.

Finally, let's turn to the dimensionality of colluminations. As an abstraction from surfaces, illuminants, and media, collumination varies in fewer dimensions than chromatic experience overall. Does it vary in as many dimensions as, for example, the visual appearances of surfaces vary? Light sources? Media? Hilbert (2005, following an earlier edition of Fairchild 2013) points out that surfaces do not just vary in colour but also in whether they are metallic, matte, or shiny. Do colluminations vary in this way, too? Facts about chromatic surrogacy at least point to an answer, though it's beyond the scope of this chapter to figure this out in detail. Alan Lee suggests that naturalistic pictures, while requiring nothing more than the gamut of colours, are able to depict problematic colour-like qualities, such as gold, amber, and blonde, which are not to be found in colour space. Moreover, the complex finishes that have become fashionable on cars can be captured in colour photographs.

(2005, 52)

Pictures, whose surfaces are not metallic, blonde, or pearlescent, manage to be good chromatic surrogates for surfaces that are. The pictures themselves do not seem metallic, even though they are good surrogates for metallic surfaces. This suggests that colluminations vary in the three dimensions of the traditional colour solid. Other chromatic features, like shine and sheen relate to how objects interact with light across the range of visible frequencies, unlike surface colour per se, which concerns variable responses to different frequencies.

5 Perspective and constancy

The surface colours of things seem rather stable across viewing conditions. Some lights are so odd that they make it impossible to discern objects' colours, but the snow looks white throughout the day, even in the reddish light at dusk. Similarly, surface colour seems relatively stable even when things are viewed through sunglasses or other selectively filtering media. This is colour constancy, or what I will call surface colour constancy. Surface colours seem to endure changes in the spectral makeup and intensity of illuminants and filters. Though rarely mentioned, similar claims hold for the chromatic features of illuminants and media. The colours of filters seem rather stable across changes in illumination and the other opaque objects seen through them. And dawn light seems reddish in winter, when all is snow, and summer, when green predominates.

Constancy figures in arguments about the nature of colour. Alex Byrne and David Hilbert (2003, 9), for example, argue as follows. Some chromatic features of scenes seem to endure changes in illumination and medium. Perceptual experience can presumably be accurate, at least under reasonably good conditions. So, some chromatic features of scenes endure changes in illumination and medium. The way in which objects reflect and absorb visible light is independent of illumination and medium, and affects chromatic experience. So, the way in which objects reflect and absorb visible light is a good candidate for the chromatic feature of scenes that endures changes in illumination and medium. That is, constancy is deployed in defence of accounts that identify colours with objective surface features of objects. Byrne and Hilbert's argument schema also supports the claim that we perceive objective features of illuminants and media, since they too seem to endure changes in other features of the visual scene.[14]

As mentioned earlier, standard examples in the colour literature tend to involve simple scenarios in which only one of surfaces, illuminants, or media is chromatically interesting. This has not been true in the history of psychology (Gilchrist 2006), and as we have seen these are precisely cases in which collumination is at its least salient. Recent work in philosophy provides an interesting range of options for accommodating complex chromatic experience, and it is here that collumination can contribute to the discussion.

David Hilbert (2005, 2012) and René Jagnow (2009) suggest adding a dimension to the experience of surface colour. Illuminants, on this view, affect the appearance of surface colour but are not perceived on their own terms. "What we see as changing with the illumination is an aspect of the object itself, not the light source or the space surrounding the object" (Hilbert 2005, 151). Jagnow (2009, 569) suggests that a proposal along these lines can handle chromatic surrogacy. Specifically, a white surface in red light seems similar to a red surface in white light because the apparent colours for each are very close to one another in the 4d quality space we get when we add illumination to the mix as a dimension of surface colour. He worries that adding illumination to perceptual experience in a manner separate from surface colour cannot account for chromatic surrogacy, for reasons to which we will return.

Unlike Hilbert and Jagnow, Jonathan Cohen understands chromatic experience to vary in only three dimensions. The other dimensions of chromatic appearance are not present in experience so much as inferred on its basis. Cohen thinks constancy is *not* simply "invariance of apparent color across changes in illumination" (2008, 64). While we are happy to see the white paper as white all over, even when partly in shadow, we also judge the differently illuminated parts of the scene as different in colour. The similarity and difference judgements subjects make in constancy experiments actually depend on the instructions they are given (Cohen 2008, 66 citing Arend and Reeves 1986). In some cases, they identify the white paper as uniform in colour, and in others as different across the luminance boundary. Following Bäuml (1999), Cohen suggests that when a surface is seen half in shadow the halves differ in apparent colour but are alike in surface colour.[15] Stable features of surfaces and illuminants are inferred from apparent colours. The white paper looks white all over because it seems as though all of it would have the same apparent colour if it were viewed under a uniform illuminant (Cohen 2008, 80). These other possible appearances are present perceptually in just that way: as possibilities. Because of how it involves something like inference, it is fair to identify this approach as Helmholtzian—e.g.: "we learn to judge how such an object would look in white light" (Helmholtz 1867, 408)—even though it is not fully in line with Helmholtz's view (Hilbert 2012).[16]

The other popular approach is to suggest that we are visually aware of both illumination and surface features at once. Helmholtz (1867, §24, esp. 409–10) suggested that in many cases the best thing we can say about chromatic experience is that we are aware of two colours at once, one of them seen, as it were, through the other. And we have already seen that Hering suggested of shadowed surfaces that "the darkness, however, which appears on the white as a shadow, is perceived as a separate something lying over the white, through which we think we still see white" (Hering 1964 [1920], 223). Ralph Evans, whose work was important for Hardin (1988) but has not been taken up in detail by many other philosophers, suggested that "we *always* see at least two colors from any stimulus except in the very simplest and usually artificial situations" (1974, 197). And Rainer Mausfeld (2003a, 2003b, 2010) stresses that such a view was fairly commonplace in the descendants of Helmholtz and Hering, including, most prominently, Katz (1935) and Koffka (1935). Mausfeld's own "dual coding" approach to perception, and colour in particular, is built around the thought that such experiences should guide the development of theories of perception. Finally, Reinhard Niederée suggests that "the visual system decomposes the locally three-dimensional input into *two* trivariant components (layers, scissions) for each direction in the visual field" (2010, 114–15; see also Gilchrist 2005).

Derek Brown represents this line of thought in philosophy: "we can experience two colours along a single line of sight, one (opaque) colour through the other (transparent) colour" (2014, 11). He suggests that this not only helps with understanding the perception of coloured transparencies, but also colour constancy. Perception of illuminant features is like the perception of a transparency in that there are two coloured things before one at once: the light source reflected from the surface and the surface itself.

Each of the preceding views has advantages and disadvantages. The notion of collumination provides an alternative that, I suggest, consolidates the gains of each without as many attendant problems.

On the one hand, there is the early modern temptation, exemplified by Cohen, to claim that awareness of colour is captured completely by three dimensions of variation, which in some mediated way relates perceivers to features of surfaces, illuminants, and media. Put differently, the early modern temptation is to identify what I have been calling colluminations with colours simpliciter. The primary chromatic features of which we are visually aware do not exhibit constancy, for example, and in that sense they seem highly dependent on perceivers and the scenes they see. Collumination, as an abstraction over features of surfaces, illuminants, and media, is an excellent candidate for being that of which Cohen thinks we are aware.[17] One worry about views like Cohen's is that they distance us from the stable features of objects, illuminants, and media that seem saliently present in a typical chromatic experience. These stable features, for Cohen, are at one remove from experience.

That worry leads to a strong temptation to complicate chromatic experience by making surface, illuminant, and medium features present all at once. This is not so much an early modern thought as a classical one (pseudo-Aristotle; Kalderon 2015, e.g.), which casts all chromatic experience as complex and impure. Surface, illuminant, and medium are not inferences away from, so much as uncomfortably amalgamated within, awareness. These views have little room for the highly inconstant features that Cohen, for example, finds central to chromatic experience. But by leaving these features out, as I will show, the classically inspired accounts have a difficult time dealing with chromatic surrogacy.

Brown (2014), for example, suggests that we are aware of two colours at once at any given location in the visual field. In chromatic surrogacy cases, however, we notice that one amalgam of surface, illuminant, and medium is a good surrogate for another. What explains this, if the two amalgamated experiences have nothing—neither surface nor illuminant features—in common?

Jagnow (2009) recognizes this worry, and uses it to motivate his 4d account of surface appearance. Because illuminants are dimensions of colour appearance, they affect the quality space into which the colours fit. And quality spaces organize perceived qualities with respect to their similarities and differences. His proposal is that "white the way it looks in red light is more like red the way it looks in neutral light than, say, white the way it looks in neutral light" (2009, 569). But why is the quality space organized in that manner? Jagnow does not so much explain chromatic surrogacy as suggest that he could, given his proposal. But the proposal itself is problematic. For example, how is it that illuminants, whose appearances can vary in just about as many ways as the appearances of surfaces, constitute a single dimension of surface appearance? And what should we do about intervening media? Brown's (2014) proposal is on much firmer ground here.

Hilbert (2005, 2012) makes a case for adding a single dimension to surface appearance largely by focusing on intensities of illuminants and not their chromatic features since he thinks, properly speaking, illuminants are not coloured (Byrne and Hilbert 2003). But, of course, to the extent that he neglects their chromatic features, he neglects an aspect of ordinary chromatic experience.

In sum, the early modern move implausibly distances perceivers from the features that seem constant in perceptual experience. The classical move leaves little room for explaining the manifest inconstancies, which are also the source of chromatic surrogacy. Colluminations are a way to consolidate the gains of both proposals without their attendant problems. We are visually aware of chromatic features of surfaces, illuminants, and media in a typical visual experience. We are *also* aware of colluminations, which are abstractions over all three. Adding collumination to the mix does not commit one to yet another independent dimension of chromatic experience, because the collumination is fixed by a combination of surface, illuminant, and medium.

Some philosophers and psychologists offer accounts closely related to the collumination proposal. Niederée, who makes a proposal much like Brown's, suggests in addition that "in each direction of visual space, a field color appears to be associated with the corresponding bundle of segmented colors" (2010, 115). Field colours are, I suggest, just colluminations. Though it is less clear than in Niederée's case, Mausfeld (2010, 136) also seems to suggest we might be aware of surface, illuminant, medium and a non-disambiguated amalgam of all three, all at once.

In philosophy, David Chalmers channels Hering: "there is a respect in which any objects with perfect shadowed white and perfect unshadowed gray are similar to each other. One might say that both of these properties entail perfect superficial grayness, for example" (2006, 88). He doesn't endorse, so much as sketch the possibility of, such a view. And Schellenberg, who is closest to the account advocated here, thinks that "it is conceivable that, say, a blue couch under yellow lighting conditions has the very same situation-dependent color property as a green couch under standard lighting conditions" (2008, 61). What Schellenberg calls situation-dependent colour properties are, I suggest, colluminations: abstractions over features of surfaces, illuminants, and media.

6 Conclusion

Pictures can be excellent chromatic surrogates for the scenes they depict. But pictures seen in ordinary circumstances need not share surface colours or features of illuminants and media with their subjects. The painting is shades of blue, uniformly illuminated, seen in clear museum conditions, while the scene it depicts involves a white surface, partly shadowed, and seen through haze. Much the same is true for pictures' spatial features. The picture has a trapezoidal region, seen head-on, which depicts a rectangular table, seen obliquely. Pictures are good spatial and chromatic surrogates because they share perceptually available, perspective-dependent features with their objects.

Perspective-dependent spatial features have long been understood and given an important place in discussions of spatial experience and depiction, but colour has somehow been left out of these discussions. Colluminations, I suggest, play a role in chromatic experience akin to that played by visible figures spatially. The idea is not new, as the historical work above should make clear, but it has not been at all prominent in contemporary work on colour. Colluminations make sense of chromatic surrogacy, and they figure in an overall account of chromatic experience that does justice to both the early modern and classical impulses behind contemporary discussions of colour constancy.[18]

Notes

1 Though a plane is two-dimensional, it is a 2d surface embedded in a 3d space, so seeing such a scene is seeing a scene in three-dimensions. Those 3d situations can present the same pattern to the eye as others, like landscapes, might.
2 Dominic Lopes (1999, 420–1) suggests that not all pictures of things as coloured satisfy the above claim and he might be right about that. For now, however, accounts of depiction are beside the point. What is important is that some coloured planes are good surrogates in the sense just outlined.
3 The following assumes that visible figures are perceptually available in much the same way that ordinary shapes and orientations are. Other models are possible. Perhaps they are only available indirectly, in virtue of awareness of shape and orientation, or perhaps shape and orientation only become perceptually available in virtue of awareness of visible figure. The latter view is early modern, while the former might have more contemporary appeal. This chapter explores a model according to which all of these features are available in the same way.
4 This line of thought is also pursued, in different ways, by Michael Tye (1995), Kathleen Akins and Martin Hahn (2000), Alva Noë (2004), Susanna Schellenberg (2008), and Berit Brogaard (2010).
5 Brad Thompson (2006, 82) appeals to cases like this in discussing representationalist accounts of chromatic experience.

6 Translations of Helmholtz are my own. I consulted Kahl (1971), and I thank Timothy Rosenkoetter for his advice.

7 The author actually uses two words, both of which get translated as 'colour' here. The first, χρόας (chroas), picks out something like experienced colours, or apparent colours, while the second, χρωμάτων (chromaton), indicates surface colours. Thanks to Christie Thomas for helping with the Greek.

8 The chromatic features of surrounding things affect the colours they seem to have (see Albers 2013 [1963] for vivid illustrations). This proposal about collumination raises no special worries about such simultaneous contrast effects. They figure in both the surface colours and the colluminations things are seen to have.

9 Dual reference theories of colour—Peacocke (1984), Rosenthal (1999), Brown (2006)—suggest that colour terms name both surface colours and "colour appearances" (Brown 2006) and these are plausibly identified with what Reid calls apparent colours and I am calling colluminations. I am neither defending nor attacking such views of colour, but I suggest that colour appearances are just colluminations, and not merely the appearances of surface colours. In fact, they are deeply related to the perception of surfaces, illuminants, and media, and might not best be thought of as appearance qualities.

10 Here Berkeley is, as usual, a bit subtler than Locke, who suggested that the visual idea, at any given time, is "only a Plain variously colour'd, as is evident in Painting" (1975 [1690], 145). Compare Noë (2004) and Alan Lee (2005, 50–51), who seem to follow Locke.

11 Schellenberg (2008) develops an account of situation dependent qualities that fits very well with the way I suggest we understand colluminations. She also argues that they play an important epistemological role in perception.

12 This case and Wittgenstein's response to it lean heavily on Ewald Hering, a critic of Helmholtz who nonetheless shared his views on the complexity of chromatic experience:

> The darkness seen in the gray is completely fused with the whiteness simultaneously contained in it into a sensation of a particular quality; the darkness, however, which appears on the white as a shadow, is perceived as a separate something lying over the white, through which we think we still see white.
>
> *(Hering 1964 [1920], 223)*

John Hyman (2006) suggests that pictures resemble their subjects not in surface colour, illumination, or medium, but in aperture colour. Collumination is a feature of which we are aware in ordinary perception, which abstracts over surfaces, illuminants, and media. Aperture viewing does not permit parsing into surfaces, illuminants, and media, and in that way it relates to collumination. It would bring us beyond the scope of this chapter to compare these two proposals in detail.

13 Ralph Evans (1974, Ch. 11) stresses the artificiality of the circumstances that many take to be exemplary for developing theories of colour perception. We return to Evans in the next section.

14 This isn't to say how such arguments figure overall in defending an account of colour. It might be, for example, that other facts about colour perception, like interpersonal variability (Cohen 2009; Kalderon 2007), carry more weight. Also, Byrne and Hilbert (2003) do not think that illuminants have colours. They might nevertheless agree that we can perceive features of illuminants, even though those features are not colours.

15 I am using terms in a way Cohen might not find congenial in order to discuss his views within the framework developed here. More along his lines, the two regions have many colours in many contexts. When viewed in shadow, they have different colours, and are judged to have the same colour in another salient context, viz. one in which the surface is uniformly illuminated. This all plays a role in Cohen's defence of his specific account of colour (2009) but for present purposes those issues should be kept to one side.

16 Though their accounts of colour properties differ quite a bit from Cohen's, and each other's, Martine Nida-Rümelin (2006), Joshua Gert (2010), Vivian Mizrahi (2006, 2010), Brad Thompson (2006), and Mohan Matthen (2005, Ch. 11; 2010) endorse similar accounts of colour experiences. They vary in three dimensions, and they relate perceivers to stable features of surfaces, illuminants, and media, which might not, themselves, be colours.

17 Cohen's account of the colours is not early modern by any means, but accounts of colour here take a back seat to the discussion of colour experience. This claim about the relationship between collumination and other features does not fix which features of surfaces, media, and illuminants we represent.

18 Versions of this chapter were presented at the University of London, the University of Michigan, and the 2015 annual meeting of the American Society for Aesthetics. Thanks to the audiences for useful feedback. I thank Cynthia Freeland for her very helpful comments at the ASA, and Derek Brown for his comments on the full draft.

References

Akins, K. and M. Hahn. 2000. The peculiarity of color. In *Color Perception: Philosophical, Psychological, Artistic and Computational Perspectives*. S. Davis, ed. New York: Oxford University Press: 215–47.

Albers, J. 2013 [1963]. *Interaction of Color*. 50th Anniversary Edition. New Haven, CT: Yale University Press.

Alberti, L. 1435/1991. *On Painting*. C. Grayson, trans. London: Penguin.

Anscombe, G.E.M. 1965. The intentionality of sensation: A grammatical feature. In *Analytic Philosophy*. R.J. Butler, ed. London: Blackwell: 158–80.

Arend, L. and A. Reeves. 1986. Simultaneous color constancy. *Journal of the Optical Society of America A* 3: 1743–51.

pseudo-Aristotle. 1936. *De Coloribus*. W.S. Hett, trans. Loeb Classical Library, vol. 307: *Aristotle: Minor Works*. Cambridge, MA: Harvard University Press.

Armstrong, D. 1961. *Perception and the Physical World*. London: Routledge.

Bäuml, K. 1999. Simultaneous color constancy: How surface color perception varies with the illuminant. *Vision Research* 39: 1531–50.

Berkeley, G. 2009 [1732]. Essay towards a new theory of vision. *George Berkeley: Philosophical Writings*. D. Clarke, ed. Cambridge: Cambridge University Press: 1–66.

Brogaard, B. 2010. Strong representationalism and centered content. *Philosophical Studies* 151: 373–92.

Brown, D. 2006. On the dual referent approach to colour theory. *Philosophical Quarterly* 56(222): 96–113.

Brown, D. 2014. Colour layering and colour constancy. *Philosophers' Imprint* 14(15): 1–31.

Byrne, A. and D. Hilbert. 2003. Color realism and color science. *Behavioral and Brain Sciences* 26: 3–21.

Chalmers, D. 2006. Perception and the fall from Eden. In *Perceptual Experience*. T. Gendler and J. Hawthorne, eds. Oxford: Clarendon Press: 49–125.

Cohen, J. 2008. Colour constancy as counterfactual. *Australasian Journal of Philosophy* 86(1): 61–92.

Cohen, J. 2009. *The Red and the Real*. New York: Oxford University Press.

Cohen, J. and M. Matthen, eds. 2010. *Color Ontology and Color Science*. Cambridge, MA: MIT Press.

Evans, R. 1974. *The Perception of Color*. New York: John Wiley and Sons.

Fairchild, M. 2013. *Color Appearance Models*, 3rd ed. Chichester: Wiley.

Gert, J. 2010. Color constancy, complexity, and counterfactuals. *Noûs* 44(4): 669–90.

Gilchrist, A. 2005. Lightness perception: Seeing one color through another. *Current Biology* 15(9): R330–2.

Gilchrist, A. 2006. *Seeing Black and White*. New York: Oxford University Press.

Gombrich, E. 1960. *Art and Illusion*. Princeton, NJ: Phaidon.

Hardin, C.L. 1988. *Color for Philosophers*. Indianapolis, IN: Hackett.

Harman, G. 1990. The intrinsic quality of experience. *Philosophical Perspectives* 4: 31–52.

Helmholtz, H. 1867. *Handbuch der physiologischen Optik*. Leipzig: Leopold Voss.

Helmholtz, H. 1903. *Vorträge und Reden* (2 vols), Friedrich Vieweg und Sohn Verlag.

Hering, E. 1964 [1920]. *Outlines of a Theory of the Light Sense*. Trans. L. Hurvich and D. Jameson. Cambridge, MA: Harvard University Press.

Hilbert, D. 2005. Color constancy and the complexity of color. *Philosophical Topics* 33(1): 141–58.

Hilbert, D. 2012. Constancy, content, and inference. In *Visual Experience: Sensation, Cognition, and Constancy*. G. Hatfield and S. Allred, eds. New York: Oxford University Press.

Hopkins, R. 1998. *Picture, Image, and Experience*. Cambridge: Cambridge University Press.

Hyman, J. 2006. *The Objective Eye*. Chicago: University of Chicago Press.

Jagnow, R. 2009. How representationalism can account for the phenomenal significance of illumination. *Phenomenology and Cognitive Science* 8: 551–72.

Kahl, R. 1971. *Selected Writings of Hermann von Helmholtz*. Middletown, CT: Wesleyan University Press.

Kalderon, M. 2007. Color pluralism. *Philosophical Review* 116(4): 563–601.

Kalderon, M. 2015. *Form Without Matter*. Oxford: Oxford University Press.

Katz, 1935. *The World of Colour*. London: Kegan Paul, Trench, Trubner & Co. Ltd.

Kemp, M. 1989. *Leonardo on Painting*. New Haven, CT: Yale University Press.

Koffka, K. 1935. *Principles of Gestalt Psychology*. New York: Harcourt, Brace, and Company.

Kulvicki, J. 2006. *On Images: Their Structure and Content*. Oxford: Clarendon Press.

Lee, A. 2005. Colour and pictorial representation. *British Journal of Aesthetics* 45(1): 49–63.

Locke, J. 1975 [1690]. *An Essay Concerning Human Understanding*. P. Nidditch, ed. Oxford: Clarendon Press.

Lopes, D. 1999. Pictorial color. *Phil. Psychology* 12(4): 415–28.

Matthen, M. 2005. *Seeing, Doing, and Knowing*. Oxford: Clarendon Press.

Matthen, M. 2010. Color experience: A semantic theory. Cohen and Matthen, eds.: 67–90.

Mausfeld, R. 2003a. Competing representations and the mental capacity for conjoint perspectives. In *Looking into Pictures*. H. Hecht, R. Schwartz, and M. Atherton, eds. Cambridge, MA: MIT Press: 17–60.

Mausfeld, R. 2003b. 'Colour' as part of the format of two different perceptual primitives. In *Colour Perception: Mind and the Physical World*. R. Mausfeld and D. Heyer, eds. Oxford: Oxford University Press: 381–430.

Mausfeld, R. 2010. Color within an internalist framework. In Cohen and Matthen, eds.: 123–47.

Maynard, P. 2005. *Drawing Distinctions*. Ithaca, NY: Cornell University Press.

Mizrahi, V. 2006. Color objectivism and color pluralism. *dialectica* 60(3): 283–306.

Mizrahi, V. 2010. Color and transparency. *Revista di Esthetica* 43(1): 181–92.

Moore, G.E. 1922. *Philosophical Studies*. London: Routledge.

Nida-Rümelin, M. 2006. A puzzle about colors. *dialectica* 60(3): 321–36.

Niederée, R. 2010. More than three dimensions: What continuity considerations can tell us about perceived color. In Cohen and Matthen, eds.: 91–122.

Noë, A. 2004. *Action in Perception*. Cambridge, MA: MIT Press.

Peacocke, C. 1984. Color concepts and color experience. *Synthese* 58: 365–81.

Pirenne, M. 1970. *Optics, Painting, and Photography*. Cambridge: Cambridge University Press.

Reid, T. 1801. *Inquiry into the Human Mind*. 5th ed. Edinburgh: Bell and Bradfute.

Rosenthal, D. 1999. The colors and shapes of visual experiences. In *Consciousness and Intentionality*, D. Fisette, ed. Dordrecht: Kluwer: 95–118.

Schellenberg, S. 2008. The situation-dependency of perception. *Journal of Philosophy* 105(2): 55–84.

Shoemaker, S. 1994. Phenomenal character. *Noûs* 28(1): 21–38.

Teller, D. 2003. Color: A vision scientist's perspective. *Behavioral and Brain Sciences* 26: 48–9.

Thompson, B. 2006. Colour constancy and Russellian representationalism. *Australasian Journal of Philosophy* 84: 75–94.

Tye, M. 1995. *Ten Problems of Consciousness*. Cambridge, MA: MIT Press.

Wittgenstein, L. 1977. *Remarks on Color*. G.E.M. Anscombe, trans. Berkeley: University of California Press.

7

THE ANALOGY BETWEEN COLOUR AND VALUE

Joshua Gert

The analogy between colour and value has typically been employed in order to shed light on the nature of value, primarily because of a (naïve) sense that the nature of colour is clearer than that of value. That is, philosophers have often appealed to colour to support their views about normative or evaluative properties, rather than the other way around.[1] Alas, it turns out that the underlying views about the nature of colour are no less controversial, and those who appeal to the analogy have not generally given any real account of the nature of colour. As a result, even if one is convinced of the general claim that there is a strong analogy between colour and value, this by itself does little to settle issues as to the nature of value. For virtually every dispute about value has its counterpart in the domain of colour. Despite this, the analogy is of course useful. A well-defended and plausible view of colour will lend some of its plausibility to the corresponding account of value, unless some relevant disanalogy can be identified. Moreover, the analogy may well suggest various theses about value, and provide lines of defence, that might not otherwise even have been visible.

This chapter has three main sections and a brief conclusion. In the first section I give a very brief sketch of the positions that philosophers have taken towards evaluative properties and colour properties. One of the things the sketch should indicate, despite the obvious simplifications of the views represented, is that the two domains really do have some interesting structural parallels. The second section then points to some disanalogies between the two domains, indicating, where appropriate, how these disanalogies might be expected to impact the usefulness of an appeal to colour when theorizing about value. The third section then explores in a little more detail some of the ways in which theorizing about value can be aided by thinking about the analogy with colour.

1 Four versions of the analogy

Philosophical accounts of value fall, very broadly speaking, into four camps, which I will call sentimentalism, realism, relativism, and error theory. Of course, my way of carving up the territory is sure to offend the sensibilities of some value theorists. But for present purposes there is no harm in regarding my labels as stipulative, so that, for example, my understanding of realism excludes relativism. What is important and notable is that all four of the views about value—whatever labels we choose to associate with them—have counterparts in the philosophy of colour. This by itself constitutes an analogy worth remarking.

1.1 Sentimentalism

First let us consider what I will call 'sentimentalist accounts'. According to one kind of sentimentalism, claims that superficially seem to ascribe a certain value to an object or action are actually best interpreted as *saying something about* the speaker's attitude towards that object. A distinct kind of sentimentalism replaces the phrase 'saying something about' with 'expressing'. It is unclear how deep the difference between the two kinds of sentimentalism really is.[2] Still, if one uses the former phrase, the view is subjectivism; if the latter, it is expressivism.[3] But both subjectivists and expressivists deny that pain, pleasure, freedom, knowledge, ability, death, and so on actually have any intrinsic properties that could straightforwardly be called 'evaluative properties', and the nature of which could fruitfully be investigated by focusing our attention outward, on the members of such a heterogeneous class of good and bad things. On such views, the place to look for insight into the nature of value is, if anywhere, in the attitudes of the people whose utterances seem to attribute them to other things. One classic source of this kind of view is David Hume. Hume explicitly sees moral and personal virtues as similar to colours in this respect.[4] Unsurprisingly, he also denies colours to external objects and holds that we merely 'gild' the world with qualities that, properly speaking, belong to our sensations or attitudes. It is significant that Hume can be read either as a subjectivist or as an expressivist about moral judgements, and that he himself did not take any pains to distinguish the two possible interpretations.

Sentimentalism has its counterparts in philosophy of colour. To begin, consider C. L. Hardin's *Color for Philosophers*. In this book Hardin argues for what he calls subjectivism about colour: the thesis that it is not really *objects* that have colours, and that assertions that seem to attribute colours to objects are best understood as expressing or reporting facts about our subjective *experiences*. One of the most powerful arguments Hardin has at his disposal is the very surprising degree of interpersonal variability in the perception of very specific colours such as shades of unique blue or unique green. And in fact there are data that some philosophers, including Hardin, have taken to suggest that judgements even about very broad colour terms exhibit a degree of interpersonal variability sufficient to undermine the idea that we should locate colours of any sort—not just highly determinate colours—in external objects.[5]

1.2 Realism

I will call the second kind of account of value 'realism'. On this view, evaluative claims are truth-apt, are often literally true, and concern what they seem to concern: the possession, by actions, agents, or other things, of evaluative properties. One of the most prominent realists about value is G. E. Moore, who held that goodness was a simple, unanalysable property, with which we have direct acquaintance.[6] In attempting to make it more plausible that we could have such knowledge of simple unanalysable properties, Moore compared goodness with a colour property: yellow. This comparison has been taken as a defining feature of Moore's view, and it has been vigorously attacked, and vigorously defended.[7] Moore's own particular version of realism suffers from a host of problems, many having to do with ontological and epistemological issues. How, for example, do we come to have reliable knowledge of the values of things? Moore appealed to the idea of 'direct apprehension', but gave us no account of this capacity. Some contemporary realists about value seek to keep the spirit of Moore's position—its non-reductive aspect—while mitigating these philosophical problems.[8] Others, including the so-called "Cornell Realists", defend a version of evaluative realism that tries to make evaluative properties less problematic by situating them in the mundane causal world.[9] Still others defend a version of realism that includes reference to a certain subjective response: for an item to be good, for example, might be for it to be such as to provoke desire under conditions of full imaginative acquaintance.[10] This last view resembles the subjectivist view described in the previous section; it holds that claims about value have, as their truth-makers, facts about the subjective responses of a certain class of people. But it differs in that this version of realism need not vindicate the idea that an evaluative claim is a *report* about those responses. Moreover, because the relevant response is one that *would* occur under certain possibly counterfactual conditions, there is a very real possibility that a sincere evaluative claim might turn out to be a mistake. This possibility of sincere, competent, but mistaken claims is part of what qualifies this particular view as a realistic one, as opposed to a sentimentalist one. On the other hand, since one need not hold that all rational creatures, or all human beings, would have the same responses under the relevant counterfactual condition, this sort of view might not have the sort of stance-independence that is sometimes taken to be a hallmark of realism. It might instead be a form of relativism, which is described in the following section.

Turning to the analogous view about colour, two of the most prominent contemporary colour realists are Alex Byrne and David Hilbert. They argue that colours should be understood as classes of surface spectral reflectances.[11] This position parallels that of the Cornell Realists about value. A different kind of realist view—more closely resembling Moore's own non-reductive account—refuses to reduce colour properties to other physical properties in the way that Byrne and Hilbert do. This anti-reductionist version of realism is often called 'primitivism', though there are anti-realist versions of primitivism as well.[12]

1.3 Relativism

A third sort of view of evaluative properties is relativism. Like the realists described in the previous section, philosophers who take this view hold that the things that seem to have evaluative properties do indeed (at least quite often) have them. When I now say that freedom is good, for example, what I say is literally true. However, these philosophers do not hold that it follows from this that the sentence 'Freedom is good' is *always* true, no matter who says it, or under what conditions. In this respect 'Freedom is good' is much like the claim 'It's raining' or 'There's a gas station nearby'. Such claims are indeed often either true or false, and they are about what they seem to be about: precipitation and the location of a gas station. However, the truth or falsity of these utterances depends crucially on the context in which they are made. So, if the speaker is in a location where it is in fact raining, the first sentence expresses something true. For normative claims, relativistically understood, a central part of the relevant context is determined by the identity of the speaker, perhaps because this fixes facts about the group or society to which the speaker belongs, which then fixes the relevant set of norms.[13]

Colour relationalism is the view that most closely corresponds to the position I have just described and labelled relativism.[14] Colour relationalists hold that the basic colour properties are relational, and take the form 'red-for-subject-S-in-circumstances-C'. That is, there is, on such a view, no such property as 'plain old red', and if one claims that a certain object—say, an apple—is red, the truth of what one says cannot be determined unless we know, as we typically do, what the relevant subjects and circumstances are. One central virtue of relationalism, according to its advocates, is that it exempts us from the need to decide whose visual responses to count as authoritative when determining the colour of an object, and which conditions to take as revelatory of an object's true colours to such privileged subjects. Both relationalism and realism about colour can allow that our everyday colour claims are quite often true.[15] While we might be able to decide between realism and relationalism by looking for cases in which they differ in their assessments of such everyday claims, it is also likely that this strategy will not yield a verdict. It is true that the relationalist will sometimes interpret two superficially contradictory colour claims as true, while a realist will refuse to ascribe a determinate truth value at all, instead making the weaker claim that both speakers are competently applying a vague term. But the two views will always agree in what we can call 'clear everyday cases'. The debate between realists and relationalists will primarily concern, therefore, other sorts of cases: the utterances of the colour blind, or of those who are viewing objects under non-standard illumination, for example. And even in these cases the relationalist will be able to say things that minimize the conflict: for example, by interpreting claims made by the colour blind as involving relational colour properties such as 'red-to-normal-viewers-in-normal-circumstances'.

1.4 Error theory

A final view in the evaluative domain is error theory. On such a view, our concepts of goodness and badness, or the status of being a reason for action or of being the thing one ought to do, are such that nothing could actually be good or bad, or a reason, or the thing we ought to do. Take, for example, the property of being a reason. According to one frequently cited error theorist, John Mackie, if a certain kind of fact is to count as a reason for someone to perform an action to which it is relevant, it follows that it will be impossible, if one recognizes that the fact has this special property, to remain unmoved by it.[16] But there is no such inherently motivating property to be found in the world as we now know it to be. Although it is not clear how much weight Mackie really put on this particular form of argument, it illustrates the general strategy of the error theorist: to point out that normative properties entail further properties that nothing could (or does) in fact have. Our normative beliefs therefore count as genuine beliefs, and as beliefs that have the form they appear to have: the attribution of a normative property to some event, or to some kind of thing. But these beliefs are all guaranteed to be as false as the claim that walking under a ladder brings bad luck.

Error theory is also an option in the domain of colour. It need not take precisely the form that an error theory takes in the normative domain. Error theorists about normative properties typically hold that *nothing* has such properties. Indeed, they often hold this because they think that nothing even *could* have such properties, at least in a world at all like ours. Some colour theorists certainly hold an analogous position. Paul Boghossian and David Velleman, for example, hold that nothing in this world could possibly have the properties that colours seem to us to have: the properties of being categorical properties of external physical objects and of being directly presented in visual phenomenology.[17] On the other hand, it is also at least possible to think that the right account of colour vision is *projective* in the sense that, in seeing things as coloured, we are projecting onto external objects properties that actually belong to something else: to our visual fields, or perhaps to some other element that plays a role in our representational economy. This interesting view is defended by Edward Averill.[18] On such a view all of our colour ascriptions (or, at any rate, all ascriptions except those of Averill and the philosophers he has managed to convince) will be false. It therefore counts as an error theory, even though it does hold that some mental or neurophysiological entities are coloured.

2 Possible disanalogies

In this section I canvass some of the more significant putative differences between colours and values. Of course there will be differences between the two sorts of properties; otherwise we would have an identity, rather than an analogy. Because of this, not all disanalogies will have the same theoretical consequences. Some may simply be irrelevant for philosophical purposes. Others may undermine the usefulness of the analogy. And still others may actually augment the usefulness of the analogy by helping explain other sorts of differences between colours and values.

2.1 Causing responses and meriting responses

One claimed difference between colours and values appears in the context of response-dependent approaches to realism about these properties. Colours, if one takes such an approach, are typically understood as properties that are such as to *cause* or *elicit* their corresponding responses, at least in a statistically high proportion of cases that meet some descriptively specified conditions. But a similar descriptive and statistical causal claim seems much more controversial in the case of value. That is, it certainly seems possible that there is widespread error even in *normal* human evaluative responses. For example, it seems possible that most of us are misguided about what is genuinely important in life, or that we wrongly take morality to be much less demanding than it really is. The genuine possibility of these sorts of evaluative errors means that we cannot plausibly make the same descriptive statistical causal claim about all values that we do about colours. Rather than saying that evaluative properties *do in fact* cause or elicit the relevant responses in relevantly normal people, perhaps the strongest claim we can make is that such properties *ought to* cause or elicit the relevant responses in relevantly normal people—though they often, or even usually, fail to do so.[19] If this is right, then since the notion of meriting is itself evaluative, it looks as though the two sorts of properties—colours and values—are significantly different. Moreover, if the analysis of evaluative notions requires other evaluative notions—such as the notion of meriting or being fitting—it looks like the possibility that those analyses will be reductive is significantly undermined. An analysis of colour concepts, on the other hand, might still hope to be reductive, in that it might not require the use of any colour concepts in the *analysans*.

There are a number of possible responses to the claim that the meriting/eliciting distinction undermines a useful analogy between colours and values. One is that even in the case of colours, a correct account will not appeal to a purely descriptive statistical claim about how and when a certain response is elicited. Rather, an appeal to the notions of *normal* conditions and *normal* observers will have to make an appearance, yielding an account such as the following:

X is red ↔ X elicits a red visual response in normal human beings under normal conditions.

It is possible to argue that the notion of normality that appears here cannot be understood in purely descriptive and statistical terms.[20] After all, in the statistical sense it is (for example) quite normal for those over 40 to suffer some yellowing of the macula, which distorts the colour of an object. And at some future point, after global warming has forced us all to live underground, it might well be *statistically* normal for us to view objects under the sort of cheap efficient illumination that makes some red things look greyish. Rather than try to patch together a non-normative account of normal conditions or observers, a viable strategy would be to draw attention to the fact that we human beings, beyond having a certain characteristic way of extrapolating from a few examples of a colour, also have certain characteristic ways of discounting the responses of those who disagree with us (including our former selves) when we learn about the circumstances under which those others formed their colour judgements. Such circumstances are deemed 'distorting' or 'abnormal', and their absence is what qualifies a set of circumstances as normal, regardless of whether or not those circumstances are quite common or not.[21] It can be argued that the same understanding of normalcy will also serve in an account of evaluative properties.

A second response to the relevance of a meriting/eliciting distinction to the analogy between colours and values is to suggest that for the most basic evaluative properties—harm and benefit, for example—a statistical account that makes use only of the notion of eliciting, and not the notion of meriting, is just as plausible as it is in the case of colour. That is, one might claim that human motivational responses to such things as death, pain, injury, and imprisonment *for the agent* are just as reliable—if not more so—than our visual responses to grass, blood, snow, and so on. Indeed, this seems very plausible, given the differential evolutionary importance of having proper attitudes towards these harms, as against having perfect colour vision. And this uniformity in response might underwrite the basic normative property of being a harm. This response to the challenge to the analogy can accommodate the suggestion that our responses to *other* evaluative properties—not basic ones—is not as reliable. These other properties might be more complex, and might be defined in terms of the basic evaluative properties. For example, we might define a term that means 'producing the least harm for *everyone affected*'. But since those harms are not merely for the agent, it is an open question whether and how particular agents will respond to the news that a certain course of action has the normative property this term denotes. This response to the causing/meriting disanalogy also serves to address, at least partially, a distinct disanalogy: that variation in evaluative response (and belief) is far greater than variation in chromatic visual response (and belief). The implicit response to this latter disanalogy is to concede it for some evaluative properties, such as being beautiful or being morally wrong, but to deny it in the case of certain *basic* evaluative properties, such as being irrational, or a harm, or a reason.[22]

2.2 The role of responses in determining extensions

Crispin Wright argues against the prospects of a useful colour/value analogy by suggesting, surprisingly, that if we try to force evaluative properties into the mould of either primary or secondary qualities, then it looks as though we regard values more along the lines of primary qualities than secondary ones.[23] This doesn't entail that evaluative properties are primary qualities, but it does undermine the colour/value analogy. In order to develop the argument, it is first necessary to present Wright's suggestion for how to draw the primary/secondary quality distinction. Let us use 'square' and 'red' as representatives of these two types of qualities, as Wright does. Now consider the following two biconditionals:

1   x is red $\leftrightarrow$ any relevantly normal human being would, if in the right sort of conditions, form the belief that x is red.
2   x is square $\leftrightarrow$ any relevantly normal human being would, if in the right sort of conditions, form the belief that x is square.

Even though the phrase 'the right sort of conditions' occurs in both (1) and (2), it does not refer to the same thing in the two biconditionals. In (1) it needs to pick out conditions in which such things as lighting and context are normal for the perception of colour, such as typical daylight. In (2), on the other hand, it needs to pick out such conditions for the perception of shape, such as the absence of distorting mirrors or prisms, and so on. In both (1) and (2), 'relevantly normal' can be taken to mean 'with statistically normal vision'. It may be worth noting that the relevant response in both (1) and (2) is a belief, rather than a visual experience. This both helps to avoid standard circularity objections to response-dependent accounts of colour that need to use colour concepts to characterize the visual response, and also facilitates the analogy with response-dependent accounts of value, since a sensory model for evaluative experience is highly contentious.

Wright holds that something like (1) will be true *a priori*, even if we also understand 'the right sort of conditions', as it occurs there, in descriptive and statistical terms that make no reference to the colour of *x*. But Wright holds that the relevant conditions in (2) will be impossible to specify without making reference to shape properties. For it will need to be stipulated, if (2) is to be true, that the shape of *x* does not change—since very many objects do indeed change their shape even during the quite short intervals in which they might be observed. To put the point in slogan form, the extensions of colour terms depend on our best beliefs about what objects have what colours, whereas the extensions of shape terms do not depend on our best beliefs about what objects have what shapes. This is the essential difference between primary and secondary qualities, on Wright's account.

Wright uses his way of marking the primary/secondary quality distinction to show that we will be unable to provide a response-dependent account of moral value that represents them as secondary qualities. For a plausible-seeming biconditional for moral value, along the lines of (1) and (2) above, would run something like the following:

3   *x* is morally correct ↔ any relevantly normal human being would, if in the right sort of conditions, form the belief that *x* morally correct.

The problem for the analogy with colour is that an explanation of the sense of either 'relevantly normal human being' or 'the right sort of conditions' will have to make reference to some moral properties of the subject. And there no is prospect, Wright believes, of doing this while using only morally neutral language. It is because of the appearance of moral notions in the right-hand side of (3) that it is impossible to see our best beliefs about moral properties as determining the extensions moral terms. But the only alternative realist understanding of the truth of (3) seems to require that we should see the extensions of moral terms as independent of our best beliefs. That is, as Wright would say, our understanding of moral properties seems to show that we regard them as primary qualities, not secondary, at least if we insist on choosing one of those two models.

2.3 Perceptual availability of bases

Another difference between colours and values has to do with the perceptual availability of the properties on which colours and values supervene. When we respond to an object visually by having an experience in which it appears red to us, we have no perceptual access to the reflectance properties, or microscopic physical properties, of that object. As a result, the *only* immediately available evidence as to its colour is supplied by the phenomenology of our visual experience of the object. It is arguable, on the other hand, that the basis for our evaluative responses to objects or events is typically available to us, either perceptually or through some other route. For example, when we judge an act to be irrational—which is a negative evaluative judgement—this is typically because we are aware of the features on which its irrationality depends: the likely consequences of the act, for example. This explains why we can typically quite spontaneously explain which features of the act make it irrational.

It is not clear what the impact of the above disanalogy would be. One consequence might be that it accounts for the fact that we can form justified beliefs not only about the evaluative properties of certain things, but also about what the grounds of those properties are. This second sort of belief is not available in the case of colour. If we think of our acquisition of competence with both colour and value concepts as based on ostension and correction (liberally understood to include more than explicit teaching episodes), then noting this particular disanalogy allows one to preserve the primary analogy while acknowledging a significant difference in the nature of our beliefs about the grounds of the two sorts of properties.

2.4 *The reliability of the relevant response mechanism*

Hagit Benbaji has pointed out that the visual system presents us with both colours and shapes. She argues that this makes for an important disanalogy with anything one might wish to call a moral sense.[24] Very few people deny that shapes are genuine properties of external objects, and that vision often accurately reveals them to us. Benbaji argues that the reliability of vision with regard to shape helps explain why we trust vision with regard to colour, and thereby helps discharge the burden of a projective error theory of colour: to explain the temptation to error. But this explanation undermines the analogy with value, if that analogy is meant to support a similar sort of projective error theory. As Benbaji notes, her point here is consistent with the analogy remaining useful if one is defending any other sort of account of colour and value: primitivist or dispositionalist ones, for example.

What precisely is the problem supposed to be for someone who wishes to extend the projectivist account of colour to the case of value? Suppose that there is some sort of faculty or sense that produces moral or evaluative seemings. In order for an appeal to this faculty to explain a widespread projective error about the moral or evaluative, on the model the projectivist uses in the case of colour, that same faculty would have to produce clearly reliable information about some other sorts of properties, just as vision clearly delivers reliable information about shape. But there does not seem to be any such faculty. Against the suggestion that the relevant faculty in the case of evaluative properties might be nothing other than reason and reflection, Benbaji suggests that if this were true, the analogy with colours would no longer help support the error theorist. Rather, what would then become necessary would be some explanation of the *particular* error in reasoning that tempts us to believe in evaluative properties. This makes clear that for the analogy between colour and value to support the error theorist in the way Benbaji describes, the faculty that underwrites the moral appearances must be something quasi-perceptual.

3 Uses of the analogy

So far we have seen that there exist broadly analogous positions within philosophy of colour for the major sorts of views one encounters in value theory. And we have also seen that there are some differences between the two domains that might undermine the usefulness of certain versions of the analogy. To the degree that the analogy is a good one, the defence of a particular sort of view in one domain provides a *prima facie* case for the same sort of view in the other domain. But the analogy can be exploited in order to do more detailed work than this—illuminating particular issues in one domain because that same issue arises in the other. In what follows I briefly sketch some of the ways in which the analogy between colours and values has been used in this sort of way.

3.1 *Essential contestability*

Much has been made of the possibility of normative disagreement in the face of full agreement on "the facts".[25] These phenomena have been taken to require special explanations, and have even been taken by some philosophers to be incompatible with a realistic account of normative notions.[26] But the same phenomena appear in the domain of colour, and even realists about colour acknowledge this. Happily, people do not typically come to blows when they find themselves involved in ineliminable disagreements about the colour of someone's socks. This makes the phenomenon of ineliminable disagreement less problematic not only in the sense that there are fewer fights, but in the sense that the lack of strong feelings about the matter allows for a more dispassionate philosophical scrutiny. And it also allows for a diagnosis of at least some of these disagreements. They may, for example, have their source in a distinction between the highly determinate nature of our conscious responses to particular instances of colours and values, and the possibly less determinate nature of (a) the chromatic and evaluative properties of the objects and acts to which those responses are in fact responses, or (b) the meanings of the public-language terms that refer to these properties. That is, just as I see a green object in a way that I can describe very precisely in terms of a location in colour space, my affective response to a particular action might have a determinate phenomenology or motivational intensity. And just as variation in human phenomenal visual response to the green object may underwrite a certain vagueness in the term 'green', so too might variation in affective response underwrite a certain vagueness in terms such as 'morally justified' or 'worthwhile'. Admittedly, there are those who hold that the scope of faultless disagreement in the case of value, or colour, or both, is too great to make this appeal to vagueness plausible. But if we restrict attention to the certain basic evaluative notions, such as the notion of personal harm mentioned in section 2.1, such scepticism seems misplaced. And if we take care to distinguish colour from colour appearance, in the way to be described in section 3.3, it seems misplaced in the case of colour as well.[27]

3.2 The relation to human nature, and the possibility of objectivity

A worry is sometimes expressed about views of evaluative notions that make them dependent on contingencies of human nature.[28] Surely the basic evaluative facts are not to be equated with sociological facts! Surely they cannot change over time! All this seems quite plausible. But if we consider analogous issues in the domain of colour these sorts of worries can be addressed in various ways. There can hardly be any doubt that the extensions of human colour words—assuming for the moment that they have extensions—depend in a very important way on contingencies of the human visual system. If we had only two kinds of colour receptors in our retinas, we could not see binary hues such as orange or purple, and therefore would not have concepts of them. And if our middle-wavelength receptors had a spectral absorption profile that peaked near 500nm rather than 540nm then the extension of our word 'red' would be different. But these kinds of contingencies in the meanings of human colour words do not underwrite any particularly surprising colour claims. That is, even though it is a contingent matter that the word 'orange' refers to the property it actually refers to (a property had by carrots, but not by tomatoes), this does not have any obvious implications as to the nature of that property. So this sort of contingency allows for it to remain a necessary truth that orange is a binary hue: in particular, a mix of yellow and red. The relevant contingency simply does not qualify the truth values of the propositions expressed with the colour words we happen to have: rather, the contingency is a matter of our having words with the relevant meanings in the first place. Thus, though it is a contingent truth that that the flesh of a ripe mango is orange, the basis of this truth is to be found in pomology, not in linguistics.

3.3 Multiple-aspects

Advocates of so-called 'fitting-attitude' accounts of value defend accounts that centrally feature a biconditional of the following form:

> x has value V $\leftrightarrow$ it would be appropriate for subjects of kind S in circumstances of kind C to have response R to x.

It is typically assumed that for each value V—moral rightness, non-moral goodness, beauty, and so on—there will be a uniquely appropriate attitude R, which would be appropriate or fitting for the right sort of subjects in the right sort of circumstance. A problem for such accounts has been to defend specific accounts of the attitude, subject, and circumstances, since the attitudes that one can appropriately take towards instances of various values will vary quite widely depending on the relation one has towards those instances. For example, the fitting attitude to take towards an episode of pain (an instance of non-moral badness or harm) can be expected to be very different depending on whether that pain is past, present, or future. Similarly, the fitting attitude to take towards one's own present pain might be very different from the fitting attitude towards someone else's present pain—especially since that other person might be a distant stranger, or one's own child, or the person who harmed one's child.

The analogy with colour can help the fitting-attitude value-theorist deal with the problems presented by variability in the appropriate response to instances of various values.[29] It is easy to see that the appropriate visual response to a coloured object will also vary considerably with one's viewing circumstances. Consider, for example, the appearance of a uniformly-coloured tabletop that is partially illuminated by sun coming in through a window. The differently illuminated parts of the tabletop will look quite different. And it is extremely difficult to justify the selection of one of the illumination conditions as revealing the *true* appearance. Rather than say that an object with a certain colour will appear in one specific way to the right sort of observer under the right sort of conditions, what we can say instead is that an object with a certain colour will exhibit a certain *pattern* of appearances, depending on viewing conditions.[30] And, in analogous fashion, we can say that the appropriate responses to episodes of pain fall into a certain characteristic pattern: for example, *fear* for one's own future pain, *relief* about past pain, *indignation* at pain unjustly caused to someone one cares about, or *satisfaction* at someone else's pain if it is richly deserved.

4 Conclusion

On reflection it should be no surprise that the analogy between colour and value has been a recurrent one in normative and ethical theorizing. Both colours and values seem obviously to be related to contingent features of human nature in some way: to the nature of our visual equipment in the case of colour, and to our emotional profiles, social nature, and particular vulnerabilities, in the case of value. There is no reason to think—and plenty of reason not to think—that animals see the colours we see, for those animals that see any colours at all. Similarly, there is no reason to think that a moral system that applied to angels would be like ours, since it is not clear that it makes sense to apply our moral system to omniscient or invulnerable beings. And though of course there may be some dissenters, it does not seem that animals are sensitive to moral properties, or to evaluative properties more generally. So—unlike shapes and chemical elements—the colours and values with which we are acquainted are plausibly regarded as strongly anthropocentric.

Admittedly, the very same dependence on human nature that suggests an analogy between colour and value might, from a different perspective, give rise to doubts that the analogy will be particularly deep or striking. After all, dependence on human nature can take many different forms, and may therefore underwrite the semantics of terms such as 'red' and 'right' in a corresponding variety of ways. Happily, even if the analogy between colour and value turns out to be flawed in various ways, these ways can function as "natural experiments" that may help in the broader philosophical search for a more general theory of the ways in which human thought and talk function, and their relation to a world populated by physical objects and by people.

Notes

1 For purposes of this chapter I make no distinction between the normative and the evaluative.
2 For doubts about the significance of the difference, see Jackson and Pettit (1998).
3 Expressivism is currently enjoying a period of relative flourishing. See Alan Gibbard (1990; 2003), Simon Blackburn (1993; 1998), and Michael Ridge (2006). Avowed subjectivists are now thin on the ground. One expression of subjectivism, under the label 'Speaker Relativism', is Dreier (1990), though Dreier no longer endorses the view. It is also possible to read Prinz (2007) and Goldman (1987) in subjectivist ways.
4 Hume (1975, pp. 285–94; 1985).
5 The data that purportedly supports this conclusion is presented in Malkoc *et al.* (2005), and is cited by Hardin and his co-authors in Cohen *et al.* (2006). See Gert (2017), pp. 114–15 for doubts about their interpretation of the data.
6 See Moore (1993), p. 7.
7 For one of the most concentrated attacks, see Blackburn (1993), pp. 159–61. For defences of various degrees of strength, see McDowell (1985), Johnston (1989), and Wiggins (1998).
8 Shafer-Landau (2005).
9 Sturgeon (1988); Brink (1986); Boyd (1988).
10 This is similar to the view expressed in Lewis (1989), though Lewis prefers the response of second-order desire: desire to desire.
11 Byrne and Hilbert (2003).
12 Yablo (1995); Broackes (1997); Watkins (2005); Gert (2008).
13 See Harman (1975).
14 Jonathan Cohen (2009) is perhaps the most vehement defender of relationalism. See also Jackson and Pargetter (1997) and McLaughlin (2003).
15 I say 'can allow' because it is possible for relationalists to hold that the actual semantics of our everyday colour claims are not relational, but realistic. Such relationalists are error theorists about our everyday claims, but advocate a revisionary position that would, if incorporated into everyday language, allow most colour claims to be true.
16 Mackie (1977), chap. 1. See also Joyce (2001).
17 Boghossian and Velleman (1989; 1991).
18 Averill (2005).
19 McDowell (1985), p. 118.
20 Gert (2011).
21 Pettit (1999).
22 Gert (2012), chap. 4.
23 Wright (1988).
24 Benbaji (2015).
25 See, e.g., Gibbard (1990), p. 198.
26 See Foot (1958) for critical discussion of this view.
27 See also note 5 regarding the data that some philosophers have appealed to in support of an overly strong claim about the degree of relevant disagreement.
28 Blackburn (1993), p. 160.
29 Gert (2010).
30 See Broackes (1997), Noë (2004).

References

Averill, Edward, 2005, 'Toward a Projectivist Account of Color', *Journal of Philosophy* 102, pp. 217–34.

Benbaji, Hagit, 2015, 'Two Uses of the Analogy Between Colors and Values', *Journal of Philosophical Research* 40, pp. 171–88.

Blackburn, Simon, 1993, 'Errors and the Phenomenology of Value', in *Essays in Quasi-Realism*. New York: Oxford University Press, pp. 149–65.

Blackburn, Simon, 1998, *Ruling Passions*. Oxford: Oxford University Press.

Boghossian, Paul, and J. David Velleman, 1989, 'Colour as a Secondary Quality', *Mind* 98, pp. 81–103.

Boghossian, Paul, and J. David Velleman, 1991, 'Physicalist Theories of Color', *The Philosophical Review* 100, pp. 67–106.

Boyd, Richard, 1988, 'How to be a Moral Realist', in Sayre-McCord 1988, pp. 187–228.

Brink, David O., 1986, 'Externalist Moral Realism', *Southern Journal of Philosophy* 24 (Supplement), pp. 23–40.

Broackes, Justin, 1997, 'The Autonomy of Color', in Byrne and Hilbert 1997, pp. 191–225.

Byrne, Alex, and David R. Hilbert, 1997, *Readings on Color 1: The Philosophy of Color*. Cambridge, MA: MIT Press.

Byrne, Alex, and David R. Hilbert, 2003, 'Color Realism and Color Science', *Behavioral and Brain Sciences* 26, pp. 3–21.

Cohen, Jonathan, 2009, *The Red and the Real: An Essay on Color Ontology*. New York: Oxford University Press.

Cohen, Jonathan, C. L. Hardin, and B. McLaughlin, 2006, 'True Colors', *Analysis* 66, pp. 335–40.

Dreier, James, 1990, 'Internalism and Speaker Relativism', *Ethics* 101(1), pp. 6–26.

Foot, Philippa, 1958, 'Moral Arguments', *Mind* 67, pp. 502–13.

Gert, Joshua, 2008, 'What Colors Could Not Be: An Argument for Color Primitivism', *Journal of Philosophy* 105(3), pp. 128–57.

Gert, Joshua, 2010, 'Color Constancy and the Color/Value Analogy', *Ethics* 121(1), pp. 58–87.

Gert, Joshua, 2011, 'Fitting-Attitudes, Secondary Qualities, and Values', *Philosophical Topics* 38(1), pp. 87–105.

Gert, Joshua, 2012, *Normative Bedrock: Response-Dependence, Rationality, and Reasons*. Oxford: Oxford University Press.

Gert, Joshua, 2017, *Primitive Colors: A Case Study in Neo-Pragmatist Metaphysics and Philosophy of Perception*. Oxford: Oxford University Press.

Gibbard, Allan, 1990, *Wise Choices, Apt Feelings*. Cambridge, MA: Harvard University Press.

Gibbard, Allan, 2003, *Thinking How to Live*. Cambridge, MA: Harvard University Press.

Goldman, Alan, 1987, 'Red and Right', *Journal of Philosophy* 84, pp. 349–62.

Harman, Gilbert, 1975, 'Moral Relativism Defended', *Philosophical Review*, 84, pp. 3–22.

Hume, David, 1975/1748, *Enquiries Concerning Human Understanding and Concerning the Principles of Morals*, 3rd ed., ed. L. A. Selby-Bigge and P. H. Nidditch. Oxford: Clarendon.

Hume, David, 1985/1752, 'The Sceptic', in *Essays Moral, Political, and Literary*, ed. Eugene F. Miller. Indianapolis: Liberty Classics, 1985, p. 166.

Jackson, Frank, and Philip Pettit, 1998, 'A Problem for Expressivists', *Analysis* 58, pp. 239–51.

Jackson, Frank, and Robert Pargetter, 1997, 'An Objectivist's Guide to Subjectivism about Color', in Byrne and Hilbert 1997, pp. 67–79.

Johnston, Mark, 1989, 'Dispositional Theories of Value', *Aristotelian Society Supplement* 63, pp. 139–74.

Joyce, Richard, 2001, *The Myth of Morality*. Cambridge: Cambridge University Press.

Lewis, David, 1989, 'Dispositional Theories of Values', *Proceeding of the Aristotelian Society Supplementary* 63, pp. 113–37.

Mackie, J. L., 1977, *Ethics: Inventing Right and Wrong*. Harmondsworth: Penguin.

McDowell, John. 1985, 'Values and Secondary Qualities', in *Morality and Objectivity: A Tribute to J. L. Mackie*, ed. Ted Honderich. Boston: Routledge and Kegan Paul, pp. 110–29.

McLaughlin, Brian, 2003, 'The Place of Color in Nature', in *Colour Perception: Mind and the Physical World*, ed. R. Mausfeld and D. Heyer. New York: Oxford University Press.

Malkoc, G., P. Kay, and M. A. Webster, 2005, 'Variations in Normal Color Vision. IV. Binary Hues and Hue Scaling', *Journal of the Optical Society of America* A 22, pp. 2154–68.

Moore, G. E., 1993/1903, *Principia Ethica*, 2nd ed., ed. Thomas Baldwin. Cambridge: Cambridge University Press.

Noë, Alva, 2004, *Action in Perception*. Cambridge, MA: MIT Press.

Pettit, Philip, 1999, 'A Theory of Normal and Ideal Conditions', *Philosophical Studies* 96, pp. 21–44.

Prinz, Jesse, 2007, *The Emotional Construction of Morals*. Oxford: Clarendon Press.

Ridge, Michael, 2006, 'Ecumenical Expressivism: Finessing Frege', *Ethics* 116, pp. 302–36.

Sayre-McCord, Geoffrey, ed., 1988, *Essays on Moral Realism*. Ithaca, NY: Cornell University Press.

Shafer-Landau, Russ, 2005, *Moral Realism: A Defense*. Oxford: Clarendon Press.

Sturgeon, Nicholas, 1988, 'Moral Explanations', in Sayre-McCord 1988, pp. 229–55.

Watkins, Michael, 2005, 'Seeing Red: The Metaphysics of Colours Without the Physics', *Australasian Journal of Philosophy* 83, pp. 33–52.

Wiggins, David, 1998, 'A Sensible Subjectivism'. In *Needs, Values, Truth*, 3rd ed. New York: Oxford University Press.

Wright, Crispin, 1988, 'Moral Values, Projection and Secondary Qualities', *Aristotelian Society Supplemental Volume* 62, pp. 1–26.

Yablo, Stephen, 1995, 'Singling Out Properties', *Philosophical Perspectives* 9, pp. 477–502.

PART II

Interlude
The science and spaces of colour

8

THE SCIENCE OF COLOUR AND COLOUR VISION

Alex Byrne and David R. Hilbert

1 Colour vision and colour science

Colour science concerns the process of colour vision and those features of the environment that affect the colours that we see and how we see them. Colour vision has been studied systematically from a variety of points of view since the nineteenth century. The science we discuss below draws on optics, psychology, neuroscience, neurology, ophthalmology, and biology. And, although the relevant basic facts of optics and physiology and their contribution to colour vision have been known for at least a century and half, there are still many aspects of colour vision—including some quite fundamental ones—that are poorly understood. In what follows we will provide an overview of what is known and indicate matters of current controversy. We will concentrate on giving the background necessary to understand those parts of colour science that are potentially relevant to philosophical work on colour. Our account is necessarily quite sketchy and we won't be able to do more than provide a starting point for those interested in the topic.[1]

2 The optical process

The process of vision typically begins with a source of light that illuminates the objects in a scene. The light is reflected from the surfaces of objects and some of it enters the eye where the cornea and lens combine to focus the light and produce an image of the scene on the retina. This textbook scenario oversimplifies in numerous respects but it captures two central truths about vision. First, it is light as modified by the surfaces and objects in the environment that enables vision, including colour vision. Differences between objects that don't affect light (or aren't correlated with differences that affect light) are not visible. Accordingly, it is the variable effects of different parts of the scene on the light falling on them that enables us to see objects and their colours. Second, a crucial part of the visual process is the formation of an image in the back of the eye. The retinal image is important because it separates the light coming from the different parts of the scene, enabling spatial vision and with it the ability to visually attribute different colours to different locations within the scene. Although we will temporarily set aside the fact that the immediate stimulus for vision is an image of the scene before the eyes, it will re-emerge when we turn to the important topic of the interaction between spatial vision and colour vision.

2.1 Light

Light is a form of electromagnetic radiation, and so can be described in both wave and particle terms. The particles of light, photons, are usefully characterized in terms of their energy (the usual unit is the *electron-volt* (eV), 1.6×10^{-19} joules) while the waves associated with the photon are usefully characterized by their wavelength (the usual unit is the *nanometer* (nm), 10^{-9} metres). These are not independent characterizations: specifically, the energy of a photon is inversely proportional to its wavelength. The *intensity* or *power* of a light is the amount of energy it delivers per unit time. Most light sources emit light at a variety of wavelengths so a complete characterization of a light in these terms requires describing how its power is distributed across wavelengths. The *spectral power distribution* (SPD) of a light specifies the proportion of the total power of that light that is carried by the photons at each wavelength. For many purposes in colour science, overall intensity is held fixed and it is the varying SPD that is the explanatory variable.

Only a very small segment of the total electromagnetic spectrum is relevant to most questions in colour science because the receptors in the eye only respond directly to a narrow range of wavelengths. The precise boundaries are somewhat arbitrary but the visible spectrum runs roughly from 400 nm (3.1 eV) at the violet end to 700 nm (1.8 eV) at the red end. The range of intensities that are relevant is much larger—the ratio of the intensities of the illumination provided by direct summer sunlight to that available on a moonless night is about 10 billion to one. Normal indoor lighting typically lies somewhere near the centre of this range.

The light sources that initiate the process of vision can be described in terms of two kinds of characteristics: spatial and spectral. First, light sources can be divided into those that are of significant spatial extent, like the sky on an overcast day or a bank of fluorescent tubes behind a diffusing panel, and those that approximate point sources, like the sun or a street lamp. An extended source can provide much more uniform illumination across the scene while a point source illuminates objects in a way that depends much more strongly on their position and orientation with respect to the source and the other objects in the scene. Second, as just noted, the light emitted by a source can be characterized in terms of its overall intensity and spectral power distribution. The SPD of light sources is critical to understanding how the process of colour vision works.

3 Colour in the environment

3.1 Objects

When light falls on an object some proportion of the light at each wavelength is reflected, some proportion is absorbed and—for transparent and translucent objects—some proportion is transmitted. Reflection can be quite complicated but for many purposes it is useful to separate the reflected light into two components. First, a diffuse component, in which the intensity of the reflected light displays relatively little dependence on the angle between the eye, the object's surface, and the light source. Second, a specular component in which the reflection is mirror-like and highly directional. Typically, the diffuse component is much more influenced by characteristics of the object, while the specularly reflected light often approximates the SPD of the light source. A number of the characteristics of an object affect the way in which it modifies the light it reflects, most notably its chemical composition and the roughness of its surface. Since many objects are heterogeneous in their composition the reflecting characteristics of an object are typically variable and the variation often is found at several different spatial scales, giving rise to both visible patterns and visible texture.

124

The *reflectance* of an object (or surface) at a given wavelength is the ratio of the light (number of photons) it reflects at that wavelength to the incident light at that wavelength. The *surface spectral reflectance* (SSR) of an object is the reflectance of the object at each wavelength (in practice narrow bands of wavelengths) in the visible spectrum. Displaying an object's SSR graphically results in its *spectral reflectance curve*. In order to achieve a widespread system of colour measurement the illuminants need to be standardized. The most important of these is *CIE illuminant C*—an approximation to average daylight that has the virtue of being reproducible in the laboratory using a standard light source and filter.

The visible light reaching the eye from an (opaque, non-luminous) object is the joint product of its SSR and the SPD of the incident light. Ignoring the effects of scene composition, these exhaust the physical characteristics of objects and light relevant to predicting colour appearance.[2] What is missing, however, from this physical description is any way of relating this information to perceived colour. First, not all differences in the SSR of the object or the SPD of the illuminant are perceptually detectable. Second, and more importantly, a pair of spectral reflectance curves is little help by itself as to whether or not the corresponding two objects will appear to match in colour when viewed in a given illuminant. Unsurprisingly, the physics of light and its interaction with objects is not enough to explain how we perceive colour.

4 Basic physiology of colour vision

Perceived colour is, in complicated ways, dependent on the spectral power distribution of the light reaching the eye from the objects in the scene. This entails that there are mechanisms in the eye/brain that respond differentially to light of different wavelengths. A large amount of research in colour science, going back to the early nineteenth century, concerns the properties of those visual mechanisms that generate the differential response to wavelength.

The process of vision is initiated by the absorption of light by specialized cells in the retina called *photoreceptors*. A given photoreceptor will respond strongly to light at some wavelengths and much less strongly at other wavelengths, keeping intensity constant. The specification of how strongly a photoreceptor responds to light in the visible spectrum is known as the *spectral sensitivity* of the photoreceptor. Displaying a photoreceptor's spectral sensitivity graphically results in its *spectral sensitivity curve*—very roughly a bell shape, with the peak centred over wavelengths to which the photoreceptor is maximally sensitive, and tails of diminishing sensitivity on either side. In spite of responding differently to light of different wavelengths, the behaviour of a single photoreceptor does not by itself contain any information about the SPD of the light to which it is responding. Photoreceptors provide the same response to an absorbed photon, no matter what its wavelength. Although photons of different wavelengths have different probabilities of being absorbed, the response of a single photoreceptor is the same to a dim light at a wavelength to which it is highly sensitive and a brighter light at a wavelength to which it is less sensitive. Since colour vision requires the ability to distinguish between lights with different wavelengths, that means that colour vision requires contributions from at least two types of photoreceptors that differ in their spectral sensitivity. In fact, as we will discuss in the next section, human colour perception is primarily driven by three distinct photoreceptor types.

4.1 Rods and cones

The human retina contains two morphologically and physiologically distinct classes of photoreceptors. The *rods*, so-called because of their characteristic shape, are active mainly at low light levels and play little role in colour vision.[3] The photoreceptors that play the major role are the *cones* (similarly so-called), active mainly at high light levels. The cones are subdivided into three types on the basis of their differences in spectral sensitivity. One type has a peak sensitivity in the short-wavelength end of the visible spectrum and the other two types have closely spaced peaks near the middle of the spectrum. The three cone-types are morphologically indistinguishable, and although their existence was inferred in the nineteenth century in order to explain the observed characteristics of human colour vision, it was only in the late twentieth century that direct measurements of their spectral sensitivities were made, and the light absorbing *photopigments* they contain were isolated (see Merbs and Nathans 1992).

Since the ability to discriminate between spectrally different stimuli depends entirely on the differences in spectral sensitivity among the three cone-types it is possible to compare the spectral sensitivities required to explain discrimination performance to the measured characteristics of the cones and their photopigments. The agreement is in general very good and simple colour discrimination tasks are an unusual case in which human behaviour (of a very specialized kind) can be predicted on the basis of knowledge of basic neurophysiology. This is possible because the later stages of visual processing preserve the information present in the cone responses and the behavioural response (under carefully controlled conditions) makes use of all the information available.

Although the cone spectral sensitivities largely determine the ability to discriminate among coloured stimuli, their relation to colour appearances is much more complicated. Since the visible spectrum, under ordinary viewing conditions, has a characteristic colour appearance, it is tempting to apply colour labels to the individual cones based on the appearance of the region of the spectrum to which they are most sensitive. The usual labels are "blue" for the short wavelength receptors (*S-cones*), "green" for the middle wavelength receptors (*M-cones*), and "red" for the long wavelength receptors (*L-cones*). This labelling can suggest the theory—sometimes found in popular discussions—that the perceived colour of a light is the result of mixing blue, green, and red, in proportion to the excitation of the corresponding cone-type. However, the usual labelling is misleading and the theory is incorrect. One reason why the labelling is misleading is that the wavelength of peak sensitivity for the L-cones is actually in the yellow-green part of the spectrum. And even if the "red" cones were well-named, the idea that all colours are mixtures of blue, green, and red doesn't fit the phenomenological facts. Admittedly, purple is, in some intuitive sense, a mixture of red and blue, but what about yellow? That seems to be just as basic as red, green, and blue. In any event, yellow doesn't appear to be a mixture of these colours in the way that purple appears to be a mixture of red and blue. Further, how does the mixing theory explain the appearance of a green light that is neither yellowish or bluish? Presumably this is because the light excites only the "green" cones—but because of the overlap in the spectral sensitivities of the three cone-types, there is no such light. As we will see, the problem of explaining colour appearance is a difficult one that does not yet have a fully satisfactory solution.

One important fact about photoreceptors, and neurons in general, helps explain one of the difficulties in predicting colour appearance given just the characterization of the stimulus. Although the relative sensitivity of the photoreceptors to light of different wavelengths is fixed, the absolute sensitivity of the photoreceptors dynamically adjusts to the light level. This adaptation allows the cones to provide usable signals at the very wide range of light intensities that we encounter as we move about the environment. One consequence of this is that the cone outputs provide relatively little information about the absolute intensity of the light stimulating them. The darkest areas of a scene lit by direct daylight are comparable in absolute intensity to the brightest areas of a scene viewed under a typical reading light, even after correcting for the change in pupil size. Another consequence is that the same stimulus can produce very different cone outputs depending on the recent history of stimulation of the cones. After adaptation to short-wavelength light the S-cones will have decreased sensitivity and a given stimulus will tend to look less blue than it would if the adapting stimulus had consisted of long-wavelength light. Adaptation of various kinds is not unique to the cones but plays a role throughout visual processing.

4.2 *Chromatic processing in the retina*

The processing of visual information begins within the retina itself and its output neurons, the *ganglion cells*, have very different response properties, both spatial and spectral, from the photoreceptors themselves.[4] A ganglion cell receives inputs (via other cells) from multiple photoreceptors arranged in a patch on the back of the retina—the cell's *receptive field*. Ganglion cells have *centre-surround* receptive fields, meaning that they are excited/inhibited by light in the centre of the receptive field and inhibited/excited by light in the periphery or surround. Importantly for understanding colour vision, the centre and surround can also differ in their sensitivity to light of different wavelengths. In *foveal* or *central* vision, where both spatial and spectral discrimination are best, in many cases the centre response is driven by a single photoreceptor while the surround draws on inputs from neighbouring photoreceptors. Consequently, ganglion cells respond best to spectral and spatial contrast. For example, a +L–M cell—one whose centre is excited by L-cone input and whose surround is inhibited by M-cone input—will respond well to a small red or white spot on a dark or blue background, less well to uniform red light (which will stimulate the M-cones to some degree) and poorly to uniform white light. Cells with this kind of opponent structure transform the original three cone channels into new channels based on contrast.

Retinal processing also begins a tendency towards specialization that continues through later stages of the visual system. The most important is the subdivision of retinal ganglion cells into two separate processing streams known as the parvocellular (P) and magnocellular (M) streams. The P-stream carries chromatic information[5] and information about sustained, high spatial resolution aspects of the retinal image. The M-stream is responsive to rapidly changing stimuli, has lower spatial resolution, and is relatively insensitive to chromatic information. These two pathways are driven by the M- and L-cone outputs; the S-cone signal is carried by a separate pathway whose properties are less well understood.

It is important to note that there is no purely chromatic channel originating in the retina. Not only are the outputs of the three cone-types subject to an opponent transformation almost immediately, but the cells in the P-stream combine spectral, intensity, and spatial information. It is only by comparing the responses of multiple cell-types to the same stimulus that it is possible to separate the chromatic information from the spatial and intensity information. It is not until the cortex that cells are encountered whose responses disambiguate the spatial and spectral information that jointly determines the activity of cells earlier in the visual pathway.

5 The psychophysics of colour

So far we have looked at colour vision from the point of view of physiology. Alternatively, we could look at how people (and other animals) behave in response to coloured stimuli. This kind of approach, in which very constrained responses to carefully constructed and varied stimuli are measured and analysed, has been central to colour science. As we saw in discussing the cone sensitivities, the physiology is intimately connected with measures of psychophysical performance, like spectral discrimination. Colour science has been traditionally characterized by an unusually integrated approach to its subject matter with studies of animal behaviour motivating and justifying physiological theorizing and vice versa. To give just two examples, the most widely used values for the cone spectral sensitivities derive from behavioural data, and what is known about the colour discrimination behaviour of many non-human animals is largely based on properties of the photopigments found in their eyes.

5.1 *Trichromacy, primaries, and colour spaces*

Any colour can be matched with an appropriate mixture of only three primaries. As might be suspected, this is a consequence of trichromacy, that exactly three types of photoreceptors contribute to human colour vision.

The claim about matching needs to be qualified, in large part because of the many complicated effects of the viewing context on perceived colour. These effects can be largely discounted if we create a very simple perceptual situation, e.g. a bisected circle on a uniform neutral background. The two halves of the circle will appear identical in colour if and only if the light reaching the eye from each half produces the same output from each of the three cone-types. In this (somewhat artificial) situation, we can choose three lights such that, for any light projected on to the left half of the circle, an appropriate weighted mixture of the three lights projected on to the right half will result in uniform cone output across the circle's retinal image.

All this only applies to *additive* mixtures, like mixtures of lights in which each element of the mixture simply adds to the light reaching the eye. In *subtractive* mixtures, like pigment mixtures, the contributions of the components of the mixture to the visual stimulus are much more complicated and it may take more than three elements to match an arbitrary stimulus. Another qualification is that some matches will require the addition of one of the primaries to the light to be matched rather than to the other two primaries—in effect, negative amounts of one of the primaries. A final point to note is that there are numerous sets of primaries. In fact, *any* three lights, no two of which can be mixed to match the others, will serve as primaries. The traditional red, green, and blue additive primaries used in television and computer screens have the virtue of matching a very large set of lights without using any negative amounts, but this is only of technological significance.

These facts about matching and primaries lead to an obvious method for a systematic representation of colour stimuli: represent the colour of each stimulus by the amounts of a certain set of primaries required to match it. In such a system, stimuli with the same coordinates will appear the same colour (at least in highly constrained viewing conditions). And given the coordinates of a stimulus in such a system, it will be possible to produce a new stimulus that will be an exact match by adding together the specified amounts of the three primaries. Since coordinates in one system can be transformed into corresponding coordinates in any other, the new stimulus need not even be constructed using the original primaries to guarantee a match. Many of the standard colour spaces used in science and industry employ this basic method. For example, the widely used CIE XYZ space is just a set of functions that take the spectral power distribution of a light into the amounts of three specially chosen primaries that match that light. These functions are based on colour-matching data collected on a relatively modest number of individuals in the early twentieth century. Many other more recent standards have a similar structure. RGB coordinates use an idealized set of monitor primaries to represent colour and although the primaries are very different the basic principle is the same.

Such systems for representing colour based on three primaries are very useful for many purposes in research and industry, but they have two significant drawbacks. First, they do a relatively poor job of representing perceived colour similarity, especially for stimuli that are distant from each other in the space.[6] Second, a system based solely on matching will fail to capture perceived colour since two stimuli may change their colour appearance substantially while still remaining matched. The fundamental problem is that the simple colour matching experiment that motivates these systems idealizes away from many factors that profoundly affect perceived colour.

5.2 Colour appearance and opponent-process theory

Neither the physics of light, nor the cone outputs, nor the primaries used in matching provide an adequate basis for understanding colour appearance. One very influential attempt to provide the outlines of a theory of colour appearance involves combining psychophysical experimentation with speculative physiology. As we saw earlier (section 4.1), attempting to account for colour appearance in terms of the three cone-types leaves us with one too few basic colours. Red, yellow, blue, and green all have a plausible claim to being basic colours, unlike purple, orange, turquoise, and olive which appear to be mixtures (in some intuitive sense) of the basic colours. In addition, these four basic colours are naturally sorted into two "opponent" pairs: red and green on the one hand and blue and yellow on the other. Red and green are opposed in the sense that there are no reddish greens or greenish reds, and similarly for yellow and blue. Red and green are so famously opposed that there is a significant philosophical literature devoted to explaining the nature of the opposition.[7] Opponent-process theory is a physiological hypothesis put forward to explain these observations, together with many others.

The core of opponent-process theory is that information about the spectral characteristics of a stimulus is carried by two opponent channels (plus a non-opponent channel for intensity). In the simplest model, one channel is generated by subtracting the M-cone signal from the L-cone signal (L-M) while the other channel results from subtracting the sum of the L- and M-signals from the S-cone signal (S-(L+M)). The L-M (or red-green) channel results in the perception of reddishness when positive and greenishness when negative, while the S-(L+M) (or yellow-blue) channel results in the perception of bluishness when positive and yellowishness when negative. Thus a stimulus that looks bluish-red will produce a high positive value for the L-M channel and a (less high) positive value for the S-(L+M) channel. Since no channel can produce a signal that is both negative and positive, the hue incompatibilities mentioned above are explained. This framework, motivated by phenomenological observations about basic colours and opponency, proved to be a powerful unifying tool that allowed a simple and intuitive understanding of diverse set of colour phenomena. When the chromatic opponency of cells in the peripheral visual pathway was first discovered in the 1960s it seemed as if direct experimental support for the hypothetical opponent processes had been found. Unfortunately, in the subsequent decades the status of opponent-process theory has become less clear. Although chromatic information is encoded in the visual pathways using opponent coding, the response properties of these cells don't match the characteristics of the psychophysically characterized opponent-processes. Unlike the good fit between the measured cone spectral sensitivities and the hypothesized sensitivities required to explain the psycho-physical discrimination data, the hoped-for match between physiology and psychophysically characterized opponent processes has failed to materialize. Although this is an area of current controversy it seems safe to say that the simple opponent-process model that seemed so promising in the late twentieth century is at best a very rough approximation.

The uncertain status of opponent-process theory leaves the field with no unified physiological account of the elementary facts about colour appearance that helped motivate it. Although there have been claims to find some basis for the special status of the unique hues in the response properties of some cortical neurons, the claims are controversial and anyway don't provide the kind of unifying framework that earlier looked to be on the cards (see Stoughton and Conway 2008; Conway and Tsao 2009; Mollon 2009; Wool *et al.* 2015). Further, the phenomenological foundations have themselves been disputed, with some claiming that there are more than four basic colours, or even that the notion of a basic colour is suspect (Saunders and van Brakel 1997).

These controversies aside, there is still a need for colour order systems that capture central facts about colour appearance and that provide a more natural representation of colour similarity than the primary based models that were discussed in section 5.1. There are a number of such systems and they all share one significant feature: the colours are represented in terms of three dimensions. It is tempting to assume that this is because the three-dimensionality that originates with the cones is maintained in the ultimate cortical representation of colour, but if so this is a peculiarity of colour vision, not an instance of general truth about perception. The human auditory system samples the frequency spectrum much more densely, but the representation of pitch is essentially one-dimensional. Moreover, there are reasons to doubt that three-dimensions are, in fact, capable of fully capturing all of the variation in colour appearance (Fairchild 1998). Nevertheless, three dimensions do an efficient job for most practical purposes.

One way to construct an ordering system that reflects colour appearances starts with the phenomenological claims that underpinned opponent-process theory. The Natural Colour System (NCS) is an example of a system with this structure (Hård *et al.* 1996a, 1996b; Kuehni 2003: 301–9). The NCS represents colour using two opponent axes (red-green and blue-yellow) and a non-opponent lightness axis. No physiological interpretation is associated with this system, and it is not directly tied to any system of primary-based matching. To classify colours with the NCS, samples are matched to standards generated in accordance with the underlying opponent model. As the name suggests, the system is intended to be a better fit to our perceptual representation of colour than other alternatives. In this form, the representation of colour embodied in opponent-process theory can be maintained independently of its success or failure as a physiological theory.

A widely used alternative is to represent colour in terms of three dimensions of hue, brightness, and saturation (HBS). These representations give rise to the familiar colour solid with hue being represented by a circle around the origin, brightness by the vertical axis, and saturation by horizontal distance from the origin. The popular Munsell system is a variant of the HBS system with its three dimension of hue, value (brightness), and chroma (a relative of saturation). One reason for the popularity of the Munsell system is that brightness and saturation are very difficult to estimate visually and the Munsell system has a physical realization that allows colours to be placed in the system by comparison to samples. Although the system was constructed to do a good job of capturing perceived similarity, the visual inaccessibility of the brightness and saturation dimensions suggest that it is not a good match for the way colour is represented by the visual system.

5.3 Contrast, adaptation, and other psychophysical effects

As we saw in the discussion of basic physiology above, the cones do not provide a fixed response to a fixed stimulus, and the channel carrying chromatic information from the retina to the brain combines spatial and spectral information. These and other physiological features have measurable (and sometimes very large) effects on how we perceive colour.

To start with a simple example, we are all familiar with the large changes in perceived lightness and colour when going inside on a bright day. Many parts of the visual system (pupil, cones, retinal ganglion cells, etc.) have adapted to the bright light and, at varying speeds, will then adapt to the much dimmer (and spectrally different) illumination indoors. The initial perception of dark and desaturated colours gradually moves back towards the brighter and more saturated colours perceived outside and there may be shifts in hue as well. One way to understand the overall effect of adaptation at the various levels of visual processing is that the visual system changes to maximize the amount of information it can extract from the visual stimulus. For example, as noted in section 4.1, the range of responses that the cones can produce is orders of magnitude smaller than the variation in the intensity of the stimulation they receive. If the cones did not adapt to changes in light intensity then they would provide useful information about only a very narrow range of stimuli. By becoming less sensitive as the stimulus intensity increases and more sensitive as it decreases, the cones preserve their ability to signal differences in stimulation across a much broader range of stimuli. One consequence of the various forms of adaptation is that large changes in the stimulus (resulting from changes in the illumination) typically produce much smaller changes in perceived colour once adaptation has run its course. Adaptation contributes to the relative stability of perceived colour across changes in illumination known as *colour constancy* (discussed in more detail in section 5.4 below).

As we have seen, the chromatic and spatial characteristics of stimuli interact in early colour processing. One illustration of this fact can be found in the familiar phenomena of colour contrast. If a neutral grey square is viewed surrounded by a larger coloured background it will appear tinted with a hue contrary to that of the background: reddish backgrounds thus induce greenish tints and greenish backgrounds induce reddish tints. Not all spatial effects involve the induction of a contrasting hue and, in *assimilation*, the colour of thin, but clearly visible, lines spreads to neighbouring areas. It needn't be only the directly adjacent regions of a scene that influence perceived colour. In the watercolour illusion, the colour of an appropriately chosen border spreads to large areas of the white space it encloses (Pinna *et al.* 2001). Even simple patterns, like a disc surrounded by concentric rings, can produce greater effects on perceived hue than a uniform background (Monnier and Shevell 2003). The causes of these kinds of effects are understood to varying degrees but in general they fall into two overlapping classes. First, there is averaging over stimulus areas at different spatial scales resulting from the underlying physiology. For example, assimilation is due, in part, to the fact that the visual system has higher resolution for achromatic contrast than for chromatic contrast. The dark lines in a typical stimulus that produces assimilation are visible to the luminance channel but not resolvable by the chromatic channels which then averages their lower lightness in with surrounding areas. Similar effects can occur with hue alone since there are many fewer S-cones than there are L- and M-cones so the averaging occurs over larger areas for the S-cone input than for the other two cone-types.[8] A different way of looking at these kinds of effects is that they are consequences of the visual system's attempt to use all of the information available to it in arriving at a representation of the spatial layout of the perceived scene and to assign visual features to different regions of it. Chromatic information is useful in extracting the spatial features of the scene from the stimulus and the spatial layout is useful in generating stable and useful colour assignments to the different areas of the scene. We will return to some of these issues later in the discussion of colour constancy.

The variety and quantity of informative and sometimes surprising interactions known to exist between perceived colour and various features of the stimulus other than the SPD of the light coming from an object is much too large to catalogue here. There are two important points worth keeping in mind with respect to the large literature on the psychophysics of colour vision. First, the psychophysics is often very informative as to the underlying physiological mechanisms, and much of the empirical literature in colour psychophysics is aimed at illuminating the underlying physiology using behavioural data collected in response to carefully controlled stimuli. Knowledge of the existence and response characteristics of the three human cone-types was almost entirely based on psychophysical data. For these purposes, the choice of stimuli need not reflect important features of the kind of stimuli encountered outside the laboratory. Second, the fact that many factors other than the character of the light reaching the eye from an object can influence its perceived colour should not be surprising. The point of vision is not to accurately characterize the proximal stimulus but rather to guide action. For the purpose of guiding action the properties of a distal object are important, and so to ignore factors other than the light an object sends to the eye would be to throw away valuable information about it.

5.4 Colour constancy

We have already mentioned *simultaneous contrast*, in which the perceived colour of an object is influenced by the colour of its surround. This phenomenon illustrates the important point that the relation between stimuli and perceived colour cannot be fully understood by taking each point in the scene before the eyes in isolation. Holding the subject's perceptual apparatus constant, the perceived colour of an object is determined by the character of the light produced by the entire scene before the eyes.

Colour constancy, the stability of perceived colour across alterations in the character of the illuminant, is another manifestation of these non-local influences.[9] Recall that the light reaching the eye from an area of a surface is the joint product of the SPD of the illuminant and the SSR of the surface. As the illuminant varies, so does the SPD of the light reaching the eye. In spite of this variation in the local visual stimulus, under many conditions the perceived colour of an object will not appreciably change. However, it is an important (although entirely unsurprising) fact that colour vision (in humans and other animals) is only approximately colour constant. (Similarly, shape constancy is only approximate.) It is easy to devise scenes and viewing conditions for which constancy effects are minimal or non-existent and, as it happens, these kind of viewing conditions are favoured for colorimetric and many experimental tasks. An interesting but virtually intractable question is how much colour constancy human colour vision displays under natural conditions. The difficulty is partly conceptual: is it constancy in colour phenomenology or colour judgement that we are attempting to measure? It is also partly technical: how can we construct a representative sample of natural viewing conditions and scenes in order to make laboratory measurements? In spite of these problems there has been a great deal of both experimental and theoretical work done on the nature of the constancy mechanisms.

One important but controversial approach to colour constancy treats it as the result of the visual system's attempt to estimate object reflectances from the light reaching the eye. The perceived colour of objects is approximately constant under many conditions because under those conditions the reflectance estimate generated by the visual system is reasonably accurate. In this framework, the most common strategy is to first generate an estimate of the SPD of the illumination in a scene and use that estimate to compute the reflectance of an object from the light reaching the eye from that object. A simple example of a theory of this kind involves the assumption that the environment, on average, is grey. That is, if the reflectances of the objects in a scene are averaged together the resulting curve will be flat across the visible spectrum and approximately ½. Given this assumption, averaging the light reaching the eye across the entire scene and dividing at each wavelength by ½ gives an estimate of the illuminant on the scene. Unfortunately, the grey world assumption is false for many scenes in which humans have reasonably good constancy, so this cannot be the entire explanation. More sophisticated theories of this kind have been developed and this is still an area of active research.

A wide variety of other factors have been invoked to explain constancy effects in various circumstances. Comparing the ratios of cone outputs across a scene contains important information about whether changes in the retinal image are due to changes in the illumination or to changes in the surface (although not about the absolute reflectance) (see Foster 2003). There are many different types of contrast, spatial and spectral, that seem to have some relationship with colour constancy. There can also be a powerful influence of perceived scene geometry on how the visual system disentangles illumination and surface properties. Although human colour vision displays some degree of several different kinds of constancy there is no current consensus on the best explanation of the various constancy phenomena or even of the best way to characterize those phenomena.[10]

6 Colour in the cortex

6.1 *The role of chromatic information in the cortex*

Chromatic discrimination is extraordinarily precise in some ways and extraordinarily coarse in others. Extremely small differences in SPD are discriminable in the right circumstances and, by some measures, the visual system is better at detecting this type of chromatic contrast than achromatic contrast (differences in the overall intensity of illumination). On the other hand, the spatial and temporal resolution for chromatic contrast is much worse than for achromatic contrast, and consequently chromatic contrast makes hardly any contribution to high-resolution spatial or temporal vision. This and other factors lead to a picture of cortical colour processing in which chromatic and achromatic information are combined in the eye and mid-brain areas but separated in the cortex, and contribute very differently to visual processing. In particular, chromatic contrast does not contribute to spatial vision in ordinary contexts and only plays a role in perceiving colour (and via that in tasks like object identification). Contrariwise, information derived from the achromatic signal plays only a minimal role in perception of colour. The one thing that's safe to say about colour in the cortex is that this picture has been rejected, at least in anything like its original form. In cortical area V1, the first cortical visual area, there are very few cells that are responsive only to chromatic signals and even that small minority are also orientation sensitive, so their behaviour reflects both chromatic and spatial information. The overwhelming majority of cells in V1 are sensitive to both chromatic and achromatic inputs. S-cone input, which does not contribute to the achromatic pathway, is found throughout the visual areas that receive inputs from V1 including areas that have nothing to do with perceiving colour, like area MT which is thought to play a role in motion perception. Similarly, chromatic contrast plays a role in spatial vision and vice versa, as can be shown using psychophysical methods. Although the precise details are still a matter of controversy, it's clear that colour is a cue used by the brain to perform a variety of tasks and that the information about the SPD of the stimulus delivered by the cones is utilized for many purposes other than that of discriminating and recognizing colour.[11]

6.2 *The organization of cortical colour processing*

There are two central issues involved in accommodating this new understanding of the role of chromatic information in the cortex. The first is partly conceptual. The results of the previous section are often described as showing that colour vision contributes to spatial vision. Although all that is intended is that chromatic information contributes to spatial vision, it can be read as implying that colour *as perceived* contributes to spatial vision—and this is a much more controversial claim. It's important to keep separate the role of chromatic information in, for example, the perception of shape and the perception of hue. It is unlikely that perceived hue is an input to the perception of shape even though both draw on the chromatic signal originating in the cones. This is supported by studies of *achromatopsia* (colour blindness resulting from cortical damage). Some achromatopsics can continue to perceive shapes that are defined solely by chromatic information even though they cannot discriminate, sort, or recognize hues at all. They have lost the ability to see colour but not the ability to utilize chromatic information for other visual functions.[12]

The second issue is primarily empirical. Although the explanation of why human beings experience colour as they do is presumably to be found in the cortex, the identified cortical cells and cortical areas do not seem well-suited to explaining the details of how we visually represent colour. Related to this is the extended controversy over whether there is a cortical area specifically dedicated to colour and, if so, where it is. Much of this controversy has centred on Zeki's controversial identification of the human analogue of macaque V4 as the brain area responsible for the perception of colour (Lueck *et al.* 1989). What does seem clear is that there are neurons responsive specifically to chromatic information in V1 and there are clusters of such neurons in areas outside of V1 as well. Our ability to discriminate and identify colour presumably relies on these neurons but going beyond that is highly speculative. Cortical processing of colour, beyond the clarification of the role of chromatic information in spatial vision, remains a confused (and confusing) topic. (For recent overviews see Conway 2014 and Johnson and Mullen 2016.)

7 Defects of colour vision and naming

Colour vision, like any other biological characteristic, varies from individual to individual. A familiar and extreme example of such variation is that a non-negligible proportion of human beings are colour "blind", most of them being specifically insensitive to the difference between red and green. In light of the salience of colour and, in particular, the striking difference between red and green for those of us with normal colour vision, it is a surprising fact that colour blindness was first clearly characterized around 1800. Thus colour blindness does not appear to be a functionally significant problem in most practical contexts.

Colour blindness is of great theoretical interest. Study of such defects has proven very illuminating in understanding normal colour vision and also raises some interesting questions about the contribution of the photoreceptors to the character of colour experience. Most colour blind individuals are not, in fact, colour blind in any strict sense of the phrase. Rather their colour vision differs from that of colour normal individuals in several well-defined respects, none of which amount to a complete loss of colour vision. The most common form of colour blindness is *dichromacy*. Dichromats require only two primaries in matching experiments, and lack the ability to discriminate some stimuli that are readily discriminable by normal (trichromatic) subjects. For example, all dichromats will accept a match between some monochromatic lights and a white light. Dichromacy results from a loss of function of one of the three cone photoreceptor types, and comes in three corresponding forms.[13]

What is commonly called red-green colour blindness actually consists of two different defects depending on whether it is the long or middle wavelength receptor whose function has been lost. *Protanopes* have no functioning long wavelength receptor and *deuteranopes* have no functioning middle wavelength receptor. They can be differentiated by, among other methods, the loss of long wavelength sensitivity relative to normals that is found in protanopia but not in deuteranopia. Although both protanopes and deuteranopes are unable to distinguish spectral lights in the middle to long wavelengths that appear green to red to normal observers, thus the name red-green colour blind, their ability to discriminate non-spectral lights is substantially different. Subjects having any of the three forms of dichromacy will accept all matches made by a normal observer, although not vice versa. Protanopia and deuteranopia are the overwhelmingly most common forms of dichromacy, and most cases are the result of recessive inherited abnormalities in genes on the X chromosome which code for the photopigments contained in the long and middle wavelength photoreceptors. Consequently, red-green colour blindness is much more common among males than among females. The third form of dichromacy, *tritanopia*, is much less common and is due to the loss of function of the short wavelength receptor. *Monochromacy* is much rarer than dichromacy and is most often due to the loss of all cone function. Monochromatic individuals are only able to make light-dark distinctions and are strictly speaking colour blind.

The genes coding for the three cone photopigments have now been isolated and sequenced. This achievement has provided new methods for understanding the early stages of colour vision and also for investigations of the evolution of colour vision. It is now known precisely what genetic abnormalities are responsible for the two varieties of red-green dichromacy and how these abnormalities affect the spectral sensitivity of the photopigments in colour blind individuals. The genetics has also helped in the discovery of the detailed structure of the photopigment proteins themselves which in turn has led to a more detailed understanding of normal variation in human colour vision (Neitz and Neitz 2011). In addition, it is now possible, using the methods of molecular genetics, to trace evolutionary relationships among the photopigments found in different species.

With the precise characterization of the different forms of colour blindness in the nineteenth century arose a puzzle as to what the visual experience of colour blind individuals is like. Protanopes and deuteranopes, for example, perceive only a single hue in the regions of the spectrum between 550 and 700 nm, but it is difficult to get empirical evidence for which hue it is. Opponent process theory suggests that, as protanopes and deuteranopes have no functioning red-green opponent channel, they should see only yellow, blue, black, and white. But colour blind subjects talk about colour just like the rest of us, only making mistakes normal observers would never make. They know that grass is green and tomatoes are red and although deuteranopes may have trouble telling the difference between ripe and unripe tomatoes, they will not say they are yellow or blue. Some very unusual individuals have normal vision in one eye and a colour deficiency in the other. These subjects might seem ideal, since they are familiar with the full range of colour experience due to their normal eye, and so can report on what they see through their colour-deficient eye. Unfortunately, the small but much discussed literature on such subjects has produced more controversy than consensus. (For a brief review see Boynton 1979: 380–2).

Most defects of colour vision are due to receptoral abnormalities. These cases are in most respects well understood, partly because there are many examples to study and partly because the role the photoreceptors play in colour vision is well understood. But receptoral abnormalities are not the only cause of defects of colour vision: as mentioned in section 6.2, damage to areas of the visual cortex is another cause. These achromatopsic disorders are, in general, less well characterized and understood than the much more common disorders discussed above. In addition, there is very little understanding of what contribution the damaged areas make to normal colour vision.

In some well studied cases of achromatopsia it has been established that all three cone-types are present and contributing to visual functioning. Even more striking is that serious impairments of colour vision can be accompanied by essentially normal perception of luminance resulting in subjects who appear to perceive the world in shades of white, grey, and black. Not all cases of achromatopsia are total and there is a great deal of variation in the severity of the impairment. There can be some remaining degree of colour vision and the defect may even be limited to some areas of the visual field. However, the specific characteristics of the colour abnormality in at least some cases of achromatopsia are very different from the forms of dichromacy.

Cortical damage can cause other kinds of colour-related deficits where the pattern of which abilities are spared and which are preserved is complicated. *Colour agnosia* is an inability to recognize the colours of seen objects with other aspects of colour vision remaining apparently intact. One colour agnosic performed normally on many non-verbal tests of colour perception, had a normal colour vocabulary and was able correctly to remember common colour associations, for example that grass is green and blood is red. When presented with an object and asked for its colour he would reply with a colour term, but his performance was no better than chance. He performed well on tasks that involve arranging colour samples in terms of similarity but poorly on sorting them into categories on the basis of similarity (van Zandvoort *et al.* 2007).

8 Animal colour vision

Some degree of colour vision is widely distributed throughout the animal kingdom, and appears to have evolved independently in several groups. Almost all vertebrates that have been studied possess some form of colour vision, although many only have a rudimentary ability which may not play a significant role in guiding behaviour. Although comparatively few have been tested, many invertebrates also possess colour vision, which in some (e.g. bees) is highly developed. The number of photoreceptor types and the spectral characteristics of the photoreceptors varies from species to species. Among mammals only (some) primates are known to have trichromatic colour vision. All other species of mammal that have been studied are dichromats with possibly a few, such as rats, lacking colour vision altogether. Some birds and fish are *tetrachromats*.[14] Further, the spectral range over which their vision extends is broader, particularly into the ultraviolet. Colour vision in these groups is phylogenetically older, and some respects more highly developed, than it is among mammals.

An organism is said to have colour vision if and only if it is able to discriminate between some spectrally different stimuli that are equated for brightness (or luminance).[15] There are two basic methods for determining the presence or absence of colour vision in non-human organisms. The first is behavioural: the organism's ability to discriminate equiluminant stimuli is tested directly. A complication arises because stimuli that are equiluminant for a human observer will not, in general, be equiluminant for a non-human observer. The luminance of stimuli for an organism can be equated if its *spectral sensitivity function* (the function from stimulus wavelength to stimulus brightness) can be determined. Alternatively, the relative luminance of the stimuli can be randomly varied over a wide range, assuming that consistently successful discrimination can only be based on colour differences. (For a review of these techniques see Jacobs 1981: 5–11.) Both techniques are somewhat tedious, and consequently have only been used to investigate a relatively small number of animals. The second method is physiological: the visual capacities of an organism are inferred from information about the physiological characteristics of its visual system. For example, it is possible to measure the *absorption spectra* of individual photoreceptor cells using a technique known as *microspectrophotometry*. Establishing the existence of two cone photoreceptor types in this way provides reasonably good evidence that the organism in question is a dichromat. These measurements, and other physiological techniques, although not easy to perform, are often less time-consuming than behavioural methods.

What selective advantages does colour vision confer? This is a large and complex question, but it is broadly accepted that the selective advantages for colour vision systems like ours include object recognition, detection of targets against variegated backgrounds, and perceptual segregation of figure from ground by similarity in colour. An even larger and more complex question is how variation in colour vision across species is connected with variation in the visual environment and more generally the species' ecological niche. As we have also seen the sensitivity to the SPD of stimuli that is crucial to colour vision also plays a role in spatial vision. Any explanation of the evolution of colour vision will have to consider the full range of visual tasks in which chromatic information is involved.

Notes

1 Two notable omissions from this chapter include the science behind technologies like paint systems and colour reproduction systems, and colour language, which displays interesting patterns across the world's languages, and whose connection to perception is disputed. The second is of more relevance to philosophy: for recent reviews and further references see Kay and Regier 2006; Regier and Kay 2009.

2 Also ignored is the fact that some surfaces have direction-dependent reflectances, and the phenomenon of *fluorescence*—the absorption of light at one wavelength and its re-emission at a longer wavelength.

3 Although it is standard to ignore rod input into colour vision, rods do influence perceived colour at intermediate and low light levels. We will follow the usual practice and ignore rod intrusion. See also footnote 5 below.

4 Very recently it has been discovered that some ganglion cells are intrinsically photosensitive and although the primary function of this sensitivity is synchronizing circadian rhythms with the day-night cycle they may, under some conditions, influence perceived colour (Horiguchi *et al.* 2013).

5 That is, information about wavelength. Chromatic or wavelength information may be used for detecting features other than colour, for instance edges.

6 There are modifications of the CIE standard, like the CIE L*AB space, that attempt to correct for this problem but they are only partially successful and almost entirely ad hoc.

7 See Hardin 1993: x–xii. As Hardin points out, the perception of reddish-green (and bluish-yellow) can be induced under special conditions. See Crane and Piantanida 1983; Billock and Tsou 2010.

8 The sparse distribution of S-cones has other consequences for vision. There are no S-cones at all in the very centre of the fovea rendering all normal human observers yellow-blue colour blind for small, centrally presented stimuli. This is presumably an adaptation to support high-resolution spatial vision which is driven by the L- and M-cone inputs. One benefit of the low-resolution of the S-cone channel is that it substantially mitigates the very high chromatic aberration of the optics of the eye.

9 Strictly speaking this is illumination-independent colour constancy, not full colour constancy. Full colour constancy requires constancy as both the illuminant and the arrangement of objects that make up the scene are varied (Brainard and Maloney 2011: 4). (For completeness one can also add constancy as the viewing medium is varied: see Brown 2003: 253–4.)

10 For a survey of the illuminant estimation approach see Brainard and Maloney 2011. For a recent theoretical challenge to that approach see Logvinenko *et al.* 2015. For more general survey of what is and isn't known about colour constancy see Foster 2011; Olkkonen and Ekroll 2016.

11 A useful recent overview is Johnson and Mullen 2016. For the S-cone picture see Conway 2014.

12 For more discussion of these issues see Akins and Hahn 2014.

13 More common than dichromacy is *anomalous trichromacy*. Although anomalous trichromats have three functioning receptor types, one of the receptors has its spectral sensitivity shifted from the normal position. Typically, this results in poorer than normal colour discrimination performance as well as other abnormalities. Corresponding to each form of dichromacy described below there is a form of anomalous trichromacy.

14 The receptoral story for birds and non-mammalian vertebrates generally is particularly complex. Their cones contain oil droplets through which light is filtered before interacting with the photopigments, and different types of droplet may be found in combination with the same type of photopigment. (See, for example, Bowmaker 1977.)

15 There has been some discussion of the adequacy of this criterion as a sufficient condition for possession of colour vision. See Hilbert 1992; Thompson *et al.* 1992; Thompson 1995: 141–214.

Alex Byrne and David R. Hilbert

References

Akins, K. A., and M. Hahn. 2014. More than mere colouring: the role of spectral information in human vision. *British Journal for the Philosophy of Science* 65: 125–71.

Billock, V. A., and B. H. Tsou. 2010. Seeing forbidden colors. *Scientific American* 302: 72–7.

Bowmaker, J. K. 1977. The visual pigments, oil droplets and spectral sensitivity of the pigeon. *Vision Research* 17: 1129–38.

Boynton, R. M. 1979. *Human Color Vision*. New York: Holt, Rinehart and Winston.

Brainard, D. H., and L. T. Maloney. 2011. Surface color perception and equivalent illumination models. *Journal of Vision* 11: 1–18.

Brown, R. 2003. Background and illuminants: the yin and yang of colour constancy. *Colour Perception: Mind and the Physical World*, ed. R. Mausfeld and D. Heyer. Oxford: Oxford University Press.

Conway, B. R. 2014. Color signals through dorsal and ventral visual pathways. *Visual Neuroscience* 31: 197–209.

Conway, B. R., and D. Y. Tsao. 2009. Color-tuned neurons are spatially clustered according to color preference within alert macaque posterior inferior temporal cortex. *Proceedings of the National Academy of Sciences* 106: 18034–9.

Crane, H. D., and T. P. Piantanida. 1983. On seeing reddish green and yellowish blue. *Science* 221: 1078–80.

Fairchild, M. D. 1998. *Color Appearance Models*. Reading, MA: Addison-Wesley.

Foster, D. 2003. Does colour constancy exist? *Trends in Cognitive Sciences* 7: 439–43.

Foster, D. H. 2011. Color constancy. *Vision Research* 51: 674–700.

Hård, A., L. Sivik, and G. Tonnquist. 1996a. NCS, natural color system—from concept to research and applications. Part I. *Color Research & Application* 21: 180–205.

Hård, A., L. Sivik, and G. Tonnquist. 1996b. NCS, natural color system—from concept to research and applications. Part II. *Color Research & Application* 21: 206–20.

Hardin, C. L. 1993. *Color for Philosophers (expanded edition)*. Indianapolis: Hackett.

Hilbert, D. R. 1992. What is color vision? *Philosophical Studies* 68: 351–70.

Horiguchi, H., J. Winawer, R. F. Dougherty, and B. A. Wandell. 2013. Human trichromacy revisited. *Proceedings of the National Academy of Sciences* 110: E260–9.

Jacobs, G. H. 1981. *Comparative Color Vision*. New York: Academic Press.

Johnson, E. N., and K. T. Mullen. 2016. Color in the cortex. *Human Color Vision*, ed. J. Kremers, R. C. Baraas, and N. J. Marshall. Cham, Switzerland: Springer.

Kay, P., and T. Regier. 2006. Language, thought and color: recent developments. *Trends in Cognitive Sciences* 10: 51–4.

Kuehni, R. G. 2003. *Color Space and Its Divisions: Color Order from Antiquity to the Present*. Hoboken, NJ: Wiley-Interscience.

Logvinenko, A. D., B. Funt, H. Mirzaei, and R. Tokunaga. 2015. Rethinking colour constancy. *PLoS ONE* 10: e0135029.

Lueck, C. J., S. Zeki, and K. J. Friston. 1989. The colour centre in the cerebral cortex of man. *Nature* 340: 386–9.

Merbs, S. L., and J. Nathans. 1992. Absorption spectra of human cone pigments. *Nature* 356: 433–5.

Mollon, J. D. 2009. A neural basis for unique hues? *Current Biology* 19: R441–2.

Monnier, P., and S. K. Shevell. 2003. Large shifts in color appearance from patterned chromatic backgrounds. *Nature Neuroscience* 6: 801–2.

Neitz, J., and M. Neitz. 2011. The genetics of normal and defective color vision. *Vision Research* 51: 633–51.

Olkkonen, M., and V. Ekroll. 2016. Color constancy and contextual effects on color appearance. *Human Color Vision*, ed. J. Kremers, R. C. Baraas, and N. J. Marshall. Cham, Switzerland: Springer.

Pinna, B., G. Brelstaff, and L. Spillmann. 2001. Surface color from boundaries: a new 'watercolor' illusion. *Vision Research* 41: 2669–76.

Regier, T., and P. Kay. 2009. Language, thought, and color: Whorf was half right. *Trends in Cognitive Sciences* 13: 439–46.

Saunders, B. A., and J. van Brakel. 1997. Are there nontrivial constraints on colour categorization? *Behavioral and Brain Sciences* 20: 167–79.

Stoughton, C. M., and B. R. Conway. 2008. Neural basis for unique hues. *Current Biology* 18: R698–9.

Thompson, E. 1995. *Colour Vision*. London: Routledge.

Thompson, E., A. G. Palacios, and F. J. Varela. 1992. Ways of coloring: comparative color vision as a case study for cognitive science. *Behavioral and Brain Sciences* 15: 1–74.

van Zandvoort, M. J. E., T. C. W. Nijboer, and E. de Haan. 2007. Developmental colour agnosia. *Cortex* 43: 750–7.

Wool, L. E., S. J. Komban, J. Kremkow, M. Jansen, X. Li, J.-M. Alonso, and Q. Zaidi. 2015. Salience of unique hues and implications for color theory. *Journal of Vision* 15: 1–11.

9

COLOUR SPACES

David Briggs

1 Introduction

The *International Lighting Vocabulary* of the *Commission Internationale de L'Eclairage (CIE)*, whose terminology is widely accepted as standard in science and technology, defines a colour space simply as a "geometric representation of colour in space, usually of 3 dimensions" (CIE, 2011, 17–226). Kuehni and Schwarz (2008) described and illustrated more than 170 historical and modern colour spaces, more than 30 of which remain in current use. Even within a single graphics program such as *Adobe Photoshop*, many different colour spaces are used as alternative frameworks for specifying, manipulating, and managing colour (Figure 9.1A, 9.1B, 9.1D, 9.1F, 9.1J, 9.1K, 9.1L). This diversity contrasts strikingly with such (admittedly, one-dimensional) qualities as length, mass, and temperature, which we generally specify using only two or three alternative systems interrelated by simple conversions.

CIE terminology admits two meanings of the word "colour", as a psychological perception (*perceived colour*) and as a specification of a class of physically varied stimuli that match in perceived colour under identical conditions (*psychophysical colour*). Purely conceptual colour spaces qualitatively represent relationships among perceived colours in terms of their psychological attributes, but most colour spaces are quantitative representations of relationships among psychophysical colours. Some of these quantitative spaces are of the "recipe" type, representing psychophysical colours according to amounts of components that may be physical (Figure 9.1A, 9.1D), imaginary (Figure 9.1B, 9.1C), or theoretical (Figure 9.1E), while others are of the psychometric type, arranging psychophysical colours according to quantitative measures of perceived-colour attributes that range from sophisticated (Figure 9.1F, 9.1G, 9.1H, 9.1I) to crude but computationally simple (Figure 9.1J, 9.1K, 9.1L). We will examine the six attributes of perceived colour defined by the CIE (*hue, brightness, lightness, colourfulness, saturation,* and *chroma*), and conclude with a brief historical survey of colour spaces that will go some way towards accounting for their remarkable diversity.

2 Spaces of what, exactly?

Demonstrations of contrast phenomena such as Figure 9.2 can be described either by saying that the influence of the background changes the colour of the squares, or by saying that the squares

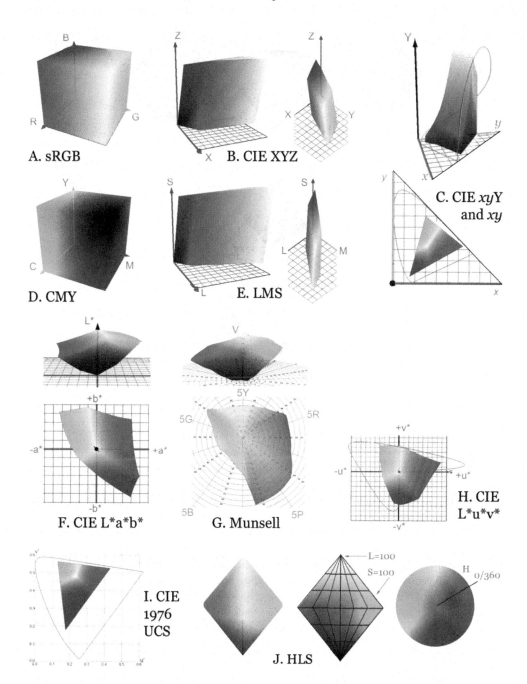

Figure 9.1 Cubic space of sRGB colours and its representation in other colour spaces. A, sRGB. B, CIE XYZ, two views. C, CIE xyY, perspective view (above) and plan projection, also known as the CIE xy chromaticity diagram (below). D, ideal CMY. E, LMS, two views. F, CIE L*a*b*, perspective view and plan projection. G, Munsell system, perspective view and plan projection. H, CIE L*u*v*, plan projection. I, CIE 1976 UCS. J, HLS, oblique view, vertical section, and equatorial section. K, HSB, oblique view, vertical section, and plan view. L, YCbCr, perspective view and plan projection. 9.1A–F, H and L and 9.2B–D (below) generated using ColorSpace program by Philippe Colantoni. 9.1G and 9.5A–F (below) generated using drop2color program by Zsolt Kovacs-Vajna.

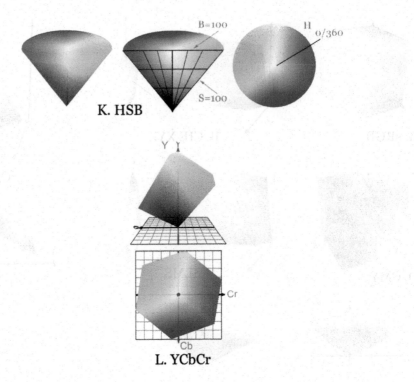

Figure 9.1   Continued.

in Figure 9.2A *appear* to be different colours, but are actually the same colour. The first description is a report of immediate visual *appearance* in which the word "colour" refers to an aspect of that appearance; the second is a statement of belief, in which the referent of the word "colour" and the precise belief being expressed depend on the viewpoint of the speaker. Based on the "common sense" assumption that colours are intrinsic in lights and objects, one speaker might mean that they believe that both squares in Figure 9.2A possess the same *veridical intrinsic colour*, presumably a particular shade of greyish red, despite these perplexing appearances. When contrast phenomena are taken into account, the intrinsic colour that "common sense" attributes to lights and objects takes on an indirect relationship to visual appearance; the colours we actually see here are just how this elusive veridical greyish red appears in various contexts. Another speaker, without assuming that any colour appearance is uniquely veridical, might mean by "the same colour" only that they expect that both squares have the same *colour specification*, that is, that these apparently different colours would both *match* the same colour chip from a system like the Munsell system placed directly alongside them. A third speaker, adopting a physicalist definition of "colour", would use the word to refer not to an appearance like greyish red but to a particular spectral reflectance/transmission, and by saying that the squares are the same colour would specifically mean that they expect that their spectral energy transmissions are identical.

The *International Lighting Vocabulary* defines two distinct conceptions of "colour", both said to be specifiable using sets of three attributes or values. The first, "*(perceived) colour*", corresponds to colour as an aspect of *appearance*, and is defined as a "characteristic of visual perception that can be described by attributes of hue, brightness (or lightness) and colourfulness (or saturation or chroma)" (CIE, 2011, 17–198). The second, "*(psychophysical) colour*", aligns with colour

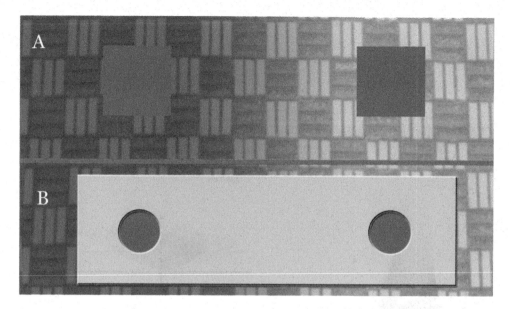

Figure 9.2   Two squares having the same psychophysical colour specification (P₂ in Figures 9.3, 9.5–9.7) appear different colours in different contexts (A) but match when viewed in the same context (B).

specification in the preceding paragraph, and is defined as a "specification of a colour stimulus in terms of operationally defined values, such as 3 tristimulus values" (CIE, 2011, 17–197). *Tristimulus values* are in turn defined as the "amounts of the 3 reference colour stimuli, in a given trichromatic system, required to match the colour of the stimulus considered", for example RGB and XYZ values in the CIE colorimetric system (CIE, 2011, 17–1345). Applying CIE terminology to Figure 9.2A, the same psychophysical colour evokes two different perceived colours.

In referring to tristimulus values, the definition of psychophysical colour embodies the colloquially and scientifically held viewpoint that two visually indistinguishable lights are considered to have the same colour even if we know that they have different distributions of energy among the wavelengths of the spectrum (called *spectral power distributions* or *SPDs*); that is, that we do not normally require a spectrometer to describe the colour of a light. Because our colour vision relies on input from just three classes of receptors (called L, M, and S cone cells), light stimuli having very different SPDs can match in perceived colour to a human observer. Such visually indistinguishable lights are called *metamers*, and it has been found empirically that any test stimulus can be matched by mixing just three suitably chosen primary lights in measured amounts, sometimes including negative amounts, that is, amounts of one primary added to the test stimulus to obtain the match. In Figure 9.3A, P_2 can be matched directly by a mixture of the CIE RGB primaries $(r_1 + g_1 + b_1)$, but an amount of the red primary, r_2, must be added to the 485 nm light to match a mixture of g_2 and b_2. Metameric matches of lights are conventionally determined against a dark or uniform surround, but persist to a good approximation when conditions are changed (Brainard and Stockman, 2010, p. 10.9) provided that both lights appear in the same context. (As Figure 9.2 shows, even physically identical lights can cease to match when presented in differing contexts.)

Because metameric matches vary somewhat from person to person, tristimulus values are specified with reference to a "standard observer" defined by a set of *colour matching functions*

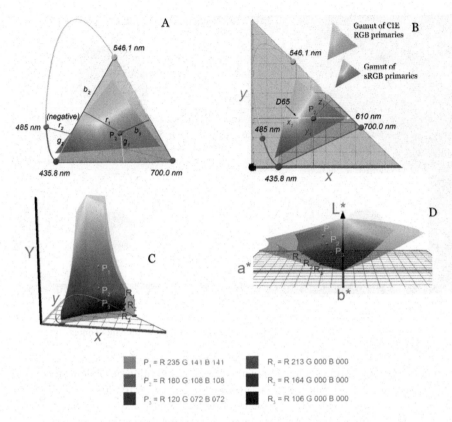

Figure 9.3 A, "Maxwell triangle" chromaticity diagram, B, CIE xy chromaticity diagram, C, perspective view of CIE xyY space, and D, perspective view of CIE L★a★b★ space, all showing gamut of CIE RGB and sRGB mixtures. r_1 g_1 b_1 and x_1 y_1 z_1 are the CIE RGB and CIE XYZ tristimulus values for P_2. 610 nm is the dominant wavelength of P_2 in relation to white point D65.

(CMFs). The most important of these are the CIE 1931 and 1964 standard colorimetric observers, whose somewhat different colour matching functions are designed for specifying colours occupying small and large areas of the visual field respectively. Figure 9.4A shows the amounts of the CIE RGB primaries that the 1931 observer would use to match the colour of each wavelength of the spectrum. To obtain the CIE RGB tristimulus values of a broad-spectrum light, each of these amounts is multiplied by the amount of that wavelength present, and the results summed. Figure 9.4B shows the corresponding CMFs for three convenient imaginary primaries, CIE X, Y, and Z, that are mathematical transformations of the CIE RGB primaries, and which are applied in the same way to obtain the XYZ tristimulus values of a broad-spectrum light. These imaginary primaries were chosen by the CIE in order to avoid negative tristimulus values and also to have one of the primaries (Y) equal to *luminance* or *visible* energy of light, that is, light energy weighted according to the wavelength-by-wavelength response of the human visual system. The *relative* proportions out of their total of the X, Y, and Z tristimulus values (*x, y,* and *z*) can be shown on a two-dimensional *chromaticity* diagram that represents the colours of lights independent of their brightness. Figure 9.3B is known as the *CIE xy chromaticity diagram*, in which all chromaticities possible for actual lights occupy the area enclosed by the horseshoe-shaped path of the spectral colours (the *spectral locus*) and the straight line connecting the ends of this path. Adding the dimension of luminance (Y) to the xy diagram produces the *CIE xyY*

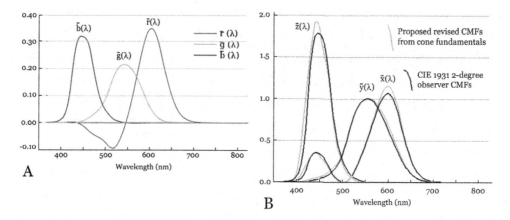

Figure 9.4 A, CIE RGB colour matching functions (CMFs) for the 1931 standard observer. B, XYZ CMFs for the 1931 standard observer and recently revised XYZ CMFs based on cone fundamentals (CVRL, 2012).

colour space (Figure 9.3C). For some purposes primaries representing the theoretical L, M, and S *cone fundamentals* (cone sensitivities at cornea level; Figure 9.1E) are more useful than the convenient but arbitrary XYZ primaries. Modern data on cone fundamentals have recently been used as the basis for a refinement of the XYZ colour matching functions (Figure 9.4B) that gives improved matches for colours of LED lights (Schanda, 2011).

Colours of objects can be specified psychophysically by the tristimulus values of the light they reflect/transmit under a given lighting (*illuminant*). As these tristimulus values depend on the illuminant used, it is necessary to indicate the latter (normally a "white" daylight illuminant such as CIE D65 or the older standard Illuminant C) when reporting tristimulus values for objects.

On my computer screen the squares in Figure 9.2 are specified by the tristimulus values R 180 G 108 B 108 in *sRGB* colour space (P_2 in Figures 9.3, 9.5, 9.6, and 9.7). sRGB is a standard implementation of the RGB colour model for screen colours (Figure 9.1A) that specifies the chromaticities and scaling of the RGB lights, the brightness and balance of RGB lights taken to be white, and the environmental viewing conditions (ICC, 2010). As Figure 9.2 demonstrates, a set of sRGB tristimulus values like R180 G108 B108 does not translate to a unique *perceived* colour, which will vary according to the context, but it does specify stimuli that we will see as having the same "common sense" intrinsic colour if we are given the opportunity to compare them in the same context. Similarly, a set of the corresponding CIE XYZ tristimulus values, X 26.9 Y 21.5 Z 16.9, does not tell us the *perceived* colour of a stimulus, but it does specify a class of stimuli that the CIE 1931 standard observer, if she possessed "common sense", would see as having *the same intrinsic colour*, because they would appear identical to her in the same context. While a tristimulus specification/psychophysical colour/intrinsic-colour stimulus class does not translate to a unique veridical perceived colour, it *can* be translated to a specification in a psychometric colour space such as the Munsell system or (given a reference white) CIE L★a★b★. Psychometric spaces represent the appearance of a psychophysical stimulus class under specified standard conditions in terms of dimensions designed to function as quantitative measures of the psychological attributes of perceived colour. Thus the Munsell designation 5R 5/6 (Figure 9.5B) specifies P_2 in terms of a Munsell hue of 5R, a Munsell value (lightness) of 5, and a Munsell chroma (colour strength) of 6, while the CIE L★a★b★ designation 53.5 27.2 1.9 (Figure 9.3D) specifies P_2 in terms of a different measure of lightness (L★) and chromatic dimensions

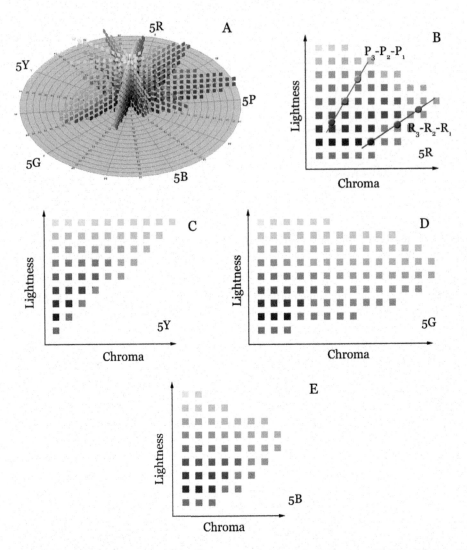

Figure 9.5 A, perspective view of Munsell colour space, showing theoretical limits of light-reflecting objects for the five principal hues. B–F, hue pages for the five principal hues, showing colour chips included in the current Munsell Book of Colour (Glossy Edition) and the remaining theoretical colours greyed out. Chroma intervals are two Munsell chroma steps. The uniform saturation series P_3–P_1 and R_3–R_1 are projected onto the 5R hue page.

(a⋆ and b⋆) that can be directly converted to CIE measures of hue and chroma. It should not be assumed that psychometric colour spaces are of the familiar Euclidean type, in which a given distance in any direction represents the same amount of perceived-colour difference. Because of the phenomenon of *hue superimportance* (Judd, 1970), no perceptually-even colour space can be Euclidean.

Use of the word "colour" in the physicalist sense of a specific spectral reflectance/transmission is not sanctioned by the CIE or by common usage. Many such *"maximally specific colours"* (Byrne and Hilbert, 1997) would appear identical to a human observer, who thus could not identify a "colour" without using a spectrometer. A space of maximally specific colours (that is, of spectral reflectance/transmission distributions) would require a potentially unlimited number of dimensions, depending how finely the spectrum is split into wavelength bands. Care should be taken not to assume that scientific terms like "colour constancy" are intended to apply to "colour" in this non-standard usage.

3 Attributes and spaces of perceived colour

Both the sufficiency of three suitably chosen lights to match any isolated light and the three-dimensional character of perceived-colour spaces are widely considered to be consequences of the dependence of our colour vision on input from three classes of receptors. A species with a single class of receptors can detect variations in light intensity but not variations in spectral composition, and so can perceive only a one-dimensional range of brightness. Three classes of receptors with sensitivities peaking at different wavelengths create a range of potential responses with three degrees of freedom, which *could* be experienced by an organism as three simultaneous perceptions of brightness, just as we separately distinguish the notes of a musical chord. Mantis shrimp evidently process the responses of their 16–21 receptor types something like this (Thoen *et al.*, 2014). In trichromatic humans however the three cone responses are *compared* with each other in a process known as *cone-opponency*, such that a light that evokes L, M, and S cone responses in the mutual balance evoked by average daylight is seen, not as a mixture of three perceptions, but as *colourless* (white) light having a single overall brightness. Departures from this mutual balance have a two-dimensional circuit of possibilities (that is, L or L + M or M or M + S or S or S + L dominant), and evoke a range of chromatic perceptions generally seen as a circuit of hues at various degrees of saturation. Dichromatic mammal species have two receptor classes and thus two degrees of freedom in their possible responses, which is thought to result in a one-dimensional range for spectral imbalance relative to daylight, perceived as two hues at various saturations. The situation can be more complex for dichromatic-testing individuals of a trichromatic species, including human protanopes and deuteranopes (Broackes, 2010).

In contrast to what is sometimes deemed the "standard" view of colour, the CIE definition of perceived colour quoted earlier implies that colour does not have a single set of three attributes regardless of mode of appearance. Four of the six colour attributes listed in the definition depend on the appearance of a single area without comparison with other areas. Any patch of the visual field can be considered without reference to the rest of the field simply as light having the three colour attributes of *hue*, *brightness* and either *colourfulness* or *saturation*, and self-luminous objects are normally seen in this way. (Saturation is defined as colourfulness relative to brightness, so specifying both colourfulness and saturation is redundant.) Colours seen in this way have been distinguished as unrelated colours according to one interpretation of the current CIE definitions (CIE, 2011, 17–1376, 17–1080), but note that other writers interpret these definitions to restrict the term "unrelated colour" to lights viewed in physical isolation through an aperture.

The two remaining attributes listed in the definition of perceived colour, *lightness* and *chroma*, refer to areas seen as light-reflecting/transmitting objects and judged in relation to other such objects. Light-reflecting/transmitting objects, unless viewed in physical isolation through an aperture, are normally seen as having these *relative* colour attributes, and their colours when viewed in this way can be described in terms of the three attributes of *hue*, *lightness*, and *chroma*. Though understandable from an evolutionary point of view, it is nevertheless remarkable that most areas of the visual field are instantly, effortlessly, and unconsciously interpreted as a combination of an *object colour* (CIE, 2011, 17–831) of this kind and an *illumination colour* (CIE, 2011, 17–560). More complex scenarios may involve an illumination colour and two kinds of object colour: a *surface colour* (CIE, 2011, 17–1285) seen through an intervening *volume colour* (CIE,

2011, 17–1421). On the other hand even a stimulus as simple as a bipartite field in which the two parts do not match is sufficient for perception of relative colour attributes (Evans, 1974).

Most patches of the visual field thus have more than one colour and thus more than three colour attributes involved in their appearance. For example, a glossy red billiard ball under a spotlight has an object colour of constant hue, value, and chroma over the whole ball, but seen as unrelated light has various colours that change in saturation and possibly hue between the specular highlight and the remainder, and in brightness and colourfulness between the lit and shadowed sides. Some patches of the visual field have additional perceived colours that depend on the attitude of the perceiver. For example on my computer screen area W$_2$ in Figure 9.6 can be seen as unrelated white light, or related to the other colours on my screen as a middle grey surface, or related to the other colours in Figure 9.6 as an image of a white surface reflecting white illumination, or related to my physical surroundings as a self-luminous white surface.

Perceived object colours show a high degree of *constancy* under varying levels of illumination (as illustrated in Figures 9.6–9.7) and a variable degree of constancy under illumination of different colours. In all cases the colour perceived as belonging to the object tends towards the perceived colour in average daylight. For example, a sheet of white paper clearly visible under coloured lighting is generally still seen as *being* white, even though the area of the visual field it occupies appears coloured; that is, the viewer attributes the chromatic appearance of the area to the illumination colour instead of the object colour. Since all major psychometric colour spaces specify perceived colour under an average daylight illuminant, these specifications in effect describe the seemingly intrinsic colour that colour constancy with varying degrees of accuracy recovers.

We can now review the six attributes of perceived colour defined by the CIE, along with their physical correlatives and some factors involved in their quantification as dimensions of colour spaces.

Hue: Hue is defined as the "attribute of visual perception according to which an area appears to be similar to one of the colours: red, yellow, green, and blue, or to a combination of adjacent pairs of these colours considered in a closed ring" (CIE, 2011 17–542). This definition attributes the cycle of hues to successive combinations of what are identified elsewhere (CIE, 2011 17–1373) as the four "unique" or "unitary" hues, in recognition of the concept of colour-opponency proposed by Ewald Hering. It remains controversial how these yellowish/bluish and

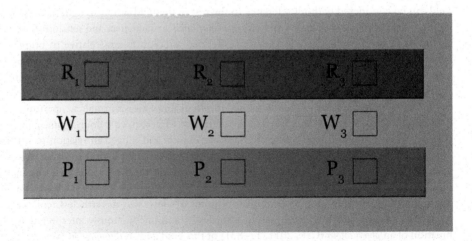

Figure 9.6 Digital illustration of uniform red (R) and pink (P) stripes on a white (W) background under a gradient of neutral white illumination.

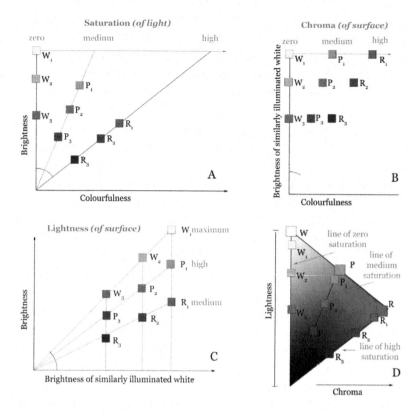

Figure 9.7 A–C, CIE definitions of saturation, chroma, and lightness illustrated in terms of patches R_1–R_3, P_1–P_3 and W_1–W_3 from Figure 9.6. D, lightness and chroma of R, P, and W, the red, pink, and white surface colours depicted in Figure 9.6, and of patches R_1–R_3, P_1–P_3, and W_1–W_3 considered as surface (image) colours. Note that the depictions of uniformly coloured surfaces in Figure 9.6 use image colours of varying chroma but uniform saturation.

reddish/greenish colour-opponent perceptions or "signals" arise from the circuit of trichromat cone-opponent responses (Hardin, 2014). Physically, the circular dimension of hue corresponds to the varieties of spectral imbalance of lights and of object reflectances, relative to daylight and unselective reflectors respectively, that can be detected by an organism having three receptor types and cone-opponent processing. Yellowishness, greenishness, and bluishness are each evoked by imbalances favouring wavelengths of a discrete range, while reddishness is evoked by imbalances favouring wavelengths from either of two unconnected bands at opposite ends of the range visible to humans. Measures of hue used in different colour spaces vary in the hues used as a frame of reference (sometimes designated "primary colours" of various kinds) and in the criteria used to place hues opposite each other, which may involve colour-opponent pairs, additive-mixing or paint-mixing complementary pairs, perceptually even spacing, or a compromise or confusion between two or more of these.

Brightness: Brightness is the "attribute of a visual perception according to which an area appears to emit, or reflect, more or less light" (CIE, 2011, 17–111). Brightness is our perception of physical luminance, as conditioned by the brightness adaptation of the observer. The brightness of the RGB components of a digital colour are recorded relative to their maxima either in linear units (proportional to luminance) or more commonly in non-linear units (using a power function) in order to approximately equalize contrast between increments (Poynton, 2009). In the scale associated with sRGB space an R 128 subpixel has about 22 per cent of the luminance of R 255.

Lightness: When a light-reflecting object is increasingly strongly illuminated, both its brightness and the brightness of a white object under the same illumination increase proportionately (Figure 9.6, 9.7C), so that the intrinsic brightness or *lightness* of the object can be defined perceptually as the "brightness of an area judged relative to the brightness of a similarly illuminated area that appears to be white or highly transmitting" (CIE 2011, 17–680). Lightness (also known as value or greyscale value) is our perception of the efficiency of an object as a reflector/transmitter of light, and has an upper limit of 100 per cent reflectance/transmission that cannot be exceeded unless the object physically generates light. Quantitative lightness scales are non-linear (generally logarithmic or power) functions of physical reflectance in order to achieve approximate perceptual equality of increments.

Colourfulness and *saturation*: Colourfulness is the "attribute of a visual perception according to which the perceived colour of an area appears to be more or less chromatic" (CIE 17–233). A coloured object reflects light of increasing colourfulness as it is increasingly strongly lit, but unless it is very bright its "colourfulness ... judged in proportion to its brightness", called its *saturation* (CIE, 2011 17–1136), remains about the same (Figure 9.6, 9.7A). By these definitions, colourfulness is the *strength* of colour of the light from an area, while saturation is the *purity* or relative freedom from whitishness of that colour. Uniform-saturation series of RGB colours (Figure 9.3) have a fixed *ratio* of the RGB components, varying only in brightness. Such series occupy a single point on a chromaticity diagram, vertical lines in CIE xyY space (P_3-P_2-P_1 and R_3-R_2-R_1 in Figure 9.3C), and lines radiating from near the black point in CIE $L\star a\star b\star$ and Munsell space, where they cut sharply across the vertical lines of uniform *chroma* (Figures 9.3D, 9.5B). Saturation is our perception of the unevenness of the SPD of a light *as detected by our visual system*: physical unevenness in the SPD of a light does not evoke hue and saturation if (like the white light from a fluorescent tube or computer screen) it does not produce a relative imbalance in the three receptor responses.

Chroma: When a chromatic light-reflecting object is increasingly strongly illuminated, its colourfulness and the brightness of a white object under the same illumination increase proportionately (Figures 9.6, 9.7B), so the intrinsic strength of colour or *chroma* of the object can be defined perceptually as its colourfulness "judged as a proportion of the brightness of a similarly illuminated area that appears white or highly transmitting" (CIE, 2011, 17–139). Chroma is our perception of an object's efficiency as a *spectrally selective* reflector/transmitter; high-chroma objects reflect/transmit high-saturation light in large quantities. Since a high-chroma object must strongly absorb some wavelengths and not others, it follows that an object that reflects *all* wavelengths either very strongly (white) or very weakly (black) must have very low or zero chroma. For each hue therefore, the chroma of common object colours (roughly indicated by the colours represented in the *Munsell Book of Colour*) and of *optimal colours* (colours at the theoretical limits possible for light-reflecting objects) both peak at an intermediate lightness level, resulting in a roughly triangular or rounded-triangular wedge of colours on each *hue page* (Figure 9.5B–F). This maximum chroma varies considerably in its magnitude and in the lightness at which it occurs for different hues.

The *International Lighting Vocabulary* does not claim that hue, brightness, lightness, colourfulness, saturation, and chroma are the exclusive "natural" attributes of colour, but states only that perceived colour can be described in terms of them. As alternatives to chroma and lightness, a hue page can be divided up using various other sets of attributes (Figure 9.9B–D) that have been quantified in some of the systems discussed in the next section. For further details of the systems mentioned below and many others the reader should consult the outstanding survey by Kuehni and Schwarz (2008).

4 The diversity of colour spaces

From its invention by Aristotle in the fourth century BC through to the Renaissance, the predominant model of colour order was the one-dimensional or *linear* system, with three or more colours intermediate between black and white (Figure 9.9A). Alongside these linear systems, *multilinear* systems with two to seven paths through "families" of intermediate colours between black and white (Figure 9.9B) began to appear in the eleventh century with Avicenna. One such system described in the short but difficult thirteenth-century text *De Colore* by Robert Grosseteste consists of seven paths between "blackness" and "whiteness" through unspecified colours arising from three "bipolarities" singly and in combination: *purum/impurum, clara/obscura,* and *multa/pauca* (Dinkova-Bruun et al., 2013). These combinations suggest a three-dimensional array that Grosseteste *might* have visualized as a cube, as Dinkova-Bruun et al. suggest, or as one of the other geometric models later used to represent combinations of yellow, red, and blue primary colours (e.g. Figure 9.9F, 9.9H), but in any case they entail three degrees of freedom. Alberti (1435) mentions that "philosophers" had formulated conflicting *linear* systems of seven colours arising from the mixing of "rare and dense", "warm and dry", and "cold and moist", but that speaking as a painter there are four families of colours, passing between black and white through red, green, blue, and "grey and ash" respectively. Comparable multilinear systems were described and illustrated by Forsius in 1611 and Glisson in 1677. The second of Forsius' two systems, with five paths, has been interpreted by some as a spherical colour space whose implied equator would be the oldest *hue* circle, but neither the diagram nor the accompanying text provide convincing evidence that Forsius intended this (Kuehni and Schwartz, 2008, pp. 45–6).

A continuous circuit of hues can first be traced in the arcs representing mixtures of successive pairs of yellow, red, and blue in the oldest diagram to represent these as "primary colours", published by Francois D'Aguilon in 1613 (Figure 9.9C). D'Aguilon's diagram ingeniously reconciles this trichromatic mixing system in its lower half with a linear system in the middle and a multilinear system of paths through yellow, red, blue, and grey in its upper half. Boyle's (1664) explanation of the concept of primary colours adds the implication that all hues in nature can be matched by the hues mixed from the primaries (Figure 9.9D). In 1677 Glisson proposed that any object colour could be specified quantitatively according to proportions of white, black, yellow, red, and blue components, but did not illustrate this idea in the form of a three-dimensional space. This step was taken much later by Tobias Mayer in an unpublished lecture of 1758, in the form of a triangular dipyramid showing numerically specified quantities of red, yellow, blue, black, and white pigments (Figure 9.9F). The scheme was only published posthumously and Mayer may have abandoned it as unworkable in practice; Boyle had been correct in conceding that some colours in nature are beyond the "Splendor" obtainable from paints of just five colours.

Newton arrived at the circuit of hues based on the mutual resemblance of the colours of the ends of the spectrum, and on his experiments on the mixing of spectral lights, which showed that the colours of lights, excluding their brightness, could be represented using a simple two-dimensional chromaticity diagram with white at the centre, his well-known hue circle from the *Opticks* of 1704 (Figure 9.9E). Newton's light-mixing circle is the first graphical representation of the dimensions of both hue and saturation, and is also the first representation of the technologically and philosophically important concept of *metamerism*: except for the fully saturated colours, a given colour of a light can result from an indefinite number of different combinations of "rays" (wavelengths). Taylor (1735) seems to have been the first to explicitly conclude that object colours could be described in terms of the three attributes of the hue, saturation ("perfection"), and relative brightness ("strength of light and shadow") of the light that they reflect.

As Kuehni and Schwarz have noted, Newton's study marks the beginning of the psycho-physical concept of colour, but this idea proved to be ahead of its time. Based on colourant-mixing experience, and on the "common sense" assumption that colours reside and mix in colourants themselves, so that for example yellow and blue paints make a green mixture because the colour green "contains" yellow and blue, the historical primary colours yellow, red, and blue, along with white and sometimes black, continued to be widely regarded as the funda-mental components colour until the mid-nineteenth century. All colour spaces (e.g. Figure 9.9F–9.9H) and almost all two-dimensional "colour wheels" from this period represent colours as if they are composed of varying proportions of these historical primaries. Some scientists, including Mayer in the eighteenth century and Brewster in the nineteenth century, rationalized this view with Newton's apparently continuous spectrum by arguing that light consists of sepa-rate red, yellow, and blue rays that create the intermediate colours of the spectrum by intermix-ture. In this enviably simple view of colour, the historical artists' primaries coincide with the primaries for mixing coloured lights, with the sensitivities of the visual receptors, and with the psychological primaries of perception, and colour is, if not physical, at least directly correlated with a species-independent physical property, the proportions of the red-, yellow-, and blue-looking components.

The three-ray hypothesis was decisively overturned by Hermann von Helmholtz in 1852, allowing resurrection of Thomas Young's suggestion of 1801 that colour vision relies on three receptor types creating three "fundamental sensations" in response to a physically continuous spectrum. James Clerk Maxwell's triangular chromaticity diagrams, of the type shown in Figure 9.3A, marked the beginning of the first phase of modern colorimetry, which culminated in the derivation of the CIE standard observer and the CIE XYZ and xyY colour spaces in 1931. In this phase the colour appearance of lights and objects was specified using physical measures (luminance, dominant wavelength, and spectral purity) related only loosely to the attributes of perceived colour.

Modern object-colour spaces began with the system of hue, value, and chroma introduced by Albert Munsell (Munsell, 1905), and further tested and refined after Munsell's death by the Munsell Color Company. Earlier systems by Klotz and Gregoire, conceptually based on dimen-sions of hue, lightness, and relative chroma, were a step towards the Munsell model, but had very limited influence (Kuehni and Schwarz, 2008, 80–3). The Munsell system was further refined by the Optical Society of America, culminating in the "renotation" published in 1943, which related the Munsell System to CIE colorimetry and established the CIE colorimetric coordinates of each Munsell specification out to the limits of the optimal colours (Figure 9.5).

Following and building on some earlier proposals for perceptual colour spaces derived directly from CIE colorimetry, the CIE in 1976 introduced two alternative systems, CIE L*a*b* (Figure 9.1F) and CIE L*u*v* (Figure 9.1H), based on non-linear and linear transformations respectively of CIE xyY space. The lightness dimension L* in both systems uses a non-linear transformation of luminance that differs from but is similar in effect to that used for Munsell value. The orthogonal chromatic dimensions can be directly converted to measures of hue and chroma, and those for CIE L*a*b* in particular accord moderately well with Munsell hue and chroma. CIE L*u*v* has an associated chromaticity diagram, the CIE 1976 UCS diagram (Figure 9.1I) that is recommended by the CIE as being more perceptually even than the 1931 xy diagram.

Wilhelm Ostwald (1916) devised an entirely different kind of object-colour space to Mun-sell's, inspired in part by the colour model proposed by Ewald Hering (Figure 9.8B). Hue pages are divided up according to whiteness, blackness, and chromaticness, judged in relation to "full colours" that correspond to a *"semichrome"*, the optimal colour evoked by a mixture of all

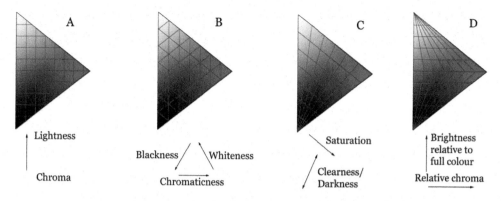

Figure 9.8 A–D, four alternative sets of attributes for describing relationships on a hue page.

wavelengths at full intensity between the two members of a complementary pair. Ostwald's hue scale was influenced by Hering's opponent hues, but is structured around additive complementaries, so that unique red and unique green as determined by most observers do not lie opposite each other. The modern *Natural Colour System (NCS)* is geometrically similar, but adheres more strictly to Hering's model, and is founded on perceptual estimations of white, black, and hue content in coloured samples. NCS chromaticness in theory is chroma relative to the perceived maximum, but lines of equal chromaticness are generally oblique to those for Munsell and CIE L*a*b* chroma for strongly chromatic colours (Billmeyer and Bencuya, 1987).

Another model for dividing up a hue page of object colours uses the saturation and the brightness relative to the maximum brightness possible for that hue and saturation of the object's reflectance (Figure 9.8C). HSB (or HSV) colour space uses this model to represent digital colours (see below). Other examples include the German DIN system, where the dimension of *darkness (D)* is measured down from the limit of optimal colours, and the systems by Johansson and Hesselgren that use an inverse of darkness, called *cleanness* or *clarity* (Kuehni and Schwarz, 2008, pp. 162–4, 107–9). Other models for dividing up a hue page involve lightness relative to the lightness of the fullest colour, and chroma relative to the maximum chroma possible at a given lightness or relative lightness (Figure 9.8D). Examples include systems by Ridgway, Ross, and Wilson (Kuehni and Schwarz, 2008, pp. 243–5, 304, 297–8) and the HLS digital colour space (see below).

Computer screens generate colour using combinations of RGB lights having 256 possible levels (000 to 255), resulting in a cubic colour space of 256^3 or about 16.8 million psychophysical colours (Figure 9.1A). Figure 9.1 shows this cube of sRGB colours transformed into some of the colour spaces discussed so far and some others developed specifically for digital applications. Figure 9.1D illustrates the theoretical *CMY* model, in which all RGB colours could be generated by subtractive mixing of ideal cyan, magenta, and yellow colourants. Actual colour printing uses *CMYK* specifications defined in relation to a specific substrate, in which the C, M, and Y dimensions represent amounts of actual CMY inks, and K specifies a black ink component (*K*) that substitutes for some of the coloured inks. *HLS* and *HSB* (or *HSV*) are two computationally simple colour models introduced in the early days of computer graphics to provide more intuitive ways of selecting colours than the RGB components. *Hue angle (H)* in both systems is based on a simple calculation that results in a perceptually very uneven measure of hue. The parameters labelled *L* and *S* in HLS are not lightness or saturation in the CIE sense, but are simple measures of lightness relative to the lightness of the fullest RGB colour (for which L = 50) and chroma relative to the maximum possible for that "L" (Figure 9.1J). *S* in HSB is a

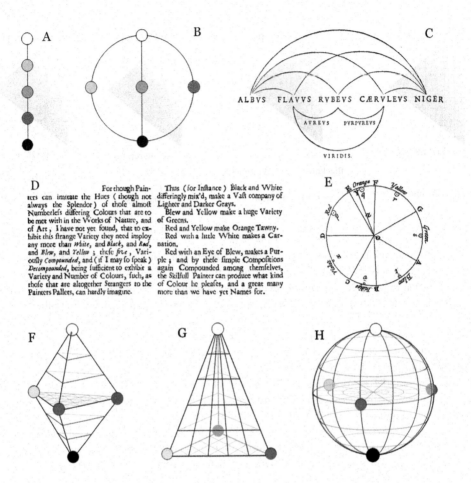

Figure 9.9 A, linear colour system. B, multilinear colour system. C, compound linear-multilinear-trichromatic system of D'Aguilon, 1613, showing mixtures of yellow (flavus), red (rubeus), and blue (caeruleus) in lower part. D, Robert Boyle's (1664) explanation of primary colours. E, light mixing diagram from Newton's Opticks (1704). F–H, three-dimensional colour spaces based on red, yellow, and blue "primary" components described by Mayer in 1758, Lambert in 1772, and Runge in 1810 (see Kuehni and Schwarz, 2008, Chapter 3).

simple measure of saturation relative to the maximum possible at a given hue angle, while B (or V in HSV) is neither brightness nor value/lightness in the CIE sense, but is a measure of brightness relative to the maximum possible for a given H and S (Figure 9.1K). YCbCr (Figure 9.1L) belongs to a family of digital colour spaces somewhat intermediate between physical spaces like RGB and psychometric spaces like CIE L★a★b★, devised to efficiently encode colour information for such purposes as image compression and television signals. Confusingly, Y here is not CIE luminance, but is a parameter informally called *luma* (Poynton, 2009) that is the sum of the non-linear R, G, and B components, weighted to allow for the relative perceived brightness of these primaries. The other two dimensions of "chrominance", Cb and Cr, are measures of yellowish/bluish and reddish/greenish chroma respectively. *Colour management* strategies to ensure consistent colour across multiple devices convert the colour spaces used by the various devices to and from a central *profile connection space*, either CIE XYZ or CIE L★a★b★.

Predicting the perceived colour of a stimulus requires information about context as well as about the stimulus itself, and takes us beyond three-dimensional colour spaces to the subject of *colour appearance models*. Although normally classed as a colour space, the 1976 CIE L★a★b★ system can also be viewed as a simple colour appearance model in that it predicts the object colour attributes of hue, lightness, and chroma from the XYZ tristimulus values of a stimulus and those of a reference white (Fairchild, 2013, p. 201). Fairchild (2013) reviews in detail various colour appearance models of increasing levels of sophistication that ultimately aim to predict the brightness and colourfulness of the light an object reflects, to incorporate background and surround dependency, and to model luminance-dependent and cognitive effects.

5 Conclusion

The CIE terminology of colour reflects a scientific orthodoxy that regards the *attributes* of colour as psychological, but regards the particular colours that we see as intrinsic in lights and objects as neither purely psychological nor purely physical, but as *ways of seeing* a physical property in terms of the psychological attributes of colour. Specified by tristimulus values as a psychophysical colour, the physical property that a "standard observer" sees as the intrinsic colour of a light/object is a spectral power distribution/spectral reflectance belonging to an objective, measurable but species-specific class united by the response evoked in the human visual system. (On a very fine-grained level these classes are likely to be individual-specific.)

Colours seen as belonging to objects can be described in terms of hue, lightness, and chroma, or various alternative sets of three attributes. Colours seen as belonging to lights, including the light reflected to the eye by an object at any given point, can be described in terms of hue, brightness, and either colourfulness or saturation. Three dimensions suffice to describe any *colour*, but most *appearances* can be seen as involving more than one colour and thus more than three colour attributes.

Spaces of psychophysical colours can be of the "recipe" type, classifying colours according to physical, imaginary, or theoretical components, or of the psychometric type, classifying colours using dimensions intended as measures of various psychological attributes of colour. The variety of alternative attributes and the variety of measures available to quantify these attributes together contribute to the great diversity of psychometric colour spaces.

6 Acknowledgements

The paper benefitted in clarity from helpful suggestions by the editors and by Dr Jean Pretorius.

References

Alberti, L. B. (1435). *On Painting*. Translated with Introduction and Notes by John R. Spencer. Revised edition, 1966. New Haven: Yale University Press.

Billmeyer, F. W. Jr and Bencuya, A. K. (1987). "Interrelation of the Natural Color System and the Munsell Color Order System". *Color Research and Application*, 12(5), 243–55.

Boyle, R. (1664). *Experiments and Considerations Touching Colours*. London: Printed for Henry Herringman.

Brainard, D. H. and Stockman, A. (2010). "Colorimetry". In the *OSA Handbook of Optics* (3rd ed., M. Bass, ed). New York: McGraw-Hill. 10.1–10.56.

Broackes, J. (2010). "What Do the Color-Blind See?" In Jonathon Cohen and Mohan Matthen (eds.), *Color Ontology and Color Science*. Cambridge, MA: MIT Press. 291–405.

Byrne, A. and Hilbert, D. R. (1997). "Colors and Reflectances". In Alex Byrne and David R. Hilbert (eds.), *Readings on Color, Volume 1: The Philosophy of Color*. Cambridge, MA: MIT Press. 263–88.

Commission Internationale de L'Eclairage (CIE) (2011). *International Lighting Vocabulary*. CIE S 017/E:2011. Searchable online at http://eilv.cie.co.at/ (accessed October 2015).

CVRL (Colour Vision Research Laboratory, University College, London) (2012). *CIE (2012) 2-deg XYZ "physiologically-relevant" colour matching functions*. www.cvrl.org/database/text/cienewxyz/cie2012xyz2.htm (accessed December 2015).

Dinkova-Bruun, G., Gasper, G. E. M., Huxtable, H., McLeish, T. C. B., Panti, C. and Smithson, H. (2013). *The Dimensions of Colour: Robert Grosseteste's* De Colore. Toronto: Pontifical Institute of Mediaeval Studies.

Evans, R. (1974). *The Perception of Color*. New York: Wiley-Interscience.

Fairchild, M. D. (2013). *Color Appearance Models* (3rd ed.). Chichester, UK: Wiley-IS&T.

Hardin, C. L. (2014). "More Color Science for Philosophers". In Dustin Stokes, Mohan Matthen, and Stephen Biggs (eds.), *Perception and Its Modalities*. New York: Oxford University Press. 379–89.

ICC (International Color Consortium) (2010). *sRGB*. www.color.org/chardata/rgb/srgb.xalter (accessed November 2015).

Judd, D. B. (1970). "Ideal Color Space". *Color Engineering* 8(2), 36–52.

Kuehni, R. G. and Schwarz, A. (2008). *Color Ordered: A Survey of Color Systems from Antiquity to the Present*. USA: Oxford University Press.

Munsell, A. H. (1905). *A Color Notation. An Illustrated System Defining All Colors and their Relations by Measured Scales of Hue, Value, and Chroma*. Boston.

Ostwald, W. (1916). "Neue Forschungen zur Farbenlehre". *Physikalische Zeitschrift* XVII, pp. 322–32, Leipzig: S. Hirzel. English translation by Rolf Kuehni available at www.iscc.org/pdf/Ostwald Farbenlehre.pdf.

Poynton, C. (2009). *Frequently Asked Questions about Color*. www.poynton.com/ColorFAQ.html (accessed October 2015).

Schanda, J. (2011). "A Colour Space Based on Advanced Colour Matching Functions". In Carinna Parraman (ed.), *Color Coded*. The Society of Dyers and Colourists. 110–27. Available at www.uwe.ac.uk/sca/research/cfpr/dissemination/publications/books.html.

Taylor, B. (1735). "A New Theory for Mixing Colours". In Joseph Jopling (ed.), *Dr Brook Taylor's Principles of Linear Perspective, A New Edition*. London: M. Taylor. 103–10.

Thoen, H. H., How, M. J., Chiou, T., and Marshall, J. (2014). "A Different Form of Color Vision in Mantis Shrimp". *Science* 343(6169), 411–13.

PART III

Colour phenomena

10

UNIQUE HUES AND COLOUR EXPERIENCE

Mohan Matthen

I Introduction

A unique hue (also called an elemental or a pure hue) is one that is experienced as not being a mixture of other hues. For trichromatic humans, there are four unique hues—unmixed shades of blue, yellow, red, and green. These shades come in opposed pairs (Figure 10.1): blue is opposed to yellow in the sense that no shade is both bluish and yellowish; red is opposed to green in the same way.

Leaving the permanently excluded opposite of each hue unsaid, we have:

Unique blue is that shade of blue that is neither reddish (in the way that mauve is reddish) nor greenish (in the way that turquoise is) [*nor whitish nor blackish*].

Unique red is that shade of red that is neither bluish (like purple) nor yellowish (like orange) [*nor whitish nor blackish*].

Similarly for unique yellow and unique green.

The reference to the achromatic elements, white and black, is usually excluded. Without their mention, shades of red on the interior of the colour solid would also count as unique. Harald Arnkill (2013, 170) explains: "When mixed with blackness, whiteness, or both, [the hues] form nuances, such as greys, browns, and olives", not to mention pastels. The **unique hues** are colour *classes*: for instance, unique red includes all of the reddish greys, browns, and pinks that do not contain any blue or yellow. The structure of these classes will be explored in Sections II–IV below. The full definitions given above define the **elementary colours**; these are singular colours. Philosophers sometimes write as if the unique hues were elementary colours. They are not always clear that to capture a single colour, they need to mention the absence of black and white.

The unique hues arise out of the opponent processing of the wavelength sensitive outputs of the three types of retinal cone-cells. As we shall see, their significance is somewhat idealized in certain representations of colour. However this might be, it is indisputable that they are phenomenologically salient in the sense that most people with normal colour vision (i.e. trichromats) can, with just a little practice, be brought to make consistent judgements of uniqueness

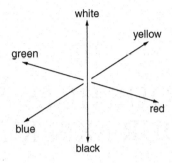

Figure 10.1 Colour oppositions: the white-black axis is orthogonal to the other two.

Source: by permission of Bruce MacEvoy.

regarding sufficiently saturated colour samples. That is, trichromats can more or less reliably identify and re-identify the same colour sample as uniquely green, etc.

This *intra*subjective consistency notwithstanding, there is surprisingly large *inter*subjective variability among trichromats about *which* samples are so identified (Webster *et al.* 2000; Kuehni 2004). Moreover, as Kuehni (*ibid*, 162) notes, individual unique hues are not rotated as a group, which means that "the perceptual distances between unique hues may vary to a smaller or larger extent by observer". This is part of a broader phenomenological feature of colour: subjects make relatively consistent judgements about the proportions of hue elements in colours, but there are substantial inter-subjective and some systematic cross-cultural differences regarding these judgements. Looking, for example, at a piece of turquoise pottery, you may consistently judge that it is equally greenish and bluish and I may consistently judge that it is rather more bluish.

It is unlikely that the magnitude of inter-subjective variation can entirely be explained by physiological differences. Webster *et al.* say that it might trace in part to "differences in the visual diets of observers" (*ibid*, 1554). Citing Webster's findings, Jules Davidoff (2001) attributes inter-subjective variation to "language", though it is unclear how he reconciles this with the fact that Webster *et al.* were using only English-speaking subjects. (Kuehni's 2004 metastudy does not mention language.)

Colour experience is surprisingly complex, and there are many ways of systematizing and representing how it varies. Some representations privilege the unique hues as basic dimensions of chromatic experience. This entry reviews some of the key issues that arise out of these representations and the alternatives.

II The structure of colour appearance[1]

1 The intensive components of colour

In every modality, perceptual qualities are experienced as more or less intense or vivid in some fundamental respect. In touch, there are pressure, temperature, and pain; in audition, pitch and volume; foods taste more or less salty, sweet, bitter, and sour. These basic intensives play a big role in perceived similarity. In colour, this kind of variation is particularly salient. Though non-basic qualities partially determine whether two flavours or two sounds are perceived as similar (for example, two flavours might be judged similar because both are "citrusy" or "earthy"), colour similarity is almost entirely determined by simple dimensions, whether or not these dimensions correspond exactly to the unique hues.[2]

Colour scientists have devised several different ways of systematizing colour similarity and its determinants, each appropriate for different purposes. I shall start by briefly considering *physical* (or, more accurately, *psychophysical*) colour systems, though these are not our primary concern here. These systems are componential representations of *external sources* of colour with respect to their effects on the visual system.

The CIE system represents external *light* in terms of the effects it has on the three different cone-cell types present in the retina. These cells are each sensitive to different, but overlapping, wavebands of visible light. Colour vision can differentiate two beams of light *only if* they differ in their effect on at least one of these cell-types. Thus, colour can be represented as a tristimulus value: one level for each cell. This basic idea is operationalized in different ways. The CIE RGB system is based on mixing lights of three primary wavelengths (700nm, 546.1nm, 435.8nm, often described, rather imprecisely, as red, green, and blue). Subjects are asked to adjust the strength of these primary lights to match a given colour—when presented with yellow, for example, they will turn red and green up and blue down. It turns out that any colour is express-ible as a triplet of RGB values (e.g. greenish yellow = R235, G235, B0). (It's a bit more com-plicated, but we can leave it at this.) This system is particularly useful for designing colour monitors and television screens, which use combinations of light emitting elements to produce colour.

The more commonly used CIE XYZ system is a modification of the RGB system, to reflect the fact that the three dimensions of the latter can be reduced to two variables without signi-ficant loss of information, with luminance being represented in the third dimension. The famil-iar horseshoe shaped representation of the spectral colours, found in many textbooks, is a luminance-constant plane in the CIE XYZ diagram.[3]

Other systems for representing physical colour sources provide guidance to designers using paint or ink. Mixing ink for printing is different from mixing light, because ink gets its colour by selectively absorbing some wavelengths and reflecting the remainder. A mixture of inks absorbs what each component absorbs; it is thus subtractive, and the mixture reflects less than each component. A mixture of lights, by contrast, contains the wavelengths of each component and is thus additive. Subtractive mixing requires at least four primaries: standard colour printers produce nearly 3,000 different colours with cyan, magenta, yellow, and black; the Pantone system uses many more than four inks for fine matching.

The RGB and Pantone systems are based on methods of creating physical sources of colour by mixing. Although the primary concern is with how these creations look, the basic compon-ents of these systems are the lights or inks needed to produce a physical specimen of a given colour. *Perceptual* systems, by contrast, aim to systematize the intensive variation of colours as they are *experienced*. The unique hues play a fundamental role in such systems because these are *experienced* as the components of perceived colour.

2 *Similarity spaces for colour*

A similarity space is a representation of colour in terms of the basic intensives discussed above. It is a multidimensional graphic representation of qualities in which the nearness of two qualities is proportional to their similarity (Goodman 1970; Clark 1993, chapter 4; Matthen 2005, chapter 4; Raffman 2015). With colour, perceptual similarity is exceedingly difficult to map in this way. The CIE spaces represent colour, as we have seen, by the activation of the colour-sensitive cone cells. Colour *appearance* does not match the activation of the receptors. In the first place, a differ-ence of activation levels might be too small to register. Second, because of opponent processing, colour experience corresponds not to cone-cell activation triplets, but to *differences* of cone-cell

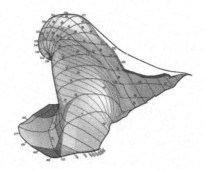

Figure 10.2 A chromaticity diagram that equalizes just noticeable differences. Notice that the plane is folded over at the top right, one reason why the total space in which it is embedded has dimensionality greater than 3. (From Mohan Matthen 2005: 111. Adapted from David L. Macadam 1944: 203.)

Source: by permission of Elsevier.

activation—for example, yellow corresponds to a small positive difference between the output of the long-wave cone and that of the medium-wave cone.

Figure 10.2 illustrates the difficulty with regard to just noticeable differences. It shows the plane corresponding to just noticeable differences for combinations of coloured lights of equal luminance. The figure is taken from a photograph of a three-dimensional model, which was constructed from a single equal-luminance place in the CIE XYZ chromaticity diagram in such a way as to equalize just noticeable differences: the plane was printed on a flat sheet of paper, just-noticeable-difference intervals were drawn on it, and then the sheet was pinched and folded to equalize these intervals. The distance between two colours in this model inversely tracks perceptual similarity. The result is a plane that is curved in three dimensions. To get *all* the colours, variations of luminance have to be added. David Macadam (1944), who made the Figure 10.2 model, estimates that the totality of colours occupies a six-dimensional Euclidean solid, which cannot be drawn or physically modelled.

Different colour spaces model different aspects of colour similarity. Figure 10.1 takes as basic the unique hues (plus black-white) and their opposition. These give us the three axes of a simpler perceptual similarity space. This figure systematizes colour-similarity in terms of the combinations of these components. It is an idealization based on what are taken to be the underlying processes of colour vision.

3 *The unique hues as absolute locations in colour space*

The unique hues are given absolute position in colour spaces that are based on Figure 10.1; they mark definite phenomenal qualities, not positions specified only relative to others. To see the difference, think of a map of the world. Longstanding convention marks the Greenwich longitude as 0°, but there is nothing qualitatively distinct about either Greenwich or the designation zero that mandates this choice. Delhi could just as easily have been marked as 0, provided that the in-betweenness relation of Greenwich-Delhi-Tokyo was maintained. By contrast, the phenomenally unmixed character of the unique hues gives them a non-arbitrary position in colour similarity space. A colour that looks reddish-yellow is naturally placed in between red and yellow; by the same token, red is naturally placed in between yellow-red and red-blue. However, yellow-red and red-blue cannot be treated as simple components of experienced colour—they are experienced as compound. It is because the unique hues are experienced as simple that they have a special place in colour similarity spaces. Maintaining in-betweenness relations is not enough. (Remember, though, the inter-personal variation in marking the poles.)

4 Colour and colour experience

The unique hues are experientially defined: they are the hues that *appear* unmixed or pure. This has important methodological consequences. The initial formulation of psychological theories of colour structure and underlying perceptual processes rested on the careful visual assessment of colour by nineteenth-century theorists such as Thomas Young, Hermann von Helmholtz, and (most successfully) Ewald Hering. These men made inferences about the underlying processes of colour perception simply by reflecting on the structure of colour experience. This was a matter of principle, not of necessity. As Hering wrote:

> For a systematic grouping of colours the only thing that matters is *colour* itself. Neither the qualitative (frequency) nor the quantitative (amplitude) physical properties of the radiations are relevant.
>
> *(Quoted by Arnkill 2013, 168)*

Hering wants to say that it is colour experience—not physical fact—that determines *perceptual* similarity spaces such as that sketched in Figure 10.1.

Spectral similarity is a kind of physical similarity. Colours that are spectrally similar have similar effects on us. Thus, any colour similarity space will track physical, i.e. spectral, similarity *over small regions*. This is true both of physical similarity spaces such as CIE RGB space, which indexes colours by cone-cell activation, and perceptual spaces such as those based on Figure 10.1 and even the massively complex and weirdly shaped space of Figure 10.2. The *large-scale* topology of perceptual colour spaces is, however, different from that of any physical measure, and also different from one another. The axes of CIE space do not correspond to those of perceptual colour; there is no natural representation within this space of the opposition of red-green and blue-yellow, which are the opposite poles of two dimensions of hue. Moreover, there is no natural position for the unique hues—yellow is a mixture of three non-zero RGB values, though it is phenomenally experienced as unmixed. The CIE spaces provide numerical indices of all the colours we experience, but not in a way that matches colour experience.

On the other side of the coin, the perceptual spaces do not track additive mixing of lights and the subtractive mixing of paints. Here are two examples. The additive mixing of red and green *lights* yields yellow; however, red and green are experiential opposites and cannot be experientially mixed. Second, different additive or subtractive mixtures may be experienced as the same colour: such perceptually equivalent mixtures are known as *metamers*.

The NCS and Munsell systems are based on colour experience. However, these systems are constructed on slightly different principles. The Munsell system takes just noticeable differences of colour as basic, and constructs colour similarity space to preserve them. There are more just-noticeable-difference steps between red and green through blue, than in the other direction around through yellow. In consequence, the blue-yellow and red-green oppositions have no special significance in this system, which does not grant the unique hues special significance. The NCS system takes the unique hues plus whiteness and blackness as defining the basic dimensions of colour experience, and orders the colours accordingly. This difference of approach leads, as we shall see, to topological and terminological differences between the two spaces. It is good to keep this in mind: though phenomenologically salient, unique hue mixtures are only one way of systematizing colour similarity.

III Colour and hue

Colour is experienced as hue *plus* an achromatic component. The achromatic component is differently defined in different systems. In Munsell's system, it is called "value" and corresponds to how bright a colour looks. A saturated yellow looks a lot brighter than a saturated blue of the same luminance. (This is because yellow excites two cone cell types, while blue excites only one.) Thus, the Munsell system gives yellow a value closer to white, whereas a maximally saturated blue falls closer to black. Thus, the blue pole in Figure 10.1 above, which corresponds to unique blue, would be lower in Munsell space than the yellow pole.

The Swedish Natural Colour System (NCS), which is based on Hering's system of opponent hues, defines the achromatic colour component as the axis of variation between white (W) and black (S for the Swedish *swart*, to distinguish it from B for blue). In this system, the hue circle consists of colours that do not contain any admixture of either white or black. Since these colours are zero white and zero black, the hue circle, Figure 10.3, is *by definition* orthogonal to the achromatic dimension. In the NCS system, there is no way even of *saying* that yellow is

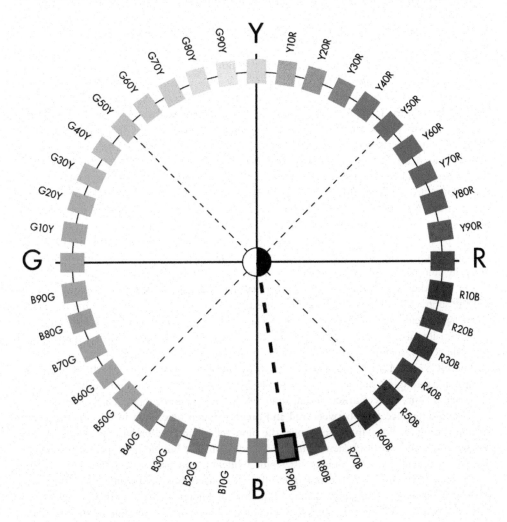

Figure 10.3 The NCS hue circle. By permission of NCS Colour AB, Stockholm www.ncscolour.com.

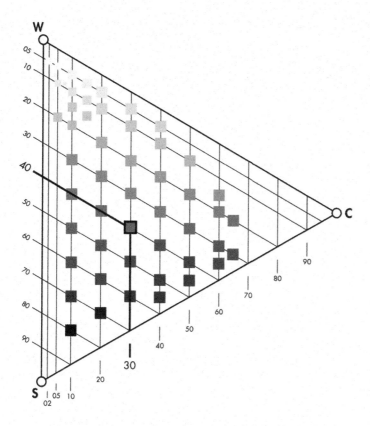

Figure 10.4 A grey-scale rendering of a vertical section of NCS space corresponding to a single radius, R90B on the hue circle, Figure 10.3. The squares mark physical samples provided by NCS. By permission of NCS Colour AB, Stockholm www.ncscolour.com. See http://tinyurl.com/nvutols for full colour versions of figures like 10.3 and 10.4.

brighter than blue. Correspondingly, there is no way, in the Munsell system, of saying that blue is the opposite of yellow. 180° separation in the Munsell hue circle does not correspond to exclusion.

Colours on the NCS hue circle have maximum chromaticness or vividness, as shown in Figure 10.4, where the C vertex corresponds to maximal chromaticness. ("Chromaticness" is a technical term in the NCS glossary. It is different from "chromaticity", which is a measure of colour content as a mixture of primary lights.) Chromaticness is understood experientially for each hue; its peak value attaches to the most vivid shade of that hue. It does not make sense to compare absolute chromaticness across hues. You cannot ask whether maximally chromatic yellow is more or less chromatic than maximally chromatic blue; both have chromaticness 1, by definition. Spectral colours are maximally chromatic, but the hue circle also spans purple, which is not a spectral colour. *There is no candidate for physical equivalency*—the criterion is experiential. A colour is maximally chromatic if its hue content cannot be intensified.

Figure 10.4 shows what happens when a single hue (such as 10 per cent red and 90 per cent blue—see the marked colour on Figure 10.3) interacts with the achromatic axis. All of the colours in Figure 10.4 correspond to the same mixture of the fundamental hue-components. The maximally chromatic C pole is singular—there is only one colour there. Hering says that

165

colour is "veiled" by black and by white; in other words, adding white or adding black reduces chromaticness. Accordingly, the C-vertex contains no white and no black. In particular, the elementary colours contain no white and no black.

When white is added to a maximally chromatic colour, we move away from C toward the W pole along the upper flank of the triangle, thereby increasing the white component and reducing chromaticness, but leaving the black component constant at zero. (Again, do not confuse physical mixing of lights or inks with experiential mixing.) The lines parallel to the upper flank mark colours of the same blackness. Adding black is another way to reduce chromaticness, but in this case we move along the lower flank of the triangle from C to S, gradually increasing the black component and leaving whiteness constant at zero. Lines parallel to this lower flank (not shown in Figure 10.4) mark equal whiteness. NCS gives numerical values to the colours by implementing Hering's equation:

$$w + s + c = 1.$$

The numbers along the left of Figure 10.4 give the blackness (s) component, and the numbers along the lower flank give chromaticness (c). The vertical lines indicate equal chromaticness.

As mentioned earlier, the NCS system is constructed on principles taken from Hering's system of the opponent hues. It treats the maximally chromatic unique hues as pure colours. The Munsell system diverges from this by giving the chromatic elementary colours different values—as mentioned before, maximally chromatic yellow is lighter than maximally chromatic blue, and green is lighter than red. On the other hand, the Munsell system treats lightness and darkness as opposite poles of a single intensive variable. NCS is different in this regard; as Hering's equation above shows, there is a three-way inter-dependency of white, black, and chromaticness in this system.

It should be clear that though they are based on phenomenal qualities, the colour similarity systems we have mentioned are idealizations. Even when you construct a similarity space out of a phenomenally meaningful measure such as a just noticeable difference or simplicity of experience, there is no guarantee that the axes of the space you construct will have a precise phenomenal meaning. Thus, there is a degree of idealization in such concepts as the unique hues and saturation.

IV Colour as a unity

Though colour has perceptual components, we experience each colour, whether simple or compound as *one* phenomenal whole, not as many phenomenal qualities bound together. Colours are, we might say, phenomenally unified. Figure 10.5 illustrates the point. The vertical lines mark colours of the same hue, but differing in lightness. Each such line is roughly equivalent to an NCS "triangle" like Figure 10.4, defined by a single radius on the hue circle of Figure 10.3. Notice how the unique hues are vertical lines in Figure 10.5, and triangles like that in Figure 10.4 in the NCS system. As we remarked at the beginning, we have to factor in the achromatic component to get a singular colour.

It is not always easy to discern sameness of hue. As Figure 10.5 shows, certain shades that people call yellow have the same hue content as certain shades that they call orange and certain others that they call brown. These shades differ only in lightness—i.e. in Munsell "value", or NCS blackness/whiteness.[4] It is very difficult to recognize that these shades are same in hue. This is a case where the components of colour are intimately mixed together: brown and orange seem like different colours, and the sameness of their components is not evident. The difference

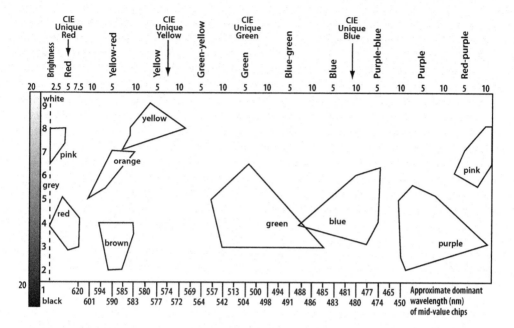

Figure 10.5 The basic colours. The pairs pink and red, and orange and brown differ little in hue. (From Mohan Matthen 2005: 76. Adapted from Berlin and Kay 1969: 9.)

Source: by permission of Paul Kay.

in their names is just one indication of this.[5] If the darkness of these colours were easily separable from their hue, it would be easy to recognize brown as a blackened orange.

This said, it should also be acknowledged that in important ways, the components of colour are separable. It is certainly possible to discern hue components in colours of high chromaticness. It is easy, for example, to see that orange is yellow–red and that turquoise is a greenish blue. It is also easy to discern which of two shades of brown is more yellow and which more red. And when the difference of lightness is not too great, it is relatively easy to discern sameness of hue: an example would be a pale and a dark magenta. Moreover, the visual system itself uses the components of colour separately. The lightness or black/white component of colour is wholly or dominantly responsible for perceptions of depth and motion (Livingstone and Hubel 1988; Livingstone 2002), while fine spatial resolution depends on colour independently of lightness. This shows that even though colour is phenomenologically a unity, the visual system has some access to the separate components.

Taking the unity of colour into account, *hues* are not colours—different colours can have the same hue. Accordingly, we speak of elementary *colours*, thereby including white and black alongside the four elemental hues (Arnkill 2013, 168), the latter pair being defined as possessing no hue element.

J. D. Mollon (2006), however, goes further:

> Discussions of the unique hues rather seldom include white as one of the unique hues. Yet white is the mother of all unique hues, and its phenomenological purity and simplicity were historically an obstacle to the acceptance of the Newtonian theory … white is *neither reddish nor greenish nor yellowish nor bluish.*
>
> *(ibid, 305; emphasis added)*

Notice that the way Mollon defines it, "neither reddish not greenish nor yellowish nor bluish", white is a class of colours that runs from pure white through various shades of grey to black. When he mentions "phenomenological purity and simplicity", he is presumably talking about an elementary colour defined by adding "nor blackish" to the above definition. If this is right, then he should have noted that black is phenomenologically pure in just the same sense as white (it too admits none of the other unique hues). Note: The apparent disagreement with Newton came from a failure to recognize the difference between mixed light and mixed sensations. White light is a mixture of wavelengths; white is, however, an unmixed colour as far as experience goes.

Mollon's point is significant. Is there a yellow that is unique in the same sense as white is unique? In one way of systematizing things, yes—the NCS system defines maximally chromatic unique yellow as lacking whiteness and blackness. However, yellow is lighter than its opponent blue. This comes out well in the Munsell system, which gives yellow a higher lightness value than blue. Arguably, white is pure in a way that yellow is not: pure white contains none of the hues, but the elementary colours contain non-zero lightness or darkness. (There is no way to say this in the NCS system, however—an indication of how it idealizes the Hering components of colour.)

One complication to be noted here is that white and black are contrast colours. Two complementary (but not quite equivalent) conditions are significant. First, white is the colour that reflects all of the colours of the illuminate; black is that which reflects none. Second, white is the lightest colour in any scene; black is the darkest. The visual system treats as white and black the patches in any scene that best conform to these conditions taken together. (The treatment of self-luminous objects is somewhat different.) Consequently, the white-black level of a colour patch can be raised or lowered depending on how light it is relative to a given presentation. Viewed through an isolation tube in which it is the only thing seen, a pink will appear more saturated and closer to red, and a brown will appear orange. It makes sense, therefore, to ask whether black and white are qualities of objects independently of the conditions in which they are viewed. It is beyond the scope of this entry to discuss this question.

A final point to be made here is that hue consists of a red-green and a blue-yellow component. In Figure 10.3, the bottom right quadrant of the figure consists of hues that vary from 100 per cent red and 0 per cent blue through all possible combinations of red and blue to 0 per cent red and 100 per cent blue at the bottom. This way of putting it, however, risks confusion by suggesting that the *colour* red is an intensive quality. *Colours* are regions in colour space such as those marked in Figure 10.5. The colour that lies halfway between red and blue in Figure 10.3 is, at maximum chromaticness, *magenta*. Magenta, the colour, is different from the colours we call "red" and "blue"; however, it is *reddish* and *bluish* to equal degrees. There is a difference between red-the-colour and red-the-hue-dimension.

V Does unique hue have a physiological counterpart?

C. L. Hardin (2014) writes:

In the early 1990s ... I asked Peter Lennie when he expected the locus of unique hues to be discovered. He then believed it would be in the next five years. It has taken twenty years, but the end appears to be in sight ... Recently, Stoughton and Conway claimed to have found a brain locus for the unique hues.

(*ibid. 379*)

So far we have been emphasizing the phenomenal basis for the unique hues and their phenomenal interaction with white/black. Hardin assumes a neural basis. Mollon (2006), however, writes:

> [W]hat are the unique hues? Are they determined within us, by the organization of our visual system? Or are they ecologically significant, identifying for us particular subsets of spectra in the world? Let us call answers of the former type "constitutional" hypotheses, and answers of the second type, "ecological". *The two types of account are not necessarily exclusive, because our visual categories may have evolved to match some feature of the world.*
>
> *(304, emphasis added)*

Hardin's question assumes a constitutional account; Mollon takes an ecological line.

For colour scientists, the status of the unique hues has not been settled satisfactorily. As we have repeatedly had reason to notice, they have a phenomenal basis. This phenomenal basis is inferred from subjects' qualitative descriptions of their sensations, descriptions that are more subjective than the more usually employed judgements about the qualitative identity of sensations. There is considerable doubt in the scientific community what kind of credence should be attached to qualitative descriptions of this kind (Mollon and Jordan 1997). Some, however, think that they are indispensable. Neitz and Neitz (2008) put it this way: "Understanding the brain requires a kind of thinking outside the main tradition of natural science: the biology has to be linked to something intangible, a private experience."

There was considerable excitement in the early 1960s, when Russell De Valois and co-workers (De Valois *et al.* 1966) found cells in precortical brain areas (specifically the lateral geniculate nucleus, LGN) that indicated opponent processes. A couple of decades later it began to become apparent that LGN is the site of spatial analysis using brightness, and that the colour-sensitive cells there do not, for the most part, correspond to the Hering red-green/blue-yellow opponencies. More complex opponent processing models were proposed as time went on; it came to be believed that the cortex extracted opponent information from the rather differently structured LGN opponent signals. Neitz and Neitz (2008, R702) remark:

> The simplest idea is [that] additional processing stages in the cortex would further transform LGN opponent signals, with the wrong spectral signatures into ones that match perception; however, even the most well thought out versions of this idea (for example [De Valois and De Valois 1993]), raise more questions than they answer. It is not clear how, and even more puzzling why, the cortex would recombine the cone signals.

In 2008, this situation changed again. Chris Tailby, Samuel Solomon, and Peter Lennie (2008) were able to identify cells in LGN that show the right spectral signature. More or less simultaneously, Cleo Stoughton and Bevil Conway (2008) reported cell populations in the inferotemporal cortex that are specific to red, green, and blue, and much more weakly to yellow. (Neitz and Neitz 2008 provide an upbeat overview from the constitutionalist perspective.) However, none of these studies are conducted in ecologically realistic situations—they are all based on single cell recordings of macaques viewing lights. And there are anomalies in the result: yellow, for example, does not evoke as pronounced a peak. As Stoughton and Conway (2009) acknowledge in response to a critical note by Mollon (2009, R443): "It remains unclear how the brain encodes the inter-connectedness and nonlinearity of these dimensions."

Mollon's ecological account is even more elusive, though it rests on some intriguing phenomena. He points out, first, with regard to white objects that they reflect light that matches the illuminant. (His proposal is actually a little more complicated and a lot more interesting than this—"an achromatic surface is one that exhibits no variation in chromaticity across its surface" (2006, 306)—but we can simplify for present purposes.) Thus white has a special ecological significance. As well, he says, light from the sky is unique blue, while direct sunlight is unique yellow (both with a considerable admixture of white); thus, as he says (attributing the point to Roger Shepard), "the yellow-blue axis of human color experience corresponds to the two predominant illuminants in our world" (*ibid*, 306). This is an interesting observation, but it is unclear how it matches up with the unique hue structure of colour vision. Why, after all, is it functionally advantageous for the blue-yellow axis to match the skylight-sunlight dimension? All that Mollon offers on this point is this: "This is a rather provocative coincidence", (*ibid*, 306) but this is not exactly an argument, much less a theory. Second, as Mollon admits, "It is less obvious that unique red and unique green can be directly related to properties of illuminants as such" (*ibid*, 307).

It is hard to judge the current state of play. On the one hand, the "constitutional" position (that the unique hues arise from the organization of the visual system) has received dramatic new support, though this support rests on somewhat shaky quantitative analysis. On the other hand, the ecological account seems so far to rest on a few suggestive "coincidences". Perhaps, we should content ourselves with the observation that the opponent structure of colour and colour processing has clear neurophysiological support, but the unique hues have less. This complements our earlier observation that the unique hues are somewhat idealized. (See also Jameson and D'Andrade 1997 and Valberg 2001.)

VI The variability of unique hue perception

Though perceivers tend to be quite consistent with regard to which physical colours they identify as unique, there is (as we noted earlier) a certain amount of variability *among* subjects—of the total amount of variability with regard to unique hue choice, only about a third is intra-observer (Hardin 2014).

Michael Tye (2006) makes a philosophical puzzle out of this variability. Let a certain object O be perceived by John as uniquely blue and by Jane as greenish blue. "Intuitively", he says, it cannot be both: to suppose otherwise "is to accept a view that is implausible from the start" (173–4). At most one of John and Jane is right. The question Tye raises is whether experiencing something differently implies experiencing it as having different (and in this case, incompatible) properties. Clearly, this is so for a single subject: if I experience the same thing colour-wise differently in similar circumstances, then I experience it as having different colours. Is the same true inter-subjectively? And how do we determine whose unique blue is the true one?

Tye acknowledges that there is no way to tell whether O is *truly* unique blue, but this, he insists, does not imply that there is no fact of the matter:

> God knows precisely which hue chip 527 has, but we may very well never know.[6] Our only access to the colours of things is via a single sense and the colour detectors nature has endowed us with are limited. We do not suppose that objects do not have precise lengths because of the limitations of our measuring equipment. Why suppose that the situation is fundamentally any different for the case of colour?

(177–8)

The analogy with length is inconclusive. Length is the quantity that determines how long light takes to traverse an interval, that determines the gravitational force between two masses, and so on. To be wrong about length is to be wrong about this quantity. Suppose I attach the number 1 to a certain length, and you attach the number 39 to the same length. Are we disagreeing? Not necessarily, because I might be using metres and you might be using inches. Let us say, for the sake of argument, that colour is reflectance. Then, to be wrong about colour is to be wrong about reflectance. Must at least one of Jane and John be wrong about reflectance? Could it not be that the difference between them is *merely* about how their colour vision systems represent one and the same quality?

Colour experience is the product of opponent processing. Something looks bluish when the response it gets from the short-wave cone is greater than the response it gets from the long- and middle-wave cones. What if two subjects have differently tuned short-wave cones, so that something that looks bluish to one looks yellowish to the other? Do these experiences tell the two subjects different things about the *external* world? Byrne and Hilbert (2003) say that it is right to perceive O as unique blue if blue is the sole contributor to its "hue magnitude". The problem is that "hue magnitude" means nothing in physics; Byrne and Hilbert define it by working backward from the perceptual qualities through cone responses to a physical quality/illuminant pair. Like the RGB and Pantone systems mentioned earlier, hue magnitudes are properties of external objects with respect to appearance.

The standard view of the function of opponent processing is this:

> Color opponency … is an attempt to remove correlations in the signals of different cone cell types that are introduced by the strong overlap of the cone spectral sensitivities. [As well] naturally occurring spectra are known to be fairly smooth … and therefore may contribute substantially to redundancies in the cone signals.
>
> *(Lee et al. 2002, 2095)*

The point is that there is a strong correlation in the response levels of the cone cells; to achieve maximum discrimination in such circumstance, it is functionally advantageous to throw away the common response level and keep the differences. Subtracting one response level from another is the best way to do this (Hardin 1988, 30–2).

Keep in mind that the information contained in opponent colours is exactly the same as that contained in the tristimulus values of CIE colours. Opponent processing adds no new information. The role of the opponent colour components then is merely to achieve maximum legibility—to "remove correlations in the signals of different cone cell types", and not to extract information about external qualities. Opponent processing also arrays colours in dimensions that are easy to combine into a unified percept as described in Section IV above.

There is, therefore, a big difference between opponent processing and processing for colour constancy. The latter uses permanently stored environmental information (genetically acquired during the course of evolution) to apportion the light signals differentially to (a) the source object's reflectance, and (b) the light incident on the source. In short, constancy processing adds information to the incident signal, while opponent processing is informationally neutral. Colour constancy processing pulls apart signals that were the same on the retina and identifies signals that were retinally different. Beyond enhancing discrimination, opponent processing does not do this: signals that are different in NCS space are different CIE space, and vice versa. Moreover, such phenomena as the mutual exclusion of the bluish and the yellowish have no physical counterpart.

The reader might think that Mollon offers us a different opinion: light from the sky is unique blue. There are two problems with this. The first is that it simply begs the question about intersubjective differences regarding unique blue: as Kuehni (2004) says, it is not justified to assume that mean unique hue values can be "considered representative of humans". The second is that even if they are, and even if Mollon is right, the question would arise: is the sky "really" unique blue because "we" experience it that way, or is such experience "true" because the sky really is unique blue? The second position is dubious because, as noted above, blue is not a *physical* kind—it has no place in physics; it is not a term in any physical law.

In effect, Tye, Byrne, and Hilbert think that the opponent colours constitute a *physical* similarity space (though, as noted above, Byrne and Hilbert define it psychophysically). The point that emerged in sections II and III above is that it is properly defined by reference to *perceptual* systems. The visual system can be seen as doing two things with incoming light—(a) it detects what wavelength/reflectance range this light belongs to, and (b) it tags this physical property with a certain colour experience. (The point of the multistage opponency theory of De Valois and De Valois 1997 is that the second function occurs surprisingly late.) (a) is a physical measure of a particular stimulus; (b) is a correspondence between this physical measure and experience that is a permanent or acquired feature of the visual system itself. Variation with respect to (b) has been attributed to variations in cone-cell distribution and eye-colour, past visual "diet", and language.

Suppose that a light of 510 nm, most often seen in industrial societies as green, happens to be seen by members of the Berinmo tribe in Papua New Guinea as blue. There are two possibilities here. The first is that the Berinmos' visual system *wrongly* measures the light as belonging to the 480 nm range, and consequently as blue because (in common with industrial societies) it tags *this* range as blue. The second is that their system correctly measures the light as belonging to the 510 nm range, and tags this range as blue. In the second scenario, the same physical stimuli are tagged with different qualia—and to treat it as *wrong* is to assume that there is something non-arbitrary about such tagging. The system can be wrong about colour, but only by getting its physical characteristics wrong. As far as the Berinmo are concerned, the difference is a matter only of *how* colour is experienced (Matthen 2009). The intersubjective variability of the unique hues is due to this sort of permanent differences among visual systems. It is a shifted spectrum phenomenon (Nida-Rumelin 1996). Differences of colour qualia tagging are never about the world outside the perceiver.

VII Conclusion

Colour appearance is the product of a number of underlying processes. Ewald Hering and the Swedish Natural Colour System focus on opponent colour processing as fundamental among these. The result is a codification of each colour experience as consisting of a triple of values along the three fundamental dimensions of the opponent process. Probably, this is philosophically the most neat and tidy way of systematizing colour appearance, but we should not lose sight of the facts that it is one of several alternative idealizations. It (a) simplifies the phenomenology of colour vision to some degree, (b) omits important elements of colour appearance such as perceived lightness, and (c) has not as yet been neurophysiologically validated. The unique hues are privileged in the Natural Colour System. Though they are phenomenologically salient, the above caveats apply.

Opponent colour phenomena, i.e. the phenomena that arise from the subtraction of cone-cell outputs in colour processing, have no informational value about the world outside the perceiver over and above the tristimulus representation of colours in the retina. (Or so I have argued.) The function of opponent processing is non-informational: to enhance discriminability and to format colour in a way that admits of combining distinct elements. This indicates that individual differences that relate to the opponent representation of colour—the unique hues, the proportion of hue magnitudes in perceived colour, the colour categories—have no significance regarding external reality. Some philosophers have suggested that some things in the world are uniquely blue independently of any perceptual system. This contradicts the function of opponent processing as I have presented it.

VIII Acknowledgements

I am very grateful to Berit Bergström of the Swedish Natural Colour System, David Briggs, author of *Dimensions of Colour* (www.huevaluechroma.com/), Derek Brown, Larry Hardin, and Yasmina Jraissati for detailed comments and corrections.

Notes

1 Information for this and the next section has been distilled from a number of sources. I am most in debt to Hardin (1988) and Arnkill (2013).
2 Colour language can influence colour similarity judgements, but linguistic colour terms are not, of course, components of colour experience. Roberson *et al.* 2000 and Davidoff 2001 offer important experimental data, but are confused about this important distinction.
3 The diagram can be found on the Hyperphysics site of Georgia State University http://tinyurl.com/nn4utgt.
4 The appearance of blackness/whiteness depends on contrast with other colours present in the same scene. When these contrasts are removed by looking at brown through an isolation tube, it looks very much like orange. The component analysis of NCS is an attempt to regiment such variation.
5 Davidoff (e.g. 2001) would write "cause" in place of "indication".
6 I am sure the "God knows" argument goes down well in Texas.

References

Arnkill, Harald (2013) *Colours in the Visual World*. Helsinki: Aalto Art Books.
Berlin, Brent and Kay, Paul (1969) *Basic Color Terms: Their Universality and Evolution*. Berkeley: University of California Press.
Byrne, Alex and Hilbert, David R. (2003) "Color Realism and Color Science", *Brain and Behavioral Sciences* 26: 1–21.
Clark, Austen (1993) *Sensory Qualities*. Oxford: Clarendon Press.
Davidoff, Jules (2001) "Language and Perceptual Categorization", *Trends in Cognitive Sciences* 5: 382–7.
De Valois, R. L. and De Valois, K. K. (1993) "A Multi-stage Color Model", *Vision Research* 33: 1053–65.
De Valois, R. L., Abramov, I., and Jacobs, G. H. (1966) "Analysis of Response Patterns of LGN Cells", *Journal of the Optical Society of America* 56: 966–77.
Goodman, Nelson (1970) "Seven Strictures on Similarity", in L. Foster and J. W. Swanson (eds.) *Experience and Theory*. Boston: University of Massachusetts Press.
Hardin, C. L. (1988) *Color for Philosophers: Unweaving the Rainbow*. Indianapolis, IN: Hackett Publishing.
Hardin, C. L. (2014) "More Color Science for Philosophers", in D. Stokes, M. Matthen, and S. Biggs (eds.) *Perception and Its Modalities*. New York: Oxford University Press. 379–89.
Jameson, Kimberly and D'Andrade, Roy G. (1997) "It's Not Really Red, Green, Yellow and Blue: An Inquiry into Perceptual Color Space", in C. L. Hardin and Luisa Maffi (eds.) *Color Categories in Thought and Language*. Cambridge: Cambridge University Press.
Kuehni, Rolf G. (2004) "Variability in Unique Hue Selection: A Surprising Phenomenon", *Color Research and Application* 29: 158–62.
Lee, Te-Won, Wachtler, Thomas, and Sejnowski, Terrence J. (2002) "Color Opponency Is an Efficient Representation of Spectral Properties in Natural Scenes", *Vision Research* 42: 2095–2103.
Livingstone, M. and Hubel, D. (1988) "Segregation of Form, Color, Movement, and Depth: Anatomy, Physiology, and Perception", *Science* 240: 740–9.

Livingstone, Margaret (2002) *Vision and Art: The Biology of Seeing.* New York: Harry N. Abrams.

Macadam, David (1944) "On the Geometry of Color Spaces", *Journal of the Franklin Society* 238: 195–210.

Matthen, Mohan (2005) *Seeing, Doing, and Knowing: A Philosophical Theory of Sense Perception.* Oxford: Clarendon Press.

Matthen, Mohan (2009) "Truly Blue: An Adverbial Aspect of Perceptual Representation", *Analysis* 69: 48–54.

Mollon, J. D. (2006) "Monge: The Verriest Lecture, Lyon, July 2005", *Visual Neuroscience* 23: 297–309.

Mollon, J. D. (2009) "A Neural Basis for Unique Hues?" *Current Biology* 19: R441–2.

Mollon, J. D. and Jordan, Gabriele (1997) "On the Nature of the Unique Hues", in C. Dickinson, I. Murray, and D. Carden (eds.) *John Dalton's Colour Vision Legacy.* London: Taylor & Francis.

Nida-Rumelin, Martine (1996) "Pseudo-normal Vision: An Actual Case of Qualia Inversion?" *Philosophical Studies* 82: 145–57.

Neitz, Jay and Maureen Neitz (2008) "Colour Vision: The Wonder of Hue", *Current Biology* 18: R700–2.

Raffman, Diana (2015) "Similarity Spaces", in M. Matthen (ed.) *Oxford Handbook of the Philosophy of Perception.* Oxford: Oxford University Press.

Roberson, Debi, Davies, Ian, and Davidoff, Jules (2000) "Colour Categories Are Not Universal: Evidence from a Stone-Age Culture", *Journal of Experimental Psychology: General* 129: 369–98.

Stoughton, C. M. and Conway, B. R. (2008) "Neural Basis for Unique Hues", *Current Biology* 18: R698–9.

Stoughton, C. M. and Conway, B. R. (2009) "Response: Towards a Neural Representation for Unique Hues", *Current Biology* 19: R442–3.

Tailby, C., Solomon, S., and Lennie, P. (2008) "Functional Asymmetries in Visual Pathways Carrying S-Cone Signals in the Macaque", *Journal of Neuroscience* 28: 4078–87.

Tye, Michael (2006) "The Puzzle of True Blue", *Analysis* 66: 173–8.

Valberg, Arne (2001) "Unique Hues: An Old Problem for a New Generation", *Vision Research* 41: 1645–57.

Webster, M. A., Miyahara, E., Malkoc, G., and Raker, V. E. (2000) "Variations in Normal Color Vision. II. Unique Hues", *Journal of the Optical Society of America A* 17: 1545–55.

11

NOVEL COLOUR EXPERIENCES AND THEIR IMPLICATIONS[1]

Fiona Macpherson

> One evening, in summer, he went into his own room and stood at the lattice-window, and gazed into the forest which fringed the outskirts of Fairyland ... Suddenly, far among the trees, as far as the sun could shine, he saw a glorious thing. It was the end of a rainbow, large and brilliant. He could count all seven colours, and could see shade after shade beyond the violet; while before the red stood a colour more gorgeous and mysterious still. It was a colour he had never seen before.
>
> *From George MacDonald (1867) "The Golden Key" in his Dealing with the Fairies,*
> *London: Alexander Strahan, pp. 250–1*

In his writings for children, George MacDonald (1867) portrays the exhilaration and wonder that would likely accompany experiencing beautiful colours that one has not experienced before. One reason it would be exciting, I proffer, is that we tend to think that we have experienced all the colours that we can experience, and the idea that there are other colour experiences to be had seems rather far-fetched. It is no coincidence that MacDonald's protagonist experiences the novel colours in Fairyland.

Part of the reason that the idea of experiencing novel colours seems a remote possibility is that most people report that they cannot visually imagine what it would be like to experience colours other than those they have already seen.[2] Contemplation of such experiences cannot be done by conjuring up images in the mind's eye of unfamiliar colours but, instead, is limited to a rather abstract contemplation of the fact that there could be such colours. This, no doubt, contributes to the sense of mystery that MacDonald invokes in his description of the colours of Fairyland.

For philosophers, the question of whether there could be experiences of colours that you have not experienced before is an exciting one for additional reasons. The existence of such colour experiences promises to substantially inform our theories of colours and colour experiences. It is therefore of great interest that some psychologists have recently claimed to create experiences of new colours.

This chapter explores the evidence for the existence of such new colour experiences and what their philosophical ramifications would be. I first define the notion of 'novel colours' and discuss why I think that this is the best name for such colours, rather than the numerous other names that they have sometimes been given in the literature. I then introduce the evidence and arguments for thinking that experiences as of novel colours exist, along with objections that people have had to that evidence and to those arguments. To do so, I outline some facts about ordinary, non-novel colours before considering whether experiences as of novel colours, exist. Then I discuss the potentially significant ramifications the existence of novel colour experiences would have for theories of the metaphysics of colour, theories of the nature of colour experience, and for theories of the nature of perception more generally.

1 What are novel colours and what should we call them?

When we contemplate experiences of colours that an individual has not had before, we have to take into account the fact that different people have different colour experiences. Colour blindness exists in many forms. If a person had a form of colour blindness that meant that they experienced all the colours that someone who was not colour-blind experienced except for the fact that they did not experience any shades of red, it would likely be very exciting for him or her, personally, if we could circumvent their colour blindness and give them an experience of red that they had not had before. However, from an impersonal, philosophical point of view this would not be a particularly interesting occurrence. We typically think that the colour red exists (if any colours do) and experiences of it are ubiquitous, even if not had by everyone.

What is really interesting, from a philosophical point of view, is whether there are experiences of hues of colour in addition to those that the standard colour theory says that humans (with what is defined to be "normal" tri-chromatic vision[3]) have in standard viewing conditions. If there are such experiences, as I hereby define them in this essay, there are experiences of 'novel colours'. Evidence from a wide variety of sources has been adduced to support the existence of experiences as of novel colours.

One thing to note about this definition of novel colours is that there is a lack of precision in it. What counts as standard viewing conditions? Different theorists offer different accounts of these. However, I don't think that we need to choose between these, or that we need be overly concerned by the vagueness that thereby remains in the definition. In almost all cases that I will examine, the conditions for experiencing novel colours fall well outside of the broad range of everyday viewing conditions: those that occur on account of detecting reflected light in the standard sorts of environments that humans typically view objects. And in those cases that are less clear cut, we can simply note that they are so, and note that whether the term 'novel' colours applies in these cases is less clear cut too.

The reason for focusing on hues of colour in this definition, rather than just colours, is that not everyone thinks that the standard colour theory captures all of the colours. For example, Saunders and van Brakel (1997) claim that the standard colour theory fails to capture properties like glossiness, lustre, sparkle, glitter, insistence, pronouncedness, brilliance, fluorescence, glow, iridescence, and colourfulness. They believe that some colours have these properties and thus they fall outwith the colours described by standard colour theory. By focusing my definition of novel colours so that it requires that they be novel hues of colours, compared to that which the standard colour theory holds there to be (in humans with normal trichromatic vision in standard viewing conditions), I want to define novel colours as properties besides those which standard colour theory says exists, but also besides the colours that have the properties that Saunders and van Brakel claim exist—which are properties that are commonplace and ubiquitously experienced by people. The novel colours that are discussed by philosophers and psychologists certainly are ones that fall outwith standard colour theory, but they are also taken to be ones that fall outwith the further list of colours and colour properties that Saunders and van Brakel take to exist.

I will take it that it does not follow simply from the fact that there are experiences of novel colours that novel colours themselves exist. This is on account of two related facts. First, to make a metaphysical stipulation, I will take it that for novel colours to exist in the actual world—or in a possible world—those colour properties have to be instantiated (at least at some point in time) in the actual world—or the possible world.[4] Second, I take it to be a possibility that experiences of novel colours could be always non-veridical and purely illusory or hallucinatory. Nonetheless, the existence of experiences as of novel colours, particularly when held together with the view that at least some colours exist, will sometimes provide evidence that novel colours exist. If there are such colours, they would fall outwith the classic colour space as defined by opponent process theory.

Other names besides 'novel colours' have been used to refer to these colours whose existence we are contemplating. They have been referred to as 'impossible',[5] 'forbidden',[6] 'alien'[7] 'Martian'[8] and 'chimerical'[9] colours. I believe that we have good reason to use the term 'novel', rather than any of these alternatives. I dislike the use of the first four of the alternative names as they are misleading in one way or another, while the fifth name properly refers only to a subset of novel colours.

I disapprove of the adjective 'impossible' to describe novel colours as it is a question of substantive philosophical debate what the modal status of novel colours is. Whether such colours are actual, or whether they are nomologically, metaphysically, conceptually, or logically possible or impossible is therefore not a matter to be stipulated by fiat. This is particularly the case because what one takes the modal status of novel colours to be will be highly dependent on the details of the theory of colour one holds to be true. For example, sense-data theorists hold that, when one has a perceptual experience as of an object having a property, there always exists a mental object that really does have that property. Sense-data theorists will therefore think that novel colours exist (in the sense of being instantiated) just so long as experiences of novel colours exist, because they will take them to be instantiated properties of sense-data. In contrast to this, if one thinks that colours are surface reflectance properties of physical objects, and if experiences of novel colours do not correspond in the right way to any surface reflectance properties then the mere existence of such experiences would not guarantee the existence (that is the instantiation) of novel colour properties. Whether, on this view, we should think of novel colours as nomologically impossible, or also as metaphysically impossible, will depend on one's further commitments. Given that there is no consensus on which theory of colour is correct, it is at least premature, and certainly biased in favour of some theories of colour at the expense of others, to label novel colours 'impossible'.

I am also not in favour of calling novel colours 'forbidden'. The only things that, plausibly, might 'forbid' them are certain theories of colour—theories that rule out the existence of such colours or colour experiences. However, as I have explained above, it is a matter of ongoing debate which theory of colours we should adopt so, again, I believe that it is best not to label these colours in a way that prematurely seems to take a stance on a debate that is as yet unsettled.

I also have an aversion to calling novel colours 'alien' or 'Martian'. These terms are often used when people are referring to the novel colours reported by some people who experience synaesthesia.[10] However, in every instance that these synaesthetic colours are discussed, the topic is whether terrestrial creatures experience or could experience these colours. There is no discussion of whether these colours exist on Mars or other alien locations within our universe or are experienced by alien creatures with a physiology unlike ours—a physiology that could not exist on Earth. So, these names are rather misleading.

In contrast to these other names for novel colours, the term 'chimerical' colours has, following Paul Churchland (2005), come to be used to refer to a distinct class of novel colours. These are colours that fall outside the classic colour space as defined by opponent process theory and that it is claimed can be experienced by inducing coloured after-images in a particular way. The after-images are induced by prolonged fixation on a colour stimulus and then by subsequent experiencing the after-images projected on a particular coloured background.[11] 'Chimerical' colours is a perfectly good name for this subset of novel colours, and I will use it to refer to that subset, in addition to using the more inclusive 'novel' colours nomenclature. I will discuss chimerical colours at greater length below.

Thus, in light of the above considerations, I will use the term 'novel' colours, to refer to all of the (alleged) colours under consideration and urge others to do the same.

2 The non-novel colours

Before considering novel colours any further, consider the 'non-novel colours'. Those are the colours that humans with normal tri-chromatic vision see just on account of detecting reflected light in the broad range of everyday viewing conditions. These colours are often thought of in terms of their location in a space of relations known as the classical colour space.[12] The three-dimensional space has six basic colour qualities that come in three sets of pairs that form the three axes of the space: black and white, red and green, and blue and yellow. The axes intersect at a mid-grey point.

There are two ways to build a colour space. The first is based on the judgements of subjects about the colours that they make based simply on the appearance of the colours—that is based on what it is like to experience the colours. In more philosophical terminology, the judgements are based on the phenomenal character of colour experience and on the phenomenal nature of the colours. According to the standard account of colour, black and white appear to people to be opposites and not to contain any chromatic colour. Moreover, within the colours it is claimed there are shades of certain colours, namely, black, white, red, green, blue, and yellow, that are unique in that they look to contain no other colours. That is, there are shades of these colours, that look that colour, simpliciter, and not to contain any other colour. For example, there is a shade of black and a shade of white that are unique that don't look to contain grey or any chromatic colour. There is a shade of red that looks not to contain any blue or yellow or green. Apart from these unique shades of colours all the other colours are said to look to contain a mixture of colours and, in particular, all the other chromatic colours look to contain a mixture of two of the four basic chromatic colours—they are said to be binary colours. For example, orange will always look to contain both red and yellow; purple always looks to contain red and blue; aquamarine looks to contain blue and green; and lime green looks to contain yellow and green. In addition, construction of the space uses judgements of resemblances that are noted between colours by a large number of observers. (For example, judgements of the form that orange is more similar to red than it is to green, or that one particular shade of colour is more similar to a second than a third.) The colour spaces that result, such as the Munsell Colour System[13] and the Natural Colour System,[14] model how the colours appear to observers—thus they serve as a model of the phenomenal character of colour experience, even if they are sometimes primarily intended as a model of surface colours.[15] To a first approximation, the colours form a sphere. However, if the space is built so that the distance between colours represents their subjective similarity then they don't form a sphere but an irregular solid or spindle. (See Figures 11.1 and 11.2).

A second way to build a colour space is to start from the details of the physiology of the colour vision system. These details are outlined in Hurvich and Jameson's (1957) theory of colour. Their theory ends up combining the ideas of the trichromatic theory of colour vision

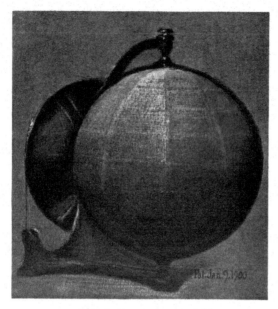

A BALANCED COLOR SPHERE

Figure 11.1   The colour frontispiece from Munsell (1905). Later, Munsell discovered that if hue, value, and chroma were to be kept perceptually uniform, actual surface colours could not be forced into a regular shape. [This figure is in the public domain due to date of publication.]

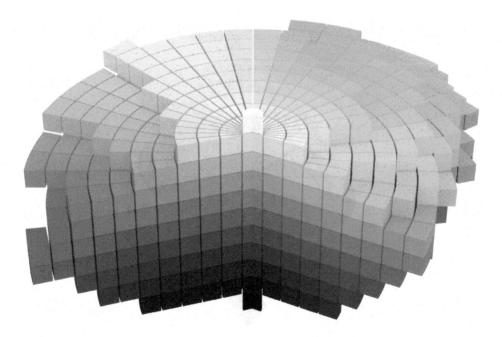

Figure 11.2   The irregular Munsell 1943 colour solid as outlined in Newhall et al. (1943) in which ensuring psychological equispacing of the colours yields an irregular figure. [Image by SharkD [CC BY-SA 3.0 (https://creativecommons.org/licenses/by-sa/3.0)]]

propounded by Young (1802) and built upon by Helmholtz (1856, 1860, and 1867), and Hering's (1878/1964) opponent theory of colour. A standard observer's eye contains three different
types of cone cell: shortwave, medium wave, and long wave. (A "standard observer" is defined
as someone who has the average human's chromatic response.) Inputs to these cells is then combined in various ways to yield three opponent processes: black-white (a lightness dimension),
red-green, and blue-yellow (two chromatic dimensions). This means that response to the colour
at one end of the dimension is antagonistic to the response to the colour at the other end. This
means that detection of red is at the expense of detection of green, and vice versa, and detection
of blue is at the expense of yellow, and vice versa.[16] The resulting space is roughly illustrated in
Figure 11.3, although details of the modelling that go beyond the scope of this essay reveal it to
be slightly more irregular in shape.

What is revealed by these two types of model—each constructed in a different way—is one
of the greatest successes of psychophysics. The second way of building up a colour space via
consideration of the nature of the colour visual system in the eye and brain yields a space that is
isomorphic to the colour space that is built up via consideration of how the colours appear to
subjects. The phenomenal facts about the nature of the colours are taken to be beautifully mir-
rored by, and therefore to be explained, to some degree at least, by the physiological facts.
Indeed, this is the best example we have of the phenomenal character of experience—what it is
like to have that experience—being apparently explained—at least to some degree—by the
physical nature of the brain.

To be precise, it is the structural or relational features of the phenomenal character that seem
to be explained—not the intrinsic features, for example the particular quality of the redness of
red. An entirely different set of qualities that bore the same structural or relational features to
each other would be equally well explained by the physiological facts. However, on account of

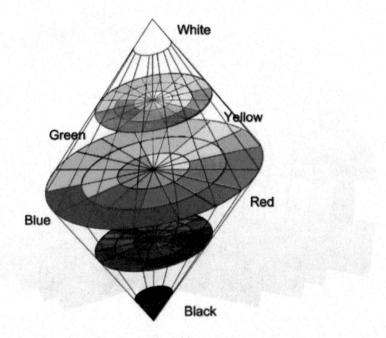

Figure 11.3 Idealisation of the classic colour space as built up from modelling the colour visual system.
Taken from Churchland (2005: 531).

the isomorphism, and the fact that it is our colour experiences to which there is this isomorphism, "speculative thoughts of intertheoretic identities [are] likely to be born" (Churchland, 2005: 538). In other words, there is some reason to think that the best and simplest explanation of the isomorphism is that the experiences simply are the relevant states of the visual system. However, this thought will be resisted by many for a large number of reasons: (1) as just mentioned, it is only the structural or relational features that are explained, (2) it is not easy to see how a physical state could be a conscious state, and (3) the numerous reasons well-rehearsed in standard philosophy of mind opposing the reduction of the mental to the physical, such as the potential multiple realization of the mental by the physical.

The colour space—conceived of now as something that reflects both the phenomenal character of colour experiences and the underlying physiology of the visual system—is also taken to explain what many people take to be a fact, namely, that we do not experience binary colours that appear as if they are made up of unitary hues that lie at opposite ends of the two chromatic dimensions of the colour space—that is reddish-green or bluish-yellow colours. The explanation for this on the phenomenal level is that there could be no appearance of reddish–green for that colour does not appear in colour space. To travel from red to green through colour space one either has to go via the central vertical lightness axis where the saturation of the red colour falls to zero and thus becomes grey before taking on greenish hues, or one has to travel by skirting around that axis. But in that case, the red hue will change to blue or to yellow before it takes on green hues. The same goes for bluish-yellow. The explanation on the physiological level is that, in line with the opponent nature of the way in which we detect colour—the fact that when we detect red it is at the expense of green and vice versa, and similarly for blue and yellow, discussed above—provides a reason to think that we could not experience reddish-green or bluish-yellow shades of colour.

Of course, whether or not there can be experiences of reddish-green and bluish-yellow forms a central topic of investigation in this chapter, for whether there can be such experiences forms the main debate about whether there can be novel colours. The question that will concern us is whether it is possible to have such experiences. The explanations I have just outlined explain why it is standardly taken to be the case that there cannot be experiences of reddish-green or bluish-yellow novel colours: the colour space, conceived of as above, predicts that there cannot, in principle, be such experiences.

3 Sources of evidence for experiences of novel colours

There are seven sources of evidence for the existence of experiences of novel colours.

1   Literary Sources
2   Colour Blindness
3   Tetrachromats
4   Chimerical Colours
5   Synaesthesia
6   Filling-In Experiments
7   Painting

I examine each in turn.

3.1 Literary sources

Experiences of novel colours have been referred to in works of fiction. One example is George MacDonald's "The Golden Key" (1867: 251), a quotation from which opens this chapter. He describes a character who is looking towards Fairyland and experiences—indeed sees—a colour that he has never seen before.

Another example comes in the writing of H. P. Lovecraft "The Colour Out of Space" (1927). He describes a meteor strike on Earth that causes things to take on new colours around the area of the impact:

> All the orchard trees blossomed forth in strange colours, and through the stony soil of the yard ... No sane wholesome colours were anywhere to be seen except in the green grass and leafage; but everywhere those hectic and prismatic variants of some diseased, underlying primary tone without a place among the known tints of earth.

These examples attest to the thought that we can conceive of the experience of novel colours. Indeed, the authors go further than this. They conceive of the existence of novel colours, not merely experiences of such. This is because the experiences of the protagonists are conceived of as veridical. According to MacDonald, Fairyland really does contain new colours, and according to Lovecraft, the meteor really has caused things to really take on a new "primary tone". Thus, they are conceiving of the instantiation of instances of new colours.

Does conceivability entail possibility? That is a question that has vexed philosophers for a long time. It seems reasonable to think that it does not—at least in a straightforward sense. This is because there are apparent counterexamples in which something at least seemed to be conceived of by some people, say some mathematical theorem, which then was proved to be false, and hence impossible. However, a good number of philosophers think that at least some forms of ideal, rational conceivability entail some forms of possibility. Some think that it entails logical and conceptual possibility, and others that it also entails metaphysical possibility. To my knowledge, no one, for good reason, thinks that it entails a nomological possibility. (Something is nomologically possible if it is possible given that the actual laws of nature hold, and something is metaphysically possible if it is possible under some set of laws of nature. Something is logically possible if it does not entail a contradiction, and something is conceptually possible if it, together with conceptual truths (such as vixens are female foxes), does not entail a contradiction.) Discussion of these highly complex debates would take me too far from my aims in this chapter, and I refer the interested reader to Chalmers (2002) and Ichikawa and Jarvis (2012) for extended discussions of these topics.

The view that novel colours are possible stands in stark contrast to the position commonly attributed to Wittgenstein that they are not possible—not even logically or conceptually possible. In a variety of writings, Wittgenstein discussed the questions of whether there could be colours other than the ones we see and whether the concept of such colours even makes sense. He is particularly vexed by the question of how we would know that a newly experienced property was a colour. He also discusses whether specific alleged novel colours like reddish-green could be perceived or experienced, or whether the idea of such colours is coherent. Lugg (2010) makes a careful summary of Wittgenstein's remarks and suggests that while the popular interpretation of Wittgenstein has been that at least at some points in his career he claimed that there could be no perceptual experiences of reddish-green, instead, Wittgenstein "is genuinely puzzled, [and] ... he is pulled in both directions and cannot commit himself either way" (Lugg, 2010: 172). Nonetheless, inspired by reading some of Wittgenstein's remarks, some philosophers, for example Brenner (1987), have held that there simply could be no experiences as of a reddish-green on conceptual grounds.

I have little sympathy for this type of view. The justification that is sometimes given for it is that our language, as we know it at present, excludes there being other colours. But I don't find this claim at all plausible. The fiction writers, some of who were discussed above, who use our language to talk about novel colours demonstrate that this claim is false. Moreover, while there could be some instances in which we might worry whether an alleged novel colour was a colour, it would seem that there could be clear cases where that worry could be easily assuaged. For example, if the alleged novel colour was a uniform quality that seemed to adhere to the surface of an object in place of any of the non-novel colours, and if it bore some similarity to the non-novel colours in core ways, such as phenomenally looking to contain red and/or green, or light/dark, or various levels of saturation, then there would be no doubt in my mind that we should classify it as a colour. For example, some of the candidates for being non-novel colours are shades of non-novel colours, such as the shade of red that one might speculate that one could see if one's visual system could respond to more of the electromagnetic spectrum than that which humans can, namely the infra-red. It is tempting to think that the classic colour space could be extended to include such a novel infrared colour by a continuous series of shades of colour leading away from red towards the novel infrared colour. Likewise, as we have seen, another candidate novel colour is reddish-green. Recall that opponent process theory predicts that we could not see or experience such a shade as signalling of red is at the expense of green and vice versa. However, if this turns out to be false, then a reddish-green colour would share certain features of the non-novel colours. For example, the classic colour space could be extended to include a new continuous series of shades of colour from red to green that doesn't go via grey or yellow or blue, that would capture that reddish-green colour, by increasing the dimensions of the colour space.[17] Being able to extend the colour space in a continuous fashion to include alleged novel colours would show that they shared important features with non-novel colours, for example having some saturation and lightness and similarity in hue, that I believe would warrant the judgement that they are colours. (It is interesting to note that this methodology of extending the range of visible colours by postulating an extension to their series in a continuous fashion is precisely how MacDonald introduces his Fairyland novel colours in the quote above.)

Before closing I would like to note that Nida-Rümelin and Suarez (2009) offer an interesting argument that while there can be novel colours there are limits on what possible types of novel colours there can be. For example, they claim that there could not be a shade of violet that did not look to contain both red and blue—and they argue that we can know this based on what we can conceive and imagine. Whether this is indeed the case, I leave to the reader to decide.

Finally, the holder of the view that novel colours are logically or conceptually impossible has to wrestle with the empirical evidence that has been adduced that there actually are such colours or experiences of such colours. I will come back to examine that evidence in later sections of this chapter.

3.2 Colour blindness

There are a variety of different forms of colour blindness and impairment in humans. In simplistic terms, and looking only at extreme forms of colour blindness rather than more mild impairments, there is red-green colour blindness and blue-yellow colour blindness, which affect the red-green opponent channel and the blue-yellow opponent channel respectively. This is caused by a lack of one of the three cone types: short, medium, or long wavelength, and so people with this form of colour blindness are called dichromats, as opposed to people who are not colour-blind who are called trichromats. There is also achromatopsia, a condition in which people (called monochromats) have, in effect, only a light/dark opponent channel and so are insensitive to chromatic colours. It is testament to the strength of the colour space that it predicts these patterns of colour blindness that we discover in the world.

The traditional view of the nature of colour blindness is that people who have it experience a subset of the colours that those with standard vision who lack colour blindness see. I will call this the 'traditional subset view'. Which colours those are will vary depending on the type of colour blindness. It was often thought, for example, that people with red-green colour blindness simply failed to experience reds and greens and just had chromatic experiences of yellow and blue. So the colour space of a red-green colour-blind person would consist of a two-dimensional area formed by a white and black axis and a blue and yellow axis, entailing that the person would be able to see blues and yellows of different lightness and brightness and saturation, in addition to white, black, and various greys (and note that thereby they would be curtailed so that they see only unique shades of blue and yellow).[18] We now know that this is likely to be a too simplistic account of what colours the colour-blind can experience. So what alternatives are there to the traditional subset view?

One important source of evidence about what colour-blind people see comes from those who are colour-blind in one eye and not the other. Evidence from this source has typically been taken to support the traditional subset view. However, Broakes (2010) shows that far from settling the matter, these reports raise more questions. For a start, these reports are, actually, highly variable. They range, in the case of red-green colour blindness, from reports of just blue and yellow chromatic colours, to reports of blue and yellow and in addition reds or greens or both, at least to some degree. (Broakes, helpfully, goes to great length to explain how it might be possible for red-green colour-blind people to have experiences of reds and greens.). Nonetheless, this evidence still points towards the idea that colour-blind people experience— to a greater or lesser degree—a subset of the colours that those without colour blindness experience.

In contrast to the subset view of colour blindness, a new account of colour blindness has arisen recently in the philosophical literature. According to this new theory, people with colour blindness see and experience none of the colours that those with normal colour vision experience.[19] Consider a red-green colour-blind person. The new account would say that not only does that person not see red or green, they don't see yellow or blue either. Instead, they see some other colours entirely—some less determinate colours. Byrne and Hilbert (2010) discuss this view, and call these other colours "alien". As I explained in section one, I think that there is good reason to avoid this name and so I will stick with calling these 'novel' colours.

In order to motivate the new theory of colour blindness, Byrne and Hilbert explicate a major problem with the standard view of colour blindness. They claim that, according to the standard view, a colour-blind person will see almost every colour incorrectly (supposing that physical objects do have the colours that we normally take them to have). To explain why, let's take red-green colour blindness again as an example. On the standard view people who are red-green colour-blind are limited to only seeing shades of unique blue and unique yellow (more or less saturated shades and more or less light shades) because they lack one of the cone types that feed into the red-green channel. Byrne and Hilbert speculate that these people therefore lack the red-green opponent process. If that is right, then any object that does not have either of the precise unique hues of blue or yellow (so nearly every object) will be misperceived—unless we can argue that objects can have multiple colours at the same time. This is a highly unwelcome consequence of the standard view. Moreover, the same would be true of a great deal of the animal kingdom, for many animals are dichromats. And, in addition, we know that dichromatic colour vision evolved before trichromatic vision, so we would have to say either that before trichromatic vision evolved, colour perception was mostly inaccurate—or that objects can have multiple different colours at the same time. These seem very hard bullets to bite.[20]

On the alternative view, we should think of colour-blind people as simply detecting different colour properties from any of those colour properties that those who are not colour-blind detect. And, given Byrne and Hilbert's specification of those colours, the colour-blind will turn out to be right a good deal of the time about those colour properties that they do detect, which would make this view exceptionally attractive.

Byrne and Hilbert's particular version of this view is that if you lack a red-green opponent channel, then any signalling of what we would otherwise think of as yellow or blue by the blue-yellow opponent channel does not actually amount to the signalling of yellow or blue. Consider that when a person with normal colour vision has their blue-yellow opponent channel signal for what we would normally think of as yellow, then that signal alone does not determine the over-all signalling of colour. There will be a contribution by the red-green opponent channel too. It will either be signalling for what we typically think of as red or green to some degree or, be neutral with respect to those (in this latter case, it signals a balance of red and green, by staying silent and failing to send a signal about red or green). So, in a person with normal colour vision, what needs to occur for unique yellow to be signalled for is both the blue-yellow opponent channel to be signalling for what we normally think of as yellow and for the red-green opponent channel to signal for neither of what we normally think of as red or green.

Now, Byrne and Hilbert argue that there is good reason to think that many dichromats will simply lack a red-green channel, particularly congenital dichromats (2010: 282). Let us suppose that this is true (although it certainly could be questioned, and no physiological evidence backs up their specific claim here). In that case, argue Byrne and Hilbert, the signalling in a red-green colour-blind person of what we normally think of as yellow by their blue-yellow opponent channel does not amount to a signalling that yellow is present. Because for that to happen the red-green opponent process must signal a balance of red and green (by neither signalling red nor green). But they lack such an opponent process. Therefore, the idea is that nothing is sig-nalling that red and green are in balance in a red-green colour-blind person—even though this is signalled in someone who has red-green channels by a failure to signal either red or green. In short, the lack of signalling for red or green in someone who has red-green opponent pro-cesses is not the same as the lack of signalling for red or green in someone who lacks red-green opponent processes. So, what gets signalled for in a red-green colour-blind person when their yellow-blue channel fires is that something *yellowish* is present, namely, that something that lies in the half of the hue circle between (but excluding) unique red and unique green going through lime green and yellow and orange is present. And, likewise, in the case of signalling what we normally think of as blue, what is really being signalled is that something *bluish* is present: something that lies in the half of the hue circle between (but excluding) unique red and unique green going through turquoise and blue and purple is present. And Byrne and Hilbert claim that the property of yellowish is a determinable of which unique yellow, oranges, and lime greens are determinates. And bluish is a determinable of which unique blue, tur-quoise, and purple are determinates. Thus, their idea is that red-green colour-blind people see colours that are less determinate than people who are not colour-blind. The people who are not colour-blind see colours that are more determinate than the colours that red-green colour-blind people see. So, in fact, red-green colour-blind people see none of the same colours as those who are not colour-blind see.

Finally, Byrne and Hilbert argue that the evidence from people who are colour-blind in one eye who testify to seeing either blue or yellow (and as we saw, sometimes red and green) can be set aside, for these are special people who due to their non-colour-blind eye will have red-green opponent channels in their cortex, which receives signals from both eyes, that will be signalling either for red or green or neither, even when they are seeing using only their colour-blind eye. This allows them to neatly side-step the empirical evidence that would otherwise prove problematic for their view.

Byrne and Hilbert's view is ingenious and has a lot to recommend it. If it is right, we would have identified some novel colours of a particular form: colours that are determinables of the determinates that those with normal colour vision see.[21] And, moreover, as I will discuss in the next section, as it is likely that there are people and animals who have more sensitive forms of colour vision than statistically normal humans, we will be able to identify other novel colours. If Byrne and Hilbert's view can rightly be applied to them then people and animals who have more sensitive forms of colour vision than humans with normal colour vision will have experiences of more determinate colours than those of statistically normal humans. And to reiterate, on this view, the vision of all of these different sorts of colour perceivers can be correct about the colours that are represented to be present, for what is different is simply how determinately the colours present are represented to be. (It should be noted that colour perceivers could also be correct about the colours that they represent to be present on a surface, even if they represent different colours, and not simply different as to how determinately the colours present are represented to be, contra Byrne and Hilbert and in line with the traditional theory of colour blindness articulated above, so long as we allow that objects can simultaneously have two distinct colours. (See footnote 20.)

As I said previously, Byrne and Hilbert's view depends on holding that dichromats lack a second opponent channel and that a colour experience as determinate as those that people with normal human trichromatic vision have cannot occur with only one active channel, and while Byrne and Hilbert offer plausible reasons for their view, they are not conclusive. However, when we turn to thinking about human tetrachromats, as I will do in the next section, we will find conclusive reasons for thinking that there are novel colours, as it is overwhelmingly plausible that human tetrachromats see colours in addition to those that people with normal trichromatic colour vision do. So, a more secure source of novel colours can be found. In addition, we will see that just as there were two accounts of the nature of dichromatic vision in comparison to trichromatic vision, there are two parallel accounts of the nature of tetrachromatic vision. Thus, both the standard account of dichromacy and Byrne and Hilbert's alternative view will be hugely useful in thinking about the nature of the relationship between trichromatic and tetrachromatic colour vision.

3.3 *Tetrachromacy*

As previously discussed, standard human colour vision involves three cone types that detect short, medium, and long wavelengths. And these signals are combined to yield three opponent channels: an achromatic light/dark one, and two chromatic ones, a red-green one and a blue-yellow one. And we have just been looking in detail at forms of dichromacy—they involve having only two cone types and hence, we speculated, only one achromatic and one chromatic opponent channel.

In the animal kingdom, and surprisingly in humans too, we also find tetrachromacy: colour vision that operates via four cone types. Birds, reptiles, and several freshwater fish have four colour receptors.[22] (Indeed, in the animal kingdom we find creatures—mantis shrimp and butterflies—that possess up to 12 spectral sensitivities in their eyes. Mantis shrimp have 20 receptor types in total: 12 for colour, 6 for polarization, and 2 with overlapping function for luminance tasks.) Marshall and Arikawa (2014: R1150) state that three factors determine the nature of a creature's colour vision: "the number, shape and chromatic spacing of the spectral sensitivities; second, behind the retina, how interneuronal channels encode a chromatic message to the brain; and third, the behaviour of the animal relative to spectra (light and reflectance) in its environment". We should add to that the nature of the colour processing that takes place in the brain. Some animals have different types of receptors in different parts of their eyes, as opposed to those receptors being spread out evenly throughout their eyes. Some combine information from all of their different receptors, some pool information from some of their receptors in groups, others do not. The richly different forms of colour vision to be found in the animal kingdom are extremely likely sources of novel colour experiences of one sort or another—the reason being that these different visual systems will give rise to sensitivity to, and behavioural response to, lightwaves reflecting from surfaces that is vastly different from that of humans with normal vision—and indeed that of any human.

Exactly how information is pooled from different receptors in animals is the area in which human knowledge is most limited in animal colour vision science. For this reason, and for the reason that we can get the best behavioural data and verbal reports from humans, I will now limit my discussion to human tetrachromacy. But, as we will see, that case illustrates the point that many different visual systems in the animal kingdom also make.

Due to the genetics of colour vision, mothers or daughters of males who are anomalous trichromats—meaning that either their medium wave receptor is replaced with one closer to their long wave receptor or vice versa—turn out to have a shortwave, a medium wave, and a long wave receptor, and an additional receptor either close to the medium wave or long wave receptor. While there has been reason to believe that there were such women for a long time, it was not known whether those women's brains exploited the extra information from the extra receptor—and hence were tetrachromats. In other words, as is the case with our present knowledge of animals, it was not known how the interneuronal channels encoded chromatic messages to the brain. However, in a recent study by Jordan *et al.* (2010) 24 such women were studied. Of these women, 23 did not exhibit behaviour that suggested that they were tetrachromats, but 1 did.

The subject, known as 'cDa29', passed a number of tests that indicated that she was a tetrachromat. The most important test was the Rayleigh match test—a test in which subjects are asked whether they can discriminate—pick out—one light that is different from two others. On each trial, two of the three lights were a monochromatic orange light and the third was of a mixture of a red and a green light. The task was to identify the odd one out. Humans with normal vision—trichromacy—can't do this. But this one subject could do so—and could do so quickly, and with that same speed given different versions of the stimulus. The authors of the study conclude that they have found "one person, a carrier of deuteranomaly, who satisfies the criteria for behavioural tetrachromacy on all our tests" (2010: 15).

What this study tells us is that if a human with normal colour vision and the human tetrachromat identified in the study looked at certain patches of colour, they would look the same to the human with normal vision, but they would look different to the tetrachromat. In fact, there is a whole extra dimension of colour experience that the tetrachromat has that humans with normal trichromatic colour vision lack. In this respect, the relationship between humans with normal trichromatic colour vision and this tetrachromatic woman are like the relationship between a dichromatic red-green colour-blind person and a normal trichromatic human. In the last section, we saw that there were two options for how to conceive of this relationship. First, we could think that the dichromat sees a subset of the colours that the trichromat sees. Likewise, we could think that trichromats see a subset of the colours that the tetrachromat sees.

A downside of this view is that we have to say that (at least) two out of these three types of perceivers—dichromats, trichromats, or tetrachromats—see most colours incorrectly. Or, second, we could think, with Byrne and Hilbert, that the dichromat, the trichromat, and the tetrachromat see different colours from each other—different in that they see different determinates and determinables of the same shades of colour. And a virtue of this view is that, as these colours are not incompatible, we need not say either that any of the three types of perceivers mostly perceive colours incorrectly.

Whichever of these views we adopt, each entails that tetrachromats see colours that normal human trichromats do not. Thus, there are novel colours: experiences of hues of colour in addition to those that the standard colour theory says that humans (with what is defined to be "normal" tri-chromatic vision) have in standard viewing conditions.

An alternative view would be that tetrachromats see qualities other than colour qualities when they look at a surface. One version of this view would be that they don't see colours at all—that they see novel non-colour properties. As discussed in section 3.1, I find this view highly implausible. If the alleged novel properties were uniform qualities that seemed to adhere to the surface of an object, if they could be lighter and darker, more or less saturated, then there would be no doubt in my mind that we should classify it as a colour. To back up this view it would be good to gather detailed phenomenal descriptions of the qualities that human tetrachromats describe, and their relation to what human trichromats describe the colours as having. A second version of this view would be that human tetrachromats see the colour qualities that trichromatic humans see but that the tetrachromats see extra non-colour properties in addition to those. This is something that could be empirically tested in part—we would have to ensure that the phenomenal descriptions of the colour experiences of the tetrachromats bore out this interpretation. However, the question would again rise, why these extra properties should not be taken to be colour qualities. I have already articulated my view on this matter, so I shall not continue discussion of this matter further.

I turn now to discuss the evidence for novel colours by looking at evidence about chimerical colours.

3.4 Chimerical colours

As we have seen, the standard colour space, underpinned by the opponent process theory, outlined in section two, is said to have explanatory power regarding colour blindness. It is also said to have explanatory power with respect to after-images. This will be the major topic of investigation of this section, for it is claimed that there are a variety of novel colours, called 'chimerical' colours, that are induced by projecting after-images onto coloured surfaces.

To begin, I will explicate what proponents of the standard colour space say about after-images in general, before looking at the specific form of after-images that are said to produce chimerical colours. I will then examine objections both to the standard account of after-images and to chimerical colours in particular.

It is frequently reported, by numerous philosophers and psychologists, following Hurvich and Jameson (1957), that fixation of tens of seconds on a patch of red gives rises to an after-image of green when one subsequently looks at a white or grey surface, and vice versa.[23] And, similarly, fixation on blue gives rise to a yellow after-image, and vice versa, and similarly for black and white. I will take these claims for granted at the moment, but I will return to question them later in this section.

The explanation of this, derived from the standard colour space and the opponent process theory that lies behind it, is that as you fixate on a colour, say red, the opponent cells fatigue in their ability to signal for red, so that when you look at a neutral white or grey surface that contains neither red or green, rather than signalling for both a lack of red and green, the opponent cells signal the presence of green. Thus, you see a green after-image. The three opponent processes, red-green, blue-yellow, and white-black, therefore, apparently account for why we experience after-images, and why we experience the particular colours that we do subsequent to looking at differently coloured stimuli.

Elaborating on another suggestion in Hurvich and Jameson (1957), Johnston (2004) and Churchland (2005) used the opponent process theory to predict that certain colours that do not appear in the standard colour space should be experienced (by those with normal trichromatic vision) when certain after-images are projected onto certain coloured back grounds. These are colours that don't have instances in the physical world, for no combination of wavelengths stimulating the eye alone could produce experiences of these colours. They can only be experienced by stimulating the eye with certain wavelengths and, in addition, doing so when the opponent processes have been fatigued in the right sort of way.

Recall the idealization of the classic colour space, as illustrated in Figure 11.3. The space, it is claimed, depicts the colours that are instantiated in the world. The idea is that you couldn't have a colour that was lighter than white, for to travel up the vertical axis to the maximum, you reach white and leave behind the chromatic hues, all of which have less lightness than white. Similarly, you couldn't have a colour that is darker than black, for to travel down the vertical axis as far as one can go, one leaves behind the chromatic hues, all of which have more lightness than black. And finally, one cannot travel out beyond the most saturated versions of each colour: red, green, orange, purple, and so on, that can be caused by light entering the eye.

But recall that these explanations, based on the colour space, are based on a model constructed by noting the colours that people report when stimulated by the various different combinations of wavelengths, in typical viewing conditions. Can we create further colour experiences in people by dispensing with typical viewing conditions? Hurvich and Jameson (1957), Johnston (2004), and Churchland (2005) claim that we can. Between them, they claim that there are three new types of colour experience that can be had in the following ways:

1   **Stygian colours** look maximally dark, as dark as black, yet they have a chromaticity. It is claimed that one such colour can be seen by fixating on a patch of yellow, and then projecting the subsequent blue after-image onto a black surface, or, equally, by fixating on a patch of white, and then projecting the subsequent black after-image onto a patch of blue. What is experienced is said to be "fully as dark as the darkest possible black … but nevertheless is of an obvious and distinctive [blue] hue" (Churchland, 2005: 544). He goes on to say (2005: 545), this is "a color that you will absolutely never encounter as an objective feature of a real physical object, but whose qualitative character you can nonetheless savor in an unusually produced illusory experience".

2   **Self-luminous colours** look maximally light, thus as light as white, yet they have a chromaticity. For example, if you fixate a patch of red and project the subsequently experienced green after-image onto a white surface you will see that "the bright green(ish) after-image seems positively self-luminous, as if it were a colored light bulb or a colored LED (light emitting diode)" (Churchland, 2005: 547). Such a colour experience can be had veridically, for example, by looking at a coloured LED. But the standard colour space predicts that when looking at a non-self-luminous surface, as one in in the specified condition, this colour cannot be seen.

3   **Hyperbolic colours** look to be supersaturated—more saturated than the maximal saturation that standard colour space would anticipate is possible. They are said to be experienced when, after fixating on a maximally saturated chromatic patch, say a shade of blue-green, one then projects the subsequent orange after-image onto a maximally saturated orange patch. Churchland (2005: 553) claims that one then experiences, "an orange that is more 'ostentatiously orange' than any (non-self-luminous) orange you have ever seen, or ever will see, as the objective color of a physical object". While Churchland thinks that only binary colours can be experienced as supersaturated, Johnston (2004: 141), following Hurvich and Jameson (1957), claims that unitary colours can be too. He says that if one projects one's red after-image onto a red surface after "being exposed to bright monochromatic unique green light (500 nanometers in wavelength) in an otherwise dark room for about twenty minutes", then one will experience supersaturated red.

If there are experiences of chimerical colours—at least stygerian and hyperbolic chimerical colours—then there are experiences of novel colours. (The case of self-luminous colours is a tricky one, and I will leave the reader to decide whether it should count as being a case of a novel or not.) But are there such experiences? Some doubts about them have recently been raised in the literature.

One doubt is whether the opponent process theory underlying the standard colour space, can account even for simple non-chimerical after-images that are projected onto white or grey surfaces. There are two sources of worry. One is physiological, the other is phenomenological.

Jameson and D'Andrade (1997) summarize the mounting physiological evidence that while opponent processes have been found in the cortex and LGN (lateral geniculate nucleus) of primates, the opponency does not correspond to the red-green and the blue-yellow axes.

With regards to phenomenology, there is a major problem: after-images don't seem to follow the patterns predicted by the opponent process theory. A red stimulus does not produce a green after-image but a blue-green (cyan) one. A green stimulus produces not a red after-image but a blue-red (magenta) one. Lest one think that this is a new observation, Jameson and D'Andrade (1997: 307) also point out, "As early as 1907 Hering's student, A. von Tschermak, reported that, 'under usual conditions of observation, in order to produce a colorless appearing mixture (of lights) one needs for a unique (urfarben) red not a pure green but a somewhat bluish-green' (Tschermak 1907: 478)." And this observation has been subsequently and repeatedly made since.[24]

It is notable that this counter evidence to the opponent process theory has mostly been ignored in textbook and research papers on this subject, as Jameson and D'Andrade (1997) and Pridmore (2011) explicitly remark. Nor has it reduced the use of the opponent process model in cognitive psychology research. One reason might come from the observation by Pridmore (2011) that when researchers found colour opponent cells in fish and primates that amounted to red-cyan opponent processes, they kept calling them 'red-green', nonetheless. Researchers seemed to be so pleased to find opponent processes, at a time when the theory was not universally accepted, that the fact that the antagonists were a little bit different (blue-green, rather than green)) from what was predicted seemed a minor point.

The latest research into this matter suggests that after-images obey rules corresponding to complementary colours, rather than the traditional opponent colours. Complementary colours are those that when mixed in suitable proportions yield a colour match to some achromatic stimulus (black, white, or shade of grey).[25] Thus, different opponent processes are needed to account for the after-images that humans perceive. Pauli (2010) argues that red-cyan, orange-blue, yellow-violet, and green-magenta opponent processes are required, in addition in a white-black one. Pridmore (2011) argues that red-cyan, blue-yellow, and green-magenta opponent processes are required, in addition to a white-black one. Just as Hurvich and Jameson (1957) combined the tri-chromatic and opponent process theories arguing that at an earlier stage of processing there are trichromatic processes and at a later stage opponent processes, so Pridmore combines that idea with his results about complementary colours. He holds that the levels and types of processing that Hurvich and Jameson posited exist, and account for many facts about the colours, but he posits a third stage of processing that involves complementary opponent processes, which take place after the first two posited by Hurvich and Jameson.

If the opponent theory is incorrect with respect to the colour of simple after-images projected onto white or grey surfaces, as the recent scientific work on the topic indicates, what, if anything, does this tell us about chimerical colours that were posited as an extension of opponent process theory? Does the science affect the reasons to think that there are chimerical colours?

Manzotti (2017) goes to great lengths noting and recording all those who explain after-images in terms of the traditional opponent theory and points out that it does not accord with phenomenological observations about which after-image colours are experienced in different situations, as I described above. He too holds that after-images work according to complementary colour rules. And he tries to press these facts into service of his theory of perception, according to which, instances of what are traditionally called illusions and hallucinations, are really instances of seeing something, and seeing something accurately, in the world. In the case of illusion, we are seeing something here and now; in the case of hallucination we are seeing something that we have seen in the past. Manzotti treats after-images as if they were veridical perceptions. He claims that when I see a cyan after-image in response to fixating on a red figure and then looking at a white surface, the fatiguing of the cells that signal for red mean that I no longer perceive the redness of the white surface. I now see the component other than red that is left within the white: cyan. This argument supposes that a white surface either always, or—what seems to be Manzotti's preferred account—sometimes (when it is viewed in the right way), has the property of being cyan and being red, and has other colour properties when viewed in other ways. This is a highly controversial premise and one that will be resisted by many. That white objects reflect wavelengths, which if reflected alone from a surface would lead us to say that the surface had a (non-white) colour corresponding to those wavelengths, does not entail that a white surface always or sometimes has those colours too. Standardly, surfaces are thought to have just one colour at a time, and don't change their colour depending on what perception is occurring of them. White surfaces are white, not (perhaps also) cyan when one's red receptors are fatigued.

This strategy of accounting for after-images as veridical perceptions does not fare well on two other accounts. First, one case of simple after-images seems to provide a counter example to Manzotti's account. If one fixates on a black stimulus then one will have a white after-image if one projects the subsequent after-image onto a black surface. If we apply Manzotti's account of after-images to this case then the explanation of what is occurring that we should give is that one is failing to see some of the black surface's aspects—by a filtering or subtracting process caused by the lesser sensitivity of the visual system to white—revealing the black surface's white aspect. But that can't be right. There is no white aspect in the black surface that a lack of sensitivity to some elements of the black surface would reveal. A black surface is black because it absorbs wavelengths of light, unlike white which reflects them. If we become less sensitive to wavelengths of light due to fatigue then we should not be more sensitive to white. Thus, this case presents a serious problem to Manzotti's account of after-images.

Second, if there are chimerical after-image colours, these too would pose a problem for Manzotti. This is because they are not colours that are somehow contained in surfaces and that can be revealed by subtraction. Supersaturated red, for example, is not an element of an ordinary red surface and not one that can be seen by subtraction.

Manzotti has a reply to this second problem case. He denies the existence of supersaturated red. He does so by falling back on the observation that red is not the colour of the after-image one experiences after fixating on green and then looking at a white or grey surface. It is magenta, according to the complementary colours theory. Thus, if one tries to do what the traditional opponent theorists have said will produce hyperbolic colours, such as supersaturated red, by fixating on green and then projecting the subsequent after-image onto a red surface, this will not produce an experience of supersaturated red, but an experience of magenta on a red background. "Supersaturated red is a perceptual myth" quoth Manzotti (2017: 171).

However, this argument is too quick. That magenta, and not red, is the colour of the after-image obtained by a green stimulus means only that one cannot experience supersaturated red by projecting a magenta after-image onto a red surface. But what if one produced a red after-image by fixating on a cyan stimulus, and then projected that red after-image onto a red surface? Would one then not experience supersaturated red? Or what if one produced a magenta after-image by fixating on a cyan stimulus, and then projected that magenta after-image onto a magenta surface? Would one not experience a supersaturated magenta? Nothing Manzotti has said would show that these methods would not produce supersaturated hyperbolic colours. Thus, as he has not ruled out the existence of chimerical colours, his theory is still under threat.

Nonetheless, it is clear that in light of the confusion about the colours of after-images, further empirical work is required to establish more conclusively the existence of chimerical colours.

3.5 Synaesthesia

Synaesthesia is a condition in which people report idiosyncratic sensory or other experiential pairings. For example, they might report that whenever they experience a taste they feel a shape, or whenever they hear sounds, they see certain shapes.[26] Following Macpherson (2007), synaesthesia is a condition in which either:

(i) an experience in one sensory modality, or
(ii) an experience not in a sensory modality, such as an experience of emotion, or
(iii) an imagining or thought of what is so experienced, or
(iv) a mental state outlined in either (i)–(iii), together with recognition of what the mental state represents

is either a sufficient automatic cause of, or has a common sufficient automatic cause (lying within the central nervous system of the subject) with, an experience or element of experience that is associated with some sensory modality and is distinct from (i).

This synaesthetic experience or element of experience can be associated with the same or a different sensory modality from that which may be ordinarily associated with the mental state in (i)–(iv).

Several forms of synaesthesia involve experiencing colour in response to some other stimulus. (In these cases, colour is known as the "concurrent", rather than the "inducer".) One inter-modal form is experiencing colours in response to hearing sounds. Another, intra-modal form, grapheme-colour synaesthesia, is triggered by seeing letters or numerals and they are experienced as having a colour, that they typically lack. For example, '5's printed in black ink might look green, and '4's printed in black ink might look orange. Synaesthetic pairings are typically stable across time.

Ramachandran and Hubbard (2001: 26) discuss cases in which synaesthetes report that their "induced colours are somehow 'weird' or 'alien' and don't look quite the same as normal 'real world' colours". In some cases, these are colour-blind subjects, in which it is surmised that they are experiencing colours that people who are not colour-blind experience, but which they typically don't experience due to their colour blindness. Ramachandran and Hubbard suggest that the synaesthetic colours by-pass the limitations of the colour-blind retinal system to activate the cortex directly, causing experiences of colours not usually seen. In other cases, they are people with normal trichromatic colour vision. In those cases, Ramachandran and Hubbard suppose that unusual activation of the cortex may occur due to its stimulation by an other sensory modality, rather than by stimulation of the retina.

As we will see in section 3.6, this is a very similar explanation to that given by Crane and Piantanida for the experience of novel colours caused by filling-in. I will therefore abstain from further discussion of this type of novel colour and subsume it under the following section, 3.6. I end this section simply by noting that further work on this topic, eliciting as detailed as possible phenomenological reports of these synaesthetically induced novel colours, would be very helpful for those considering the nature of these experiences.

3.6 *Filling-in*

I turn now to examine evidence for the final type of novel colours: reddish-green and bluish-yellow novel colours. It has been claimed by some psychologists that experiences of these colours have been produced in the lab by exploiting the 'filling-in' phenomenon.[27]

Normally the colours we see objects as having depends to a large extent on the wavelengths of light emitted from those objects. In some situations, however, the colour perceived does not in any way so correspond. It has been noted by many psychologists that an image that is stabilized on the retina fades from view, and the brain then 'fills in' the faded region—that is, produces in the subject an experience of that area—in a manner determined by the surrounding unstabilized area.[28] The psychologist Krauskopf (1963), for example, stabilized a green disk on subjects' retinas. This disk was surrounded by an unstabilized orange area. At first the subjects reported seeing a green disk on an orange background, but within several seconds reported that the green disk faded from view to be replaced by a uniformly orange surface. When retinal cells receive no change in the information that they detect, they cease to respond. The device used to stabilize an image on the retina is called an 'eye-tracker'. It is important to note that what gets 'filled-in' depends on the area surrounding the stabilized area. A similar, but not quite so prominent, effect can be seen by fixating one's eyes in the centre of a green disk on an expansive, uniform orange background. After a time, the green disk fades from view and is 'filled-in' with orange. This is the Troxler effect.[29]

Exploiting the filling-in phenomenon, Crane and Piantanida (1983) presented subjects with a red vertical stripe abutted to a green vertical stripe. The top and bottom of the stripes extended beyond the subjects' field of view. The outer edge of each stripe was formed by a black occluder. Crane and Piantanida stabilized the red-green boundary area using an eye-tracker but they ensured that the black occluders were not stabilized.

The thought behind the experiment was that the area that was to be filled-in was surrounded not by one colour, as in the Krauskopf filling-in experiment, but by two opposing colours, therefore providing conflicting information to the brain, when it tried to fill-in the area corresponding to the stabilized part of the image. Observers of the image reported different things that they saw in the stabilized area, which fell into the following three categories:

1   The entire field was covered in a regular array of very small (just resolvable) red and green dots;
2   The field contained either islands of red on a green background or vice versa;
3   The field contained a novel hue that subjects reported never having seen before.

The experiment was repeated with blue and yellow areas, with corresponding results.

The response that is of interest to us is the third one. Crane and Piantanida describe that response further:

> some observers indicated that although they were aware that what they were viewing was a color (that is, the field was not achromatic), they were unable to name or describe the color. One of these observers was an artist with a large color vocabulary.
>
> *(1983: 1079)*

Other observers of the novel hues described the novel colour as a reddish-green. Crane and Piantanida's description of the colour is that it appeared to have the characteristics of a binary colour, one phenomenally composed of red and green, in the way that other binary colours seem to be so composed. For example, orange seems to be phenomenally composed of yellow and red, and purple seems phenomenally to be composed of red and blue. The colour was not uniform across the field though, as it was "greener near the unstabilized green boundary and redder near the unstabilized red boundary" (1983: 1079)—just as a field of orange could be a more reddish orange on one side, transitioning smoothly to a more yellow orange on the other.

Such results appear in conflict with the opponent-process model of colour vision, which predicts that one cannot have experiences of reddish-greens because when responding to redness, one is simultaneously responding negatively to green. However, Crane and Piantanida speculate that the opponent-process model applies only in cases where the retina is stimulated by light and not to those cases that involve the filling-in phenomenon, where the retina is not stimulated. They believe that the filling-in phenomenon results from purely cortical activity, unrestrained by lower-level retinal-cortico processes that display opponency. In other words, experiences of colour produced by the filling-in phenomenon are not restricted to opponent channels and thus can appear reddish-green or bluish-yellow.

If Crane and Piantanida's experimental reported results are true then we would have instances of experiences of novel colours—and the most convincing instances out of all of those that I have examined in this chapter. However, Crane and Piantanida's conclusions have been challenged.

Hsieh and Tse (2005) complain that Crane and Piantanida reply solely on subjects' verbal reports of the colour. They argue that Crane and Piantanida cannot rule out the idea that the subjects saw a non-novel colour—a brownish colour in the case of alleged reports of reddish-green, and a yellowish colour in the case of bluish-yellow. Hsieh and Tse carried out an experiment that didn't use an eye-tracker to produce filling in but that relied on Troxler fading during fixation. Cleverly, they got subjects to produce a match to the filled-in colour that was experienced by adjusting another patch of colour that was at the same time in the subjects' field of view. In the case of reddish-green subjects matched a perfectly possible brownish colour; in the case of filling-in in response to a red and green stimulus. Thus, Hsieh and Tse failed to replicate Crane and Piantanida's results and they are sceptical that novel colours were produced in their experiment.

However, Crane and Piantanida's experiment was replicated more faithfully by Billock *et al.* (2001). Unlike Hsieh and Tse, Billock *et al.* used an eye-tracker for stabilization. In the version of the experiment that they conducted, they conducted trials in which they ensured that, for each participant, the shades of red and green chosen were isoluminant for that subject.[30] With this modification, they could reliably elicit reports of novel colours in six out of seven observers—the seventh observer's vision only experienced grey (Billock and Tsu, 2010). Sometimes those who saw the novel colour reported "a gradient of color that ran from, say, red on the left to green on the right with a large region in between that seemed both red and green" (Billock *et al.*, 2001: 2398). At other times they experienced "a homogeneous mixture color whose red and green components were as clear and as compelling as the red and blue components of a purple" (Billock *et al.*, 2001: 2399). In the trials in which non-equiluminant colours were used, they obtained only reports similar to the first two sorts of reports made by Crane and Piantanida: very small (just resolvable) red and green dots or islands of red on a green background or vice versa.

This replication and refinement of Crane and Piantanida's experimental results lends weight to those results, and provides a potential explanation of why Hsieh and Tse didn't replicate the results: they didn't use an eye-tracker or equiluminant stimuli. Yet, one element of Hsieh and Tse's worry remains: Billock *et al.* didn't test to see if subjects could match a possible surface colour to the allegedly impossible one that participants said that they experienced. We would clearly be in a stronger position to claim that there can be experiences of novel colours elicited in the filling-in experimental set-up if evidence could be provided that this cannot not be done. I will return to consider this objection in the next section. Nevertheless, there is fairly substantial and replicated evidence in favour of there being experiences of reddish-green and bluish-yellow novel colours.

In the next section—the final section in which I will look at evidence for the existence of experiences of novel colours—I turn to discuss the cutting-edge, as yet unpublished, work of the aesthetician Michael Newall—with his permission—on the subject of novel colours in paintings.

3.7 Painting

Newall (unpublished) was provoked by a question from a painter: is it possible to paint a continuous fade of yellow colour to blue, without going through green or red (or an achromatic colour) using acrylic paint? Basing an answer on the traditional colour space, we have already seen, would provide a negative answer to the question. However, Newall knew that some people thought that some painters had achieved this effect, and that some people thought that it must be possible, because sometimes they said that they saw the sky as a gradation going from blue to yellow (vertically downwards), without green or red or other hues featuring in what they saw. For example, Rulon Larsen said:

> I know why the sky is blue during the day, and why it turns yellowish to reddish at sunrise and sunset. My question is; why doesn't the sky ever look green? Why does the color go from blue to yellow?
>
> *(on physlink.com)*

And James Elkins in *How to Use Your Eyes*, New York: Routledge, Fig. 26.1, p. 197 (2000), produced a series of images illustrating the colour of the sunset in a clear sky. (See figure 11.4.) Looking east, at half an hour before sunset he describes pale blue fading into pale orange (the shade just beyond yellow), and at ten minutes after sunset he describes a "yellow-blue" shade of colour between blue and orange.

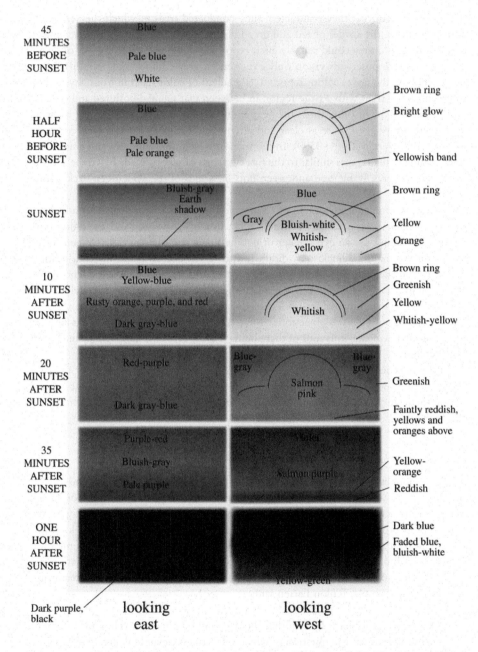

Figure 11.4 From Elkins, J. (2000) *How to Use Your Eyes*, New York: Routledge, Fig. 26.1, p. 197)

Of course, this does not provide conclusive proof that this is how the sky can look, but such detailed observations from colour experts are certainly suggestive.

Newall explains that the effect in question—the fading from blue to yellow directly, without going through other hues of colour—does seem to be achieved in some acrylic paintings.

One can see such a painting being made in the YouTube video by Sean Ryans "How to Paint a Sky—Acrylic Painting Lesson", published 17 August 2013, www.youtube.com/watch?v+ Zr9kMc25bPI, still of which appears in Figure 11.5. In the top two-thirds of the painting there is a gradation from blue to yellow that does not seem to go through any other shade of colour.

Figure 11.5 A portion of a still from Ryans, S. (2013) "How to Paint a Sky - Acrylic Painting Lesson" YouTube Video, published on Aug 17, 2013, www.youtube.com/watch?v=Zr9kMc25bPI.

Figure 11.6 A portion of a still from Ryans, S. (2013) "How to Paint a Sky - Acrylic Painting Lesson" YouTube Video, published on Aug 17, 2013, www.youtube.com/watch?v=Zr9kMc25bPI.

Newall also cites several well-known paintings in which this effect is achieved, including Claude Lorrain's c.1757 *A Mediterranean port at sunrise with the Embarkation of Saint Paula for Jeru-salem*, private ownership, J.M.W. Turner's 1815 *Dido Building Carthage*, The National Gallery, Charles Cuisin's 1815 *Effet de crépuscule, environs de Troyes. La chaussée du Vouldy*, Musée du Louvre, and Charles Gleyre's 1843 *Evening or Lost Illusions*, Musée du Louvre.

Newall asks us to consider in an area of apparent bluish-yellow and how far up the yellowish effect goes, however faintly. And how far down does the bluish effect go, however faintly? He claims that "if those areas overlap, you are experiencing a yellowish bluish colour" (unpublished, slide 20). He notes that the effect can be strengthened by blurring the image by, for example, squinting.

At the same time, Newall notes that "in the area where the blue grades into yellow *the paint itself is a pale grey*—maybe slightly bluish, or slightly yellowish, but never both" (unpublished, slide 27). He says that this can be illustrated by removing a slice from the relevant area of the painting, which is illustrated in Figure 11.6, which is a slice of Figure 11.5.

Thus, Newall concludes that there is no bluish-yellow paint. So, any experience we have of bluish-yellow must be an optical illusion. Newall thinks that a variety of filling-in is taking place. "Where there is a limited stimulus (here a soft, unmodulated, grey with unclear boundaries), the visual system fills it in with information from both the surrounding (yellow and blue) areas" (unpublished, slide 29).

This is an interesting suggestion. The idea is that the bluish-yellow that we experience isn't a colour that physical objects can have or be painted. It is a purely illusory novel colour—the same bluish-yellow that is also claimed to be created by filling-in in the Crane and Piantanida experiments. But the version that we see in the painting is easily available to people (at least those with normal trichromatic vision) to view. It doesn't take an eye-tracker and equiluminant stimuli matched specifically to every subject.

We have here a nice example of neuroaesthetics—an unusual experience predicted and created in the lab by psychologists and neuroscientists—that turns out to have been produced and studied for centuries by artists. I leave it to the reader to assess the merits of Newall's proposal, but for what it is worth, it appears phenomenologically plausible to me.

4 The philosophical significance of experiences of novel colours

Thus far, I have presented a variety of evidence about the existence of experiences of novel colours by looking at an assortment of visual phenomena. I now examine the philosophical significance of experiences of novel colours. While, in previous sections, I have tried to weigh up the evidence in favour and against the existence of these colour experiences, in this section I will simply assume, for the sake of argument, that there are such experiences, and attempt to map out what follows from that claim. This means that most of the claims in this section should be taken to be conditional claims—conditional on experiences of these novel colours existing.

Different kinds of experiences of novel colours have different significance. I start by looking at the conception of experiences of novel colours posited by Byrne and Hilbert in colour blindness. I then go on to discuss the experiences of chimerical colours and reddish-green and bluish-yellow novel colours from the filling-in experiments. It is this latter kind of novel colours that are the most philosophically interesting, so the greater part of this section will be on these.

Recall that Byrne and Hilbert (2010) think that when, say, a red-green colour-blind person looks at a blue object, they will not have an experience that represents it as blue, but "bluish"—because, in order to represent something as blue, the red-green opponent channel must be in balance and hence signalling "neutral" (i.e. neither reddish nor greenish). But red-green colour-blind people lack a red-green opponent channel, therefore they cannot represent that red and green are in balance. 'Bluish' is a technical term, here, the meaning of which is stipulated as being what is represented when the blue-yellow opponent process signals for blue and when there is no signal from a red-green opponent process. Thus, a normal trichromat cannot represent that an object is bluish, in this technical sense, as their red-green opponent process will always be signalling something (even if it signals neither red nor green by signalling a balance between red and green). According to Byrne and Hilbert, neither the red-green colour-blind person nor the normal trichromat are misrepresenting the colour of the object. The object is blue, and the object is bluish.

It therefore follows that, on Byrne and Hilbert's view, the same part of the same object simultaneously has multiple colours—both blue and bluish. And it will have other colours too, given that normal human trichromatic vision will represent something less determinate than a person, or creature, with tetrachromatic vision, who will in turn represent something less determinate than a person, or creature, with pentachromatic vision, and so on.

This view is a variety of pluralism. As outlined in the introductory chapter to this volume by Brown and Macpherson, it is a form of pluralism according to which a ripe banana may be yellow all over, but it is also other colours all over at the same time. Yet it is not an unrestricted pluralism because it doesn't allow that an object can be any two colours all over at the same time. It is restricted to certain determinates and determinables, such a blue and bluish. One might think, therefore, that this view is not too far from a common-sense view. After all, you might think that when a normal trichromat experiences that something is a particular shade of red, say crimson, they also experience that the thing is, less determinately, red, and less determinately still, coloured.

However, the view does depart quite significantly from that common-sense position. In light of the fact that there are tetrachromats and pentachromats, and so on, this means that normal human trichromatic vision will only represent colours that are determinables—determinables of the more determinate colours that those with more colours receptors see. And normal human trichromatic vision won't represent the determinables that the colour-blind represent—determinables of the more determinates that normal human trichromats represent.

A striking concomitant of this view—one that few philosophers have traditionally held—is that in light of the existence of perceivers with more types of receptors, normal trichromatic humans only ever see determinables of some more determinate colour. The view that most philosophers hold is that this is not what our experience is like. It is well represented by David Hume:

> 'tis confest, that no object can appear to the senses; or in other words, that no impression can become present to the mind, without being determin'd in its degrees both of

quantity and quality. The confusion, in which impressions are sometimes involv'd, proceeds only from their faintness and unsteadiness, not from any capacity in the mind to receive any impression, which in its real existence has no particular degree nor proportion.

(1740/1978: 1.1.7)

One philosopher who holds that Hume's view is wrong is Stazicker (2018). In an ingenious paper, he argues, on independent grounds, that we only ever experience determinables and not determinates (and indeed that this is true of every property that we visually experience). It is interesting to note that two separate lines of argument—Byrne and Hilbert's and Stazicker's—both end up concluding that there is only determinable colour experience, a conception that is quite at odds with that of common sense. Greater investigation of this matter would be fruitful territory for further philosophical endeavour.

The novel colours advocated by Byrne and Hilbert on the one hand, differ from the chimerical colours and the reddish-green and bluish-yellow novel colours, on the other, in that only the former are posited to be colours that physical objects can have. Only the former are posited to be perfectly possible, indeed actual, colours of physical objects. I turn now to consider the latter types of novel colours as they present a different set of philosophical ramifications for theories of colour and theories of colour experience.

Chimerical colours and reddish-green and bluish-yellow have in common that they are colours that fall outwith the standard colour space. And they are almost without exception taken to be colours that no physical objects could have because there is no set of wavelengths that a physical object could reflect that would cause a normal perceiver in normal conditions to experience them.[31] This is one reason for thinking that such colours are nomologically impossible. Given the laws of nature, there could not be instances of such colours in the physical world. However, this reasoning supposes that for a colour to be instanced it must be instanced by a physical object, on account of its reflecting certain wavelengths corresponding to the colour. If one doesn't hold that view, then one could think that such colours are perfectly possible, indeed actual. For example, if one thought that colours are distinctly non-physical mental qualia or properties of sense-data (properties of non-physical mental objects), then one could hold that these novel colours are nomologically possible, indeed actual, as they are instantiated in the non-physical mind when people experience them.[32] Or if one thought, as Manzotti (2017: 172) does, that if a perceiver experiences an object to have a colour it thereby makes it the case that that object has that colour then one might think that these novel colours are nomologically possible, indeed actual, as they can be instantiated in physical objects when people experience those objects as having those colours. And if one further thinks, as Manzotti does, that, if multiple perceivers perceive an object to have two different colours on the same part of the same object simultaneously, then that part thereby has both of those colours simultaneously, then this view is a form of unrestricted pluralism.

Going back to consider the view that these novel colours are nomologically impossible, a further question arises whether they are metaphysically possible. The answer to that question will be determined by whether one is an objectivist about colour. As Brown and Macpherson laid out in the introduction to this volume, objectivists think that the nature of colour does not require appeal to perceivers at all. A prominent version of this theory, defended by Byrne and Hilbert (this volume, Chapter 17), draws on contemporary colour science and identifies each colour with a class or disjunction of surface spectral reflectances (SSRs). According to that view, once we have singled out the physical properties that in our world are responsible for colour, those physical properties are the colour properties in all possible worlds. Colour words are taken to refer rigidly to the physical properties so identified, and thus, in all other possible worlds, the judgments of any perceivers are irrelevant to the identity of the colours. Byrne and Hilbert (1997: 282, fn. 8), suggest that the best description of a world with a very different physics from our own is that in such a world objects merely look coloured. Thus, defenders of this type of objectivism will hold that the novel colours under consideration are both nomologically and metaphysically impossible. However, those who are not objectivists and who tie the identity of the colours in a possible world to the judgements of colour perceivers in that world could hold that these novel colours are not nomologically possible, but that they are metaphysically possible. I said "could hold", and not "will hold" in the last sentence, as some such philosophers might hold that these novel colours are nomologically possible too, for a world with our laws of nature might contain very different perceivers who might issue forth the judgements that according to those philosophers determine that some physical objects did have these novel colours.[33]

We can see then that the modal status one takes these novel colours to have is highly dependent on the theory of colour that one holds. This means that theories of colour can be assessed for the treatment that they give of these novel colours—and whether we find it satisfactory. Let me give one example.

One problem that faces those philosophers who think that novel colours are not actual is that they face a particular explanatory burden that the philosophers who think that they are actual do not. The philosophers who think that novel colours are not actual have to come up with an explanation of why having an experience as of those novel colours seems to give people knowledge of what those colours are like. After all, if a colour is not instantiated in virtue of having the experience, then how can having the experience allow people to know what it would be like to see an instance of that colour?

It has long been noted that if one has not perceived a certain thing then, unless one has seen closely related things of the right sort, it is impossible to know what it would be like to see that thing. For example, if one has not seen the colour red, then it is tempting to think that one cannot know, or even visually imagine, what it is like to see red. (Frank Jackson (1986) famously articulated this temptation with his thought experiment about Mary who has never seen red.) What sorts of closely related things would one have to see in order to know what it would be like to see something that one has not? Take the example of having never seen a golden mountain. One could come to know what it is like to see a golden mountain if one has seen a mountain and if one has seen gold, and one can combine these ideas together in the imagination. Another example would be a case in which one has not seen something, say a shade of blue, but one has seen all the other shades of blue laid out in order with a gap in the right place for the shade that one has seen.[34]

An interesting feature of cases in which people have claimed to experience reddish-green and bluish-yellow that is noted in all the papers cited above on the topic, is that after people took part in the experiments that tried to induce those experiences, they said that before having the experience of the novel colours they could not imagine what those colours were like, but after having experienced the colours they could imagine them.

If, in having an experience as of a novel colour, that colour is in no way instantiated—even in the experience or in mental sense-data that one is aware of (if one is aware of any)—then it is mysterious how having such an experience could confer knowledge on one of the nature of the uninstantiated property. If the property is instantiated, and if one comes to be aware of it, then of course that provides a simple explanation of the knowledge that one comes to have. But if the property is not instantiated, and one does not therefore see the property, how can one come to know what it would be like to see the property? Simply stating that one is in a state that represents the property is not a good explanation. Before experiencing reddish-green, I can represent reddish-green by thinking about it and by having beliefs about it. But in virtue of representing it like that I don't come to know what it would be like to see it. One might think that what seems special about visual representation, and that makes it more powerful than representation in thought or belief, is that it makes one visually aware of an instance of the property—but what I am pointing out is that those who endorse this thought need to come up with some reason to believe that this is true in the case of these novel colours if no instances of them exist.

Perhaps the main reason that philosophers have been interested in experiences of these novel colours—the chimerical kind and the reddish-green and bluish-yellow kind—is that they threaten to provide a counterexample to some theories of perception and perceptual experience. Deciding between philosophical theories of perception and perceptual experience is very difficult indeed. One reason is that most philosophical theories of perception are built to accommodate as wide a set of empirical possibilities as possible. That is, to some degree, what makes them philosophical, rather than empirical theories. Thus, it is rare that philosophical theories of perception can be ruled out by discovery of empirical fact. However, I think that some philosophers assumed that there could not be experiences of these sorts of novel colours and so did not build theories that accommodated them. I suspect that many philosophers had ruled out this possibility due to what they found it possible to visually imagine. Let me explain.

Some philosophers seem to use what they cannot visually imagine as a guide to what is impossible. Here is one example, in a case that is not about novel colours. In Macpherson (2015), I point out that Aristotle made the claim that all visual experience must be experience of chromatic or achromatic colour. That is what it is to be a visual experience on his account. That idea has rattled down the centuries with many philosophers repeating the same claim, and citing Aristotle on the matter. But Aristotle gave no reason for the claim. And nor do the philosophers that repeat it. Why? Perhaps they are appealing to Aristotle simply as a wise authority. But I suspect that they also think that a priori reflection on the matter reveals it to be so—it is self-evidently true. And I suspect that many philosophers think that because when they imagine having a visual experience, all they can imagine is experiences that have chromatic or achromatic colour—for they themselves have had no other type of visual experience. However, as I explain in detail in that paper, modern evidence suggests that people can have visual experiences when they are not experiencing colour. I can't imagine what it is like to have such experiences, but I have good reason to believe that such experiences exist and that they are visual, given that they are caused by light entering the eyes and they inform people about the distal environment. In general, it is a mistake to infer from the fact that you can't imagine something to thinking that that thing is impossible.

I think that this sort of faulty reasoning has probably guided philosophers theorizing about perceptual experience. When considering whether there are experiences of hues of colour beyond those that the standard colour space indicates exist, philosophers—like everyone else who has not experienced them—have not been able to imagine any. Thus, I think that they have falsely thought that this is good evidence for believing that there cannot be such experiences. However, as I have shown earlier in this chapter, there is quite strong evidence to think that this is false and that there can be experiences of such novel colours.

Manzotti (2017) provides a different reason for thinking that there are no experiences of these novel colours. He argues that when we examine all the visual experiences that we ever have, perceptual, illusory, or hallucinatory, we cannot find one that isn't composed of solely of elements that we have experienced when seeing the world. We can find evidence of illusions or hallucinations of scenes that we have not seen, but not of scenes that are not composed from elements that we have previously seen. He claims:

all our experiences—be they a perception or a dream or a hallucination—are made of stuff we encounter in the external world. We do not see or hallucinate colors we have not encountered in the real world. We do not imagine a hue of blue we have never seen. We do not hallucinate or dream of anything that has not been part of the world we have lived in. *We do not experience anything but the physical world in various combinations.*

(2017: 149)

By induction, one might argue that there are no such experiences.

So, if, contra these views, there can be experiences of these novel colours, then those experiences have a good chance at helping us test philosophical theories of perception and perceptual experience because they provide examples of experiences that most philosophical theories did not set out to accommodate from the outset, on account of people not believing that their theories had to accommodate such experiences.

Theories that struggle to accommodate experiences of novel colours are ones which explain the phenomenal character of experience in terms that make essential reference to the actual or possible occurrence in the world, of that which one seems to be aware of. I will give two examples of such theories of perception and perceptual experience that are prominent in the current philosophical literature.

The first example is externalist versions of representational theories of phenomenal character. According to representationalism, when we have an experience in which we veridically see the world, that is because we represent the world to be a certain way, the world is that way, and the world is hooked up to the experience in the right way—it is often claimed that the experience is caused by the world in an appropriate, non-deviant, non-lucky way. When one has an illusion or a hallucination, this is experienced because the subject represents the world to be a certain way when the world is not that way, or if it is that way, it is so by chance.

Externalist versions of representationalism are ones which hold that what it is for a state to represent something is for it to bear a certain relationship to that thing. For example, your experience must track that thing in ideal conditions, or it must have the function of tracking that thing, which it gained by actually tracking that thing in the past and then being selected for on the grounds of the usefulness of tracking that thing. There are different versions of externalist representationalism, but core to them all is the thought that the thing that is represented exists or existed and experiences get to represent that thing by bearing a relationship to it.[35]

Novel colours of the sort that don't actually exist thus pose a problem for this theory. Our experiences of those colours represent those colours, but they can't have been hooked up to instances of that colour in the right way, for such instances don't exist.

Of course, there are ways for externalist representationalists to try to rebut this argument. These are explored at length in Macpherson (2003), but I argue that ultimately experiences of novel colours do present a counterexample to externalist representationalist theories.

The second example is certain versions of naïve realism. To understand what these theories are, I will compare and contrast them to other central philosophical theories of perception.[36]

According to the sense-datum theory, when one either sees an apple, has an illusion as of an apple, or hallucinates an apple, one is in the same mental state—a state in which one is aware of some mental object that has the properties that one seems to be aware of. Such a view is a variety of "common-kind" view, for the same sort of mental state is postulated to exist when veridically seeing (the good case) and when one is undergoing an illusion or hallucination (the bad cases). Some versions of representationalism are common-kind theories—according to them, in the good case and in the bad cases, one is in the same type of mental state: one that represents an apple. Some representationalists have started to distance themselves from this view arguing that there are some mental differences in the good case and the bad cases. Different versions of this view outline different differences, but what they are needn't be a matter of concern here.[37] Views according to which there are mental differences in the good and bad cases are "disjunctive" views and they stand opposed to common-kind theories.

One brand of disjunctivism is not representationalist. According to this view, when one is in the good case one is not in a state that represents the world being a certain way. Instead, one is directly aware of that portion of the world, and not in virtue of being aware of a representation or having a representation. Rather, one is simply directly aware of the world. The world is presented to one, and so a representation of the world in not required. Indeed, when the world is presented to one, the state that one is in could not stand for the way that the world is in a manner that could be judged correct or incorrect, true or false. The state encompasses the world being the way that it is: the relevant part of the world is a constituent of the state. This view is naïve realism, and naïve realists claim that the phenomenal character of your experience is not to be identified with a mental-proxy—a representation, representational content, or sense-datum—rather it is to be identified with the very state of the world itself.[38]

If one gives such an account of the good case, then what account can one give of the bad case? The core thought that forms the answer that disjunctive naïve realists give is that in the bad case you are not in direct contact with the world. In some sense, it seems to you as if you are, but this seeming is incorrect. Because the phenomenal character of the good case is constituted by the world, then the disjunctive naïve realist has to say that the bad case does not involve this phenomenal character. It either involves no phenomenal character, or at least a different one.[39]

Another form of naïve realism abandons disjunctivism and claims that in the bad case one is in the same mental state as the good case—it is one in which one is aware of the world too. How could that be? The answer proffered is that one is aware of previously seen objects and properties.[40]

One can see straight away that the latter non-disjunctive form of naïve realism will fail to account for experiences of these novel colours if it is true that they are not actual, for in that case, they are not seen now, and they have not previously been seen in the past. As previously mentioned, Manzotti (2017), who holds a view bearing a very close affinity to this one, tries to overcome this objection by claiming that if there are experiences of these novel colours then physical objects actually come to have those novel colour properties when they are so experienced. Thus, he overcomes this problem by becoming non-objectivist about colour properties. But this moves Manzotti's view away from a naïve realism, towards a non-realist position.

What of the disjunctive form of naïve realism? Recall that, according to that view, in the bad case it seems to you as if you are seeing the world when you are not. In what sense does it seem to you that way? According to Fish (2009) it seems to you that way because you are in a mental state that has all the same cognitive effects as a state of seeing the world. This view is troubled by these novel colours, for if such colours are not actual, then there isn't a state of seeing the world that is the state of seeing such colours. So, there can't be a hallucinatory state that has all the same effects as this state.

Martin's disjunctive naïve realism is less committal about the nature of hallucinations than that of Fish. On principle, Martin holds a 'negative epistemic' account of hallucinations because he holds that any positive characterization of hallucination leads the disjunctive naïve realist into the screening-off problem. This is the problem of being able to give the experience in the good case an explanatory role—an explanatory role that explains the phenomenal aspects of the experience—that is distinctive from the experience in the bad case, and shows that we need to posit a different sort of mental state in the good case, rather than just the mental state that we posit in the bad case. If one does not need to posit a distinctive good case experience, then the need for the disjunctive naïve realist account of hallucination vanishes. Martin's account of what makes it the case that one's hallucinatory experience is as of an apple is just that it is an occurrence which is indiscriminable from—cannot be told apart, solely on the basis of introspection, from—a veridical perception of an apple.

Can this negative epistemic account of hallucination deal with the sorts of experience of novel colours under discussion—ones that don't exist and must be non-veridical, if we are to remain realists and objectivists about the properties that we take ourselves to perceive? I find this question hard to answer. On the one hand, there seems to be a reading on which it cannot, for if there can be no veridical perception of a certain colour how could one be in a state which is indiscriminable, solely on the basis of introspection, from it—a state that does not (and, depending on your view, perhaps cannot) exist? To see this, consider the following analogy: suppose we are told that there is a creature that lives in the forests of Scotland which is such that it is impossible to tell it apart from a unicorn. And, at the same time, it is true that there are no unicorns. How could there be such a creature? How could it be impossible to tell apart a creature from one that does not exist? What criteria could one use to know whether one had not told it apart, rather than that one had? But, on the other hand, there seems to be a reading on which there could be a state indiscriminable, solely on the basis of introspection, from a state that does not exist, such as a state of seeing reddish-green. If, when you are in that state, you cannot know whether, just on the basis of introspection, you are in it, or in the state of seeing reddish-green, then the actual fact that you must merely be in the indiscriminable state, seems not to matter. One (at least often) does not know, just by introspection, which states of seeing do and do not exist, or could and could not exist.

Which reading should we give of the negative epistemic account, and which reading does the naïve realist intend, or which does he or she have intend to make best sense of their view? These are interesting questions that lie at the very forefront of our thinking about the impact the existence of experiences of novel colours should have on which theories of perception and perceptual experience we should accept.

5 Summary

The topic of novel colours is fascinating. Weighing up the evidence about whether there are experiences of such colours necessarily takes us deep into both philosophical and scientific territory. A detailed understanding of how normal and unusual human colour perception works, and that of other creatures, is essential. And all of this is contested and not yet fully understood. Furthermore, experimental work that has been taken to reveal experiences of novel colours is less developed than we would ideally like it to be.

Nonetheless, there is evidence from multiple empirical sources that there are experiences of novel colours. That such evidence converges is helpful for those who wish to argue that there are such experiences.

If there are such experiences, they present very powerful, interesting examples with which to test, explore, and examine the various theories of colour, colour perception, and perceptual experience of colour, that form the core of philosophy of perception. I have indicated various ways in which this can be done and indicated directions for future study.

Notes

1 Thanks to Derek Brown for very helpful comments on a draft of this chapter.
2 Hume's missing shade of blue is a likely counterexample here, but one that lacks any bite as its novel nature is so slight.
3 This is discussed in section 2.
4 Some metaphysicians hold that properties exist even if never instantiated. That is not the sense of existence that I am interested in contemplating in this chapter.
5 This title is mostly found in popular media. See, for example, Helmsteine (2018) and Wikipedia contributors (2018).
6 See Billock *et al.* (2001), Billock and Tsou (2004) and (2010), and Hsieh and Tse (2006).
7 See Ramachandran and Hubbard (2001).
8 See Ramachandran and Hubbard (2001) and Gatzia (2008).
9 See Churchland (2005), Helmsteine (2018), and Wikipedia contributors (2018).
10 See Ramachandran and Hubbard (2001) and Gatzia (2008).
11 Such after-images are often called 'negative' after-images or 'complementary' after-images, terms which are used to signal that they are induced by a hue on the opposite side of the hue circle, as opposed to 'positive' after-images which are induced by the very same colour. See Macpherson (September 2017).
12 Colours spaces are discussed at length in David Brigg's chapter on that topic in this volume (Chapter 9).
13 See Munsell (1905).
14 Hård *et al.* (1996).
15 Surface colours are colours that are perceived as being on an opaque surface of an object, as opposed to colours seen in translucent volumes or radiant colours. Surface colours are also distinguished from aperture colours. Surface colours are seen in conditions in which it is possible to distinguish the colour of the surface from that of the ambient light. In contrast, aperture colours are perceived by looking though a small aperture formed by an achromatic colour, which makes it impossible to distinguish the colour from that of the ambient light. See Maund (2019).
16 See Churchland (2005) for technical details.
17 See Macpherson (2003).
18 See Broakes (2010) and Byrne and Hilbert (2010).
19 In this chapter, I discuss only the new theory as it pertains to dichromatic colour blindness. However, the interested reader should look at Akins (2014) for a similar new account of rod achromatopsia (the condition of having only the visual system that operates in low light that utilizes rod cells in the eyes rather than the cones cells that we have discussed thus far that operate in greater lighting conditions). In the past this condition has been treated as being monochromatic vision. But Akins' exceptional work drawing on a very detailed knowledge of the latest colour science and what that tells us about the nature of experience argues that it is not like black and white vision.
20 The suggestion that objects can have multiple colours at the same time is explored at length in Mark Kalderon's chapter (Chapter 20) for this volume on "Monism and Pluralism", and in Keith Allen's chapter (Chapter 14) on "Interspecies Variations". Colour relationalists are likely to hold this view—see Jonathan Cohen's chapter (Chapter 19) on "Colour Relationalism" in this volume too.
21 See Stazicker (2018) for an excellent discussion of why the view that we only perceive determinates and not determinables is wrong and why we should hold the view that we see only determinables of one sort or another, rather than determinates.
22 See Keith Allen "Interspecies Variations" (Chapter 14, this volume) for more on animal colour vision. See also Marshall and Arikawa (2014) from whom I take the details of animal colour vision in this section. We also find trichromatic animals whose three different types of cells are attuned to different wavelengths than those of humans: they are shifted towards and into the ultraviolet. I will not discuss this type of colour vision, but it is interesting to speculate what it would be like to have it.
23 See Manzotti (2017: 168) for a table listing many of those who have claimed this, including Macpherson (2013).
24 See Jameson and D'Andrade (1997: 308).
25 See Wyszecki and Stiles (1982: 176).
26 More details can be found of synaesthesia in Berit Brogaard's chapter (Chapter 12) in this volume.

27 Some of this section and the next presuppose the opponent-colour theory that I questioned in section 3.4. I will set aside questioning that theory for the rest of this chapter. First, I have already covered that topic. I leave it to the reader to decide whether anything of substance would have to change in articulating the issues of the rest of these sections in terms of opponent complementary colours, rather than in terms of the traditional opponent colours. I believe it would not.

28 See, for example, Krauskopf (1963) and Yarbus (1967).

29 See Troxler (1804) and Thomson and Macpherson (July 2017).

30 Which colours are isoluminant varies from subject to subject.

31 As noted previously, self-luminous chimerical colours are somewhat different from the other chimerical colours. The other chimerical colours (stygerian and hyperbolic colours) are not colours that any physical object could have. This matter is more nuanced in the case of self-luminous chimerical colours. Of course, physical objects can really be self-luminous and those will typically look the way self-luminous chimerical colours look. What makes a self-luminous chimerical colour is that it looks self-luminous, but it appears to be on the surface of an object that is in fact not self-luminous. I will leave aside this complication in the main text and speak as if all chimerical colours are straightforwardly colours that no physical object can have, and leave out the extra nuance noted here.

32 See Howard Robinson's chapter (Chapter 21) in this volume, "Mentalist Approaches to Colour".

33 The interested reader may wish to consult Gierlinger and Westphal's chapter (Chapter 5) in this volume on "The Logic of Colour Concepts" for further discussion of the modal force of various claims about colour.

34 See Hume's (1740/1978: 6) discussion of the "missing shade of blue".

35 See, for example, Dretske (1995) and Tye (1995).

36 See also Brown and Macpherson in this volume, "Introduction to the Philosophy of Colour", and John Campbell in this volume, "Does That Which Makes the Sensation of Blue a Mental Fact Escape Us?" (Chapter 25).

37 One clear example is Schellenberg (2013).

38 See Crane and French (Spring 2017).

39 See, for example, Martin (2004 and 2006) and Fish (2009).

40 See, for example, Weir (2004), MacGregor (2015), and Manzotti (2017).

References

Akins, K. (2014). "Black and White and Colour", in R. Brown (ed.), *Consciousness Inside and Out: Phenomenology, Neuroscience and the Nature of Experience. Studies in Brain and Mind*, Vol. 6. Dordrecht: Springer.

Billock, V. A. and Tsou, B. H. (2004). "What Do Catastrophic Visual Binding Failures Look Like?", *Trends Neurosci*, 27(2): 84–9.

Billock, V. A. and Tsou, B. H. (2010). "Seeing Forbidden Colors", *Scientific American*, 302(2): 72–7.

Billock, V. A., Gleason, G. A., and Tsou, B. H. (2001). "Perception of Forbidden Colors in Retinally Stabilized Equiluminant Images: An Indication of Softwired Cortical Color Opponency?", *J Opt Soc Am A Opt Image Sci Vis*, 18(10), 2398–403.

Brenner, W. (1987). "'Brownish-Yellow' and 'Reddish-Green'", *Philosophical Investigations*, 10(3), 200–11.

Broackes, J. (2010). "What Do the Colour-Blind See?", in J. D. Cohen and M. Matthen (eds.), *Color Ontology and Color Science*, Cambridge, MA: MIT Press, pp. 291–405.

Byrne, A. and Hilbert, D. R. (1997). "Colors and Reflectances", in A. Byrne and D. R. Hilbert (eds.), *Readings on Color Volume 1: The Philosophy of Color*, Cambridge, MA: MIT Press.

Byrne, A. and Hilbert, D. R. (2010). "How Do Things Look to the Color-Blind?" in J. Cohen and M. Matthen (eds.), *Color Ontology and Color Science*, Cambridge, MA: MIT Press.

Chalmers, D. J. (2002). "Does Conceivability Entail Possibility?", in T. Gendler and J. Hawthorne (eds.), *Conceivability and Possibility*, Oxford: Oxford University Press, pp. 145–200.

Churchland, P. (2005). "Chimerical Colors: Some Phenomenological Predictions from Cognitive Neuroscience", *Philosophical Psychology*, 18(5): 527–60.

Crane, T. and French, C. "The Problem of Perception", in E. N. Zalta (ed.), *The Stanford Encyclopedia of Philosophy* (Spring 2017 Edition), https://plato.stanford.edu/archives/spr2017/entries/perception-problem/.

Crane, H. D. and Piantanida, T. P. (1983). "On Seeing Reddish Green and Yellowish Blue", *Science*, 221(4615): 1078–80.

Dretske, F. I. (1995). *Naturalising the Mind*, Cambridge, MA: MIT Press.

Elkins, J. (2000). *How to Use Your Eyes*, New York: Routledge.

Fish, W. (2009). *Perception, Illusion and Hallucination*, Oxford: Oxford University Press.

Gatzia, D. E. (2008). "Martian Colours", *Philosophical Writings*, 37: 3–16.

Hård, A., Sivik, L., and Tonnquist, G. (1996). "NCS Natural Color System—from Concepts to Research and Applications. Part I and II", *Color Research and Application*, 21: 180–220.

Helmholz, H. v. (1856, 1860, and 1867). *Handbuch der physiologischen Optik*, 3 vol., Heidelberg. Eng. tr. by J. P. C. Southall, *Treatise on Physiological Optics*, 3 vol., (from the 3rd ed.) for the *Optical Society of America* (Rochester, NY, 1924–5).

Helmsteine, A. M. (2018). "Impossible Colors and How to See Them", *ThoughtCo.*, 19 October 2018, accessed 6 November 2018, thoughtco.com/impossible-colors-introduction-4152091.

Hering, E. (1878/1964). *Outlines of a Theory of the Light Sense*, translated by L. M. Hurvich and D. Jameson, Cambridge, MA: Harvard University Press.

Hsieh, P.-J. and Tse, P. U. (2006). "Illusory Color Mixing Upon Perceptual Fading and Filling-in Does Not Result in 'Forbidden Colors'", *Vision Research*, 46: 2251–8.

Hume, D. (1740/1978). *A Treatise of Human Nature*, ed. L. A. Selby-Bigge, revised by P. H. Nidditch, Oxford: Oxford University Press.

Hurvich, L. M. and Jameson, D. (1957). "An Opponent-Process Theory of Color Vision", *Psychological Review*, 64(6, Pt.1), 384–404.

Ichikawa, J. and Jarvis, B. (2012). "Rational Imagination and Modal Knowledge", *Nous*, 46(1): 127–58.

Jackson, F. (1986). "What Mary Didn't Know", *Journal of Philosophy*, 83: 291–5.

Jameson, K. and D'Andrade, R. G. (1997), "It's Not Really Red, Green, Yellow, Blue: An Inquiry into Perceptual Color Space", in C. L. Hardin and L. Maffi (eds.), *Color Categories in Thought and Language*, Cambridge: Cambridge University Press, 295–319.

Johnston, M. (2004). "The Obscure Object of Hallucination", *Philosophical Studies*, 120(1): 113–83.

Jordan, G., Deeb, S. S., Bosten, J., and Mollon, J. D. (2010). "The Dimensionality of Color Vision in Carriers of Anomalous Trichromacy", *Journal of Vision*, 10(8): 12, 1–19.

Krauskopf, J. (1963). "Effect of Retinal Image Stabilization in the Appearance of Heterochromatic Targets", *Journal of the Optical Society of America*, 53: 741–3.

Lovecraft, H. P. (1927). "The Colour Out of Space", *Amazing Stories*, 2(6): 557–67. Reprinted online: www.hplovecraft.com/writings/texts/fiction/cs.aspx, accessed 7 May 2018.

Lugg, A (2010). "Wittgenstein in Reddish Green: Logic and Experience", in A. Marquest and N. Venturinha (eds.), *Wittgenstein on Forms of Life and the Nature of Experience*, Bern: Peter Lang.

MacDonald, G. (1867). "The Golden Key", in *Dealings with the Fairies*, London: Alexander Strahan.

MacGregor, A. S. (2015). *A Natural View of Perceptual Experience*, University of Glasgow PhD Thesis, http://theses.gla.ac.uk/6361/.

Macpherson, F. (2003). "Novel Colours and the Content of Experience", *Pacific Philosophical Quarterly*, 84(1): 43–66.

Macpherson, F. (2007). "Synaesthesia, Functionalism and Phenomenology", in M. de Caro, F. Ferretti, and M. Marraffa (eds.), *Cartographies of the Mind: Philosophy and Psychology in Intersection*, Series: Studies in Brain and Mind, Vol. 4, Dordrecht: Kleuwer, 65–80.

Macpherson, F. (2013). "The Philosophy and Psychology of Hallucination: An Introduction", in F. Macpherson and D. Platchais (eds.), *Hallucination: Philosophy and Psychology*, Cambridge, MA: MIT Press.

Macpherson, F. (2015). "The Structure of Experience, the Nature of the Visual, and Type 2 Blindsight", *Consciousness and Cognition*, 32: 104–28.

Macpherson, F. (September 2017). "Positive Afterimages", in F. Macpherson (ed.), *The Illusions Index*. Retrieved from www.illusionsindex.org/i/positive-afterimages.

Manzotti, R. (2017) *Consciousness and Object: A Mind-Object Identity Physicalist Theory*, Amsterdam/Philadelphia: John Benjamins Publishing Company.

Marshall, J. and Arikawa, K. (2014). "Unconventional Colour Vision", *Current Biology*, 24(24): R1150–4.

Martin, M. G. F. (2004). "The Limits of Self-Awareness", *Philosophical Studies*, 120: 37–89.

Martin, M. G. F. (2006). "On Being Alienated", in T. S. Gendler and J. Hawthorne (eds.), *Perceptual Experience*, Oxford: Oxford University Press, 354–410.

Maund, B. (2019). "Color", in E. N. Zalta (ed.), *The Stanford Encyclopedia of Philosophy* (Spring 2019 Edition), https://plato.stanford.edu/archives/spr2019/entries/color.

Munsell, A. H. (1905). *A Color Notation*, Boston: G. H. Ellis Co.

Newhall, M. (unpublished). "Painting With Impossible Colours", slides of a talk delivered at the 'Depiction, Pictorial Experience, and Vision Science' conferences, Centre for the Study of Perceptual Experience, University of Glasgow, 15–17 November 2018.

Newhall, S. M., Nickerson, D., and Judd, D. B. (1943). "Final Report of the O.S.A. Subcommittee on the Spacing of the Munsell Colors★", *J. Opt. Soc. Am.*, 33: 385–418.

Nida-Rümelin, M. and Suarez, J. (2009). "Reddish Green: A Challenge for Modal Claims About Phenomenal Structure", *Philosophy and Phenomenological Research*, 78(2): 346–91.

Pauli, R. (2010). "Opponent Processes in Colour Vision: What Can Afterimages Teach Us?", literature review and practical report, University of Birmingham.

Pridmore, R. W. (2011). "Complementary Colors Theory of Color Vision: Physiology, Color Mixture, Color Constancy and Color Perception", *Color Res. Appl.*, 36: 394–412.

Ramachandran, V. S. and Hubbard, E. M. (2001). "Synaesthesia—a Window into Perception, Thought and Language", *Journal of Consciousness Studies*, 8(12): 3–34.

Ryans, S. (2013). "How to Paint a Sky—Acrylic Painting Lesson", YouTube Video, published on 17 August 2013, accessed 19 November 2018, www.youtube.com/watch?v=Zr9kMc25bPI.

Saunders, B. A. C. and van Brakel, J. (1997). "Are There Nontrivial Constraints on Colour Categorization?", *Behavioral and Brain Sciences* 20(2): 167–228.

Schellenberg, S. (2013). "Externalism and the Gappy Content of Hallucination", in F Macpherson and D. Platchias (eds.) *Hallucination*, Cambridge, MA: MIT Press, 291–311.

Stazicker, J. D. (2018). "The Visual Presence of Determinable Properties", in F. Dorsch and F. Macpherson (eds.), *Phenomenal Presence*, Oxford: Oxford University Press.

Thomson, G. and Macpherson, F. (July 2017). "Troxler Effect", in F. Macpherson (ed.), *The Illusions Index*. Retrieved from www.illusionsindex.org/i/troxler-effect.

Troxler, D. (1804). "Über das Verschwinden gegebener Gegenstände inner-halb unsers Gesichtskreises", in K. Himly and J. A. Schmidt (eds.), *Ophthalmologische Bibliothek II*, Fromman: Jena, 51–3.

Tye, M. (1995). *Ten Problems of Consciousness: A Representational Theory of the Phenomenal Mind*, Cambridge, MA: MIT Press.

Weir, A. (2004). "An Ultra-Realist Theory of Perception", *International Journal of Philosophical Studies*, 12(2): 105–28.

Wikipedia contributors. (2018, 29 September). "Impossible Color", *Wikipedia, The Free Encyclopedia*. Retrieved 6 November 2018, from https://en.wikipedia.org/w/index.php?title=Impossible_color&oldid=861736985.

Wyslecki, G. and Stiles, W. S. (1982). *Color Science*, 2nd ed. New York: Wiley.

Yarbus, A. L. (1967). *Eye Movements and Vision*. Trans. Haigh. New York: Plenum.

Young, T. (1802). "On the Theory of Light and Colours", *Phil. Trans. R. Soc. Lond.*, 92: 12–48.

12

COLOUR SYNAESTHESIA AND ITS PHILOSOPHICAL IMPLICATIONS

Berit Brogaard

1 Introduction

Synaesthesia is an unusual way of perceiving the world, comprising cases in which an experience of one thing in one sensory or cognitive stream causes a non-veridical experience (or image or thought) of another thing in a different sensory or cognitive stream (Baron-Cohen *et al.*, 1987; Cytowic, 1989; Rich and Mattingley, 2002; Sagiv and Ward, 2006). For example, seeing the number 9 may lead to an experience of dark imperial blue, hearing the word "Swiss" may flood the mouth with the flavour of old bread soaked in Tuscan tomato soup, and hearing the key of C# minor may elicit a bright purple helix discharging from the middle of the visual field.

The object of the experience that causes the non-veridical experience is called 'the inducer', whereas the apparent object of the experience it elicits is called 'the concurrent' (Grossenbacher and Lovelace, 2001). In visual synaesthesia, the concurrent may be seen as projected out into space and experienced as located in the visual scene outside the subject's mind, or it may be merely imagistically or semantically associated with the inducer (Dixon *et al.*, 2004). The former is known as 'projector synaesthesia', whereas the latter is called 'associator synaesthesia'. Projection is some-times experienced much like veridical perception, that is, the apparent concurrent objects are experienced as located in the visual scene outside of the synaesthetes' mind (Dixon *et al.*, 2004). While some synaesthetes who experience projection report seeing concurrents that hover above their inducers, others describe their experiences as similar to seeing after-images or phosphenes.

Synaesthetes who associate inducers and concurrents imagistically or semantically describe seeing or feeling synaesthetic concurrents within their "mind's eye", or they report simply "knowing" that the inducers are strongly connected to or associated with their concurrents (Dixon *et al.*, 2004). For example, grapheme-colour synaesthetes might view a black letter 'A' yet describe it as having the quality of the colour blue, even though they do not actually have the perceptual experience of seeing a blue 'A'.

Regardless of whether synaesthesia is of the projector or associator type, the many different forms exhibit two main characteristics. (i) It involves an aberrant co-occurrence or binding of features from different sensory or cognitive streams that are associated with atypical conscious experiences or thoughts and (ii) these experiences or thoughts are automatic, that is, synaesthetes cannot suppress the association between an inducer and its concurrent. Other characteristics of the condition are specific to the different forms.

According to Grossenbacher and Lovelace (2001), synaesthesia comes in three main varieties: (1) Developmental, or genuine, (2) Acquired, and (3) Drug-induced. Developmental synaesthesia, the most common type, is a form of the condition that has persisted since birth or early childhood (Tilot *et al.*, 2018) and that remains relatively stable and systematic over time (see Figure 12.1): each inducer has a highly specific concurrent (Baron-Cohen *et al.*, 1987; Mattingley *et al.*, 2001; Simner *et al.*, 2006). It also seems to be prevalent in many members of the same family (Baron-Cohen *et al.*, 1996).

For the most common forms of developmental synaesthesia, the Synesthesia Battery, an automated online test, allows for rigorous testing of both the tightness of the synaesthetic association and its stability and systematicity over time (www.synesthete.org/; Eagleman *et al.*, 2007).

Acquired synaesthesia is a form of the condition that emerges after brain injury or disease or during use of technologies such as sensory substitution (Ward and Wright, 2012). It has been reported following stroke (Ro *et al.*, 2007; Beauchamp and Ro, 2008; Thomas-Anterion *et al.*, 2010; Schott, 2012), traumatic brain injury (Brogaard *et al.*, 2013; Brogaard and Marlow, 2015), neuropathology involving the optic nerve and/or chiasm (Jacobs *et al.*, 1981; Armel and Ramachandran, 1999; Afra *et al.*, 2009), seizures (Jacome and Gumnit, 1979), migraine (Alstadhaug and Benjaminsen, 2010), hypnotic or post-hypnotic suggestion (Cohen Kadosh *et al.*, 2009; Anderson *et al.* 2014), and sensory substitution (Ward and Wright, 2012). Audio-visual synaesthesia has been reported to be the most common acquired type (Afra *et al.*, 2009). Like developmental synaesthesia, the acquired form tends to be automatic and systematic over time, though in some cases it only persists for a limited time period (Jacome and Gumnit, 1979; Lessell and Cohen, 1979; Afra *et al.*, 2009). Phenomenally, acquired synaesthesia may be indistinguishable from the developmental type, though it can be less inducer-specific, that is, the same concurrent sometimes has several different inducers (Brogaard *et al.*, 2013). Cases have also been reported in which the acquired form is simpler than the developmental counterpart, often similar to light flashes (phosphenes) or pure colour experiences (Afra *et al.*, 2009).

Drug-induced synaesthesia is a blending of sensory or cognitive streams that occurs during peak exposure to a hallucinogen (psilocybin, LSD, mescaline, peyote; Shanon, 2002; Friedrichs, 2009; Sinke *et al.*, 2012). Unlike the developmental and acquired varieties, the drug-induced form is usually limited to the most intense phases of intoxication, though in some cases it continues for weeks or months after exposure to the drug (Abraham, 1983; Ffytche, 2007). Reports of coloured music are particularly frequent (Shanon, 2002, 2003; Sinke *et al.*, 2012). In other cases experiences take the form of complex, surrealistic landscapes consisting of, for example, oddly shaped objects with multicoloured contours or images with ornamental or kaleidoscopic compositions (Hintzen and Passie, 2010).

					Grapheme					
		0	1	2	3	4	5	6	7	8	9
	3	/	B	Y	G	P	R	Bl	W	Br	R
	4	/	B	Y	G	P	R	Bl	W	Br	R
	5	Go	B	Y	G	P	R	DBr	W	Br	R
Age (in years)	6	Go	B	Y	G	P	R	DBr	W	Br	R
	7	B	B	Y	G	P	R	Br	W	Br	R
	8	B	B	Y	G	P	R	Bl	W	Br	R
	...	B	B	Y	G	P	R	Bl	W	Br	R
	14	B	B	Y	G	P	R	Bl	W	Br	R

Figure 12.1 Example of test-retest reliability of synaesthetic experience in an associator grapheme-colour synaesthete from ages 3 to 14 (**B**lue, **Bl**ack, **Br**own, **D**ark **Br**own, **G**reen, **Go**ld, **P**urple, **R**ed, **W**hite, and **Y**ellow).

211

Colour synaesthesia is a form of the condition in which either the inducer or the concurrent is a colour. The two most commons forms are weekday-colour synaesthesia, in which the days of the week are conceived of as coloured, and grapheme-colour synaesthesia, in which numbers or letters are perceived or envisaged as having a particular colour with a highly specific hue, brightness, and saturation. Other forms include music-colour synaesthesia, in which musical notes are experienced as coloured; lexical-colour synaesthesia, in which spoken words are experienced as coloured; and colour-touch synaesthesia in which colours are felt on specific locations of the body. Furthermore, coloured experiences in response to emotions or bodily sensations like pain, itches, and orgasms are not uncommon (Nielsen *et al.*, 2013).

It is unlikely that there is a single mechanism underlying all forms of colour synaesthesia. Even with the breadth of recent research and interest in the condition, the underlying mechanism is still unknown. Any accurate neural mechanism should accommodate at least two factors: whether the neural connection associating inducer and concurrent is direct or indirect, and whether this connection is structural or functional (Bargary and Mitchell, 2008; Ward, 2013). The first factor is concerned with whether unimodal brain regions interact by feed-forward mechanisms alone (direct) or whether they influence regions that influence other brain areas through feedback (indirect) (Ward, 2013). Both types of mechanisms exist in the neurotypical brain, but in synaesthesia they are aberrant compared to what we see in the normal brain (Driver and Noesselt, 2008; Ward, 2013). The second factor turns on whether neural networks that give rise to synaesthetic experiences have additional synaptic connections (structural) or merely exhibit excessive disinhibition or hyper-excitement of neurotypical connections through a change in neurotransmitters (functional) (Ward, 2013).

There has been an ongoing debate in philosophy about whether synaesthesia can provide any insight into the philosophical question of the nature of perception. There is some evidence suggesting that some forms of projector synaesthesia provide a challenge for direct representationalism, the view that the phenomenal character of perceptual experience ("what it is like to have the experience") is exhausted by how the experience represents the world. It has also sometimes been argued that synaesthesia presents a problem for functionalism, the view that a given type of mental state is definable by the role it plays in the cognitive system. However, a convincing watertight argument for this position has yet to be provided. Finally, synaesthesia may present a problem case for colour physicalism, the view that colours are surface spectral reflectances, i.e. the percentage of the light at each wavelength across the visible spectrum that is reflected by a surface (or disjunctions of these). In what follows I will begin by covering some research on grapheme-colour and sound-colour synaesthesia, two of the most common forms, and then look at some of the potential philosophical implications of these phenomena.

2 Neural mechanisms

While the precise neural mechanism underlying grapheme-colour synaesthesia is unknown, several hypotheses have been offered (Baron-Cohen *et al.*, 1993; Grossenbacher and Lovelace, 2001; Ramachandran and Hubbard, 2001a; Nunn *et al.*, 2002; Weiss *et al.*, 2005; Hubbard and Ramachandran, 2005; Hubbard *et al.*, 2005; Rouw and Scholte, 2007). The different proposed mechanisms can be divided into groups based on two factors: whether the mechanism responsible for the binding of colours to graphemes (or co-occurrence of colours and graphemes) operates directly or indirectly and whether such a mechanism suggests structural or functional differences from the neurotypical brain (Bargary and Mitchell, 2008; Rothen and Meier, 2009; Ward, 2013). In regard to the first factor, direct mechanisms take unusual connectivity to be the result of an atypical feed-forward connection between form processing areas and colour areas, whereas the indirect mechanisms suggest that the connectivity originates in aberrant feedback from, say, number or word processing areas to colour areas. In regard to the second factor, structural mechanisms take the cause of unusual connectivity to be the underlying brain structure whereas functional mechanisms take it to be grounded in a difference in how an otherwise neurotypically structured brain processes perceptual information through normal channels.

An influential hypothesis of the direct structural type is the local cross-activation hypothesis, according to which grapheme-colour synaesthesia is a genuine form of low-level perceptual experience that arises due to cross-activation between colour areas in the visual cortex and the adjacent visual word form area (Ramachandran and Hubbard, 2001a, 2001b; Hubbard *et al.*, 2005). This suggestion is inspired by the observation that local crossover phenomena may explain other illusory and hallucinatory experiences, such as phantom limb sensations (Ramachandran *et al.*, 1992; Ramachandran and Hubbard, 2003b). This model is most plausible as an explanation of developmental forms of projector synaesthesia, as these forms are most like ordinary visual perception neurologically and phenomenologically (Ramachandran and Hubbard, 2001a, 2001b). One data point suggesting that projector grapheme-colour synaesthesia is a genuine form of perception that arises as result of direct projection to the occipital cortex is brain imaging evidence. Several recent studies support the theory that the aberrant binding of features occurs via direct connectivity between the adjacent form and colour regions in areas overlapping the occipital cortex and the temporal lobe (Rouw and Scholte, 2007; Jancke *et al.*, 2009; Hanggi *et al.*, 2011; see also Zamm *et al.*, 2013).

Another data point comes from the phenomenology that projector grapheme-colour synaesthetes report in connection with their experiences (Brogaard, 2016). An overwhelming number of projectors report that their experiences are more like seeing that something is the case than imagining it, visualizing it or thinking about it. However, there is a variety of different ways in which they report experiencing the relationship between the inducer and the concurrent. Some report that they experience the concurrent as transparent and as being located just on top of the inducer grapheme's true colour. When asked to shift overt attention by moving their eyes without moving their head, some report that they experience the synaesthetic colour as staying in the same location just on top of the grapheme until it is out of sight. Others report that experiencing the concurrent as an after-image floating quite some distance above the grapheme or as a blob similar to the after-images that might float in front of your eyes following exposure to bright light. Some synaesthetes report that the transparent blob moves with their eyes the way that an after-image moves with your eyes when you shift your gaze. Others report the after-image-like blob as being locationally tied to the grapheme. There haven't yet been any scientific reports of synaesthetes who have claimed that they experience graphemes printed in back as instantiating both black and the concurrent colour in exactly the same way. The majority report not experiencing the concurrent colour as literally instantiated by the grapheme the way that the grapheme's true colour is instantiated. However, on rare occasions projector synaesthetes will insist that they "see" the concurrent colour as instantiated by grapheme, despite also insisting that they "see" it as hovering over the grapheme.

The best known hypothesis of the indirect functional type posits that the unusual crosstalk originates in feedback processes as a result of disinhibited feedback from an area of the brain that binds information from different senses (Armel and Ramachandran, 1999; Grossenbacher, 1997; Grossenbacher and Lovelace, 2001; Smilek *et al.*, 2001; Myles *et al.*, 2003). The main piece of evidence cited in favour of this hypothesis comes from an analogous case in which a patient PH reported seeing visual movement in response to tactile stimuli following acquired blindness (Armel and Ramachandran, 1999). As PH was blind and hence had impaired visual pathways, he could not have received the information via standard visual channels. It is plausible that the misperception was a result of disinhibited feedback from brain regions that receives information from other senses.

This model would explain why visual context and meaning typically influence the phenomenal quality of synaesthetic experience (Myles *et al.*, 2003; Dixon and Smilek, 2005, Brogaard *et al.* 2014, 2016). In Figure 12.2, for instance, some grapheme-colour synaesthetes assign different colours to the shared letter depending on whether they interpret the string of letters as spelling the word 'POT' or the word 'JACK'. For example, one of our child subjects, a 17-year old female, experiences the shared letter as lemon-coloured (**O**) when she reads the word 'pot' and as bright pink (**C**) when she reads the word 'Jack'. This suggests that it is not the shape of the letter that gives rise to the colour experience but the category or concept associated with the letter (Cytowic and Eagleman, 2009: 75).

The observation that the very same grapheme can elicit different colour experiences in synaesthetes depending on the context in which it occurs suggests that these individuals need to interpret what they visually experience prior to having a synaesthetic experience. There are other cases pointing to an indirect mechanism in some cases of the condition. Ramachandran and Hubbard (2003a) presented the sentence 'Finished files are the result of years of scientific study combined with the experienced number of years' to a subject and asked her to count the number of 'f's' in it. Most normal subjects count only three 'f's' because they disregard the high-frequency word 'of', and even though the synaesthete eventually spotted six 'f's', she initially responded the way normal subjects do. One explanation of this result is that high-level processing of low-level perceptual information is required for synaesthetic experience to occur.

There are also models that indicate that some cases of grapheme-colour synaesthesia may consist in special kinds of automatized memory associations (Brogaard *et al.*, 2014; Rothen and Meier, 2010, 2014; Ásgeirsson *et al.*, 2015). Brogaard *et al.* (2014) and Brogaard (2017) propose that the automatic association between graphemes and colours in some cases of the condition may be akin to the automatic association between smell and negative memories. For example, the smell of chlorine may automatically induce visual images of a particular negative event. In

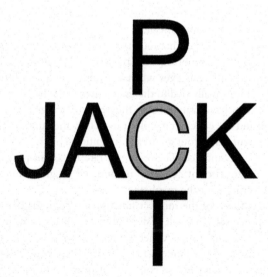

Figure 12.2 Synaesthetes interpret the middle letter as a 'C' when it occurs in 'Jack' and as an 'O' when it occurs in 'pot'. The colour of their synaesthetic experience will depend on which word the grapheme is considered a part of.

the case of smell, the tight association presumably is formed immediately as a result of the negative valence of the event. Presumably hyperactivation of the amygdala leads to the formation of connections between the adjacent olfactory bulb and visual areas.

On the memory model, synaesthesia is the result of an indirect mechanism (see Figure 12.3). The hippocampus would at some point have generated synaptic connections between visual colour and grapheme areas owing to the advantage of these conditions in early learning. Exposure to achromatic grapheme-stimuli might trigger both recognition of the grapheme *as* a particular grapheme (e.g. the numeral '2') and memory retrieval of synaesthetic colours to executive areas of the brain. The renewed activity in the colour areas taking place in order for memory retrieval of synaesthetic colour information to occur may simultaneously give rise to a conscious projection of synaesthetic colour from visual colour areas either via functional hyperactivity or structural changes in the visual cortex. In synaesthetes in which graphemes and colours truly are bound together to the extent that graphemes literally are seen as having colours, the hippocampus may be treating the distinct neural networks the way it normally would with form and colour that belong together (e.g. tomato and red). In cases in which the grapheme and colour are not tightly bound together, the hippocampus must be treating the neural networks more like involuntary quick associations, such as the association between the striking of a match and its being lit.

One virtue of the LTP model is that it straightforwardly can account for cases in which there is not a true binding of graphemes and colours. Some grapheme-colour synaesthetes report that graphemes merely are felt as inducers of colours either projected out into the world or seen in

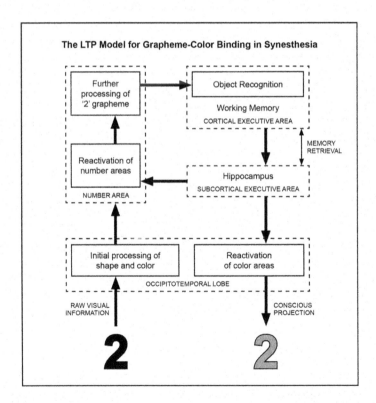

Figure 12.3 Graphic illustration of the LPT model for grapheme-colour binding in synaesthesia.
Source: from Brogaard *et al.* (2014).

the mind's eye. On the LTP model, information stored in memory about graphemes and their synaesthetic colours need not be as tightly connected as the characteristic features of objects (e.g. red hearts). There are also synaesthetes that merely know the colour of graphemes but have no corresponding visual experience associated with the grapheme. Ward (2013) suggests that the visual experience may have faded over the years (see also Tilot *et al.*, 2018). The LTP model offers a simple explanation of this type of fading. Memories tend to fade in their vividness over time. So, if synaesthetic binding is stored in memory, we should expect some fading to occur. Another virtue is that it can make sense of recent studies showing that in some cases grapheme colour-synaesthesia is triggered by exposure to the inducer-concurrent connections during early learning processes (Blake *et al.*, 2005; Hancock, 2006; Witthoft and Winawer, 2006, 2013; Meier and Rothen, 2015). In a widely debated study, Witthoft and Winawer (2013) looked at the letter-colour associations in 11 grapheme-colour synaesthetes whose letter-colour connections were remarkably similar. On the basis of battery tests, subjective reports, and market investigations, the researchers were able to provide strong evidence that the 11 subjects acquired their synaesthesia while learning the alphabet using refrigerator magnets. It's important to emphasize, however, that memory alone doesn't explain why only a small percentage of individuals who play with refrigerator magnets develop synaesthesia. Presumably individuals must already be predisposed to develop synaesthetic experiences, for example, by having hyperexcitable visual areas.

An independent model has been proposed for drug-induced sound-colour synaesthesia, the most common form of the drug-induced form of the condition (Brogaard, 2013). The suggestion is that drug-induced synaesthesia, like hallucinations, originates in hyperactivity in the occipital cortex. Psilocybin, the active ingredient in magic mushrooms, is one of the most commonly used drugs in studies of hallucinogens because its neurotransmitter activity is more specific than other hallucinogens, such as LSD. Psilocybin is believed to activate layer V pyramidal cells in the visual cortex, while destabilizing connections between visual areas and the thalamus (Kim and McCormick, 1998; Markram *et al.*, 2004). Projections from the visual cortex to the thalamus play a role in discriminating among incoming information and integrating information from different sensory channels. Destabilization of these connections can result in random information from the thalamus being processed in the hyperactivated visual areas. In normal multisensory perception, low-level multisensory binding of incoming signals from visual and auditory channels occurs spontaneously in the auditory cortex via thalamocortical feedback loops, when the spatial and temporal attributes of incoming signals match (Schroeder and Foxe, 2005). So, it is plausible that the random information from the thalamus is bound together with auditory information in the auditory cortex, resulting in experiences of coloured sounds (see Figure 12.4).

It is highly unlikely that there is just one correct model of synaesthetic association that applies to all forms of synaesthesia, or even colour synaesthesia. Most likely all the proposed models have some application to different cases of the condition. Synaesthesia, including colour synaesthesia, then is best thought of as an umbrella term covering a number of related but mechanistically and phenomenally distinct conditions (Simner, 2012).

3 Synaesthesia and strong representationalism

One of the reasons that philosophers have been interested in synaesthesia is that it may present a counterexample to a popular view about perceptual experience, known as 'representationalism' (see, e.g., Chalmers, 2004). Representationalism is the view that the phenomenal character of experience ("what it is like to have the experience") is exhausted by its representational

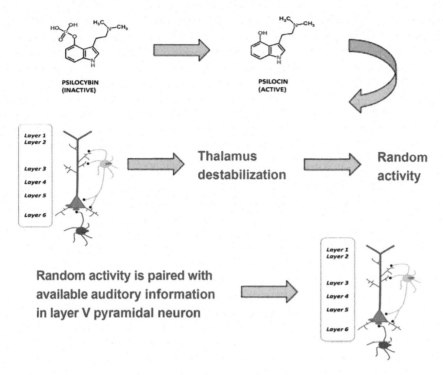

Figure 12.4 Psilocybin, which is inactive, is metabolized to the active ingredient psilocin. Psilocin then triggers a 5-HT2A serotonin receptor excitability response in layer V pyramidal neurons and an inhibitory response in GABAergic interneurons. This leads to thalamic destabilization, which triggers random thalamic activity. The occipitally processed random activity is paired with available auditory information in layer V pyramidal neurons, which yields synaesthetic experience.

Source: from Brogaard (2013).

content ("the information conveyed by the experience"); for a perceptual experience to have a phenomenal character just is for it to have a representational content (Dretske, 1995; Tye, 1995; Lycan, 1996, 2001). On this view, the phenomenal character supervenes on, or flows from, the representational content. So, it is not possible for two experiences that have the same representational properties to vary in their phenomenal properties. Like most naïve realists, representationalists ordinarily think that their theory should be able to accommodate illusory experiences, viz. experiences in which an external object is presented as having a property it does not have (Brewer, 2011). Unlike most naïve realists, however, representationalists hold that hallucinations are genuine perceptions (Tye, 2002).

As has been pointed out on many occasions in the past, synaesthesia seems to present a counterexample to representationalism (see, e.g. Wager, 1999, 2001; Rosenberg, 2004). Consider grapheme-colour synaesthesia as an example. Although inducer-concurrent pairings are not completely random, there is nonetheless still a considerable degree of idiosyncrasy in terms of which concurrents are triggered by which inducers. So, two synaesthetes who both perceive the number 3 printed in black may have synaesthetic experiences with different phenomenal properties. The grapheme may trigger an experience of blue in John but an experience of green in Mary. According to representationalism, John and Mary's experiences nonetheless represent an object with the very same properties, viz., *being the grapheme 3* and *being black*. As representationalism entails that two experiences with the same representational content have the same phenomenal properties, grapheme-colour synaesthesia presents a counterexample to this position. Or so the argument goes.

The argument, as it stands, is unconvincing, however. As Torin Alter (2006) has argued, there are countless ways that the representationalist might circumvent this simple argument. Since a number of synaesthetes do indeed perceive the inducer as instantiating the concurrent, their perceptual experience might be taken to represent the inducer as instantiating the concurrent. Of course, the inducer doesn't actually have the property in question, but if the experience can be properly said to represent it as having the property, then synaesthesia does not present a difficulty for representationalism. The experience can simply be taken to have an illusory property. So, synaesthesia, in general, does not present a counterexample to representationalism. A different argument is thus called for.

There is indeed a quite simple argument in support of the view that the phenomenology of certain forms of projector synaesthesia cannot be fully understood in terms of the experience's representational content (see Brogaard, 2016). I will first introduce a characteristic of ordinary visual experience inspired by Siegel's (2006) view that ordinary visual experience represents things as mind-independent (see Brogaard, 2018). The expanded criterion for the representation of mind-independence may be articulated as follows:

Mind-independent representation

S's experience represents property *F* as a mind-independent feature of her environment just in case:

(i) It phenomenally seems to *S* that *F* is in front of her eyes, or in her field of vision, as opposed to being a feature in her mind's eye.
(ii) If *S* closes her eyes, she no longer has an experience that represents property *F*.
(iii) If *S* moves her eyes without moving her head, it does not phenomenally seem to *S* as if *F* moves with her eyes.

Mind-Independent Representation entails that projector synaesthesia may represent a concurrent property without representing it as mind-independent. Consider one of our projector synaesthetes B. When B has a visual experience of the grapheme 3 printed in black, this triggers an experience of an after-image-like bitter-lime greenish-yellowish projection (Brogaard, 2016). B's synaesthetic experience satisfies condition (i): it phenomenally seems to B that the synaesthetic concurrent is in front of her eyes as opposed to being a feature in her mind's eyes. It also satisfies condition (ii): if B closes her eyes, she no longer has a synaesthetic experience that represents the synaesthetic concurrent. However, it does not satisfy condition (iii). If she moves her eyes without moving her head, it phenomenally seems to her that the synaesthetic concurrent moves with her eyes.

B's synaesthetic experience thus fails to represent the concurrent as mind-independent, except in the minimal sense of satisfying (i) and (ii). But this presents a problem for strong representationalism. Representationalism holds that the phenomenology of experience is exhausted by its representational content. This does not seem to hold for B's synaesthetic experience. Suppose we were to say that the relevant content of B's experience is *there is a bitter-lime greenish-yellowish volume floating some distance above the grapheme 3*.

This content, however, is not a genuinely representational content of the experience. A minimal constraint on genuine representational content is that it has truth-conditions. It can be true as well as false. Consider an illusory experience of a white table illuminated by red light.

Although the representational content *the table is red* is false, there are normal conditions in which it is true. For example, the content would be true, were you to paint the table. By contrast, there are no normal conditions in which someone has a veridical experience with the content *there is a bitter-lime greenish-yellowish volume floating some distance above the grapheme 3*. Granted, some bitter-lime greenish-yellowish smoke might happen to float above a grapheme 3, but the phenomenology of B's synaesthetic experience is not the same as the phenomenology of the experience of coloured smoke. Unlike B's synaesthetic experience, an experience of coloured smoke represents the coloured smoke as mind-independent. As B's synaesthetic experience and an experience of coloured smoke do not have the same phenomenology, representationalism predicts that they do not have the same content. As there are no normal conditions in which the content *there is a bitter-lime greenish-yellowish volume floating some distance above the grapheme 3* is true, it is not a genuinely representational content. So, the phenomenology of B's experience is not exhausted by its representational content.

Note that it is plausible that B's synaesthetic experience is best understood as a co-occurrence of a veridical experience of the inducer (the graphema printed in black) and a pure property hallucination triggered by the inducer (in the sense of Macpherson and Batty, 2016). This way of capturing the experience, however, is not a way for representationalists to bypass the objection, as they treat hallucinations as genuine perceptual experiences.

The representationalist may, however, attempt to ward off the objection by saying that synaesthesia is the result of a brain abnormality. Hence, we should not expect representationalism to be able to account for it. There are several problems with this sort of reply. It is widely acknowledged at least in the scientific community that a complete account of perception will require an account of projector synaesthesia, because at least some forms of projector synaesthesia are so similar neurologically and phenomenally to ordinary sensory perception that it would be ad hoc to rule it out on a priori grounds. Furthermore, it is doubtful that projector synaesthesia should be regarded as non-perceptual as opposed to a manifestation of perceptual variation across individuals.

4 Synaesthesia and functionalism

A second reason that philosophers have been interested in synaesthesia is that it may present a counterexample to a popular view about mental states, known as functionalism. Functionalism about the mind is the view that what makes something a particular kind of mental state depends on the way it functions in a cognitive or behavioral system (Hurley and Noë, 2003). A classical example in the literature is that of pain. A functionalist may treat pain as, for instance, any state which (normally) produces the belief that something is wrong with the body and a desire for the state to disappear and which tends to give rise to anxiety, moaning, whining, or screaming. If this functional role is played by C-fibre stimulation, then a person is in pain when she undergoes C-fibre stimulation. The functional role property is the property of having something occupy the pain role. So, role functionalists would identify the pain property with the functional role property itself, not the C-fibre stimulation. Realizer functionalists, on the other hand, identify pain with C-fibre stimulation.

Jeffrey Gray has argued that synaesthesia may provide a counterexample to functionalism about conscious mental states (Gray, 2003; Gray *et al.*, 1997, 2002, 2006). The idea is that the different sensory modalities are functionally distinct. For example, seeing is defined by a different function than hearing. But cases of synaesthesia show that one and the same type of colour experience can be the result of auditory processing or visual processing (Gray, 2003). As two distinct functions are associated with the same type of experience, synaesthesia shows that experience cannot be adequately functionally defined. Sound-colour synaesthesia present a further difficulty for the functionalist, it is argued, because functionally it is a kind of hearing but phenomenally it is both a kind of seeing and a kind of hearing. So, distinct experiences are defined by the same function.

The first argument attempts to show that one and the same experience can correspond to two distinct functional properties. As Fiona Macpherson points out, however, this is only a potential problem for views that take functions to be defining of experiences (Macpherson, 2007). But a functionalist might merely take experiences to supervene on functional properties. This would allow merely to rule out that the same function could correspond to distinct experiences but not that one and the same experience could involve different functions.

When thought of as ammunition against strong functionalism, the argument is equally problematic. It assumes that synaesthetic colour experiences are exactly similar to ordinary (illusory) colour experiences. It seems quite clear that they are not. Some forms of synaesthesia are not even sensory. But if we focus on the experiences that do seem to be sensory—those of projector synaesthetes—we have seen that many projectors do not experience the concurrent as instantiated by an external entity but is rather hovering over it or floating in from of their eyes like after-images (Brogaard, 2016, 2017; Brogaard *et al.*, 2014, 2016). Coloured hearing, too, comes in two distinct forms: projector and associator. Like grapheme-colour projectors, sound-colour projectors often describe the colours as floating in their visual field or hovering over the source of the sound. Few describe the colour as instantiated by the sound in the same way that pitch is instantiated by a musical note. So, it is in all likelihood incorrect that synaesthesia shows that *the same type* of sensory experience can involve distinct functional properties.

In making his argument Gray (2003) focuses on the colour qualia that are presented to subjects in synaesthetic experiences and normal experiences rather than the experiences in their entirety. It is perhaps the focus on qualia that prompts him to see synaesthesia as a counterexample to strong functionalism. As Gray puts it, "there should be no cases in which one quale is associated with two disparate functions. Yet that is just what happens in coloured-hearing synaesthesia. Colour qualia, affirmed by the synaesthete herself to be closely alike, occur in response to both heard words and seen coloured surfaces" (2003: 194). Focusing on qualia is unlikely to help, however. Qualia just are phenomenal properties. They are not the private, ineffable, intrinsic, and directly apprehensible features of experience that Daniel Dennett (1988) made a big deal out of rejecting. As we have seen in the previous section, phenomenal properties, such as phenomenal red and phenomenal green, are representational in cases of ordinary visual experience but not in reported cases of projector synaesthesia. Phenomenal colour properties in synaesthesia may even represent more richly than ordinary phenomenal colour properties. In colour-touch synaesthesia, for example, phenomenal colour properties represent colours and localized tactile pressure on the body. So, even if we redirect our focus from experience to qualia, we do not get the result that colour qualia in neurotypical individuals and synaesthetes are of the same kind.

The second argument, too, is also deeply problematic. It attempts to show that one and the same functional property can be instantiated by distinct experiences. In doing so, it makes the illicit assumption that sound-colour synaesthesia is a product of the realizer of ordinary auditory function or that it can be defined by the property of playing the auditory role. But as we have seen in the previous section, coloured hearing is likely the result of processing in both the auditory and visual areas. As auditory and visual neurons are the realizers of different functions in the case of colour-sound synaesthesia (auditory versus visual), coloured hearing cannot be defined solely in terms of the realizers of ordinary auditory function. Gray's argument does not fare any better if we assume that hearing is a functional role property. Coloured hearing functions very differently from ordinary hearing. For example, coloured hearing often facilitates perfect pitch, which is not something the average mature auditory system is capable of. In some reported cases coloured hearing has induced temporary impaired vision, or blindness, in very noisy environments, because the synaesthetic colours cloud up the visual field. So, if coloured and ordinary hearing can be defined by certain functional role properties, then the two instances of hearing correspond to different role properties. Gray's argument thus does not succeed in establishing that synaesthesia makes it impossible to define 'experience' functionally.

5 Synaesthesia and theories of colour

A third reason that philosophers have been interested in synaesthesia is that it may present a counterexample to a popular view about colours, known as colour physicalism (Armstrong, 1961, 1968; Hilbert, 1987; Tye, 2000; Byrne and Hilbert, 2003). This view is not always explicitly defended but is very often assumed in the philosophy of mind literature. One form of colour physicalism holds that colour properties are surface spectral reflectance properties. A surface spectral reflectance property is the percentage of the light at each wavelength across the visible spectrum that is reflected by a surface. One well-known problem for this view is that there exist so-called metamers. Metamers are objects with different surface spectral reflectance properties that appear to have the same colour under different illuminations. For example, a surface that has a peak in reflectance at 500 nm and a second peak at 650 nm gives rise to the same green colour appearance in daylight as a surface with a peak in reflectance around 550 nm. A version of physicalism that takes the colours to be surface spectral reflectance properties cannot explain this, as it would predict that metamers should have different colours.

Whereas Hilbert (1987) bites the bullet, Byrne and Hilbert (2003) avoid the problem of metamers by denying that colour types (e.g. red, yellow, green, and blue) are surface spectral reflectance properties. The colour types, they say, are sets of these surface spectral reflectance properties. So, metamers whose spectral properties correspond to those of monochromatic light of 580 nm and a mixture of light of 540 nm and 670 nm have the same colour, viz. unique yellow, because their reflectance properties belong to the same reflectance type, viz. that for unique yellow.

Colour synaesthesia, however, may present a more intricate challenge for colour physicalism than the issue of metamers (Brogaard, 2012, 2015). Some forms of synaesthesia seem to imply that there are colours that are not relevantly causally connected to any set of surface spectral reflectance properties, a scenario which seems to undermine colour physicalism. An example of this is the so-called Martian colours perceived by some synaesthetes, particularly colour blind synaesthetes (Ramachandran and Hubbard, 2003a). As these kinds of synaesthetic colours are never instantiated in the physical world, there is no set of surface spectral reflectance properties that regularly triggers them (for a more detailed argument, see Brogaard, 2015).

6 Conclusion

In this chapter I have argued that some forms of colour synaesthesia can be considered to be a genuine form of low-level perception. These experiences, I have argued, present a problem for representationalism, but not for functionalism. Colour synaesthesia also provides a challenge for colour physicalism, because it seems that there are synaesthetic colours that aren't causally connected to surface reflectance properties in the external environment and hence cannot be reduced to the latter.[1]

Note

1 For helpful comments and discussion, I am grateful to Hazel Anderson, Daniel Bor, Ophelia Deroy, Fiona Macpherson, Beat Meier, Nicolas Rothen, Thomas Alrik Sørensen, and audiences at Johns Hopkins University, NYU, and Stanford University.

References

Abraham, H. D. (1983). "Visual phenomenology of the LSD flashback", *Arch. Gen. Psychiatry*, 40, 884–9.

Afra, P., Funke, M., and Matuso, F. (2009). "Acquired auditory–visual synesthesia: A window to early cross-modal sensory interactions", *Psychol. Res. Behav. Manag.*, 2, 31–7.

Alstadhaug, K. B., and Benjaminsen, E. (2010). "Synesthesia and migraine: Case report", *BMC Neurol.*, 10, 121.

Alter, T. (2006). "Does synesthesia undermine representationalism?", *Psyche*, 12(5).

Anderson, H. P., Seth, A. K., Dienes, Z., and Ward, J. (2014). "Can grapheme-color synesthesia be induced by hypnosis?", *Front. Hum. Neurosci.*, 8, 220. 10.3389/fnhum.2014.0022.

Armel, K. C., and Ramachandran, V. S. (1999). "Acquired synesthesia in retinitis pigmentosa", *Neurocase*, 5, 293–6.

Armstrong, D. (1961). *Perception and the Physical World*, London: Routledge and Kegan Paul.

Armstrong, D. (1968). *A Materialist Theory of Mind*, London: Routledge and Kegan Paul.

Ásgeirsson, Á. G., Nordfang, M., and Sørensen, T. A. (2015). "Components of attention in grapheme-color synesthesia: A modeling approach", *PLoS ONE*, 10(8), e0134456. https://doi.org/10.1371/journal.pone.0134456.

Bargary, G., and Mitchell, K. J. (2008). "Synaesthesia and cortical connectivity", *Trends Neurosci.*, 31, 335–42.

Baron-Cohen, S., Wyke, M., and Binnie, C. (1987). "Hearing words and seeing colors: An experimental investigation of synesthesia", *Perception*, 16, 761–7.

Baron-Cohen, S., Burt, L., Smith-Laittan, F., Harrison, J., and Bolton, P. (1996). "Synaesthesia: Prevalence and familiality", *Perception*, 25, 1073–9.

Beauchamp, M. S., and Ro, T. (2008). "Neural substrates of sound-touch synesthesia following a thalamic lesion", *J. Neurosci.*, 28, 13696–702.

Blake, R., Palmeri, T. J., Marois, R., and Kim, C.-Y. (2005). "On the perceptual reality of synesthetic color". In L. C. Robertson and N. Sagiv (Eds.), *Synesthesia: Perspectives from Cognitive Neuroscience*. New York: Oxford University Press, 47–73.

Brewer, B. (2011). *Perception and Its Objects*, Oxford: Oxford University Press.

Brogaard, B. (2012). "Colour eliminativism or colour relativism?", *Philosophical Papers*, 41(2), 305–21.

Brogaard, B. (2013). "Serotonergic hyperactivity as a potential factor in developmental, acquired and drug-induced synesthesia", *Front. Hum. Neurosci.*, 7, 657. doi: 10.3389/fnhum.2013.00657.

Brogaard, B. (2015). "The self-locating property theory of color", *Minds and Machines*, 25(2), 133–47.

Brogaard, B. (2016). "Synesthesia as a challenge for representationalism". In W. Buckwalter and J. Sytsma (Eds.), *Blackwell Companion to Experimental Philosophy*, Oxford: Wiley-Blackwell, 306–17.

Brogaard, B. (2017). "Synesthetic binding and the reactivation model of memory". In O. Deroy (Ed.), *Sensory Blending: On Synaesthesia and Related Phenomena*, Oxford: Oxford University Press, 126–50.

Brogaard, B. (2018). *Seeing and Saying: The Language of Perception and the Representational View of Experience*, New York: Oxford University Press.

Brogaard, B., and Marlow, K. (2015). *The Superhuman Mind*, New York: Penguin/RandomHouse.

Brogaard, B., Vanni, S., and Silvanto, J. (2013). "Seeing mathematics: Perceptual experience and brain activity in acquired synesthesia", *Neurocase*, 19(6), 566–75.

Brogaard, B., Marlow K., and Rice, K. (2014). "The long-term potentiation model for grapheme-color binding in synesthesia". In D. Bennett and C. Hill (Eds.), *Sensory Integration and the Unity of Consciousness*, Cambridge, MA: MIT Press, 37–72.

Brogaard, B., Marlow K., and Rice, K. (2016). "Do synesthetic colors grab attention in visual search?", *The Review of Philosophy and Psychology*, 7(4), 701–14.

Byrne, A., and Hilbert, D. R. (2003). "Colour realism and colour science", *Behavioural and Brain Sciences*, 26, 3–21.

Chalmers, D. (2004). "The representational character of experience". In B. Leiter (Ed.), *The Future for Philosophy*, Oxford: Oxford University Press, 153–81.

Cohen Kadosh, R., Henik, A., Catena, A., Walsh, V., and Fuentes, L. J. (2009). "Induced cross-modal synaesthetic experience without abnormal neuronal connections", *Psychol. Sci.*, 20, 258–65.

Cytowic, R. E. (1989). *Synesthesia: A Union of the Senses*, New York: Springer Verlag.

Cytowic, R. E., and Eagleman, D. M. (2009). *Wednesday is Indigo Blue*, Cambridge, MA: MIT Press.

Dennett, D. C. (1988). "Quining qualia". In A. J. Marcel and E. Bisiach (Eds.), *Consciousness in Contemporary Science*, Oxford: Oxford University Press. Reprinted in W. Lycan (Ed.), *Mind and Cognition*, New York: Basil Blackwell, 1990, 519–47.

Dixon, M. J. and Smilek, D. (2005). "The importance of individual differences in grapheme-color synesthesia", *Neuron*, 45, 821–3.

Dixon, M. J., Smilek, D., and Merikle, P. M. (2004). "Not all synaesthetes are created equal: Projector versus associator synaesthetes", *Cogn. Affect. Behav. Neurosci.*, 4, 335–43.

Dretske, F. (1995). *Naturalizing the Mind*, Cambridge, MA: MIT Press.

Driver, J., and Noesselt, T. (2008). "Multisensory interplay reveals crossmodal influences on 'sensory-specific' brain regions, neural responses, and judgments", *Neuron*, 57, 11–23.

Eagleman, D. M., Kagan, A. D., Nelson, S. S., Sagaram, D., and Sarma, A. K. (2007). "A standardized test battery for the study of synesthesia", *Journal of Neuroscience Methods*, 159, 139–45.

Ffytche, D. H. (2007). "Visual hallucinatory syndromes: Past, present, and future", *Dialog. Clin. Neurosci.*, 9, 173–89.

Friedrichs, H. (2009). *Die Psychologie des Meskalinrausches*, Berlin: Verlag für Wissenschaft und Bildung.

Gray, J. A. (2003). "How are qualia coupled to functions?", *Trends in Cognitive Sciences*, 7(5), 192–4.

Gray, J. A., Williams, S. C. R., Nunn, J., and Baron-Cohen, S. (1997). "Possible implications of synaesthesia for the question of consciousness". In S. Baron-Cohen and J. Harrison (Eds.), *Synaesthesia: Classic and contemporary readings*, Cambridge, MA: Blackwell, 173–81.

Gray, J. A., Nunn, J., and Chopping, S. (2002). "Implications of synaesthesia for functionalism: Theory and experiments", *Journal of Consciousness Studies*, 9(12), 5–31.

Gray, J. A., Parslow, D. M., Brammer, M. J., Chopping, S. M., Vythelingum, G. N., and Ffytche, D. H. (2006). "Evidence against functionalism from neuroimaging of the alien colour effect in synaesthesia", *Cortex*, 42(2), 309–18.

Grossenbacher, P. G. (1997). "Perception and sensory information in synaesthetic experience". In S. Baron-Cohen and J. E. Harrison (Eds.), *Synaesthesia: Classic and contemporary readings*, Malden, MA: Blackwell Publishers, Inc., 148–72.

Grossenbacher, P. G., and Lovelace, C. T. (2001). "Mechanisms of synesthesia: Cognitive and physiological constraints", *Trends Cogn. Sci.*, 5, 36–41.

Hancock, P. (2006). "Monozygotic twins' colour-number association: A case study", *Cortex*, 42, 147–50.

Hanggi, J., Wotruba, D., and Jäncke, L. (2011). "Globally altered structural brain network topology in grapheme-color synesthesia", *J. Neurosci.*, 31, 5816–28.

Hilbert, D. (1987). *Colour and Colour Perception: A Study in Anthropocentric Realism*, Stanford, CA: CSLI.

Hintzen, A., and Passie, T. (2010). *The Pharmacology of LSD*, Oxford, New York: Oxford University Press.

Hubbard, E. M., and Ramachandran, V. S. (2005). "Neurocognitive mechanisms of synesthesia", *Neuron*, 48, 509–20.

Hubbard, E. M., Arman, A. C., Ramachandran, V. S., and Boynton, G. M. (2005). "Individual differences among grapheme-color synesthetes: Brain-behavior correlations", *Neuron*, 45(6), 975–85.

Hurley, S., and Noë, A. (2003). "Neural plasticity and consciousness", *Biol. Philos.*, 18, 131–68.

Jacobs, L., Karpik, A., and Bozian, D. (1981). "Auditory–visual synaesthesia: Sound-induced photism", *Arch. Neurol.*, 38, 211–16.

Jacome, E., and Gumnit, R. J. (1979). "Audioalgesic and audiovisuoalgesic synesthesias: Epileptic manifestation", *Neurology*, 29, 1050–3.

Jancke, L., Beeli, G., Eulig, C., and Hanggi, J. (2009). "The neuroanatomy of grapheme-color synesthesia", *Eur. J. Neurosci.*, 29, 1287–93.

Kim, U., and McCormick, D. A. (1998). "The functional influence of burst and tonic firing mode on synaptic interactions in the thalamus", *J. Neurosci.*, 18, 9500–16.

Lessell, S., and Cohen, M. M. (1979). "Phosphenes induced by sound", *Neurology*, 29, 1524–6.

Lycan, W. G. (1996). *Consciousness and Experience*, Cambridge, MA: Bradford Books/MIT Press.

Lycan, W. G. (2001). "The case for phenomenal externalism", *Philosophical Perspectives*, 15, 17–35.

Macpherson, F. (2007). "Synaesthesia, functionalism and phenomenology". In M. de Caro, F. Ferretti, and M. Marraffa (Eds.), *Cartographies of the Mind: Philosophy and Psychology in Intersection Series*: Studies in brain and mind (Vol. 4, pp. 65–80). Dordrecht, The Netherlands: Springer.

Macpherson, F., and Batty, C. (2016). "Redefining illusion and hallucination in light of new cases", *Philosophical Issues*, 26, 263–96.

Markram, H., Toledo-Rodriguez, M., Wang, Y., Gupta, A., Silberberg, G., and Wu, C. (2004). "Interneurons of the neocortical inhibitory system", *Nat. Rev. Neurosci.*, 5, 793–807.

Mattingley, J. B., Rich, A. N., Yelland, G., and Bradshaw, J. L. (2001). "Unconscious priming eliminates automatic binding of colour and alphanumeric form in synaesthesia", *Nature*, 410, 580–2.

Meier, B., and Rothen, N. (2015). "Developing synaesthesia: A primer", *Front Hum Neurosci.*, 2015, 9: 211. Published online 2015 Apr 20. doi: 10.3389/fnhum.2015.00211.

Myles, K. M., Dixon, M. J., Smilek, D., and Merikle, P. M. (2003). "Seeing double: The role of meaning in alphanumeric-colour synaesthesia", *Brain Cognition*, 53, 342–5.

Nielsen, J., Kruger, T. H. C., Hartmann, U., Passie, T., Fehr, T., and Zedler, M. (2013). "Synaesthesia and sexuality: The influence of synaesthetic perceptions on sexual experience", *Front. Psychol.*, 16 October 2013. doi: 10.3389/fpsyg.2013.00751.

Nunn, J. A., Gregory, L. J., Brammer, M., Williams, S. C. R., Parslow, D. M., *et al.* (2002). "Functional magnetic resonance imaging of synesthesia: Activation of V4/V8 by spoken words", *Nature Neuroscience*, 5, 371–5.

Ramachandran, V. S., and Hubbard, E. M. (2001a). "Psychophysical investigations into the neural basis of synaesthesia", *Proc. R. Soc. B Biol. Sci.*, 268, 979–83.

Ramachandran, V. S., and Hubbard, E. M. (2001b). "Synaesthesia: A window into perception, thought and language", *J. Conscious. Stud.*, 8, 3–34.

Ramachandran, V. S., and Hubbard, E. M. (2003a). "The phenomenology of synaesthesia", *Journal of Consciousness Studies*, 10, 49–57.

Ramachandran, V. S., and Hubbard, E. M. (2003b). "Refining the experimental lever: A reply to Shanon and Pribram", *Journal of Consciousness Studies*, 10, 77–84.

Ramachandran, V. S., Stewart, M., and Rogers-Ramachandran, D. C. (1992). "Perceptual correlates of massive cortical reorganization", *Science*, 258, 1159–60.

Rich, A. N., and Mattingley, J. B. (2002). "Anomalous perception in synaesthesia: A cognitive neuroscience perspective", *Nat. Rev. Neurosci.*, 3, 43–52.

Ro, T., Farne, A., Johnson, R. M., Weeden, V., Chu, Z., Wang, Z. J., *et al.* (2007). "Feeling sound after a thalamic lesion", *Ann. Neurol.*, 62, 433–41.

Rosenberg, G. (2004). *A Place for Consciousness: Probing the Deep Structure of the Natural World*, Oxford: Oxford University Press.

Rothen, N., and Meier, B. (2009). "Do synesthetes have a general advantage in visual search and episodic memory? A case for group studies", *PLoS ONE*, 4(4), e5037. https://doi.org/10.1371/journal.pone.0005037.

Rothen, N., and Meier, B. (2010). "Grapheme–colour synaesthesia yields an ordinary rather than extraordinary memory advantage: Evidence from a group study", *Memory*, 18(3), 258–64.

Rothen, N., and Meier, B. (2014). "Acquiring synaesthesia: Insights from training studies", *Front. Hum. Neurosci.*, 8, 109. 10.3389/fnhum.2014.00109.

Rouw, R., and Scholte, H. S. (2007). "Increased structural connectivity in grapheme-color synaesthesia", *Nat. Neurosci.*, 10, 792–7.

Sagiv, N., and Ward, J. (2006). "Crossmodal interactions: Lessons from synesthesia", *Prog. Brain Res.*, 155, 259–71.

Schott, G. D. (2012). "Pictures as a neurological tool: Lessons from enhanced and emergent artistry in brain disease", *Brain*, 135, 1947–63.

Schroeder, C. E., and Foxe, J. (2005). "Multisensory contributions to low-level, 'unisensory' processing", *Curr. Opin. Neurobiol.*, 15, 454–8.

Shanon, B. (2002). *The Antipodes of the Mind*, Oxford: Oxford University Press.

Shanon, B. (2003). "Three stories concerning synaesthesia: A commentary on the paper by Ramachandran and Hubbard", *J. Conscious. Studies*, 10, 69–74.

Shea, N. (2013). "Naturalising representational content", *Philosophy Compass*, 8(5), 496–509.

Siegel, S. (2006). "Subject and object in the contents of visual experience", *Philosophical Review*, 115(3), 355–88.

Simner, J. (2012). "Defining synaesthesia", *British Journal of Psychology* 103(1), 1–15.

Simner, J., Mulvenna, C., Sagiv, N., Tsakanikos, E., Witherby, S. A., Fraser, C., *et al.* (2006). "Synaesthesia: The prevalence of atypical cross-modal experiences", *Perception*, 35, 1024–33.

Sinke, C., Halpern, J. H., Zedler, M., Neufeld, J., Emrich, H. M., and Passie, T. (2012). "Genuine and drug-induced synesthesia: A comparison", *Conscious. Cogn.*, 21, 1419–34.

Smilek, D., Dixon, M. J., Cudahy, C., and Merikle, P. M. (2001). "Synaesthetic photisms influence visual perception", *Journal of Cognitive Neuroscience*, 13, 930–6.

Thomas-Anterion, C., Creac'h, C., Dionet, E., Borg, C., Extier, C., Faillenot, I., *et al.* (2010). "De novo artistic activity following insular-SII ischemia", *Pain*, 150, 121–7.

Tilot, A. K., Kucera, K. S., Vino, A., Asher, J. E., Baron-Cohen, S., and Fisher, S. E. (2018). "Rare variants in axonogenesis genes connect three families with sound–color synesthesia", *Proceedings of the National Academy of Sciences*, 2018; 201715492 doi: 10.1073/pnas.1715492115.

Tye, M. (1995). *Ten Problems of Consciousness: A Representational Theory of the Phenomenal Mind*, Cambridge, MA: The MIT Press.

Tye, M. (2000). *Consciousness, Colour, and Content*, Cambridge, MA: MIT Press.

Tye, M. (2002). "Representationalism and the transparency of experience", *Nous* 36(1), 137–51.

Wager, A. (1999). "The extra qualia problem: Synaesthesia and representationalism", *Philosophical Psychology*, 12(3), 263–81.

Wager, A. (2001). "Synaesthesia misrepresented", *Philosophical Psychology*, 14(3), 347–51.

Ward, J. (2013). "Synesthesia", *Annual Reviews of Psychology*, 64, 49–75.

Ward, J., and Wright, T. (2012). "Sensory substitution as an artificially acquired synaesthesia", *Neurosci. Biobehav. Rev.* doi: 10.1016/j.neubiorev.2012.07.007.

Weiss, P. H., Zilles, K., and Fink, G. R. (2005). "When visual perception causes feeling: Enhanced cross-modal processing in grapheme–color synesthesia", *Neuroimage*, 28, 859–68.

Witthoft, N., and Winawer, J. (2006). "Synesthetic colors determined by having colored refrigerator magnets in childhood", *Cortex*, 42, 175–83.

Witthoft, N., and Winawer, J. (2013). "Learning, memory, and synesthesia", *Psychological Science* Jan 10; doi: 10.1177/0956797612452573.

Zamm, A., Schlaug, G., Eagleman, D. M., and Loui, P. (2013). "Pathways to seeing music: Enhanced structural connectivity in colored-music synesthesia", *Neuroimage*, 74, 359–66.

13

SPECTRUM INVERSION

Peter W. Ross

Introduction

The fundamental idea of spectrum inversion is that the way a particular object looks with respect to colour can vary radically—as radically as the difference between what it's like to see red and green—between two perceivers in the same viewing conditions (or a single perceiver over time in similar viewing conditions). This idea can occur to people independent of philosophical or scientific discussion of colour and colour perception, often with an interest in whether such differences could be undetectable. The philosophical treatment of the spectrum inversion idea examines its presuppositions and its implications for accounts of colour and colour experience. In what follows, I'll focus on the current philosophical treatment of the spectrum inversion idea as this idea is expressed in a general form of argument, often called the inverted spectrum hypothesis. (Locke's use of the spectrum inversion idea is often noted as an important example of a philosophical treatment, but since Locke's theoretical purposes in using spectrum inversion were so different from current theoretical purposes, I'll set Locke's views aside; for a historical examination of Locke's purposes, see Allen, 2010.)

Characterized as a general form of argument, the inverted spectrum hypothesis has instances which compose a family of objections to certain kinds of account of colour experience. These objections are typically presented in thought experiments which envision a difference in colour experience as being radical and systematic, even while properties relevant to colour experience are the same. A simple illustration of the radical difference in colour experiences that these thought experiments present is this: suppose that two people see a particular ripe strawberry, and one (helpfully named Nonvert) experiences the strawberry as red (that is, as we experience ripe strawberries), while the other (helpfully named Invert) experiences the strawberry as green (that is, as we experience ripe limes). This radical difference in colour experience is systematic in that, for example, as they look at a variety of objects together, Invert experiences objects as red just in case Nonvert experiences them as green, and Invert experiences objects as green just in case Nonvert experiences them as red, and that this sort of inversion occurs for a wide range of colours. (One might presume that 'a wide range of colours' means every colour in the spectrum. The term 'spectrum inversion', while standard in the literature, is misleading. What's typically meant is a shift in the psychological colour space—a representation of qualitative relations among colours with respect to hue, saturation, and lightness—that flips one or both of the red-green and yellow-blue poles.)

As described so far, this instance of the hypothesis provides a challenge for an account of differences in colour experiences in terms of differences in the properties of objects experienced (for example, properties of the ripe strawberry) and viewing conditions (including lighting), since the differences in colour experiences occur while Nonvert and Invert are looking at the same object in the same viewing conditions. But the hypothesis has many other instances.

For example, the hypothesis is commonly presented in a thought experiment elaborated to suppose that relevant functional (or causal) properties of Nonvert's and Invert's colour experiences are the same despite their radical and systematic difference in colour experiences. Such functional properties include how perceivers interact with, think about, and communicate about red and green objects. To illustrate this further supposition, consider that Nonvert's experience caused by a French absinthe causes her to say "What a lovely green", while Invert's experience caused by the same absinthe causes him to say "What a lovely green", despite the radical difference in their colour experiences, and that, more generally, the difference in colour experience isn't manifested in anything that Nonvert and Invert say or do. This instance of the hypothesis provides a challenge for the standard functionalist account of colour experience, since differences in colour experience occur even while Nonvert's and Invert's colour experiences are equivalent in their causal relations to stimuli, other mental states, and behaviour, precisely the factors by which the standard functionalist account characterizes colour experience.

To set up a discussion of the inverted spectrum hypothesis and some of the main differences among its instances, I'll explain some terminology. By 'colour experience' I'll mean a kind of perceptual state. I'll assume that these states can be characterized as representational states, since this is widely assumed in the literature having to do with spectrum inversion. (By a 'representational state' I mean a mental state that conveys a content, that is, a way things are, where this content can be accurate or inaccurate.) Adopting useful terminology from Byrne and Hilbert (1997b and 1997c), I'll call the aspect of the experience often described as what it's like to be conscious of colour the 'colour-feeling' aspect, and I'll call the aspect of the experience of colour that represents colour as a property of objects the 'colour-representing' aspect (Shoemaker, 1982, pp. 647–8 draws the same distinction in terms of the qualitative character and the intentional content of colour experience; the colour-feeling aspect is sometimes called the phenomenal aspect). (Because some theorists who support the inverted spectrum hypothesis, for example, Ned Block, claim that the colour-feeling aspect of experience is ineffable and so cannot be specified in language as, for example, red feeling as opposed to green feeling, I won't use determinate colour terms—red, green, etc.—to express the colour-feeling aspect.)

The centre of attention for all instances of the inverted spectrum hypothesis is the colour-feeling aspect. All instances strive to show that the colour-feeling aspect cannot be accounted for in terms of some other properties relevant to characterizing colour experience, and all instances strive to show this by means of hypothesizing the separation of the colour-feeling aspect from these other properties.

However, there are two importantly different ways in which the inverted spectrum hypothesis is deployed, either objecting to a direct account of the colour-feeling aspect of colour experience in terms of some candidate non-qualitative property, or objecting to an account of the colour-feeling aspect in terms of the colour-representing aspect. According to the first type of objection, the colour-feeling aspect cannot be explained in terms of non-qualitative properties, in particular, some range of physical (including neurophysiological) or functional properties. In this case, instances of the hypothesis are used to distinguish the colour-feeling aspect from the candidate physical or functional property—as, for example, an instance was just used against the standard functionalist account of colour experience. Used this way, an instance of the hypothesis is a *direct objection* to an attempted account.

According to the other type of proposal, the colour-feeling aspect cannot be explained in terms of the colour-representing aspect (or, in other words, in terms of representational content, since the colour-representing aspect is characterized in terms of content); this type of account of the colour-feeling aspect is often called representationalism. By itself, representationalism does not claim that the colour-feeling aspect can be accounted for in non-qualitative terms. Thus, an objection to representationalism does not directly object to such an account. However, a well-known strategy for explaining the colour-feeling aspect in non-qualitative terms combines representationalism with an account of mental representation in functional terms (in particular, in terms of some specified causal relation that determines content) and an identification of colours included in content with physical properties of objects. (This strategy has been prominent recently, but it has been around at least since the 1960s; see, for example, Armstrong 1968/1993, and in particular pp. xviii–xix, and pp. xxi–xxii for a brief summary.) Instances of the inverted spectrum hypothesis are used to undermine this strategy by distinguishing the colour-feeling aspect from representational content. In this case, the route to an account of colour feeling in non-qualitative terms is blocked. When the inverted spectrum hypothesis is used in this way, it is an *indirect objection* to the attempt at a non-qualitative account.

After explaining the reasoning involved in use of instances of the hypothesis as direct objections in section 1 and as objections to representationalism in section 2, I'll briefly take up the issue of the kind of possibility involved with the hypothesis in section 3 and the methodologies used to assess possibilities in section 4. I'll then describe some general considerations that are commonly used against the inverted spectrum hypothesis in section 5, and in section 6 I'll discuss attempts to support it with findings from colour science. I'll end with an opinionated conclusion.

1 Direct objections to non-qualitative accounts of colour feeling

Many theories of the nature of mind since the second half of the twentieth century attempt to account for mind in physical or functional terms, and so attempt to account for colour experience—a kind of mental state—in these terms. In offering an explanation of colour experience, each of these attempts has faced its own instance of the inverted spectrum hypothesis. I'll centre my discussion on instances opposing different versions of functionalism.

1.1 The inverted spectrum thought experiment

Consideration of spectrum inversion typically involves a thought experiment. Such thought experiments have been depicted in many ways, but the gist is to suppose circumstances which make plausible the claim that while some range of properties relevant to characterizing colour experience are the same, the colour-feeling aspect can vary. When the inverted spectrum hypothesis is used directly against an attempted account of colour feeling in non-qualitative terms, the range of properties is some specified range of physical or functional properties offered to explain the colour-feeling aspect. As I'll explain in section 2, when the hypothesis is used against representationalism, the range of properties is a range of colour-representing properties (characterized in terms of content) offered to account for the colour-feeling aspect.

Ned Block offers a widely known presentation of the inverted spectrum thought experiment (I'll focus on his 2007, pp. 91–100 presentation of the thought experiment, but this presentation is similar to those in his 1990, pp. 681–2, and his 1994, p. 516; also, it is interesting to see the similarity in general outline between Block's presentation and Armstrong's 1968/1993, pp. 259–60). The thought experiment involves putting you, the reader, in the shoes of a subject of an experimental colour inversion surgery, and the story is intended to get you to consider a series of events from the first-person perspective. (Block's 2007 presentation can be used against functionalism, as Block notes on p. 93 and as I'll discuss in this section, but its primary aim is to argue for the existence of ineffable colour-feeling aspects of experience, which Block calls colour qualia (2007, p. 74). In section 2, I'll give additional background for the argument for ineffable colour-feeling aspects.)

At Stage 1 of the thought experiment you are a normal colour perceiver. As a normal colour perceiver, your colour experiences are veridical (or accurate) in normal viewing conditions. (In this context, veridicality has to do with accurately identifying the determinate colour attributed to objects—as red or green, for example. This claim need not conflict with eliminativist views, which, as Boghossian and Velleman, 1989, pp. 98–101 contend, can give an account of the veridicality of colour attribution.)

Stage 2 occurs a day after (elective) colour inverting surgery (which, as far as Block's description specifies, flips the red-green poles of the psychological colour space). At this point, some things seem to have changed colours. It seems that ripe strawberries have turned green, but your experiences of red and green are not veridical; red things look as green things had before the surgery, and green things looks as red thing had.

Decades later, at Stage 3, red things still look as green things had before the surgery, and you acknowledge this as an odd sort of colour illusion. In the meanwhile, a few years after the surgery, to fit in with your peers' use of colour language, you *say* that red things are red, even though they still look as green things used to look. Thus, you effortfully mimic your pre-surgical use of colour language. Eventually, mimicking becomes effortless, and your beliefs about red things, as well as your experiences of red things in normal viewing conditions, become red representing. But you continue to acknowledge that red things look as green things had prior to the surgery. Thus, even though your experiences of red objects are red representing, you still acknowledge that you have an odd sort of colour illusion.

Finally, yet another decade later at Stage 4, you develop amnesia with respect to the period of time up to Stage 3, and thus you have no memory of the surgery or the way things had looked prior to it with respect to colour. You continue to say that red things are red, and so you continue to effortlessly mimic your pre-surgical behaviour, and your experience continues to be red representing. But, since you no longer remember the surgery or the way things used to look, you no longer acknowledge that red things look the way green things had looked. Consequently, even though you are still colour inverted, there's no difference between your thought and talk about colour and a normal colour perceiver's. You are, Block claims, a normal perceiver again (2007, p. 94).

This thought experiment can be expressed as a general form of argument. Given a range of properties A that's offered to account for the colour-feeling aspect of colour experience, the thought experiment advances the hypothesis that:

1   Colour experiences of ripe strawberries are equivalent with respect to A at Stages 1 and 4, and
2   colour experiences of ripe strawberries at Stage 4 are inverted relative to colour feeling at Stage 1.

If an instance of this hypothesis objecting to an attempted account of colour feeling is plausible, it provides a powerful counterexample to the account.

1.2 *Formulation of direct objections to particular accounts of colour feeling*

Direct objections to particular accounts of the colour-feeling aspect are formulated by replacing A in the argument form with the range of non-qualitative properties proposed by the particular account. For example, the standard version of functionalism replaces A with causal relations of experience to stimuli, other mental states, and behaviour. Thus, the objection to the standard version of functionalism is that at Stages 1 and 4, colour experiences of ripe strawberries are equivalent in their causal relations to stimuli, other mental states, and behaviour, but inverted with respect to colour feeling.

Of course, for this objection to be convincing it has to be plausible that at Stages 1 and 4, colour experiences are inverted with respect to colour feeling. But, arguably, this is plausible. Block's presentation of the thought experiment differs from the presentation involving Nonvert and Invert in that it has you think through a series of events from the perspective of your experience—that is, *intra*-subjectively—so that the events of the thought experiment can be considered from the first-person perspective. And an inversion of the colour-feeling aspects of your experience seems to be a plausible description of what your experience would be like as a result of the surgery (2007, p. 81; 1990, pp. 681–2). In addition, the first-person perspective seems to be authoritative about the colour-feeling aspect of actual experience, as well as authoritative about what the colour-feeling aspect would be in the supposed circumstances.

Also, for the objection to be convincing the functional equivalence at Stages 1 and 4 has to be plausible. Again, arguably, it is plausible. Since at Stage 4 you mimic the thought and talk of a normal colour perceiver, it seems plausible that causal relations of your colour experiences to stimuli, other mental states, and behaviour are equivalent at Stages 1 and 4 (Block, 1990, p. 681). (Empirical findings that the human psychological colour space is irregularly shaped have been used to argue that colour-inverted human perceivers would not be functionally equivalent. I'll describe this argument in section 5.)

Crucial to this equivalence in functional properties is the epistemological idea of undetectability. Spectrum inversion is commonly specified as involving undetectable inversion, where undetectability is used as evidence of the equivalence of colour experiences with respect to A, the range of properties that are proposed to account for the colour-feeling aspect. Since the replacement of A differs with different instances of the hypothesis, the relevant undetectability does as well. Against the standard version of functionalism, undetectability is often specified with respect to a range of properties that's detectible in ordinary situations, in particular, behaviour such as verbal communication about coloured objects (Shoemaker, 1982, pp. 648–9). For example, in Block's argument against the standard version of functionalism, undetectability is with respect to such behaviour. In contrast, undetectability is not with respect to neurophysiological properties, since these properties are not detectable in ordinary situations, and Block allows that inversion is neurophysiologically detectable (2007, p. 86; also see Shoemaker, 1982, pp. 648, 651–4 for this position).

But if one is convinced that the objection to the standard version of functionalism succeeds, the hypothesis allows for exploration with respect to alternative replacements for A. In particular, A can be replaced by alternative functionalist characterizations of colour experience.

For example, while Austen Clark accepts that the standard functionalist characterization is vulnerable to the inverted spectrum hypothesis (1993, pp. 200–2), he proposes a different functionalist characterization of colour experience which is both limited to causal relations among states in the head and scientifically informed. Clark claims that long-arm functionalism (called long arm because its characterization of mental states includes stimuli and behaviour; see Block, 1990, p. 680 for this terminology) fails because the same external stimulus can produce radically different colour experiences. He points out, however, that even if the same stimulus can produce (subtly or radically) different colour experiences among human perceivers (or the same perceiver over time), perceivers share largely the same qualitative similarity relations among colour experiences (such as that an experience of red is qualitatively more like an experience of orange than it is like an experience of green) (1993, pp. 169–70). This intersubjective similarity is the basis for Clark's short-arm functionalism, where explanations of qualitative similarity relations are to be provided in terms of psychophysics and neurophysiology. Furthermore, Clark contends that such an explanation of qualitative similarity relations provides an explanation of the colour-feeling aspect of experience (1993, pp. 202–9).

Yet it's not clear that Clark's short-arm functionalism does explain the colour-feeling aspect of experience. The relations among internal states described in scientific terms might explain qualitative similarity relations, but without capturing the individual (or determinate) colour feelings that are related. Thus it seems that at Stages 1 and 4, colour experiences equivalent in their internal causal relations could be inverted in their colour-feeling aspects. (For criticisms of this sort, see Chalmers, 1996, p. 235; Levine, 2001, pp. 97–8, 100.)

Conceding aspects of the standard functionalist account in a different way, Sydney Shoemaker's classic article, "The Inverted Spectrum" (1982), precedes Clark in proposing to explain the qualitative similarity relations among colour experiences in terms of functional properties (realized in neurophysiology). Shoemaker's considerations in favour of explaining qualitative similarity relations are not scientific, but rather considerations about the effects of qualitative similarities and differences on beliefs and behaviour (the sorts of beliefs and behaviour that a science such as psychophysics can employ as evidence in the attempt to develop a scientific account of colour experience). Nevertheless, Shoemaker concedes that an explanation of qualitative similarity relations doesn't capture the individual (or determinate) colour feelings related, and that an instance of the inverted spectrum hypothesis, where colour experiences are equivalent with respect to qualitative similarity relations but inverted in colour feeling, shows that functionalism fails to account for individual colour feelings (1982, pp. 650–1). However, Shoemaker claims that the individual colour-feeling aspects of experience are identifiable with neurophysiological properties (1982, pp. 651–2).

An objection to Shoemaker's account is that scientific descriptions of neurophysiological properties don't seem sufficient for *explaining* the colour-feeling aspect any more than do scientific descriptions of internal causal relations. It seems that a description of a neurophysiological property doesn't tell us why one has an experience with one determinate colour feeling rather than another (see Chalmers, 1996, pp. 99–101 for this point).

Furthermore, the inverted spectrum hypothesis can be used against neurophysiological identity. To see this, modify Block's thought experiment as follows: at a post-op examination at Stage 3, your neurosurgeon is astonished to find that your brain's plasticity has managed to reverse the inversion surgery. But, even so, red things continue to look as green things had before the surgery. Consequently, it seems that at Stages 1 and 3, colour experiences that are physically identical could be inverted in colour feeling. (Stage 4 gets dropped, since your testimony claiming colour inversion plus the examination attesting to neurophysiological identity is all that's needed to make the point.) This instance of the inverted spectrum hypothesis pushes us toward the claim that the colour-feeling aspect of experience is a non-physical property.

1.3 Spectrum inversion and the explanatory gap

Nevertheless, many who support use of the inverted spectrum hypothesis against functionalism—Block and Shoemaker, for example—also hold fast to the claim that colour-feeling aspects are identifiable with neurophysiological properties, and so don't consider use of the inverted spectrum hypothesis against neurophysiological identity to be plausible. In order to better understand why, it is helpful to make a connection between the inverted spectrum hypothesis and the so-called problem of the explanatory gap.

As Joseph Levine, the primary formulator of the problem of the explanatory gap, poses this problem: it seems there can be no explanation of the colour-feeling aspect in physical or functional terms. (By 'explanation', Levine has in mind the deduction of what is to be explained from scientific laws. Applied to the colour-feeling aspect of experience, this would involve a deduction of colour feeling from scientific laws. However, what is involved in explanation is controversial. See Levine, 2001, pp. 70–6 for a brief discussion.)

Levine thinks of the inverted spectrum hypothesis as a manifestation of the problem of the explanatory gap, and so as an *epistemological* problem for materialism about mind, as opposed to a reason to reject materialism altogether (2001, pp. 78–9). According to this way of understanding the inverted spectrum hypothesis, materialism, and in particular neurophysiological identity, is plausible (for example, due to reasons presented by Levine, 2001, chapter 1); nevertheless, the colour-feeling aspect of colour experience is strongly resistant to explanation in neurophysiological terms.

2 Objections to representationalism

So far, I've discussed the inverted spectrum hypothesis as a direct objection to theories that attempt to explain the colour-feeling aspect of experience in terms of some range of physical or functional (and so non-qualitative) properties. Against representationalism—which accounts for the colour-feeling aspect of experience in terms of representational content—the inverted spectrum hypothesis is not a direct objection to an explanation of colour feeling in non-qualitative terms. Representationalism by itself does not offer an account of colour feeling in non-qualitative terms, but rather leaves open both whether mental representation and whether colours included in content can be accounted for in physical or functional terms.

One version of representationalism accounts for the colour-feeling aspect in terms of the colour-representing aspect to the extent that a difference in colour feeling requires a difference in the colour-representing aspect. Thus, the idea is that the colour-feeling aspect of experience supervenes on the colour-representing aspect. A more ambitious claim, which is the focus of a great deal of the discussion of representationalism in the literature, is so-called strong representationalism, which claims that the colour-feeling aspect of experience is identified with the colour-representing aspect. (In what follows, what I'll mean by 'representationalism' is the supervenience thesis, unless stated otherwise.)

Those who support representationalism form a motley group. Many supporters of *strong* representationalism, including David Armstrong (1968/1993), Fred Dretske (1995), William Lycan (1996), and Michael Tye (2000), try to explain the colour-feeling aspect of experience in physical or functional (and so non-qualitative) terms by proposing a functional account of mental representation along with an identification of the colours included in content with physical properties of objects (Dretske, 1995, p. 72 and pp. 88–90, gives a brief statement of this strategy).

But not all supporters of representationalism have this aim. For example, Shoemaker claims that colour experience represents not only colours (understood as physical properties of objects) but also phenomenal properties (or appearance properties) which are dispositional properties of objects to cause colour experiences, and Shoemaker holds that the colour-feeling aspect supervenes on phenomenal properties. Thus, he accepts a version of representationalism.

Nevertheless, Shoemaker allows for spectrum inversion, by contending that experiences with the same objective-colour-representing aspects can have inverted phenomenal-colour-representing aspects. And, appealing to the explanatory gap, Shoemaker denies that the colour-feeling aspect can be explained in physical or functional terms while holding that it can be identified with neurophysiological properties (2000, pp. 458–9).

In addition, Jeff Speaks (2011) defends representationalism against the inverted spectrum hypothesis, but at the same time offers a strategy for arguing that neither the colour-feeling nor colour-representing aspects can be explained in physical or functional terms. Along with defending representationalism, he considers whether instances of the hypothesis can be used as *direct* objections to the explanation of the colour-feeling aspect of experience in physical or functional terms (2011, p. 357). If a particular direct objection is plausible, then this objection combined with representationalism can be used as an objection to a physical or functional explanation of the colour-*representing* aspect. Against an account of the colour-representing aspect, the objection can apply to its physical or functional account of mental representation (2011, pp. 358–9).

On the other side of the debate, philosophers who use the inverted spectrum hypothesis against representationalism often accept that mental representation can be explained in physical or functional terms, but claim that the colour-feeling aspect cannot be explained in this way. Therefore, their contention is that the colour-feeling aspect cannot be accounted for in terms of the colour-representing aspect. For these philosophers, the objection to representationalism is motivated by the same concern as that which motivates the direct objection to a functionalist account of colour feeling: the colour-feeling aspect of experience cannot be explained in physical or functional—and so non-qualitative—terms. But since the objection opposes representationalism rather than accounts of colour feeling in physical or functional terms, its opposition to the latter accounts is indirect.

The objection against representationalism can be stated using the same argument form as that used as a direct objection, namely the hypothesis that:

1   Colour experiences of ripe strawberries are equivalent with respect to A at Stages 1 and 4, and
2   colour experiences of ripe strawberries at Stage 4 are inverted relative to colour feeling at Stage 1.

Against representationalism, A is replaced by some range of colour-representing properties (characterized in terms of content) that is offered to account for the colour-feeling aspect of experience. Plausible instances of this argument provide counterexamples to representationalism. Against even the representationalist supervenience claim, they show that a difference in colour feeling (the inversion) is consistent with sameness of the colour-representing aspect of experience.

To successfully press an instance of the inverted spectrum hypothesis against representationalism, it has to be plausible that at Stages 1 and 4, colour experiences are inverted with respect to colour feeling. And again, from the first-person perspective, the inversion seems plausible.

However, for an instance of the objection to be successful, it also has to be plausible that colour experiences are representationally equivalent (that is, equivalent in content) at Stages 1 and 4. In particular, it has to be plausible that the colour-representing aspect doesn't simply invert along with the colour-feeling inversion. If the colour-representing aspect does invert, then the colour-representing and colour-feeling aspects co-vary. In this case, the suggestion is that the colour-representing aspect accounts for the colour-feeling aspect, and that representationalism is correct.

If the colour-representing aspect does invert along with the colour-feeling inversion, experience comes to *misrepresent* the colours of things (given the strawberry is red, not green). Thus, use of the inverted spectrum hypothesis against representationalism involves giving reasons that your experience *doesn't* misrepresent colours at Stage 4 relative to Stage 1, supporting the idea that the colour-representing *hasn't* inverted. Consequently, the inverted spectrum hypothesis against representationalism is often put in terms of colour inversion without misrepresentation. (In this section, I'll focus on general considerations about representational equivalence without taking up exploration of alternative replacements for A. I'll take up that dimension of variation in connection with the Inverted Earth thought experiment in section 2.1.)

But support for the claim of colour inversion without misrepresentation is controversial. Going back to Block's description of the inverted spectrum thought experiment, if an instance of the hypothesis is used against representationalism, it is crucial that at Stage 4 (after amnesia has struck) your experience of red things isn't illusory. Block tries to establish that your experience of red things isn't illusory at Stage 4 by arguing that at this stage you are a normal colour perceiver again.

According to Block, being a normal colour perceiver cannot be characterized in terms of colour feeling—which he claims is ineffable—but instead in terms of colour representing (2007, p. 82). Normal colour perceivers are perceivers who acquire colour terms in the normal way (2007, p. 80). In his (2007) presentation of the inverted spectrum thought experiment, Block appeals to what he calls the Principle of Normality. This principle states that normal perceivers in normal viewing conditions perceive veridically (2007, p. 94). But from Block's standpoint that is just to say that the standard for accurate application of colour terms is set by people who have acquired colour terms in the normal way. Abnormal perceivers, by contrast, are perceivers for whom "color terms have to be used relative to normality" (2007, p. 94). An example of an abnormal perceiver is a person who, as a result of colour inversion surgery, says 'red things look green'. This does not indicate that red things produce green-feeling experiences in the colour-inverted perceiver—'green' doesn't express the green-feeling aspect of experience. Instead, it indicates that for the colour-inverted perceiver, red things produce the feeling that green things used to produce prior to the colour inversion surgery. Assuming that the colour-inverted perceiver had been a normal colour perceiver prior to the surgery, the colour-inverted perceiver— if aware of the colour-inversion—uses colour terms relative to normality. At Stage 4, amnesia dispenses with your awareness of colour inversion. Thus, you no longer use colour terms relative to normality. You are a normal colour perceiver.

However, Block's Principle of Normality won't be acceptable to many representationalists (Block, 2007, p. 84, notes it would be acceptable to Shoemaker). In particular, representationalists need not think that colour illusion is judged relative to normality. Thus, Armstrong (1968/1993, p. 258) argues that even if the population of colour perceivers was evenly split between two radical and systematic differences in colour experience, one of the groups would be misrepresenting colour, even though in this situation considerations about normality wouldn't help determine which group (1968/1993, p. 258). According to Armstrong, what determines which group is misrepresenting is the colour of objects, which is a mind-independent matter (1968/1993, p. 260). But whether, and in what sense, colour is a mind-independent property is controversial.

In the context of a wide-ranging defence of representationalism against the inverted spectrum hypothesis, David R. Hilbert and Mark Kalderon (2000, section 4) argue that there are no arguments which succeed in showing that an inversion in colour-feeling aspects of experience wouldn't be accompanied by an inversion in colour-representing aspects. Consequently, they claim that there is no reason to accept that there is colour inversion without misrepresentation.

At the same time, it's difficult to *support* the claim that misrepresentation accompanies colour inversion. To make a claim of misrepresentation compelling, a representationalist requires independent justification in terms of a theory of mental representation or a theory of colour, or both, and these sorts of theory are (as just noted with respect to Armstrong's theory of colour) controversial.

2.1 The Inverted Earth thought experiment

Block has sought to bring more clarity to the debate with a related thought experiment which he calls the Inverted Earth thought experiment. To aid understanding of this elaborate thought experiment, I'll start by describing its aim in contrast with the aim of the inverted spectrum thought experiment (as it is used against representationalism). The aim of the inverted spectrum is to make plausible the idea that colour experiences could be the same in their colour-representing aspects but inverted in their colour-feeling aspects. The aim of the Inverted Earth thought experiment is to make plausible the converse: that colour experiences could be the same in their colour-feeling aspects but inverted in their colour-representing aspects.

The Inverted Earth thought experiment is tailored to the latter aim. Inverted Earth is a place where everything *has* inverted colours—ripe strawberries are green (and unripe ones are red), the sky is yellow, and so on. Also, on Inverted Earth, colour language is systematically switched so that red is referred to by the word 'green' and yellow is referred to by the word 'blue', and so on. The thought experiment proceeds as follows: asleep one night, you are abducted by Inverted Earthlings and transported to Inverted Earth. While unconscious during the trip, you have been given 'inverting lenses'. When you awake, you have no awareness of the trip or the lenses, and you have been fitted into an environment that (apart from colours) matches your home environment. As far as you are aware, you had an ordinary night's sleep (perhaps with some odd dreams). Most pertinently, due to the combination of inverted colours and inverting lenses, as well as the switched colour language, everything about colours seems normal (Block, 1990, pp. 682–3).

In your early days on Inverted Earth, when you look at a ripe strawberry, you see it as red, and say and think 'what a bright red'. But you are misrepresenting its colour, which is in fact green. According to Block, it is plausible (given his assumed theory of mental representation, which I'll describe below) that the colour-representing aspect of your experience, as well as your representation of colour in thought and speech, will eventually shift to be in line with your environment. After perhaps a decade, even though your inverting lenses continue to invert the colour-feeling aspects of experience, when you see ripe strawberries, your representation of their colour by experience, thought, and speech will match that of your Inverted Earth companions. When this occurs, the thought experiment advances the Inverted Earth hypothesis that:

1 Colour experiences of ripe strawberries are the same with respect to colour-feeling aspects on Earth and Inverted Earth, and

2 colour experiences of ripe strawberries are inverted with respect to A on Earth and Inverted Earth.

(Note that instances of this form are counterexamples to the idea that a difference in the colour-representing aspect of experience requires a difference in colour feeling. This is the converse of the representationalist supervenience claim stated earlier. However, such counterexamples still count against strong representationalism. Also, it's easy to formulate a counterexample to the representationalist supervenience claim with Inverted Earth resources: the colour-representing aspect of your experience of ripe strawberries on Earth is equivalent to that of your experience of ripe limes on Inverted Earth (where, of course, limes are red), but these experiences are inverted in colour feeling.)

For this new objection to be convincing, it has to be plausible that colour experiences are inverted with respect to representational content. As Block presents the thought experiment, he replaces A—the range of colour-representing properties characterized in terms of content—with the normal causes in your environment of colour experience. Thus, Block assumes a normal cause theory of mental representation (where the normal cause of mental states determines content; in Block's presentation, deference to your linguistic community on Inverted Earth also plays a role in determining content) (1990, p. 683). But A need not be replaced this way.

While it's true that Block's normal cause theory of mental representation would have it that the colour-representing aspect of your experience would eventually conform to the environment and linguistic community of Inverted Earth, alternative theories of mental representation would not. Thus, exploration can commence with respect to A's alternative replacements. According to Dretske's (1995) theory, contents are not determined by normal causes of colour experience, but by causes which colour experience has an evolutionarily determined biological function to represent. This content does not change with your long stay on Inverted Earth, since the evolutionarily determined biological function doesn't change, and your experiences' colour-representing aspects will not invert. However, there are objections to Dretske's theory of content. Furthermore, as Fiona Macpherson (2005) argues, any theory of content determination for experience will have to mesh with a theory of content determination for belief. If one were to accept a theory of content determination of experience that gets around the Inverted Earth thought experiment by disallowing an inversion in content on Inverted Earth, but also hold a theory of content determination for *belief* that allows an inversion in belief contents on Inverted Earth, then it seems that when beliefs invert and so come to correctly attribute colours to objects, one's reports of one's current colour experiences (which haven't inverted) become false. For example, when one's beliefs eventually come to correctly attribute green to ripe strawberries (which are green on Inverted Earth), and one is asked the colour of ripe strawberries, one will say—expressing an introspective belief—that they look red (which means green on Inverted Earth). But then this report of one's experience is false—beliefs attribute green while the colour experience hasn't inverted in colour-feeling or colour-representing aspects. Yet it seems implausible that introspective beliefs could be systematically wrong about current colour experience (Macpherson, 2005, p. 138; but see Hilbert and Kalderon, 2000, section 4(b) for a response to this sort of worry).

For the Inverted Earth hypothesis to be convincing, it also has to be plausible that colour experiences are the same with respect to colour-feeling aspects on Earth and Inverted Earth. The events of the thought experiment are to be considered intra-subjectively, and from the first-person perspective, the sameness of colour feeling—that you wouldn't notice any change in the colour feeling on Inverted Earth—seems plausible.

2.2 Some strengths of the Inverted Earth hypothesis compared to the inverted spectrum hypothesis

What clarity does the Inverted Earth thought experiment bring to the debate? Block claims that a major advantage of Inverted Earth over the inverted spectrum thought experiment is that in addition to your first-person testimony of sameness in colour feeling, we can also suppose that you are *physically* the same in relevant ways on Earth and Inverted Earth (1990, p. 684). Here, Block appeals to a supervenience claim called phenomenal internalism, which claims that colour feeling supervenes on internal physical properties. Since this claim implies that perceivers who are the same with respect to internal physical properties must be the same with respect to the colour-feeling aspects of their experiences, it supports (1) of the Inverted Earth hypothesis. Thus, the Inverted Earth thought experiment brings some clarity to the extent that phenomenal internalism is plausible.

Also, this supervenience claim can be used to support the claim that there is a plausible *inter-subjective* version of the Inverted Earth hypothesis. If Nonvert (on Earth) and Invert (on Inverted Earth) are physically the same, phenomenal internalism holds that they have the same colour feeling (1990, p. 686). Since a comparison in colour feeling between perceivers cannot be made on the basis of introspection, this significantly strengthens the case for (1) of an inter-subjective version of the hypothesis—again, to the extent that phenomenal internalism is plausible.

3 What kind of possibility is involved?

Because the thought experiment has us consider a hypothetical, it has us consider a possibility rather than (what's known to be) an actuality. Because attempts to account for the colour-feeling aspect of experience are metaphysical—they offer a proposal about the nature of colour experience—the kind of possibility that's focused on in the literature is typically metaphysical possibility. (Metaphysical possibility is often characterized by contrast with logical possibility and possibility according to scientific laws, called nomological possibility. Accordingly, metaphysical possibility includes all nomological possibilities, but excludes some logical possibilities due to the nature of things.) The idea is that a proposal about the nature of colour experience rules out certain situations as metaphysically impossible. If what the proposal rules out is plausibly found to be metaphysically possible, then that indicates that the proposal is mistaken.

Some discussions of the hypothesis suggest that consideration of metaphysical possibility is merely an indulgence in ignorant speculation. C. L. Hardin (1997, pp. 299–300) suggests this attitude. But if it is his attitude, it is too dismissive toward the role of considering metaphysical possibilities in philosophy. Metaphysical theories are, in fact, distinguished from science in part by the depth of our ignorance of the subject matter. But with respect to issues such as the nature of the colour-feeling aspect of experience, we face a combination of deep ignorance and compulsion to attempt a better understanding. Metaphysical theories help to advance thinking about problems which, due to our ignorance, are scientifically intractable, so that they might eventually become scientifically tractable (see Ross and Turner, 2013, pp. 4247–50 for general characterization of the distinction between philosophical and scientific existence problems). Since we aren't at a point where the colour-feeling aspect of experience is scientifically tractable, it is important to consider whether certain metaphysical possibilities are plausible.

It might be that Hardin's point isn't that we shouldn't *consider* metaphysical possibilities, but that proposed possibilities need to be constrained by findings from colour science. If that is his point, it is one about methodology, which I'll take up in the next section.

Block asserts the stronger claim that spectrum inversion is nomologically possible. He contends that spectrum inversion can be achieved by switching the pigments of the M and L cones, and, he points out, colour science indicates that this switching of pigments is nomologically possible. Thus, he claims that there is scientific support for the inverted spectrum hypothesis (2007, p. 86, pp. 97–9). I'll say more about this in section 6.

4 What kind of methodology is involved in affirming a possibility as being plausible?

When should we consider the claim that a situation is metaphysically possible to be plausible? One methodological approach characteristic of philosophical theorizing is use of armchair methods. A common armchair method is the use of conceptual analysis in addressing problems, and this method can be conspicuous when thought experiments are used to set the stage for conceptual analysis. In philosophy of mind, another armchair method involves use of introspection as an authoritative source of information about the nature of mind. Over the past number of decades, philosophy of mind, and philosophy of colour and colour perception in particular, has largely moved away from addressing problems solely through armchair methods. In the philosophical literature on colour and colour perception, C. L. Hardin (and especially his 1988/1993) has been a leader in this shift away from exclusive use of armchair methods by incorporating scientific findings from psychophysics and neuroscience into his philosophical work. Thus, current standard methodology includes use of scientific findings mixed with use of armchair methods.

However, there are important disagreements about methodology, a prominent one being with respect to the authority of introspection. The use of introspection is standard, and presumably ineliminable in addressing questions about the nature of the mind. But the question remains whether introspection is authoritative about the nature of the mind—and, in particular, about the nature of the colour-feeling aspect of experience—and has an authority that trumps science. This question is important with respect to the inverted spectrum hypothesis because from the standpoint of introspection, it seems quite plausible that colour-feeling aspect of an experience can be varied while its physical or functional properties remain constant. If introspection is considered authoritative about the nature of the colour-feeling aspect, the plausibility of the inverted spectrum hypothesis might be taken to mark an insuperable limit on science with respect to the mind. The visual scientist Stephen E. Palmer provides a clear statement of the view, which is held by many philosophers, that introspection is authoritative with respect to colour feeling (1999a, pp. 627–8), and he argues that this authority does set a potentially insuperable limit on science, which he calls the subjectivity barrier (1999a, pp. 656–63; also see Palmer, 1999b for a more complete presentation of Palmer's views, and see the peer commentary and Palmer's responses that follow this article for a useful discussion).

But many philosophers consider introspection to often be misleading about the nature of the mind, and so judge it to not be authoritative about the nature of the colour-feeling aspect of experience. These philosophers are sceptical that introspection of the colour-feeling aspect of experience can establish a potentially insuperable limit on science, and treat the plausibility of the inverted spectrum hypothesis as an indicator of how misleading introspection can be about the nature of the mind when it has not yet been understood scientifically (Rosenthal, 1999, pp. 149–52 states this scepticism about the authority of introspection). Given that one's attitude toward the authority of introspection provides a basis for one's judgements about the plausibility of the inverted spectrum hypothesis, the basis for these judgements is disputed.

5 Common considerations against the inverted spectrum hypothesis

A common general objection to the inverted spectrum hypothesis is an epistemological worry about undetectability (this objection is general because it applies to the hypothesis used either as a direct objection or as an objection to representationalism). As Shoemaker (1982, p. 648) explains, the relevant undetectability in the context of the instance of the hypothesis used against the standard version of functionalism is behavioural undetectability, not neurophysiological undetectability. Even so, if there are behaviourally undetectable inversions in colour feeling among people, then it seems that the problem of other minds—the problem of knowing if and when you have mental states of the same types as others—is a serious problem. As Shoemaker admits, behavioural differences are the ordinary ways in which we detect others' mental states (1982, p. 648). If brain science is needed to know other minds, we don't have the knowledge of other minds we think we have. And if a lack of knowledge of other minds seems implausible, this provides a serious objection to the inverted spectrum hypothesis.

Shoemaker's response is that the epistemological problem does not apply to aspects of mental states that are functionally characterized and so (on the standard version of functionalism) are characterized in part by behaviour. Thus, beliefs, desires, the colour-representing aspect of experience, and even (for Shoemaker) qualitative similarity relations among colour experiences, are behaviourally detectable. The only aspect of mind to which behavioural undetectability applies, and thus the only place where the problem of other minds gets a grip, is with respect to the colour-feeling aspect of experience. Shoemaker (1982, p. 656) admits the problem but emphasizes that this is a limited problem of other minds.

Another common general objection to the hypothesis contends that according to colour science any inversion would in fact be detectable. Since the undetectability of inversion is used as evidence for either the functional or representational equivalence required for the hypothesis to be plausible, detectability leaves the required equivalence unsupported.

As noted in the Introduction, what's called spectrum inversion is typically taken to be a shift in the psychological colour space where either the red-green poles are flipped, the yellow-blue poles are flipped, or both. However, Hardin (1997) explains that according to colour science, the human psychological colour space is irregularly shaped (also see Hilbert and Kalderon, 2000, section 6.1 for this explanation). For example, the yellow and blue regions of the colour space are not symmetrical. A saturated yellow is much lighter than a saturated blue (Hardin, 1997, pp. 296–7; Palmer, 1999a, p. 626). Thus, Invert's inversion of saturated yellow and saturated blue would be detectable—for Nonvert a saturated yellow of a lemon is lighter than a saturated blue of a blueberry, but for Invert, the blueberry would be lighter than the lemon.

However, Palmer (1999a, p. 626) claims that this asymmetry could be corrected by inverting black and white along with yellow and blue, and that in any case, a red-green inversion would work better since saturated red and green are not grossly different in lightness. Justin Broackes (2007) argues to the contrary that saturated red and green are different enough in lightness to make an inversion detectable, and thus that a correction on the white-black axis would also have to accompany red-green inversion (p. 173). But, Broackes argues, any inversion of white and black would be detectable. (Palmer, 1999a, p. 626, note 2, seems to dismiss detectability of white-black inversion, but says very little to support this point.) The upshot, according to Broackes, is that the science of colour and colour perception indicates that any colour inversion very likely would be detectable.

One response to this objection is that the inverted spectrum hypothesis provides a tool to get at the nature of the colour-feeling aspect of experience. Our actual visual systems have various contingent characteristics that might mislead us about the nature of colour feeling. Thus, considerations about the nature of colour feeling should not be limited to considerations about our actual visual systems (Shoemaker, 1982, pp. 648–9; Block, 1990, pp. 683–4).

Another general objection to the inverted spectrum hypothesis, as well as an objection to the Inverted Earth hypothesis, targets the assumption of phenomenal internalism (that is, the claim that the colour-feeling aspect of experience supervenes on perceivers' internal physical properties). Phenomenal internalism is denied by phenomenal externalism, which holds that the supervenience base of the colour-feeling aspect encompasses both external and internal physical properties. Phenomenal externalism, held by many strong representationalists including Dretske (1995), Lycan (1996), and Tye (2000), claims that it is possible for perceivers with the same internal physical properties to have experiences with different colour-feeling aspects, due to being related to different external physical properties of objects, such as reflectance properties of their surfaces. If this is the case, it might be that perceivers with systematically switched neuro-physiological properties (as is supposed with colour-inverting surgery) do not undergo an inversion in colour feeling at all. Instead, switched neurophysiological properties provide different physical realizations of colour experiences, the colour-feeling aspects of which are determined at least in part by physical properties of objects in perceivers' surroundings (Byrne and Hilbert, 1997c, p. 271 note this problem for the inverted spectrum hypothesis). Interestingly, if this objection is right, my description of Nonvert and Invert in the second paragraph of the Introduction was already misguided, for it indicated that the physical properties of strawberries play no role in determining colour feeling. I'll discuss the debate between phenomenal internalism and phenomenal externalism further in relation to the use of colour science to support the inverted spectrum hypothesis.

6 The use of colour science to support the inverted spectrum hypothesis

Palmer (1999a, p. 626) claims that a behaviourally undetectable red-green inversion is plausible from the standpoint of colour science. In support of this, he points out that the psychological colour space is not grossly asymmetrical with respect to flipping the red-green poles. In addition, he claims that an important factor in the scientific plausibility of red-green inversion is that "a good biological argument can be made that there should be some very small number of seemly normal trichromats who should be red-green reversed" (Palmer, 1999a, p. 626). According to Palmer, a biological case can be made for what's called pseudonormal vision as well as for spectrum inversion.

A widely accepted neurophysiological explanation of red-green blindness is that genetic abnormalities result in the M and L cones containing the same photopigment, rendering red and green indiscriminable. As it turns out, M and L cones contain the same photopigment sometimes because the photopigment normally contained in the M cones is also contained in the L cones, and sometimes because the photopigment contained in the L cones is also contained in the M cones. With the right combination of genetic abnormalities, the photopigments in the M and L cones could switch. The condition of this switch is called pseudonormal vision (Boynton, 1979, p. 356; Nida-Rümelin, 1996, pp. 99–100; Palmer, 1999a, pp. 626–7). This condition has not been detected (Palmer, 1999a, p. 627), but its possibility is supported by widely accepted science. This science indicates that pseudonormal vision is nomological possible, and, as Palmer indicates, that it is likely actual.

Nevertheless, pseudonormal vision by itself does not imply that this science indicates that *spectrum inversion* is likely actual. Instead, as Palmer makes admirably clear, phenomenal internalism is also needed to conclude that pseudonormal vision results in red-green inversion (1999a, p. 662; also see Nida-Rümelin, 1999, p. 571). But how do we decide the debate between phenomenal internalism and phenomenal externalism? Martine Nida-Rümelin claims that phenomenal internalism is fundamental to colour science, and so the success of colour science provides substantial support for it (1999). But this isn't so. Phenomenal internalism is a claim about the nature of the colour-feeling aspect (or other qualitative-feeling aspect) of experience. While colour scientists such as Palmer make claims about colour feeling, their claims are not grounded in science; as I stated in section 4, Palmer's claims assume controversial philosophical views about the authority of introspection. We don't know enough about the nature of colour feeling for it to be scientifically tractable.

Palmer's biological argument is plausible for pseudonormal vision. But the argument for red-green inversion is not a biological argument (see Ross, 1999a and 1999b for more discussion of this point).

6.1 An opinionated conclusion

Many supporters of the inverted spectrum hypothesis, for example, Block and Shoemaker, use the hypothesis to argue (directly, indirectly, or both) that the colour-feeling aspect of experience cannot be explained in non-qualitative terms. Nevertheless, by relying on independent support for materialism, they claim that colour feeling is a neurophysiological property. Spectrum inversion is, for them, a manifestation of the problem of the explanatory gap understood as an epistemological problem rather than a reason to deny a materialist theory of mind. Many theorists find this combination of a materialist metaphysics and the explanatory gap attractive.

However, independent support for materialism is controversial, making identification of colour feeling with a neurophysiological property vulnerable to the inverted spectrum. For example, Block (1994, p. 517) appeals to phenomenal internalism as independent support for materialism, but phenomenal internalism isn't an adequate defence of materialism for property dualists such as Chalmers. Indeed, Chalmers uses the inverted spectrum hypothesis to argue that materialism is false.

Alternatively, materialists can object to phenomenal internalism from the standpoint of phenomenal externalism. I'll conclude with some remarks from the standpoint of phenomenal externalism. From this standpoint, the problem of the explanatory gap, at least in its standard formulation, is mistakenly framed. In its standard formulation, the problem of the explanatory gap concerns how the colour-feeling aspect of experience can be explained in *internal* physical or functional terms, that is, it assumes phenomenal internalism. However, according to phenomenal externalism, the physical properties of external objects are part of what makes a visual experience red-feeling as opposed to green-feeling. If external properties are left out, the problem is mistakenly framed.

If physical properties of external objects are part of what makes a visual experience red-feeling as opposed to green-feeling, then phenomenal externalism must explain how external physical properties are involved in making that difference. Whether an explanation is possible has yet to be seen. From the standpoint of phenomenal internalists who assume that introspection is authoritative about the nature of the colour-feeling aspect of experience, phenomenal externalism will seem like a non-starter. Since introspection isn't authoritative about the nature of external physical properties, phenomenal externalism might even seem perverse from this standpoint. But the view that introspection is authoritative about the nature of colour-feeling is controversial, and questioning its authority might be necessary for explaining colour feeling in non-qualitative terms. If this turns out to be the right direction, then the inverted spectrum will serve as a reminder of how misleading introspection can be about the mind.

Acknowledgements: I am tremendously grateful to Derek Brown for helpful comments, and to Janet Levin for extremely valuable feedback on two drafts of this chapter.

References

Allen, Keith (2010). "Locke and the Nature of Ideas", *Archiv für Geschichte der Philosophie*, Volume 92, Issue 3 (January 2010): 236–55.

Armstrong, D. M. (1968). *A Materialist Theory of the Mind*. Revised Edition 1993. London: Routledge.

Block, Ned (1990). "Inverted Earth", *Philosophical Perspectives, 4: Action Theory and Philosophy of Mind*, edited by James E. Tomberlin. Atascadero, Cal.: Ridgeview Publishing Company, 53–79. Reprinted in Block, Flanagan, and Güzeldere, 1997, 677–93. Page numbers refer to reprint.

Block, Ned (1994). "Qualia", in *A Companion to the Philosophy of Mind*, edited by Samuel Guttenplan. Oxford: Blackwell Publishers, 514–20.

Block, Ned (2007). "Wittgenstein and Qualia", *Philosophical Perspectives*, Volume 21, Issue 1 (December 2007): 73–115.

Block, Ned, Owen Flanagan, and Güven Güzeldere (Editors) (1997). *The Nature of Consciousness: Philosophical Debates*. Cambridge, Mass.: The MIT Press.

Boghossian, Paul A. and J. David Velleman (1989). "Colour as a Secondary Quality", *Mind*, Volume 98, Number 389 (January 1989): 81–103. Reprinted in Byrne and Hilbert, 1997a, 81–103.

Boynton, Robert M. (1979). *Human Color Vision*. New York: Holt, Rinehart and Winston.

Broackes, Justin (2007). "Black and White and the Inverted Spectrum", *The Philosophical Quarterly*, Volume 57, Number 227 (April 2007): 161–75.

Byrne, Alex and David R. Hilbert (Editors) (1997a). *Readings on Color, Volume 1, The Philosophy of Color*. Cambridge, Mass.: The MIT Press.

Byrne, Alex and David R. Hilbert (1997b). "Introduction", in Byrne and Hilbert (1997a), xi–xxviii.

Byrne, Alex and David R. Hilbert (1997c). "Colors and Reflectances", in Byrne and Hilbert (1997a), 263–88.

Chalmers, David J. (1996). *The Conscious Mind: In Search of a Fundamental Theory*. New York: Oxford University Press.

Chalmers, David J. (Editor) (2002). *Philosophy of Mind: Classical and Contemporary Readings*. New York: Oxford University Press.

Clark, Austen (1993). *Sensory Qualities*. Oxford: Clarendon Press.

Dretske, Fred (1995). *Naturalizing the Mind*. Cambridge, Mass.: The MIT Press.

Hardin, C. L. (1988). *Color for Philosophers: Unweaving the Rainbow*. Revised Edition 1993. Indianapolis: Hackett Publishing.

Hardin, C. L. (1997). "Reinverting the Spectrum", in Byrne and Hilbert (1997a), 289–301.

Hilbert, David R. and Mark Eli Kalderon (2000). "Color and the Inverted Spectrum", in *Color Perception: Philosophical, Psychological, Artistic and Computational Perspectives*, edited by Steven Davis. Oxford: Oxford University Press, 187–214.

Levine, Joseph (2001). *Purple Haze: The Puzzle of Consciousness*. Oxford: Oxford University Press.

Lycan, William G. (1996). *Consciousness and Experience*. Cambridge, Mass.: The MIT Press.

Macpherson, Fiona (2005). "Colour Inversion Problems for Representationalism", *Philosophy and Phenomenological Research*, Volume LXX, Number 1 (January 2005): 127–52.

Nida-Rümelin, Martine (1996). "Pseudonormal Vision: An Actual Case of Qualia Inversion?" *Philosophical Studies*, Volume 82, Number 2 (May 1996): 145–57. Reprinted in Chalmers, 2002, 99–105. Page numbers refer to reprint.

Nida-Rümelin, Martine (1999). "Intrinsic Phenomenal Properties in Color Vision Science: A Reply to Peter Ross", *Consciousness and Cognition*, Volume 8, Number 4 (December 1999): 571–4.

Palmer, Stephen E. (1999a). *Vision Science: Photons to Phenomenology*. Cambridge, Mass.: The MIT Press.

Palmer, Stephen E. (1999b). "Color, Consciousness, and the Isomorphism Constraint", *Behavioral and Brain Sciences*, Volume 22, Number 6 (December 1999): 923–43.

Rosenthal, David M. (1999). "Sensory Quality and the Relocation Story", *Philosophical Topics*, Volume 26, Numbers 1 and 2 (Spring and Fall 1999): 321–50. Reprinted in his *Consciousness and Mind*, 1995, Oxford: Oxford University Press, 149–74. Page numbers refer to reprint.

Ross, Peter W. (1999a). "Color Science and Spectrum Inversion: Further Thoughts", *Consciousness and Cognition*, Volume 8, Number 4 (December 1999): 566–70.

Ross, Peter W. (1999b). "Color Science and Spectrum Inversion: A Reply to Nida-Rümelin", *Consciousness and Cognition*, Volume 8, Number 4 (December 1999): 575–6.

Ross, Peter W. and Dale Turner (2013). "Existence Problems in Philosophy and Science", *Synthese*, Volume 190, Issue 18 (December 2013): 4239–59.

Shoemaker, Sydney (1982). "The Inverted Spectrum", *Journal of Philosophy*, Volume 79, Number 7 (August 1982): 357–81. Reprinted in Block, Flanagan, and Güzeldere, 1997, 643–62. Page numbers refer to reprint.

Shoemaker, Sydney (2000). "Introspection and Phenomenal Character", *Philosophical Topics*, Volume 28, Issue 2 (Fall): 247–73. Excerpt reprinted in Chalmers, 2002, 457–72. Page numbers refer to reprint.

Speaks, Jeff (2011). "Spectrum Inversion without a Difference in Representation Is Impossible", *Philosophical Studies*, Volume 156, Issue 3 (December 2011): 339–61.

Tye, Michael. (2000). *Consciousness, Color, and Content*. Cambridge, Mass.: The MIT Press.

14

INTERSPECIES VARIATIONS

Keith Allen

Colour vision varies significantly across the animal kingdom, and these differences raise a number of interesting and important philosophical questions about the nature of colour and colour perception. After outlining some of the salient differences in §1, §2 considers their bearing on the question of what colour vision is. §3 considers the implications of interspecies differences for our account of what colours are. Finally, §4 considers the nature of conscious experience, and 'what it is like' to perceive colour as members of different species do.

1 Interspecies variations

There are a number of ways in which colour vision differs between species. First, animals differ physiologically in the number of types of photoreceptor (differing in the region of the electromagnetic spectrum to which they are sensitive) that their eyes contain.[1] Some animals, such as octopuses and sea mammals, have retina that contain only one type of photoreceptor. Animals with only one type of photoreceptor are generally considered to lack colour vision altogether, since they are, at a minimum, unable to distinguish differences in light intensity from differences in light wavelength (see §2). Many animals have eyes that contain two types of photoreceptor, including many species of mammal and certain types of 'colour blind' human. 'Normal' human retina contain three types of cone; the same is also true of many primates and bees. Members of other species, however, have eyes with four or more photoreceptor types: for example, goldfish and pigeons have four types of photoreceptor, some butterflies have at least five types, and mantis shrimp appear to have at least twelve.[2]

Second, different species differ in the nature and extent of their sensitivity to the electromagnetic spectrum. Humans are sensitive to light of around 400–700nm. Some species, including honeybees and jumping spiders, are sensitive to light in the ultra-violet region of the electromagnetic spectrum (lower than 400nm); some species, such as sturgeon, are sensitive to light in the infra-red region of the electromagnetic spectrum (over 700nm); and some species, including pigeons and turtles, are sensitive to light in both the ultra-violet and the infra-red regions of the electromagnetic spectrum (Kelber *et al.* 2003). At the same time, different species also differ in the 'amount' or acuity of their sensitivity at different parts of the spectrum. For instance, whereas humans normally tend to have greatest wavelength discrimination around 470nm and 580nm, for bees it is around 400nm and 490nm, for goldfish it is around 400nm, 500nm, and 610nm, and for pigeons it is around 390nm, 450nm, 540nm, and 600nm (Thompson *et al.* 1992: 10).

Third, different species differ psychophysically in the 'dimensionality' of their colour vision. Dimensionality is defined in terms of the number of spectral lights that are needed to match any given spectral light. The dimensionality of a visual system is typically related to the number of photoreceptor types that the eye contains: monochromats normally have one type of photo-receptor, dichromats normally have two types of photoreceptor, trichromats three, and so on. However, although the dimensionality of colour vision cannot exceed the number of receptor types the eye contains, the number of receptor types that an organism's eye contains does not necessarily correlate straightforwardly with the dimensionality of its colour vision. For instance, although some species have retina that contain five or more types of photoreceptor, it is unclear whether their colour vision (or indeed, any colour vision systems) are pentachromatic or greater: different photoreceptor types may be used as parts of distinct mechanisms, as in the case of the swallowtail butterfly (*Papilio xuthus*) which has eight types of photoreceptor but uses only four for colour discrimination (Koshitaka *et al.* 2008; Kelber and Osorio 2010).

Fourth, different species are likely to differ in the way that the signals from their retinal recep-tors are processed. In humans, the outputs of the three types of photoreceptor are processed in opponently organized psychophysical channels. This results in a colour space standardly repres-ented by the three dimensions of hue, saturation, and brightness (or lightness), and in which there is a fundamental distinction between *elementary* colours (the hues green, blue, yellow, red, and the achromatic colours black, and white) some instances of which are phenomenologically 'pure' or 'unique', and *compound* colours (such as orange, cyan, chartreuse, brown, and grey) all instances of which appear to be composed of unique instances of the elementary colours. It cannot simply be assumed that differences in the dimensionality of a visual system will correspond to the number of dimensions needed to represent the associated quality space. But it seems reasonable to suppose that whilst some species will perceive properties that have a quality space that can be represented using two dimensions, others may perceive properties that have quality spaces that can be repres-ented using four, or more, dimensions. Correspondingly, these quality spaces will presumably contain more elementary colours and a larger set of compound colours. Indeed, they might even contain different types of colours: whereas human colour space contains binary hues—like orange, cyan, chartreuse, and purple—which appear to be phenomenal mixtures of two unique hues, a four dimensional colour space might contain ternary hues, which would appear to be phenomenal mixtures of three unique hues—the equivalent of seeing something as a phenom-enal mixture of red, yellow, and green (e.g. Thompson *et al.* 1992: 15).

2 What is colour vision?

Are these variations across the animal kingdom variations in *colour* vision? Early researchers into the visual abilities of other species often struggled to convince their contemporaries that non-human animals possessed colour vision (Kelber and Osorio 2010: 1621). Although colour vision is now widely attributed to other species, exactly what colour vision *is*—and hence which species possess it—remains controversial.

Colour vision is often operationally defined in the empirical literature as involving, at a minimum, an ability to respond to differences in the wavelength of stimuli independent of differences in their relative intensity (e.g. Menzel 1979; Goldsmith 1991; Kelber *et al.* 2003; this operational definition was employed by von Frisch in his pioneering work on bees and fish in the early twentieth century, cf. Kelber and Osorio 2010: 1617). According to this definition, monochromats, with only one type of photoreceptor, lack colour vision.[3]

The bare ability to discriminate light on the basis of wavelength is a widely accepted necessary condition for possessing colour vision, but it is more controversial whether it is sufficient. First, some plants, bacteria, and fruit sorting machines would count as having colour vision by this criterion: for instance, some species of plants avoid shade by comparing the ratio of red to far red light (Skorupski and Chittka 2011: 251). However, it is doubtful that these things have *vision*, let alone colour vision. Second, colour vision is also often contrasted with mere 'wavelength-dependent' (or 'wavelength-specific') behaviour, in which very specific types of behaviour are triggered by responses to particular types of light: for example, the increased movement of *Daphnia* under predominantly blue light, or the flight, escape, and 'open space' reactions often triggered by ultra-violet light in insects (Menzel 1979: 552–8). Wavelength-dependent behaviour can be exhibited by creatures that plausibly possess colour vision: for instance, bees exhibit wavelength-dependent behaviour in being attracted to UV light, but apparently employ trichromatic colour vision in feeding (Menzel 1979; Goldsmith 1991: 75). Wavelength-dependent behaviour itself, however, is often considered to be distinct from— although a possible evolutionary precursor to—colour vision. At least in part this is because the photoreceptor responses associated with wavelength-dependent behaviour cause particular motor responses directly, or at any rate without appropriate processing of the responses of different photoreceptor types by distinctively visual systems (Goldsmith 1991: 74; cf. Skorupski and Chittka 2011); as such, these motor responses are hard-wired and unresponsive to training.

One of the problems with taking the bare ability to discriminate stimuli based on wavelength as sufficient for colour vision is that it does not require information about the chromatic properties of a stimulus to be available for use by an organism: for instance, as a means of identifying or reidentifying objects, or as a way of conveying biologically important information about them (cf. Mollon 1989; Hilbert 1992: 356). Colour vision, by contrast, is therefore often taken to require some kind of internal representation of colour, generated in response to opponent processing of responses from different types of photoreceptor. An ability to learn (or a susceptibility to operant conditioning) provides evidence for the occurrence of internal representations of colour. This criterion is standardly used in empirical studies as a way of determining whether members of different species possess colour vision: if an animal can learn to associate a particular colour with a reward, then they will be able to identify an appropriate stimulus in a different context. In his pioneering work on animal colour vision, for instance, von Frisch found that if a bee is trained to feed on cards of a particular colour, then it can pick a card of that colour from amongst a range of grey cards differing in lightness, and so differing in the intensity of the light they reflect (cf. Skorupski and Chittka 2011: 254). But although the ability to learn provides evidence for an internal representation of colour, it is more controversial whether it is strictly essential for colour vision, as opposed to merely being a way of testing for the presence or absence of colour vision (Goldsmith 1991: 74; Thompson 1995: 142).

To say that colour vision requires internal representations leaves open exactly what form those representations must take. Hilbert (1992), for instance, argues that colour vision has the function of representing certain kinds of distal mind-independent properties of physical objects: specifically, surface spectral reflectances (SSRs). SSRs are illumination-independent properties of physical objects, that determine the proportion of the incident light that an object reflects at each visible spectral wavelength. If this is the function of colour vision, it follows that a necessary condition on possessing colour vision is that the visual system exhibit colour constancy with respect to changes in the illumination (exhibiting constancy is also suggested as a necessary condition by Thompson *et al.* 1992: 14; Thompson 1995: 145; Bradley and Tye 2001; Burge 2010; Allen 2016: 73).[4] Colour constancy is found across the animal kingdom: in invertebrates, fish, amphibians, birds, and mammals (Neumeyer 1998). By exhibiting colour constancy, representations of the subject's environment achieve a certain kind of objectivity: they represent properties of the subject's environment independent of the particular circumstances in which they are encountered (cf. Burge 2010: 396–416).

Still, Hilbert's account is controversial. On the one hand, it might appear too permissive. It is debatable whether some animals that exhibit colour constancy—bees, for example—are *consciously* aware of their environment (e.g. Hardin 1993: 151; see also §4). Some degree of colour constancy might be attained even in very simple systems simply by virtue of the automatic adaptation of photoreceptors (Neumeyer 1998; Kelber and Osorio 2010: 1620; Skorupski and Chittka 2011: 255). Indeed, there is evidence from humans for the possibility of exhibiting colour constancy whilst lacking conscious experience: for instance, patients with cerebral achromatopsia, who have suffered cortical damage that impairs their ability to enjoy chromatic colour experiences, are not only able to distinguish borders between coloured stimuli on the basis of wavelength, but in doing so exhibit some degree of colour constancy (Cowey and Heywood 1997; Skorupski and Chittka 2011; cf. Thompson 1995: 144; Kentridge *et al.* 2004). Yet given the distinctive phenomenology of *our* colour experiences, there may be reluctance to ascribe colour vision to those who lack conscious experiences of this general kind.

On the other hand, Hilbert's account might appear too restrictive. Hilbert (1992: 365) claims that species inhabiting environments relevantly similar to our own normally need to be at least trichromatic in order to have colour vision. This is because at least three types of photoreceptor are necessary for achieving colour constancy given the types of reflective objects and the nature of the illumination that these environments typically contain (cf. Maloney and Wandell 1986; Shepard 1990). This, however, might seem overly restrictive. Now, it need not automatically follow from this that human dichromats or patients with extrastriate cortical lesions in whom colour constancy is impaired thereby lack colour vision, if they can count as having colour vision by virtue of sharing their evolutionary history with normal colour human perceivers (Hilbert 1992: 369, fn. 15). Moreover, the extent to which this criterion will rule out members of species as possessing colour vision will depend upon the degree of constancy required, as at least some minimal degree colour constancy might be attainted simply by virtue of the way that photoreceptors function. Still, setting the bar for possession of colour vision too high is liable to seem *ad hoc*. Colour constancy comes in degrees, and even in humans, colour constancy is not perfect: for instance, it often breaks down under strongly chromatic illuminants. Requiring too great a degree of constancy runs the risk of arbitrarily ruling out too many species as possessing colour vision.

More generally, tying colour vision too closely to the representation of SSRs threatens to show insufficient recognition of the functions that colour vision plays in other species. There is, for example, evidence that pigeons are able to use colour vision to detect directions in space: pigeons are sensitive to UV light, and light coming from a direction perpendicular to the sun has a higher concentration of UV light than light of longer wavelengths because UV light is more likely to be scattered by the atmosphere (cf. Nuboer 1986; Matthen 2005: 173). To say that in doing this pigeons are not strictly speaking employing colour vision, but at best visual abilities related to colour vision (cf. Hilbert 1992: 364), might seem *ad hoc* and unacceptably anthropocentric. Is there a principled reason for denying that these abilities are properly characterized as colour vision? (cf. Matthen 2005: 171–6).

The two criticisms of Hilbert's account—on the one hand it is too permissive, on the other it is too restrictive—suggest different ways in which accounts of colour vision can be developed. One response to the problem of over-permissiveness is to require that possessing colour vision requires an ability to enjoy *conscious* experiences with a phenomenological character that is suitably similar to our own (e.g. Thompson *et al.* 1992; Stoerig and Cowey 1992). One advantage of this view is that it satisfies pretheoretical intuitions that we might have about what is required for colour vision: after all, talk of 'colour' and 'colour vision' have their home in familiar cases, and it is perhaps not entirely unreasonable to restrict their (literal) application beyond cases that exhibit a suitable similarity to those with which we are familiar.

Nevertheless, this view is not unproblematic. One problem with this requirement from an empirical perspective is that it becomes difficult, if not impossible, to determine which species possess colour vision (e.g. Kelber and Osirio 2010: 1617); operational definitions of colour vision are clearly preferable in this respect. A second problem is to specify the nature of the 'suitable similarity' to our own experiences that is required for a creature to possess colour vision. On the one hand, if colour vision is tied too closely to the colour experiences that we enjoy—experiences of colours such as red, green, yellow, brown, black, etc., differing amongst themselves in terms of hue, saturation, and brightness—then it becomes difficult to make sense of different creatures perceiving novel colours that have no place in human colour space. On the other hand, generalizing from other features of our colour experience is also problematic. Human colour vision, for example, exhibits perceptual constancy. But we might wonder whether this is an essential characteristic of anything that we are prepared to call a 'colour experience': compare, for instance, the experience of the shifting unstable colours on the back of a CD, which is still recognizably a colour experience, even though the colours do not appear to remain constant. Similarly, human colours exhibit an opponent structure: red-green, yellow-blue, and black-white are antagonistic pairs. But must all experiences have this feature in order to count as colour experiences? It might at least seem conceivable that there could be experiences of properties that lack opponent structure but which are still experiences of colour. Finally, normal human colour vision is categorical, as manifested in the 'banding' seen in the rainbow. But is this an essential feature of colour experience? This claim is at least hostage to empirical fortune: whilst there is evidence for categorical colour perception in pigeons, there isn't in goldfish (Kelber and Osorio 2010: 1622).

One response to the apparent over-restrictiveness of Hilbert's view, by contrast, is to relax the constraints on the type of stimulus that can be represented as coloured, so that it can include, amongst other things, light sources and directions. According to Matthen, for instance, colour vision is 'the visual discrimination capacity that relies on wavelength-discriminating sensors to ground differential *learned* (or conditioned) responses to light differing in wavelength only' (2005: 187). Whereas Hilbert's account of colour vision is (self-consciously) anthropocentric, Matthen's functional definition is pluralistic: there is no single type of phenomenology associated with colour vision, and no one mind-independent property that different colour perceivers detect or track.[5]

Indeed, it might be wondered whether Matthen's pluralism goes far enough. In making learned or conditioned responses to light differing in wavelength an essential feature of colour vision, Matthen accepts the traditional distinction between wavelength-specific behaviour and colour vision. But this might itself seem *ad hoc* and overly anthropocentric. Perhaps in humans and other more sophisticated species, colour vision involves some kind of internal representation of the stimulus. But is this sufficient reason for denying that wavelength-dependent behaviours are themselves examples of colour vision? Such behaviours at least reliably track mind-independent properties of the organism's environment. An even more inclusive alternative would be to distinguish different 'levels' or 'grades' of colour vision, of which wavelength-dependent behaviour is a common, but relatively crude, example (cf. Kelber and Osorio 2010).

3 What is colour?

Questions about the nature of colour vision are closely related to questions about what colours themselves are. Interspecies variations again raise interesting issues when addressing this question.

In the first instance, variations across the animal kingdom provide a dramatic illustration of 'the Argument from Perceptual Variation'. The argument from perceptual variation is directed principally against views according to which colours are mind-independent properties of the physical environment: properties whose nature and existence are constitutively independent of the experiences (or psychological responses more generally) of conscious subjects, as they are according to various forms of physicalism and primitivism. If the same physical objects appear different in colour to different subjects (and in different conditions), then which subjects (in which conditions) perceive objects to be the colours that they really are? In the absence of any non-arbitrary reasons to privilege the experiences of one set of perceivers (in one set of conditions) over those of the others, it might seem gratuitous to suppose that colours are really mind-independent properties of physical objects that different perceivers are attempting to track.[6]

Interspecies variations provide a particularly dramatic illustration of the argument from perceptual variation for at least two reasons. First, the interspecies differences appear to be so large: members of different species don't just disagree about which of a range of lights or objects instantiate a very specific colour (such as 'unique green'), but potentially perceive completely different kinds of colour. Second, and especially given that the differences are so large, there is strong pressure towards adopting an ecumenical response to the variation.

Ideally, any attempt to non-arbitrarily identify one set of privileged perceivers should include 'normal' humans as amongst those who perceive physical objects to be the colours that they really are; otherwise, the defence of the mind-independence of colour will be at the expense of the veridicality of normal human colour perception, and this would likely seem a pyrrhic victory.

Perhaps the most direct way of pursuing this response would be to argue that only humans, and non-human animals with similar colour vision (e.g. great apes), *veridically* perceive colours. This might seem more plausible when comparing trichromatic colour perceivers with dichromatic colour perceivers, assuming that in general dichromatic perceivers stand in a similar relationship to trichromatic human colour perceivers as their dichromatic ('colour-blind') human peers. Even so, it is likely to seem less plausible when comparing trichromatic human colour vision with, say, the tetrachromatic colour vision of the pigeon. Although it cannot automatically be assumed that the pigeon's colour vision is veridical with respect to the extra types of colour distinctions it makes, the idea that there are distinctions to which we are insensitive is a familiar one, and it might seem tempting to suppose that normal trichromatic humans in fact stand to pigeons as dichromatic humans stand to the normal human population.

In the case of intra-species variations, such as variations in the perception of the unique hues, it is sometimes suggested that human colour perception is at least roughly veridical: for instance, veridical at the level of determinable colours, such as red, green, blue (e.g. Gert 2006; Tye 2006; Allen 2016). However, given the extent of the differences between species, there is less scope for this type of response in the interspecies case: pigeons, bees, and normal human perceivers are likely to disagree about even the determinable colours of objects. Similarly unattractive, given the extent of the interspecies differences, is the claim that there are knowledge-transcendent facts about colour, also sometimes suggested in the case of intra-species variations (e.g. Byrne and Hilbert 2007a).[7] Whatever the merits of knowledge-transcendent facts about colour in general (cf. Hardin 2004), this response is more palatable if the supposedly knowledge-transcendent facts pertain just to the very fine-grained, super-determinate, colours that objects instantiate. However, accounting for interspecies variation along these lines would seemingly require ignorance even at the level of coarse-grained determinable colours, such as blue, 'bee ultra-violet', 'pigeon ternary hue a', and so on.

A second general way of trying to privilege human colour perception would be to argue that only humans strictly speaking *perceive* colour: other species may have colour *vision*, but perhaps colour vision falls short of conscious colour perception (see §2). This line of defence, however, is hostage to empirical fortune. Whilst it may be plausible that some simple creatures who have colour vision lack conscious perception, it may seem less plausible for more complex creatures like large mammals or primates (see §4 for further discussion). Yet if they perceive physical objects to be different colours than normal human perceivers, then this is sufficient to run the argument from perceptual variation.

A related response is to argue that only humans strictly speaking perceive *colour*. Colour terms have their primary application to the properties perceived by humans, and it may be suggested that we are under no obligation to extend their use to the properties perceived by members of other species. (Compare Wittgenstein's claim that the question of whether others could perceive colours that we do not does not admit of an unambiguous answer because 'There is, after all, no commonly accepted criterion of what is a colour, unless it is one of our colours', 1977: III.42.) This response avoids holding out hostages to empirical fortune, since the possibility of other species perceiving colours is ruled out *a priori*. Nevertheless, the refusal to extend colour talk beyond the human case is liable to seem chauvinistic and *ad hoc*, given similarities, for instance, in the general type of stimuli to which animals are sensitive, their neurophysiological make up, the behaviour they exhibit, and perhaps the experiences that they enjoy. (Indeed, as Wittgenstein goes on to say, 'And yet we can imagine circumstances under which we would say, "These people see other colours in addition to ours".')

Given the problems identifying a non-arbitrary reason for privileging particular types of colour perceiver, interspecies variations in colour perception might be taken to motivate one of a range of broadly subjectivist theories of colour. At one extreme, eliminativists may see interspecies variations as evidence that physical objects are not really coloured at all (e.g. Hardin 1993). Alternatively, interspecies perceptual variation might be used to motivate dispositionalist, or more generally relationalist, theories of colour, according to which colours are dispositions to produce particular kinds of subjective responses in particular perceivers (e.g. Johnston 1992), or properties that are constituted in terms of relations to different kinds of perceivers in different kinds of conditions more generally (e.g. Cohen 2009; see Cohen 2009: 26–9 on interspecies variation in particular). Of particular note in this context is the 'ecological' theory of colour defended by Thompson and colleagues, which is motivated by detailed consideration of differences in colour vision across the animal kingdom. According to the ecological view, colours are relations between active exploring animals and non-neutral 'environments' (Thompson *et al.* 1992; Thompson 1995: Chapters 4–5). According to Thompson, this view is relationalist but not dispositionalist (in the standard sense) both because colours are 'ecological-level' dispositional properties, not 'physical-level' dispositional properties, and because perceivers and their environments are inter-dependent and not merely extrinsically related (Thompson 1995: 245; but contrast Whitmyer 1999; Byrne and Hilbert 2003: 8).

A common objection to broadly subjectivist theories of colour is that they entail a potentially unattractive error theory about the way colours are represented in perception and thought: the way colours are represented is best explained by the view that colours are mind-independent properties of physical objects, and other things being equal we should prefer a philosophical theory of the nature of colour that respects this. This objection is not uncontroversial: on the one hand, it might be suggested that the way colours are presented in perception and thought is at best silent on the question of whether they are mind-independent, and perhaps even supports a broadly relational theory of colour (e.g. Thompson 1995: 249–50; Cohen 2009; Chirimuuta 2011); on the other hand, it might be suggested that other things are not equal, and despite convicting experience and common sense of systematic error broadly subjectivist theories of colour can nevertheless be defended on other grounds (e.g. Boghossian and Velleman 1989; Johnston 1992). However, consistent with the claim that colours are mind-independent properties of the environment, an alternative response to the argument from perceptual variation is the 'pluralist' or 'selectionist' view that physical objects instantiate a plurality of mind-independent colour properties that different species, in virtue of differences in the perceptual mechanisms, select between (e.g. Hilbert and Kalderon 2000; Bradley and Tye 2001; Mizrahi 2006; Kalderon 2007; Allen 2009, 2016). But even if it does provide a way of taking the appearances at face value, selectionism is nevertheless controversial. For one thing, it is at best ontologically luxuriant, if not downright ontologically profligate. For another, it threatens to overgeneralize, thereby making perceptual error impossible: if any disagreement between perceivers (or perhaps even within perceivers, across perceptual conditions) can be used to motivate the introduction of different sets of mind-independent colours that each veridically perceive, then it becomes difficult to make sense of the possibility that any perceivers (in any conditions) are misperceiving the colours of objects (for further discussion see e.g. Kalderon 2007 and Chapter 20 in this volume; Allen 2009, 2016; Cohen 2009: 78–88).

Interspecies variations in colour perception not only provide a dramatic illustration of the argument from perceptual variation; they have also been used to argue against particular theories of the nature of colour on more specific grounds. Matthen (2005), for instance, appeals to the ability of pigeons to navigate using celestial colour gradients to argue against reductive forms of physicalism that identify colours specifically with SSRs (e.g. Hilbert 1992; Byrne and Hilbert 2003; see also §2). Byrne and Hilbert (2007b), meanwhile, use interspecies variations in colour perception to raise a problem for primitivist theories of colour according to which colours are *sui generis* non-physical properties. Byrne and Hilbert argue that primitivists are committed to 'Revelation', the thesis that the essential (or intrinsic) nature of the colours is revealed in a standard visual experience as of a coloured thing. However, it is difficult to make sense of the idea that different species perceive novel colours if Revelation is true: careful reflection on human colour space suggests that human colour space is a closed space, in which all regions are occupied, and as such Revelation appears to preclude the possibility of novel colours that have no location in human colour space (but see Allen 2016 for a response).

4 What is it like?

Some of the most intriguing questions raised by interspecies variations in colour perception relate to the nature of conscious experience, or 'what it is like' to be a pigeon, goldfish, or mantis shrimp. Do members of other species enjoy phenomenally conscious colour experiences? If so, what are their experiences like? Can we know? And what, if anything, does this tell us about the nature of consciousness?

Most people would probably accept that there is nothing it is like to be a plant, bacterium, or fruit sorting machine that is able to respond to differences in the wavelength of a stimulus independent of its relative intensity. It is similarly tempting to suppose that there is nothing it is like to be a creature than exhibits merely wavelength-dependent behaviour, like a *Daphnia* whose movement increases under predominantly blue light or a male glow-worm that is attracted to green light that matches that emitted by females of the species (Booth *et al.* 2004). Indeed, there are good reasons to suppose that possessing colour vision in a more demanding sense need not imply the occurrence of conscious experience. It is sometimes suggested that some of the simpler organisms that possess colour vision, like honeybees, might nevertheless lack conscious experience (e.g. Hardin 1993: 151), and we know from pathological human cases like blindsight that possessing colour vision does not necessary entail the capacity to enjoy conscious experience (Stoerig and Cowey 1992; see also §2 above).

The capacity to enjoy phenomenally conscious experiences plausibly requires at least a certain degree of neurophysiological complexity (lacking in plants and perhaps simple organisms) and particular kinds of neurophysiological structures (of the sort damaged in blindsight patients). As such, neurophysiological investigation can provide one source of evidence that non-human animals are (or are not) conscious. On this basis, for instance, the authors of the 'Cambridge Declaration on Consciousness' suggest that there is convergent evidence that many non-human animals, including all mammals and birds, possess 'the neurological substrates that generate consciousness' (Low *et al.* 2012).

Behavioural evidence can also be taken to bear on the question of whether non-human animals are conscious. The capacity to enjoy conscious experiences is often associated with the capacity to learn and exhibit seemingly intentional, flexible, behaviour. Tye (2000: 171–85), for instance, argues that the best explanation of the apparently purposive behaviour of creatures like fish and bees—such as bees' ability to associate coloured stimuli with food—is that there is 'something it is like' to be a fish or a bee.

The neurophysiological and behavioural evidence for the presence of conscious experience in non-human animals is, of course, contentious. On the one hand, there can be disagreement about exactly what kinds of neurophysiological organization are required to realize phenomenally conscious experience, and exactly what kinds of behavioural response provide adequate evidence for its occurrence. As we saw in §2, for instance, the capacity to learn, and thereby exhibit flexible behaviour, might be taken to provide evidence for the existence of internal representations of an animal's environment; however, it is, on the face of it, a further question whether the presence of internal representations entails the existence of conscious experience. On the other hand, it might be suggested that animals need to meet further conditions in order to enjoy conscious experience. According to higher-order thought (HOT) theories of consciousness, for instance, the capacity to enjoy conscious experiences requires at least an ability to think about your mental states, if not the actual occurrence of higher-order thoughts (e.g. Carruthers 1998). It is often thought to follow from higher-order thought theories that the majority of non-human animals (except perhaps the great apes) lack phenomenally conscious experiences altogether—although clearly whether this is an acceptable consequence of the view is debatable (see e.g. Allen and Trestman 2014 for further discussion).

Assuming that non-human animals do enjoy conscious experiences, what is it like to perceive ultra-violet light, novel hues, or directions in heliocentric space as coloured? Empirical investigation allows for a certain degree of speculation. It is possible to experimentally determine, amongst other things, the number of photoreceptor types that an animal's eye contains, the dimensionality of their colour vision, the presence of spectrally opponent neural mechanisms which could realize opponently organized colour experiences, the degree to which their visual system exhibits colour constancy, and the spectral location of categorical colour boundaries. These factors give some indication of the ways in which other species' colour experiences may be similar to, and different from, our own; as such, they allow for some speculation about the specific form others' colour experiences could take. For instance, assuming that the signals from the retinal receptors of tetrachromatic pigeons are processed along three opponently organized psychophysical channels, it seems reasonable to suppose that pigeons experience six unique hues, a corresponding number of binary hues and perhaps even ternary hues, which would be like our binary hues but a perceptual mixture of three unique hues.

However, it is important to approach the empirical evidence with a certain degree of caution. Without a complete understanding of ways visual processing mechanisms function, it is easy to be misled by neurophysiological and psychophysical evidence. So, for instance, although the number of photoreceptor types constrains the dimensionality of an animal's colour vision, you cannot infer from the fact that an animal has four or more types of photoreceptor that their experience is at least tetrachromatic, since some of the receptor types might play different functions (see §1). Similarly, the dimensionality of an organism's colour vision does not fully determine the nature of their visual experience, which depends in addition on the way that the retinal signals are subsequently processed. For a concrete illustration of some of the problems here consider a comparable human case. Opponent cells in the lateral geniculate nucleus (LGN) discovered in the 1960s were initially thought to be the neural realizers of the psychophysical opponent channels hypothesized by Hering to explain (amongst other things) the unique-binary structure of the hues. Based on this evidence, however, you would be forgiven for thinking that the human unique hues are chartreuse, violet, teal, and cherry, since this is what the peak responses of the opponent cells would lead you to predict. Given that this does not accord with the more direct psychological evidence that the unique hues are red, green, blue, and yellow, however, it has since been suggested that there must be a third stage of processing, the neural basis for which has yet to be identified (e.g. De Valois and De Valois 1993).

Besides, even if the empirical evidence allows us to conceive in abstract terms of how pigeons or mantis shrimp see the world, it is unclear that they allow us to fully imagine 'what it is like'. It may be tempting to assume that other species have experiences that are basically much like ours, but with some more or less minor modifications such as the addition of an extra hue category or categories. There are reasons, however, for thinking that non-human colour experiences differ more radically than this. Consider, for instance, a bee's sensitivity to UV light. We cannot simply assume that bees' experiences of UV-reflective objects are the same as our experiences of objects when they are illuminated solely by UV light. According to Bradley and Tye (2001: 473, fn. 10), for instance, a human trichromat's experience in these conditions is comparable to that of a human monochromat perceiving an object that only reflects long wavelength (red) light against the background of an object that reflects only short wavelength (blue) light, when both are illuminated only by long wavelength (red) light: although the monochromat would still be able to distinguish the brighter red object from its background, it seems unlikely that their experience of the red object would be the same as ours. More generally, it is not clear that we can simply think of 'bee purple' (as it is sometimes called) as a straightforward addition to the set of colours that we perceive. The colours that we perceive can be represented in a colour space that represents in external spatial terms internal relations of similarity between the colours. Human colour space, however, is a closed space in which every region is occupied. As such, there is no way of simply slotting extra colours into our colour space: we cannot, for instance, add an extra colour into the hue circle without fundamentally changing the nature of the colours around the hue circle (cf. Westphal 1987: 100–1; Thompson 1995: 272–3; Allen 2009: 205). Finally, even in areas of the visible spectrum where there is overlapping sensitivity, there is evidence that different species perceive the same stimuli differently. Wright and Cummings (1971), for instance, found that whereas humans generally perceive 540nm light as green-yellow, 540nm light marks a categorical boundary for pigeons (cf. Hardin 1993: 152–4; Thompson 1995: 150–1).

The claim that we cannot imagine 'what it is like' to perceive the world as other creatures do famously formed part of Nagel's (1974) argument that conscious experience is irreducibly subjective, and cannot (at least, not currently) be reductively explained in objective, physical, terms. Nagel's central example was the ability of bats to perceive using echolocation, although the seemingly novel colours perceived, for instance, by pigeons provide an equally striking illustration of Nagel's point. In a similar spirit, Jackson (1982) uses the example of Fred, who is able to perceive novel hues, to illustrate his version of the knowledge argument for the existence of facts that are not physical facts (the discussion of Fred comes after the much more widely discussed example of the super-scientist Mary, who has been locked in a black and white room and never before seen (chromatic) colours). In Jackson's example Fred is a human perceiver, but non-human perceivers potentially provide actual examples of the kind of case Jackson considers. Needless to say, Nagel's and Jackson's arguments against physicalist theories of conscious experience are controversial, and have generated an extensive literature (see e.g. Ludlow *et al.* 2003). Nevertheless, these examples illustrate the importance of considering interspecies variations in colour perception when addressing wider questions about the nature of conscious experience.

Notes

1 There are two basic types of photoreceptor: cones are standardly associated with colour vision, whereas rods are normally associated with vision in very low intensity lighting conditions. The claim that rods make *no* contribution to colour vision is arguably an over-simplification, at least for some species (e.g. Jacobs 1981: 87–9; Kelber *et al.* 2003). However, I will set aside the role of rods in colour vision here.
2 See e.g. Jacobs 1981 and Kelber *et al.* 2003 for an overview. In addition, some species' retina contain filters and oil droplets, the precise function of which is controversial but which appear to tune the spectral sensitivity of the photoreceptors (Jacobs 1981: 39–45; Goldsmith 1991: 84; Kelber *et al.* 2003: 87).
3 Although creatures with two types of photoreceptor do not thereby automatically possess colour vision, if the responses of the two types of photoreceptor are not compared but merely increase the sensitivity to the electromagnetic spectrum (Goldsmith 1991: 74; Skorupski and Chittka 2011: 252).
4 Exhibiting colour constancy is closely related to a susceptibility to colour contrast phenomena (Neumeyer 1998), which could constitute a further necessary condition on the possession of colour vision.
5 For a related suggestion, see Skorupski and Chittka (2011), who require at a minimum that colours be attributed to things, and as such colour vision requires spatial vision.
6 For a contemporary presentation of the argument, see Cohen (2009). The argument, of course, has a much older history, and a version of the argument can be traced back at least as far as Protogaras (cf. Kalderon 2007).
7 Assuming a suitable externalist theory of knowledge, this approach need not deny that can we know what the colours of physical objects are if, as a matter of fact, we are appropriately sensitive. However, it does at least imply that we cannot know that we know (if we do) what the colours of physical objects are.

References

Allen, C. and Trestman, M. 2014. 'Animal Consciousness', *Stanford Encyclopedia of Philosophy*: http://plato.stanford.edu/entries/consciousness-animal/.
Allen, K. 2009. 'Inter-Species Variation in Colour Perception', *Philosophical Studies* 142: 197–220.
Allen, K. 2016. *A Naïve Realist Theory of Colour*. Oxford: Oxford University Press.
Boghossian, P. and Velleman, D. 1989. 'Colour as a Secondary Quality', reprinted in A. Byrne and D. Hilbert eds. *Readings on Color, volume 1*, Cambridge, MA: MIT Press, 1997.
Booth, D., Stewart, A.J.A., and Osorio, D. 2004. 'Colour Vision in the Glow-Worm *Lampyris noctiluca* (L.) (Coleoptera: Lampyridae): Evidence for a Green-Blue Chromatic Mechanism', *Journal of Experimental Biology*, 207: 2373–8.
Bradley, P. and Tye, M. 2001. 'Of Colors, Kestrels, Caterpillars, and Leaves', *Journal of Philosophy* 98: 469–87.

Burge, T. 2010. *The Origins of Objectivity*. Oxford: Oxford University Press.

Byrne, A. and Hilbert, D. 2003. 'Color Realism and Color Science', *Behavioural and Brain Sciences* 26: 3–21.

Byrne, A. and Hilbert, D. 2007a. 'Truest Blue', *Analysis* 67: 87–92.

Byrne, A. and Hilbert, D. 2007b. 'Color Primitivism', *Erkenntnis* 66: 73–105.

Carruthers, P. 1998. 'Animal Subjectivity', *Psyche* 4: http://psyche.cs.monash.edu.au/v4/psyche-4-03-carruthers.html.

Chirimuuta, M. 2011. 'Touch-Feely Colour', in C.P. Biggam, C. Hough, and D.R. Simmons eds. *New Directions in Colour Studies*. Amsterdam and Philadelphia: John Benjamins.

Cohen, J. 2009. *The Red and the Real*. Oxford: Oxford University Press.

Cowey, A. and Heywood, C. 1997. 'Cerebral Achromatopsia: Colour Blindness despite Wavelength Processing', *Trends in Cognitive Sciences* 1: 133–9.

De Valois, R.L. and De Valois, K.K. (1993). 'A Multi-Stage Color Model', *Vision Research* 33(8): 1053–65.

Gert, J. 2006. 'A Realistic Colour Realism', *Australasian Journal of Philosophy* 84: 565–89.

Goldsmith, T.H. 1991. 'The Evolution of Visual Pigments and Colour Vision', in P. Gouras ed. *Vision and Visual Dysfunction, 6: The Perception of Colour*. London: Macmillan Press.

Hardin, C.L. 1993. *Color for Philosophers*. Indianapolis: Hackett.

Hardin, C.L. 2004. 'A Spectral Reflectance Doth Not a Color Make', *Journal of Philosophy* 100: 191–202.

Hilbert, D. 1992. 'What Is Color Vision?' *Philosophical Studies* 68: 351–70.

Hilbert, D. and Kalderon, M. 2000. 'Color and the Inverted Spectrum', in S. Davis ed. *Vancouver Studies in Cognitive Science, 9*. Oxford: Oxford University Press.

Jackson, F. 1982. 'Epiphenomenal Qualia', *The Philosophical Quarterly* 32: 127–36.

Jacobs, G. 1981. *Comparative Color Vision*. New York: Academic Press.

Johnston, M. 1992. 'How to Speak of the Colors', *Philosophical Studies* 68: 221–63.

Kalderon, M. 2007. 'Color Pluralism', *The Philosophical Review* 116: 563–601.

Kelber, A. and Osorio, D. 2010. 'From Spectral Information to Animal Colour Vision: Experiments and Concepts', *Proceedings of the Royal Society B* 277: 1617–25.

Kelber, A., Vorobyev, M., and Osorio, D. 2003. 'Animal Colour Vision: Behavioural Tests and Physiological Concepts', *Biological Review* 78: 81–118.

Kentridge, R.W., Heywood, C.A., and Cowey A. 2004. 'Chromatic Edges, Surfaces and Constancies in Cerebral Achromatopsia', *Neuropsychologia* 42: 1555–61.

Koshitaka, H., Kinoshita, M., Vorobyev, M., and Arikawa, K. 2008. 'Tetrachromacy in a Butterfly that has Eight Varieties of Spectral Receptors', *Proceedings of the Royal Society B* 275: 947–54.

Low, P., Panksepp, J., Reiss, D. Edelman, D., Van Swinderen, B., and Koch, C. 2012. 'Cambridge Declaration on Consciousness' http://fcmconference.org/img/CambridgeDeclarationOnConsciousness.pdf.

Ludlow, P., Nagasawa, Y., and Stoljar, D. 2003. *There's Something About Mary: Essays on Phenomenal Consciousness and Frank Jackson's Knowledge Argument*. Cambridge, Mass.: MIT Press.

Maloney, L.T. and Wandell, B.A. 1986. 'Color Constancy: A Method for Recovering Surface Spectral Reflectance', *Journal of the Optical Society of America A* 3: 29–33.

Matthen, M. 2005. *Seeing, Doing, and Knowing*. Oxford: Oxford University Press.

Menzel, R. 1979. 'Spectral Sensitivity and Color Vision in Invertebrates', in H. Autrum ed. *Handbook of Sensory Physiology, 6A: Vision in Invertegrates*. Berlin: Springer.

Mizrahi, V. 2006. 'Color Objectivistm and Color Pluralism', *dialectica* 60: 283–306.

Mollon, J.D. 1989. '"Tho' She Kneel'd in that Place Where They Grew …" The Uses and Origins of Primate Colour Vision', *Journal of Experimental Biology* 146: 21–38.

Nagel, T. 1974. 'What Is It Like to Be a Bat?', *Philosophical Review* 83: 435–50.

Neumeyer, C. 1998. 'Comparative Aspects of Color Constancy', in V. Walsh and J Kulikowksi eds. *Perceptual Constancy*. Cambridge: Cambridge University Press.

Nuboer, J.F.W. 1986. 'A Comparative View on Colour Vision', *Netherlands Journal of Zoology* 36: 344–80.

Shepard, R.N. 1990. 'Possible Evolutionary Basis for Trichromacy', in M.H. Brill ed. *Perceiving, Measuring, and Using Color*. Santa Clara, Calif.: Proceedings of the SPIE.

Skorupski, P. and Chittka, L. 2011. 'Is Colour Cognitive?' *Optics and Laser Technology* 43: 251–60.

Stoerig, P. and Cowey, A. 1992. 'Wavelength Processing and Colour Experience', *Behavioural and Brain Sciences* 15: 53.

Thompson, E. 1995. *Colour Vision*. London: Routledge.

Thompson, E., Palacios, A., and Varela, F. 1992. 'Ways of Coloring: Comparative Color Vision as a Case Study for Cognitive Science', *Behavioural and Brain Sciences* 15: 1–74.

Tye, M. 2000. *Consciousness, Color, and Content*. Cambridge, Mass.: MIT Press.

Tye, M. 2006. 'The Puzzle of True Blue', *Analysis* 67: 335–40.

Westphal, J. 1987. *Colour: Some Philosophical Problems from Wittgenstein*. Oxford: Blackwell.

Whitymer, V. 1999. 'Ecological Color', *Philosophical Psychology* 12: 197–214.

Wittgenstein, L. 1977. *Remarks on Colour*, ed. G.E.M. Anscombe. Oxford: Blackwell.

Wright, A. and Cummings, W. 1971. 'Colour-Naming Functions for the Pigeon'. *Journal of the Experimental Analysis of Behaviour* 15: 7–17.

15

COLOUR ILLUSION[1]

Michael Watkins

A perceptual illusion occurs whenever someone perceives something to have some property when, in fact, it doesn't have that property. Illusions and the possibility of illusions have long concerned philosophers of perception and knowledge. How are cases of illusion and cases of veridical perception related? Am I perceptually aware of something in both types of cases, for instance? Am I perceptually aware of the same thing in both cases? Given the possibility of illusion, how can perception advance knowledge? If what I seem to see might be an illusion, what justifies my claim to know by perception that it is? And so forth. For philosophers of perception and knowledge, colour illusions are somewhat ho-hum examples of a more general phenomenon. Such philosophers are concerned with *illusions*, but not with *colour* illusions, per se.

For scientists interested in colour perception, the challenge is to explain the causal mechanisms involved in colour-illusory experiences. For example, a scientist might wish to explain why, when a Benham disc spins at certain speeds and is viewed under tungsten light, bands of various chromatic colours appear, even though the disc is patterned black and white. Such a phenomenon is interesting for scientists, especially to the extent that the phenomenon is not fully understood, but their interest does not concern its being an illusion, if indeed it is one. Scientists are interested in colour experiences, understood very broadly, and so in colour illusions, but not with colour *illusions*, per se.

So caring about illusions may cause us to care about colour illusions (as is the case with the philosopher of perception). And so caring about colour experience may cause us to care about colour illusions (as is the case with the scientist). But why care about *colour illusions qua colour illusions just for themselves*? What, if anything, makes colour illusions philosophically interesting above and beyond what might be interesting about any other kind of illusion or any other kind of experience?

To see why colour illusions might seem to pose a special challenge, I begin the first section of this chapter with the kind of case that can be treated as we would treat other standard cases of illusions. Here I lean on Mark Eli Kalderon's excellent paper on colour illusion (2011). I will not defend Kalderon's position, although I am generally sympathetic. What will matter is only that, for certain kinds of purported colour illusions, whatever you say you can say about illusions generally.

In the second section I begin to look at the role that colour illusions play in the (philosophical) colour literature and argue that that role is very different than the role played by illusions elsewhere in philosophy. Elsewhere, the concern is with illusions, and not with what the illusion is an illusion of. But in the colour literature, the concern is with colours. Here, illusions are supposed to tell us something about what they are illusions of. And so even if Kalderon is correct generally about illusions, it may well seem that his treatment of illusions, indeed any treatment of *illusions*, leaves a particular, residual problem concerning *colour illusions*.

I aim both to isolate that residual problem—to show why philosophers have worried about *colour illusions*—and to suggest, in the third section, that those worries have been exaggerated.

1 Illusion

Imagine that we walk into a room with white walls and blue lighting. We might, at least until some mix of philosophy and science unsettles our common sense, expect one of two things to happen: either we will realize that the walls are white (although we might say that they look bluish) or we will be led to believe, mistakenly, that the walls are actually blue. What should we say about these cases, with respect to illusions?

In the first case, where we realize that the walls are white, we might be tempted to conclude that our experience is still illusory; that we see the white walls as blue, even though we are not misled by that illusion. That seems to me a mistake. At the very least, while focusing on our experiences of colours, we should not forget that our perceptual experiences are representationally complex. While looking out my window at the trees, I see the trees and the green leaves, lit by the afternoon sun, occasionally shadowed by passing clouds, and moving in the wind. As the leaves are shadowed by the passing clouds, someone might be tempted to say that I now see the leaves as being more darkly coloured; it is only that I'm not led to believe that they are. But saying this ignores the fact that I see, not only leaves, but also the leaves being lit by the afternoon sun and the leaves as they are shadowed by the clouds. To insist that the leaves appear darker in the shadows is to ignore that I see the shadows. The leaves do not appear darker in shadow. Arguably, and even most plausibly, the leaves while shadowed appear the same colour as before, only now shadowed.[2]

Likewise, when I look at a wall I see not only the wall and its colour, but also a coloured wall under certain lighting. When I see a wall as white under blue lighting, I might very well be said to see just that: a white wall under blue lighting. It isn't that *white walls* under blue lighting always look different than *white walls* under white lighting. It is just that *white walls under blue lighting* look different than *white walls under white lighting*, and that is because the lighting is different and we see that it is.

The position being suggested is reminiscent of J.L. Austin's criticism of the claim that straight sticks in the water appear bent (1962). Austin responds that the experience is not illusory, and not because the stick *is* bent in the water, but because it doesn't look bent. It looks the way that straight sticks look in the water. Someone might respond to Austin that the straight stick in the water and the bent stick in the water have the same *look*. We may not be able to tell, even when the stick is in the water, whether it is bent or not. And even when we can tell, the *looks* are similar. Likewise, when we look at the white wall under blue lighting, it may have the same *look* as a blue wall under white light. We may not be able to tell whether the wall is white or blue. And even when we can tell, the *looks* are similar.

As Kalderon points out, however, when we say something like "the wall looks blue", we might either be saying, of the wall, that it looks to be blue (and so, if it is white, we are mistaken) or we might be saying of the way it *looks*, that it is similar to the way a blue wall looks. In the first, 'blue' qualifies the wall; in the second, 'blue' qualifies the look of the wall. My daughter looks like her mother when she smiles, you might say, which isn't to say that you suffer an illusion, that you cannot tell them apart, that you have somehow made a mistake, or that your visual experience misrepresents the way the world is whenever you see my smiling daughter.[3]

The better candidates for actual illusions are when we are confused about the colours of objects, as when we mistakenly think that the white wall under the blue lighting is blue. Here, surely, we might think, we suffer a colour illusion. But even here it is not obvious. What we say will likely depend in large part on our favoured theory of perception, and that takes us outside the scope of this article.[4] Regardless, it is not clear that even when we are mistaken about the colour of the object, that our mistake is best understood as resulting from a perceptual illusion. Once we remember that we never visually represent something as having a particular colour *simpliciter*, that we are always visually presented with (or represent) something as having a particular colour under a particular lighting condition, as being in a particular location and at a particular distance from us, and so forth, it is not clear where in perception the illusion is to be located.[5] What is true is that white objects under blue lighting *look* as certain blue objects under white lighting *look*. It is sometimes hard to tell which we are seeing, just as it is sometimes hard to tell identical twins apart. They look so much alike. But it isn't an illusion to see the one and think it is the other. It's a mistake, true enough, but not an illusion. And so it is no surprise that, at times, even when experience doesn't fail us, we get things wrong. It is easy to get it wrong when it is hard to tell; it is easy to get things wrong because visual experience sometimes fails to provide us with enough information, not because it provides us with false information. At least, in many cases where we are mistaken about the colours of objects (or their shapes, etc.), it is plausible to hold that, even if perception has misled us, it has not misinformed us.

2 Illusion and the nature of colours

The kinds of standard cases of illusions that we have looked at thus far are not obviously illusions at all. In any case, they are not the kinds of cases that philosophers interested in colour have tended to care about. For philosophers interested in the metaphysics of colours, illusions have not been of interest in their own right. These philosophers have not been concerned to explain illusions (that's a problem for the philosophy of perception), but rather to use illusions or purported illusions to shed light on the nature of colours. And this highlights something interesting about the role colour illusions have played for philosophers. After all, if we wanted a better understanding of the nature of being straight or being bent, reflecting on how sticks look while under water would be of no help. We need to understand what it is to be straight or bent (or at least to know already whether something is bent or straight) to know when an experience of something's being bent is veridical or illusory, and not the other way about. That many philosophers have thought that illusions tell us something about the nature of colours is one reason, perhaps the principle reason, that philosophers have been concerned with *colour illusions*.

How are colour illusions to inform us about the nature of colours? It cannot be merely that illusions serve as data to be accommodated by a theory of colour. It is true, of course, that if a particular colour experience is illusory, then that is evidence against any theory of colour that treats the experience as veridical. And so it is *prima facie* a problem for any account according to which we are never mistaken about the colours of objects, and it is *prima facie* a problem for any account according to which we are never correct. *Prima facie*, such accounts are wrong about when our colour experiences are veridical (and so getting things right) and when our colour experiences are illusory (and so getting things wrong). And so, at least *prima facie*, it counts against a theory of colours that it has us getting things wrong far more often or far less often than we intuitively do. But the same might be said about being straight or being bent. An account must get the facts right, and we must begin with what the facts seem to us to be.

What gives colour illusions pride of place in discussions about the nature of colours, and what might be thought the *sine qua non* of the so-called secondary properties, is the additional concern that there might be no way independent of our experiences to understand what colours are, and so perhaps no way to determine which experiences are illusory and which are not. The special interest that philosophers have in colour illusion, then, goes hand in hand with worries about the nature of colours, and so debates about whether colours are objective or subjective, primary or secondary, relative or non-relative. If we know what it is to be coloured, if we at least know when it is that something has a colour (as we presumably knew, in the example above, that the wall was white and the light blue), then colour illusions or purported colour illusions can apparently be handled as any other kind of illusion. Otherwise, we would seem not so much at a loss to explain colour illusions, but at a loss to determine which of our experiences are illusory in the first place.

John Locke's classic example of how blood looks differently coloured under a microscope helps to illustrate how reasoning about colours might shape our views about illusions, or purported illusions, and how that in turn might shape our views of colours. Locke tells us that a drop of blood looks red to the naked eye, but under a microscope it "shews only some few Globules of Red, swimming in a pellucid Liquor" (1975/1690, II.xxiii.21). Since nothing can be both uniformly red and mostly not red, someone might argue, either the appearance of blood to the naked eye is illusory or its appearance under the microscope is illusory. Either answer seems arbitrary, and so both appearances are illusory. And since what is true of the drop of blood can be generalized—if the microscope is powerful enough, any object will look differently coloured under that microscope as compared with how it looks to the naked eye—all colour experiences are illusory.

Of course, someone might instead conclude that neither experience is illusory, and conclude that the colour of something is relative to an observer and to a viewing condition. Or someone might think instead that colours are dispositions of objects to appear a certain way under the right, or normal, or optimal viewing conditions to the right or normal observers, and conclude that the blood's appearance under the microscope is illusory (microscopic vision not being normal) or that its appearance with the naked eye is illusory (the naked eye not being optimal).

Pointillist paintings serve as a similar example. When viewed from a distance, a part of a painting might appear green. On closer inspection, however, the scene is painted with only blue and yellow paint; not a speck of green is present. Again the question is raised: which experience is illusory, the one of the painting from a distance (in which case the relevant part of the canvas appears green) or the one of the painting from close on (in which case the relevant part of the canvas is blue and yellow)? Both seem normal.

At one time, even while philosophers disagreed about what positive lessons we should learn from these cases and cases like them, even while disagreeing about which experiences were illusory and which veridical, they tended to agree that these cases demonstrate the implausibility of thinking of colours as objective properties of objects, properties that objects have independent of how they are perceived. They tended to agree that colours are at best "secondary" properties, properties importantly different than primary properties like the property of being straight or bent. But it is not at all clear that these cases either force us to favour one experience (with the naked eye or under the microscope, say) over the other or show us anything interesting about the nature of colours. As David Hilbert points out, there's reason to deny that the object we see under the microscope is the same object as that seen with the naked eye (1987, pp. 29–42). With the naked eye, we see a drop of blood. Under the microscope, we see components of that drop of blood. Since the objects that we see under the microscope are different than the object we see with the naked eye, we might conclude that the drop of blood is red and its parts are mostly yellow. Some philosophers have objected that, even if we are dealing with different objects, it is plausible to think that if something is uniformly a particular colour, then all of its parts must be (e.g., Armstrong, 1961). However, it is worth noting, and Hilbert does, that as plausible as this principle might sound, it gains little support from our common sense interactions with colour. To use Hilbert's example, we think little of treating a fabric as pink, even after we notice that it is made of red and white threads. And so for Hilbert, none of these cases count as illusory. The philosophical arguments intended to show that they are illusory fail, he contends, and so these cases do not motivate any particular theory of colours.

Again, the interesting feature of Locke's example, as well as pointillist paintings, is that they are unlike what we ordinarily think of as cases of illusion. In the ordinary case, we know well what it is for something to have a feature (or at least we know well whether it has it), and we are presented with a case in which we are mistaken about whether that thing has that feature. In the case of microscopes and pointillist paintings, however, we are being led by arguments, whether probative or dubious, to conclude that there must be an illusion because some experiences (under the microscope or close-on) are incompatible with other experiences (with the naked eye or further away). We are not being given a purported illusion—a case where we all agree that we are getting things wrong—and being asked to explain it in the context of providing a theory of perception, as is the case with Austin's submerged stick. We are instead given examples that presumably force us to treat some experiences as illusory, even where it is not clear when we are getting things right or wrong.

The same is true with most of the cases now commonly appealed to in debates about colour. Take two objects that match metamerically. (Two objects match metamerically if and only if they appear the same colour to an observer under some lighting condition even though they do not reflect the same light, and so do not look the same in colour under all lighting conditions.) Here the arguments commonly offered are similar to what we have seen, except that here there can be no question about the number of objects involved. The very same object appears one colour under one lighting condition and a different colour under another, different lighting condition. Moreover, an object might appear one colour to many seemingly normal observers and another colour to other seemingly normal observers. Again the question arises, are the experiences of each set of observers veridical? Are the experiences of both illusory? Is the one group having veridical experiences while the other suffering illusions?

Here, once again, we might think that we face a choice point, having to decide which experiences are illusory and which are not. And we might think that any particular answer about which cases are illusory forces our hand, or at least severely limits our choices, about which philosophical theory of colour to accept. If we conclude that an object that looks blue to one set of observers and green to another is actually both blue and green, then how do we avoid being relativists about colour? Unlike with the case of microscopes and pointillist paintings, there seems no way to claim that different objects are being observed and so, unless we wish to conclude that an object might be simultaneously two different colours all over at the same time, it looks like we must relativize the colour of an object to an observer and a lighting condition.[6] And if we conclude that the object is neither blue nor green, perhaps because we think it can't be both and the choice of either is arbitrary, then we might seem on our way to denying that any object is colored.[7] At the very least, these various cases, cases that I will call cases of "perceptual difference", have long been thought to challenge the commonsense view that colours are objective properties of objects, properties that objects have regardless of how they would be perceived.[8]

Earlier I discussed a way of thinking about illusion in order to illustrate what we might think is special about colour illusions, why it is that *colour* illusions present a philosophical problem of their own. That problem, I suggested, is that without an independent handle on when something has a particular colour, it is not clear which of our experiences are illusory and which are veridical. The problem is not simply that what we take to be a perceptual illusion might not be. Kalderon shows why, even where we are mistaken about the colour of an object due to the way it appears, it does not follow that our experience is illusory. The problem, instead, is that it is not clear when we are mistaken. When normal observers under normal conditions disagree about the colour of an object, how do we determine who is right? How do we determine which experiences are veridical and which illusory? It would seem that we could settle these questions only if we know already when something has a particular colour. But the philosophical debate has often gone in the opposite direction. Rather than depend upon our ordinary understanding of what is coloured to determine which experiences are veridical and to then determine the nature of that property that we see—which is exactly what we would do for our experiences of the so-called "primary properties—we have instead focused on the problem cases to guide us in determining the nature of colours. That, I believe, is a mistake.

Of course, if nothing is coloured, if an error-theory of colours is true, then it must be the case that all colour experiences are illusory. And if something's colour is relative to perceivers and viewing conditions, if something has whatever colour it appears to have to any observer under any viewing condition, then it must be the case that no colour experience is illusory. But this is to get things backwards. Of course it is true that, once we know the nature of colours, we can then determine which of our experiences are veridical and which illusory. That is just as it is with experiences of primary properties. But what is often assumed, what I contend to be a mistake, is that perceptual differences, and the colour illusions those differences seem to force upon us, tell us something about the nature of colours.

To show that this is false, I will begin by sketching an objectivist account of colours, an account developed by Alex Byrne and David Hilbert (2003).[9] I will not argue for the account. It doesn't matter, for my purposes here, whether that account is correct or not. I will not aim to show that, if the account is right, then we can determine which experiences are illusory and which are not. I assume that that is true for any account, once that account is sufficiently developed. I will instead show that any answer we might give to cases of perceptual difference is perfectly compatible with the objectivist position that I sketch. Perceptual differences and the illusions they portend, I will argue, cannot tell us about the nature of colours. Perceptual difference, no matter what we say about it, leaves the field open. The residual problem of colour illusions, if there is one, cannot be solved without our first settling questions about the nature of colours, or at the very least settling the question of which things are coloured what.[10]

3 Perceptual difference, illusion, and the nature of colours

According to Byrne and Hilbert, the ultimately determinate colours—the finest shades of colours—are spectral reflectance properties. Two objects have the same ultimately determinate colour if and only if they reflect all and only the same light across the visible spectrum. Objects that are different shades of the same determinable colour, or objects that match under some lighting condition, share a reflectance type.[11] A similar story can be told for determinable colours, each a type of reflectance.

There are many reflectance types, since there are very many colours that we and other animals see, and perhaps many more reflectance types that could be seen were the right kind of creature around to see them, and each particular determinate reflectance property belongs to (or constitutes, or has instances that realize the instances of) very many, perhaps infinitely many, reflectance types. And so an object might be said to have very many different colours, some of which are at the same determinable level, though perhaps it will be that at any determinable level an object will have only one "human colour", that is a colour that humans see.[12] Bee colours and human colours are not the same, after all, but the very same reflectance property might be determinate of that object's human colour—that colour we correctly see it as having—and its bee colour—that colour that bees correctly see it as having.

Of course, a similar story is available to the philosopher wishing to treats colours as those underlying physical properties responsible for objects' having the reflectance properties that they have, and so for those inclined to be more reductive than Byrne and Hilbert a similar story is available.[13] Likewise for those inclined to be less reductive than Byrne and Hilbert.[14] Colours might be thought of as primitive properties, as properties that are perhaps realized by various physical properties, but not reducible to them. Consistent with such a view we might hold that what realizes a human colour likewise realizes a bee colour. As far as I can tell, the position sketched thus far is available, *mutatis mutandis*, to any objectivist.

Now back to the problem of perceptual difference. Here is a striking case and the kind of case commonly encountered in the colour literature: subjects are given a series of coloured cards ranging from reddish-blue to reddish-yellow and asked to select the card that is unique red, that is that shade of red with no blue or yellow in it. It is well documented what will happen, given a sufficiently large and random sample of subjects.[15] Although each subject will select the same card or a nearby neighbour on every occasion that she takes the test, considerable disagreements will arise between subjects. Different subjects will select a wide range of different cards as unique red. What some perceive as unique red will to others appear quite bluish or quite yellowish. Each card, of course, has a different reflectance property. Indeed, each belongs to many different reflectance types. But which of these is unique red? Which of our perceivers experience the unique red card as unique red, and which suffer unique-red-shade illusions? Any answer will seem arbitrary. What to do?

Jonathan Cohen (2009) argues that since different perceivers, and even the same perceiver under different viewing conditions, will sometimes visually represent an object's colour differently, and since we at times have no good reason to favour the one as veridical as opposed to the others, we should conclude that each is veridical. We should, as Cohen puts it, be "ecumenical" about colour perception. And the best way to reach that conclusion, the best way to be ecumenical, is to think of colours as relational properties.

So let us assume, with Cohen, that different perceivers sometimes perceive the same object as having different colours, and let's assume further that those perceptions are veridical. Is this enough to motivate Cohen's relationalism? Would it give us reason to abandon the kind of objective account of colours that I sketched above? No. Colours are, for Byrne and Hilbert, reflectance properties and types. If they were to agree with Cohen that we should be ecumenical, then the Byrne and Hilbert conclusion should be that the property you veridically experience as unique red and the property that I veridically experience as bluish-red are different reflectance types realized or partly constituted by the same reflectance property. If you think it absurd that an object simultaneously has more than one colour, then that's a reason not to be ecumenical. It's no reason to be a relationalist.

Indeed, it is generally overlooked that relational accounts like Cohen's treat colour properties as compatibles. Cohen's response to the problem of perceptual difference is, after all, to treat each observer's colour experience as veridical, but about different colour properties. The object that is unique red (relative to you) is bluish-red (relative to me). As Cohen admits, "it is true that, according to relationalism, ordinary objects have infinitely many colors" (2004, p. 472).

It might also be thought that the relationalist has a way of explaining how colours might be compatibles whereas the objectivist does not. But this claim requires support, and it won't be found. Remember the Byrne and Hilbert view of colours. The colours that we see, on this view, are reflectance types constituted by more determinate reflectance properties. There is nothing about this view, to this point, that prevents Byrne and Hilbert from claiming that the same reflectance property is a constituent of more than one reflectance type. Indeed, they claim this already since for them the same reflectance property that is a constituent of scarlet is also a constituent of red (and of colour and of whatever colour a bee sees when it sees something having that reflectance property). And so there's nothing to prevent them from treating some of the reflectance properties constitutive of unique red as also constitutive of bluish-red, at least nothing but that it violates the colour incompatibility claim. Ecumenicalism is perfectly compatible with objectivism.

If being ecumenical is to accept more than one judgement as correct, then being non-ecumenical is to accept no more than one as correct. Although it is not required of their general theory of colours, Byrne and Hilbert are non-ecumenical, or at least less ecumenical than Cohen. If one subject sees square 32 as unique red and the other doesn't, then at least one is suffering an illusion. Byrne and Hilbert argue that, even if we do not have a good reason to conclude that either is suffering an illusion, we have a good reason to conclude that at least one is. It might be (and has been) objected that we not only do not know which of our subjects is correct, but we also have no idea how it might be determined. It might also be objected that, if Byrne and Hilbert are correct, then most of us suffer colour-shade illusions much of the time. If Byrne and Hilbert are right that there is a unique red that most of us are getting wrong, then it is almost certainly the case that most of us suffer shade illusions pretty consistently. Our experiences may be generally veridical about colour determinables—we generally see red things as red, for instance—but our experiences of the particular shades we see things as having will generally be illusory. In any case, the view that there is a unique red that most of us misrepresent is obviously compatible with the objectivist view that I sketched above. We needn't worry more about it here.

So far we've looked at the possibility that both of our observers are correct and the possibility that at most one is correct, and we've seen that neither possibility threatens objectivity. What if we conclude that both observers are (and even must be) suffering an illusion? The argument for such a view might go like this. Nothing about the two observers, and nothing about their viewing conditions, makes it plausible to favour the one experience over the other. Since nothing can simultaneously be unique red and reddish blue, they cannot both be correct. Thus, neither perceiver is correct. And now a more radical conclusion is within reach. Since no other perceiver or condition can reasonably be favoured over our two perceivers or their viewing conditions, no perceiver can be correct in concluding that the square is unique red. Everyone is mistaken whenever she concludes that something is unique red. All such experiences are illusory.

Notice, however, that even if we are convinced by this argument, it at best gives us reason to conclude that nothing is unique red, and the average person on the street will hardly be shocked by that. If I see an object as being unique red and you see it as bluish-red, and if I recognize that we are both normal perceivers under normal conditions, and if I accept the colour incompatibility claim, then perhaps I should not judge that the object is unique-red. Indeed, perhaps nothing is unique red. It is red, of course, and coloured. It is also *that* colour, as I point, and not another. But just as the category of "best" perhaps fails to apply to works of art, we might conclude that the category of "unique red", as a shade of objective colour, fails for us.[16] If you believe that the standard for any object's colour is the way it appears to normal perceivers under normal conditions, and if you insist on the truth of the colour incompatibility claim, then where normal perceivers under normal conditions disagree, you are committed not only to being non-ecumenical, but to concluding that none of those perceivers are correct. But this gives us no reason to conclude that they are not correct when and where they agree. And an objectivist will have a story to tell about what they are correct about when they are correct about it.

Of course, disagreements arise not only for the unique shades, but also for borderline cases and cases of metameric matches, cases where objects appear the same under some lighting conditions but not others, or to some observers but not others. But this does not call into question the general strategy on offer. These, too, will be cases where, at certain determinable levels, colour categories may not apply to certain objects. Those objects will, of course, have the ultimately determinate shades that they have, where for Byrne and Hilbert those are the reflectance properties that they have. And certain determinable categories will apply; at the very least they are all coloured. It is sometimes assumed, I suppose, that every determinate colour must belong to some determinable colour or other at every determinable level. But I see no reason to assume this. Compare with shapes. An object has whatever determinate shape it has and, of course, it is shaped. But it might not be quite cubical, or quite round, or quite more cubical than round, and so forth. We rarely find, in the world of ordinary objects, the precision we find in geometry. Likewise, an object might be some determinate colour and coloured, but not red or blue (though it appears more red to some and more blue to others, or it appears more red under some lighting conditions and more blue under other lighting conditions, or it appears more blue against certain backgrounds and more red against others, and so forth).

And so when faced with the problem of perceptual difference, when faced with a case in which two (or more) observers make different perceptual judgements about the colour of an object, we might be moved by any of the following three arguments. First, the standard for whether an object is a particular colour is how it would appear to the right kind of observer under the right kind of condition. And so, since the right kinds of observers under the right kinds of conditions judge the same object to be different colours, we should conclude that it is different colours. We should be ecumenical. We should conclude that both observers are correct. Second, the best standard we have for whether an object is a particular colour is how it would appear to the right kind of observer under the right kind of condition. And so, since the right kinds of observers under the right kinds of conditions conclude that the same object is different colours, and since no object can be two colours at the same time, we should conclude that both observers are wrong about the colour of those objects. Third, since the observers make different judgements about the colour of the object, and since no object can simultaneously be different colours, we should conclude that at most one of those observers is correct, even if we do not know which observer to favour. Each argument has its proponents and I've said nothing here aimed at settling that dispute. My aim has been merely to show that regardless how the problem of perceptual difference is solved, there's an objectivist strategy for doing so. Of course, for any particular case of perceptual difference, only one answer can be correct. Taken together, they are logically incompatible. We can't be ecumenical here. But we can be meta-ecumenical: we can happily accept any of them, while remaining objectivists.

So why have philosophers taken the problem of perceptual difference to implicate objectivism? In the case of colours, one reason, perhaps, is that we have confused objectivism with the naïve theory of colour that includes objectivism as a proper part. The naïve theory of colours, we might think, is the conjunction of three theses:

1   Colours are objective surface features of objects.
2   The right kinds of perceivers under the right kinds of conditions are epistemically privileged with respect to colours; those perceivers under those conditions cannot be mistaken about the colours of objects.

3   Colours are incompatibles; nothing can simultaneously have two different colours all over at the same time.

The naïve theory is perfectly coherent. The three theses might live happily hand in hand. But empirical evidence that seemingly equally apt perceivers under seemingly equally ideal conditions have different colour experiences directly challenges the view.

We have three options. First, we might deny that equally apt perceivers under equally ideal conditions have different colour experiences. We might insist that some of these perceivers are more apt than others, even if we do not know which they are. This is the option defended by Byrne and Hilbert, and the only path to save our naiveté. Second, we might deny the epistemic privilege of any particular colour perceiver under any particular condition, at least where the observers disagree. This is the option defended by Hardin. This option allows that the judgement made by any perceiver under any condition might be undermined by the judgement of another equally apt perceiver or judge. Finally, we might deny the colour incompatibility claim. This is the option chosen by Cohen, and it allows that equally apt judges might be equally correct even where their experiences or judgements differ. And so when the naïve theory faces the empirical challenge of perceptual differences, we might either deny that those differences undermine the naïve theory, or we might deny the epistemic privilege of any particular perceivers or judges, or we might deny the incompatibility claim. But what goes untouched, what is not denied by any of our three options, is the objectivist thesis. Abandoning objectivism is not a way to solve the problem of perceptual difference. Objectivism is beside the point.

Now I hasten to remind the reader that I have not aimed here to defend objectivism. My focus has been on colour illusion and the role colour illusion has played in discussions about the nature of colours. That objects appear differently coloured under different lighting conditions or to different observers has long played a central role in arguments for the conclusion that colours are not real, or that they are "secondary", subjective, relational, or transitory. These arguments contend that if colours are objective and non-relational features of objects, then we face the challenge of determining which of our perceptual experiences are getting it right and which are getting it wrong. And they assume that perceptual differences and the illusions they portend tell us something important about the nature of colours. I suspect that this places the cart before the horse.[17]

Notes

1 My thanks to Derek Brown and Fiona Macpherson for many helpful suggestions and probative comments, some of which deserve far more attention than space allowed me to address. I also thank Kelly Jolley, James Shelley, Jody Graham, Sheldon Wein, and Duncan MacIntosh for helpful discussions and suggestions.
2 See Hilbert (2005) and Brown (2014) for discussions of colour perception in general sympathy with this point.
3 The "looks" debate is, of course, long and contentious. See Kalderon (2011) and Breckenridge (this volume, Chapter 26).
4 But see the articles in this volume under Part V, "Colour Experience and Epistemology".
5 A promising suggestion is that illusions result from deviant causal chains. See Cohen (2007) for one way to develop this idea.
6 See, for example, Cohen (2009, and this volume, Chapter 19).
7 See, for example, Hardin (1988) and Wright (this volume, Chapter 22).
8 For discussions of objective accounts of colour, see Byrne and Hilbert (this volume, Chapter 17) and Gert (this volume, Chapter 18).

9 Also see Hilbert (1987) and Tye (2000).

10 Perhaps it would be better to start neither by focusing on perceptual differences and illusions (as I think we too often do) nor with common sense and the metaphysics of colours (as I recommend), but with an eye firmly on both. Perhaps. I am convinced, however, that the philosophy of colour is in need of a corrective. The focus on, even the obsession with, cases of perceptual difference is motivated largely by the idea that they inform our metaphysics; in particular, that such differences provide a direct challenge to objectivists accounts of colour. I argue below that such differences do not force our hand, regardless what we decide to say about them.

11 We might think of these reflectance types as disjunctive properties having the relevant reflectance properties as disjuncts. We might, instead, think of them as properties that are realized by, or supervene upon, the particular reflectance properties. Nothing that I say below depends upon any particular characterization of these properties.

12 For accounts of colour that are both pluralistic and objective, see Byrne and Hilbert (2007), Kalderon (2007), and Watkins (2002).

13 See Jackson (1996).

14 See Gert (2008) and Watkins (2002, 2005).

15 See Webster and Webster (2000).

16 Gert (2006) defends such a view about colours. For a similar position in aesthetics, see Shelley (2013).

17 This is obviously not the final word on the importance of perceptual difference for debates about the metaphysics of colours. Indeed, it is not entirely the next word, which would minimally require more of a response to Cohen (2009, Chapter 3) and Hardin (2003). For that, see Kalderon (this volume, Chapter 20), Byrne and Hilbert (2004), and Watkins (unpublished).

References

Armstrong, David. 1961. *Perception and the Physical World*. New York: Routledge and Kegan Paul.

Austin, J.L. 1962. *Sense and Sensibilia*. Oxford: Clarendon Press.

Brown, Derek. 2014. "Colour Layering and Colour Constancy", *Philosophers' Imprint*, 14(15).

Byrne, Alex and Hilbert, David. 2003. "Color Realism and Color Science", *Behavioral and Brain Sciences*, 26: 3–64.

Byrne, Alex and Hilbert, David. 2004. "Hardin, Tye, and Color Physicalism", *Journal of Philosophy*, 101: 37–43.

Byrne, Alex and Hilbert, David. 2007. "Color Primitivism", *Erkenntnis*, 66: 73–105.

Cohen, Jonathan. 2004. "Color Properties and Color Ascriptions: A Relationalist Manifesto", *The Philosophical Review*, 113: 451–506.

Cohen, Jonathan. 2007. "A Relationalist's Guide to Error about Color Perception", *Nous*, 41: 335–53.

Cohen, Jonathan. 2009. *The Red and the Real*. Oxford: Oxford University Press.

Gert, Joshua. 2006. "A Realistic Color Realism", *Australasian Journal of Philosophy*, 84: 565–89.

Gert, Joshua. 2008. "What Colors Could Not Be: An Argument for Color Primitivism", *Journal of Philosophy*, 105: 128–55.

Hardin, C.L. 1988. *Color for Philosophers*. Indianapolis: Hackett Publishing Company.

Hardin, C.L. 2003. "A Spectral Reflectance Doth Not a Color Make", *Journal of Philosophy*, 100: 191–202.

Hilbert, David. 1987. *Color and Color Perception*. Stanford: Center for the Study of Language and Information.

Hilbert, David. 2005. "Color Constancy and the Complexity of Color", *Philosophical Topics*, 33: 141–58.

Jackson, Frank. 1996. "The Primary Quality View of Color", in Tomberlin (ed.), *Philosophical Perspectives*, Vol. 10. Blackwell: Cambridge, MA: 199–219.

Kalderon, Mark Eli. 2007. "Color Pluralism", *Philosophical Review*, 116: 536–601.

Kalderon, Mark Eli. 2011. "Color Illusion", *Noûs*, 45: 751–75.

Locke, John. 1975/1690. *An Essay Concerning Human Understanding*. New York: Oxford University Press.

Shelley, James. 2013. "Hume and the Joint Verdict of True Judges", *Journal of Aesthetics and Art Criticism*, 71: 145–53.

Tye, Michael. 2000. *Consciousness, Color, and Content*. Cambridge, MA: MIT Press.

Watkins, Michael. 2002. *Rediscovering Colors: A Study in Pollyanna Realism*. Dordrecht: Kluwer.

Watkins, Michael. 2005. "Seeing Red: The Metaphysics of Colours without the Physics", *Australasian Journal of Philosophy*, 83: 35–52.

Watkins, Michael. unpublished. *From Blue to the Blues*.

Webster, M.A. and Webster, S.M. 2000. "Variations in Normal Color Vision, III: Unique Hues in Indian and United States Observers", *Journal of the Optical Society of America A*, xix, 10: 1951–62.

16

COLOUR CONSTANCY

Derek H. Brown

At first pass, colour constancy occurs when one sees a thing in one's environment to have a stable colour despite differences in the way it is illuminated at a time (simultaneous constancy) or over time (successive constancy). The phenomenon is intuitively grounded in everyday experiences in which something is partly shadowed but, in some sense, looks to be uniformly coloured (simultaneous constancy), and in which one views something indoors then outdoors and the thing looks to be stably coloured (successive constancy). The concept is established in vision science, where it traditionally refers to any efforts visual systems take to separate surface and incident illuminant contributions to the colour signal (i.e. the light reaching the eye) and stably represent the surface contributions. However, one can broaden the concept in various ways (e.g. Brown 2003), for example to include efforts visual systems take to stably represent colour across changes in viewing angle, the medium through which one is viewing, and other aspects of scene composition. I largely adhere to narrower conceptions, but comment on broader ones where appropriate.

After a brief introduction to the colour constancy concept (§0) and the science of colour constancy (§1), my focus is on the significance of colour constancy for two intertwined philosophical issues. The first is colour ontology, where constancy has been used to argue for the objectivity of colour, and in particular for a reductive form of it (see §2). The second is colour constancy's complicated connection to colour experience and colour epistemology. Colour constancy is a subtle phenomenon: it is situated at the intersection of perceptual experience and judgement; it is influenced by myriad forces within our visual-cognitive systems; and is likely a composite of interestingly disparate phenomena. I approach this suite of issues from the perspective of the *given* in colour perception (§3). As will become plain, the ontological and epistemic issues are related in important ways. This does not, however, detract from the value of focusing on each individually.

§0 What is colour constancy?

Here is a brief sample of various ways to develop the rough idea that colour constancy occurs when one sees a thing in one's environment to have a stable colour despite differences in the way it is illuminated over or at a time. Note that the *thing* in question is typically taken to be a material surface in one's environment (though see §0.4 below).

§0.1 What is the relevant sense of 'sees'? Some one or more of 'visually represents', 'experiences', 'is acquainted with', or 'judges' may be appropriate instead of or in addition to a success-verb notion of 'sees'. If colour constancy is a perceptual phenomenon then it arguably cannot merely arise through judgement. By default, I will assume it is perceptual, and that 'visually represents' and 'experiences' are both acceptable terms for describing the relation between perceiver and the target stable colour. Typically, I default to 'experiences'. This issue is central to (§3).

§0.2 What is meant in saying that the target thing's colour is experientially 'stable' across the illumination variations? Is the experienced colour (a) exactly the same, or (b) of the same colour category (say blue) but perhaps of a different shade within that category (say darker blue)? Alternatively, is colour constancy (c) the ability to experience stable relations between colours across illumination variations, regardless of stabilities of experienced colour itself (Foster 2003)?

Option (a) has intuitive appeal, but it is difficult to defend. Instead, colour constancy is typically regarded as a *tendency* to experience a thing as having a stable colour despite the presence of illumination variations, a fact sometimes summarized by referring to colour constancy as *approximate* (e.g. Bradley & Tye 2001, Byrne & Hilbert 2003). This implies that some degree of colour sameness (at least categorical sameness) is experienced during constancy, but typically not *exact* sameness. The latter is usually associated with *perfect* colour constancy, a rare occurrence (see also §1, esp. note 1). As we will see, there are means of trying to preserve (a), but I will in general assume that colour constancy involves (b), that the degree of sameness that is experienced during colour constancy at least stays within a colour category. I briefly remark on (c) in §3, but otherwise leave this intriguing option in the background.

§0.3 The target object is differently illuminated over or at a time. What contribution do these illumination variations make to colour experience? If perfect constancy were the norm, then one could assume that the illuminant contribution to the colour signal is generally *discarded* and hence neither experienced nor represented during colour constancy. All else being equal this would result in colour constancy experiences only involving experiences of perfectly stable surface colours. This was perhaps the hope of early constancy theorists, arguably an assumption in Land's pioneering work on the topic (e.g. Land & McCann 1971), and central to early idealized computational models (e.g. Wandell 1989). However, given that imperfect constancy is now recognized as the default kind of colour constancy, it is generally understood that various aspects of the illuminant contribution, though often not all, are experienced and represented in colour vision. As pretheoretic evidence think of the above examples, of shadows, scattering effects, the visual difference between seeing the world in daylight versus twilight, et cetera. Two qualifications are important.

First, it remains to explain the *manner* in which illumination enters into colour experience during colour constancy. For example, is it a modifier of the experienced surface colour (and if so what form of modification takes place), or is illumination experienced to have its own colour? This question will return throughout. Second, the idea that colour constancy involves discounting or minimizing the experiential impact of illumination changes is not bankrupt. For example, low level light adaptation mechanisms exist and to some extent *do* discount illumination variations. Intuitively, one experiences this form of adaptation when moving from dimly (/brightly) illuminated areas to brightly (/dimly) illuminated ones: the initially sharp contrast in experienced illumination is to some degree normalized by our visual systems. This thus remains a viable form of colour constancy.

One challenge is to build a colour constancy model that incorporates both the partial discounting of illumination variations via mechanisms like adaptation, and the vivid experiential impact of illumination variations familiar from shadowing and the like. As a first step, adaptive effects typically apply to changes in *overall* illumination (i.e. illuminant changes that bound toward spanning one's field of view). This is entirely compatible with more local illumination variations due to partial shadowing, scattering, et cetera being left largely perceptible under changes in overall illumination. In this vein, Wright (2013) has usefully suggested that we recognize two fundamentally different kinds of colour constancy. I will be focusing on the constancies in which illumination variations are experienced (in some manner or other). This is in part because it follows standard practice and in part because such cases are the most illuminating and challenging to work with.

§0.4 As mentioned at the outset, it is conceptually straightforward to broaden our understanding of colour constancy beyond "experienced stabilities in surface colour across illumination variations". First, one can simply invert the traditional model and ask about experienced stabilities in *illumination* conditions across changes in *surfaces*. Second, in theory a surface can be experienced to have a fairly stable colour not only across illumination variations, but also for example across variations in the medium through which one is looking (air versus water; one pair of sunglasses versus another pair; etc.), and across variations in surfaces surrounding a target surface. Surely these modest feats are "approximately" achieved in human colour vision, there is no reason to disregard them as insignificant, and it is likely that the same or similar mechanisms are involved in them as are involved in securing approximate surface colour stabilities across illumination variations (see again, e.g. Brown 2003). To capture these generalizations, one might conceive of colour constancy as efforts visuals systems make to disentangle and track stable contributions to the colour signal (be them stable surfaces, illuminants, or whatever) as other contributions vary.

To be sure, colour constancy *purists* will resist such deviations from the traditional "experienced stabilities in surface colour across illumination variations" picture, though from my perspective there are few to no philosophically important reasons for doing so. I will nonetheless focus on the traditional conception, as this contains enough to chew on for unfamiliar readers. With luck, what follows will generate some interest in exploring these generalizations of colour constancy in future work.

§1 Colour constancy science

The science of colour constancy has developed immensely in the last 30 years. The details are complicated, and I can only provide a broad, selective outline.[1] First, it is important to note that some degree of colour constancy has been observed in many species, including not only in various land animals but also in birds, insects, and water creatures. The phenomenon is therefore widespread and seems critical to understanding colour perception. Neurally, there is evidence of processing relevant to colour constancy occurring in the retina, in V1 and in V4. The emerging picture is thus that colour constancy isn't achieved by a single mechanism at a distinctive neural location, but instead that different facets of constancy are achieved by different mechanisms at differing levels of neural processing (see also §0.3). In many respects we are at an early stage of research with regard to how these pieces fit together. Of most relevance to our discussion is the psychophysical evidence drawn from human subjects.

There are four main types of psychophysical experiments, those involving: asymmetric colour matching; achromatic adjustment; colour naming; and surface and illuminant change attribution (see Foster 2011, 681–90). Before remarking on them, it is worth highlighting that within each type are tokens that vary in numerous ways. For example, the experiment can test for simultaneous or successive constancy, or it can utilize stimuli that are briefly presented (adaptation minimal) or stimuli that presented for an extended duration (adaptation significant). The nature of the stimuli can also vary greatly. Stimuli can be depicted on computer monitors or actually presented to subjects. Stimuli can be presentations/depictions of natural or artificial kinds, of recognizable things or unfamiliar geometric structures, et cetera. The most influential "measure" of colour constancy is the Colour Constancy Index (CCI), which provides a decent measure of the extent to which what a subject identifies as matching surfaces, despite being differently illuminated, deviates from a perfect physical match (introduced in Arend et al. 1991, p. 665). The index ranges from 0–1, with 1 representing perfect colour constancy, and 0 representing the opposite (i.e. something like perfect constancy failure or perfect colour variation—there is no standardized term).

The asymmetric colour matching paradigm is arguably the most influential. It involves two stimuli either simultaneously or sequentially presented under different illuminants (i.e. simulated on a monitor). The stimuli are traditionally collections of abstract colour patches (*Mondrians*) though have also been more natural scenes. Subjects are asked to adjust a patch on the test stimulus (*test patch*) so that it matches a corresponding patch on the target stimulus (*target patch*). Since the test and target patches are presented under different illuminants, a difference that is apparent in experience, the task is non-trivial. Interestingly, the task is subject to significant instructional effects. An influential design (Arend & Reeves 1986) involves two separate instructions:

> *Appearance Match Condition*: adjust the test patch to match the target patch's hue and saturation.

> *Surface Match Condition*: adjust the test patch so that it looks like it is cut from the same piece of paper as the target patch.

While Surface Match responses contain evidence of approximate colour constancy (often ranging from 0.6–0.8 CCI), Appearance Match responses contain evidence of substantive colour change (often ranging from 0.2–0.4 CCI).[2] This has led to difficult interpretational questions (see §2 and esp. §3).

Like the asymmetric colour matching paradigm, the surface and illuminant change attribution experiments typically present to subjects (either simultaneously or sequentially) Mondrian stimuli under different illuminants. However, a crucial facet of these experiments is that subjects are asked to assess whether a given colour-perceptual change is due to a difference in illumination or surface conditions. This task can be paired with Appearance and/or Surface Match instructions and the results compared. Perhaps not surprisingly, changes identified as being due to surface conditions correlate well with Surface Match results, and are linearly separable from Appearance Match results (Reeves *et al.* 2008).[3]

§2 Colour constancy and ontology: the path to colour objectivism and beyond

One can naturally seek justification for the objectivity or mind-independence of colours in folk psychology ('spinach is green') or in naïve experience (green looks to be *of* or *in* spinach and not for example in or part of 'the perceiver'). Colour constancy is a tempting additional anchor for colour objectivists, especially those seeking a more naturalized source of justification. The idea that colour experience is to a reasonable degree invariant across illumination conditions is an instance of something being stable as some variable changes values. This makes colour ripe for study through controlled experimentation, setting at least the tone for a naturalized colour epistemology. Ontologically, if experienced colour is fairly invariant across illumination changes, then, assuming colour experience is broadly veridical, colour is an illumination-independent property. Further, if colour is experienced as a property of things in one's environment (often on/in their surfaces), then, again assuming colour experience is broadly veridical, colour is an illumination-independent property of things in one's environment.

The step from here to colours being mind-independent is tempting. After all, light gets to directly strike things in one's environment all the time, certainly more directly than vision does. Thus, if colour is an illumination-independent feature of those things, it is independent of us. Also tempting is the reductive and more precise postulate that the nature of colour is critically tied to the ways surfaces reflect light (their SSRs) and more generally to the ways things interact with light. SSRs are fairly stable features of things, and are directly relevant to the causal chain from light source to surface to eye that gives rise to colour perception. Colour constancy is therefore a naturalistically respectable anchor for colour objectivism and in particular a reductive form of it like reflectance physicalism (Chapter 17).

Although there are various means of formalizing this reasoning, the following simple rendering is useful for our purposes:

1 *Colour Constancy:* experienced(/represented) colour is fairly stable across illumination variations and is experienced(/represented) as a feature of things in one's environment.
2 *Veridicality:* our colour experiences(/representations) are generally veridical.

Thus,

3 *Illumination-independence:* colour is an illumination-independent property of things in one's environment.

And more precisely,

4 *Reflectance physicalism*: the ways objects reflect light, their SSRs, are plausible candidates for colours.

The simplicity and elegance of the argument are impressive.[4] For centuries colour subjectivists have used colour variation, illusion, and hallucination as a basecamp from which to defend their view. If nothing else this straightforward argument provides a much-needed counterweight, grounded in a phenomenon—colour constancy—that has roots in common sense perception and is naturalistically respectable. The argument can thus serve as a basecamp from which to defend colour objectivism, in this case reflectance physicalism.

§2.1 Objections and replies

Many challenges to reflectance physicalism have been put forward that do not focus on the role of constancy in what motivates the view (see again Chapter 17). Others focus precisely on it. Cohen (2008) contends that colour constancy data do not support the illumination-independence of colour in any straightforward way, an idea discussed in §3. Chirimuuta (2008) argues roughly that "ontologically neutral" experimentation on colour constancy is unavailable. Instead, constancy data that seem to support reflectance physicalism do so because antecedent theoretical assumptions to that effect are built into the experimental approach, and similarly for different assumptions/experimental approaches. Though these are excellent contributions, I focus on evaluating the above argument.

To begin, the two premises contain important qualifiers: experienced colour is *fairly* stable and colour experience is *generally* veridical. The premises thus provide at best defeasible justification for (3) and (4). Much hinges on how to interpret the impact of illumination variations on experienced colour and on the veridicality of colour experience. For example, an opponent might argue that, via (1), illumination variations are often experienced to at least some degree, and that (2) the general veridicality of colour experience implies that colour is to some degree illumination dependent. The defender of the above argument thus needs to justifiably "contain" illumination's impact on colour ontology.

One strategy is to prevent Veridicality from applying to colour experiences of illuminants on grounds that such experiences are rare or anomalous. This is roughly the strategy of Byrne and Hilbert (2003): we sometimes experience light to be blue, say that of a blue laser, but these are exceptional situations and the blueness we experience is illusory. They propose that the experienced blue is actually the blue of the light source, not of the light beam itself. However, even if this strategy has merit in some cases, it is difficult to generalize given the widespread presence of shadowing and scattering effects and the fact that lights drastically change the 'tones' of experienced colours in everyday scenes (e.g. more bluish tones at sunrise and more reddish at twilight). Illuminants impact colour experience in seemingly every scene. Thus, if Veridicality is in force, colours are routinely illumination dependent and so colours cannot be confined to SSRs.

A different strategy concedes that illuminants regularly impact colour experience, but maintains that they do so in such a way as to preserve illumination-independent colour. This requires developing an interesting account of colour experience, the latter being the topic of §3. In this context it is worth rehearsing how the strategy has been used to help bolster the argument for colour objectivism. As a start, one could offer the plausible idea that illuminants *illuminate* colours in various ways, and thereby treat experienced illuminants as an additional dimension in colour experience beyond the traditional three of hue, saturation, and lightness (Hilbert 2005, 2011; Jagnow 2010). Thus, when one experiences a given surface colour one experiences the colour's hue, saturation, and lightness, plus a manner of illumination, where the latter is distinct from the former. How should we understand the *way* in which illuminants enter into colour experience? One option is to suppose, as is plausible, that illuminants can and often do serve an epistemic role, making surface colour more or less visible (e.g. very visible in bright light versus barely visible in low light). Suppose in addition that, controversially, this epistemic role is "marked" in experience. One can explicate this "mark" in numerous ways, but for simplicity (setting aside obvious confounds) assume it is through the vivacity or faintness of the experienced colour, where a vivacious colour is indicative of its being highly visible, and a faint colour is indicative of its being poorly visible. On this account, the only colours typically experienced are surface colours, and thus Veridicality can perform its original function of securing them. In addition, Veridicality can be extended to the new machinery. Thus, experiencing the degree of vivacity/faintness of a colour is both experiencing the level of illumination of the colour and experiencing (in some sense of the term) the degree of epistemic access one has to that colour.

A third strategy combines the first two, allowing illumination to enter colour experience in two distinct ways. Sometimes illumination is experienced as coloured (e.g. laser case)—these experiences are non-veridical. Other times illumination makes surface colours more or less visible by making us experience those colours more or less vividly. In theory illumination can serve both functions in a given perception, generating an illusory colour perception at one location in the scene, and modifying the vivacity of the experienced colours at other locations. Perhaps both functions can even be served by the same sample of light. Suppose a blue laser strikes a wall. The experienced blueness of the laser could be illusory. At the same time the surface colour "behind" the laser might nonetheless be faintly experienced and thus to some degree veridically experienced. This hybrid strategy can thus be a powerful view.

One worry about the hybrid strategy stems from the thought that illuminants regularly—not rarely—impact experienced colour itself. Illuminants often directly impact experienced hue, and arguably saturation and lightness. As mentioned above, sunrise often generates more bluish tones throughout the scene, and twilight more reddish ones. These illuminant colours can arguably vary in richness or saturation (e.g. an intense red twilight versus a pale red one), and can be lighter or darker (e.g. a light red sunset versus a somewhat darker one). More scientifically, recall that in the Appearance Match condition subjects are instructed to adjust the test patch to match the hue and saturation of the target. It is hard not to read this as an instruction to match colour in some basic sense. Yet the reports deviate significantly from surface colour constancy (CCI = 0.2–0.4). Presumably this is because the illumination variation impacts experienced colour proper, not merely how "vividly" colours are experienced.

The problem for the hybrid strategy is straightforward. If illuminants only have occasional impact on experienced colour proper, then that impact can be classified as non-veridical by appeal to something like statistical irregularity. But if illuminants have widespread impact on experienced colour proper, then we need a different justification to classify that impact as non-veridical. The truth of reflectance physicalism would provide such justification, were reflectance physicalism not what we are trying justify in this context. Therefore, if studying colour constancy teaches us that illuminants have widespread impact on experienced colour proper, then constancy suggests that colours depend on illuminants (Cohen 2008). Fortunately, there is another route.

§2.2 A more liberal "dual-colour" alternative

A simple way forward supposes that we experience both surfaces *and* illuminants to be coloured. If these two colour types are distinctly experienced, then when the illuminant (/surface) colour varies and the surface (/illuminant) colour remains stable, and one experiences precisely that, one experiences a constant colour while also experiencing a variable one. A natural model for developing the thought is in terms of colour layering (Brown 2014), and the rough idea is defended by Mausfeld (2003), Tokunaga and Logvinenko (2010), and Davies (2016). This approach can accommodate the ideas from the account just discussed. Illuminant colours can be viewed as ways of experiencing surface colours, and we can have better or worse access to surface colours depending on illumination conditions. We can also posit the converse, that we have better or worse access to illuminant colours depending on surface conditions.

By positing surface and illuminant colours, this view undermines the argument for reflectance physicalism. This is an unfortunate outcome if one seeks an argument for reflectance physicalism. It is not an unfortunate outcome if one seeks an argument for some form of colour objectivism, for illuminant colours are in theory as objective as surface colours.

Independently of one's ontological interests, views admitting surface and illuminant colours can maintain a crucial role for colour constancy, when we conceive of colour constancy as efforts visual systems make to disentangle and track stable surface and illuminant contributions to the colour signal. This requires departing from the traditional conception of colour constancy as efforts to isolate stable surface colours across illumination variations, but the departure is minimal. The departure is certainly not a rejection of the spirit of the traditional conception colour constancy, as would for example obtain if illuminants and surfaces collectively impact a single type of colour, say relational surface colour (as in Chapter 19). We will shortly see an analysis of colour constancy that proposes this kind of more radical break.

The dual-colour view receives anecdotal support from naïve perceptual judgements that distinguish surface and illuminant parameters, for example claims that we can experience different surfaces as similarly illuminated, and uniform surfaces as differently illuminated. But such reports must, under scrutiny, buttress the idea that both illuminants and surfaces impact distinctly experienced colours. Unfortunately, traditional colour constancy experiments are not designed to test this idea. They perhaps come closest in the surface and illuminant change attribution experiments (§1). There is additional evidence that we are very good at identifying changes in overall illumination, as opposed to not noticing it (e.g. because it is "adapted out") or conflating such changes with changes in surface colour (Gerhard & Maloney 2010). However, further empirical work would be needed to assess the viability of the dual-colour proposal.

§2.3 *Other colour ontologies*

Independently of whether or not colour constancy can be used to *justify* some form of colour objectivism, one might wonder how *compatible* constancy is with other colour ontologies. It is very compatible. While some evidence of this can be drawn from the differing analyses of constancy covered below, it is perhaps useful to reflect on the general idea that experiencing colour to be constant across illumination variations only demands a stable colour *experience* [or *representation*] across changes in the illumination parameter. There is no antecedent barrier to our visual systems *constructing* such experiences [/representations], regardless of whether or not they are veridical. This opens the door to consistency between constancy and various subjectivist ontologies (Chapters 21 and 22), although some form of error-theory about colour perception is plausibly required. There is also no antecedent barrier to the experienced stable colour being a *sui generis* property, and thus colour primitivist views are consistent with constancy (Chapter 18). It is much trickier to incorporate constancy into colour relationalism (Chapter 19), but we will soon consider a way of closing this gap. None of this diminishes the interest of the above argument, but it is worth keeping in mind that above argument uses colour constancy to *justify* colour objectivism, and in particular a reductivist form of it, and doesn't try to show that constancy requires objectivism.

§3 Colour constancy and epistemology: the given in colour perception

What do subjects receive from the world via perception? With a bit more precision, suppose a subject reports on a perception in speech, thought. or non-verbal behaviour with the intent simply to state or act on what it is that she perceives. Call these *perceptual reports*, and what they express the *contents* of those reports.[5] How much of the content of a report reflects what is *given* to her in perceptual experience, and how much reflects information or hypotheses that outstrip what perceptual experience itself makes available?[6] This is a central question in philosophy of perception, a key issue in perceptual epistemology, and it informs our understanding of the mind-body-world relation. It is also a very difficult question to assess.

Colour constancy is a fascinating case study of this basic struggle. Suppose a thing has a uniform surface. When we see the thing to be partly in shadow, in some sense we experience it to have a constant colour, in some sense we experience the shadowed part to be darker in colour than the unshadowed part. How can the same experience elicit tendencies to report both colour constancy and colour variation? Two broad proposals are found in the literature, at their core differing on what we are perceptually given in this kind of case. One proposal asserts that one of the reports (variation or constancy) reflects what is experienced and the other (constancy or variation) reflects something else, for example a non-experiential perceptual output or a post-perceptual judgement. This is a two-component approach to the puzzle (§3.1). The other proposal asserts that each constancy and variation report reflects a different part of the same experience. This approach seeks to resolve the puzzle by complicating our account of what is perceptually given (§3.2).

The core psychophysical evidence for colour constancy—data from asymmetric matching experiments—informs this discussion in two direct ways. First, how should we interpret the divergent data elicited by the Appearance Match and Surface Match instructions, given that both data sets emerge from subject efforts to perceptually match the same stimulus? According to the first 'two-component' proposal, one of these reports reflects what is perceptually experienced, and the other reflects something else. According to the second proposal, both reports pick up on different aspects of the same perceptual experience. Second, it is important to note that neither set of responses is near "perfect": Surface Match responses deviate significantly from perfect constancy (CCI = 0.6–0.8; 1 being perfect), and Appearance Match data deviate significantly from perfect variation (CCI = 0.2–0.4; 0 being perfect). Taken at face value, this means that subjects experience neither a surface colour that is fully separated from illumination contributions (considering Surface Match data), nor a colour that fully blends the surface and illuminant contributions (considering Appearance Match data). So, what is given to subjects?

There is no simple way out of this quandary. Nonetheless, the following sketch outlines some solutions that contain fruitful insights. The first two accounts propose a two-component— phenomenal and non-phenomenal—analysis of colour constancy, while the second two aim for a more purely phenomenal analysis.

§3.1 Two-component solutions

Two component accounts of colour constancy propose one component to capture colour experience and the other, non-experiential component, to explain residual constancy data (Cohen 2008; Wright 2013). In theory, the second component might be perceptual or cognitive. If cognitive, the second component is something akin to a post-perceptual judgement. If perceptual, the idea is that our perceptual systems, in addition to facilitating colour experiences, generate non-experiential outputs that impact subjects' dispositions to formulate constancy reports (i.e. dispose subjects to formulate thoughts, words, actions with colour constancy contents). Both two component accounts I consider opt for a perceptual (but non-experiential) interpretation of the second component. Most likely this is because they wish their accounts of constancy to preserve constancy's status as a perceptual phenomenon. This means that post-perceptual judgement is not used to fill any gaps between perception and perceptual reports.

Cohen (2008) argues that constant colours are not given in perceptual experience. Instead, what is given are variable, illumination-dependent colours. A second, *counterfactual* component, explains constancy reports. This content is of the form <surface$_1$ would match surface$_2$ were both similarly illuminated>, and is a non-experiential, perceptual output. The rough idea is as follows. Colour experience varies across illumination changes (in-line with Cohen's colour relationalism—see Chapter 19), and thus there is no experienced colour constancy. Appearance Match data reflects these variable experienced colours. Evidence of colour constancy from both Surface Match and pretheoretic sources is explained by appeal to counterfactual contents. Interestingly, *even here* colour attributions are illumination-dependent, that is, reports of constant colours are reports of colours matching (experientially or counterfactually) under similar conditions of illumination. Cohen thus generally rejects the very idea that constancy involves illumination-independent colour. Although this provides a straightforward analysis of the divergent data sets from asymmetric matching experiments, it substantively departs from the traditional conception of colour constancy—indeed one could argue that it is an attempt to redefine colour constancy from scratch. If the justification for colour relationalism is strong enough, this redefining may be warranted. It is worth noting that to this point the account does not illuminate why both Appearance and Surface Match data are imperfect. However, in theory Cohen's relationalism does not commit him to colour outputs being perfectly variable across illumination variations, it only commits him to colour outputs being variable across those variations.

Wright (2013) argues for two perceptual constancy mechanisms: a phenomenal and a non-phenomenal (in his terminology *projective*) mechanism. Both can contain approximate colour constancy, though to different extents, via different internal mechanisms, and in response to different kinds of stimuli. Phenomenal approximate constancy occurs most notably when low-level adaptive mechanisms are able to factor-out some of the shift due to changes in overall illumination conditions. We experience this when sunshine changes to cloud cover and our visual systems partially accommodate to the new illumination conditions. However, within these experiences many sharp changes in illumination conditions are still experienced and experienced as variations in colour. Shadowing effects are a prime example. Thus, while there is some degree of constancy in colour experience (e.g. regarding changes in overall illumination conditions), there is still robust colour variation (e.g. regarding local illumination contrasts). This colour variation is used to explain the Appearance Match data. However, even here Wright believes that there can be a powerful sense of surface colour constancy—this is what Surface Match data illustrates. Projective constancy is postulated to explain this phenomenon. It is a non-experiential, perceptual output of an approximately constant colour that explains why the partially shadowed thing in some sense looks to have a constant colour. Thus, like Cohen, Appearance Match data is explained by appeal to colour experience, and Surface Match by appeal to a non-phenomenal perceptual output. Since both of Wright's constancy mechanisms yield at best approximate constancy, the colour "outputs" from both are to some degree illumination-dependent. This provides a direct account of the imperfect responses from both Appearance and Surface Match conditions.

Both Cohen's and Wright's accounts propose two perceptual outputs, a phenomenal and a non-phenomenal output. Subject reports can be informed by one or both of these, and are not readily dissectible to determine which or how much of each component informs a given report. It is in the first instance the task of empirical researchers to try to tease out these disparate contributions to perceptual reports. However, the task is extremely difficult. Part of Cohen's argument is that asymmetric matching data doesn't and likely won't straightforwardly favour a traditional conception of constancy over a relationalist-friendly counterfactual one. Instead the matter is arguably to be settled by appeal to broader considerations. I don't detect a similar commitment in Wright to the underdetermination of theory by evidence, but he certainly agrees that teasing apart the various contributions to perceptual reports is horribly challenging.

Interestingly, although both authors propose two colour outputs that are to some degree illumination-dependent, there is an important difference. Cohen's approach is designed to minimize if not excise our commitment to illumination-independent colours in perception, for both experienced colour and counterfactual contents ascribe illumination-dependent colour to things. By contrast, Wright's account is designed to recover a considerable degree of illumination-independent colour in perception, since both phenomenal and projective components express different forms of approximate constancy (i.e. different forms of colour stability across illumination variations). It would be worthwhile to work through this difference in future work.

§3.2 *Solutions from phenomenology*

The second type of account tries to explain colour constancy via perceptual experience, as opposed to in part via a non-experiential component. This is achieved by making colour experience more complex in the following respect. It is often tacitly assumed that in typical visual perceptions a uniform surface is simply experienced to have a single, straightforward colour (perhaps with a determinate hue, saturation, and lightness value). By contrast the views under consideration hold that when one perceives a uniform surface, the purported surface colour is experienced, not *simpliciter*, but in some *way* or from some *perspective*. These perspectives qualify, in some manner, the experienced colour, creating the conceptual space for illumination variations to enter into experience without thereby altering the underlying surface colour. Although views of this sort are in theory compatible with a two-component approach, what is distinctive of them is their attempt to explain more with colour experience than their rivals. Numerous approaches fall into this broad category.[7] Some of them treat perspectives on colour as primitive (arguably Kalderon 2008 and Gert 2010). Others explicate perspectives on colour by appeal to more basic elements. I briefly outline two options of the latter sort. Both views were introduced in §2, but here the emphasis is on their approach to colour experience, as opposed to their approach to colour ontology.

One approach (Hilbert 2005, 2011; Jagnow 2010) proposes that illumination often enters into colour experience as a non-coloured entity that helps reveal colours to us (e.g. perhaps by making colours more or less vivid). Thus, during colour constancy perceptions, when one perceives a uniform surface that is differently illuminated, one experiences that surface colour to be differently illuminated. The sameness in colour is part of what is experienced, but the same colour is experienced from different perspectives, specifically under different illuminants. Notably, while the experienced illumination variation can impact our epistemic access to colours (seeing them better or worse), it is not typically a variation in colour *proper* (e.g. hue, saturation, lightness).

Since there is a sameness in experienced colour across illumination variations, this approach can explain constancy reports, including Surface Match data, in terms of experienced colour. That said, the degree of imperfection in Surface Match data isn't straightforwardly explained. It is also unclear how the account explains Appearance Match data, where there is robust constancy failure. In Appearance Match conditions subjects are asked to match the hue and saturation of the target and test colours. Thus, it seems straightforward that in at least this regard illumination variation impacts experienced colour.

Another alternative proposes that illumination typically enters into colour experience and enters it as a coloured entity alongside surface colours (Brown 2014). During surface colour constancy perceptions, one experiences a stable surface colour and variable illuminant colours. Similarly, during illuminant colour constancy perceptions, one experiences a stable illuminant colour and variable surface colours. It is supposed that in some sense we experience surface colours through illuminant colours, a natural conceptualization being that we experience colour layers along a line of sight. Regardless, one's experience of each is *interdependent* on one's experience of the other, and thus during colour constancy subjects are perceptually given two distinct colours along a given line of sight.

This yields several notable consequences. First, an experience of a surface colour under two distinct illuminant colours can be interpreted as one having two different *perspectives* on that surface colour, each perspective facilitating distinctive means of accessing that colour. In this regard the epistemic role of illuminants familiar from the Hilbert-Jagnow approach can be incorporated into the view. Second, since during colour constancy subjects are perceptually given two distinct colours along a line of sight, any reports about a single experienced colour require that subjects perform a dissection of what is given that seeks to isolate the colour of interest. Such dissections invariably involve some form of post-perceptual activity (e.g. judgement, mental imagery) on the part of subjects and, without training, are likely fallible. This permits an interesting interpretation of Surface and Appearance Match conditions.

In Surface Match conditions subjects are asked to select the surface contribution to experienced colour and match for it, ignoring the illuminant contribution. However, because the illuminant colour is nonetheless experienced on both the test and target patches a kind of guess is required, and the post-manipulation test patch (presented under one illuminant) should not be expected to perfectly match the target patch (presented under a different illuminant). This provides a means of explaining the imperfection in Surface Match data and the fact that subjects often report being unable to perfectly perform a surface match.

Appearance Match conditions effectively ask subjects to adjust the test patch so that it matches a fusion or mixture of the surface and illuminant colours from the target patch. However, it is not obvious that a fusion of the surface and illuminant colours from the target patch is perceptually given to subjects—indeed if the target patch is inducing a colour constancy experience then on this view such a fusion is *not* experienced. The same holds for the test patch. In this regard the Appearance Match instructions presume a perceptual given that may not obtain.[8] This account thus also provides a means of explaining the imperfection in Appearance Match data.

The view can be developed in various ways, including by allowing for non-constancy experiences that fuse aspects of surface and illuminant contributions, and by allowing for experiences of *partial colours* (see Brown 2014). Such developments create the conceptual space to consider that there may be varying extents to which illuminant and surface contributions are experienced, and are distinctly experienced, in response to a stimulus. This is useful because it may be that the extent to which we experience, and distinctly experience, surface and illuminant contributions is sensitive to a host of factors, including not only the nature of the current stimulus, but also previous experiences, stimuli, cognitions, et cetera. Postulating that our colour experiences are sensitive in such ways might help explain the perplexing data that has arisen from constancy research. As stated above, while such an account is consistent with there being non-experiential perceptual outputs influencing subject reports, the account is distinguished by creating numerous avenues within perceptual experience to explain disparate phenomena.

§3.3 Additional considerations

There are important issues about colour experience in the vicinity, some of which were highlighted in §0. To what extent are constancy reports of determinable or *coarse-grained* colours as opposed to determinate or *fine-grained* ones and what does this tell us about what is given in colour experience? Evidence for the existence of *unconscious* colour constancy tendencies has recently been offered (Norman *et al.* 2014). To what extent do these tendencies impact constancy reports offered in response to conscious colour constancy perceptions?

Also of interest is the idea of *relational* colour constancy, roughly that colour constancy only reflects a perceived stability in some relation(s) between colours across illumination variations, as opposed to a stability in colour itself (Foster 2003). For example, under one illuminant one might perceive the colour in one region to be (say) 20% lighter than the colour of another region. That lightness relation might be preserved under a different illuminant, even though the perceived colour of each region has changed. In this case variable colours are perceptually given in constancy experience, but those variable colours maintain at least some stable relations between other (variable) colours in a scene. Physiologically, the idea is grounded in a stability in cone excitation ratios across illumination variations. It is also readily applicable to constancy reports, where <x and y match in colour> is interpreted to mean the weaker claim <x and y relate to other perceived colours in the same way>. This can be offered as the correct interpretation of our reports, as a rational reconstruction of them, or of what our reports should be.

As plausible as this might sound, there are key limitations. We typically regard the "stability" in colour constancy as at least involving experiencing a thing's colour across illumination variations to be in the same colour category. This is arguably supported both by reflection on everyday experience and empirical data. On its own relational constancy does not mandate this constraint and so cannot explain what seems to be a central feature of colour constancy. Nonetheless, the relational conception is a potentially important ingredient to constancy processing and maybe to constancy experience.[9]

§4 Conclusion

Colour constancy is of interest to colour ontologists largely because it can be used to construct an argument for colour objectivism that is particularly attractive to naturalistic philosophers. While there are difficulties with the argument, it serves as an important basecamp to counter familiar arguments from variation, illusion, et cetera that have created a safe space for subjectivist colour ontologies. It is noteworthy that a more liberalized objectivist ontology, one that admits not only surface but also illuminant colours, overcomes the core difficulty the argument faces from the routine impact illumination has on experienced colour.

Colour constancy is also of interest to perceptual epistemologists, as it illustrates how difficult it is to capture what is given in colour experience, how that informs colour perceptual reports, and how to interpret the meanings of those reports. The plethora of disparate accounts on offer is testament to these difficulties, and we have only partially come to grips with the depth of the challenge.

Beyond this, there is much to be gained from exploring wider conceptions of colour constancy as opposed to merely focusing on the narrow conception ('experienced colour is fairly stable across illumination variations'). Colour constancy mechanisms are not hostage to illumination variations and surface stabilities, but can to some extent be triggered via variations in media/filters (e.g. looking through air versus tinted glasses versus water) and variations in background/surrounding objects. The concept *colour constancy* as it is employed in vision science is typically not understood this broadly (an exception is Brown 2003). However, if the same or similar mechanisms are triggered in these broader contexts, philosophers should at least be open to the *phenomenon* demanding a broader treatment.

There are also worthwhile connections outside the microcosm of philosophy of colour. For example, little work has been done to examine how colour constancy impacts debates between rival theories of perceptual experience (e.g. naïve realism, representationalism, sense-datum theory). There is ample to chew on here, as is revealed by reflection on the different one- and two-component accounts of constancy. In addition, the relation between colour constancy and other perceptual constancies (e.g. shape and size constancy) is understudied, despite being important for broader projects. Consider two brief examples. The idea that colour and other constancies are substantively similar is critical to some of Gert's (2017) arguments for his preferred account of colour. Outside colour, the idea that constancies can be treated *en masse* to motivate significant philosophical theses is central to Smith (2002) and Burge (2010). Yet, given our discussion, colour constancy is difficult to interpret, and many of its perplexing features at least seem to be peculiarities about colour. Thus, any presumption in favour of there being a uniform treatment of constancies that reflects a consensus view should give us pause. Suffice to say, colour constancy is a rich phenomenon that we understand well-enough to use to illuminate core question in philosophy of colour and perception more widely, and that we understand poorly enough to motivate future endeavours.[10]

Notes

1 Helpful recent review articles include Foster (2011) and Shevell & Kingdom (2008). An earlier but insightful review is Jameson & Hurvich (1989).

2 Recall (§0.2) that colour constancy is rarely perfect and instead typically viewed as a tendency of visual perception. CCIs ranging from 0.6–0.8 in the Surface Match condition are a good empirical indication of this. Perfect constancy (CCI = 1) is rarely observed. Instead, we observe reports that fall far short of perfect constancy, but nonetheless imply that some degree of experienced colour stability is achieved. Thus approximate (as opposed to perfect) colour constancy emerges as a robust, empirically supported phenomenon. The CCI = 0.2–0.4 results from Appearance Match conditions demonstrate a robust failure of colour stability in these conditions.

3 A brief remark about the other two kinds of experiments. In achromatic adjustment experiments subjects are presented with a stimulus (e.g. a Mondrian) and asked to adjust a test patch so that it appears achromatic. This is not a measure of surface colour constancy, but can provide useful information about the locally experienced illuminant colour, and about the influence of memory on colour experience. Colour naming paradigms ask subjects to identify colours in different illumination conditions using a selection of colour names. There is a naturalness to the appeal to colour names, but this is at times counteracted by struggles with defining adequately fine-grained terminology.

4 See Chapter 17, Bradley and Tye (2001, 479–80), and Byrne and Hilbert (2003, 8–9) for this kind of argument. Two qualifications might be helpful. The first concerns Byrne and Hilbert's colour ontology. They maintain that surface colours are identifiable with *classes* of SSRs. Colours more broadly, which they take to include surfaces colours, volume colours, and the colours of light sources, are identifiable with classes of what they call *productances*. Light itself, as opposed to light sources, is explicitly excluded from their colour ontology. Second, a crucial premise in Hilbert (1992), also mentioned in Chapter 17, ties colour constancy to the *function* of colour vision, and seeks to reach conclusions about colour ontology from said function. I will set this issue aside (see Brown 2017, for commentary).

5 Although it might initially seem odd to talk about the contents of non-verbal behavioural reports, as opposed to the contents of thought or speech reports, it is fairly common to do so. For example, a subject might believe that blue things contain food and when hungry reach for the blue container. This is a reasonable expression of the content <that is blue> and that expression may but need not coincide with the formation of a thought or utterance to that effect. More directly, if a subject is asked to match two colours then push 'Enter', her pressing of 'Enter' following her manipulation of colours is naturally taken to be an expression of <those colours match>. Readers should at minimum admit that it is rational for us to ascribe such contents to these actions. This is enough to motivate what follows.

6 The classic discussion of the perceptual given is Sellars (1956). Recent work includes Gupta (2006), Crane (2013), and Montague (2016). I take the *given* in perception to refer to what a subject perceptually *experiences*. I do not mean to imply that what is given in perception is non-inferentially knowable or yields infallible knowledge, but merely that the perceptual given is what perception itself makes consciously available to perceivers for use in perceptual reports. There are other valuable ways of construing the idea that are not as tied to experience. For example, one could take the perceptual given to be what perceptual systems "deliver", via experiential or non-experiential channels, to subjects for use in reports, or what perceptual systems make available to other neural/cognitive systems for use in their processing. Such construals make no critical link between the perceptual given and perceptual experience, and thus I set them aside. My commitment to a given-experience link doesn't prevent there from being non-experiential contributions to perceptual reports (see below). It merely prevents such contributions from being part of the perceptual given.

7 E.g. Hilbert (2005, 2011), Kalderon (2008), Gert (2010), Jagnow (2010), Brown (2014), Davies (2016).

8 In slightly more detail, in Appearance Match conditions subjects are potentially asked to mentally construct a blend of the surface and illuminant target patch colours, and manipulate the test patch to a state presenting surface and illuminant colours that, if blended, would match the first construct. That is, they are asked to match for two surface-illuminant colour blends, neither of which are perceptually given.

9 Will Davies (in progress) is working through ways to develop the relational conception of colour constancy.

10 I am indebted to Keith Allen, Mazviita Chirimuuta, and Will Davies for helpful comments on an earlier draft. My sincere thanks to the Templeton Foundation, via The University of Cambridge and

Tim Crane's *New Directions in the Study of Mind* project, for financial assistance. This publication was made possible through the support of a grant from the John Templeton Foundation. The opinions expressed in this publication are those of the author and do not necessarily reflect the views of the John Templeton Foundation.

References

Arend, L., & Reeves, A. 1986. Simultaneous color constancy. *Journal of the Optical Society of America A—Optics Image Science and Vision*, 3, 1743–51.

Arend, L.E., Jr, Reeves, A., Schirillo, J., & Goldstein, R. 1991. Simultaneous color constancy: Papers with diverse Munsell values. *Journal of the Optical Society of America A—Optics Image Science and Vision*, 8, 661–72.

Bradley, P., & Tye, M. 2001. Of colors, kestrels, caterpillars, and leaves. *Journal of Philosophy*, 98, 469–87.

Brown, D. 2014. Colour constancy and colour layering. *Philosophers' Imprint*, 14(16), 1–31.

Brown, D. 2017. Colouring for and colour relationalism: A critical notice of *Outside Colour* (M. Chirimuuta. 2015. MIT Press). *Analysis Reviews*, 77(2), 433–49. doi:10.1093/analys/anx025.

Brown, R. 2003. Background and illuminants: The yin and yang of colour constancy. In R. Mausfeld & D. Heyer, eds., *Colour Perception: Mind and the Physical World*, pp. 247–72. Oxford, UK: Oxford University Press.

Burge, T. 2010. *Origins of Objectivity*. Oxford, UK: Oxford University Press.

Byrne, A., & Hilbert, D. 2003. Colour realism and colour science. *Behavioral and Brain Sciences*, 26, 3–64.

Byrne, A., & Hilbert, D. 2007. Color primitivism. *Erkenntnis*, 66, 73–105.

Chirimuuta, M. 2008. Reflectance realism and colour constancy: What would count as scientific evidence for Hilbert's ontology of colour? *Australasian Journal of Philosophy*, 86(4), 563–82.

Cohen, J. 2008. Colour constancy as counterfactual. *Australasian Journal of Philosophy*, 86, 61–92.

Crane, T. 2013. The given. In J. Schear, ed., *Mind, Reason and Being-in-the-World: The McDowell-Dreyfus Debate*, pp. 229–49. London: Routledge.

Davies, W. 2016. Colour constancy, illumination, and matching. *Philosophy of Science*, 83(4), 540–62.

Davies, W. 2017. Relational colour constancy. Lecture delivered at the *Philosophy, Psychology and Neuroscience Research Seminar* at the University of Glasgow, 27 November.

Foster, D. 2003. Does colour constancy exist? *Trends in Cognitive Sciences*, 7, 439–43.

Foster, D. 2011. Color constancy. *Vision Research*, 51, 674–700.

Gerhard, H., & Maloney, L. 2010. Detection of light transformations and concomitant changes in surface albedo. *Journal of Vision*, 10(9), 1–14.

Gert, J. 2010. Color constancy, complexity, and counterfactual. *Noûs*, 44(4), 669–90.

Gert, J. 2017. *Primitive Colours*. Oxford, UK: Oxford University Press.

Gupta, A. 2006. *Empiricism and Experience*. Oxford, UK: Oxford University Press.

Hilbert, D. 1992. What is color vision? *Philosophical Studies*, 68(3), 351–70.

Hilbert, D. 2005. Colour constancy and the complexity of colour. *Philosophical Topics* 33(1), 141–58.

Hilbert, D. 2011. Constancy, content, and inference. In G. Hatfield & S. Allred, eds., *Visual Experience: Sensation, Cognition, and Constancy*, pp. 199–211. Oxford, UK: Oxford University Press.

Jagnow, R. 2010. Shadow-experiences and the phenomenal structure of colors. *Dialectica*, 64(2), 187–212.

Jameson, D., & Hurvich, L.M. 1989. Essay concerning color constancy. *Annual Review of Psychology*, 40, 1–22.

Kalderon, M.E. 2008. Metamerism, constancy, and knowing which. *Mind*, 117, 935–71.

Land, E., & McCann, J. (1971). Lightness and Retinex theory. *Journal of the Optical Society of America*, 61, 1–11.

Mausfeld, R. 2003. 'Colour' as part of the format of different perceptual primitives: The dual coding of colour. In R. Mausfeld & D. Heyer, eds., *Colour Perception: Mind and the Physical World*, pp. 381–430. Oxford: Oxford University Press.

Montague, M. 2016. *The Given: Experience and its Content*. Oxford, UK: Oxford University Press.

Norman, L., Akins, K., Heywood, C., & Kentridge, R. 2014. Colour constancy for an unseen surface. *Current Biology*, 24, 2822–66.

Reeves, A.J., Amano, K., & Foster, D.H. 2008. Color constancy: Phenomenal or projective? *Perception & Psychophysics*, 70, 219–28.

Sellars, W. 1956. Empiricism and the philosophy of mind. In H. Feigel & M. Scriven, eds., *Minnesota Studies in the Philosophy of Science*, vol. I, pp. 253–329. Minneapolis, MN: University of Minnesota Press.

Shevell, S.K., & Kingdom, F.A.A. 2008. Color in complex scenes. *Annual Review of Psychology*, 59, 143–66.

Smith, A.D. 2002. *The Problem of Perception*. Cambridge, MA: Harvard University Press.

Tokunaga, R., & Logvinenko, A.D. 2010. Material and lighting dimensions of object colour. *Vision Research*, 50, 1740–7.

Wandell, B. 1989. Color constancy and the natural image. *Physica Scripta*, *39*, 187–92. Reprinted in Byrne & Hilbert, eds. 1997. *Readings in Color Volume 2: The Science of Color*, pp. 161–75. Cambridge, MA: MIT Press.

Wright, W. 2013. Color constancy reconsidered. *Acta Analytica*, 28, 435–55.

PART IV

Colour ontology

17

OBJECTIVIST REDUCTIONISM

Alex Byrne and David R. Hilbert

1 Objectivist reductionism

Physical objects like lemons, canaries, and lumps of sulphur have a myriad of physical-chemical properties. Some of these properties are shared: all three kinds of objects have mass, for example. Some are unique: only lumps of sulphur are composed of a single element, give or take a few impurities. Some are partly shared: lemons and canaries both contain carotinoid pigments. We may assume that "physical-chemical properties" are specified in a relatively restricted language—in particular, one that does not contain colour words like "yellow". Now imagine an uncountably large book in which all and only the shared physical-chemical properties of lemons, canaries, and lumps of sulphur are inscribed in this restricted language. Since objects of these three kinds are yellow, a question arises: Is yellowness among the properties mentioned in the book? Because the word "yellow" does not appear in the book, the answer isn't obviously yes. But neither is it obviously no: there's no problem in principle with expressions lacking colour words referring to colours. So which is it? According to *Objective Reductionism*, or *(colour) physicalism*, it is yes: yellowness is identical to physical-chemical property Y, and so on for the other colours.[1]

Objective Reductionism stands opposed to *Subjective Reductionism*, or *(colour) dispositionalism*, the view that yellowness is identical to a disposition or tendency to affect perceivers in a certain way.[2] In an older and more traditional terminology, Objectivism Reductionism identifies yellowness with a *primary quality*, and Subjective Reductionism identifies it with a *secondary quality*. Objective Reductionism also stands opposed to *Primitivism*, on which yellowness is an irreducible property, and *Eliminativism*, the view that no physical objects are yellow.[3]

The terminology of "Objective/Subjective Reductionism" is not ideal, mainly because "Subjective" can suggest "less than fully real", or "not part of the Absolute Conception of reality", or something along equally obscure lines.[4] Subjective Reductionism is simply committed to *subjects* (i.e. perceivers) figuring in the most perspicuous account of what the colours are, not anything more metaphysically heady. Conversely, the Objective Reductionist is simply committed to the identity with physical-chemical property Y, not the additional claim that Y figures in the Absolute Conception or anything of that sort.

2 Motivations

One might motivate Objectivist Reductionism as an instance of a more global claim, something like the contemporary doctrine of physicalism, that the world is (in some sense) "entirely phys-ical". But Objectivist Reductionism can be motivated in a much more local (and much more convincing) fashion.

First, we can start by noting that colours are *properties* or *qualities* that have their own special vocabulary in natural languages ("green", "vert", "grün", ...). They are not *relations*, and there is no obvious reason why they are relational properties (like, say, poisonousness). These prop-erties are among the ways external objects like cucumbers and avocados appear or look and plainly are very closely tied to vision. Since, as every child knows, cucumbers and avocados *are* green, vision enables us to detect the colours of things.

Second, changing the illumination, even quite dramatically, often does not change apparent colours significantly. A tomato appears to be stably red when we remove it from under the halogen kitchen light, take it outside into direct early morning daylight, and then put it in shadow. (This is the well-known phenomenon of *colour constancy*.[5]) That suggests that colours are illumination-independent properties: changing the ambient light does not (typically) change the colours of things.

Third, we aren't the only animals with colour vision. Even without getting into any details about eyes, wavelength selectivity and so forth, a glance around the natural world strongly sug-gests that a lot of animal colouration is the result of natural selection, and moreover can only be selected because other animals can detect colours. Males' exotically coloured plumage would be pointless if it were lost on females; similarly, camouflage often involves precise colour matching, a puzzle if the predators are oblivious to colour differences. As Darwin put it:

> When we see leaf-eating insects green, and bark feeders mottled grey, the alpine ptar-migan white in winter, the red-grouse the colour of heather, and the black-grouse that of peaty earth, we must believe that these tints are of service to these birds and insects in preserving them from danger.
>
> (Darwin 1859: 84)

This third point, that we colour-seeing humans are not alone, has a number of consequences. It shows that colours are ecologically significant (in different ways to different animals), which reinforces the second point. Properties of objects that do not change with constantly changing illumination are generally much more useful to know about. It also shows that the detection of colours simply requires an appropriate visual system, not any kind of conceptual sophistication. Finally, if we add in some facts about the design of other visual systems, the third point suggests that the familiar human colours are just a parochial subset of all the colours.

Summing up, the colours, on initial inspection:

a   are (largely) illumination-independent properties of objects;
b   are ecologically significant;
c   are detectable by perceptual systems alone, without assistance from higher cognition;
d   form a large family of properties, only some of which are detectable by human vision.

Human colour vision works by sampling the image at the back of the eye with three kinds of broad-band receptors spanning the visible spectrum, followed by specialized processing to extract information about, among other things, the light-altering properties of objects. In general, colour vision systems across the animal kingdom appear to be well-suited to detect ways in which objects alter light.

Thus the natural hypothesis is that colours *are* ways of altering the light. If we restrict attention to colours as they appear to qualify surfaces, then the hypothesis is that colours are *surface spectral reflectances* (SSRs)—dispositions to reflect incident light.[6] (In the case of humans, the pertinent kind of light is in the visible spectrum, but it need not be so restricted for other animals). Since this is the most plausible kind of Objective Reductionism, we will take this hypothesis, *reflectance physicalism*, as our central example.

Objective Reductionism is not the product of an ideology to "naturalize" everything that moves, or a doctrine whose main motivation is distinctively "philosophical". Rather, it falls naturally out of some elementary observations about language, biology, physiology, and phenomenology. For Martian scientists and philosophers, lacking any kind of colour vision, Objective Reductionism (specifically, reflectance physicalism) would seem pretty boring. What could possibly be wrong with it?

3 Objections

As it turns out, quite a lot. To judge by the philosophical literature on colour, Objective Reductionism is widely supposed to suffer from a number of fatal problems. We now discuss the most prominent of these, ranging from those that are easily dismissed to those that deserve serious discussion.

3.1 *Metamers*

Objects that alter light in quite different ways can nonetheless look to have exactly the same colour in, say, daylight (more exactly, daylight of a specific kind). This is the phenomenon of *metamerism*: objects that differ in the amount of light they reflect at each wavelength—that is, in their reflectance—can nonetheless perceptually match under certain illuminants (including natural illuminants like daylight). Metamerism is a consequence of the fact that the cones in the eye are sensitive to wavelengths over a wide range, and so will respond identically to light of different wavelengths, if appropriately adjusted for intensity. Suppose x and y are a metameric match (in daylight); specifically, x and y both look exactly the same shade of magenta. We may further suppose that x and y *are* that shade. Yet (we may further suppose) the reflectance curves of x and y are quite different. (Say, x reflects 70 per cent of light around 500nm, while y reflects none.) If the slogan "colours are reflectances" is understood as identifying the shades that are (visibly) maximally determinate with specific reflectances, then this example shows that the slogan is wrong. x and y have the same (visibly) maximally determinate shade but different specific reflectances. So such shades are not specific reflectances.

However, this is a non-issue. Plainly determinables like red and blue, and less than maximally determinate shades like magenta and crimson, cannot be identified with specific reflectances. They must instead be identified with *types* or *kinds* of specific reflectances, or (in perhaps better terminology), *general* reflectances. A general reflectance stands to a specific reflectance as *being a rectangle of area > A* stands to *being a rectangle of area exactly A + n*. Once it is clear that red and magenta cannot be specific reflectances, there is no need for the Objective Reductionist to make an exception for red_{29}, a (visibly) maximally determinate shade, and every reason for her not to.

Although metamerism is not best thought of as providing an *objection*, it does bring out a distinctive feature of Objective Reductionism, namely that it recognizes invisible colours, in particular specific reflectances. According to the Objective Reductionist, what we intuitively think of as maximally determinate shades are in fact determinables in their turn, with absolute determinates only being reached at the level of specific reflectances. And we do not see specific reflectances—no object looks to us to have an absolute determinate colour (rather, objects look to have one of the determinables of which specific reflectances are determinates). That result will be unacceptable to those who, like P. F. Strawson, think that "colours are visibilia, or they are nothing" (Strawson 2011: 142), but a clear case for treating colours differently from shape or motion is hard to find. Strawson, for instance, claims that a "logical divorce" between a thing's being a colour and its looking that colour "produces nonsense", but omits to explain why.

3.2 Normal conditions and standard observers

The Objective Reductionist identifies colours with general reflectances. But *what* general reflectance is to be identified with, say, yellowness? There are enormously (perhaps infinitely) many to choose from. Take some general reflectance G. Since the motivation for Objective Reductionism relies crucially on the idea that the colours of objects are (frequently) *detectable*, if G is a serious candidate for yellowness, it had better be a feature of many objects that we ordinarily see as yellow, like lemons. For if not, then many of our perceptual beliefs about yellowness, for instance that this lemon is yellow, would be in error. G, then, is a property of objects like lemons, canaries, and lumps of sulphur. But what unites these objects? The answer might be thought to lie in us, because:

> there seems to be no perceiver-independent way of specifying the disjunction of surface reflectance properties to which a particular colour shade is to be reduced. The different surface reflectance properties involved bear no intrinsic resemblance to each other; they form a disjunction simply because of the colour experiences they cause in perceivers.
>
> *(Gow 2014: 806)*[7]

Lemons, canaries, and lumps of sulphur all *look* yellow to normal perceivers, so presumably the Objective Reductionist will identify yellowness with the general reflectance shared by all and only those objects that look yellow to normal perceivers (or, more carefully, normal perceivers in normal conditions). But now there is ...

> ... the problem of identifying, in a non-arbitrary way, *normal conditions*, and *normal observers*. The objectivist account requires that we identify the 'real' color for object X as a certain causal basis (e.g., the reflectance profile) for the way it appears, to normal observers and in normal conditions. The problem is that, as Hardin has persuasively pointed out ... this cannot be done except in a highly arbitrary way. Not only is there a minority of color perceivers who are anomalous (only slightly, but appreciably so) with respect to normal observers, but there is a considerable statistical spread even within the group of normal observers. For example, the reflectance profile for unique green[8] will differ for different members of the 'normal group'. One can decide, of course, on a standard and fix one reflectance profile as green, but the procedure is highly arbitrary.
>
> *(Maund 2012: sect. 6.3)*[9]

This is a common complaint against the Objectivist. And there is indeed a serious problem, if the Objectivist is unwise enough to specify the colours in terms of "normal" perceivers and conditions.[10] However, there is no reason to accept this poisoned pawn. True, perceptible properties are only detectable because of the effects they have on us, but to move from that to the conclusion that they are *definable* in terms of these effects is arguably the classic operationalist mistake.

Consider, for example, the word "craggy" as applied to mountain peaks and such. This word plausibly picks out a certain idiosyncratic shape property, of interest mainly to human climbers and hikers, possessed by Scafell Pike in the Lake District and not by Sugarloaf Peak in New Mexico. In other words, "Objectivist Reductionism" about cragginess is plausible: cragginess is identical to shape property S, a property canonically characterized in geometrical terms. S is some kind of "general" shape property, a type or kind of specific shape property. But what is S, canonically characterized?[11] Since our judgements of cragginess are (we may assume) often correct, we can use this to narrow down the candidates significantly, but since (we may also assume) error cannot be eliminated entirely, there will be numerous ones remaining. One of these must be S, but which is it? No one knows. It does not help to retreat from Objective Reductionism and try to analyse cragginess in terms of its effects on us—for one thing, the selection of the pertinent kinds of perceivers and conditions seems considerably more "arbitrary" than in the colour case. And it is anyway quite unclear why the failure to supply S, in its geometrical guise, should embarrass the Objective Reductionist. Presumably "craggy" picks out S in virtue of complicated facts involving our use of the word, but we only have outlines of how this might work—certainly nothing that would enable us to expose S in geometrical terms. But our inability to produce a detailed theory of how we do such-and-such is no argument against us actually doing such-and-such. We may reasonably conjecture that cragginess is a certain shape property, even though we can only gesture towards it.

Objectivist Reductionism about colour should be understood in an analogous fashion: if there is no pressure to reveal S, there is no pressure to reveal the general reflectance that is identical to yellowness.[12]

3.3 *Variation among normal perceivers*

As Hardin famously pointed out (see the previous quotation from Maund), there is significant variation among those with normal colour vision, for instance variation with respect to which objects appear unique green. A question then naturally arises:

> [Imagine that all of the] hue chips manufactured by the Munsell Company covering [the] 5 Blue-Green to 2.5 Green range were randomly spread out before you to be separately viewed on a dark gray background in North Daylight. One of them would be your considered choice for unique green. Your colleague might make a different choice. If so, which of the chips is unique green?
>
> *(Hardin 1993: 80)*

Reading between the lines, Hardin's answer is evidently "none". What is not clear is why this—or, indeed, any noteworthy claim about colour—is motivated by the dispute between you and your colleague. It's quite astonishing that our colour vision systems are able to recover the colours of things at all; it should come as no surprise that there is variation between two "normal" colour vision systems when pushed to their limits of resolution. If you and your colleague get slightly different results from your respective desk thermometers nothing alarming or noteworthy follows about the temperature of the office. Perhaps your thermometer is correct, and the temperature is 70°, or perhaps hers is, and the temperature is 68°. It may be in practice imposs-ible to tell, but at least you both know that it's in the comfortable range. Similarly (or so one might think) with your dispute about the colours of the chips. Perhaps your colour vision system is correct, and this chip is unique green, or perhaps hers is, and it's slightly bluish-green. It may be in practice impossible to tell, but at least you both know that it's in the middle-green range.

Those who think that variation does rule out Objective Reductionism have responded by questioning any analogy with measuring instruments (e.g. Cohen 2009: 47–52), and by taking up the challenge of turning the facts about variation into an argument (e.g. Cohen *et al.* 2006; Cohen 2009: ch. 2).[13] There seems little sign of a consensus, but in any case the objection from variation has nothing in particular to do with the "reductive" nature of Objective Reduction-ism. If the objection works at all, it works against any view of colour on which only one of Hardin's chips is unique green, which includes the most natural form of Primitivism.

3.4 Boghossian and Velleman

In "Physicalist theories of color" (1991), Boghossian and Velleman launch a sustained attack on "physicalism about color", the view that "the colors of material objects are microphysical prop-erties of their surfaces" (67); that is, Objective Reductionism.[14] Summarizing a rich and intricate paper, their main argument is the following. Divide Objective Reductionist views into two kinds. First, those on which:

> visual experiences like yours represent colors only as a matter of contingent fact. Under the terms of these theories, an experience internally indistinguishable from your experience of seeing something as red might fail to represent its object as having that color. The reason is that red is represented by your experience, according to these the-ories, only by virtue of facts incidental to the internal features of the experience.
>
> *(Boghossian and Velleman 1991: 87)*

One simple version of Objective Reductionism of this first kind is that "your experience of seeing something as red" represents its object as having the property P that is the normal cause of such experiences. (We may suppose that, as things have turned out, P is a certain general reflectance G⋆, and likewise for the other colours.)

Objective Reductionist views not of the first kind are of the second kind. On these views, "an experience internally indistinguishable from your experience of seeing something as red" cannot fail to represent its object as being red.[15]

Having made this distinction, Boghossian and Velleman argue against both kinds of Objective Reductionism in turn. Their argument against the first kind is that it fails to meet certain simple epistemological constraints, for instance that, "simply in your capacity as a subject of visual experience", you know that "red and orange are different properties, though of the same kind—different determinates of the same determinable" (85). This is because, on theories of the first kind:

> [a] bizarre possibility is that visual experience might represent only two color proper-ties—one when things look either red, orange, or yellow, and another when they look either green, blue, or violet. The correlational or causal facts could certainly be arranged in such a way as to give these experiences one of only two contents ... These theories

[of the first kind] therefore imply that one cannot always tell without investigation whether red and orange are different colors, the same color, or no color at all.

(91)

Let us agree that this consequence is unacceptable. What is wrong with theories of the second kind, which do not have this consequence? Most current Objective Reductionists are also *intentionalists* or *representationalists* (examples include Byrne and Hilbert 1997 and Tye 2000; see also Chapter 23 by Pautz), which basically means that they deny that "an experience internally indistinguishable from your experience of seeing something as red" might fail to represent its object as being red.

However, Boghossian and Velleman argue against only one particular theory, and their argument against it does not extend to theories of the second kind of the sort currently in vogue.[16] Provided representationalism is viable, Objective Reductionists can escape Boghossian and Velleman's argument.

3.5 Chirimuuta

In *Outside Color* (2015), Chirimuuta makes a number of objections to Objective Reductionism—specifically in the guise of reflectance physicalism or, in her terminology, "reflectance realism". We shall consider one of the most prominent, that there is "no-theory independent reason to assert that SSR detection is the primary function [of color vision] and that the others are secondary" (99). Other functions she mentions include the perception of depth, texture, edges, and object boundaries. For example, as she notes (91), colour vision is particularly useful for determining object boundaries because they are much better correlated with reflectance boundaries than with luminance boundaries (which could be caused by a shadow cutting across an object).

We may take the "function" of some adaptive subsystem in an organism to be its *biological function*—roughly, the features of the system that were selected for (see, e.g., Millikan 1984: ch. 1). Thus the function of the heart is to pump blood, or to deliver oxygen to the body, or something along similar lines; at any rate, it is not to make a thumping noise. How do we get from this multiplicity of functions of colour vision to the conclusion that Objective Reductionism is false? It would certainly be an embarrassment if SSR detection was not *one* of the functions of colour vision, for then there would be no obvious reason why selective pressure would have produced a system that could accurately recover (general) reflectances. Admittedly, there would presumably have been selection for accurate recovery of *differences* in reflectances (as in the example of object boundaries above), but that could have been accomplished while getting the reflectances themselves wrong or, more simply, by not attempting to recover such information in the first place. However, Chirimuuta's claim is that SSR detection is not the "primary function" of colour vision; the experimental work she cites does not suggest that it is not a function at all.

There thus remains a gap between Chirimuuta's premise and her conclusion. Pending some clarification of the notion of a "primary function", the Objective Reductionist need not insist that SSR detection is the *primary* function of colour vision—*a* function of colour vision will do. In fact, Chirimuuta's discussion in effect reinforces the position she intends to attack. If evolution could have equipped us with an SSR detection system, it would have. Not only is the detection of SSRs useful in itself, but such a system is handy for all sorts of other things. And if we have an SSR detection system, then what else could it be other than our colour vision system? Reflectance physicalism then becomes hard to avoid.[17]

3.6 Similarity, and the unique/binary distinction

The quotation from section 3.4, in which Boghossian and Velleman mention some things you know about red and orange "simply in your capacity as a subject of visual experience", continues:

> you know ... that they are not as different from one another as they are from blue ... A property that wasn't ... similar to red—such a property simply wouldn't be orange.
>
> *(1991: 85)*

In the same vein, Boghossian and Velleman could have mentioned the distinction between the unique and binary hues—a property that wasn't a binary hue wouldn't be orange either. These elementary facts about similarity and the unique/binary distinction give us an argument against Objective Reductionism, as Hardin pointed out:

> [Objective Reductionism] fails because nothing in the domain of objects, properties and processes beyond our skins is both causally connected with our colour experiences and models the essential characteristics of colours.
>
> *(1984: 496)*

Imagine a Martian physicist, well versed in optics but entirely lacking colour vision, cataloguing the general reflectances that the Objective Reductionist identifies with the colours. The Martian might well classify them by similarity, putting the reflectances with a high peak towards the long wavelength end together, say. The Martian might also classify some reflectances as combinations or mixtures of others, in a variety of mathematically natural ways. But we can be quite sure that none of this is going to "model the essential characteristics" of colours. The unique/binary distinction, and the similarity relations between the hues, will remain entirely beyond the Martian's ken.

Focusing on the more straightforward case of similarity, we can set out the argument as follows. Let G^o be a reflectance that is, according to the Objective Reductionist, a candidate to be orange (likewise G^r (red) and G^b (blue)):

P1. Orange is more similar to red than it is to blue.

P2. G^o is not more similar to G^r than it is to G^b.

C. Either $G^o \neq$ orange, or $G^r \neq$ red, or $G^b \neq$ blue.[18]

The argument appears to be of the valid form: Rabc, ~Rdef, hence a ≠ d v b ≠ e v c ≠ f. Since we may assume that P2 is equally plausible for any candidates to be orange, red, and blue, if C is warranted so is the stronger conclusion that Objective Reductionism is false.

Arguments in this style are quite widely endorsed. Here is Pautz, for example:

> [T]he thesis that colours are literally identical with reflectance properties cannot be correct because it entails that certain obvious claims about colour structure are false: for instance, that red is a unitary colour while purple is a binary colour, and that blue resembles purple more than green. The reason is that reflectance properties do not have the requisite structural features.
>
> *(2006: 536)*

And Chirimuuta:

> Physicalism is vulnerable to a line of attack that, broadly speaking, points out the great dissimilarities between features of color as we experience them, such as the structure of color space, and what is known of physical properties, such as SSR.
>
> *(2015: 46–7)*

It is hard to deny the premises of the argument as just set out. If the argument really is valid then Objective Reductionism is sunk; nevertheless, it is invalid. Compare the following argument:

P1★. Peter Parker is more similar to Clark Kent than to Bruce Wayne.

P2★. Spiderman is not more similar to Superman than he is to Batman.

C★. Either Clark Kent ≠ Superman, or Peter Parker ≠ Spiderman, or Bruce Wayne ≠ Batman.

The first premise is true. Peter Parker is a freelance photographer for the *Daily Bugle*; Clark Kent is a reporter for the *Daily Planet*; Bruce Wayne is a billionaire and playboy. The second premise is also true: Spiderman and Batman are both men with a fetish for animal-inspired costumes; Superman is a space alien.[19] Despite the truth of the premises, the conclusion is false, as all philosophers of language know.

The argument is invalid because different respects of similarity figure in (the natural interpretation of) the two premises. P1★ says (roughly) that three people are comparatively similar *with respect to their ordinary lifestyles and occupations*; P2★ says that the same trio are comparatively similar *with respect to their superhero identities*. The argument is not of the valid form: Rabc, ~Rdef, hence a ≠ d v b ≠ e, or c ≠ f. Rather, the comparative similarity predicate is four-place: x is more similar to y than it is to z in respect i. The argument is thus of the invalid form: Rabcg, ~Rdefh, hence a ≠ d v b ≠ e v c ≠ f. And if validity is restored by keeping the respects of similarity constant between P1★ and P2★, there is now no reason to affirm both premises. Interpreted with shifting respects of similarity, the argument is invalid; interpreted with constant respects of similarity, it is unsound.

Similar remarks go for the similarity argument against Objective Reductionism, although here there is much more to be said. What is the respect in which orange is more similar to red than to blue? Putting it intuitively but not particularly helpfully, orange "has some red in it", and "has no blue in it". The task is to explain what that means, in such a way that we can assess whether there is any difficulty in supposing that G° "has some red in it".

Byrne and Hilbert (2003: 14; see also 2010: 280–1) proposed that the visual perception of an object as orange involves representing the object as having a roughly equal proportion of the two "hue magnitudes" reddishness and yellowishness, which are themselves identified with light-altering magnitudes. (Since the account is inspired by the phenomenological observations that motivated the opponent process theory of colour vision, there are two other hue magnitudes, blueishness and greenishness.) According to Byrne and Hilbert, a property P will "have some red in it" just in case having P partly consists in having some proportion of reddishness. Since there is no obstacle to taking reddishness to be a physical magnitude, the supposition that G° "has some red in it" is, they say, unproblematic.

Byrne and Hilbert's positive account is controversial.[20] However, whatever its fate, that does not alter the fact that the argument from similarity against Objective Reductionism is invalid.

Validity could be restored by keeping the respects of similarity constant between P1 and P2—a likely candidate would be "natural respects", in something like Lewis's sense of "natural" (Lewis 1983). But now the similarity objection to Objective Reductionism is far from straightforward, hinging on metaphysical speculations that are easy to dispute. First, it is not clear that the colours are similar in natural respects; second, the need for the Lewisian apparatus of natural properties is disputable. If Objective Reductionism is a natural hypothesis given established science,[21] then appeal to the darker regions of contemporary metaphysics is unlikely to overturn it.

Notes

1 Objective Reductionists include Armstrong (1969), Smart (1975), Hilbert (1987), Jackson (1996), Tye (2000), McLaughlin (2003), Byrne and Hilbert (2003).

2 As defined in the text, Objectivism and Subjectivism are actually compatible. A Subjective Reductionist might also hold that all properties are physical, in which case she would be an Objective Reductionist too. For our purposes, this awkwardness doesn't matter: the Objective Reductionists mentioned in this chapter are invariably opposed to the Subjective kind, and so here the two positions can be treated as incompatible.

3 Another pair of distinctions, relativist/non-relativist and relational/non-relational, basically cuts across the distinctions just mentioned. For a relativist view, see Brogaard 2010; for a relational view see Cohen 2009. (Cohen's alternative taxonomy of positions is also helpful: see 2009: ch. 1.) For criticism of both relativism and relationalism, see Byrne and Hilbert forthcoming. We will not discuss either of these positions in this chapter.

4 For the Absolute Conception, see Williams 1978: 64–8 (and for Williams' views on its connection to color, 237–44).

5 See Chapter 8, section 5.4, in this volume, on the science of colour.

6 To cover the case of coloured lights and volumes, Byrne and Hilbert (2003: 11–12) identify the colours with *productances*, defined similarly but more generally than reflectances. This refinement can be ignored for present purposes.

7 This quotation might uncharitably be read as suggesting that the SSRs that correspond to the familiar colours look like a completely random selection, with no commonalities in how they alter light. In any event, that suggestion is quite wrong.

8 Unique green is that shade of green that is neither yellowish nor bluish.

9 For uniformity, we have silently replaced two occurrences of "standard" in this quotation with "normal".

10 One problem is this: since there is no reasonable interpretation of "normal" on which *anything* is disposed to look unique green to normal perceivers in normal conditions, the proposed specification has the unwanted consequence that nothing is unique green (see Byrne and Hilbert forthcoming: section 2.2). Whether there is anything to the charge of "arbitrariness" is not obvious. If the winning lottery ticket number = 4985743, that is "arbitrary" in one standard sense, but of course that is not an objection to the identity! On another interpretation, the charge is that we have no way of knowing what the correct definition of "normal" is. But again, this does not appear to be an objection, at least not without further premises: the winning number may be 4985743 even though we have no way of knowing it.

11 Competing theories of vagueness are not to the point. If, say, "craggy" somehow indeterminately picks out a range of shape properties, rather than a single one, then the corresponding question concerns this range, and the same issues will arise.

12 For another example, take the old Smart/Place "identity theory", that "sensations are brain processes" (Smart 1959: 144). Interestingly, the leading objections to this theory did not include the complaint that neither Smart nor Place revealed the particular brain processes that are identical to such-and-such sensations.

13 See also Byrne 2006, Tye 2006, Byrne and Hilbert 2007, Cohen *et al.* 2007, Gert 2008.

14 For the purposes of this chapter, we are eliding Boghossian and Velleman's distinction between "identity-physicalism" and "realization-physicalism" (1991: 73), analogous to the similarly named views familiar from debates about functionalism in the philosophy of mind.

15 Although being "internally indistinguishable" is an epistemic matter (which raises unnecessary complications due to the fact that this relation is not transitive), we take it that this was not Boghossian and Velleman's primary intent: "identical with respect to phenomenal character" would be better.

16 In fact, the theory they argue against, "that objects are visually characterized as having properties that normally cause color sensations, and that colors are the higher-order properties expressed by these characterizations" (104), is better classified as a version of Subjective Reductionism.

17 For more discussion of Chirimuuta, see Cohen 2015.

18 Here is the parallel argument using the binary/unique distinction:

> P1. Orange is binary.
> P2. G° is not binary.
> C. G° ≠ orange.

The reason why this argument is less straightforward is that it is not immediately obvious how to determine whether G° is "binary" in the intuitive sense in which orange is. In his exposition of this argument, Hardin writes: "If hues are physical complexes, those physical complexes must admit of a division into unique and binary complexes" (Hardin 1993: 66), but gives little guidance on what this division comes to. For discussion see Byrne and Hilbert 2003: 13–15.

19 Needless to say, quibbling over details of superhero interpretation is not to the point.

20 The simple account of colour phenomenology used by Byrne and Hilbert is at best an oversimplification (for some of the complexities see Allen 2015). However, it is unclear whether the complications significantly affect the basic idea. See also Chapter 23 in this volume, n. 10.

21 Of course, this is not to say that colour scientists themselves embrace Objective Reductionism.

References

Allen, K. 2015. Colour physicalism, naïve realism, and the argument from structure. *Minds and Machines* 25: 193–212.

Armstrong, D. M. 1969. Colour realism and the argument from microscopes. *Contemporary Philosophy in Australia*, ed. R. Brown and C. Rollins. New York: Humanities Press.

Boghossian, P. and J. D. Velleman. 1991. Physicalist theories of color. *Philosophical Review* 100: 67–106.

Brogaard, B. 2010. Perspectival truth and color primitivism. *New Waves in Truth*, ed. C. Wright and N. Pedersen. Basingstoke: Palgrave Macmillan.

Byrne, A. 2006. Comments on Cohen, Mizrahi, Maund, and Levine. *Dialectica* 60: 223–44.

Byrne, A. and D. R. Hilbert. 1997. Colors and reflectances. *Readings on Color, Volume 1: The Philosophy of Color*, ed. A. Byrne and D. R. Hilbert. Cambridge, MA: MIT Press.

Byrne, A. and D. R. Hilbert. 2003. Color realism and color science. *Behavioral and Brain Sciences* 26: 3–21.

Byrne, A. and D. R. Hilbert. 2007. Truest blue. *Analysis* 67: 87–92.

Byrne, A. and D. R. Hilbert. 2010. How do things look to the color-blind? *Color Ontology and Color Science*, ed. J. Cohen and M. Matthen. Cambridge, MA: MIT Press.

Byrne, A. and D. R. Hilbert. forthcoming. Color relationalism and relativism. *Topics in Cognitive Science*.

Chirimuuta, M. 2015. *Outside Color*. Cambridge, MA: MIT Press.

Cohen, J. 2009. *The Red and The Real: An Essay on Color Ontology*. Oxford: Oxford University Press.

Cohen, J. 2015. Review of M. Chirimuuta, *Outside Color. Notre Dame Philosophical Reviews* 2015.10.21.

Cohen, J., C. L. Hardin, and B. P. McLaughlin. 2006. True colours. *Analysis* 66: 335–40.

Cohen, J., C. L. Hardin, and B. P. McLaughlin. 2007. The truth about 'the truth about true blue'. *Analysis* 67: 162–6.

Darwin, C. 1859. *On the Origin of Species*. London: John Murray.

Gert, J. 2008. What colors could not be: An argument for color primitivism. *Journal of Philosophy* 105: 128–55.

Gow, L. 2014. Colour. *Philosophy Compass* 9: 803–13.

Hardin, C. L. 1984. Are 'scientific' objects colored? *Mind* 93: 491–500.

Hardin, C. L. 1993. *Color for Philosophers* (expanded edition). Indianapolis, IN: Hackett.

Hilbert, D. R. 1987. *Color and Color Perception: A Study in Anthropocentric Realism*. Stanford, CA: CSLI Press.

Jackson, F. 1996. The primary quality view of color. *Philosophical Perspectives* 10: 199–219.

Lewis, D. 1983. New work for a theory of universals. *Australasian Journal of Philosophy* 61: 343–77.

Maund, B. 2012. Color. *Stanford Encyclopedia of Philosophy*, ed. E. Zalta. http://plato.stanford.edu/archives/win2012/entries/color/.

McLaughlin, B. 2003. The place of color in nature. *Colour Perception: Mind and the Physical World*, ed. R. Mausfeld and D. Heyer. Oxford: Oxford University Press.
Millikan, R. G. 1984. *Language, Thought and Other Biological Categories*. Cambridge, MA: MIT Press.
Pautz, A. 2006. Can the physicalist explain colour structure in terms of colour experience? *Australasian Journal of Philosophy* 84: 535–64.
Smart, J. J. C. 1959. Sensations and brain processes. *Philosophical Review* 68: 141–56.
Smart, J. J. C. 1975. On some criticisms of a physicalist theory of colors. *Philosophical Aspects of the Mind-Body Problem*, ed. C. Cheng. Honolulu: University Press of Hawaii.
Strawson, P. F. 2011. Perception and its objects. *Philosophical Writings*. Oxford: Oxford University Press.
Tye, M. 2000. *Consciousness, Color, and Content*. Cambridge, MA: MIT Press.
Tye, M. 2006. The puzzle of true blue. *Analysis* 66: 173–8.
Williams, B. 1978. *Descartes: The Project of Pure Enquiry*. Harmondsworth, UK: Penguin Books.

18

PRIMITIVIST OBJECTIVISM

Joshua Gert

Primitivist Objectivism (or simply 'Primitivism' for the remainder of this chapter) is the view that colours are irreducible, mind-independent, *sui generis* properties of objects, and that any normal eight-year-old in the developed world knows which of the objects they see have which ones. Proponents of Primitivism take it to be distinctive of their view that it supports virtually all of the simplest and most commonsensical beliefs about colour. It is no coincidence that one of the early defences of Primitivism bears the title 'A Simple View of Color'.[1] The following list gives the flavour of the claims at issue:

1   Red, Green, Yellow, and Blue are colours.
2   For the four colours just mentioned, if a patch has one of them, it doesn't have any of the others.
3   Blood is red, snow is white, and grass is green.
4   We can typically perceive the colour of an object by looking at it, but errors are possible too.
5   Colours are not something *else*; they have their own distinctive similarity relations and other structural features.

It is arguable that only Primitivism vindicates all of these claims. Reductive objectivism denies 5, identifying colours with microphysical properties or reflectance properties—properties that have similarity relations quite different from those of the colours. Mentalism obviously denies 3. The essence of Pluralism is the denial of 2, while Eliminativism denies 3 and 4. Relationalism we can divide into (a) dispositionalism and (b) the sort of view Jonathan Cohen defends, according to which there is no such property as simple plain-old red, but only red-for-viewer-V-in-circumstances-C and so on.[2] The latter view either denies 1, 2, and 3, or makes such claims much less straightforward than they seem to be, by claiming that they get their sense only because we are implicitly supplying a context. Dispositionalism, on the other hand, denies 4, since perception of a property requires that it play a causal role, and dispositions do not play a causal role in their manifestations.

Of course Primitivism would overshoot its target of simplicity, and become simple-minded, if *all* it put forward was a catalogue of commonsense claims. After all, there are philosophical pressures that explain why other theorists go in for more sophisticated theories, and these pressures cannot simply be ignored. So it would be nice to have some positive argument in favour of Primitivism. In fact, there are a number of such arguments. Let us begin with one argument that has typically been offered on behalf of the Primitivist by those who do not endorse it. It is not a very good argument, but it is worth discussing it, since it is often—but falsely—offered as one of the primary motivations for Primitivism.

1 The argument from revelation

Revelation is the thesis that the whole nature of the colours is revealed to us in experience of the colours; to see a particular colour, at least if one is paying attention, is to come to know everything about its essential nature (Johnston, 1992, p. 223). If it is true that the essential nature of the colours is revealed to us in experience, it follows that colours cannot have any hidden essence. Colours could not be, for example, like the property of being gold, or being water, at least if we accept the orthodoxy that gold has, as part of its essence, the possession of a certain atomic number, and that water has, as part of its nature, that it is composed of hydrogen and oxygen. Inasmuch as colour experience seems to show that certain exclusion relations hold between the colours, and that colours are properties of external surfaces, and inasmuch as it does *not* seem to reveal that colours are microphysical, or dispositional, or that they have any *other* deeper essence, it might seem as though Revelation would uniquely support Primitivism.

Perhaps Revelation does uniquely support Primitivism. As it happens, however, there is no need to decide this issue. Despite the argument from Revelation often being cited as a crucial support for Primitivism, it is in fact explicitly rejected by many of those who are most explicit in their defence of Primitivism.[3] John Campbell (2005) for example, contrasts Revelation with a much weaker doctrine he calls 'Transparency', and he endorses only the latter. Campbell's Transparency is not a matter of coming to have any sort of propositional knowledge about the colours, such as truths about their essence. Rather, it is a matter being directly acquainted with the colours in vision. Joshua Gert (2008, p. 142) also regards Revelation as much too strong to be credible, and substitutes a much weaker thesis, 'Modest Revelation', which only claims that the essential nature of *some* colours *can* be revealed in an experience of that colour, to someone who *already* has colour concepts. That is, for example, a normal English-speaking adult who never had occasion to learn what particular colour taupe was, might be taught this by being shown a pair of shoes that were taupe. And Bohossian and Velleman, who endorse a mentalist primitivism, reject Revelation as dubious grounds for the rejection of Reductive Objectivism (1991, 84–5), which they therefore oppose for other reasons.

Perhaps the most powerful argument against Revelation is an extended discussion by Keith Allen (2011). One important point Allen repeatedly stresses is that much of what we now take to be essential to the colours—that there are four primaries, that some colours are combinations of hues, while others are unmixed, and so on—were hard-won discoveries that were contested by people who met any plausible standard for having normal vision, paying adequate attention to their experiences, reflecting on them, and so on. What was required to arrive at our present grasp of the essential nature of the colours was not simply thoughtful attention to the contents of visual experience. Rather, it required a certain amount of neuroscience, a certain amount of cognitive science, a certain amount of philosophical argument, and so on.

Alex Byrne and David Hilbert have argued that the Primitivist cannot avoid a commitment to Revelation (2007, pp. 78–9). But, as Allen (2011, pp. 168–9) also points out, their argument relies on the false assumption that the Primitivist holds that all essential claims about the colours can be framed in "purely chromatic sentences". These are sentences that include only colour terms and topic-neutral terms such as the logical constants and such terms as 'similar' and so on. Contrary to this constraint on essential claims about the colours, however, the Primitivist holds that colours are non-disjunctive properties of surfaces, that they are not relational, that they are the grounds of dispositions, and perhaps also that they supervene on the physical. These claims need not be revealed in experience, according to the Primitivist.

2 Defensive views

In the absence of support by the argument from Revelation, one might simply appeal to the fact that Primitivism respects all the commonsense beliefs listed at the beginning of this chapter. Surely that fact constitutes a *prima facie* case in favour of the view, making Primitivism the position of "first resort", to be abandoned only if it can be shown to face insuperable difficulties. And one might then regard it as a sufficient defence of Primitivism simply to rebut worries that there is something suspicious or incoherent in taking these commonsense beliefs at face value. In this section I will mention some of the most common objections, and indicate how they might be dealt with.

One of the primary objections to *sui generis* colour properties is the claim that our knowledge of physics and physiology shows that, if they existed, they would not play any causal role. According to this objection, we already know that it is the microphysical properties of surfaces that cause us to see them as coloured in the way we do, so it seems silly to claim that in *addition* to these microphysical properties, there are *also* colour properties doing the same job.[4] If this objection goes through, it might also undermine the idea that the Primitivist can hold that we *perceive* colours. Perception might be taken to require some causal relation, either in the evolutionary history of our perceptual mechanisms (Pautz, 2009, p. 154) or during actual episodes of perception (Watkins, 2005, p. 40).

Whatever rhetorical force the above objections have depends on a misleading and quite uncharitable picture of the Primitivist's view. On this picture the colour properties are thought of as *separable* from the microphysical properties on which they depend in such a way that there would be no problem conceiving of a world in which everything physical and psychological remained *exactly* as it is in this world, but the colours were differently distributed.[5] But one need not think of the colours as separable in this way. Rather, for example, one might take the colour red to be a non-physical determinable of microphysical determinates (Yablo, 1995, p. 487), which would explain the supervenience of the colours on the microphysical. No one would complain about the claim that the determinable property of weighing more than 50 pounds caused a certain scale to tip, though of course the determinate weight—54.7 pounds, as it might be—was certainly sufficient to explain the tipping. Moreover, it is the *less* determinate property here (weighing over 50 pounds) that is involved in the counterfactuals that are of interest to us: had the weight not been over 50 pounds, the scale would not have tipped, while had it not been 54.7 pounds, it well might have tipped. It is certainly not wrong to say that the cause of the scale tipping was its weighing over 50 pounds, or that the scale detects this determinable property. The moral here is that determinable and determinate need not compete for "causal honours", and if they do, the determinable may sometimes emerge as the winner.

Another criticism rests on the assumption that the only mind-independent properties are those that would appear in an "absolute conception" of the world. As John Campbell (1993, p. 258) presents it, such a conception is one that does not involve properties, the conception of which requires one to rely on features of one's own particular perspective (such as the possession of colour vision). If this is correct, colours cannot be mind-independent, as the

Primitivist requires. Campbell resists this criticism by arguing that our natural view of perception—a view that contributes to our way of thinking about, for example, the causing of a subjective experience by some particular arrangement of matter—makes it impossible to separate out the properties that would appear in the putative "absolute conception" that figures in the present criticism. Rather, mind-independence is a matter of the role a property plays in the simple view of perception: one on which our experiences of something mind-independent requires contributions both on the side of the object (e.g. its colour), and on the side of the subject (being normal, looking at the object, and so on). If one worries that we don't really need the *colour* to be making the object-side contribution, and that microphysical properties will do the job, one has simply returned to the "causal exclusion" objection of the previous paragraph. Indeed, in the case of colour it is arguable that we should only take the supposedly "excluding" microphysical explanation—the one offered in terms of wavelengths, opsins, and neural interactions—to explain the resulting *neural state*, and not to explain the *perception of redness* at all. The idea that an explanation of the former amounts to an explanation of the latter rests on the very controversial assumption that we can reduce perceptions of redness to neural states. If we reject this assumption, the explanation that appeals to colour simply explains a different but related phenomenon than that explained by appeal to microphysics. As a result, the two explanations—one at the supervening level and one at the subvening level—simply do not compete.

Another criticism of Primitivism relies on the assumption that it is just common sense to attribute the perception of colours to at least some other animals (Byrne and Hilbert, 2007, pp. 94–5). The problem this is supposed to give rise to is that the Primitivist cannot make sense of this bit of common sense, since the only colours that the Primitivist can countenance are those that make up human colour space. Why are Primitivists limited to the recognition of *human* colours in this way? Byrne and Hilbert's argument for this surprising and strong claim appeals to Revelation. They claim that if the whole nature of the colours is revealed to us in visual experience, and if part of the nature of a given colour is its relation to other colours, then we cannot even conceive (let alone visually imagine) a colour that does not stand in determinate similarity and difference relations with the colours we know (2007, p. 94). But our colour space already includes points that correspond to every possible degree of similarity and difference from every other point; it is complete. If Primitivists were indeed limited in this way, then they would have to embrace one of two quite implausible views: (a) that either non-human animals, or we ourselves, see the world in the *wrong* colours (since animals would see a different distribution of the very same colours that we do) or (b) that non-human animals see properties that might be *like* colours, but aren't *actually* colours.

Inasmuch as Byrne and Hilbert's objection from animal colour vision depends on Revelation, Primitivists who reject Revelation—and that includes most Primitivists—need not worry. Watkins (2010) also points out that the surface properties that animals perceive via their visual mechanisms are similar to our own in that they supervene on the same sorts of microphysical properties. As a result we have the materials to hand to explain why it is appropriate to regard them as the same sort of properties (i.e. colours), even if it is true—as it is—that we cannot with any confidence even imagine what they might look like to those animals.[6] Allen (2011, p. 171) makes a similar point: the properties that animals perceive will count as colours if the appearances of those properties are sensitive in the right sort of ways to changes in the illumination, but also exhibit the right sort of constancy with respect to such changes.

3 Distinct problems for each non-primitivist proposal

One strategy for supporting Primitivism simply identifies problems with existing alternatives. I hinted at this argumentative strategy in the introduction to this chapter, pointing out that the alternatives contradict various commonsense views. Moreover, there are additional problems with many of the views canvassed there. For example, all reductive physicalist theories will identify colours with quite disjunctive properties, and there are significant worries about the causal efficacy of disjunctive properties (Watkins, 2010, pp. 133–4). Mentalism faces the problem of the apparent co-location of colour and shape, and the related problem of explaining how it is that properties of the mental could even *seem* to be properties of external physical objects, given that the mental is not an object of perception. Dispositionalism has difficulties describing the mental state that coloured objects are disposed to produce without ending up relying on a non-dispositional conception of colours that those mental states represent objects to have (McGinn, 1996, p. 538). Jonathan Cohen's relational view, on which any object that looks blue to me under my present circumstances *is* blue-for-me-under-my-present-circumstances makes it very hard to understand how there could be colour illusion, except perhaps in cases of direct brain stimulation or hypnosis.[7] It must be admitted, though, that for this patchwork strategy to succeed, the arguments against each alternative must, individually, be successful. And since they are not related by any unifying idea, the success of some provides no support for the others. Moreover, the failure of all the alternative views is consistent with the failure of Primitivism as well, unless we have a compelling argument that there simply is no other view in the logical space of views.

4 A common source of problems for all non-primitivist proposals

Joshua Gert (2008) has offered an argument for the elimination of alternatives that is more principled than the above piecemeal approach. It begins by noting that for some properties, though there are extensionally equivalent properties to which we might be tempted to "reduce" them, any such reduction will involve significant problems. A classic example of this phenomenon was made famous by Paul Benacerraf in "What Numbers Could Not Be" (1983). In that paper Benacerraf made two points about attempts at set-theoretic reductions of the numbers. The first was that there are many possible reductions, with nothing to favour one over the other in anything like a decisive way. And the second was that no matter what option we picked, we would then give sense to a set of questions about the numbers that are simply ill-posed. For example, if we identify the numbers 1, 2, and 3 with the sets $\{\varnothing\}$, $\{\{\varnothing\}\}$, and $\{\{\{\varnothing\}\}\}$, it will turn out that 3 contains 2 but does not contain 1. If, on the other hand, we identify those numbers with $\{\varnothing\}$, $\{\{\varnothing\}, \varnothing\}$, and $\{\{\{\varnothing\}, \varnothing\}, \{\{\varnothing\}\}, \{\varnothing\}, \varnothing\}$, then 3 will contain both 2 and 1. But the debate about whether 3 does or does not contain 1 is not a genuine debate.

Gert admits that the Benacerraf-style anti-reductionist argument with regard to the numbers is—completely unsurprisingly—not applicable to all properties. In fact, it isn't even plausible for all properties of which we can master concepts without knowing how those properties are constituted. It is possible, for example, to master the concept of water completely without knowing anything about chemistry at all; this does nothing to undermine the fact that water is indeed nothing other than H_2O. The question, then, is whether colours are more like water and other natural kinds, or more like numbers. Gert provides a number of arguments that they are more like numbers.

One consideration in favour of taking colours to be more like numbers than like natural kinds is that in the case of colours, as in the case of numbers, there are a number of equally plausible candidates. In the case of colour, these candidates are those supported by reflectance physicalists, dispositionalists, microphysicalists, and other reductionists. In the case of water, on the other hand, H_2O is the lone candidate with any degree of plausibility. One thing that explains the difference between water and redness is that in the case of water and many other natural kinds, we have an interest in differentiating *genuine* instances of the kind from other instances that merely share a *superficial* similarity. For example, we want to use water for certain purposes, including drinking and washing, and we want to avoid drinking poisons even if they look and taste just like water. In the case of colour, on the other hand, the superficial appearance *is* what we are concerned with: it is precisely our interest in these appearances that explains why we have terms in our language that allow us to talk about them. For the purposes served by colour vocabulary, it makes no difference to us how those appearances are produced; that is why no useful purpose would be served by distinguishing real red from fools' red. So there is little reason to think that the meaning of a given colour word serves to pick out one of the many candidates, in the way that the meaning of 'water' *does* serve to pick out H_2O. Just as number words can perform their function perfectly well without any commitment to reduction, and just as the learning of number words allows anyone who has mastered them to perform those func-tions, so too do colour words perform their function perfectly well without commitment to any 'deeper essence'.[8] It is part of the *meaning* of natural kind terms that empirical investigation can reveal their essence. The same is not true for *all* terms, however: not for numbers, and not for colours.

If one does reduce colours to something else, then, just as in the case of set-theoretic reduc-tions of the integers, one endows the target of analysis with too many properties. For example, primary quality accounts of the colours will endow them with too many dimensions of similar-ity. As a result, it will turn out that for all we know a certain shade of green might be *essentially* more similar to a certain shade of red than to another shade of green, though of course it might not *look* more similar. And relational accounts will endow colours with too many relata. That is, just as set-theoretic reductions of the integers require an answer to such ill-posed questions as "How many members does five have?", so too does the relational account of colour require an answer to the ill-posed question "Relative to what viewers does that object have the colour it appears to you to have?" There are also many *modal* properties that reductive accounts end up attributing to the colours. For example, a reductive microphysicalist would have to hold that ripe tomatoes would be red in a world in which light behaves differently, or in a world in which human retinas have only two colour receptors. In this way all reductive accounts entail contro-versial and unnecessary answers to questions about the colours of objects in counterfactual circumstances.[9]

5 An argument from neo-pragmatism

Jonathan Cohen (2009, pp. 69–72) has objected to the Benacerraf-style argument offered in the previous section. In his view, the argument places too much weight on facts about the acquisi-tion of competence with colour terms, and too little on the semantics and metaphysics of colour. In brief, he accuses Gert of trying to get too much out of considerations regarding con-ceptual competence, and of moving immediately from (a) the fact that competent users may not have any view as to the colours of objects in counterfactual circumstances to (b) the claim that any such view would be false.

Cohen points out that in acquiring colour concepts we acquire a competence that allows us to apply colour terms in new contexts. And he is surely right about this. But this obvious fact is neutral on the issue of Primitivism vs. reductionism. After all, acquiring competence with integers allows us to add and subtract integers we may never have encountered before, and to say how many gold airplanes we would have in the distant possible world in which we initially had two, and they were then flawlessly duplicated by a giant three-dimensional copy machine. Cohen also complains that the usefulness of philosophical thought-experiments involving odd counterfactuals shows that when we acquire competence with concepts via ostensive teaching, this often underwrites the truth of certain modal claims we might make that involve these concepts. This is certainly true as well. In fact, it is what allows us to show that certain terms are natural kind terms. But Gert never denied this. Indeed, he noted that when we acquire conceptual competence with a new natural kind term—'water' as it might be—then certain counterfactuals we utter are true, and certain ones false, even if we have no idea which are which. But the question remains as posed above: is 'red' more like 'water', or more like 'five'? The Primitivist argument offered some considerations in favour of taking it to be more like 'five'.

Cohen takes Gert's essential question to be "[H]ow could it be that color terms latch onto property P_1 rather than property P_2, given that P_1 and P_2 come apart in extension only in cases found outside the learning scenario?" (71). He thinks the error in the Benacerraf-style argument for Primitivism is that it moves from the lack of a compelling answer to such questions, to the conclusion that there *is* no answer (71). As he also points out, his reasons for thinking this inference is invalid are by no means specific to colour. After all, many terms latch onto properties about which competent speakers—indeed, *all* speakers—might be in complete ignorance. So, in contrast to the Primitivist, he endorses a view that he correctly attributes to all non-primitivist realists: that 'color terms latch onto one rather than another property—viz., a property that is picked out by the analysans occurring in the [correct] non-primitivist theory of color' (70).

What stands behind Cohen's criticism is a view of the division of labour in philosophy. On his view, it is the job of semantics to connect terms and concepts with the right properties and individuals, the job of language-learning to bring about this connection in the heads of particular speakers, and the job of metaphysics to tell us how the properties and individuals are constituted (71). One way of opposing Cohen's objections, therefore, and of bolstering the Benacerraf-style argument for Primitivism presented in section 4, is to challenge this picture. And, though it seems to go against the dominant view among philosophers of colour, there is a coherent and compelling alternative. This opposing picture finds its clearest and most extensive expression in the work of Huw Price.[10] The resulting view, variously called neo-pragmatism, subject-naturalism, global expressivism, or linguistic naturalism, rejects the sort of representational view of language that Cohen endorses. It is this representational view that stands behind both the posing, and the "solving", of the placement problem presented by colour: the problem of finding something that is naturalistically respectable for colours to be. The same representational view also underwrites placement problems that arise when we reflect on morality, modality, the mental, the mathematical, and so on. A different view of what language is doing—the neo-pragmatist view—allows us to dismiss some—though perhaps not all—of these placement problems.

Placement problems arise when we notice that we have a set of terms that function as subjects and predicates in sentences that seem clearly to be truth-apt, but we wonder what those terms could be picking out: what, in Cohen's terms, they 'latch onto'. Reductionists seem committed to the following theses:

1   Real predicates and names latch onto properties and objects "out there" in the world via a substantive semantic relation called 'reference'.
2   Only certain sorts of things exist "out there" to be latched onto.
3   These include only the sorts of things studied by science, and constructions out of them.

Given the background of these theses, philosophical theories then come in to find something of the appropriate kind that will vindicate the truths to which we would like to remain committed. In a certain sense, the representational view is underwritten by a commitment to naturalism. But it does not take the naturalism far enough. It recognizes that language is a natural phenomenon, and seeks natural objects and properties to be the referents of names and predicates—the things they 'latch onto'. Some version may even go so far as to try to find some naturalistic relation called 'reference'. But it takes for granted that there is such a relation, and rejects out of hand the idea that an appropriate account of semantic vocabulary will be deflationary.

Opposed to the representational view is another conception of language, also naturalistic, which starts with fewer commitments, and which may well undermine the representational view just described. This version of naturalism avoids an *a priori* commitment to the *substantive* nature of semantic notions such as truth and reference, and begins by viewing human linguistic activity as the production of structured sounds and marks that serve a plurality of functions. It might explain our use of moral predicates, for example, as a means of coordinating attitudes in such a way that we can function to better effect in groups. It may also explain our use of semantic vocabulary—'true' and 'refers', for example—as disquotational devices that enable generalizations that would otherwise be impossible, or, as Price argues, as part of a linguistically mediated mechanism for bringing psychological states into agreement in domains in which such agreement is advantageous. Nothing in these explanations requires us to find properties or relations studied by science for the terms 'immoral', 'true', or 'refers' to latch onto. Similar remarks go for the counting numbers. And, given the functions that colour words have, similar remarks go for them as well.

Once one sees the attractions of the neo-pragmatist view of language, the pressure to find a naturalistic reduction of colour terms—or normative or modal terms—is lifted to such a degree that it is easy to entertain the possibility that there is no such reduction.[11] Nor does the view entail that numbers do not exist, or that moral properties and colour are not genuine properties. The very idea that it does have this unfortunate entailment rests on a lingering commitment to the idea that there is a distinction between genuine truth, genuine facts, genuine reference, and so on, and mere "quasi" versions of these things. And the neo-pragmatist denies that there is such a distinction.

6 An argument from the nature of properties

A more metaphysically oriented argument for Primitivism has been offered by Michael Watkins (2002, 2005, 2010). Watkins, following Stephen Yablo (1995) and Sydney Shoemaker (2007) defends a particular view of how properties are individuated, and applies that view to the case of colour. For Watkins, properties are picked out by the causal powers they contribute to the objects that have them. That does not mean that we should *identify* properties with causal powers, since causal powers are dispositions. Rather, we should identify properties as the categorical bases that endow objects with those dispositions.[12] Redness, for example, is realized by various quite distinct physical properties. That these physical realizers are *distinct* entails, on the view of property individuation Watkins endorses, that they contribute distinct sets of causal powers. But they also have a shared set of causal powers: those we associate with the colour red. Most salient among these powers are those related to the experience of beings like us. On Watkins' view, these causal powers serve to pick out redness. Redness is distinct from any of its realizers, since those realizers contribute *more* (and therefore a different set of) causal powers. It is true that on this account redness cannot contribute more causal powers than are contributed by any one of its realizers. But this is a virtue of the view, inasmuch as it immediately explains the supervenience of the colours on whatever properties realize them; any change in the colour of an object entails a change in the properties that realize the colour of that object. Moreover, Watkins' view explains this supervenience both on the assumption that physical properties have their causal powers *essentially* (in which case the physical facts metaphysically determine the chromatic facts) and on the contrary assumption that physical properties only have their causal powers as a matter of *physical law* (in which case the physico-chromatic laws supervene on the physical laws).

One might worry that on Watkins' view, precisely because colours are picked out in virtue of contributing a *subset* of causal powers, they will not count as "real" properties: that they are mere abstractions constructed by noting that a class of "real" (i.e. physical) properties happen to share a subset of causal powers. Against this worry we can note that the property of being quadrilateral is certainly a real property. It is realized by the property of being square, rectangular, trapezoidal, and by various other shape properties. It contributes a subset of the causal powers of each of these more determinate shapes, but it is identical to none of them. Similarly, being a metal is a real property. It is realized by being gold, iron, aluminum, and so on. And, like the property of being a quadrilateral or being red, it contributes a subset of the causal powers of its determinates, but is identical to none of those determinates. So the worry here cannot be sustained *merely* because colours are picked out by reference to a shared subset of the causal powers of its realizers.

One might attempt to object to the above analogy with shapes and elements by appeal to some sense of natural unity. Being a quadrilateral or being metal, one might hold, contribute causal powers that are naturally unified in some way, while the causal powers contributed by being red are relevant only to a certain radically contingent mechanism: the human visual system. Suppose I constructed a mechanism that classified chemical compounds into four categories—call them 'algors'—first by determining their molecular structure, and then by applying some complex and arbitrarily constructed algorithm based on the total number of protons, neutrons, and electrons to be found in one molecule. For each different algorithm, the mechanism would induce a distinct set of four algors, supervenient on the molecular structure of the substances. But the temptation in this case is not to think that each such classification reveals a distinct set of four primitive algor properties. And the human visual system can be seen as a mechanism that induces a similar sort of arbitrary classification of surfaces, based on reflectance.

One response to the above objection is to appeal to a difference in our intuitions about whether or not the algors and colours cause their distinctive effects (see Watkins, 2010, p. 128). Suppose I settled on one particular algorithm, and called the resulting algors 'eenie', 'meenie', 'miney', and 'moe'. It would not be surprising if many people wanted to resist the claim that my mechanism *detected* ceniness or meeniness. Relatedly, it would not be surprising if some people wanted to resist the claim that the mineyness of hydrogen peroxide *caused* my mechanism to classify it as miney. But realists about colour do *not* want to resist analogous claims about colour: they want to say that we *do* detect redness, and that the redness of blood *does* cause us to see it as red. Watkins can therefore say that, inasmuch as there are very significant problems regarding the disjunctive properties of reductive realist views as causing their effects, we need to appeal to a *unified* cause. This provides at least the *motivation* to think of the colours as genuine—though supervenient—properties: more like being metal and being quadrilateral than like being eenie or meenie.

John Campbell seems to endorse a version of the "causal power" view outlined above, but he includes as central to our concepts of the colours not only their effects on observers, but also their liability to change at our hands, as the result of our intentional interventions. That is, Campbell thinks that our ability to act on the colours of objects—to change their colours by painting or dying them, for example—is part of our conception of them as categorical properties that ground the dispositions of objects to produce certain experiences in viewers (Campbell 2005, pp. 108, 114, 115; 2006, p. 31). He holds that our sense that we are *directly acting* on the colour when we paint or dye makes salient the sense in which we take vision to acquaint us *directly* with the properties we are acting on, so that we know *which* properties we are acting on (2006, p. 39). This is in contrast to a case in which we manipulate some *other* variable—whether we have some idea of what that variable is, or not—and the result of acting on that variable is a change in the appearance of an object. This latter process is what goes on, for example, when we pound an almond or slap our cheeks. Campbell holds that if all changes in our chromatic experience of objects were due to causes of this sort, in which we saw ourselves as manipulating *other* properties directly, our concept of the colours would be quite different. Under such circumstances, if we had such concepts at all, they might well be dispositional.

It is not entirely clear what to make of Campbell's argument with respect to the issue of Primitivism proper, as opposed to the idea that common sense is committed to Primitivism. He admits, for example, that even in the case of a subject who lacks colour concepts, it may well be the case that 'the content of her vision includes experience of the colours' (2006, p. 32). So one might take the issue of the nature of colour to concern the properties that figure in that content, rather than the concepts we humans happen to develop once we've acquired the ability to produce dyes and paints. That is, Campbell is arguing primarily at the level of concepts, and not properties. But since he also spends a great deal of time defending our concepts from the charge of error, it is possible to take the overall thrust of his argument to be about the nature of the colours themselves, and not simply our concepts of them.

7 Summary

Among theories of colour, Primitivism is uniquely consistent with all the simplest and most basic commonsense beliefs about colour. Contrary to what some of its critics claim, it does not rest on the controversial thesis of Revelation, or rob colours of causal relevance, or exclude animals from the world of colour vision. Reductive views of colour might seem more attractive than Primitivism to some philosophers because they endorse—whether explicitly or not—a set of assumptions about what real properties must be like, and about how reference must work. But these assumptions can and have been called into question. Not all referring words need to refer to the objects and properties studied by science, or to constructions out of such objects and properties. A very plausible, very general, and very naturalistic view of language allows the truth of 'Blood is red' to express what it seems, right on the surface, to express: the simple attribution of a simple property.

Notes

1 Campbell (1993).
2 Cohen (2009) defines a concept of 'red *simpliciter*', but this is not to be confused with the simple plain-old red of common sense. Red *simpliciter*, for Cohen, is identical to the relational colour red-for-viewers-V-under-circumstances-C, where V and C are determined by conversational context. As a result, there is no red *simpliciter simpliciter*.
3 An exception is Colin McGinn, who abandons his earlier dispositionalism because 'color properties do not look much like dispositions to produce color experiences' (1996, pp. 537–8).
4 Yablo, 1995, p. 486; Campbell, 2006, pp. 39–40; and Byrne and Hilbert 2007, pp. 83–4 all present this objection in order to rebut it. See also Johnston, 1992, pp. 227–8.

5 See Byrne and Hilbert (2007, p. 96). Pautz (2009) seems to attribute this view to the Primitivist as well. Levine (2006, p. 271) explicitly considers only versions of Primitivism that fit this uncharitable picture, though he acknowledges that other versions of Primitivism are possible. Watkins (2010, p. 126) claims that all Primitivists belong to Levine's unconsidered category.

6 This has more to do with the notions of 'perception' and 'property' than with the essence of colour in particular.

7 But see Cohen (2007).

8 This point is stressed by Justin Broackes (1992), who presents an argument that is very sympathetic to Primitivism.

9 This does not mean that non-chromatic descriptions can never support chromatic ones. Given that colours supervene on the physical, a possible world that is just like this one except that my overdone steak was merely seared will be a world in which the centre of my steak is red.

10 Price has been developing and defending this view for nearly 30 years. For a nice overview, see the first three chapters of Price (2013).

11 McGinn's Primitivism also relies on suspicions about the idea that all there is is the physical and the mental. Peter Ross (1999) thinks the addition of levels of existence requires more pressure than the Revelation McGinn endorses, so he rejects McGinn's view. But the neo-pragmatist view vindicates a plurality of non-reducible properties without any aid from Revelation.

12 Although he presents it in quite different terms, this seems to be McGinn's view as well, since his 'colour impressionism' includes commitments to the *sui generisness* of Primitivism, the categorical nature of colours, and the idea that we pick out the colours by means of their dispositions to cause experiences (1996, pp. 544–5, 548, 550). On the other hand, McGinn takes colours to be *grounded in, based on*, or *consequential upon* dispositions, which all seem to be stronger relations than being *individuated by* dispositions. Moreover, while Watkins' colours are realized by a heterogeneous collection of microphysical properties, McGinn's are realized by unified dispositions, which *themselves* are realized by microphysical properties (pp. 546–7).

References

Allen, Keith (2011). "Revelation and the Nature of Colour", *Dialectica* 65:2, pp. 153–76.

Benacerraf, Paul (1983). "What Numbers Could Not Be", in Hilary Putnam and Paul Benacerraf (eds.), *Philosophy of Mathematics: Selected Readings*, New York, Cambridge, pp. 272–93.

Boghossian, Paul A. and Velleman, J. David (1991). "Physicalist Theories of Color", *The Philosophical Review* 100, pp. 67–106.

Broakes, Justin (1992). "The Autonomy of Color", in David Charles and Kathleen Lennon (eds.), *Reduction, Explanation, and Realism*, Oxford, Clarendon Press, pp. 421–65.

Byrne, Alex and Hilbert, David R. (2007). "Color Primitivism", *Erkenntnis* 66, pp. 73–105.

Campbell, John (1993). "A Simple View of Color", in John Haldane and Crispin Wright (eds.), *Reality, Representation, and Projection*, New York, Oxford University Press, pp. 257–68.

Campbell, John (2005). "Transparency vs. Revelation in Color Perception", *Philosophical Topics* 33, pp. 105–15.

Campbell, John (2006). "Manipulating Colour: Pounding an Almond", in Tamar Gendler and John Hawthorne (eds.), *Perceptual Experience*, Oxford, Oxford University Press, pp. 31–48.

Cohen, Jonathan (2007). "A Relationalist's Guide to Error about Color Perception", *Noûs* 41:2, pp. 335–53.

Cohen, Jonathan (2009). "Color", in John Symons and Paco Calvo (eds.), *The Routledge Companion to Philosophy of Psychology*, New York, Oxford University Press, pp. 568–78.

Gert, Joshua (2008). "What Colors Could Not Be: An Argument for Color Primitivism", *Journal of Philosophy* 105:3, pp. 128–55.

Johnston, Mark (1992). "How to Speak of the Colors", *Philosophical Studies* 68, pp. 221–63.

Levine, Joseph (2006). "Color and Color Experience: Colors as Ways of Appearing", *Dialectica* 60:3, pp. 269–82.

McGinn, Colin (1996). "Another Look at Color", *The Journal of Philosophy* 93:11, pp. 537–53.

Pautz, Adam (2009). "Color, Philosophical Issues", in Tim Baynes, Axel Cleeremans, and Patrick Wilken (eds.), *Oxford Companion to Consciousness*, New York, Oxford University Press, pp. 150–5.

Price, Huw (2013). *Expressivism, Pragmatism and Representationalism*, New York, Cambridge University Press.

Ross, Peter (1999). "The Appearance and Nature of Color", *Southern Journal of Philosophy* 37, pp. 227–53.

Shoemaker, Sydney (2007). *Physical Realization*, Oxford, Oxford University Press.

Watkins, Michael (2002). *Rediscovering Colors: A Study in Pollyanna Realism*, Boston, Dordrecht.

Watkins, Michael (2005). "Seeing Red: The Metaphysics of Colour Without the Physics", *Australasian Journal of Philosophy* 83:1, pp. 33–52.

Watkins, Michael (2010). "*A Posteriori* Primitivism", *Philosophical Studies* 150, pp. 123–37.

Yablo, Stephen (1995). "Singling out Properties", *Philosophical Perspectives* 9, pp. 477–502.

19

COLOUR RELATIONALISM

Jonathan Cohen

It is when I struggle to be brief that I become obscure.

—*Horace, Ars Poetica, l. 25*

1 What is it?: Exposition

Colour relationalism is the view that colours are constituted in terms of relations to perceiving subjects and perceptual circumstances.

It may be useful to compare this proposal about colour against less controversial relationalist views about other properties. Relationalism about *being a teacher* is the (plausible) view that things bear the latter property not by virtue of their intrinsic makeups, but by standing in the right (viz., pedagogical) sort of relation to relata (viz., students).[1] Or, again, relationalism about *being humorous* is the (plausible) view that things bear the latter property not in virtue of their intrinsic makeups, but by standing in the right sort of relation (viz., the relation of bringing about in the relata certain kinds of amusement reactions) to relata (viz., appropriately equipped sentient beings). So, too, relationalism about colour is the view that things bear the latter not by virtue of their intrinsic makeups, but by standing in the right sort of relations to (the right sorts of) perceivers and (the right sorts of) perceptual circumstances.[2]

So exactly what, for a relationalist, counts as the right—i.e. colour constitutive—sorts of relations, perceivers, and circumstances? Because there is a wide range of answers to these questions, about which reasonable relationalists will disagree, it is probably best to think of relationalism as a view family, rather than a single specific view. Perhaps the most historically important form of colour relationalism, sometimes associated (controversially) with great moderns including Galileo, Boyle, Newton, and Locke, holds that the relevant relations are dispositions to cause colour sensations, and the relata are normal perceivers in normal circumstances. Contemporary defenders of related views include McGinn (1983), Peacocke (1984), and Johnston (1992). Moreover, a number of philosophers, including Thompson *et al.* (1992), Thompson (1995), Cohen (2003, 2009), Matthen (2005), have more recently defended a range of non-traditional forms of colour relationalism that differ from dispositionalism and from one another largely in just how they understand the colour-constitutive relation.[3] For present purposes, however, it will be useful to think of relationalism broadly, as there is much that can be said about the strengths and weaknesses of the general view—i.e., the claim that colours are constituted in terms of relations to perceivers and circumstances—independently of the more particular commitments that divide relationalists.

2 Why believe it?: Motivation

The leading motivation for colour relationalism, in both its historical and contemporary forms, is a non-deductive argument form concerning perceptual variation. Though this argument form generalizes over a very wide set of intrapersonal, interpersonal, and interspecies phenomena, it is best appreciated, at least initially, in its application to single cases.

Thus, we can begin with a case of intrapersonal variation that involves our perceptual reactions to the central strips in the left and right halves of Figure 19.1. The strips in the two halves of the figure are intrinsically (qualitatively) identical. (Indeed, with scissors and glue, we could generate the same effect with a single strip rather than two qualitatively identical copies.) But if you are like most normally sighted subjects, your visual system will react differently to the strip depending on the background against which it is set: it will look lighter and more greenish against the yellowish background on the left, and darker and more yellowish against the greenish background on the right. There is, then, variation in your perceptual reaction to the one stimulus (the strip) as a function of the circumstances in which you perceive it.

Now, on standard assumptions, each of your variant perceptual reactions is a representation of the strip and its properties—each represents the way the distal object is.[4] If so, then we can ask: which of the variant reactions is a *veridical* representation of the way the distal object is, and why? This question is intended metaphysically, not epistemically: we are asking not 'how do we know which is veridical?' but 'which of the variant perceptual effects really is veridical, and what makes that the case?'. The logically possible answers (in a case with two variants) are: (i) neither veridical, (ii) one veridical at the expense of the other, (iii) both veridical.

Figure 19.1 The two centre strips are qualitatively identical, but visual systems react differently to them as a function of the backgrounds against which they are set.

Which of the logically possible answers should we select? The neither veridical option is coherent, but unduly sceptical: the case can be elaborated so as to make it as conducive to veridical visual apprehension of the world as we like without thereby eliminating the possibility of perceptual variation, so choosing this answer is uncomfortably close to holding that no one ever perceives any colour veridically. The one right option is also coherent, but objectionably stipulative given the symmetry between variants: every physical or psychological fact that can be cited in a description of either variant can be met by a corresponding physical or psychological fact that can be cited in a description of the other, and there's no obvious reason why the facts cited in one of these descriptions (and not others) should make it count as veridical to the exclusion of others. Hence, it's hard to imagine what could count as a non-stipulative, non-question-begging reason for counting any one variant as uniquely veridical.[5] This leaves the ecumenicist answer, on which both variants are veridical; this answer has the advantage over other answers that it avoids forms of undue scepticism and unmotivated stipulation that, I take it, we should want to avoid.

But accepting this kind of ecumenicism is a short inference to the best explanation away from colour relationalism.[6] Relationalism explains how it could be, in a situation where a given stimulus a brings about different perceptual effects in perceiver S in circumstance C_1 and in S in circumstance C_2—i.e. a looks red to S in C_1 and does not look red to S in C_2—that both perceptual effects can veridically represent a. The crucial observation here is that if an object bears relation R to a sequence of relata $\langle r_1, r_2 \ldots \rangle$, that says nothing at all about whether it does or does not bear R to some other sequence of relata $\langle r'_1, r'_2 \ldots \rangle$ or whether it does or does not bear some different relation $R^\star$ to either one of those sequences of relata. Thus, if Aristotle is the teacher of Alexander, this neither requires nor precludes that Aristotle is the teacher of Cleopatra. (Nor, indeed, does it require or preclude that Aristotle bears some other relation to either Alexander or Cleopatra.). So, too, if colour relationalism is true, and a is red to S in C_1, this neither requires nor precludes that a is red to S in C_2. Consequently, relationalists can hold both that (i) a's effect on S in C_1 is a veridical representation because a is red to S in C_1, and (ii) a's effect on S in C_2 is a veridical representation because a is not red to S in C_2.

In short, then, the facts about perceptual variation motivate colour relationalism via a pair of non-deductive inferences—the first from the empirical data (plus standard canons of rationality) to ecumenicism, and the second from ecumenicism to relationalism.

As indicated above, this argumentative pattern generalizes widely, and can be applied, in a consistent way, to interspecies, intrapersonal, and interpersonal instances of perceptual variation.

Interspecies: Perceivers of different species differ considerably in their colour vision: the chromatic effects that a single stimulus has on these perceivers vary widely as a function of many parameters of their visual systems—retinal cone type populations (and population ratios), cone tuning curves, macular and lens pigmentation, and on and on. While there may be principled grounds for saying that some such variants represent the stimulus colour erroneously, there remains significant variation between variants in organisms that pass standard comparative psychophysical criteria for normal colour vision; as such, it would be objectionably *ad hoc* to treat these variants as systematically misrepresenting the colours of objects. The relationalist holds that all of these variants are veridical, thereby avoiding undue scepticism and *ad hoc* stipulation, by holding that the stimulus exemplifies (simultaneously, all over) one colour with respect to perceivers of kind K_1, another colour with respect to perceivers of kind K_2, and so on.

Interpersonal: Human perceivers differ considerably in their colour vision: the chromatic effects of a single stimulus on these viewers vary widely as a function of many parameters of their visual systems—retinal cone populations (and population ratios), cone tuning curves, macular and lens pigmentation, and on and on. While there may be principled grounds for saying that some such variants represent the stimulus colour erroneously, there remains significant interpersonal variation among perceivers who pass standard tests for normal colour vision; as such, it would be objectionably *ad hoc* to treat these variants as systematically misrepresenting the colours of objects. The relationalist can hold that all of these variants are veridical, thereby avoiding undue scepticism and *ad hoc* stipulation, by holding that the stimulus exemplifies (simultaneously, all over) one colour with respect to perceiver S_1, another colour with respect to perceiver S_2, and so on.

Intrapersonal: The chromatic effects of a single stimulus on a single perceiver vary widely as a function of many parameters of the viewing circumstance—surround, lighting, viewing angle, viewing distance, state of adaptation of the perceiver, and on and on. While there may be principled grounds for saying that some such variants represent the stimulus colour erroneously, there remains significant perceptual variation within ecologically normal circumstances; as such, it would be objectionably *ad hoc* to treat these variants as systematically misrepresenting the colours of objects. The relationalist holds that all of these variants are veridical, thereby avoiding both undue scepticism and *ad hoc* stipulation, by holding that the stimulus exemplifies (simultaneously, all over) one colour with respect to circumstance C_1, another colour with respect to circumstance C_2, and so on.

Combining these considerations, and ignoring many niceties (also assuming that each perceiver falls in exactly one relevant perceiver type), leads to the relationalist proposal that colours are constituted in terms of relations to both perceivers and perceptual circumstances—that colours are not monadic properties like *red* or *green*, but rather relational properties like *red for S_1 in C_1* or *green for S_2 in C_2*.

3 No, really?: Objections

3.1 Colour representation

There is a mismatch between the relationalist's colours and the form of ordinary linguistic (and, plausibly, mental) representation of colour. Ordinary linguistic/mental colour attributions typically don't contain overt specifications of the perceiver and circumstance parameters—and certainly not overt specifications of perceivers or circumstances that are as fine-grained as apparently needed to cope with the observed range of perceptual variation per the relationalist strategy above. So it's not clear how ordinary predications could genuinely (non-gappily) have relationalist's colours as semantic values.

But this problem can be solved by two independently plausible ideas. The first is that ordinary colour predicates pick out "coarse-grained colours"—relational properties analogous to the fine-grained colours discussed above, but whose parametric positions are filled by relatively coarse-grained specifications of perceivers and perceptual conditions. This idea allows that the contents expressed by ordinary uses of colour predicates need not attain the high levels of determinacy of the fine-grained colours; it simultaneously allows that the contents expressed by ordinary uses of colour predicates can be multiply instantiated. The second independently plausible idea needed is a version of semantic contextualism for colour language and thought—roughly, that contextual enrichment adds to the information overtly encoded in ordinary colour attributions. Combining these two ideas results in the view that the predicate 'is red', as uttered/thought in context K, expresses the property *red for the perceivers relevant in context K under the perceptual circumstances relevant in context K.*[7] (Similarly for other colour predicates.)[8]

3.2 Disagreement

One might worry that the relationalist's implementation of ecumenicism, which involves the idea that different variants ascribe properties relativized to different parameters, deprives distinct ascriptions of a common subject matter, and so precludes intrapersonal and interpersonal disagreement about colour.[9]

But this worry can be answered by appeal to the relationalist's coarse-grained colours. Even if the distinct fine-grained colours *unique yellow for S_1 in C_1, greenish-yellow for S_2 in C_2* attributed by S_1's and S_2's visual systems are compatible, we can account for the disagreement between S_1 and S_2 by claiming that S_1 verbally/cognitively attributes, while S_2 verbally/cognitively forebears, a common coarse-grained colour (viz., one whose perceiver/circumstance parameters are assigned to the very same values). It would seem, then, that relationalism has the capacity to describe individuals as disagreeing about the colours of objects—it is just that the descriptions in question will involve representations of coarse-grained properties at the cognitive/linguistic level rather than representations of the fine-grained properties by the visual system.[10]

3.3 Error

It is also possible to worry that the relationalist's embrace of ecumenicism—designed, as it is, to make veridical many different representations of colour—leaves her without a way of saying that *any* variant colour representation is erroneous, and so without an account of colour misrepresentation. But this worry is misplaced: relationalism makes room for several forms of colour misrepresentation.

A first involves hallucination. If, in hallucinatory experience, I perceptually represent an elephant exemplifying *pink (for myself in the circumstances I am in)* even though there is no local elephant, I am thereby entertaining a perceptual representation that misascribes a colour to an individual. Admittedly, here blame for the representation's non-veridicality lies, in the first instance, with the absence of an individual answering to the subject term, and not with some more limited problem about the colour property it attributes—that's what makes the case an instance of hallucination rather than illusion. Notwithstanding this point, it seems fair to describe the case as one in which the perceiver perceptually entertains a non-veridical colour representation, viz., a colour misrepresentation. And there's no reason a relationalist cannot recognize colour misrepresentations of this kind.

A second relationalist-friendly form of colour misrepresentation involves deviant causal chains. Thus, to return to a fanciful example from Cohen (2007), if a telekinetic tomato stimulates my visual cortex without affecting my retina, and my subsequently attending to that tomato causes in me the reaction I normally get when looking at ordinary, non-telekinetic, ripe tomatoes, then my perceptual representation of its colour is obtained through a deviant causal chain. But if that's so, then even a committed ecumenicist about perceptual variation is within her rights to say that *this* colour representation should be excluded rather than treated as veridical. The point generalizes: while accepting ecumenicism about perceptual variation means treating

Jonathan Cohen

as veridical whatever colour ascriptions can't be set aside for principled and non-question-begging reasons, this is compatible with thinking that there are some variants that *can* be set aside for reasons independent of our commitments about colour. There's surely room for disagreement about what counts as deviant, but it's plausible that cases involving telekinetic tomatoes and blunt instrument head trauma fall into this class on anyone's story, and therefore that relationalists can describe the colour representations arising in such cases as erroneous, notwithstanding their general ecumenicist sympathies.

A third way in which relationalism makes room for erroneous colour representation involves errors in the representation of the coarse-grained colours described above. Suppose you encounter *a* when it is illuminated in an unusual way you are not aware of—say, in the psychophysics lab, or, as happens frequently around my university, in parking lots with low pressure sodium vapour lamps, and that you (veridically) perceptually represent *a* as exemplifying the fine-grained colour *grey for you in the circumstance you are in*. You have no reason to believe that there is anything odd about the spectral composition of the illumination, and so hold rational but false beliefs about what sorts of perceiver you are/what sort of perceptual circumstance you are in. Thus, the perceiver and circumstance types relevant in your context K are the ordinary ones you take yourself to exemplify and occupy, rather than the unusual ones you in fact exemplify and occupy. Consequently, you infer/compute, in the ordinary way, from your veridical perceptual representation that *a* bears the fine-grained colour *grey for you in the circumstance you are in* to the erroneous conclusion that *a* bears the coarse-grained colour *grey for the perceivers relevant in context K under the perceptual circumstances relevant in K*. In so doing, you misrepresent *a*'s colour.[11]

3.4 Colour constancy

As we have seen, colour relationalism takes differences in colour perception very seriously, and indeed (to a first approximation) treats differences in colour perception as strong evidence of differences in colour properties. But one might object that this treatment ignores a kind of stability that comes out in garden-variety instances of colour constancy, such as that depicted in Figure 19.2, where a materially uniform coffee cup is partially illuminated by direct sunlight and partially shaded (there is a luminance edge on its facing surface). Though there's much that is puzzling and controversial about such cases, it surely seems natural to say that there's some good sense in which patches of the cup on opposite sides of the luminance edge are alike in colour. Of course, relationalists will want to say that there is perceptual variation, hence a colour difference, across the luminance edge: the patch on one side looks and is lighter white to perceiver S_1 in its condition involving direct sunlight illumination, while the patch on the other side looks and is darker white to perceiver S_1 in its condition involving indirect illumination. Are relationalists, therefore, unable to account for the phenomenon of colour constancy?

They are not. Recall that, for relationalists, objects (including surface patches) simultaneously exemplify multiple colours. In particular, relationalists will say that a patch of the coffee cup exemplifies not only the colour that it is occurrently manifesting (to S_1 in C_1), but also colours that it is not occurrently manifesting. Thus, the relationalist can hold that the occurrently darker patch of the cup now in C_1 exemplifies the non-manifest colour *brighter white to S_1 in C_2*. Of course, she will say that that is the very colour the lighter patch of the cup both exemplifies and occurrently manifests. Therefore, she can acknowledge a colour property that is constant/shared between the two patches, even though (she will say) it is a colour that only one of them occurrently manifests.[12] And she can describe mechanisms of colour constancy as delivering verdicts about whether patches occurrently manifesting different colours would match visually if,

Figure 19.2   Canonical instance of colour constancy.

counterfactually, the two were presented under the conditions that one of them is occurrently in.[13]

3.5 Visual access to fine-grained colours

Though this will depend on the broadly empirical question of which differences in visual systems and perceptual circumstances result in faultless psychophysical variation, it seems that the relationalist's fine-grained colours are likely to be quite fine-grained indeed. Some have worried that, consequently, such colours will be inaccessible to vision or visual representation, or otherwise unsuited to the purposes colour vision serves in creatures like us.

Thus, Byrne and Hilbert (2017) object that the properties in question are both too determinate to be recovered by visual systems and ecologically insignificant because too fine-grained to stand in even local correlations with ecologically/adaptively useful object properties (say, being tasty, being nutritious, etc.).[14] Pautz (2010b) builds on this criticism by objecting that the fine-grained colours fit poorly with standard views of the psychosemantics of sensory representation (e.g. Millikan 1984; Dretske 1995; Tye 1995, 2000), on which (roughly) state-types are assigned as content whatever they have the functional role of indicating among the general population under optimal conditions. The problem, Pautz urges, is that it's hard to see how any state type could have the function of indicating in the general population under optimal circumstances such extremely finely individuated, non-recurring, and ecologically insignificant properties as the relationalist's fine-grained colours. If so, such standard psychosemantic views would entail that no visual state type has any fine-grained colour as its content.

I believe relationalism withstands these worries.

It's unclear what to make of Byrne's and Hilbert's worry about the unrecoverability of the fine-grained properties. For, while the relationalist's fine-grained properties will plausibly depend on many parameters of the perceiver and circumstance, relationalists won't take any parameter to individuate colours without empirical evidence that visual systems are sensitive to its value. Of course, the computational techniques visual systems employ to estimate such values are quite complicated, highly interactive, dependent on endogenously fixed assumptions about the world (Shepard 2001), and as yet imperfectly understood. But this is no reason for supposing that these parameters are beyond the reach of visual systems.

I accept Byrne's and Hilbert's additional point that the relationalist's fine-grained colours may lack ecological significance (when considered on their own). On the other hand, and as they note (p. 183) there's no reason to doubt that the relevant ecologically salient properties are locally correlated with the coarse-grained colours relationalists already have reason to recognize (cf. Cohen 2009, pp. 126–7: ripe fruits exemplifying different fine-grained colours plausibly share the property *crimson for the perceivers relevant in context K under the perceptual circumstances relevant in K* for a suitable choice of *K*. So long as our theory of colour allows (as relationalism does) that organisms can be responsive to ecologically significant properties or their local correlates in one way or another, the fact of this responsiveness presents no obstacle for that theory.[15]

Pautz's psychosemantic concern can be answered as well. It should be uncontroversial to parties in this dispute that there is *mental* representation of relational properties (say, *humorousness*) and of fine-grained relational properties (say, *nutritious to a creature with narrowly specified metabolism type M, conspecific to a creature with narrowly specified reproductive type R,* and even *red for creature with a narrowly specified visual system type S in narrowly specified perceptual circumstances C*). But if so, then it's open to relationalists to hold that whatever accounts for the mental representation of such properties can also serve as an account of states of the visual system represent the very same properties. Now, one might insist that the story about the mental representation of fine-grained relational properties won't extend to sensory representation—that, though such properties can be mentally represented, they can't be represented by sensory systems. But why accept that insistence? Surely not simply because standard psychosemantic theories don't extend to fine-grained relational properties. For one thing, the mental representatability of such properties already shows that the theories in question can't be the whole story about mental representation (*a fortiori*, about representation in general); so it is up for grabs that whatever amounts to the rest of the story for mental representation (some extension of current theories? some completely different theory?) is applicable to sensory representation as well. For another, the psychosemantic theories at issue are themselves beset with serious difficulties even with respect to the simple non-relational properties they typically use as starting places (Cohen 2004); as such, it would seem inadvisable to treat compatibility with these theories as an adequacy condition for anything.[16]

3.6 Determinables without determinates?

As we have seen, the principal motivation for relationalism is to allow us to accept as veridical the multiple ways objects look in respect of their colours; hence, its proponents will accept instances of the schema (**R**):

(**R**) *a* is *F* to perceiver *S* in circumstance *C* iff *a* looks (/is disposed to look) *F* to *S* in *C*

(where ⌜F⌝ is the name of a colour). Cutter (2019) urges that this principle (which is naturally understood as nothing more than an expression of the relationalist's ecumenicism) is problematic when applied to cases of peripheral colour perception. Because the density of retinal cone cells mainly responsible for colour vision drops off significantly outside the fovea, colour perception in the periphery of the visual field is much less determinate than in foveal regions. Consequently, subjects often report that stimuli presented in the periphery look (as it might be) reddish without looking any determinate shade of red. Taking these reports at face value, the relationalist's commitment to (R) would seem to entail that peripherally seen objects bear determinable properties without bearing any of their determinates.

Cutter objects that this conclusion clashes with a traditional view about the metaphysics of determination (henceforth, "Determination")—the principle that, necessarily, nothing can have a determinable without having one of its determinates (cf. Johnson 1921; Prior 1949; Funkhouser 2006). Indeed, as he points out, many have rejected sense data accounts because their description of our perception of Ryle's famous speckled hen, involving a sense datum that has many speckles but no determinate number of speckles, offends against Determination (Armstrong 1968). If the clash with Determination is a reason for rejecting sense data views, Cutter suggests, it should likewise be a reason for rejecting colour relationalism.

But this objection is unpersuasive.

First, as remarked in §3.3, while the relationalist's ecumenicism about perceptual variation requires her to accept as veridical whatever colour ascriptions can't be set aside for principled and non-question-begging reasons, this is compatible with holding that some variants *can* be set aside given appropriately principled reasons. Much will turn on what reasons one is prepared to accept, but one can surely imagine that, for some relationalists, the abundant evidence of the anomalous character of peripheral colour vision amounts to sufficient theory-independent reason for setting aside—for not treating as veridical—variants arising in peripheral vision. The point here is not that peripheral colour vision is statistically infrequent or ecologically contrived (it is neither). Rather, it is that peripheral perception is anomalous in important psychophysical respects: e.g. in the periphery discrimination is poorer and more sensitive to contrast (Strasburger *et al.* 2011), cortical projections fewer in number (Gattass *et al.* 1997), flicker fusion thresholds lower (Hartmann *et al.* 1979), illusory conjunctions more common (Prinzmetal *et al.* 1995), and crowding more frequent (Levi and Carney 2009). (Peripheral perception's exceptional status presumably explains why (i) it would be misleading to answer questions about the limits on human visual discrimination or flicker fusion by providing data about the periphery, and (ii) perceivers nearly always preferentially employ foveal vision when stakes are high.) To the extent that one takes these considerations as principled reasons for setting aside such variants (I take no official stand on this question), the relationalist is within her rights to regard them as falling outside the scope of (R). If so, these variants will not lead to conflict with Determination.

Second, even for relationalists prepared to accept variant colour representations arising in peripheral vision as veridical, there is reason, stemming from the same psychophysical considerations just adduced, for regarding the consequent violations of Determination as far less objectionable than those to which sense data theorists are committed, and not reasons for rejecting the view. What makes the sense data theorist's description of the speckled hen so odd is (in part) that the property she thinks violates Determination (viz., the sense datum's number of speckles) is free-standing and non-visual-system-involving. Ordinary visual-system-independent properties plausibly obey Determination, and there's no motivated reason for thinking that the property at issue should be an exception. By contrast, given colour relationalism, there *is* a reason for expecting that peripherally perceived colours will behave quite differently from ordinary visual-system-independent properties. Again, even granting the current assumption that visual states arising in peripheral colour vision are veridical, we still have reasons (see above) for regarding the latter as oddly behaved (relative to our expectations about foveal visual perception). But if these visual states are unusual, it's unsurprising (even predictable) that relations built from such oddly behaved relata are themselves odd: if you put visual systems in unusual states, it's unsurprising that the relations constituted partly by them will be similarly unusual (relative to our expectations about relations to visual systems engaged in foveal perception). To be sure, failing to conform to generalizations about determinable-determinate structure (even if formed from reflection on ordinary cases of properties not constituted in terms of relations to visual systems) goes against standard expectations. But since the nomologically necessary facts about the case under consideration provide theory-independent reasons for expecting that the relational properties arising here are likely to behave exceptionally, the discovery that they do is not, by itself, a reason to reject the identification between them and the colours.[17]

3.7 Phenomenology

For many, phenomenology is relationalism's "Achilles' heel" (Maund 2010)—a source of evidence that runs directly counter to the view. Many have held that, with notable exceptions such as the colours of holograms and glossy or shimmering materials (e.g. the backs of CDs), colours just do not look the way that relationalism says they are. Here is one especially direct expression of this idea:[18]

> ... when we see an object as red we see it as having a simple, monadic, local property of the object's surface. The color is perceived as intrinsic to the object, in much the way that shape and size are perceived as intrinsic. No relation to perceivers enters into how the color appears; the color is perceived as wholly *on* the object, not as somehow straddling the gap between it and the perceiver. Being seen as red is not like being seen as larger than or to the left of. The "color envelope" that delimits an object stops at the object's spatial boundaries. So if color were inherently relational, ... then perception of color would misrepresent its structure—we would be under the illusion that a relational property is nonrelational. Contraposing, given that perception is generally veridical as to color, colors are not relational.
>
> *(McGinn 1996, pp. 541–2)*

This objection is at least initially puzzling, since it is not immediately obvious whether and how phenomenology might provide evidence about the relationality or non-relationality (or any other aspect of the metaphysics) of the properties whose instances we perceptually experience. Indeed, the very idea that phenomenology is potentially informative about the metaphysics of, say, *being water* or *being a tiger* is surprising. So we should ask: just why does the proponent of the objection we are considering believe that phenomenology bears on the metaphysics of colour in particular?[19]

A clue comes from consideration of the notable exceptions mentioned earlier and allowed by the objectors—the colours of holograms and the backs of CDs, which, according to the critics, *do* look relational. The distinguishing feature of such objects is that the colour phenomenology they generate is (intrapersonally) unusually fragile: even very slight and involuntary changes in viewing angle of a sort that are almost impossible to avoid in ordinary circumstances alter the resulting colour phenomenology dramatically. So it would seem that proponents of the phenomenological objection against relationalism are treating the colours of these (according to them, exceptional) objects as looking relational on the grounds that we all have (indeed, cannot avoid having when visually attending to them) evidence of intrapersonal variation in the phenomenology they occasion. Whereas, in contrast, says the objector, we lack analogous evidence of intrapersonal phenomenal variation when visually attending to the steady colours of ordinary matte objects.

The explanation just contemplated has in its favour both that it begins to make sense of how phenomenology might bear on the relationality of colours, and that it initially seems to distinguish the exceptions from the non-exceptions in the way intended.

But on second thought, the latter distinction appears not to survive scrutiny. For if evidence of phenomenal variation counts as support for the relationality of unsteady/shimmering colours, then, presumably, phenomenal variation, if it exists, should likewise count in favour of the relationality of the steady colours of matte objects. And there *is* phenomenal variation—both intrapersonally and interpersonally—with respect to the steady colours of matte objects: as we saw in §2, colour phenomenology varies dramatically along a large number of parameters of the perceiver and the viewing condition (including, *inter alia*, the viewing angle parameter cited in support of the relationality of unsteady colours).

If there is a difference between the forms of phenomenal variation accepted as evidence of relationality by the critics (viz., intrapersonal variation as a function of viewing angle for unsteady colours) and the rest, it appears to be a difference only in obviousness. Intrapersonal phenomenal variation across changes in viewing angle is hard *not* to observe with unsteady colours, while it takes somewhat more effort (how much varies between cases) to catalogue the intrapersonal variation present with steady colours. Interpersonal phenomenal variation is ordinarily even less obvious to single observers without access to psychophysics labs, though, as we have seen, no less real. In short, once we accept that phenomenal variation gives a way of understanding how phenomenology can speak to questions about relationality at all, we have reason for treating the wide range of evidence of interpersonal and intrapersonal phenomenal variation with respect to colour perception, whether obvious or not, as evidence of the relationality of colours.

Why, then, have so many thought that phenomenology is at odds with a relationalist metaphysics for steady colours? Plausibly, this is because the very fragility of intrapersonal phenomenology for unsteady colours hides the fact, emphasized by Levin (2000, p. 157), that intrapersonal phenomenology bears on questions about relationality only when we engage in comparisons between multiple phenomenal episodes, together with reflective ratiocination on those comparisons—and not just the application of introspection to individual, punctate phenomenal glances. Unsteady colours, by their very unsteadiness, make phenomenal comparison so automatic that it is easy to lose sight of the need for comparison and ratiocination, and to believe falsely that relationality must reveal itself in the non-comparative, unreflective phenomenology of punctate glances. Critics are correct to observe that non-comparative, unreflective phenomenology does not reveal the relationality of steady colours. The mistake, fostered by the false belief at issue, is to treat this absence of evidence as evidence of absence.[20]

In sum, it appears that phenomenology is not the decisive obstacle to relationalism that many have supposed it to be. So long as we remain careful to use phenomenology in a way that allows it to speak to the question of relationality, it turns out that phenomenological evidence supports, rather than detracts from, the case for colour relationalism.

4 Conclusion

Colour relationalism merits philosophical interest not only because of its continuity with historically important positions, but because it attempts to respect and to reconcile the deliverances of two of our most important pictures of the world: that supplied by our best broadly scientific theories, and that supplied by our manifest experience. Moreover, as I have argued, several of the most pressing objections against the view can be answered. There is, of course, much more to be said about colour relationalism, about the many different more specific forms it can take, and about their respective virtues and vices. However, I hope to have made the case that relationalism is a view, or family of views, worth taking seriously.[21]

Notes

1 Here I pass over all sorts of complications about the metaphysics of intrinsicness; see, e.g., Weatherson and Marshall (2014).
2 One could, of course, consider a more general form of relationalism requiring that colours are constituted in terms of relations, but not that they are constituted in terms of relations to perceivers and circumstances, in particular. I'm formulating relationalism in the more restrictive way so as to make the relationalist/non-relationalist distinction coincide with the most important and historically salient divisions in philosophical space. (On the more general construal, the view that colours are (classes of) surface spectral distributions—which are ways of affecting light—would be no less relationalist than the classical dispositionalist view that colours are (roughly) dispositions to cause certain sensations in normal perceivers in normal circumstances; a taxonomy that lumps these positions together seems like not the most useful way of carving the space of options.)
3 For discussion and comparison, see Cohen (2009, ch. 8).
4 Such standard assumptions are rejected by Smith (2002); Travis (2004), and defended by, e.g., Byrne (2009); Pautz (2010a); Siegel (2010a, 2010b).
5 Some authors (e.g. Byrne and Hilbert 2003, p. 17, 2007, pp. 88–89; Byrne 2006, p. 337; Tye 2006, p. 175, 2012, pp. 2–3; Byrne and Hilbert 2017, p. 179–80) disagree, and claim that it is relatively easy to say what makes it the case that a given variant is veridical: it is veridical just in case it (i) represents the colour of the stimulus as F, and (ii) the colour of the stimulus is indeed F. That does indeed amount to a correct statement of what it means for a variant to be veridical. But it does nothing to explain what makes it the case that one variant meets this condition at the expense of the others, which is the question facing us.
6 The colour pluralism of Kalderon (2007, and Chapter 20 in this volume) and Mizrahi (2007) can be thought of as denying this inference to the best explanation by supplying a non-relationalist way of accepting ecumenicism. Colour pluralism is the view that objects have multiple non-relational colours, to different ranges of which different perceivers in different circumstances are selectively responsive. For pluralists, distinct variants selected by different perceivers/circumstances are compatibly veridical because objects indeed compatibly exemplify multiple colours.

Briefly, I worry that this non-relationalist form of ecumenicism is unsuccessful because there remain cases of perceptual variation, grounded in differences in post-receptoral processing, between perceivers who access/are selectively responsive to exactly the same ranges of (what it recognizes as) non-relational colours. The pluralist can't describe such cases of perceptual variation ecumenically, since here the perceivers access the very same ranges of non-relational colours. For discussion, see Pautz (2006, 2008) and Cohen (2009, pp. 78–88).
7 Analogy: Ordinary motion attributions don't contain overt specifications of reference frames, so it's not clear how ordinary predications could genuinely have properties constituted in terms of relations to reference frames as their semantic values. But we can reconcile these predications with a relativistic ontology of motion properties by construing the former as making tacit reference to a contextually salient reference frame, holding that 'is moving at 60 miles per hour', as uttered/thought in context K, expresses the property *moving at 60 miles per hour relative to the reference frame relevant in context K*.
8 Two points about coarse-grained colours are worth noting. First, as defined, they are no less relational than fine-grained colours, so fit into a thoroughly relationalist ontological inventory. Second, though they are designed to serve our conversational/explanatory needs by being relativized to contextually relevant types of perceivers and circumstances, such choices are not therefore metaphysically principled: it would be absurd to attempt to break symmetries between perceptual variants by holding that the variant arising in perceivers/circumstances contextually relevant to us is distinguished from others in any metaphysically significant way. (Analogy: we might be speaking in a context in which having fewer than 100 hairs on one's head makes one count as bald; but it would absurd to treat this contextual standard as a metaphysically principled distinction between the positive and negative extension of 'bald'.) So the acceptance of coarse-grained colours is not at odds with relationalist's claim (crucial to her argument from perceptual variation) that perceptual variants are metaphysically symmetric.

9 What I say here and below applies to both agreement and disagreement.

10 Objection: This solution buys the relationalist an account of disagreement in colour representation, but it inappropriately precludes perceptual disagreement about colour (Brogaard 2010, pp. 13–14, 2012, pp. 317–18, 2015; Pautz 2010b; Allen 2011, p. 318, 2012; Egan 2012; Tye 2012).

Response: Evidence of agreement and disagreement in colour representation (e.g. matching judgements, verbal attributions) involves contributions from cognitive/linguistic as well as perceptual levels of representation. Hence it shouldn't be taken for granted that we must seek explanations of the phenomena exclusively in terms of perceptual representations. (Analogy: It's reasonable to demand that an adequate overall account of language understanding should predict the unacceptability of strings like those in (1).

(1)   a. Le silence vertébral   indispose la voile licite (Tesnière 1959, ch. 20).
           The vertebral silence indisposes the licit sail.
    b. Buffalo buffalo Buffalo buffalo buffalo buffalo Buffalo buffalo (Pinker 2000, p. 210).

But it's not reasonable to demand that a theory of syntax, in particular, should be the component of the overall account of language understanding from which such predictions are derived.) It's fair game to demand that the explanatory labour get done—but not to insist in advance on a particular theoretical distribution of the labour.

11 Objection: This third route to error locates the error at cognitive/linguistic levels, so doesn't make room for specifically *perceptual* colour misrepresentations.

Response: As noted, relationalists have other resources for describing perceptual misrepresentations of colour, in case that is wanted. Moreover, and once again, while I agree we should want an account of colour that makes room for misrepresentation, I also think it should be potentially up for grabs just what kind of theoretical descriptions of misrepresentation we offer (cf. note 10).

12 Objection:

> … if … the perceptually distinguishable regions … manifest different colors, then, on Cohen's account of color, they actually *look* different colors. According to Cohen, then, there isn't color constancy (in the relevant sense). This seems wrong to me and to miss the point. I take color constancy for the purposes of this objection to be constancy in how things *look* color-wise through different lighting conditions. It isn't constancy, period. Cohen fixes up something that gets the latter but he doesn't get the former.
>
> *(Tye 2012, p. 303)*

Response: Why assume that an adequate description of colour constancy must allow that what is shared is manifested colour? That is a theoretical assumption that goes far beyond the matching data that motivates taking there to be a shared/constant property, and that the relationalist description of constancy clearly respects. Relationalism may not respect the theoretical description of the phenomenon that Tye prefers; but he owes us an argument for thinking that's a shortcoming of the view. (I'd add that relationalists can also allow that the two regions share any number of occurrently manifested properties that are not colours; hence even if, counterfactually, we had a reason to believe that what is shared in the cases under dispute must include an occurrently manifest property, this still wouldn't threaten the relationalist's characterization of them. For further discussion of these and related issues, see Cohen 2012; Gert 2012.)

13 The counterfactual condition at issue is neither (i) that they would match if presented under some or other condition (that is too weak), nor (ii) that they would match if presented under every condition (that is too strong). It is that they would match if presented under the very condition that one of them is occurrently presented in.

14 Byrne and Hilbert (2017) make the further criticism that, because the relationalist's fine-grained colours are so fine-grained as to be rarely if ever repeated, they are incapable of explaining intrasubjective colour matches in how things look (e.g. in standard psychophysical experiments). But the explanation of colour constancy in §3.4 extends directly to a general relationalist explanation of intrasubjective colour matching. On this story, matches in how things look reflect not a representation of identity between distinct fine-grained colours, but representation that the distinct fine-grained colours are appropriately related to one another given the way in which perceptual circumstances vary—i.e. that the objects *would* exemplify the same fine-grained colour were they both presented in a circumstance that in fact only one of them occupies.

15 Nor does accounting for this responsiveness in terms of representations of coarse-grained colours undercut our motivation for believing in fine-grained colours or their representation; the argument for accepting

such representations (viz., that this allows for a non-stipulative, non-sceptical, and general response to cases of perceptual variation with respect to colour) remains as strong or as weak as before.

16 I myself am already committed to denying that standard psychosemantic theories are fully adequate accounts of sensory representation for reasons having to do with the possibility of representational differences in creatures selectively responsive to exactly the same range of stimuli (see note 6). Moreover, similar commitments attend competing views. Thus, as Pautz points out (p.c.), it's unobvious that standard psychosemantic theories allow for the representation of disjunctions of reflectances (Tye 2000; Byrne and Hilbert 2004) either, since such theories typically require contents to cause the tokens that represent them, and since many have thought that disjunctions (as opposed to their disjuncts) are acausal. However, and quite apart from these perhaps idiosyncratic commitments, it's fair to say that no current psychosemantic view is fully satisfactory.

17 NB: the suggestion here is not that relational properties *tout court*, or relational properties constituted in terms of relations to visual systems *tout court*, should be excepted from metaphysical generalizations like Determination. It is, rather, that we can expect such odd behaviour from relations *to visual systems, in cases where those visual systems are in states we have independent reason to regard as exceptional.*

18 For similar sentiments, see Dancy 1986, p. 181; Armstrong 1987, p. 36; Boghossian and Velleman 1989, p. 85; Averill 1992, p. 556; Johnston 1992, pp. 226–7; Yablo 1995, pp. 489–90; Tye 2000, pp. 152–3; Chalmers 2006, p. 56; Gibbard 2006; Brogaard 2010; Hazlett and Averill 2010; Allen 2011.

A further phenomenological objection to relationalism, which I leave unaddressed here for reasons of space, contends that relationalism cannot be combined coherently with a plausible metaphysics of conscious experience (Sellars 1956; Boghossian and Velleman 1989; McGinn 1996; Stroud 2000). For further discussion and response, see Cohen (2009, pp. 163–74).

19 I ask this question not in order to motivate rejecting the relevance of phenomenology for the metaphysics of colour (after all, I myself made heavy appeal to colour phenomenology in motivating colour relationalism in §2), but because I hope that answering it will assist us in understanding and assessing the objection at hand.

20 This mistake appears to underlie the quotation above from McGinn (1996), as well as this oft-quoted passage:

> If colours looked like dispositions, however, then they would seem to *come on* when illuminated, just as a lamp comes on when its switch is flipped. Turning on the light would seem, simultaneously, like turning on the colours; or perhaps it would seem like waking up the colours, just as it is seen to startle the cat. Conversely, when the light was extinguished, the colours would not look as if they were being concealed or shrouded in the ensuing darkness: rather, they would look as if they were becoming dormant, like the cat returning to sleep. But colours do not look like that; or not, at least, to us.
>
> *(Boghossian and Velleman 1989, p. 85)*

21 Thanks to Damon Crockett, Matthew Fulkerson, E. J. Green, Eliot Michaelson, Adam Pautz, and the editors of this volume for helpful discussions on this material.

References

Allen, Keith (2011), "The Red and the Real: An Essay on Color Ontology, by Jonathan Cohen", *European Journal of Philosophy*, 19, 2, pp. 315–18.

Allen, Keith (2012), "Colour, Contextualism, and Self-Locating Contents", *Croatian Journal of Philosophy*, 12, 3, pp. 331–50.

Armstrong, David (1968), *A Materialist Theory of the Mind*, Routledge, London.

Armstrong, David (1987), "Smart and the Secondary Qualities", in *Metaphysics and Morality: Essays in Honour of J. J. C. Smart*, ed. by Philip Pettit, R. Sylvan, and J. Norman, Reprinted in Byrne and Hilbert 1997, 33–46, Basil Blackwell, Oxford.

Averill, Edward Wilson (1992), "The Relational Nature of Color", *The Philosophical Review*, 101, 3, pp. 551–88.

Boghossian, Paul A. and J. David Velleman (1989), "Colour as a Secondary Quality", *Mind*, 98, Reprinted in Byrne and Hilbert 1997, pp. 81–103.

Brogaard, Berit (2010), "Perspectival Truth and Color Primitivism", in *New Waves in Truth*, ed. by Cory D. Wright and Nikolaj J. L. L. Pedersen, Palgrave Macmillan, Basingstoke.

Brogaard, Berit (2012), "Color Eliminativism or Color Relativism?" *Philosophical Papers*, 41, 2, pp. 305–21.

Brogaard, Berit (2015), "The Self-Locating Property Theory of Color", *Minds and Machines*, 25, 2, pp. 133–47.

Byrne, Alex (2006), "Comments", *dialectica*, 60, pp. 337–40.

Byrne, Alex (2009), "Experience and Content", *Philosophical Quarterly*, 59, 236, pp. 429–51.

Byrne, Alex and David R. Hilbert (eds.) (1997), *Readings on Color, Volume 1: The Philosophy of Color*, MIT Press, Cambridge, Massachusetts.

Byrne, Alex and David R. Hilbert (2003), "Color Realism and Color Science", *Behavioral and Brain Sciences*, 26, 1, pp. 3–64.

Byrne, Alex and David R. Hilbert (2004), "Hardin, Tye, and Color Physicalism", *The Journal of Philosophy*, CI, 1, pp. 37–43.

Byrne, Alex and David R. Hilbert (2007), "Truest Blue", *Analysis*, 67, 293, pp. 87–92.

Byrne, Alex and David R. Hilbert (2017), "Color Relationalism and Relativism", *Topics in Cognitive Science*, 9, pp. 172–92. doi:10.1111/tops.12243.

Chalmers, David (2006), "Perception and the Fall from Eden", in *Perceptual Experience*, ed. by Tamar Szabó Gendler and John Hawthorne, Oxford University Press, New York, pp. 49–125.

Cohen, Jonathan (2003), "Color: A Functionalist Proposal", *Philosophical Studies*, 112, 3, pp. 1–42.

Cohen, Jonathan (2004), "Information and Content", in *Blackwell Guide to the Philosophy of Information and Computing*, ed. by Luciano Floridi, Basil Blackwell, New York, pp. 215–27.

Cohen, Jonathan (2007), "A Relationalist's Guide to Error About Color Perception", *Noûs*, 41, 2, pp. 335–53.

Cohen, Jonathan (2009), *The Red and The Real: An Essay on Color Ontology*, Oxford University Press, Oxford.

Cohen, Jonathan (2012), "Redness, Reality, and Relationalism", *Croatian Journal of Philosophy*, 12, 3, pp. 351–78.

Cutter, Brian (2019), "Indeterminate Perception and Color Relationism", *Analysis*, 79, 1, pp. 25–34.

Dancy, Jonathan (1986), "Two Conceptions of Moral Realism", *Proceedings of the Aristotelian Society*, Supplementary Volume 60, pp. 167–87.

Dretske, Fred (1995), *Naturalizing the Mind*, Originally delivered as the 1994 Jean Nicod Lectures, MIT Press, Cambridge, Massachusetts.

Egan, Andy (2012), "Comments on Jonathan Cohen's *The Red and the Real*", *Analytic Philosophy*, 53, 3, pp. 306–12.

Funkhouser, Eric (2006), "The Determinable-Determinate Relation", *Noûs*, 40, 3, pp. 548–69.

Gattass, Rocardo, Aglai P. B. Sousa, Mortimer Mishkin, and Leslie G. Ungerleider (1997), "Cortical Projections of Area V2 in the Macaque", *Cerebral Cortex*, 7, pp. 110–29.

Gert, Joshua (2012), "Crazy Relations", *Croatian Journal of Philosophy*, 12, 3, pp. 315–30.

Gibbard, Allan (2006), "Moral Feelings and Moral Concepts", in *Oxford Studies in Metaethics, 1*, ed. by Russ Schafer-Landau, Clarendon Press, Oxford, pp. 195–215.

Hartmann, E., B. Lachenmayr, and H. Brettel (1979), "The Peripheral Critical Flicker Frequency", *Vision Research*, 19, 9, pp. 1019–23, doi: https://doi.org/10.1016/0042-6989(79)90227-X.

Hazlett, Allan and Edward Wilson Averill (2010), "A Problem for Relational Theories of Color", *Philosophy and Phenomenological Research*, 81, 1, pp. 140–5.

Johnson, W. E. (1921), *Logic, Part 1*, Cambridge University Press, Cambridge.

Johnston, Mark (1992), "How to Speak of the Colors", *Philosophical Studies*, 68, pp. 221–63.

Kalderon, Mark Eli (2007), "Color Pluralism", *The Philosophical Review*, 116, 4, pp. 563–601.

Levi, Dennis M. and Thom Carney (2009), "Crowding in Peripheral Vision: Why Bigger Is Better", *Current Biology*, 19, 23, pp. 1988–93.

Levin, Janet (2000), "Dispositional Theories of Color and the Claims of Common Sense", *Philosophical Studies*, 100, pp. 151–74.

Matthen, Mohan (2005), *Seeing, Doing, and Knowing: A Philosophical Theory of Sense Perception*, Oxford University Press, Oxford.

Maund, Barry (2010), "The Red and The Real", *Australasian Journal of Philosophy*, 88, 4, pp. 755–6.

McGinn, Colin (1983), *The Subjective View: Secondary Qualities and Indexical Thoughts*, Oxford University Press, Oxford.

McGinn, Colin (1996), "Another Look at Color", *The Journal of Philosophy*, 93, 11, pp. 537–53.

Millikan, Ruth Garrett (1984), *Language, Thought, and Other Biological Categories: New Foundations for Realism*, MIT Press, Cambridge, Massachusetts.

Mizrahi, Vivian (2007), "Color Objectivism and Color Pluralism", *dialectica*, 60, 3, pp. 283–306.

Pautz, Adam (2006), "Sensory Awareness Is Not a Wide Physical Relation: An Empirical Argument Against Externalist Intentionalism", *Noûs*, 40, 2, pp. 205–40.

Pautz, Adam (2008), "A Simple View of Consciousness", in *The Waning of Materialism*, ed. by George Bealer and Robert Koons, Oxford University Press, Oxford.

Pautz, Adam (2010a), "An Argument for the Intentional View of Visual Experience", in *Perceiving the World*, ed. by Bence Nanay, Oxford University Press, New York.

Pautz, Adam (2010b), "Review of Jonathan Cohen, *The Red and the Real*: An Essay on Color Ontology", *Notre Dame Philosophical Reviews* (3).

Peacocke, Christopher (1984), "Colour Concepts and Colour Experiences", *Synthese*, 58, 3, Reprinted in Rosenthal 1991, 408–16, pp. 365–81.

Pinker, Steven (2000), *The Language Instinct: How the Mind Creates Language*, Harper Perennial Modern Classics, New York.

Prinzmetal, William, Deborah Henderson, and Richard Ivry (1995), "Loosening the Constraints on Illusory Conjunctions: Assessing the Roles of Exposure Duration and Attention", *Journal of Experimental Psychology: Human Perception and Performance*, 21, 6, pp. 1362–75.

Prior, A. N. (1949), "Determinables, Determinates and Determinants: I", *Mind*, 58, 229, pp. 1–20.

Rosenthal, David (1991), *The Nature of Mind*, Oxford University Press, New York.

Sellars, Wilfrid (1956), "Empiricism and the Philosophy of Mind", in *Minnesota Studies in the Philosophy of Science*, ed. by Herbert Feigl and Michael Scriven, University of Minnesota Press, Minneapolis, vol. 1, pp. 253–329.

Shepard, Roger N. (2001), "Perceptual-Cognitive Universals as Reflections of the World", *Behavioral and Brain Sciences*, 24, pp. 581–601.

Siegel, Susanna (2010a), "Do Experiences Have Contents", in *Perceiving the World*, ed. by Bence Nanay, Oxford University Press, New York.

Siegel, Susanna (2010b), *The Contents of Visual Experience*, Oxford University Press, New York.

Smith, A. D. (2002), *The Problem of Perception*, Harvard University Press, Cambridge, Massachusetts.

Strasburger, Hans, Ingo Rentschler, and Martin Jüttner (2011), "Peripheral Vision and Pattern Recognition: A Review", *Journal of Vision*, 11, 5, p. 13, doi: 10.1167/11.5.13.

Stroud, Barry (2000), *The Quest for Reality: Subjectivism and the Metaphysics of Colour*, Oxford University Press, New York.

Tesnière, Lucien (1959), *Éléments de syntaxe structurale*, Éditions Klinksieck, Paris.

Thompson, Evan (1995), *Colour Vision: A Study in Cognitive Science and the Philosophy of Perception*, Routledge, New York.

Thompson, Evan, Adrian Palacios, and Francisco Varela (1992), "Ways of Coloring: Comparative Color Vision as a Case Study for Cognitive Science", *Behavioral and Brain Sciences*, 15, pp. 1–74.

Travis, Charles (2004), "The Silence of the Senses", *Mind*, 113, 449, pp. 57–94.

Tye, Michael (1995), *Ten Problems of Consciousness: A Representational Theory of the Phenomenal Mind*, MIT Press, Cambridge, Massachusetts.

Tye, Michael (2000), *Consciousness, Color, and Content*, MIT Press, Cambridge, Massachusetts.

Tye, Michael (2006), "The Puzzle of True Blue", *Analysis*, 66, 291, pp. 173–8.

Tye, Michael (2012), "Cohen on Color Relationalism", *Analytic Philosophy*, 53, 3, pp. 297–305.

Weatherson, Brian and Dan Marshall (2014), "Intrinsic vs. Extrinsic Properties", in *The Stanford Encyclopedia of Philosophy*, ed. by Edward N. Zalta, Spring 2014.

Yablo, Stephen (1995), "Singling Out Properties", *Philosophical Perspectives*, 9, pp. 477–502.

20

MONISM AND PLURALISM

Mark Eli Kalderon

1 Monism and pluralism

What is colour pluralism?

Not the claim that there are a plurality of colours, if such there be. Most philosophers are colour monists, and if they are realists, they likely believe that there are a plurality of colours—that things are blue, yellow, and red, mauve and magenta, and many other colours, both named and unnamed. Nor is colour pluralism the claim that objects can be multicoloured. On the most straightforward understanding of that claim (not the only one), for an object to be multicoloured is for it to have differently coloured parts. But again the monist orthodoxy in the philosophy of colour accepts that if things are coloured they can be multicoloured in the sense of having differently coloured parts. To bring into focus the distinctive claim of colour pluralism, it will be useful to contrast it with colour monism. After all, colour pluralism just is the denial of colour monism. Though colour monism is the orthodox position in the philosophy of colour, it is rarely held explicitly with its commitments articulated clearly. So let us begin by examining the claims of colour monism.

There are a plurality of colours. Things are blue, yellow, and red, mauve and magenta, and many other colours both named and unnamed. But despite this plurality, all the colours that we see are, in some sense, generically alike. They are all colours. Specifically, they are sensible qualities of surfaces, transparent volumes, and radiant light sources that are perceptually available to sight (or would be if there were any) and that have a distinctive sensible character—a visible chromatic quality. What unites the colours that we see, if we do, as being the colours? (For an interesting sceptical case against the idea that the colours display the requisite unity see Matthen 1999.)

That there is a kind of unity manifest in a range of sensible qualities is an ancient idea. The ancients tended to think of a distinctive range of sensible qualities, such as colour or temperature, as arrayed between opposites in order of their respective similarities to these (for discussion see Lloyd 1966). Thus there are a plurality of temperatures that we can feel. These are ordered between the extremes of hot and cold depending upon their similarities to these, in order of how hot or cold these temperatures are. Notoriously, Aristotle understands the colours on this model (*De Sensu* III). The colours are visible qualities arrayed between the extremes of light and dark ordered by their similarities to these. Thus Aristotle understood the hues to be a proportion of light and dark, a view with Homeric roots (Gladstone 1858) that finds few modern defenders other than Goethe (1810). Even if, along with the early moderns, we reject the ancient view, we can hold onto the idea that the colours are generically alike. This need not be understood strictly in terms of the related notions of genus and species. Rather, the colours are generically alike, at least in part, by virtue of the relations they bear to one another.

So far, we have the idea that there are distinctive ranges of sensible qualities, the colours prominently among them, that display some unity despite their plurality. Call such a distinctive range a *family* of sensible qualities. The sensible qualities in a family display a unity in virtue of which they are generically alike. This unity is manifest in the relations the colours bear to one another. Following the ancients, in the case of the colours, this unity plausibly consists, at least in part, in the similarities and differences the colours bear to one another. We can accept at least that much, even if we reject the further ancient idea that the colours are arrayed in order of similarity to the extremes of light and dark. The colours are thus plausibly generically alike at least in the minimal sense of finding a place in a common colour-similarity ordering.

While we have extracted this much from the ancient view, we should be wary of looking no further. For there are other relations that obtain among the colours. Moreover, some of these obtain among the colours in virtue of what they are, in virtue of being the kind of sensible qualities they are (colours as opposed to temperatures, say) and having the specific sensible character that they do (a specific shade of mauve as opposed to a specific shade of magenta, say). Thus, as W.E. Johnson (1921) observed, colours stand in relations of determination, there are determinable and determinate colours (for recent discussion see Funkhouser 2006). Thus red is a determinable. There are different ways of being red, crimson and scarlet among them. Colours stand in relations of determination in virtue of what they are. Given the kind of sensible qualities they are, and given their specific sensible character, they stand in relations of determination.

Moreover, not only are there similarities and differences among the colours as well as relations of determination, but the colours also stand in exclusion relations. Being red, a thing is not green. Being mauve, a thing is not magenta. And again this seems to be in virtue of what the colours are, the kind of sensible quality they are with their specific sensible character, visible chromatic qualities.

So in addition to similarities and differences among the colours, perhaps what unites the plurality of sensible qualities in the chromatic family are relations of determination and exclusion. So far, then, we have considered three plausible candidates for relations obtaining among a plurality of sensible qualities in virtue of which they constitute a family of colours:

1   similarities and differences
2   determination relations between determinables and determinates
3   exclusion relations

For a relation to be a candidate for uniting the chromatic family, it must, at a minimum, hold of all and only the colours. Some say that red is like the sound of a trumpet. Perhaps so. Is this a problem for our first candidate relation? For it would seem that similarities obtain, not only among the colours, but among the colours and sounds. So too with differences. Aristotle in *De Anima* II maintained that we experience the difference between colours and sounds. In so doing he was self-consciously criticizing Plato who maintained, in the *Theaetetus*, that discrimination was the operation of reason, not sense. Whether or not the difference between colour and sound is apprehended by experience or reason, it remains the case that differences hold not only among the colours, but among the colours and other sensory objects as well. So similarities and differences don't hold among all and only the colours. That may be so, but what purports to unite, at least in part, the colours into a family of sensible qualities, are *chromatic* similarities and differences. The similarity of red to the sound of a trumpet, and the difference between colour and sound, are not chromatic similarities and differences. They are not similarities and differences in hue, say. Similarly determination relations obtain among properties other than colours, but it is the structure of determinates and determinables in which they stand that purport to unite the colours into a chromatic family.

Once we have identified candidate relations that might serve to unite the colours into a chromatic family, we might ask not only whether they might in fact be so related but also how they might be. Perhaps the colours stand in some relations in virtue of standing in others. Even if all of some set of candidate relations genuinely obtain among all and only the colours, some candidate relations may be explanatorily prior to other candidate relations.

Thus, for example, the colours plausibly stand in exclusion relations as a consequence of their standing in a structure of determinates and determinables. Red is a determinable way for things to be in the sense that there is more than one way of being red. Scarlet is one way for a thing to be red, and crimson is another. So determinates are ways of being some determinable way. Moreover if something is scarlet it is not crimson and *vice versa*. So distinct determinates of red, such as scarlet and crimson, are distinct ways of being that determinable way. This is why being scarlet excludes being crimson: the colours stand in exclusion relations as a consequence of their standing in a structure of determinates and determinables. It would seem then that determination relations are explanatorily prior to exclusion relations. One might concede that crimson excludes scarlet because these are distinct determinates of the determinable red, but can all exclusion relations be explained in this way? Is, for example, red excluding green a consequence of determination relations? Red, insofar as it admits determination as scarlet or crimson or some other shade, is a determinable as is green. But red and green, though determinables, are themselves determinates of the determinable coloured. Being red is a way of being coloured and is a distinct way of being coloured than being green. And so red excluding green is again a consequence of determination relations.

Similarities and differences on the one hand and the structure of determinates and determinables on the other are themselves importantly related, though it is a substantive and controversial issue which, if any, is prior to the other. Thus, for example, the structure of determinates and determinables can be represented by the geometry of the colour space (see Hilbert and Kalderon 2000 and Funkhouser 2006). Points in the colour space represent utterly determinate colours (colours for which no other colour is a determination), and determinable colours are represented by regions of the colour space. Moreover, that a colour is a determinate of a determinable, as scarlet is of red, is represented by the region of the colour space associated with the determinate colour being a subregion of the region associated with the determinable colour. And two colours are codeterminates of a determinable if they are associated with non-overlapping subregions of the broader determinable region. No doubt it is possible, at least in principle, to fully represent the structure of determinates and determinables among the colours in terms of the geometry of the colour space. However, it is doubtful whether this fact, by itself, establishes the further claim that the colours stand in the structure of determinates an determinables *because* of the similarities and differences between them. Consider the colour space. Within it there is a dragon-shaped region coiling throughout that space without quite filling it. It is doubtful whether there is a colour determinable corresponding to the dragon-shaped region. So it is not the case that for every region of the colour space there is a colour determinable that corresponds to it. So we cannot identify colour determinables with arbitrary regions of the colour space. If colour determinables are regions of the colour space, nonetheless, as they would be if colour similarity and difference were explanatorily prior to the structure of determinates and determinables, they must be distinguished regions of that space. The challenge to the claim of explanatory priority is to specify these distinguished regions purely in terms of colour similarities and differences.

It is possible, at least in principle, to represent the structure of determinates and determinables among the colours in terms of the geometry of the colour space. Another reason for doubting that this fact, by itself, suffices for the explanatory priority of colour similarities and differences is that it is consistent, as well, with the reverse explanatory priority. Suppose that colours are similar or different from one another *because* of the relations of determination in which they stand. It would be no surprise that determinates and determinables could be represented by the consequent relations of colour similarity and difference that they give rise to. So a representation of the structure of determinates and determinables in terms of the geometry of the colour space is consistent with the relations of determination having explanatory priority.

So far, we have the idea that there are distinctive ranges of sensible qualities, the colours prominently among them, that display some unity despite their plurality. Such a distinctive range is a *family* of sensible qualities. The sensible qualities in a family display a unity in virtue of which they are generically alike. This unity is manifest in the relations the colours bear to one another. Plausibly, these include similarity and difference, determination, and exclusion relations, and perhaps others. Moreover, it is an open question what the precise explanatory relationship is between these relations. Despite these open questions, we should, by now, have a reasonably clear understanding of the notion of a family of colours.

Now that we have a clear if not distinct notion of a family of colours, we are in a position to define colour monism:

Colour Monism: There is one and only one family of colours

Colour monism presupposes realism about the colours. Consider colour eliminativism, understood as the view that nothing is or could be coloured. If colour eliminativism is true, then there are no colours. And if there are no colours, there are no families of colours. And if there are no families of colours it is not the case that there is one and only one family of colour qualities. So colour monism presupposes realism about the colours. If we hold fixed this presupposed colour realism, then colour pluralism is the denial of colour monism. Since we are presupposing colour realism, we are presupposing that things are coloured. Moreover, the colours of things are related to one another in such a way that colours are generically alike. The colour pluralist concedes to the monist that there is a unity to a plurality of colours displayed in the relations of similarity and difference, determination, and exclusion in which they stand. And in virtue of standing in these relations these colours constitute a family of sensible qualities. The colour pluralist merely denies that there is one and only one family of colours. Their pluralism consists in their conviction in there being a plurality of families of colours. According to colour pluralism, then, things are multicoloured, not merely in the straightforward sense of having differently coloured parts, but also in the sense of instantiating colours from different chromatic families (how this is so much as possible will become clear in subsequent sections).

Why believe that there is a plurality of families of colours? Why depart from the monist orthodoxy? As we shall see in the next section, colour pluralism is motivated as a response to the problem of conflicting appearances. The problem of conflicting appearances is a puzzle or *aporia* at the heart of the Manifest Image of Nature. It is less a conflict between the Manifest Image of Nature and its Scientific Image (see Sellars 1963), than a conflict or incoherence within the Manifest Image of Nature itself. If the pluralist is right in contending that the *aporia* is only resolved by denying colour monism while retaining the monist's presupposed realism, then colour monism is not only false but incoherent.

2 The argument from conflicting appearances

The label "colour pluralism" was independently introduced by Mizrahi (2006) and Kalderon (2007). The doctrine so labelled has antecedents, both ancient and modern. Thus Kalderon (2007), following Burnyeat (1979), attributes this doctrine to Heraclitus. And, as we shall see, many contemporary philosophers are committed to colour pluralism, even if they have never used that label (it is, at the very least, entertained by Harman 2001). The doctrine of colour pluralism, that there is more than one family of colours, however it is labelled, is invariably introduced as a resolution of a puzzle or *aporia*. Indeed the argument for colour pluralism is a variant of the argument from conflicting appearances where the allegedly conflicting appearances are chromatic appearances. (On the argument from conflicting appearances see Burnyeat 1979; Annas and Barnes 1985.)

A schematic representation of the puzzle is both useful and misleading. It is useful in that it allows one to clearly see the alleged inconsistency at the heart of the puzzle. However, it is in one important respect misleading. We will return to the way in which it is misleading when we are in a better position to appreciate this.

At the heart of the puzzle is three seemingly inconsistent claims that can be schematically represented as follows:

1   *Variation*: o appears F to S and o appears G to S'
2   *Incompatibility*: Nothing is both F and G
3   *Veridicality*: The F-appearance and the G-appearance are both veridical

"o" is a schematic letter whose permissible substituends are singular terms, be they names or definite descriptions, denoting coloured objects. "F" and "G" are schematic letters whose permissible substituends are colour predicates. Finally, "S" and "S'" are schematic letters whose permissible substituends are singular terms denoting subjects of perception. Following a taxonomy that goes at least as far back as the *Theaetetus*, S and S' can be different perceivers from the same or different species, or they can be the same perceiver in different circumstances of perception.

Consider, then, the putative inconsistency. By *Variation*, o appears F to S and o appears G to S'. By *Veridicality*, The F-appearance and the G-appearance are both veridical. So o is both F and G. But that is straightforwardly inconsistent with *Incompatibility*, the claim that nothing is both F and G.

It would seem, then, that in order to avoid this inconsistency, at least one of *Variation*, *Incompatibility*, or *Veridicality* would have to be denied. Thus, colour eliminativists avoid the puzzle by denying *Veridicality* (see, for example, Hardin 1993 on the location problem for the unique hues; for more recent discussion see Gatzia 2010). If nothing is or could be coloured, then none of the colour appearances that normal human perceivers enjoy are veridical. So there is no way for *Variation* and *Incompatibility* to conflict.

How does colour pluralism avoid the conflict between *Variation*, *Incompatibility*, and *Veridicality*? Unlike the colour eliminativist, the pluralist retains the commitment to *Veridicality*. The colour pluralist thus retains the realism presupposed by the colour monist. Instead, the pluralist denies *Incompatibility*.

Before seeing how the denial of *Incompatibility* leads to colour pluralism, let's first consider how this is so much as possible. After all, *Incompatibility* seems, at first blush, to be merely a consequence of exclusion relations obtaining among the colours, and we have conceded that exclusion relations are plausible candidates for being, in part, what unites the colours as a family of chromatic qualities. Does denying *Incompatibility* commit one to denying that red excludes green, that being mauve excludes that thing from being at the same time magenta? (For an intriguing thought experiment that supports these latter possibilities see Harman 2001.) The pluralist maintains that one can deny *Incompatibility* without denying that exclusion relations obtain among the colours or denying even that exclusion relations are plausibly among the relations that unite the colours into a family of chromatic qualities. Recall, the candidate relations that unite the sensible qualities into a family obtain among all and *only* such qualities. Exclusion relations hold only within a family of colours. If mauve and magenta belong to the same chromatic family, then being mauve excludes being at the same time magenta. But this has no consequence for qualities outside that chromatic family. Something can be mauve and loud, say, or magenta and demure. Now suppose, the pluralist invites us to imagine, that there are plurality of families of colours. Since exclusion relations hold only within a family of colours, then while a determinate colour from within a family will exclude all other determinate colours in that family as well as all colour determinables for which it is not a determination, it will not exclude colours from distinct families, just as mauve does not exclude being loud, or magenta being demure.

According to the ancient taxonomy, S and S' can be different perceivers from the same or different species, or they can be the same perceiver in different circumstances of perception. Consider, then, what is surely the strongest argument for colour pluralism, the argument from conflicting appearances constructed on the basis of interspecies perceptual variation (see, *inter alia*, Bradley and Tye 2001; Byrne and Hilbert 2003; Mizrahi 2006; Allen 2007; Kalderon 2007). Thus, plausibly, while humans perceive one family of colours, distinct species with colour vision, such as bees and pigeons, perceive distinct families of colours. That these animals perceive distinct families of colours is made plausible by the fact that not only are distinct ranges of the electromagnetic spectrum visible (some birds and insects can see ultraviolet light invisible to normal human perceivers), but also by the fact that the colours perceived by different species can differ in dimensions of similarity. Thus pigeon colours, the colours perceptually available to pigeons, have a dimension of colour similarity that does not occur in the human colour space (Bradley and Tye 2001; Allen 2007). If humans and pigeons really do perceive distinct families of colour qualities, then since exclusion relations hold only within families of colours, something can instantiate both a pigeon colour, a colour from the family of colours perceptually available to pigeons, and a human colour, a colour from a distinct family perceptually available to humans, all over and at the same time. Thus if the variation in appearance schematically represented by *Variation* were the variation in colour appearance between a human and a pigeon looking at the same scene, these appearances would not conflict, since being a pigeon colour does not exclude being, at the same time, some human colour, and so each appearance may be veridical.

The colour pluralist, while denying *Incompatibility*, does not deny that colours from the same family exclude one another, nor that exclusion relations are among the relations that unite the colours into a family of chromatic qualities. The pluralist does not deny these things, since exclusion relations obtain only within a family, and the pluralist maintains that the variation in appearance is due to the visual presentation of colours from distinct families.

That is the abstract form of the pluralist response to the problem of conflicting appearances. Earlier I mentioned that the schematic representation of the conflict at the heart of the problem is importantly misleading. Now is a good time to explain why. There are a number of importantly different cases of perceptual variation that fit the abstract scheme. We have just discussed a case of interspecies perceptual variation, but there are also cases of intraspecies perceptual variation, such as the variation in the location of the unique hues by normal human perceivers (see Hurvich *et al.* 1968; Hardin 1993; Tye 2006a, 2006b, 2007; Cohen *et al.* 2006; Byrne and Hilbert 2007; Cohen *et al.* 2007; Kalderon 2007; for arguments for colour pluralism from intraspecies perceptual variation see Byrne and Hilbert 1997a; Tye 2000; Mizrahi 2006; Kalderon 2007). Whether the variation in appearance holds between members of the same or distinct species, each type of variation that we have so far considered is interpersonal. There is, according to the ancient taxonomy, in addition, cases of intrapersonal variation, where a scene appears differently to the same perceiver when viewed in different circumstances of perception. The way in which a coloured object will appear differently to a perceiver in different conditions of illumination would be an example. The abstract representation of the problem of conflicting appearances obscures these important differences. This is important since different forms of perceptual variation might be differently explained, and this might have consequences for how best to resolve the seeming *aporia*.

Consider a case of perceptual variation which might give rise to the problem of conflicting appearances, but where the seeming paradox is implausibly resolved by making the pluralist response. Specifically, consider the variation in appearance involved in cases of colour constancy (on the importance of constancy phenomena in the philosophy of perception see Smith 2002; Burge 2010). Suppose you go out to the garden to pick a tomato to bring inside for washing and slicing. When you see the tomato outside in broad daylight, the tomato is seen to be a particular shade of red. As you move from natural daylight to the artificial illumination of the kitchen, the appearance of the red tomato changes without the tomato itself appearing to change colour. As it travels between these differently illuminated environments, it appears to remain red, and that particular shade of red, even though it varies in appearance. This is a diachronic case of intrapersonal perceptual variation. There are synchronic cases as well (see Arend and Reeves 1986; Cohen 2008). Thus a partially shaded white wall will appear uniformly white, though the shaded part of the wall appears differently from the brightly lit part of the wall. We might reasonably describe this difference in appearance by saying that while the brightly lit part of the wall appears white the shaded part appears grey. If we now reason that since nothing is both uniformly white and partly white and partly grey to the conclusion that the variable appearances in synchronic colour constancy conflict with the appearance of a constant colour, we have our puzzle or *aporia*. The pluralist response to the problem of conflicting appearances gets going by claiming that the difference between the variable appearances is explained by their being the presentation of colours from different families. But not all variations in appearance are plausibly explained in terms of the presentation of different sensory objects. Perhaps the variation in appearance is best explained, not in terms of what is presented in appearance, but in terms of the way in which it is presented in appearance. Cases of colour constancy are cases where what's presented is the constant colour and what varies is the way that constant colour is presented. This is Austin's (1962) insight. Arguably, he inherits it from Aristotle (see Kalderon 2015). Austin's use of the Platonic example of the straight stick looking bent in a refracting medium (*Republic* X 602c–603a) is precisely a case of shape constancy. And in maintaining that while the straight stick in water looks like a bent stick it does not look exactly like a bent stick, Austin is denying that the bent appearance is the presentation of anything bent. What is presented is the constant percept, what varies is the way it is presented. (See Chisholm 1957; Kalderon 2011b. There are, of course, dissenters. For recent philosophers who claim that the variable appearances in cases of colour constancy are best understood in terms of what is presented in those appearances see Noë 2004; Chalmers 2006.)

However the variation in appearance involved in cases of colour constancy are to be understood, the methodological point remains: Given that there are distinct sources of perceptual variation, susceptible to distinct explanations, it is implausible to suppose that every putative case of conflicting appearances admits of a uniform solution. It is therefore important to look at psychological and phenomenological details of the particular kind of perceptual variation before deciding which, if any, of *Variation*, *Incompatibility*, or *Veridicality* to abandon. Insofar as the schematic representation of the problem of conflicting appearances obscures these differences thereby suggesting that all such cases should admit of a uniform solution, it is, to that extent, at least, misleading.

3 Metaphysical accounting

So far we have seen that colour pluralism maintains that there are a plurality of families of colours, that things are multicoloured, not merely in the straightforward sense of having differently coloured parts, but also in the sense that they can instantiate colours from different chromatic families all over at the same time. Thus something can have all over and at the same time a human colour, a colour perceptually available to humans, and a pigeon or a bee colour, a colour perceptually available to pigeons or bees. Moreover, colour pluralism is argued to be the best resolution of certain, if not all, cases of the problem of conflicting appearances. Now that we have a better idea what colour pluralism is and the reasons for it, let's clarify the metaphysical commitments of colour pluralism.

First, let's revisit the pluralist's alleged commitment to colour realism. The pluralist was represented as retaining the colour monist's commitment to colour realism. However, the attribution of realism to the colour monist was made on the back of a particular, and particularly strong, characterization of colour eliminativism—that nothing is *or could be* coloured. This suggests that the very existence of the colours is impossible and not merely their instantiation. The very existence of the colours would be impossible if, for example, the conditions for being coloured conflict—say, if colours must at once be qualities of the natural environment obtaining independently of the perceiver and yet have the qualitative character only possessed by sensory experience (Boghossian and Velleman 1989, 1991; Smith 1990). The denial of colour realism can take weaker and stronger forms. If qualities need not be immanent but can be transcendent, if they can exist independently of their instantiation, then it is open to claim that while the colours exist, they are uniformly uninstantiated. This is a weaker form of denial than colour eliminativism, at least as herein represented. This weaker denial of colour realism, where the colours exist albeit uniformly uninstantiated, is consistent with the existence of a family of uninstantiated colours, qualities that, while uninstantiated, are importantly related by relations of similarity, difference, exclusion, and determination. Moreover, this weaker denial of colour realism is thus also consistent with there being a plurality of families of uninstantiated colours. So perhaps colour pluralism is consistent with the denial of realism after all. However, the principle reason for believing in colour pluralism was in response to certain cases of conflicting appearances. Specifically, in certain cases, it is urged that the only way to resolve the *aporia* within the Manifest Image of Nature is to deny *Incompatibility* while retaining *Variation* and *Veridicality*. But notice, even the weaker form of the denial of colour realism is committed to the denial of *Veridicality*. If there are no Fs or Gs, then neither the F-appearance nor the G-appearance is veridical. That means that an irrealist colour pluralism, where there are distinct families of uninstantiated colours, cannot be argued for on the basis of the argument from conflicting appearances. But if not for that reason, what reason could there be for holding this position? An irrealist colour pluralism, while logically possible, seems unmotivated, at least for all that has been said (not necessarily all that can be said).

Some readers may have, by now, grown impatient. After all, it might be objected, colour pluralists aren't the only ones who would resolve the problem of conflicting appearances by denying *Incompatibility*. Perhaps *Ecumenicism*, as the denial of *Incompatibility* has been dubbed by Cohen (2009), is itself ecumenical, embracing a variety of different views, colour pluralism merely among them. Thus, for example, Protagorean relativists and relationalists more generally, deny incompatibility as well (for an important recent statement see Cohen 2009; other relationalists include, *inter alia*, McGinn 1983; Thompson 1995; Matthen 1999, 2005; Cohen 2004). Suppose that our colours, *F* and *G*, are perceiver relative. To be sure being *F* for *S* will exclude being *G* for *S*—nothing is both *F* for *S* and *G* for *S* all over and at the same time. However, being *F* for *S* is perfectly compatible with being *G* for *S'*. It is because the variable appearances involve the presentation of relational properties with different *relata* that *Incompatibility* fails. The objection, while *prima facie* plausible, is unfounded, however. Protagorean relativism about the colours is a species of colour pluralism. According to the relativist, corresponding to each perceiver is a family of colours potentially determined by that perceiver in relation with the object and circumstances of perception. While exclusion relations hold within these families, relative colours from distinct families are compatible with one another. Colour relativism is colour pluralism with the additional commitment to the colours in the plurality of families being relational in nature. Colour pluralism, considered in and by itself, has no such commitment, though it is consistent with it. (We will discuss colour relativism further in subsequent sections.)

The relativist objection has some force, however. While relationalism about the colours is a species of colour pluralism and so no genuine alternative, we have already seen a non-pluralist denial of *Incompatibility*. The pluralist denies *Incompatibility* since the variable appearances are presentations of colours from different families and exclusion relations only hold within a family. But perhaps the variable appearances can be explained in another way equally inconsistent with *Incompatibility*. Thus, for example, we entertained the suggestion that the variable appearances in cases of colour constancy are explained less by being different presentations of colours or colour-appearance properties than by being different modes of presentations of the constant colour. If this Austinian conception of perceptual constancy is right, then *Incompatibility* fails, not because the variable appearances are presentations of distinct sensible qualities or appearance properties from distinct families, than because they are different ways of presenting the constant quality. So colour pluralism can understood as the denial of *Incompatibility* only if we make the further assumption that in cases of conflicting chromatic appearances, the variable appearances are the presentations of different colours.

So far we have discussed colour pluralism's relation to realism and relativism, but what of reductionism? One central question about the metaphysics of colour is whether or not colours reduce to material or physical properties more generally. Reductionism is important since it offers the most straightforward answer to how the colours may be intelligibly realized by material surfaces, transparent volumes, and radiant light sources, thus reconciling the Manifest Image of Nature with its Scientific Image, at least with respect to our chromatic experience of the natural environment. Of course not all philosophers of colour are reductionists. And not all that deny the possibility of reduction deny as well that colours are intelligibly realized in nature. Thus whereas Hilbert (1987); Byrne and Hilbert (1997a, 2003) maintain that families of colours are families of anthropocentrically defined physical properties, most likely reflectance types, colour primitivists (such as Broackes 1997; Campbell 1997; McGinn 1996; Yablo 1995; Gert 2008; Allen 2011) deny the possibility of any such reduction but maintain that the colours may be intelligibly realized in nature (for a reductionist critique of primitivism, see Byrne and Hilbert 2006). Thus, for example, Yablo (1995) maintains that colours are non-physical, but that they can be intelligibly realized by physical things since colours are non-physical determinables with physical determinates (in contrast Byrne and Hilbert maintain that they are physical determinables with physical determinates). Colour primitivism thus contrasts with eliminativist positions such as Hardin's (1993). Like the primitivist, eliminativists deny the possibility of reduction, they differ only with respect to the consequences for the colours being intelligibly realized by the natural environment. Colour pluralism, as characterized here, is neutral between reductionism and primitivism. The colours may be susceptible to physical reduction or not, but so long as there are a plurality of families of colours, then whether or not they are reducible to physical properties, colour pluralism is true.

4 Objections and replies

In this final section, let's briefly consider the challenges and prospects of colour pluralism as a response to certain cases of conflicting appearances. Some objections to colour pluralism apply to specific forms of colour pluralism, others apply to all forms. Let's first consider an objection to a specific form of colour pluralism, before considering more general objections.

Consider, then, colour pluralism as a response to interpersonal variation in colour appearances between normal human perceivers. Though a common scene viewed in the same circumstances of perception can present different chromatic appearances to different normal human perceivers, the pluralist maintains that these appearances do not conflict since these appearances differ only in the presentation of colours from distinct families and exclusion relations hold only within a family. One way, not the only way, of understanding this is that the visual sensibilities of the distinct perceivers select from among the plurality of abundant regularities that obtain in the natural environment different ranges of properties as being the colours. The colour relativist, though no less a pluralist, does not accept the metaphor of selection and will understand the situation differently. Thus, according to the Protagorean relativist, colours are determined by the relation between the perceiver, the object of perception, and the circumstances of perception. So it is the presentation of different families of perceiver relative chromatic qualities that explains the difference in chromatic appearance of the common scene. Whether or not the pluralist response to interpersonal perceptual variation between normal human perceivers is best understood in relativist or non-relativist terms, both forms of pluralism face a common challenge. While the chromatic appearances enjoyed by normal human perceivers viewing a common scene in the same circumstances of perception may differ, if this difference is best explained by the presentation of colours from different chromatic families, how is a shared colour language so much as possible?

This is an ancient problem for Protagorean relativism. Socrates raises this objection in the *Theaetetus* 183a–b (for discussion see Burnyeat 1990). Kalderon (2007) attempts to respond to this problem by emphasizing that the vast bulk of our colour words represent colour determinables. Even very specific colour words, such as "burnt sienna", represent colours that admit of further determinate shades. Moreover, it seems that the colour words we have for determinate colours (leaving aside the artificial stipulations of philosophers in speaking of "red$_{17}$") are those that are definable in terms of colour determinables. Thus "unique green" represents a determinate shade of green, but is definable as a shade of green that is not at all bluish and not all yellowish. But green, bluish, and yellowish are all determinables. The thought is that while we may not agree about determinate shades given the interpersonal variation in colour appearance—we may disagree whether something is unique green, or bluish green, or yellowish green given how it appears in our respective experiences, nevertheless, we can agree that the perceived object is green. That is to say, there is sufficient interpersonal agreement about the use of determinable colour words to imbue them with a common sense. Cohen (2009) offers a different way out of the Socratic difficulty. Cohen combines relativism about the colours with a contextualist semantics for our colour words. Colour ascriptions are essentially relational. Made fully explicit the attribution of red to a tomato would be represented as the tomato being red for S in C, where S is the subject of perception and C the circumstances of perception. While S and C are not represented explicitly in surface grammar, context provides the values of these parameters. While contextually specified colour ascriptions may attribute relational properties to their subjects, such colour ascriptions do not represent the colours as relational. (For criticism, see Allen 2012; Gert 2012. For an alternative semantics see Egan 2006, 2010.)

While pluralists who argue on the basis of interpersonal variation among normal human perceivers must explain how their pluralism is consistent with there being sufficient interpersonal agreement in the use of colour words for these to be genuinely meaningful, other pluralists who argue on a different basis, for example, on the basis of interspecies perceptual variation, face no such challenge. However, there is a potential challenge that any variety of pluralism may face, no matter its precise motivation. The challenge derives from an argument in Shoemaker (2003) criticizing Hilbert and Kalderon (2000) and variants of that argument have been presented by Pautz (2006, 2009); Cohen (2009); Pautz (2011).

Let S and S' be perceivers with differently structured colour experience spaces. Given their differently structured colour experience spaces, S and S''s visual sensibilities select families of colours that constitute differently structured colour property spaces (where the visual sensibility of a perceiver is determined by their visual system, the nature of the natural environment, and their relation to it). Let c be a property selected to be a colour by S and S''s visual sensibilities. S and S''s visual experience of c will differ phenomenologically—what it is like for S to experience c in a given circumstances of perception will differ from what it is like for S' to experience c in the same circumstances of perception. Now suppose further that the proximate effects of the instantiation of c on S and S' are the same. Then the fact that c's instantiation elicits phenomenologically different colour experiences is entirely due to further visual processing by their respective visual systems. But it would seem, then, that the different colour appearances enjoyed by S and S' in viewing an instantiation of c in common circumstances of perception is not explained by the presentation of colours from different chromatic families, but is explained, instead, by the further visual processing involved in S and S''s perception of c's instantiation.

There is no widespread non-collusive agreement about what, if anything, the argument establishes. Let me briefly canvas some alternatives.

Kalderon (2011a) suggests that judgements about the causal structure of the process of perceiving a colour's instantiation will crucially depend upon the underlying metaphysics of experience. Thus while the proximal stimulation of sensory transducers will count as a proximal cause of S and S''s perception of c's instantiation on a conception of experience that finds its proper home in a paradigm inaugurated by the early moderns, proximal stimulation of sensory transducers will not count as a proximate cause if the perceptual experience of c's instantiation is instead understood in relational terms, as *naïve* realists and disjunctivist's maintain. (For critical discussion and an application of some of these ideas to the grammatical case see Longworth 2007.) But if S and S''s experience of c's instantiation differ in phenomenological character, what explains the difference? It could not be the presentation of c's instantiation in their respective experiences. However, c's instantiation is not merely presented to S and S', but to their distinct perspectives on c's instantiation, perspectives constituted in part by their distinct sensibilities. In general, the naïve realists and disjunctivist maintain that perception is the presentation of its object to the perceiver's partial perspective, and so the contribution to the phenomenological character of perceptual experience by its object is always perspective relative.

Pautz (2011, 429 n35) professes not to understand how claims proximal causation depends upon the underlying metaphysics of experience and offers an alternative understanding of these hypothetical cases. Pautz (2013) offers an extended case in a later paper. Pautz and Kalderon's root disagreement, however, seems to concern the metaphysics of experience. Whereas Pautz (2011) defends a conception of experience at home in the early modern paradigm (though naturalistically refined and extended), Kalderon, following Putnam (1994), is deeply sceptical about that paradigm (see especially Kalderon 2015, Preface).

Cohen (2009) presents a different kind of response to the hypothetical cases first envisioned by Shoemaker (2003). In Cohen's hands, such cases pose a challenge for non-relational forms of colour pluralism while leaving his preferred relationalism intact. Some background is useful in understanding Cohen's argumentative strategy here. In the previous section I represented colour relativism as a species of colour pluralism—as colour pluralism along with the further commitment to the colours in the chromatic families being perceiver relative. This raises a challenge for the colour relativist (Kalderon 2007). According to the pluralist, *Incompatibility* is denied since the variable appearances are explained in terms of the presentation of colours from different chromatic families. Notice that it is the claim that the perceived colours are from distinct families coupled with the claim that exclusion relations hold only within families of colours that resolves the paradox. Moreover, we needn't assume that the colours are perceiver relative for this to be so, any more than we need assume that mauve and loudness need be relational in order to explain their co-instantiation. But if, as Cohen (2009) maintains, colour relativism is established on the basis of the argument from conflicting appearances, and the best resolution of that puzzle or *aporia* is simply the denial of *Incompatibility*, then the possibility of non-relational colour pluralism undercuts the main argument for Protagorean relativism about the colours. It is against this background that Cohen argues that while non-relational forms of colour pluralism are susceptible to a variant of Shoemaker's argument, relational forms of colour pluralism are not. It is difficult to fully assess Cohen's case since he does not directly address the arguments of section 7 of Kalderon (2011a) where the response to Shoemaker is given.

5 Summary

Colours, if there are any, are sensible qualities that display a unity despite their manifest diversity. This unity is manifest in relations the colours bear to one another, such as relations of similarity and difference, determination, and exclusion. Chromatic qualities that are so related constitute a family of colours. Colour monism is the claim that there is one and only one family of colours. Colour pluralism is its denial. Colour pluralism is urged on the basis of certain cases of conflicting chromatic appearances (not all such cases) schematically represented by three inconsistent claims:

1 *Variation*: o appears F to S and o appears G to S'
2 *Incompatibility*: Nothing is both F and G
3 *Veridicality*: The F-appearance and the G-appearance are both veridical

In some cases, it is argued that the variable appearances are best explained as the presentation of colours from different chromatic families (the best such cases involve interspecies perceptual variation), and since exclusion relations hold only within families of colours, there is no genuine conflict between these variable appearances and the schematic claim *Incompatibility* fails, at least in these cases. Like the monist, colour pluralism is best understood as retaining a colour realism, at least if it is motivated by the argument from conflicting appearances by rejecting *Incompatibility* while retaining *Variation* and *Veridicality*—*Veridicality* would fail if colour realism were false. Moreover, while colour pluralism is consistent with colour relativism, it represents a more general view. Colour pluralism is also consistent with both reductionism about the colours and colour primitivism. The main challenge to colour pluralism consists in variants of an argument due originally to Shoemaker (2003). There is, at present, no shared consensus on the soundness of such arguments, or what precisely they establish.

References

Allen, Keith. Inter-species variation in colour perception. *Philosophical Studies*, 142: 197–220, November 2007. 10.1007/s11098-007-9183-z.

Allen, Keith. Revelation and the nature of colour. *dialectica*, 65 (2): 153–76, 2011. 10.1111/j.1746-8361.2011.01261.x.

Allen, Keith. Colour, contextualism, and self-locating contents. *Croatian Journal of Philosophy*, 36: 331–50, 2012.

Annas, Julia and Jonathan Barnes. *The Modes of Scepticism: Ancient Texts and Modern Interpretations*. Cambridge University Press, Cambridge, 1985.

Arend, Lawrence and Adam Reeves. Simultaneous color constancy. *Journal of the Optical Society of America*, 3 (10): 1743–51, 1986. URL http://josaa.osa.org/abstract.cfm?URI=josaa-3-10-1743.

Austin, J.L. *Sense and Sensabilia*. Oxford University Press, New York, 1962.

Boghossian, Paul A. and J. David Velleman. Colour as a secondary quality. *Mind*, 98: 81–103, 1989. Reprinted in Byrne and Hilbert 1997b.

Boghossian, Paul A. and J. David Velleman. Physicalist theories of color. *The Philosophical Review*, 100: 67–106, 1991. Reprinted in Byrne and Hilbert 1997b.

Bradley, Peter and Michael Tye. Of colors, kestrels, caterpillars, and leaves. *Journal of Philosophy*, 98: 468–87, 2001.

Broackes, Justin. The autonomy of colour. In Alex Byrne and David Hilbert, editors, *Readings on Color: The Philosophy of Color*, volume I, pages 191–225. MIT Press, Cambridge, MA, 1997.

Burge, Tyler. *Origins of Objectivity*. Oxford University Press, Oxford, 2010.

Burnyeat, M.F. Conflicting appearances. In *Proceedings of the British Academy*, volume lxv, pages 69–111, 1979.

Burnyeat, M.F. *The Theaetetus of Plato*. Hackett Publishing Company, Indianapolis, IN, 1990.

Byrne, Alex and David R. Hilbert. Colors and reflectances. In Alex Byrne and David R. Hilbert, editors, *Readings on Color: The Philosophy of Color*, volume 1. MIT Press, 1997a.

Byrne, Alex and David R. Hilbert, editors. *Readings on Color: The Philosophy of Color*, volume i. The MIT Press, Cambridge, MA, 1997b.

Byrne, Alex and David R. Hilbert. Color realism and color science. *Behavioral and Brain Sciences*, 26: 3–21, 2003. 10.1017/S0140525X03000013.

Byrne, Alex and Hilbert, David R. Color primitivism. *Erkenntnis*, 66: 73–105, 2006.

Byrne, Alex and David R. Hilbert. Truest blue. *Analysis*, 67 (1): 87–92, January 2007. 10.1111/j.1467-8284.2007.00654.x.

Campbell, John. The simple view of colour. In Alex Byrne and David R. Hilbert, editors, *Readings on Color*, volume 1, pages 177–90. MIT Press, Cambridge, MA, 1997.

Chalmers, David. Perception and the Fall from Eden. In Tamar Szabó Gendler and John Hawthorne, editors, *Perceptual Experience*, chapter 2, pages 49–125. Clarendon Press, Oxford, 2006.

Chisholm, Roderick M. *Perceiving: A Philosophical Study*. Cornell University Press, Ithaca, NY, 1957.

Cohen, Jonathan. Color properties and color ascriptions: A relationalist manifesto. *The Philosophical Review*, 113 (4): 451–506, 2004. URL http://aardvark.ucsd.edu/color/relational.html.

Cohen, Jonathan. Colour constancy as counterfactual. *The Australasian Journal of Philosophy*, 86 (1): 61–92, March 2008. 10.1080/00048400701846566.

Cohen, Jonathan. *The Red and the Real: An Essay on Color Ontology*. Oxford University Press, Oxford, 2009.

Cohen, Jonathan, C.L. Hardin, and Brian P. McLaughlin. True colours. *Analysis*, 66 (4): 335–40, October 2006. 10.1111/j.1467-8284.2006.00638.x.

Cohen, Jonathan, C.L. Hardin, and Brian P. McLaughlin. The truth about 'the truth about true blue'. *Analysis*, 67 (2): 162–6, April 2007. 10.1111/j.1467-8284.2007.00668.x.

Cooper, John M. *Plato Complete Works*. Hackett Publishing Company, Indianapolis, IN, 1997.

Egan, Andy. Appearance properties. *Noûs*, 40 (3): 495–521, 2006.

Egan, Andy. Projectivism without error. In Bence Nanay, editor, *Perceiving the World*, page 68. Oxford University Press, Oxford, 2010.

Funkhouser, Eric. The determinable-determinate relation. *Noûs*, 40 (3): 548–69, 2006.

Gatzia, Dimitria Electra. The individual variability problem. *Philosophia*, 38 (3): 533–54, 2010.

Gert, Joshua. What colors could not be: An argument for color primitivism. *Journal of Philosophy*, 105 (3): 128–55, 2008.

Gert, Joshua. Crazy relations. *Croatian Journal of Philosophy*, 12 (3): 315–30, 2012.

Gladstone, W.E. *Studies on Homer and the Homeric Age*, volume iii. Oxford University Press, Oxford, 1858.

von Goethe, Johan Wolfgang. *Theory of Colours*. MIT Press, Cambridge, MA, 1978 edition, 1810.

Hardin, C.L. *Color for philosophers: Unweaving the rainbow*. Hackett Publishing, Indianapolis, IN, expanded edition, 1993.

Harman, Gilbert. General foundations versus rational insight. *Philosophy and Phenomenological Research*, 63: 657–63, 2001.

Heraclitus. *The Art and Thought of Heraclitus*. Cambridge University Press, Cambridge, 1979.

Hett, W.S. *Aristotle, On the Soul, Parva Naturalia, On Breath, with an English Translation*. Loeb Classical Library. Harvard University Press, Cambridge, MA, 1936.

Hilbert, David R. *Color and Color Perception: A Study in Anthropocentric Realism*. Center for the Study of Language and Information, Stanford, CA, 1987.

Hilbert, David R. and Mark Eli Kalderon. Color and the inverted spectrum. In Steven Davis, editor, *Color Perception: Philosophical, Psychological, Artistic, and Computational Perspectives*, volume ix of *Vancouver Studies in Cognitive Science*, pages 187–214. Oxford University Press, Oxford, 2000.

Hurvich, Leon M., D. Jameson, and J.D. Cohen. The experimental determination of unique green in the spectrum. *Perceptual Psychophysics*, 4: 65–8, 1968.

Johnson, W.E. *Logic*, volumes i–iii. Cambridge University Press, Cambridge, 1921.

Kalderon, Mark Eli. Color pluralism. *The Philosophical Review*, 116 (4): 563–601, 2007. 10.1215/00318108-2007-014.

Kalderon, Mark Eli. The multiply qualitative. *Mind*, pages 1–22, 2011a. 10.1093/mind/fzr034.

Kalderon, Mark Eli. Color illusion. *Noûs*, 45 (4), 751–5, 2011b.

Kalderon, Mark Eli. *Form without Matter, Empedocles and Aristotle on Color Perception*. Oxford University Press, Oxford, 2015.

Lloyd, G.E.R. *Polarity and Analogy*. Cambridge University Press, Cambridge, 1966.

Longworth, Guy. Conflicting grammatical appearances. *Croatian Journal of Philosophy*, 21 (3): 403–26, 2007.

Matthen, Mohan P. The disunity of color. *Philosophical Review*, 108 (1): 47–84, 1999.

Matthen, Mohan P. *Seeing, Doing, and Knowing: A Philosophical Theory of Sense Perception*. Oxford University Press, Oxford, 2005.

McGinn, Colin. *The Subjective View: Secondary Qualities and Indexical Thoughts*. Oxford University Press, Oxford, 1983.

McGinn, Colin. Another look at the colors. *The Journal of Philosophy*, 93 (11), 1996.

Mizrahi, Vivian. Color objectivism and color pluralism. *Dialectica*, 60 (3): 321–36, 2006.

Noë, Alva. *Action in Perception*. MIT Press, Cambridge, Massachussetts, 2004.

Pautz, Adam. Sensory awareness is not a wide physical relation: An empirical argument against externalist intentionalism. *Noûs*, 40 (2): 205–40, 2006.

Pautz, Adam. A simple view of consciousness. In Robert C. Koons and George Bealer, editors, *The Waning of Materialism: New Essays*, pages 25–66. Oxford University Press, Oxford, 2009.

Pautz, Adam. Can disjunctivists explain our access to the sensible world? *Philosophical Issues*, 21 (1): 384–433, 2011.

Pautz, Adam. Do the benefits of naïve realism outweigh the costs? Comments on fish, perception, hallucination and illusion. *Philosophical Studies*, 163 (1): 25–36, 2013.

Putnam, Hilary. Sense, nonsense, and the senses: An inquiry into the powers of the human mind. *The Journal of Philosophy*, 91 (9): 445–517, September 1994.

Sellars, Wilfrid. Philosophy and the scientific image of man. In *Science, Perception and Reality*. Routledge & Kegan Paul, London, 1963.

Shoemaker, Sydney. Content, character, and color. *Philosophical Issues*, 13: 253–78, 2003. 10.1111/1533-6077.00014.

Smith, A. D. Of primary and secondary qualities. *Philosophical Review*, 99 (2): 221–54, 1990.

Smith, A. D. *The Problem of Perception*. Harvard University Press, Cambridge, MA, 2002.

Thompson, Evan. *Colour Vision: A Study in Cognitive Science and the Metaphysics of Colour*. Routledge, New York, 1995.

Tye, Michael. *Consciousness, Color, and Content*. MIT Press, Cambridge, MA, 2000.

Tye, Michael. The puzzle of true blue. *Analysis*, 66 (3): 173–8, July 2006a. 10.1111/j.1467-8284.2006.00611.x.

Tye, Michael. The truth about true blue. *Analysis*, 66 (4): 340–44, October 2006b. 10.1111/j.1467-8284.2006.00639.x.

Tye, Michael. True blue redux. *Analysis*, 67 (1): 92–3, January 2007. 10.1111/j.1467-8284.2007.00655.x.

Yablo, Stephen. Singling out properties. *Philosophical Perspectives*, ix: 477–502, 1995. 10.2307/2214231.

21

MENTALIST APPROACHES
TO COLOUR

Howard Robinson

1 Mentalism in context

I want to begin by looking at the options available for theories of colour, as very usefully set out by Barry Maund (2012). He classifies theories as follows.

1   Colors are 'primitive' properties simple, *sui generis*, qualitative properties that physical bodies possess or appear to possess: Primitivism.
2   Colors are 'hidden' properties of bodies—complex, physical properties that dispose bodies to look blue, pink, yellow, etc.: Reductive Physicalism.
3   Colors are perceiver-dependent, dispositional properties—powers to look in distinctive ways to appropriate perceivers, in appropriate circumstances: Dispositionalism.
4   Colors are subjective qualities 'projected' onto physical objects and light-sources—qualities which visual experiences represent objects as having: Projectivism.
5   Colors are subjective qualities—either qualities presented in experience or qualities of experience: Subjectivism. (Maund, 2012, #1.6)

We appear here to have five different theories of colour. The last two are *mentalist*, in the sense that they locate colour 'in the mind' of the perceiving subject—though 4 says we try to disown this subjectivism by 'projecting' them onto objects, whilst, according to 5, we accept their subjectivity. In fact, however, four of them—or perhaps four and a half—do not disagree significantly about the physical and sensational or experiential facts, only about how colour terms are used and what they refer to within that process. 2 to 5 agree that there is something physical out there which possesses some structural features which ground a disposition to cause us to have experiences of particular recognizable types. They seem to differ only on how colour terms are mapped on to this. 2 says that these terms are names for the physical structures that underlie the dispositions to cause the experiences. 3 says that the terms characterize the dispositions themselves which cause experiences of particular kinds. That there is a physical structure that underlies the disposition is not an explicit part of the theory, but that there is such a structure can generally be taken to be assumed. 4 says that we treat the way things look—the features in the experiences—as if these were intrinsic properties of the objects. Again, it is presumably assumed that the features we project are caused by dispositions in the external objects, though that this is the case is not part of the concept of colour. 5 says that the terms apply directly to the qualities in or of the experience. In this case, reference to the dispositions in the objects does not enter into the analysis of colour, but that there are such necessarily involved in the process is generally assumed to make sense of the fact that the sensations arise in an appropriately systematic way. Even 1 does not escape this net. The second disjunct in 1—'or appear to possess'—leaves open the possibility that the primitive property exists only in how it manifests in experience: again the presence of a disposition to produce such appearances is assumed. It seems that from this second disjunct to 5 all agree about what is actually happening, but dispute how colour terms apply within this process.

It might seem that it is not strictly true to say that 2–5 agree entirely about the facts, because 2—reductive physicalism—is committed to the view that the same colour is always associated with the same physical structure: if the word 'red' designates a structure, then all cases of it ought to be similar structures. This 'type identity' theory is not present in 3–5. But this type identity claim is generally disputed. It is commonly argued that there are no consistent physical properties that matches the colours as we experience them. It has proved extremely difficult, if not impossible, to specify any such properties: the unity of colours seems to work essentially through the similarity of the experience produced, rather than any non-contrived common feature of the external cause. (Maund, 2012, #6.3: Hardin, 1988, 61–7) This fact—if it is a fact—would not itself show that the reductive physicalist account is an incorrect account of our colour concepts. It suggests rather that our colour terms are failed would-be natural kind terms, like jade. The situation would be that colour terms are based on the assumption that there is some unitary physical state present when we have the same colour experience, but that assumption turns out to be false.

It is not clear to me, however, that a physicalist reductionist need be committed to the view that there is a unitary physical property for all things of the same colour. This is not because he can allow that the property is disjunctive, as some have argued, for this is just a botched form of unitariness. Rather it is because it depends on whether your reduction is functional or of a natural kind pattern. Suppose you define 'red' as

a   The redness of an object is whatever it is in that object that gives rise standardly to the appropriate red-sensation.

Then the red of objects would vary from situation to situation. It is only if you take the reduction rigidly as

b   The redness of physical objects is that particular physical property common to all red things which standardly causes red-sensations

that you are committed to the type identity problem. The fact that the reductive theory is associated with D. M. Armstrong, whose major works date from the time when type identity theories, not functional theories, were the standard forms of physicalism, no doubt influenced this bias, but it is not a necessary feature of reductive physicalism.

Perhaps it might be argued that (a) makes the identity of the colour too dependent on what the sensation is like to count as a form of colour realism, but both theories pick out the colours by how they look: they agree that the physical structure is hidden, and it is the nature of the sensation or experience behind which it lies. As we shall see below, what is at issue is whether the semantics or the phenomenology of colour is what determines the concept. The functionalist saves the realist semantics. The problem for the reductive realist comes if he wants to maintain both that the real nature of colour is hidden—as he must, given that experience itself does not tell us what the physical property is—and yet hold that this physical property also constitutes the phenomenology: that the physical structure is, in some sense, colour *as it appears*. It is unclear how this could be the case if it is 'hidden', where this latter expression seems to mean precisely that it does not present itself in appearance.

So the factual disagreements between 2–5 are not significant.

2 What is at stake between the theories?

This naturally poses the following question: granting that Maund is essentially correct about the range of theories available (as I think he is) can anything substantial be at stake between these different theories, with the exception of the first? If the rest agree about the facts, what does it matter to which part of this process a particular concept is applied? Suppose in different languages or different worlds the facts were agreed to be the same as above, but the concepts worked differently, would this be more than a linguistic difference? If the facts are agreed, what does it mean to say that they disagree about what colour *is*, rather than about how colour terms happen to be used?

In a sense, the answer to this is that the dispute is ideological. Primitivism, Projectivism, and Subjectivism all agree that our colour concepts pick out *the way things look*, or their phenomenal properties. Primitivism takes these properties to belong to the external objects themselves. Projectivism and subjectivism locate the way things look in the subject. Reductive physicalism and dispositionalism agree that primitivism is false, but want to hold on to the idea that our colour concepts refer to something external and physical, so they are obliged to abandon the idea that they designate how things look, and say instead that they designate something that lies behind and causally explains the appearances. Reid was, I think, the father of this approach. I have to admit that I can only regard this approach as either disingenuous or revisionary: that is, I cannot see how anyone can seriously hold that our colour concepts as we pre-philosophically and pre-scientifically understand them designate something other than certain ways things normally or standardly look. The reductive and dispositional theories can be nothing more than the best that direct realists can do, given scientific discoveries: they are not an attempt to 'save the phenomena' but to 'save the semantics'. Perhaps in the view of such philosophers, the semantics *are* the phenomena: that colours are attributed to objects is a more important fact than how they appear. This is why I called the dispute 'ideological': it is between those who give pride of place to what they take to be the semantics of a term and those for whom phenomenology is, for empirical concepts, central.

I shall not take up this issue directly here. It will be my assumption that those theories that make appearance fundamental are the serious ones in the case of such concepts as colour, for this assumption is what lies behind the mentalist approach. Nevertheless, there are theories which seem to be trying to have it both ways, preserving both the realist semantics and the intuitive phenomenology. Christopher Peacocke (1983) is, I think, a case of this. He argues that 'red' is a property of objects, but 'red*' is a feature of sensations, but that the latter is the phenomenal quality we recognize in experience.[1] Peacocke's general approach rests on distinguishing the representational features of experience (otherwise known as 'content') from the sensational features. The question is whether red* is different from what the primitivist, or naïve realist, calls 'red'. It could be argued that because it is a feature of sensation, it cannot possess spatial properties of the kind possessed by physical objects, which the red of the primitivist obviously does and is meant to. This does not appear to be Peacocke's view, for he says that red* occupies a 'region of one's visual field' (37) and this sounds like spatial talk. Presumably, then, whilst objects can be red and square, sensations possess the properties of red* and square*. If this is the case, then it is unclear how the latter properties differ from the former, as conceived by the naïve realist, which, if what I say above is correct, is how we naturally conceive of these properties. As far as I can see, this makes Peacocke's position—and those other philosophers who use the 'F★' manoeuvre in a similar way—indistinguishable from the sense-datum theory.

3 Varieties of mentalism

Are mentalism and the sense-datum theory the same thing? *Prima facie* they are not. There are three other mentalist options that have been adopted by some philosophers. The least popular—and one of which C. D. Broad (1923: 273–4) said 'if this be not nonsense I do not know what nonsense is'—is the view that colours are subjective, but visual shape is not: that is, one can be a direct realist about shapes whilst being a subjectivist about colour, whereas the sense-datum theory obliges one to believe that both are subjectively realized (though shape is, of course, also externally realized). The second option is adverbialism. Adverbialism is a form of mentalism, because it deems phenomenal qualities to be modes of sensings, which are mental states. The third option is the intentional theory, at least under certain interpretations.

i Colour subjectivity with direct perception of spatial properties

At first sight, this is an attractive idea—we directly perceive the shape of an object, then fill in the colour for ourselves. Only a little thought is needed to see how problematic is this idea. The subjective colour that we supply must be an extended phenomenon, so the subjective colour patch will have a shape and how can the shape of the patch itself be external if the colour is internal? It seems that this combination is not a serious alternative to the sense-datum account.

There is, nevertheless, something that might be interpreted as a version of this theory that stands in high repute, namely John McDowell's account of secondary qualities. He compares secondary qualities and ethical values, on the grounds that they are both a function of the specifically human constitution and sensibility, yet objective. We will return to McDowell's theory later.

ii Adverbialism

Adverbialism differs from the sense-datum theory because it rejects the 'act-object' analysis of sensory states. This rejection itself is rather confusing. It assumes two things. One is that if one regards sense-contents as a kind of entity, then one must also believe in acts of awareness in addition to the objects. Both Hume and maybe Berkeley deny this. The other is that it assumes that if sensory contents are modes of awareness they cannot be spatially structured in the way sense-data are. If they allow that a mode of awareness can be a spatially extended visual field, then adverbialism is not inconsistent with the sense-datum theory. In fact there is much confused history here. One strain of adverbialism starts as a response to Moore's 'refutation of idealism' (Ducasse, 1942). Moore argued that any act-object analysis allows that the object must be independent of the act, so that the idealist principle *esse est percipi* cannot apply. Adverbialism then appeared as a way of restoring *esse est percipi*, but the adverbial jargon ('sensing redly' and the like) undermines the idea that the contents are organized in a spatially extended visual field. My own view is that the truth of the act-object account is trivial, because it means only that the subject (however you understand that) is aware of the contents. These contents are 'objects' only in the grammatical sense that they are that of which one is aware, and so are the objects of awareness. The notion that they are self-standing entities does not enter into this notion of 'object'. That they are modes of the subject, in a sense that implies that the subject is qualified by them as properties does not enter into this idea, so their spatiality does not entail that the subject is spatially extended. I shall have more to say relevant to this below.

iii Intentional theories: are they mentalist?

There is a further complication. Adverbialism became prominent in the philosophy of perception through Chisholm's perceiving (1957), and it was there presented as an interpretation of what it meant to say that the contents of perception were intentional objects. As far as I can tell, most intentionalists reject the adverbial interpretation of what it means for an object to be intentional.[2] Nevertheless, probably the main stream of intentionalists are mentalists, in the sense that they accept that intentional objects are part of a common factor in experience and they reject the disjunctivism to which standard direct realists are forced to resort. (Crane, 2006). I think that this is a mistake, because, if intentionality really applied to perception it would break down the distinction between the common factor theory and disjunctivism, as a comparison with the intentionality of thought shows. If I think about the Abominable Snowman, then if there is such a creature, it is really that creature of which I am thinking, but if there is no such creature then my thought has a *merely* intentional object. The thought does, of course, have a vehicle—presumably in this case a sentence—but the intentionality lies not in the vehicle per se, but in how it is understood. The thought is both common to both cases and directly of the actual object when there is such an object. It is this trick which it is hard to pull off in the case of perception, if one allows that the common vehicle is a sensation with sensible qualities—with or without a prime as superscript. It is difficult to avoid the thought that a red★ square★ sensation which qualifies a region of the visual field constitutes a veil between oneself and direct perception of the external world (if sense-data constitute a veil), in a way that the sentence 'the Abominable Snowman must be very lonely' does not make one's reference indirect if there is such a creature.

It seems to me, therefore, that neither adverbialism nor common factor intentionalism are serious rivals to the sense-datum theory within the mentalist camp.[3]

4 Problems for the sense-datum theory (i); indeterminacy and contradiction

> The empirical evidence in favor of the indeterminacy of visual shape and color under various conditions of seeing seems overwhelming; we should take it to be a phenomenological fact ... But accepting indeterminacy into phenomenology is one thing and incorporating it into ontology is another.
>
> The sharp sensory-interpretative distinction seems to be consequent on a strict distinction between act and object of perception ... Drawing this distinction appears to be a core tactic of sense-datum theorists and leads in turn to the most damaging problem of all, the pressure to assign incompatible predicates to the same sense-datum ... It may be possible to find and articulate appropriate pairs of phenomenological predicates that will capture the relevant sensory differences and similarities between the way that the rocks in the waterfall illusion seems to move and the way in which they do not seem to move, and likewise for other paradoxical sensory presentations.
>
> *(Hardin, 1988, 108–9)*

So, according to Hardin, there are two serious objections to the sense-datum theory. They are both objections to the reification of phenomenal content on the grounds that it fails to meet the standard necessary for being an entity, namely that entities must be determinate and must not possess inconsistent properties. My response to both these points is essentially the same, namely that there is no such thing as an indeterminate or inconsistent sensation; there are only ways of characterizing sensations in physical object terms which are indeterminate or inconsistent.

Hardin, like others, makes a lot of phenomena such as the waterfall illusion but there is an example of putative contradiction much nearer home, namely feeling dizzy. If you feel dizzy, things seem to go round without actually getting any further. The experience is difficult to describe in a way that does not turn out to be incoherent, but it would not occur to many people to think of it as an incoherent experience because we think of it as just a sensation 'in the head' and not a representation of an apparent physical state of affairs. I suggest that in neither case is there anything contradictory about the experience per se, only that there is no physical interpretation of the scene that does not involve inconsistency. The situation is, I think, analogous to that of an Escher painting. What is there is not a contradiction, only if you see it as a three dimensional scene does the contradiction arise. Something similar applies to sensations: in themselves they are just as they are, but attempts to render them as representations of physical processes sometimes leads to contradiction.

A similar approach works for indeterminacy. First it might be helpful to distinguish between indeterminacy and vagueness, where vagueness is something that allows the generation of sorites paradoxes. Sorites vagueness is a phenomenon of concepts; nothing real can be vague in this way. Indeterminacy is another matter. It seems to me to be unclear what absolute *physical* determinacy is, and absolute determinacy for a secondary quality such as colour is particularly unclear. We have an absolute geometrical notion of shape and size, but whether anything quite fits it, is another matter. If I take off my glasses, I have fuzzy images of things. It would be hard, if not impossible to create physical things like that, but it does not follow that sensations cannot be like that, or if they are, that they can only be 'phenomenologically' real and not 'ontologically'.

The view that the sense-datum theorist should take is this. Our common-sense or Manifest Image conception of the world fundamentally rests on the nature of our sensations. It is fashionable to talk of the transparency of sensations or qualia. This means that their qualitative nature is merely the other side of the coin of how we take the world to be. This is clearly true for many of our sensations. What red looks like, is how we take 'naïve' (or in Chalmers's expression, 'Edenic') red to actually be like. The same goes for visual squareness and actual physical squareness, as the normally sighted hold it to be. But there are some sensations—such as dizziness—that cannot be treated in this transparent way. This is because, even though these phenomena apparently involve the external world (for example. it seems to spin) and is not like a simple bodily sensation, such as a headache, they do not fit into the organized pattern of how the world works—they are not part of the 'constancy and coherence' that Hume pointed out was what leads us to take our experience as being of an objective world.

I do not wish to claim that these remarks deal with all the problems that face the sense-datum theory, but this chapter is concerned only with the mentalist theory of *colour*, not of all sensible qualities. They do not, I think, answer the puzzle presented by Müller-Lyre lines or Adelson's checker-shadow illusion. In the former, two lines look to be of different length, but one can tell by looking carefully that they are in fact of the same length. Similarly in the checker-shadow illusion, experiences of two objects that appear to have different colours but which, when moved together, appear to have the same colour yet neither appears to change colour. In both cases one seems to have a choice between two options. Either similar physical states (lines of the same length and patches of the same colour) produced sense-data that were different (different lengths and different colours); or one misjudged the nature of the data: they seemed similar but were not. Neither of these options seems acceptable; the second more obviously so, because the whole point of sense-data is to constitute entities that embody how things appear. And the former close attention also seems to reveal their similarity.

I think that this indicates the need to distinguish two conceptions of sense-data. The generic conception is:

a   Sense-data are entities instantiating the qualitative nature of how things appear.

But there is an ambiguity here depending how one understands 'qualitative nature'. Are comparative judgements—like comparisons of size—part of the qualitative nature, or a cognitive process, however primitive, something added to the basic qualities sensed? This gives rise to the two interpretations of (a).

b   Sense-data are the qualitative content of 'mature' experience, after certain spontaneous cognitive processes have taken place, including judgements of similarity.
c   Sense-data are raw qualitative contents sensed prior to any cognitive processes beyond bare awareness itself.

The former might crudely be labelled the empiricist account and the latter is more like a Kantian approach to the given.

I do not see why the sense-datum theorist cannot say that you can use the term either way, depending on purpose and context. The essence of the sense-datum theory is that there could not be sense-experience of the kind with which we are all familiar without subject-dependent instances of standard phenomenal qualities. This applies paradigmatically to colour. As H. H. Price (1932, 3) pointed out:

> When I see a tomato there is much that I can doubt … There is one thing I cannot doubt: there exists a red patch of a round and somewhat bulgy shape …

The reality of certain qualitative features that show up through whatever further cognitive processing that there might be is something without which there could be no experience. Dennett (1991) is not wrong to say that fully mature experience involves various layers of processing: he is wrong to try to ignore the phenomenal nature of that which undergoes this refinement. The line between data and further processing might be uncertain without doubt being thrown on the need for qualitative data if there is to be experience at all.

5 Problems for the sense-datum theory (ii) the 'veil of perception'

Despite these problems, the main objection to sense-data has always been that they constitute a so-called 'veil of perception' between the subject and the physical world. The charges raised against the theory in the previous section seem really to be ways of forcing home this fundamental objection. It is as if the objectors are saying 'not merely would sense-data cut us off from the world, they are not even coherent entities'. It looks as if (putting aside for the moment my interpretation of McDowell's theory) the concession that colour is mentalistic forces one to the sense-datum theory. Would this really cut us off from the physical world?

This raises the question of how one should understand the notion of *direct perception* of the external world. The Primitivist about colour is a naïve realist and thinks that visual contact with the world consists in an awareness relation with the surface properties of objects. This theory notoriously has problems with the argument from illusion, and in the case of secondary qualities like colour, at least, with the apparent deliverances of science. But there is a possible alternative account of directness.

In some sense of the term, perception involves *judgements* about what confronts one in the world. According to most modern philosophers, the notion of judgement involves propositions or concepts and so is more sophisticated than most or perhaps any animals can manage. Animals, however, perceive the world, so perception cannot involve judgement.

Something must be wrong here, however. Animals certainly gain information about the world around them through perception, and it is information of which they are, in some sense, aware. This seems to me to constitute at least a minimal or limiting case of judgement: it need not involve any deliberation. I believe that the medium for such judgements can be sensory, not verbal.

Many writers seem to treat the divide between any kind of conceptual activity and perception as an absolute one. A. D. Smith, for example, says

> Concepts are simply irrelevant to perception as such … For when I say that concepts are irrelevant to perception, what I mean is that they are irrelevant to *what it is that makes any sensory state a perception at all*: they are irrelevant to the intentionality of perception, to its basic world-directedness.
>
> *(2002, 95)*

Despite Smith's certainty, I find it difficult to discern exactly what the debate is about. Its roots seem to be in the Wittgensteinian dogma that there can be no thought (and possibly even no consciousness) without language. It is clear that there are no concepts without thought and if there is no thought without language, then there are no concepts without language. As it is very natural to think that non-linguistic animals, including very young human beings, are perceptually conscious, then perception must be non-conceptual. But the connection between thought—and therefore concepts—and language is a nominalist dogma, as I shall now explain.

There seem to me to be a weak and a strong form of conceptualization. Any mental act that is genuinely conceptual must involve an irreducible grasping of a universal in some form. So if the kind of judgement involved in perception—including animal perception—is to be different from that involved in discursive thought, it must turn on the difference between the ways in which universals are grasped in these two cases. This difference, I believe, is between grasping a universal as it presents itself in a sensory or quasi-sensory (imagistic) form, and grasping it where it no longer depends on a sensory medium or instantiation for its apprehension: for example, as linguistic meaning or in 'pure thought', assuming there to be such. Grasping of universals only in their imagistic form is the weak sense of conceptualization. In the latter, linguistic, stronger, sense of 'conceptualization' it is intimately connected with that sense of 'thought' where thought happens naturally in the absence of *instances* of the universals that constitute its content. In the weaker form, there is still a grasping of universals, but they cannot be handled with the freedom and flexibility that 'thought in absence' allows. This is where nominalism is relevant. If you regard consciousness itself, whenever it involves even the slightest element of recognition, however fleeting, as involving the apprehension of a universal *in re*, then you will see the world as already, in a sense, conceptualized for us and apprehended as such. Put in another jargon, if perception is the reception of form, then it is at least proto-conceptual. If you are a nominalist, on the other hand, universals only enter in at the point at which a certain fairly sophisticated kind of mental activity comes into play. It seems that this is far too intellectual a level to be essential to animal perception.

The sense in which perception is a form of judgement, according to my account above, only involves the form of weak conceptualism that involves the handling of universals in their instances or quasi instances. I do not think that this should be denied to animals or babies.

This brings us back to John McDowell (1985). His generally Kantian—or even Hegelian—approach to metaphysics (somehow Janus facedly also presented as Wittgensteinian quietism) shows that it is not only secondary qualities that are dependent on the nature of human sensibility, but even primary qualities, in the form that they appear to us—visual shape, tactile shape, etc.—are also dependent on the nature of our sensibility. How can this fail to be a version of the sense-datum theory? McDowell's theory is generally classified as a form of intentionalism, and according to that theory contents do not count as instances of the qualities represented, but merely as representations of them. This cannot, I think, be McDowell's position, because anyone who thinks that some feature exists only in an intentional content is an eliminativist about that quality—there are no actual instances. This is certainly not McDowell's view, especially about ethical properties, with which secondary qualities are paralleled: they are subject dependent but perfectly real. Another reason why it might be thought to differ from the sense-datum theory is that McDowell thinks that these properties are objective, not subjective, even though they depend on our sensibility. It might seem difficult to see what this means, but one interpretation is the following. According to a conventional sense-datum view, data are logically private objects. These might be 'projected' onto the world, but they are essentially private. If one were convinced by Wittgenstein's anti-private language argument, one would believe that there can be no such private objects, so even properties dependent on our sensibility must be properties in and of external objects.

Clearly, there are tensions—if not contradictions—in such a position, but my concern with McDowell is motivated by the fact that these tensions can perhaps be resolved by the account of judgement presented above, thus suggesting that mentalism and one of the leading forms of direct realism are not that different. The perceptual judgements that are realized in states constituted by sensible qualities are judgements about an external world (whatever that means) and so the manner of appearance of those objects—how they show up in sensation—are necessarily attributed to external objects. How similar that world is 'in itself' to the way in which it is presented to our sensibility, is, however, a further question. The denial that it resembles the way it is presented in our colour experiences was the first step in a process that that can end up denying that it resembles it in any other way than at the most formal, mathematical level (e.g. Russell, 1927).

Notes

1 Peacocke uses 'red"', but 'red★' is notationally clearer.
2 One exception to this is Kriegel (2011: see 150ff).
3 For further discussion on adverbialism, see Robinson (1994, 183–6) and Robinson (2009).

References

Broad, C. D. 1923. *Scientific Thought*, New York, Harcourt Brace and Co.
Chisholm, R. 1957. *Perceiving: A Philosophical Study*, Ithaca, NY, Cornell University Press.
Crane, T. 2006. 'Is there a perceptual relation?', in *Perceptual Experience*, eds. T. Gendler and J. Hawthorne, Oxford, Oxford University Press, 126–46.
Dennett, D. 1991. *Consciousness Explained*, London, Penguin Press.
Ducasse, C. J. 1942. 'Moore's refutation of idealism', in *The Philosophy of G. E. Moore*, ed. P. A. Schilpp, Chicago, Northwestern University Press, 223–51.
Hardin, C. 1988. *Color for Philosophers*. Indianapolis, Hackett.

Kriegel, U. 2011. *The Sources of Intentionality*. Oxford, Oxford University Press.

Maund, B. 2012. 'Color'. plato.stanford.edu/entries/color/.

McDowell, J. 1985. 'Values and secondary qualities', in Ted Honderich, ed., *Morality and Objectivity*, London, Routledge and Kegan Paul, 110–29.

Peacocke, C. 1983. *Sense and Content*. Oxford, Clarendon Press.

Price, H. H. 1932. *Perception*. London, Methuen.

Robinson, H. 1994. *Perception*. London, Routledge.

Robinson, H. 2009. 'Why phenomenal content is not intentional', *European Journal of Analytic Philosophy*, 5(2), 79–93.

Russell, B. 1927. *An Analysis of Matter*. New York, Harcourt, Brace.

Smith, A. D. 2002. *The Problem of Perception*. Cambridge, MA, Harvard University Press.

22

ELIMINATIVISM[1]

Wayne Wright

Introduction

Colour eliminativism denies that colour is a real property of physical objects.[2] According to eliminativism, basketballs are not orange, stoplights are not red, snow piles are not white, and filter gels used to correct tungsten lighting to daylight are not blue. Nor are these objects any other colours. Thus eliminativists convict our everyday experience, in which colour looks to be a ubiquitous feature of the world around us, of massive and systematic error. However, by and large colour eliminativists are not in the business of telling us that we would be better off if we ceased carrying on in our daily lives as if objects are coloured. Indeed, eliminativists have stressed various benefits of seeing, thinking, and talking as though we live in a colour-filled world (Boghossian and Velleman 1989/1997; Hardin 1992; Maund 2006).

Colour eliminativism has deep historical roots. It goes back at least as far as Democritus, whose atomistic metaphysics granted a "merely conventional" existence to sensible qualities such as colour. Galileo, Descartes, Newton, Locke, and Hume are among the luminaries who expressed sentiments in the vicinity of eliminativism, although some of these figures, properly interpreted, are more likely dispositionalists than eliminativists. Contemporary eliminativists claim that there is no place for colour when we take stock of our currently best accounts from fields such as physics, chemistry, neuroscience, and psychology. No known property of objects is apt for identification with colour. Plus, while there are gaps in the scientific story about colour vision, none look suited to be filled by the addition of colours to the inventory of properties that objects have. Unless one is willing to base one's ontological commitments entirely on extrascientific considerations, it follows that there are not any colours "out there".

This chapter sets out the main motivations for and realist responses to colour eliminativism, and examines the broader significance of eliminativism to our picture of how we are connected to the world. Along the way, some new considerations will be introduced.

1 Motivations

Colour eliminativism is a minority position within philosophy, but is plausibly viewed as widely endorsed by scientists working on colour phenomena. Of course, caution is in order when attempting to discern stances on philosophical disputes from scientists' remarks, as there is always the risk that philosophers and scientists frame issues and options in different ways. In any event, as already noted, the case for eliminativism made by philosophers is grounded in the apparent empirical inadequacy of all available realist views. The empirical orientation of the contemporary colour realism debate is largely due to the fact that the philosopher most responsible for launching what is now over a quarter-century of scientifically informed philosophical discussions about colour, C.L. Hardin (1988), is a resolute advocate of eliminativism. Hardin's efforts on behalf of eliminativism form a challenge that any realist hopeful must face. Other philosophers who have recently supported colour eliminativism include Boghossian and Velleman (1989/1997), Chalmers (2006), Maund (1995, 2006), and Pautz (2006).

One can begin to get a sense of what is supposed to make eliminativism appealing by considering metamerism (Hardin 1988, p. 64) and the structural relations that are thought to hold necessarily amongst the colours (*ibid.*, p. 66). Metamers are physically different stimuli that are perceptually indistinguishable in some viewing circumstance, with some metameric pairs having pronounced physical differences. Crucially, two stimuli that are indistinguishable in one situation might be quite distinguishable in another setting. The basic problem metamers pose for realism is that metameric stimuli do not have an underlying shared objective nature. Rather, all that metameric colour stimuli have in common is that a perceiver's visual system treats them equivalently in some circumstance(s). This holds whether we consider reflectance properties of surfaces, spectral power distributions of lights, scattering properties of tiny particles, or any other physical property; see Churchland (2007) for an attempt to provide a physical unification of metameric reflectances and Kuehni and Hardin (2010) and Wright (2009) for criticism of that proposal. Furthermore, there is variation amongst "normal observers" (designated as such by tests used by researchers and clinicians) when it comes to colour perception; e.g. two stimuli that are judged to match in colour by one observer might not be a match for another observer. Also significant is that no set of viewing conditions (e.g. illuminant spectrum, surround configuration, perceiver's state of adaptation) merits being singled out as normative (Hardin 1988, pp. 67, 76; Wyszecki and Stiles 1982, p. 172). Thus even if a realist were tempted to identify a given colour with a metameric set of physically diverse (say) surface reflectances by appealing to a specific class of perceivers and privileged viewing conditions to pick them out, she could not make a principled choice of which reflectances to include (Hardin 1988, p. 81).

As for the structural relations amongst the colours, key here are the binary/unique distinction, similarity, and opponency.[3] The eliminativist's argument hinges on these structural relations being *essential* to the nature of the hues (Hardin 2003, p. 198). Phenomenological reflection is said to reveal that perceived hues contain "amounts" of component hues, with some hues admitting of unique variants; i.e. they have only one component hue. Green, blue, red, and yellow are thought to be the only four hues that can be experienced uniquely; Matthen's entry in this volume offers in-depth examination of unique hues. All other hues are experienced as weighted binary mixtures of these primary hues; e.g. there is no unique orange, as all instances of perceived orange involve red and yellow components (Kuehni 2004, p. 158). Moreover, the primary hues stand in opponent (exclusionary) relations to one another. For example, red is opposed to green in that no hue can be experienced as a combination of them, and the same is supposed to hold for blue and yellow. Lastly, there are claims about the apparent similarities of the hues, such as that aqua green is more similar to unique blue than it is to unique yellow.

Hering's (1920/1964) opponent colours theory has it that the perceived hues are organized around red/green and yellow/blue cardinal axes, with an achromatic neutral point at the origin. This perspective has broad acceptance amongst contemporary researchers and it is thought by many to account for the just-noted structural features of the hues. Psychological research on hue cancellation and hue scaling agrees with the preceding phenomenological observations and

Hering's opponent colours theory; see Hurvich and Jameson (1957) and Abramov and Gordon (2005). Hering's theory picked up neuroscientific support in the middle of the twentieth century with the discovery of opponent-processing cells in the lateral geniculate nucleus (De Valois *et al.* 1966). It turns out, though, that the response functions of the opponent cells discovered so far fail to neatly correspond to the Hering primaries (MacLeod 2010).

Eliminativists argue that the highlighted structural characteristics do not obtain for any perceiver-independent property. For example, consider the reflectance profiles of green and red surfaces. Reflectance spectra for many (certainly not all, which only complicates things for colour realists) biological and artificial green surfaces are bell-shaped with a peak in the 500 to 550 nm region of the spectrum, whereas those for red surfaces tend to be step-like functions, with low reflectance at short and middle wavelengths and a pronounced rise in the middle-long region that levels out in the vicinity of 600 nm (Maloney 2003; Wright 2009). While there are many qualitative and quantitative differences between such reflectance spectra, there are also commonalities. One would search in vain for an opponency relation in whatever patterns one might find. For much the same reason, the similarity relations that hold amongst the hues are not evident in reflectance spectra (Byrne and Hilbert 2003, p. 13), nor is the distinction between unique and binary hues; e.g. orange spectra frequently have the same sigmoidal shape as red spectra, only somewhat shifted toward shorter wavelengths. Similar examples involving spectral power distributions could be provided for lights. Since these structural relations are essential to colour and they lack physical counterparts, colour cannot be identified with a physical property. That is, colour physicalism is false. For more on colour physicalism, see Byrne and Hilbert's chapter on reductive objectivism in this volume (Chapter 17).

Of course, physicalism is not the only available realist option. Dispositionalists claim that objects really are coloured and that we are not massively in error when it comes to colour experience, cognition, and discourse. They do this by identifying colours with dispositions objects have to cause certain kinds of colour experiences; e.g. redness is the disposition to cause red experiences. The relevant dispositions (presumably) have a physical categorical basis, but the dispositionalist relies on the responses of (say) the human visual system to individuate colours without regard for the physical properties that give objects their colour experience-causing powers. This manoeuvre is supposed to allow the dispositionalist to side-step the above-noted problems stemming from metamers and structural properties. Dispositionalism has been criticized in various ways, but here attention is limited to an already-introduced issue that is at the heart of eliminativism's general opposition to colour realism.

The simple statement above that "redness is the disposition to cause red experiences" is incomplete. Whose red experiences? In what conditions? One might be tempted to appeal to "normal perceivers" and "normal circumstances" to nail down the missing details. As was noted when discussing metamers, however, perceptual variation across normal colour perceivers is empirically well-established; we can set aside related complications that might also arise from consideration of the colour experiences of non-human animals. Studies in which subjects select samples (or make settings) that they see as exemplifying the unique hues vividly illustrate this point (Kuehni 2004). Most notorious is the high degree of inter-observer variability for unique green. In some studies one subject's unique green stimulus turns out to be another subject's unique blue, while there are also observers whose unique green stimuli are unique yellow for someone else. Which normal perceivers have it right? Since we lack an independent objective standard for colour by which we might evaluate the choices made by different normal perceivers, it is unclear why we should think that any of them are correct. Moreover, considering that our epistemic access to colour begins with colour experience and there is so much variation across perceivers regarding the unique hues (which are supposed to play an anchoring role in our colour experience), one might doubt that there is anything at all about which colour perceivers might be right or wrong.

As for how to specify the relevant viewing context, even small changes to conditions can have significant effects on perceived colour. The Cornsweet effect can be nullified by placing a thin object over a pair of opposing luminance gradients in a picture, making two much larger regions immediately switch from looking markedly different to looking identical in colour (Purves and Lotto 2011, p. 32, fig.2.11). Changing illumination conditions (e.g. tungsten versus fluorescent lighting, the phases of daylight) can affect colour appearance and alter what stimuli are indistinguishable from one another (e.g. the oft-cited disagreements between how clothes look in a store and how they look at home). Because of contrast effects, a patch's colour appearance is liable to vary when it is viewed against backgrounds that are differently coloured from one another. Some colours, such as black and brown, cannot be seen except in specific contrast conditions; e.g. something that looks brown when viewed against a brighter surround will look dark orange when seen against a darker surround. Of all the different variables of viewing conditions that might vary, we are unable to say which, if any, reveal the true colours of objects.

Many more examples of such problems could be produced. We lack a legitimate basis for singling out some specific class of perceivers and some particular set of circumstances, as the "normal" or "standard" ones that would allow a realist to fill in the rest of the statement of what it is for something to be green (or some specific shade of green). There are plenty of practical matters that could justify favouring some formulation of conditions over others, just as practical considerations drove the construction of the CIE standard observers (Wyszecki & Stiles 1982, pp. 131–43; for criticism of the principles guiding the CIE system, see Fairman *et al.* 1997, p. 21 and Thornton 1999, pp. 155–6). However, it would be arbitrary to choose any single set of practical considerations as the basis for the normative details required by a realist theory of colour. Hence, like physicalism, dispositionalism fails to satisfy an important desideratum for a realist theory of colour: it cannot tell us what colour an object really has.

Some physicalists (Byrne and Hilbert 2003; Tye 2000), in recognition of these difficulties, have eschewed trying to identify what combination of perceivers and viewing conditions provides for access to the real colours of things. They insist that such perceivers and circumstances exist but are "unknowable" (Byrne and Hilbert 2003, p. 21 n.50). This manoeuvre has met stiff resistance, largely on the grounds that unless one is already working with a commitment to colour physicalism, there is nothing to recommend the idea that there are epistemically inaccessible standards of veridical colour perception (Cohen 2010; Hardin 2004; Wright 2010). A dispositionalist trying the same gambit would fare no better.

One could attempt to defuse the worries about normal perceivers and normal circumstances by giving up the goal of being able to specify *the* colour of an object. The idea here is to relativize colour properties to perceivers and circumstances and to speak of (for example) unique-green-for-subject-S-in-circumstances-C rather than unique green *simpliciter*. This leads to objects having multiple colours (pluralism). This strategy could be worked out in different ways and it is beyond the scope of this chapter to consider the details of particular views along these lines. See Cohen's chapter in this volume for discussion of both dispositionalism and relativization (Chapter 19), and Kalderon's chapter for discussion of pluralism (Chapter 20).

Eliminativists are liable to find certain common flaws across theories that relativize colours to perceivers and contexts; Cohen (2010) replies to objections from Hardin. Particularly troubling is that relativizing generates a limitless horde of colour properties. From the perspective of constructing a scientifically relevant theory of colour, this unconstrained multiplicity of colours is unwelcome (Hardin 2004, pp. 35–6). Rather than offering insight into how and why colour vision works the way it does (e.g. facilitating general conclusions about the nature of colour and colour perception), such a conception seems to muddy the waters. For instance, relativizing to perceivers and circumstances risks making all colour perception veridical, thereby greatly straining the notion of veridicality. Seeing as it is reasonable to expect colour realism to support meaningful assessments of veridicality, that result is no more palatable than the positing of standards of veridical perception that are epistemically closed off to us. While it is understandable that one might be troubled by eliminativism rendering all colour perception illusory, realists struggle to provide a robust, serviceable notion of veridicality.

Relativizing colours to perceivers and circumstances also comports poorly with a natural way realists might explain the evolution of our colour vision systems (Wright 2010; this is an extension of an intra-personal example from Byrne and Hilbert 2003, p. 58). The colours I experience are not the same ones experienced by my ancestors, as those colours were relativized to them and their circumstances. Thus the forces of selection could not have favoured creatures whose visual systems provided experiences of the colours that my visual system provides experiences of. So, we are left wondering how it is that I have come to experience the colours that I do, in the circumstances that I experience them. As a final point, considering the substantial role colour experiences play in individuating colours and the massive, seemingly fractured inventory of colours we are left with, one might doubt that any account that relativizes colours in such a prolific way qualifies as realist.

The final realist view to consider is primitivism; the pairing of eliminativism and a non-realist form of primitivism is discussed later. Primitivists understand colours as qualitative properties of objects that stand to one another in the structural relations said to be essential to the colours. These simple, *sui generis* properties are not reducible to some physical property that is causally relevant to colour experience, although it is open to hold that primitive colours supervene on a distal property such as surface reflectance. Unlike physicalists, whose view looks best understood as including the thesis that the commonsense colours have "hidden" complex essences waiting to be revealed by examination of what science tells us about the processes that lead from the interaction of light and matter to colour experience, the primitivist claims that our everyday qualitative notion of colour faithfully captures how things really are outside our heads.

Primitivism has met with a number of objections, including the now-familiar concerns based on perceptual variation. One complaint that merits mention is that positing primitive colour properties is empirically unmotivated. They do not appear anywhere in our best scientific account of colour perception and there is no causal work for them to do that would justify trying to shoehorn them into it (Chalmers 2006, p. 67; Hardin 1988, p. 61). Gert's chapter in this volume (Chapter 18) goes into much greater detail about primitivist realism.

Granting for the moment the success of the criticisms of physicalism, dispositionalism, and primitivism (those presented here and others made elsewhere), it looks like eliminativism wins by defeating all known realist challengers. Perhaps, though, since so much of the case for colour eliminativism is made *via negativa*, we should proceed more cautiously. There might be an as-yet unconceived realist view for which eliminativism lacks an answer. However, the general message suggested by the specific problems eliminativists find in extant realist theories is that there is, at best, very little room for further manoeuvring. The eliminativist's challenge to realists is to identify a property that (i) plays an appropriate role in the causal chain leading up to colour experience, (ii) accounts for the essential structural features of the colours, and (iii) allows us to make useful theoretical statements pertaining to how and why colour vision works as it does (including which colour experiences are veridical). Condition (i) is a plausible requirement on any theory of colour being worthy of the appellation "realist" and violating it would likely also compromise what one does with (iii). Condition (ii) is tough to meet without appealing to facts about colour perceivers, which would potentially complicate how one deals with either (i) or (iii). The variability of colour appearance across perceivers and contexts makes condition (iii) particularly imposing and likely a threat to any realist view that might be proposed.

Eliminativism clearly demands an answer from colour realists. The main moves available for realists are to creatively refine the details of their views in response to eliminativist objections, undermine the empirical support for eliminativism, or change the terms of the debate. The first two options are considered in the next section, with the last one taken up in the section after that.

2 Responses to eliminativism

Some ways in which realists might revise or elaborate their accounts in response to the challenge from perceptual variation have already been noted, such as relativization and arguing that the variability of colour experience justifies only an epistemic (not metaphysical) conclusion about the real colours of things. Colour physicalists have also confronted the objection from phenomenal structure. To do so, Byrne and Hilbert (2003) combine a thesis about colour experience with the prevalent beliefs that Hering opponent colours theory is true and that the opponent relations amongst the hues are rooted in neural mechanisms in the visual system; see also Bradley and Tye (2001). The claim about colour experience is that it represents objects as having colour properties. Hering's theory is used to help spell out just what those represented properties are. According to Byrne and Hilbert, colour experience represents objects as having *hue magnitudes* of reddishness, greenishness, yellowishness, and bluishness. For example, a purple object is represented as having balanced or nearly balanced magnitudes of reddishness and bluishness. The hue magnitudes are given a physical pedigree by linking them to hue-opponent neural mechanisms that compare outputs from the short, middle, and long wavelength sensitive cones in the human retina. Reddishness is the degree to which a surface tends to reflect more light at longer wavelengths than at middle wavelengths (*vice versa* for greenishness). Yellowishness is the degree to which a surface tends to reflect more light at middle and long wavelengths than at short wavelengths (*vice versa* for bluishness). Consequently, unique yellow surfaces reflect more light at middle and long wavelengths than at short wavelengths and are balanced (i.e. at a null point) in how much light they reflect at middle and long wavelengths.

Although hypothesized features of human visual processing are used to pick out the hue magnitudes (on the basis of an account at the psychological level of structural features of colour perception), the hue magnitudes are perfectly objective and physical properties. The response functions of the cones are specified in terms of wavelength and the hue-opponent neural mechanisms simply make comparisons between the levels of response in the different cone classes. All the details of visual processing used to isolate the hue magnitudes can be stated in physical and mathematical terms. We would have no interest in hue magnitudes if we did not perceive colour as we do, but that does not make hue magnitudes non-physical.

The hue magnitude proposal is not without difficulties. Chiefly, as was previously observed, there are no known neural mechanisms that neatly correspond to the Hering opponent colour axes. In fact, there is good reason to think that opponent processing mechanisms at the neural level are altogether functionally irrelevant to opponency and uniqueness at the psychological level (MacLeod 2010, p. 160). Byrne and Hilbert (2003, p. 55) chalk this up as merely a problem for the simplified example they provide in terms of cone responses and opponent processes, with no deeper consequence for their view. Their example is intended to illustrate how it is that hue magnitudes *could* be physical properties, but nothing about the nature of the hue magnitudes themselves is supposed to depend on cone responses or opponent processing (*ibid.*, p. 14). It is important to note, however, that Byrne and Hilbert's example proceeds from a starting point that takes to be true both colour physicalism and the hue magnitude proposal about the content of colour experience (*ibid.*, p. 55). They are well aware of the need to spell out in useful detail the physical *bona fides* of the hue magnitudes, in order to make good on their claim that the colour physicalist can overcome the objections from phenomenal structure (*ibid.*, p. 15). Without a compelling, workable example that provides insight into just what sort of physical property a hue magnitude actually is, it is far from clear that there is any reason to believe that they are real, physical properties of objects; Broackes (2003) pursues a similar line of criticism. From the eliminativist's perspective, the situation on this score looks similar to that regarding the idea that the challenge from perceptual variation can be met by positing unknowable standards of veridical colour perception.

Rather than try to show how the structural features highlighted by eliminativists can be accommodated within a realist framework, one might question the eliminativists' take on the structural features that they claim necessarily hold amongst the colours. In particular, concerns have been raised about the unique/binary distinction and the special status accorded to the Hering primaries. For example, some researchers contend that use of the "unique" designation has been overly restricted. According to them, when employing the usual perceptual purity criterion to assess the uniqueness or binariness of hue percepts, there are (for example) orange and purple samples that are just as unique as the four Hering primary hues (Koenderink 2010, p. 579; Wright 2011, p. 633 n.2). That is, they claim that there are hues intermediate between the canonical unique hues that are not experienced as perceptual mixtures, but as wholly orange (purple, etc.). It also has been suggested that empirical results that seem to bolster the claims that the unique hues have a special role in colour experience and that the binary hues are in some sense dependent on or subordinate to them, are an artefact of task instructions and experimental design (Jameson 2010, pp. 190–4).

These heterodoxies are not mere unconfirmable phenomenological musings or idle speculation, as they have empirical support. For one thing, the received picture of the unique hues (which draws on the Hering opponent colours theory) makes predictions that are not borne out; Jameson and D'Andrade (1997) are followed closely here. Every mixture of unique red with unique green that yields a non-reddish, non-greenish percept, appears yellowish, not achromatic. Scaling of colour similarity judgements produces a space that does not have a red/green axis. The result instead is a Munsell-like space with red sitting across from blue-green while green resides opposite a reddish purple. Significantly, hues that lie opposite one another in this Munsell-like space *are* (or are very close to) additive complements; i.e. they can be mixed to produce an achromatic percept. Some recent studies have found that red, green, blue, and yellow do not stand out (in comparison to hues standardly thought to be binary) in several of the ways one might expect, given the significance attached to them; see Bosten and Boehm (2014), Bosten and Lawrance-Owen (2014), Malkoc and Webster (2005), Witzel and Franklin (2014). Since the unique hues play such a prominent role in the eliminativist critique of colour realism—for example, Hardin (1992, p. 371) casts the absence of physical counterparts for the unique hues as the *central* reason for rejecting physicalism—perhaps these concerns about the unique hue construct provide an opening realists can exploit. For more on this line of response to eliminativism, see Wright (2019).

A relevant consideration is that there is a great deal of systematicity in the relationship between colour experience and colour-relevant physical properties. Spectral reflectances that differ from one another only slightly tend to elicit similar colour experiences, while continuous variation in the light signal reaching the eye is met with continuous variation in colour experience (Isaac 2014, p. 494). Additionally, numerous studies using dimensionality reduction techniques have found that natural and artificial surface reflectances can be approximated to a high degree of precision in as few as three dimensions. A plot of the Munsell chips in three-dimensional reflectance space bears a qualitative resemblance to their locations in Munsell colour space and linear transformations enable a mapping between the space of approximated surface reflectances and Munsell colour space (Romney 2008).

Several issues need to be dealt with in order to properly assess the significance of such results for the colour realism debate (Wright 2010). Additionally, some phenomena cited by eliminativists (e.g. contrast effects) are not addressed by the findings regarding dimensionality reduction. However, if the eliminativist's objections based on unique hues can be neutralized by some of the points raised above, that removes a major obstacle to attempts to motivate some form of realism on the basis of the systematic relations between physical properties and colour experience. As far as phenomenal similarity is concerned, the structural relations between reflectance space and Munsell colour space would go a long way toward accounting for it. The same looks to be true for opponency; e.g. the reason red and green exclude each other is that they are so far apart from one another in both reflectance space and Munsell colour space. To be clear, the suggestion is not that the (potential) downplaying of the importance of the unique hues ensures a realist victory, only that realism's prospects look much less dim with the unique hues taken off the table.

3 Standards of reality

A different approach for realists is to undermine the conception of reality the eliminativist employs. As was noted earlier, some realists, in response to eliminativist objections, appeal to facts about (individual or a special class of) perceivers as part of their account of the nature of colour. This is supposed to allow realists to unify collections of physically disparate properties and impose structure that matches that of phenomenal colour. Such views are *relationalist*, as they consider colours to be constituted by relations that obtain between features of the mind-independent world and perceivers. As Cohen (2010, pp. 239–40) discusses, Hardin finds relationalism lacking as a species of realism. Hardin's thinking is that that if realism were true, facts about colour perception would depend on (be recoverable from, etc.) facts about the colours of objects, but relationalism has the dependence the other way around; Hardin (2003, p. 198) offers a similar criticism of the physicalist hue magnitude account of phenomenal structure canvassed in the preceding section.

However, there are plenty of things that are considered real, in some significant sense, even though they depend on subjects or are not physically unified. Cohen (*ibid.*) gives the examples of being beautiful and being humorous. A different set of examples could be drawn from the special sciences; e.g. mating strategies, head-initial languages, market economies (Johnson and Wright 2006; Whittle 2003 makes related points). Regarding special science properties, the justification for counting such properties as real comes from the work they do in our best scientific theories (Johnson and Wright, p. 153). As it happens, colour plays an important role in explanations and generalizations in fields such as botany, ethology, and population biology, especially when it comes to mating behaviour, camouflage, pollination, and foraging. Whatever account of colour might emerge from careful study of the roles colours play in such scientific research is sure to depend on facts about colour perceivers and may very well address few of the standard concerns about the metaphysics of colour beyond saying that colours are real. Perhaps the most we can do is to treat colours as high-level statistical constructs. Importantly, though, that is often the case with kinds of the special sciences (*ibid.*, pp. 159–60).

Eliminativists are unlikely to be moved by these considerations. The colours we experience do not present themselves as needing us for their existence. They instead appear to be "stuck to" or "in" objects, all on their own (Boghossian and Velleman 1989/1997, pp. 93–4). As a prominent colour physicalist puts it, not only are colours not experienced as relational properties, they look to be just as non-relational as shape is (Tye 2000, p. 153). Taking this phenomenological observation to constrain theorizing about colour does not require believing that the full nature of colour is revealed in experience (Johnston 1992/1997), but only that some essential properties of colours are revealed in experience (Pautz 2006, p. 538). Mind-independence, it might be claimed, is one of them. This is to treat the apparent mind-independence of the colours the same as the structural relations amongst the colours; see Hardin's (2003, p. 201) remarks about the commitments of "common-sense realism". This makes a perceiver-dependent account of colour guilty of changing the subject. Furthermore, according to this characterization of the phenomenology of colour experience, relationalism yields a massive error theory: colours look like (are represented as, etc.) perceiver-independent properties of objects when they really are perceiver-dependent. Since avoiding a massive error theory is often thought to be an advantage of colour realism, this is an unwelcome result. Much more could be said on this topic; e.g. Levin (2000) replies to the massive error theory charge, Pautz (2006) presses the phenomenological objection even against non-relationalist realist theories.

4 Colour experience in a colourless world

This concluding section takes up how we should understand colour experience, assuming that eliminativism is true. While eliminativism is a thesis about the furniture of the physical world and not an account in the philosophy of mind, it clearly has significant, counterintuitive implications for our understanding of the relationship between the mind and the world. Thus it is fair to expect the eliminativist to say something about what we encounter in colour experience.

One option is to take colours to be mental in nature, as either properties of mental objects (such as sense data) or properties of experiences (qualia). Hume (1738/1992, III.I.I; p. 469) declared that colours are "not qualities in objects, but perceptions in the mind". Boghossian and Velleman (1989/1997, pp. 94–5) regard colours as "intrinsic sensational qualities of a [subjective] visual field" that are "projected" onto objects in experience. Vision scientists are also prone to making claims along these lines, such as Palmer's (1999, p. 95) remark that "color is a psychological property of our visual experiences". Accounts that treat colours as mental properties that objects are seen as having threaten to convict colour experience not only of massive error, but also a category mistake (Shoemaker 1994, p. 25; Tye 2000, pp. 165–6). On certain (plausibly straightforward) readings of the thesis that colours are mental in nature, colours are dubious candidates for being properties that could cover the surfaces of physical objects and so forth. One does not have to be a Cartesian about the natures of the mental and the physical to find it hard to understand how sensational (experiential, etc.) properties might cover the surfaces of physical objects. Since colours certainly look like properties that physical objects could possess, taking colours to be essentially mental properties results in the phenomenology of colour experience being grossly confused (or confusing) about the nature of colour.

Mentalist accounts of colour also take on the burden of accommodating the distinction between colour and patently mind-independent properties such as shape and size; this is related to a long-standing objection to dispositionalism that traces back to Berkeley (Byrne and Hilbert 2003, p. 7). A simple way of putting the point at issue here is that once one has stated the nature of colour in mental terms and adopted all the machinery that goes along with that, a commitment to shape (size, etc.) also being a mental property is unavoidable. It is hard to motivate a theory that turns the shapes we experience into mental qualities that no physical object can possess, although some are willing to embrace a robust idealism about the qualities we encounter in experience (Hoffman 2009). Of course, some have attempted to block the Berkeleyian objection, often by pointing to differences between the cases of colour and properties such as shape; e.g. we have an account of objective shape while an account of objective colour seems hopeless.

A more promising route for the eliminativist is to hold that there is not anything—physical or mental—that is actually coloured, but visual experience presents us with colour properties that objects *could* have, were circumstances different; it is worth noting that many mentalist views can plausibly be understood or re-cast in terms consistent with what follows (Maund 2006 illustrates this). Such a view is left open by, for example, Hardin's (1984, p. 496) remark about not having proven colour objectivism to be false in all possible worlds. Using the phenomenology of experience as a guide to the nature of these colour properties, we end up with a primitivist understanding of them: across the vast bulk of our experience, the colours we encounter look to be simple qualities of objects themselves (Chalmers 2006; Maund 1995, 2006; Pautz 2006). In the actual world, these primitive properties are uninstantiated, but they can figure in experiential contents. Fortunately for us, experiences that represent these primitive colour properties are systematically (but contingently) connected to disjunctions of physical properties. Thus although colour experience is a pervasive illusion, it is "as if" we inhabit a chromatic world (Maund 2006). In a different world (e.g. Chalmers' Eden) objects would possess these primitive properties and they would play a role in the causal chain leading up to colour experience suitable for facilitating genuinely veridical colour perception.

The pairing of eliminativism and primitivism comes with complications. One is that the Berkeleyian objection might be developed against such an account to argue that it leads to primitivism about all perceptual qualities. There is also, of course, the usual apprehension about massive error theories. More fundamental (but related) issues stem from the fact that we, our evolutionary antecedents, and all other creatures have not had any causal contact with the hypothesized primitive colour properties. It is difficult to make sense of just how it is that our visual systems evolved to represent, in a useful manner, a suite of properties that nothing in our world actually possesses (Byrne and Hilbert 2003, p. 59). Moreover, we are left to wonder how to specify the conditions under which the representation of these primitive colour properties takes place, if there are no actual instances of their veridical representation (Tye 2000, p. 166). It is a measure of the vexatious character of colour, that even with its potential to respect both phenomenology and science, this approach leaves us with further puzzles to address.

Notes

1 A debt of thanks is owed to Kimberly Jameson and A. Kimball Romney for much enlightening and engaging discussion about some of the issues treated in this chapter. I am also grateful to the editors of this volume for their useful feedback on an earlier draft of this chapter.

2 This characterization of colour eliminativism is narrower than that sometimes found in the literature; see, for example, Cohen (2011). On some broader taxonomies of theories of colour ontology, eliminativism amounts to the claim that *nothing*—physical or mental—is actually coloured. The focus here is instead on the idea that nothing in the world outside perceivers has colour, which is consistent with colours being mental properties (as discussed in Chapter 21 of this volume by Howard Robinson) and with there being nothing mental or physical with colour. These nuances are discussed in the final section of this chapter.

3 As is often done, matters are being simplified by attending mostly to hue. Also, in listing opponency among the essential structural features, experimental results suggesting that it is possible to experience "forbidden" combinations of opponent colours (e.g. reddish greens) are being set aside; see Crane and Piantanida (1983), Hardin (1988, pp. 123–7), and Macpherson's chapter in this volume (Chapter 11).

References

Abramov, L., and J. Gordon. 2005. Seeing unique hues. *Journal of the Optical Society of America A, 22,* 2143–53.

Boghossian, P., and D. Velleman. 1989/1997. Color as a secondary quality. In A. Byrne and D. Hilbert (eds.) *Readings on Color: The Philosophy of Color.* Cambridge (MA): MIT Press. 81–103.

Bosten, J., and A. Boehm. 2014. Empirical evidence for unique hues? *Journal of the Optical Society of America A, 31,* A385–A393.

Bosten, J., and A. Lawrance-Owen. 2014. No difference in variability of unique hue selections and binary hue selections. *Journal of the Optical Society of America A, 31,* A357–A364.

Bradley, P., and M. Tye. 2001. Of colors, kestrels, caterpillars, and leaves. *Journal of Philosophy, 98,* 469–87.

Broackes, J. 2003. Do opponent process theories help physicalism about color? *Behavioral and Brain Sciences, 26,* 786–88.

Byrne, A., and D. Hilbert. 2003. Color realism and color science. *Behavioral and Brain Sciences, 26,* 3–64.

Chalmers, D. 2006. Perception and the fall from Eden. In T. Gendler and J. Hawthorne (eds.) *Perceptual Experience.* New York: Oxford University Press. 49–125.

Churchland, P. 2007. On the reality (and diversity) of objective colors: How color-qualia space is a map of reflectance-profile space. *Philosophy of Science, 74,* 119–49.

Cohen, J. 2010. It's not easy being green. In J. Cohen and M. Matthen (eds.) *Color Ontology and Color Science.* Cambridge (MA): MIT Press. 229–44.

Cohen, J. 2011. Color. In J. Symons and P. Calvo (eds.) *The Routledge Companion to Philosophy of Psychology.* New York: Routledge. 568–78.

Crane, H., and T. Piantanida. 1983. On seeing reddish green and yellowish blue. *Science, 221,* 1078–80.

De Valois, R., I. Abramov, and G. Jacobs. 1966. Analysis of response patterns of LGN cells. *Journal of the Optical Society of America, 56,* 966–77.

Fairman, H., M. Brill, and H. Hemmendinger. 1997. How the CIE 1931 color-matching functions were derived from Wright-Guild data. *Color Research and Application, 22,* 11–23.

Hardin, C.L. 1984. Are 'scientific' objects colored? *Mind, 93,* 491–500.

Hardin, C.L. 1988. *Color for Philosophers: Unweaving the Rainbow.* Indianapolis: Hackett.

Hardin, C.L. 1992. The virtues of illusion. *Philosophical Studies, 68,* 371–82.

Hardin, C.L. 2003. A spectral reflectance doth not a color make. *Journal of Philosophy, 100,* 191–202.

Hardin, C.L. 2004. A green thought in a green shade. *Harvard Review of Philosophy, 12,* 29–39.

Hering, E. 1920/1964. *Outlines of a Theory of the Light Sense.* Cambridge (MA): Harvard University Press.

Hoffman, D. 2009. The interface theory of perception: Natural selection drives true perception to swift extinction. In S. Dickinson, M. Tarr, A. Leonardis, and B. Schiele (eds.) *Object Categorization: Computer and Human Vision Perspectives.* Cambridge (UK): Cambridge University Press. 148–65.

Hume, D. 1738/1992. *Treatise of Human Nature.* Buffalo (NY): Prometheus Books.

Hurvich, L., and D. Jameson. 1957. An opponent-process theory of color vision. *Psychological Review, 64,* 384–404.

Isaac, I. 2014. Structural realism for secondary qualities. *Erkenntnis, 79,* 481–510.

Jameson, K. 2010. Where in the World Color Survey is the support for the Hering primaries as the basis for color categorization? In J. Cohen and M. Matthen (eds.) *Color Ontology and Color Science.* Cambridge (MA): MIT Press. 179–202.

Jameson, K., and R. D'Andrade. 1997. It's not really red, green, yellow, blue: An inquiry into perceptual color space. In C.L. Hardin and L. Maffi (eds.) *Color Categories in Thought and Language.* Cambridge (UK): Cambridge University Press. 295–319.

Johnson, K., and W. Wright. 2006. Colors as properties of the special sciences. *Erkenntnis, 64,* 139–68.

Johnston, M. 1992/1997. How to speak of the colors. In A. Byrne and D. Hilbert (eds.) *Readings on Color: The Philosophy of Color.* Cambridge (MA): MIT Press. 137–76.

Koenderink, J. 2010. *Color for the Sciences.* Cambridge (MA): MIT Press.

Kuehni, R. 2004. Variability in unique hue selection: A surprising phenomenon. *Color Research and Application, 29,* 158–62.

Kuehni, R., and C.L. Hardin. 2010. Churchland's metamers. *British Journal for the Philosophy of Science, 61,* 81–92.

Levin, J. 2000. Dispositional theories of color and the claims of common sense. *Philosophical Studies, 100,* 151–74.

MacLeod, D. 2010. Into the neural maze. In J. Cohen and M. Matthen (eds.) *Color Ontology and Color Science*. Cambridge (MA): MIT Press. 151–78.

Malkoc, G., P. Kay, and M. Webster. 2005. Variation in normal color vision. IV. Binary hues and hue scaling. *Journal of the Optical Society of America, 22*, 2154–68.

Maloney, L. 2003. The importance of realistic models of surface and light in the study of human colour vision. In R. Mausfeld and D. Heyer (eds.) *Colour Perception: Mind and the Physical World*. London: Oxford University Press. 243–6.

Maund, B. 1995. *Colors: Their Nature and Representation*. Cambridge (UK): Cambridge University Press.

Maund, B. 2006. The illusory theory of colors: An anti-realist theory. *Dialectica 60*, 245–68.

Palmer, S. 1999. *Vision Science: From Photons to Phenomenology*. Cambridge (MA): MIT Press.

Pautz, A. 2006. Can the physicalist explain colour structure in terms of colour experience? *Australasian Journal of Philosophy, 84*, 535–64.

Purves, D., and B. Lotto. 2011. *Why We See What We Do Redux: A Wholly Empirical Theory of Vision*. Sunderland (MA): Sinauer Associates.

Romney, A.K. 2008. Relating reflectance spectra space to Munsell color space. *Journal of the Optical Society of America A, 25*, 658–66.

Shoemaker, S. 1994. Phenomenal character. *Nous, 28*, 21–38.

Thornton, W. 1999. Spectral sensitivities of the normal human visual system, color-matching functions and their principles, and how and why the two sets should coincide. *Color Research and Application, 24*, 139–56.

Tye, M. 2000. *Consciousness, Color, and Content*. Cambridge (MA): MIT Press.

Whittle, P. 2003. Why is this game still being played? In R. Mausfeld and D. Heyer (eds.) *Colour Perception: Mind and the Physical World*. London: Oxford University Press. 203–4.

Witzel, C., and A. Franklin. 2014. Do focal colors look particularly 'colorful'? *Journal of the Optical Society of America A, 31*, A365–A374.

Wright, W. 2009. The physical unnaturalness of Churchland's ellipses. *Philosophy of Science, 76*, 391–403.

Wright, W. 2010. Perception, color, and realism. *Erkenntnis, 73*, 19–40.

Wright, W. 2011. Reply to Broackes. *Review of Philosophy and Psychology, 2*, 629–41.

Wright, W. 2019. The unique hues and the argument from phenomenal structure. *Philosophical Studies, 176*, 1513–33.

Wyszecki, G., and W. Stiles. 1982. *Color Science: Concepts and Methods, Quantitative Data and Formulae*. New York: Wiley and Sons.

PART V

Colour experience and epistemology

23

HOW DOES COLOUR EXPERIENCE REPRESENT THE WORLD?

Adam Pautz

There is no call to treat illusory sensible qualities, and in particular colours, as actual qualities of actual entities.

David Armstrong (1984)

Many favour *representationalism* about colour experience. To a first approximation, this view holds that experiencing is like believing. In particular, like believing, experiencing is a matter of representing the world to be a certain way.

Once you view colour experience along these lines, you face a big question: do our colour experiences represent the world as it really is? For instance, suppose you see a tomato. Representationalists claim that having an experience with this sensory character is necessarily connected with representing a distinctive quality as pervading a round area out there in external space. Let us call it "sensible redness" to highlight the fact that the representation of this property is necessarily connected with the sensory character of the experience. Is this property, sensible redness, *really* co-instantiated with roundness out there in the space before you?[1]

Since the development of the new mathematical physics of the seventeenth century, many prominent thinkers have returned a negative answer. Galileo, for instance, famously said that "tastes, odours, colours, and so on reside in consciousness", not the external world. Following this tradition, some contemporary representationalists hold that tomatoes and other objects are just collections of particles and fields lacking sensible properties. We evolved to have experiences that habitually misrepresent objects in space as having various sensible colours, only because this helps us to discriminate them from one another.

However, other representationalists resist this radical irrealist view. They think representationalism about colour experience goes best with "realism" about sensible colours. The tomato's surface really does exemplify sensible redness. In general, our colour experiences typically represent objects as they really are.

We will look at these different versions of representationalism. But first I will explain in more detail the basic representationalist approach they share.

1 Representationalism about colour experience: the basic idea

To understand representationalism, it is best to start with non-veridical colour experience. Suppose that someone—call her "Mary"—suffers from "Charles Bonnet syndrome", a condition which involves having vivid hallucinations. Suppose in particular that she hallucinates a tomato. Intuitively, having this phenomenal experience is essentially connected with having an experience as of a *reddish* and *round* item in a certain location. But, in this case, no *physical* round and reddish thing is present. So how come it is correct to say Mary has an experience as of a *reddish* and *round* item?

Before representationalism became popular, the dominant view was the *sense datum theory*. On this approach, what Mary experiences is a *non-physical* round and reddish item created by her brain—a "sense datum" or "mental image". In general, sensible colours do not qualify ordinary physical objects, but such mental images of them created by the brain. However, this view faces well-known puzzles.[2]

Enter the representationalist alternative. On representationalism, all that is going on is that Mary's experience "represents" that there is something before her with the properties *being round* and *reddish*. This doesn't require that there really is an item—a peculiar mental "sense datum"—that has these properties. On representationalism, Mary's hallucination is like a belief in that it is a "representational" state that can represent properties belonging to no real (physical or mental) thing.

But, of course, Mary's hallucinatory experience is a representational state of a kind very different from belief. Hallucination, unlike mere belief, involves a *vivid impression* of the *real presence* of a thing. To explain this, representationalists would claim that, in having her hallucination, Mary stands in a very *unique* representational relation to the properties *being round* and *being reddish*, even though those properties are not presently instantiated before her. I will call it the "perceptual representation relation". This hypothesized relation is unique in that, when one bears it to some properties, one has the vivid impression that there is an object present with those properties. Indeed, on a simple form of representationalism, Mary having her tomato-like hallucination *is just identical with* her perceptually representing (or "perceptually predicating") a cluster of tomato-like properties such as *being reddish* and *being roundish* (where these properties can exist even if they aren't instantiated by any real thing). Representationalists, then, do not appeal "sensations", or "qualia", that are distinct from and lie behind perceptually representing the world to be a certain way (*pace* Campbell, this volume); rather, they say that experiencing is *nothing but* representing.

In general, most representationalists hold that, necessarily, if two individuals have phenomenally different visual experiences, then they perceptually represent different clusters of sensible properties. Other representationalists advocate weaker versions of representationalism that allow for some exceptions to this general principle (e.g. cases where you perceptually represent the same properties but there is a change in which ones you *attend to*).

Representationalism about colour experience has many virtues. It accommodates the undeniable fact that, necessarily, in having standard visual experiences, it seems that sensible colours are co-instantiated with certain shapes and location properties. For instance, necessarily, if one has a tomato-like experience, then one has an experience that matches the world only if a reddish, round item is present at a certain place. It also explains how both veridical and non-veridical experience can provide a subject with the capacity to think about and learn truths about sensible colours and shapes, even when they aren't instantiated by physical objects before the subject (Russell 1912, chap. X; Johnston 2004, 130; Tye 2014, 51–2). At the same time, it avoids the "sense data" of traditional sense datum theory.

For the sake of discussion, let us assume that representationalism is right. This view implies that every sensory experience has two elements: (i) the *perceptual representation relation*, and (ii) a complex of sensible properties that are the *relata* of this relation (sensible colours, shapes, audible properties, and so on).[3] So once we accept representationalism, we face a pair of difficult questions. For colour experience, they are as follows.

First, the *sensible colours question:* what is the nature of the "sensible colours". For instance, what is the nature of the "sensible redness" which Mary perceptually represents as co-instantiated with roundness? Is it a property that tomatoes and other objects sometimes really have?

Second, there is the *representation relation question*. What is the nature of "the perceptual representation relation" that we bear to sensible redness and other perceptible properties? For instance, when Mary hallucinates a tomato, she bears this relation to *being reddish* and *being round*. How does Mary's brain enable her to "reach out" and perceptually represent these properties, so that they seem present before her, even though they are not really present before her? Is this "perceptual representation relation" a spooky non-physical relation between her mind and these sensible properties? Or can it be identified with some kind of unproblematic physical relation (e.g. the kind of "tracking relation" we'll discuss in the next section)? As Mark Johnston has observed (2011, 215–16), a central puzzle about the mind is how to "explain the relation of sensory intentionality".

Let us now to turn to different versions of representationalism about colour experience. They differ in how they answer these twin questions.

2 Response-independent representationalism

I will explain *response-independent representationalism* by way of a simple argument for it based on considerations of *uniformity*. The argument starts with an account of our experience of shape, and then generalizes that account to the experience of colour.[4]

Above we supposed that Mary has a hallucination of a tomato. Let's now suppose that she has an ordinary, non-hallucinatory experience of one. Let's start with the question: how does Mary perceptually represent the shape, *being round*? This is the "representation relation question" concerning shape.

Most philosophers are realists about space as we perceive it: they think that the shapes we perceptually represent are real properties of objects that are detected by our visual systems (but see note 26 for dissent). So the simplest answer would seem to be that Mary perceptually represents this property in much the same way that a thermometer represents a temperature. Very roughly: she perceptually represents the property of being round by virtue of undergoing an internal state (namely, a neural pattern) that, under biologically normal conditions, is typically caused by ("tracks") the instantiation of that shape in the environment. (Likewise for more primitive spatial features, like edges and angles.) This is a simple version of what we might call the "tracking" theory of how we perceptually represent shape.

Once we accept this "tracking" model of how Mary perceptually represents roundness, considerations of uniformity suggest using that same model to explain how she perceptually represents the reddish quality that seems to her to be co-instantiated with roundness. On such a uniform view, sensible redness, like roundness, is a real, objective property of the tomato that our visual system causally detects or tracks. What could this property be? Our visual system tracks *reflectance properties:* that is, *dispositions to reflect certain amounts of incident light across the visible spectrum*. Objects that have different colours will have different reflectances (see Figure 23.1 below). So if we say that sensible redness *just is* a particular reflectance property of the tomato, the payoff is that we can then say that Mary perceptually represents this property *in the same way* she represents the property of being round.

This view may seem immediately implausible because sensible colours seem to be *non-dispositional, simple* properties that you can't define in other terms. But maybe this is just wrong. On the basis of ordinary experience, it doesn't seem to us that water is H_2O. But that is what water is. Similarly, maybe sensible colours are in fact complex dispositional properties involving light, even if this is not visually evident.[5]

This approach also applies to illusion and hallucination. For example, return to Mary's tomato-like *hallucination*. How can she stand in the perceptual representation relation to the property *being reddish* (and also the property *being round*), even though it is not instantiated before her? What is it for this sensible property to be *ostensibly present* to her? On the tracking view, the answer is that the property *being reddish* is just a reflectance property. And Mary stands in a *tracking relation* to this property, even though she is hallucinating and this property isn't instantiated before her. Roughly, this consists her standing in this relation to it: she undergoes a neural pattern that is *normally* caused by its instantiation (when she sees the tomato, for instance).[6]

This yields *response-independent representationalism* about colour experience. It combines representationalism with the hypothesis that sensible colours are (like shapes) real properties objects that are totally independent of how we respond to them.[7]

Response-independent representationalism is *externalist*. On this view, the characters of your colour experiences are not fixed by the intrinsic features of your neural processes. Rather, they are fixed by what reflectance properties those neural processes track in the extracranial world. For instance, Tye, a leading proponent, says that "[the brain] is not where phenomenal character is to be found" (1995, 162–3). Instead, his slogan is "phenomenal character is in the world" (2009, 119). So, for instance, the phenomenal character of your experience of red is not constituted by a neural pattern, but by a reflectance property (see Figure 23.1 below).

Response-independent representationalism, in the version we are considering, is also *reductive*. It combines representationalism with a reductive physicalist approach to experience. It holds that sensible colours are *identical with* complex physical properties (namely, reflectance properties) and the perceptual representation relation is *identical with* a complex physical relation between subjects and those complex physical properties (namely, a "tracking" relation). So it is attractively simple.[8]

However, there are also arguments against response-independent representationalism. Here we will look at two types of argument: the *structural-mismatch argument* and *arguments from variation*.

First, the *structural-mismatch* argument. To illustrate, suppose that someone—call him *Maxwell*—consecutively experiences a purple-looking grape, a blue-looking ball, and finally a green-looking leaf. Now suppose Maxwell says, "blue resembles purple more than green". This is an evident truth about the *resemblance structure* of the sensible colours.

But it is a truth that response-independent representationalists apparently cannot accommodate. For the actual reflectance types typical of such objects are shown in Figure 23.1 below. On response-independent representationalism, the sensible colours purple, blue, and green *just are* these reflectance-types. So, on this view, Maxwell's statement is true just in case the blue *reflectance type* (in the middle) resembles the purple *reflectance type* (on the left) more than the green reflectance type (on the right). But, somewhat surprisingly, this is apparently not true. In fact, if anything, the blue reflectance type resembles the *green* reflectance type more than the purple reflectance type. So the identification of the sensible colours with the corresponding reflectances types implies that Maxwell's statement "blue resembles purple more than green" is *false*. Indeed, it seems to imply that "blue resembles *green* more than purple" is true! Since these implications are incorrect, the fact of structural-mismatch shows that sensible colours must be *distinct from* the corresponding response-independent reflectance types of objects.[9]

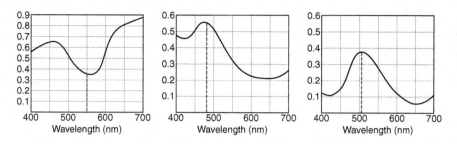

Figure 23.1 Reflectances typical of purple, blue, and green objects.

Source: from MacAdam (1985).

Why is there such a surprising mismatch between resemblances among the apparent colours of objects and the resemblances among those objects' reflectances? The answer seems to lie in our neural responses to those reflectances. For instance, even though the blue reflectance and the green reflectance are very similar, they lead to quite different neural responses in the brain, and this is why they lead to experiences of quite different sensible colours. This strongly suggests an alternative to response-independent representationalism. In particular, it suggests an account of sensible colours, and of their resemblances, in terms of our *neural responses*. We will return to these points later.

Some response-independent representationalists have tried to answer the structural-mismatch argument. In particular, Byrne and Hilbert (2003) have tried to give a response-independent account of the truth of "blue resembles purple more than green" in terms of reflectances. First, they assert that there are four basic *hue-magnitudes*, namely, *being reddish, being greenish, being yellowish*, and *being bluish*. They identify each of these four hue-magnitudes with a disjunction of reflectances (2003, 55). Thus, *being bluish* is just the disjunction of reflectances possessed by bluish objects (e.g. blue objects, purple objects, etc.). Then they say that the truth of "blue resembles purple more than green" amounts to the following: the blue reflectance-type and the purple reflectance-type, but *not the green reflectance-type*, imply a common hue-type (in this case, *being bluish*), that is, belong to one of the aforementioned disjunctions of reflectances. In short, they hold that when we say "blue resembles purple more than green", what we are saying is true just in case the relevant reflectance-types stand in the *hue-difference relation*, that is, the relation *x* and *y*, but not *z, imply belonging to a common hue-type (that is, imply having one of the aforementioned disjunctions of reflectances)*.

Byrne and Hilbert's response to the structural-mismatch argument faces several problems of detail.[10] However, here we will focus on one general worry about their discussion. Although we are focusing on sensible colours, it is important to realize that the structural-mismatch argument poses a *general* problem for response-independent representationalists. Therefore, to answer the argument, it is not enough to focus just on the case of sensible colours, as Byrne and Hilbert do.

Let's look at the experience of smell. Byrne and Hilbert (2003, 59) note that, because we expect a uniform account of different sensible properties, response-independent representationalism about the experience of colours stands or falls with response-independent representationalism about the experience of other types of sensible properties. So if response-independent representationalism is right for the experience of colour, you would expect a parallel account to apply to the experience of smell. On such an account, smell qualities (citrus, minty, etc.) are response-independent chemical types, and we perceptually represent them because our olfactory systems track them.

However, the structural-mismatch argument against response-independent representational-ism rears its head here as well. To illustrate, let's take another example based on our actual resemblance judgements. Suppose that, after seeing objects with the reflectances shown in Figure 23.1, Maxwell consecutively smells the chemical types shown in Figure 23.2 below.

As a matter of fact, even though the first two chemical types are very different, they produce very similar neural responses in us. They cause in us experiences of similar, but distinguishable, citrus-like qualities (Howard *et al.* 2009). The third chemical type smells minty. So, Maxwell will judge "the middle smell (citrus$_1$) resembles the first smell (citrus$_2$) more than the third smell (minty)". This statement is evidently true. But, again, response-independent representationalism seems to have the absurd implication that it is false. For, on this view, the smell qualities that Maxwell experiences *just are* the *external response-independent chemical types* shown in Figure 23.2, which his olfactory system tracks. And the middle chemical type does *not* resemble the first chemical type more than the third—if anything, it resembles the third more than the first. Given the empirical facts, response-independent representationalism about smell just seems clearly wrong.

Response-independent representationalists like Byrne and Hilbert haven't responded to the structural-mismatch argument in the case of smell resemblance. Nothing like their "hue-difference" account applies here. As is well-known, there simply are no privileged "basic smell categories" in the way that Byrne and Hilbert think that there are four basic hue categories.

Here is another element of the structural-mismatch problem for response-independent rep-resentationalists. To illustrate, suppose that we encounter an island where all humans lack the experience of chromatic colours—they only experience black-white-grey—and also lack the sense of smell. Still, because they do experience many *other* qualities (achromatic colours, taste qualities, audible qualities), they can acquire a general, topic-neutral concept of comparative resemblance among qualities, "quality *x* resembles quality *y* more than quality *z*". Now, suppose that we tell one of the islanders—call him "Larry" —about the colours and smell qualities I've discussed above, which are unlike any qualities he's experienced. And suppose we ask him to just guess the resemblances of these qualities that he cannot experience. Employing his general concept of comparative resemblance among qualities, he makes the following guess:

[#] Blue resembles purple more than green and the citrus$_1$ smell resembles the citrus$_2$ smell more than the minty smell.

Intuitively, Larry's guess is (determinately) *true*. Analogy: given a finite number of examples of arithmetical sums, Larry can acquire a general concept of *plus*, which he can then use to make true (or false) claims about new cases.

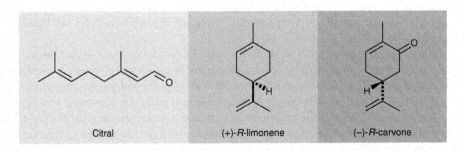

Citral   (+)-*R*-limonene   (−)-*R*-carvone

Figure 23.2 From Margot (2009).

However, response-independent representationalists cannot explain how Larry's guess [#] could be determinately true. For, on this view, the qualities his guess is about are the *reflectance-types* and *chemical properties* represented in the figures above. So, on this view, Larry's guess is true just in case the ordered-triple <the blue reflectance, the purple reflectance, the green reflectance> *and* the ordered-triple <R-limonene, citral, R-carvone> both satisfy a general, topic-neutral relation of comparative resemblance that is expressed by his use of the resemblance-predicate in [#]. But how could Larry's history on the island (his interaction with other physical properties) determine that his use of the resemblance predicate picks out a relation *that is satisfied by both of these trios of disparate physical properties, physical properties he has never interacted with*? The problem is not that there are *no* relations that are satisfied by these trios. Since relations are abundant, there are in fact *infinitely* many such relations; they are extremely disjunctive, unnatural relations, since they are instantiated by trios of disparate physical properties. Rather, the problem is that there are also infinitely many relations defined over reflectances and chemical properties *that are not satisfied by these trios*. And *since all these relations are equally unnatural and disjunctive, it's very hard how Larry's history on the island could have determined that his use of the resemblance predicate picks out a relation of the first sort rather than a relation of the second sort*. (It is not the case that relations of the first sort are more "natural" than relations of the second sort, in the way that *plus* is more natural than *quus*, and therefore easier for Larry to refer to: see Lewis 1983, 375–6.) That is why, on response-independent representationalism, it's hard to see how Larry's guess [#] could be determinately true.[11]

In the next section, we will see that alternative forms of representationalism avoid these problems concerning structural-mismatch.

Let us now turn to a second type of argument against response-independent representationalism: *arguments from variation*. We will consider a few different arguments of this kind.

Consider first an argument from *actual* cases of variation. While we are trichromats, some birds have a tetrachromatic colour vision system that is sensitive to UV light. There is reason to think that, when a human and such a bird see a tomato, they experience different sensible colours. There is also variation *among* normal humans. For instance, the colour chip might look pure blue to John and greenish blue to Jane, where John and Jane both have normal colour vision. On representationalism, such variation means that different perceivers disagree concerning what sensible colours they perceptually represent objects as having. But if so, then it looks like they are stuck with saying that some perceivers are getting it right and the others are getting it wrong. But this kind of misrepresentation is implausible. All the perceivers have equal claim to being veridical perceivers of colour.

However, this argument is unpersuasive. Response-independent representationalists have another option: they might accommodate such cases by accepting *colour pluralism* (Tye and Bradley 2001; Byrne and Hilbert 2003, 16). To explain why the tomato looks different to us and to the birds, they might say that the tomato objectively possesses the colour red *and* it also objectively possesses an alien colour that we cannot imagine constituted by UV light. We track and thereby perceptually represent the red colour while the bird tracks and thereby perceptually represents the alien colour. So there is no colour misrepresentation. Byrne and Hilbert (1997, 272–3) and Kalderon (2011) extend pluralism to variation among humans. The colour chip viewed by John and Jane is *both* pure blue and slightly greenish blue, where these shades are identical with distinct but overlapping ranges of reflectances. John and Jane's different visual systems track and thereby represent these *different* but equally real properties of the chip.[12]

Because actual cases do not clearly undermine response-independent representationalism, some rely on the conceivability of certain *hypothetical* "altered experience" cases to try to undermine the view. One prominent example is David Chalmers. To illustrate, let's turn back to the example about Suppose Maxwell. Maxwell looks at the ball with the middle reflectance shown in Figure 23.1. Then it looks *bluish* to him. Chalmers (2010, 415–16; and 400, n. 7) would say that it's conceivable that there should be another individual—call him *Twin Maxwell*—belonging to another human-like species who bears the *tracking relation* to *the very same* response-independent reflectance property of the ball as Maxwell, but who *phenomenally represents* a totally different sensible colour—say, *being greenish*. If the conceivability of this "altered experience" case shows that it is really possible, then of course the phenomenal representation relation cannot be identified with a tracking relation, and sensible colours cannot be identified with reflectance properties.

In response, response-independent representationalists like Tye (2000, 109–11) have said that, when it comes to such cases, mere conceivability doesn't establish possibility. According to this response, such altered spectrum cases are *conceivable*, but maybe they are not *really possible*. Chalmers himself concedes (2010, 152) that such conceivability arguments may fail because we are ignorant of the true nature of the physical world. So there is reason to doubt that the mere *conceivability* of hypothetical "altered spectrum" cases refutes the externalist approach of response-independent representationalism.

This brings us to a final type of argument against response-independent representationalism based on variation in colour vision. This argument is similar to the previous one, except that it relies on *research in neuroscience*, rather than mere conceivability, to argue for the possibility of a certain kind of "altered spectrum" case that is inconsistent with response-independent representationalism. This argument may succeed where the previous arguments from variation fail.

To illustrate the relevant research in neuroscience, we can use the same example that we used to illustrate the structure argument: the example where Maxwell consecutively experiences a grape, a ball, and a leaf with the reflectance-types shown in Figure 23.1. He then experiences purple, blue, and green. His colour experience of the ball resembles his colour experience of the grape more than his colour experience of the leaf. This phenomenological fact cannot be explained in terms of the reflectances of those objects tracked by his visual system: as we noted before, the reflectance of the ball does *not* resemble the reflectance of the grape more than the reflectance of the leaf. Now here is a question that we haven't looked at yet: what then *is* the explanation? Recent neuroscience supports the hypothesis that the explanation lies in his *neural responses* to those reflectances. In particular, Brouwer and Heeger (2009) and Bohon *et al.* (2016) found that, in brain area V4, neural similarity among distributed patterns of activity predicts phenomenal similarity among colour experiences. In fact, if you order these distributed neural patterns by overall similarity, then they form a circle akin to the "colour circle". So we can conjecture that the reason why *Maxwell's colour experience of the ball resembles his colour experience of the grape more than his colour experience of leaf* is that his internal *V4 neural representation* of the ball is more like his *V4 neural representation* of the grape than his *V4 neural representation* of the leaf. The explanation is to be found inside, not outside.

Now we can use this research to construct a two-step argument for the possibility of a hypothetical altered spectrum case that is inconsistent with the externalist approach of response-independent representationalism.

First step. Imagine that Maxwell has a twin, Twin Maxwell, in a hypothetical human-like community that evolved differently than humans. Just like Maxwell, Twin Maxwell consecutively experiences a grape, a ball, and a leaf with the reflectances shown in Figure 23.1. Let us suppose that Twin Maxwell's V4 neural representations of the grape and the leaf are identical with Maxwell's. However, because of naturally evolved differences in this community's postreceptoral wiring, let us suppose that Twin Maxwell's V4 neural representation of the *middle* object only—the ball—differs from Maxwell's. Specifically, while Maxwell's V4 neural representation of the ball resembles his V4 neural representation of the grape more than his V4 neural representation of the leaf, in Twin Maxwell the *opposite* his true: his V4 neural representation of the ball resembles his V4 neural representation of the *leaf* more than his V4 neural representation of the grape. As a result, while Maxwell sorts the ball with the grape, Twin Maxwell sorts it with the leaf. At the same time, we can suppose that Twin Maxwell's V4 neural representation of the ball, although it is different from Maxwell's V4 neural representation, *tracks* exactly the same reflectance-type as Maxwell's V4 neural representation, namely a reflectance-type that includes the reflectance shown in the middle in Figure 23.1. Therefore, on viewing the ball, they bear the *tracking relation* to the very *same reflectance-type*. Analogy: two people, in who belong to different language communities, can use different words to track the same type of object.[13]

So far, we have only stipulated the physical facts about the case. We have left open how Twin Maxwell's colour experiences of the objects compare to Maxwell's. That is the crucial issue.

Second step. What is the most reasonable view on this issue? Well, when it comes to the first and third objects, namely the grape and the leaf, everything is physically the same between Maxwell and Twin Maxwell: they respond to the reflectances of these objects with the very same neural processing and the very same V4 neural states. So, presumably, the grape looks *purplish* to both, and the leaf looks *greenish* to both. But what about their experience of the ball in between? We know that, while Maxwell's V4 neural representation of the ball resembles his V4 neural representation of the *purple-looking grape* more than his V4 neural representation of the green-looking leaf, in Twin Maxwell the opposite is true: Twin Maxwell's V4 neural representation of the ball resembles his V4 neural representation of the *green-looking leaf* more than his V4 neural representation of the purple-looking grape. We also know that similarity among the reflectances tracked by the colour system is a very poor predictor of phenomenal similarity and that similarity in V4 neural states is the only good predictor of phenomenal similarity. So, the most reasonable view is that, on viewing the ball, while Maxwell experiences *blue*, Twin Maxwell experiences a *greenish colour*. This verdict is also supported by their different sorting dispositions.

But this most reasonable verdict about the case is inconsistent with response-independent representationalism. On response-independent representationalism, they should have the very same colour experience, *because they bear the tracking relation to the very same reflectance-type*. The neural difference shouldn't make a difference to the character of their experiences, because it doesn't make for a difference in what they track. Since this verdict is not reasonable, we must reject response-independent representationalism. Even though they *track* the *same* response-independent *reflectance-type*, Maxwell and Twin Maxwell *experience* different *sensible colours*, contrary to response-independent representationalism.

Let us use "internal-dependence" to name the thesis that there are possible hypothetical cases in which two individuals have different experiences (and hence, given representationalism, phenomenally represent different properties) because they have suitably different neural states, even though those neural states track exactly the same response-independent properties. In general, the present argument has two steps. First, many different lines of research, across the sense-modalities, provide overwhelming support for internal-dependence.[14] Second, response-independent representationalism is incompatible with internal-dependence. Call this *the internal-dependence argument.*[15]

Notice that the internal-dependence argument against response-independent representationalism differs from the structure argument, even if we used the same example to illustrate both arguments. The structure argument was that response-independent representationalism cannot accommodate the truth of claims like [#], given the mismatch between our judgements of similarity among sensible properties and the similarity relations among the corresponding response-independent physical properties. The internal-dependence argument is different. The internal-dependence argument is that response-independent representationalism, as an externalist theory of phenomenal character, cannot accommodate an additional fact: the empirically supported role of the brain in shaping the phenomenal character of experience.

The internal-dependence argument may succeed where other arguments from variation fail. It is invulnerable to the "pluralist" response that response-independent representationalists may use to handle *actual* cases of variation. For, even if the ball has a plurality of chromatic properties, we have stipulated that Maxwell and Twin Maxwell track exactly *the same* one when they see the ball. So response-independent representationalism inevitably delivers the mistaken verdict that they experience the same sensible colour, despite the radical neural and behavioural differences between them (Cohen 2009, 86).[16] Further, the internal-dependence argument is invulnerable to the "mere conceivability doesn't entail possibility" response that can be used to answer David Chalmers' argument against response-independent representationalism. In fact, the internal-dependence argument doesn't rely on conceivability at all to establish the possibility of individuals experiencing different sensible colours while tracking the same response-independent properties. Instead, it provides a two-step *empirical argument* for this possibility.[17]

Given internal-dependence, *internal neural responses* play a big role in determining what sensible colours we perceptually represent in external space. This brings us to response-dependent representationalism.

3 Response-dependent representationalism

I will introduce *response-dependent representationalism* by way of explaining how it might accommodate "internal-dependence". Recall that, given internal dependence, Maxwell and Twin Maxwell track the same reflectance property of the ball, but nevertheless perceptually represent it as having different sensible colours, namely *being bluish* and *being greenish*, due to their differing internal neural states.

In one version, the proposal of response-dependent representationalists is that the different sensible colours that Maxwell and Twin Maxwell perceptually represent are identical with the different dispositions of the ball to cause their differing internal neural states (call them *"N1"* and *"N2"*).[18] So, the bluish sensible colour that Maxwell experiences is identical with a response-dependent property of the ball along the lines of: *normally causing neural state N1 in members of one's kind.* (Or maybe *normally causing N1 in members of some kind or other.*) By contrast, the greenish sensible colour that Twin Maxwell perceptually represents is identical with a different such property: *normally causing neural state N2 in members of one's kind.* On this view, the visual system is narcissistic: it represents how objects affect the visual system.

So response-dependent representationalism shows more promise in accommodating internal-dependence than response-independent representationalism. Unlike response-independent representationalism, it may also be able to accommodate our "structure judgements". On this view, judgements about the resemblances among sensible colours are not about response-independent reflectances properties of objects like those in Figure 23.1, as on response-independent representationalism. Rather, they are judgements about response-dependent properties of objects of the form *normally causing neural response N.* Now, such response-dependent properties resemble insofar as the responses in terms of which they are defined resemble (Johnston 1992, 240). So if, as empirical research seems to indicate (Brouwer and Heeger 2009), the resemblances among our internal neural states in the colour vision system match our judgements of resemblances among sensible colours, then those judgements come out true. Response-independent repre-sentationalists can generalize the same account to our judgements of resemblances among other sensible properties, such as judgements about the resemblances among smells considered in the previous section.

However, response-dependent representationalism faces problems of its own. We will focus on two.

First, response-dependent representationalists have focused almost exclusively on what I have called the "sensible colours question". But what is their answer to the "representation relation question" about how we *represent* sensible colours?

As noted in §2, it is natural to use a broadly "tracking" model to explain how we can per-ceptually represent spatial properties, and considerations of uniformity suggest generalizing this account of the perceptual representation of sensible colours. But response-dependent represen-tationalists cannot accept a tracking model for the perceptual representation of sensible colours.

To see this, return to the case of Maxwell and Twin Maxwell. On response-dependent rep-resentationalism, they perceptually represent the ball as having different sensible colours, identi-fied with relational properties of the form *normally causing so-and-so neural state*. But they do not in any sense *track* these different complex, relational properties. For instance, Maxwell's internal neural state *N1* is not *caused*, under biological normal conditions, by the instantiation by the ball of the relational property: *normally causing that very neural state, N1, in Maxwell's population*. For the property of *normally causing N1* isn't itself casually efficacious in causing *N1*. Our visual systems are not causally sensitive to such properties. Furthermore, *N1* arguably doesn't have the *biological function* of tracking this specific ecologically insignificant relational property. Similar remarks apply to Twin Maxwell. On the contrary, Maxwell and Twin Maxwell's different internal neural states are caused by, and have the function of tracking, the *same reflectance property* of the ball (Cohen 2009, 86), since the colour system is geared to recovering surface reflect-ances. Since response-dependent representationalists claim that they *perceptually represent* different response-dependent properties, it follows that they cannot identify the perceptual representation relation with a standard tracking relation.

But if Maxwell and Twin Maxwell's visual systems do not have the function of tracking the relevant response-dependent properties of the ball, then what is the alternative account of how they perceptually represent them? Sydney Shoemaker, a prominent defender of this approach, candidly admits, "I have no fully satisfactory answer" (1994, 37). Call this the *representational problem*.

The problem is made more difficult by the fact that the ball has *multiple* response-dependent properties of this sort involving different subjects, different responses, and different conditions: for instance, it *normally causes certain V4 neural responses in Maxwell under certain conditions*, it *nor-mally causes certain V4 neural responses in Twin Maxwell under certain conditions*, it *normally causes certain retinal activity in Maxwell*, and so on. What makes it the case that Maxwell perceptually represents one *specific* response-independent property on this list, and Twin Maxwell perceptu-ally represents another? What makes it the case that certain *specific* response-dependent prop-erties are visually represent to them?

In fact, the problem is even more difficult than this. For, in addition to perceptually repre-senting sensible colours, we of course perceptually represent *spatial properties*, such as shapes, positions, and distances. These spatial properties are evidently *not* response-dependent properties of the form: *normally causing neural response X*. So, response-dependent representationalists must answer the following question: what is the *single, uniform* reductive theory of the perceptual representation relation that implies that in some cases we perceptually represent funny *response-dependent* properties of the form *normally causing neural response X in individuals with colour system S* (or whatever response-dependent with which they identify the sensible colours), while in other cases we perceptually represent *response-independent* spatial properties of a radically different sort? It would be implausible to answer by saying that the shape–system has the function of indicating response-independent shape properties, while the colour-system has the sole function of indicating these entirely different, funny response-dependent properties (rather than, say, the function of indicating response-independent *reflectance* properties, or simply the function of guiding our behaviour in a useful way). Since the notion of "the function" of a system is unclear, it is just not at all obvious what could this mean and what could make it the case.[19]

There is a second, much simpler problem for response-dependent representationalism. Briefly, on this view, sensible colours are *relations* to types of neural states and types of perceivers. But this doesn't fit the phenomenology. Sensible colours just don't look like relations. They seem non-relational. Indeed, they seem "simple". Call this the *phenomenological problem*.[20]

So far, we have looked at one version of response-dependent representationalism. But it is not the only version. Colin McGinn (1996) has devised a complicated novel version that is designed to avoid the phenomenological problem. As a bonus, it suggests an answer to the representational problem. Let me explain.

The version of response-dependent representationalism we have so far considered is *reductive*: it *identifies* sensible colours with response-dependent, physical properties of objects (see note 8). McGinn (1999) defends a form of representationalism. But, against reductive representationalism, he insists (1996, 541–2) that, "when we see an object as red we see it as having a *simple*, monadic, local property of the object's surface", distinct from any complex physical property. He is a *non-reductive representationalist*.

Even though he thinks colours are simple, non-relational properties of objects, McGinn also holds that it is just a brute "law of metaphysics" that their instantiation by objects is tied to those objects' effects on perceivers. This is what makes his view qualify as *response-dependent*. In particular, he postulates the following general principle: it is metaphysically necessary that an object has a simple sensible colour *C* if and only if, and because, it normally causes the experience of that very sensible colour, *C*, in some normal perceivers under some normal conditions. Call this [Bicon], because it is bi-conditional claim.

Let's take an example. The ball in our example above has the property: *normally causing experiences of the property of being blue in normal humans (like Maxwell) under normal conditions*. By [Bicon], the fact that the ball has this relational property *grounds* the fact that it actually instantiates the property *being blue*. Nevertheless, according to McGinn, *being blue* is a "simple", non-relational property of the ball that is *distinct from* this relational property that always grounds it. So McGinn thinks that [Bicon] doesn't amount to a *reduction* of *being blue*. Likewise, because the ball is also disposed to normally look greenish to normal twin humans (like Twin Maxwell), it *also* instantiates the simple property *being greenish*, according to [Bicon]. In general, thanks to [Bicon], objects are guaranteed to really possess exactly those simple colours that they normally appear to possess.

McGinn's view provides a unique origin story for colour. Given [Bicon], before sentient creatures evolved, objects had no sensible colours, for the simple reason that they did not habitually look to have any colours to any individuals. Then brains evolved that have an intrinsic capacity to enable us to perceptually represent objects as having certain simple sensible colours. That is, brains evolved that in this sense "project" simple colours into objects. Thanks to [Bicon], those objects thereby *acquired those* (and only those) simple sensible colours, in addition to their scientific properties. In other words, [Bicon] guarantees a fortunate match between appearance and reality when it comes to sensible colours.

McGinn's non-reductive response-dependent view avoids the two problems with the reductive version considered above. First and most obviously, it avoids the "phenomenological problem" facing the reductive version. For, on McGinn's non-reductive version, sensible colours *themselves* are simple, non-relational properties of objects just as they appear to be, even if by [Bicon] they are *grounded in* distinct complex, relational properties of those objects.

As we saw, the reductive response-dependent theorist also faces a "representational problem". McGinn faces a question here too: how do we manage to perceptually represent these alleged "simple" sensible colours? McGinn also cannot identify the perceptual representation between subjects and sensible colours with the externally determined "tracking relation", for a couple of reasons. This goes against internal-dependence. And it requires that sensible colours are "out there" prior to our representation of them, which goes against [Bicon].

However, McGinn's view suggests an alternative answer to the "representational problem". Because he is already an anti-reductionist about sensible colours, he might provide a parallel *non-reductive* account of our ability to perceptually represent those sensible colours. In particular, he might say that this relation is irreducible, just as he thinks sensible colours are. That is, there is *no* true identity of the form: the perceptual representation relation = complex physical relation R. (Compare: it is implausible that there is a general *reduction* of the reference relation in physical terms, given that we can refer to such diverse things as chairs, numbers, and uninstantiated kinds.) Nevertheless, he might say that, whenever one bears this relation to some sensible colours, this is *grounded in* one's total internal neural state. Indeed, maybe it is possible in principle to systematically "decode" what sensible colours an individual perceptually represents from her V4 neural patterns (Brouwer and Heeger 2009; Haynes 2009, Bohon *et al.* 2016). This yields a non-reductive and internalist form of representationalism (Chalmers 2010; Horgan 2014). It might be combined with non-reductive physicalism: experiential facts are *grounded in* physical facts, even if a general reduction is impossible.

It is worth noting another virtue of McGinn's view: it nicely avoids the structural-mismatch problem that we brought against response-independent representationalism (§2). On his view, the sensible colours that we perceptually represent are *simple* properties, which are quite distinct from the types of reflectances shown in Figure 23.1. So McGinn is free to say that these simple properties generally stand in exactly the resemblance relations they seem to stand in, even if the corresponding reflectances-types do not. For instance, he might say that, when Maxwell says "this shade of blue resembles this shade of purple more than that shade of green", he is correctly reporting that the shades stand in a unique unanalysable relation of intrinsic qualitative resemblance (see e.g. Allen 2017, 124–5). Since this relation is very "natural" (in the sense of Lewis 1983), McGinn's view also accommodates the point (illustrated in §2 with the story about Larry on a remote island) that, once we experience a finite number of resembling qualities, we can easily determinately grasp this general relation. Then we can apply it to new qualities, and thereby make true or false claims.

McGinn's view also avoids a general problem that Chalmers (2010, 400) raises for all realist views of colour. Chalmers suggests that realists are led to *chromatic explosion*. Let's go back to the ball with the reflectance shown in Figure 23.1. It normally looks one colour to Maxwell. It could have looked another colour to "Twin Maxwell". Indeed, Chalmers holds that, for any colour you choose, the ball *could* normally look that colour to a possible perceiver. So, to avoid favouritism or arbitrariness, mustn't realists say that, right now, the ball has *all* of those colours? McGinn's view— which Chalmers doesn't consider—avoids this radical chromatic explosion. Given his [Bicon] principle, the ball possesses *only* those simple colours it appears to have to some *actual* normal perceiver under some normal conditions. In general, an object only has enough colours to make the experiences of *actual* perceivers generally veridical, and not more. This is a *limited* colour pluralism.

While McGinn's view avoids some problems, it also faces a few new ones. Here I will mention two.

First, the case for [Bicon] is unclear. It is not *a priori*. This is shown by the fact that the *irrealist* representationalist view to be considered in the next section rejects [Bicon], but it cannot be ruled out *a priori* (Tye 2000, 170). The only argument for [Bicon] seems to be that it allows McGinn to agree with our pre-theoretical conviction that objects have the sensible colours they appear to have. But our pre-theoretical convictions have a bad track-record.

Second, simplicity considerations count against [Bicon]. It reports a necessary connection between two highly disparate sorts of properties, namely, *simple, occurrent sensible colours* and *complex dispositions of objects* to appear to have those sensible colours. It is not derivable from logic or from any general modal principles. It would have to be accepted as an additional, brute principle—a special brute "law of metaphysics" (Rosen 2009, 133), or a "grounding dangler".

Third, [Bicon] faces a problem about borderline cases. As Hardin (1988) has emphasized, lighting conditions can radically influence colour appearance but there is no precise cutoff between normal and abnormal lighting conditions. Now suppose that you view a colour chip in lighting conditions C, where this is a *borderline* case of normal conditions. On McGinn's view, there is a specific simple shade that you determinately perceptually represent, which is somewhat different from the apparent shade of the chip in perfect daylight. Suppose you dub it "$blue_{31}$". Now, by [Bicon], the chip really instantiates $blue_{31}$ iff it looks $blue_{31}$ under normal conditions. Since in this case the right-hand side is indeterminate (since C is a *borderline* case of "normal conditions"), it follows from [Bicon] that the left-hand is indeterminate too. That is, there is this specific shade, $blue_{31}$, such that it is *indeterminate* whether the chip instantiates it. Hence [Bicon] requires "vagueness in the world", which many consider to be incoherent (Lewis 1993).

4 Irrealist representationalism

Irrealism holds that ordinary physical objects don't instantiate sensible colours. All that is out there are particles and waves and fields. It became very popular after the scientific revolution of the seventeenth century and was defended by Galileo, Newton, Descartes, and Locke. Hardin (1987) and Chalmers (2010) describe the rejection of realism in dramatic terms: they call it a "fall from Eden".

Traditionally, irrealists have said that, although sensible colours do not qualify ordinary physical objects, they do qualify *something*. For instance, if you look at a tomato, the reddish quality *is* instantiated by a round item you experience (called an "idea", a "sense datum", or a "visual field region") located in a kind of private mental arena created by your brain (Boghossian and Velleman 1989). On this view, you only ever experience such very life-like mental images, which you mistakenly believe to be physical objects. But, as I noted at the outset, such "sense data" create serious puzzles.

Representationalism has made possible a new and more defensible form of irrealism. *Irrealist representationalism* holds that, when you view a tomato, you *perceptually represent* the property *being reddish* as co-instantiated with the property *being round*. So it *seems* that these properties are instantiated together before you. But, in fact, the property of being reddish is not instantiated by *anything*. It is not instantiated by a *physical* round thing before you; and it is also not instantiated by a *mental* round thing—there is no such thing. There is no reddish thing there of any kind, even though there seems to be one. So the property *being reddish* is a bit like the property *being a unicorn*: it is an entirely uninstantiated property. When it comes to sensible colours at least, the brain is a kind of "partial virtual reality machine", which projects onto objects some features that they don't really have.[21]

In some respects, irrealist representationalism resembles McGinn's view considered above. It shares with McGinn's view the following two claims. First, we perceptually represent objects as having *simple* colour properties, which cannot be identified with reflectances or the like. Second, the brain has an intrinsic and innate capacity to enable us to perceptually represent these properties, without any contribution from the world. The difference is this: McGinn wants to accept the commonsense view that objects normally have the very simple colour properties that the brain projects onto those objects, so he posits a brute principle, [Bicon], that guarantees this result. By contrast, irrealists reject [Bicon]. They deny that objects really have the simple colour properties that the brain projects.

What is the argument for irrealist representationalism? In his influential paper, "Perception and the Fall from Eden", David Chalmers provides a mostly *a priori* defence of this view. As we saw (§2), he uses the conceivability of "altered spectrum cases" to rule out the view of response-independent representationalists that sensible colours are identical with reflectance properties. More generally, he argues that sensible colours cannot be identical with *any* physical properties, because there is an intuitive "epistemic gap" between sensible colours and all physical properties (2010, 399, 415). So, Chalmers concludes, sensible colours must be *simple, irreducible* properties. Then, as we noted before (§3), Chalmers argues that, to avoid arbitrariness, realists would need to accept the conclusion of "chromatic explosion": every object has every simple colour (p. 400)! (Allen (2017, 71–2 apparently defends this view.) Chalmers says that "this conclusion is even more counterintuitive than the [irrealist] conclusion that all color experiences are illusory" (ibid.). So, he opts for irrealism.

But this complex *a priori* rationale for irrealism faces problems. First of all, as we already noted, Chalmers' conceivability argument against externalist approaches like response-independent representationalism is open to the standard criticism that "conceivability doesn't establish possibility". In other words, response-independent representationalists might agree that "altered spectrum cases" like the case of Maxwell and Twin Maxwell are *conceivable*, but then just deny that they are possible. Second, even if representationalists accept the possibility of such cases, realism doesn't require "chromatic explosion". As we saw, McGinn's form of realism, which Chalmers does not consider, puts the brakes on chromatic explosion, and yet it is liberal enough to accommodate the veridicality of our actual colour experiences in normal conditions.

However, there is also a more *empirical* argument for irrealist representationalism. This argument has two stages. *First stage:* representationalists can rule out *reductive* theories of sensible colours on the basis of empirical arguments, without having to rely on Chalmers' *a priori* considerations. In particular, sensible colours cannot be identified response-independent *reflectance properties* of objects. For this view is undermined by the structural-mismatch argument and the internal-dependence argument (§2). Sensible colours also cannot be identified with response-dependent properties of objects of the form: *normally causing neural response N in community C.* This view is undermined by the representational problem and the phenomenological problem (§3). So if representationalists want to be realists about sensible colour, then their only option is to accept a view like McGinn's on which objects have *simple* sensible properties *over and above* their physical properties. *Second stage:* this type of view can now be argued against on the basis of *simplicity considerations* (§3). McGinn's view requires the [Bicon] principle, which posits a massive unexplained *coincidence*. In particular, [Bicon] is the conjecture that, if we evolved so that our brain projects certain simple sensible colours onto objects, then *viola* those objects thereby *acquire* those very simple sensible colours. But why should nature be so obliging? There is no overwhelming *a priori* or empirical reason to accept this principle. Of course, it *could* be true. But irrealist representationalist will say that we are obliged to reject it for the same reason we are obliged to reject other needlessly complicated empirical theories.

Another consideration in favour of irrealist representationalism about colour experience over the realist forms of representationalism is this. There are especially strong empirical and *a priori* reasons to think various *qualities* we feel in bodily regions (pain qualities, "pins and needles", etc.) cannot be identified with any real, mind-independent physical properties of those bodily regions. There are also especially strong empirical reasons to think that smell properties (discussed in §2) as well as audible properties (e.g. *phoneme-types*) cannot be identified with real physical properties of external items. These are all "projected" qualities. Why should we continue to insist that *sensible colours* are an exception? Why insist that they are really possessed by external items, if these other sensible properties are not (Locke 1869, II.viii.16)?[22]

Finally, there is an evolutionary argument for taking irrealist representationalism seriously. The primary function of the sensory systems is to enhance adaptive fitness—not to represent the way the world really is. There is every reason to expect that this should sometimes involve embellishment or error, depending on an individual's unique ecology. For instance, even if fruits are not intrinsically bright or sweet, it is understandable that we evolved to experience them as bright and sweet.

Irrealism in some form or another is the dominant view among colour scientists. For instance, Cosmides and Tooby (1995, xi) maintain that "color is an invention that specialized circuitry computes and then projects onto physically colorless objects".

While irrealism is a popular view among colour scientists, it is typically considered to be an outlandish "position of last resort" among philosophers. There is a curious disconnect between philosophy and science. Let us consider some of the philosophical objections to irrealist representationalism, together with possible replies.

Objection. The irrealist representationalist holds that, when you see a tomato, then *redness* is in some sense *ostensibly present to you*, and this is bound up with the character of your experience, even though *it is not instantiated in the world or in your experience*. But this is difficult to understand.[23]

Reply. To see that this is not an objection, consider a different example. Suppose you have the condition known as "Charles Bonnet syndrome" which involves vivid hallucinations. You hallucinate an object with a very unusual shape. In this case, everyone should admit that, necessarily, in having this experience, you in *some* sense ostensibly presented with an unusual *shape property*, and this is bound up with the character of your experience, even if this property is not instantiated in your environment or in your experience (setting aside exotic objects like "sense data"). This explains why everyone recognizes a sense in which your experience is *non-veridical*. It also explains how your experience gives you the ability to refer to this unusual shape property (a shape property you might have not recently encountered in real life). If this kind of delusory presentation of an uninstantiated property can happen with respect to shape, why can't it happen with respect to colour?

Objection. But how could such colour illusions *always* happen? How could the brain enable us to perceptually represent properties of a wholly novel sort that have *never* been instantiated in the world? Our standard models for explaining how we represent properties appeal to *tracking* real instances of those properties in the world, but irrealists cannot accept this view. In short, irrealism requires a total mystery when it comes to the "representation relation question" (Tye 2000, 166).

Reply. Irrealist representationalists can make a few points in reply. *First*, we already know from internal-dependence that tracking theories fail in the special case of perceptual representation. For instance, Maxwell and Twin Maxwell experience different sensible colours but track the same reflectance properties. In view of this, the best view of perceptual representation may be the internalist, non-reductive view we considered in connection with McGinn's approach.

And that view is consistent with irrealism. On this internalist view, the brain has an intrinsic capacity to represent sensible colours and other sensible properties, *whether or not* they are instantiated in the world.[24]

Second, we already know, independently of the colour debate, that the brain is "creative": it is not limited to representing what is there. For instance, it can represent uninstantiated kinds and abstract objects (Chalmers 2010, 417). So why not uninstantiated sensible colours?[25]

Third, the claim of irrealist representationalists that the brain has an intrinsic capacity to represent unreal sensible properties may look mysterious only because we do not know enough about the brain. Maybe, if we had a more systematic understanding of the "neural code", we would understand why one neural state is the basis of representing the colour red, while another is the basis of representing the colour orange (Brouwer and Heeger 2009; Haynes 2009, Bohon *et al.* 2016).

Objection. Suppose you view a tomato. Then you have a neural representation of sensible redness "bound" in the brain with a neural representation of *roundness*. We just saw that irrealists must accept an internalist theory of how we perceptually represent sensible redness. But previously (§2) we saw that it is very natural to accept an externalist, tracking theory of how we perceptually represent shape. So irrealist representationalists require a non-uniform theory of perceptual representation. Since the perceptual representation of shape is inextricably bound up with the perceptual representation of sensible colour, such a non-uniform theory is untenable: if the perceptual representation of sensible colour is internally determined, so too must be the perceptual representation of shape.

Reply. In fact, irrealist representationalists are not committed to a non-uniform theory of perceptual representation. Chalmers (2010, 443) and Horgan (2014) have argued the perceptual representation of spatio-temporal properties is internally determined, just like the perceptual representation of sensible colours. In fact, one might go further and argue that perceived spatial-temporal relations are no more "out there" than sensible colours. For instance, it seems obvious that the spatial-temporal relations we phenomenally represent are not frame-relative, but relativity theory shows that no such relations are out there.[26]

Objection. Irrealist representationalism requires an implausible across-the-board error theory about all of our talk of colours.

Reply. In fact, irrealist representationalism does not require this. Recall Maxwell viewing the grape, the ball, and the leaf. He judges "the blue colour resembles the purple colour more than the green colour". Remember that response-independent representationalists have trouble accommodating the truth of this judgement (see Figure 23.1). By contrast, irrealists can hold that this is a perfectly true judgement about the relevant sensible colours, even though they are not instantiated. Compare: there can be truths about resemblances among complex shapes, even if they are not instantiated. Maxwell also judges "the grape is purple, the ball is blue, and the leaf is green". Irrealists can say that he thereby expresses or implicates a truth about how these things habitually look (Boghossian and Velleman 1989; for a somewhat different conciliatory approach, see Chalmers 2010).

5 Conclusion

One general moral to draw from the preceding overview is that representationalism about colour experience is a very flexible doctrine. It is compatible with just about every major view on the metaphysics of sensible colours.[27] The hope of representationalists is that their view can simultaneously accommodate two facts: (i) the phenomenological fact that we ostensibly experience sensible colours "out there" along with shapes and locations, and (ii) the empirical fact that the experience of sensible colours is bound up with neural processing in the head.[28]

Notes

1 A note on terminology: Most representationalists, for instance Byrne and Hilbert (2003) and Tye (2000), think that ordinary colour terms in English like "the colour red", or "redness", or "that colour" refer to what I'm calling "sensible redness". If they are right (and I think that they are), then we could drop the cumbersome term "sensible redness" and simply use "redness". But other representationalists, for instance Shoemaker (1994) and Chalmers (2010, essay 12), deny that ordinary colour terms to refer to this property. So, to refer to this property, they invent special technical terms, like "phenomenal redness" (Shoemaker), or "perfect redness" (Chalmers). We all have the same property in mind; we just use different terms to refer to it. To stay neutral on this terminological disagreement, I have decided to introduce the neutral term "sensible redness" to refer to this property.

2 However, the sense datum theory of colour experience has recently been defended by Brown (2010) and Robinson (1994, 59–74), among others.

3 Here and in what follows, I work with the simple *property-complex* formulation of representationalism. See Bealer (1982, 235–9), Dretske (1995, 101–2), McGinn (1999, 319–23), Chalmers (2012, 343), Tye (2014). On another formulation, representationalism is the view that having an experience consists in standing in a special relation (the "perceptual entertaining relation") to a *complete proposition* attributing sensible properties to things.

4 Armstrong (1987, 36) and Byrne and Hilbert (2003, 7) stress the desirability of a uniform account of *colour* and *shape*. The point to be developed is that it is desirable to have a uniform answer to the question of how we manage to *represent* colour and shape ("the representation relation question").

5 Due to "metamerism", the best view in the vicinity is that colours are extremely unnatural *disjunctions* or *types* of reflectances (Tye 2000; Byrne and Hilbert 2003). There is a serious problem about how we might "track" and represent such unnatural properties (Armstrong 1987, 42 and Byrne and Hilbert 2003, 792). But, for the sake of simplicity, I will ignore this issue.

6 More exactly, proponents of the tracking model identify the dyadic perceptual representation relation between individuals and sensible properties with a complex relation along the following lines: ëxëy(x is in an internal state that is poised for cognitive access and that has the systemic biological function of tracking property y). See Dretske (1995, 19–20), Tye (2000, 62), and Tye (2014, 51–2). This is a very simple sketch. Indeed, Byrne and Hilbert (2003) claim that *all* existing accounts are too simple. (MacPherson (2003) also raises a difficult puzzle about "novel colors".) However, I will use "tracking" generically to name *whatever* physical relation it is that we bear to reflectance properties which enables us to perceptually represent them, under the assumption that colours are reflectance properties. In this generic sense, even Byrne and Hilbert hold that perceptual representation is a matter of "tracking".

7 David Armstrong (e.g. 1984) is the originator of response-independent representationalism. More recent proponents of some form of this view include Dretske (1995), Tye (2000), Lycan (2001), Byrne and Hilbert (2003), Hill (2009).

8 On one general formulation, "reductive physicalism" about some property or relation R (*being reddish, being a city*, etc.) is the view that R is identical with a *complex property* built up from the properties on some short list of "basic" physical properties and relations (e.g. the fundamental physical properties, together with various "topic-neutral" properties and relations such as *causation* and *similarity*). For different conceptions and defences of reduction, see Lewis (1994), Jackson (1998, especially 62, 123), Dorr (2008), and Sider (2011, chaps. 7 and 13).

9 Philosophers who have put forward the structural-mismatch argument include Hardin (1988, 66–7) and Thompson (1995, chap. 3). Scientists have long recognized the point when it comes to other sensible properties. For instance, Stevens *et al.* (1937) famously argued that *perceived pitches* cannot be identified with response-independent *frequencies*, on the grounds that the relations (in particular, equal intervals) among apparent pitches do not match those among frequencies.

10 Here are three main problems of detail facing Byrne and Hilbert's hue-magnitude proposal. (1) Byrne and Hilbert give no response-independent account of truths involving *degree* such as: *the degrees of bluishness and reddishness in the ball are roughly equal* (so that *the ball roughly equally resembles a pure blue object and a pure red object*). Intuitively, this is not a truth about *numbers*, any more than *the height of the rectangle is equal to (or double, etc.) to its width* is about numbers. But if degrees of hue-magnitudes are not numbers, then what are they, and what is it for them to be "equal"? Byrne and Hilbert (2003, 55) apparently hold that *the degree of reddishness* that the ball possesses is just *a certain disjunction D1* of reflectances, namely the disjunction of the reflectances of all objects (all balanced blue-red objects, all balanced blue-green objects) that are bluish to this same degree. Likewise, they hold that *the degree of bluishness* that the ball

possesses is just another *disjunction D2 of reflectances*. This implies that *the degrees of bluishness and reddishness in the ball are roughly equal iff D1 is roughly equal to D2*. But if *D1* and *D2* are just distinct (but overlapping) disjunctions of reflectances, as Byrne and Hilbert claim, then what is it for *D1* to be "roughly equal to" *D2*? (2) Byrne and Hilbert also give no response-independent theory of degrees of *brightness*. One idea would be to equate brightness with physical luminance. But this idea fails. At equiluminance, reds are brighter than greens (Corney *et al.* 2009). Indeed, a yellow patch might be brighter than a white patch, even if the yellow patch has lower luminance (Conway 2013, 11). So how would Byrne and Hilbert analyse "colour *x* is brighter than colour *y*" in response-independent terms, in particular, in terms of reflectances? (3) Finally, any adequate account must accommodate the truth of *general* claims of colour resemblance such as "every colour on the hue-circle resembles nearby colours more than farther away colours". But Byrne and Hilbert's hue-difference account of colour resemblance is unable to accommodate the truth of such a general claim (Pautz 2011, 423–4, fn. 6). For instance, there are shades of purple *P1*, *P2*, and *P3* on the hue-circle such that that *P1* resembles *P2* more than *P3*; but they certainly don't satisfy the hue-difference relation as explained in the text. In response, Byrne and Hilbert might suggest that, for arbitrary colours *x*, *y* and *z*, *x* resembles *y* more than *z* iff there is some hue-magnitude *h* such that the *degree* of *h* of *x* is more similar to the *degree* of *h* of *y* than the *degree* of *h* of *z*. (Here I'm indebted to Keith Allen.) But this too is open to counterexamples: for instance, let *x* = R60, Y40, *y* = R63, B37, and *z* = R70, Y30. For other problems with Byrne and Hilbert's proposal, see Allen (2017, chap. 6).

11 The argument here is not that response-independent representationalists must show that the truth of Larry's guess [#] can be deduced *a priori* from the response-independent character of the physical properties shown in Figures 23.1 and 23.2. In fact, they certainly should reject this *a priority* claim for standard reasons (see Davies 2014, 301–3). Rather, the argument is that, even if they do reject this *a priority* claim, they still must at least gesture at an *a posteriori* account of how Larry managed to make a *true claim*, rather than a false (or indeterminate) one. Compare: a type-type neural identity theorist for pain needs to gesture at an *a posteriori* account of truths like "my second pain was more intense than my first pain" in terms of neural firing rates or whatever, even if they deny that such truths are *a priori* deducible from truths about firing rates and the line.

12 There is evidently no formal contradiction in the pluralist view of Byrne and Hilbert (1997) that the colour chip has one colour that is completely bluish and a distinct colour that is not completely bluish but rather a bit greenish as well as bluish. But it is very counterintuitive. For this reason, more recently, Byrne and Hilbert (2003) have converted to *inegalitarianism* about this case: they now assert that the chip does *not* have both shades. So, given response-independent representationalism, either John or Jane must be misrepresenting the chip. But now a new problem arises: since John and Jane are both normal perceivers, it is hard to see what could make it the case that one but not the other is guilty of misrepresentation (Cohen 2009). Byrne and Hilbert (2007, 90) reply that this is a general problem faced by anyone who accepts that John and Jane represent fine-grained colours. But, since Byrne and Hilbert also accept inegalitarianism instead of pluralism, they do face an *additional* question about John and Jane that others (for instance, pluralists) do not face, namely: what is the general theory of perceptual representation that entails that one of them perceptually represents a reflectance-type that the chip *possesses*, while the other perceptually represents a reflectance-type that it *does not possess*?

13 Let me clarify this case a bit. As I noted before (see footnote 5), because of metamerism, response-independent representationalists identify the blue colour of the ball with a general "class" or "disjunction" of reflectances. This might be called a "reflectance-type" or "reflectance-class" (Tye 2000; Byrne and Hilbert 2003). This reflectance-class includes the reflectance of the ball shown in Figure 23.1 (call this *R1*) *and* all the other reflectances (*R2*, *R3*, *R4*) of objects that normally have the same effect on the visual system and so look the same shade of blue. So, here is a more complete description of the case I'm imagining: When Maxwell views the ball, he has a V4 neural representation that tracks (is normally caused by), and thereby represents, this *reflectance-class* (that is, it can be caused by *R1* or *R2* or *R3* or *R4*). When Twin Maxwell views the ball, his V4 neural representation, although different, tracks (is normally caused by) this very same *reflectance-class* (*R1, R2, R3, R4*).

14 For research on colour vision supporting internal-dependence, see Brouwer and Heeger (2009), Conway (2013), Schmidt *et al.* (2014), Danilova and Mollon (2016), and Forder *et al.* (2017). For research on audition, taste, smell, and pain supporting internal-dependence, see Coghill *et al.* (1999), Howard *et al.* (2009), Chang *et al.* (2010), and Crouzet *et al.* (2015). For an overview, see Kriegeskorte and Kievit (2013). Since internal-dependence is especially well-supported for non-visual modalities, it is unlikely that colour vision is an exception.

15 For the internal-dependence argument, see Pautz (1998), (2003), and (2010). For discussion, see Cohen (2009, 82–8), Kalderon (2011, 250–6), Fish (2013, 58–9), and Allen (2017, 68–73). Kalderon (this volume) suggests that Shoemaker (2003, 269) uses a similar argument. But Shoemaker's argument is quite different. In fact, Shoemaker (2003, 269) gives no argument at all thinking that the relevant kind of "altered spectrum" case is possible except that we can conceive of it (he says "we can imagine" such a case). So he seems to defend the conceivability argument discussed above. We saw that this argument is vulnerable to the response "conceivability doesn't entail possibility". By contrast, the internal-dependence argument relies on *empirical research* across the various modalities to argue that such a case is possible, not mere conceivability. Therefore, it is not vulnerable to the response "conceivability doesn't entail possibility".

16 For the same reason, the response-independent representationalist cannot in this case use the inegalitarian response that Maxwell or Twin Maxwell is *misrepresenting* the colour of the ball, contrary to Byrne and Tye (2006, 253). For this point, see Cohen (2009, 86).

17 There is another important problem for response-independent representationalism quite different from the empirical problems I have focused on. In particular, Chalmers (2010, 354–5) suggests that this view faces a problem about *experiential indeterminacy*. Here is an especially difficult case (not considered by Chalmers). Consider the well-known "inverted earth case". (For details, see for instance Lycan 2001, 30–1.) But let's add a twist. To begin with, suppose that there is an Earthian male whose neural representation S of the sky has the biological function of tracking *blue*, and an inverted Earthian female whose neural representation S of the sky instead has the biological function of tracking *yellow*. Strictly speaking, they belong to different species, which evolved on the different planets independently. However, let us suppose that, by an outstanding coincidence, they are genetically nearly identical (except for their different colour vision), so that they can interbreed and have a child. Now here is the problem: on response-independent representationalism, it will presumably be *indeterminate* whether the *child's* neural representation of the sky, S, represents yellow or blue, since it is indeterminate whether in this creature S has the *historical, biological function* of tracking yellow or blue (for we may suppose that there is nothing that could settle whether the child belongs to one parent's species rather than the other's). If so, it will *indeterminate* whether it has a yellowish or bluish colour experience. But it is deeply counterintuitive that colour phenomenology could be radically indeterminate in this way.

18 This might be called "the neural response version" of response-dependent representationalism. Harman (1996, 10) and Kriegel (2009, 90) are proponents. Shoemaker (1994) defends a different version, on which the relevant responses are *colour experiences*. But it faces a serious circularity problem that is avoided by the neural response version. For discussion of this point, see Harman (1996, 10), Kriegel (2009, 88), and Levine (2019). For these reasons, I will focus on the superior "neural response" version, which avoids the circularity problem. *Fregean representationalism about colour experience* (Chalmers 2010, essay 11) is very similar to response-dependent representationalism. It holds that one has a bluish experience iff one has an experience that represents that something has the property *having the unique property that normally causes bluish experiences*. I will not discuss it separately here.

19 For presentations of this "representational problem" for the response-dependent representationalism, see Pautz (2010, 350–5), and Byrne and Hilbert (forthcoming). For a response, see section 3.5 of Jonathan Cohen's contribution to this volume. Cohen's response is that we certainly can represent *in thought and language* fine-grained response-dependent properties. For instance, I can say "consider a property of the form *causing neural state, N1, in Maxwell's population under precise viewing circumstances C1*", and thereby refer to a property of this kind. Cohen then suggests, "if so, then it's open to [response-dependent representationalists] to hold that whatever accounts for the mental representation of such properties [*in thought and language*] can also serve as an account of how states of the *visual system* represent the very same properties". But this is mistaken. The correct account of my ability refer to such a fine-grained response-dependent property *in thought* is that I speak a *language* with a compositional semantics, and this language has symbols like "neural state", "Maxwell's population", "precise viewing circumstances". So I can form a complex predicate out of these terms in order to represent to a fine-grained response-dependent property. Contrary to Cohen, the same compositional, language-based account definitely cannot serve to explain the *perceptual* representation of these properties, for a very simple and decisive reason: the format of perceptual representation is *not* language-like but rather *iconic* (Tye 1995). Even setting this point aside, the suggestion is incredible. What evolutionary advantage would come from the visual system being innately equipped with symbols like "neural state", "my population", "precise viewing circumstances C1", and forming, whenever one enjoys a colour experience, a complex representation along the lines of "there is an object out there that causes

neural state, *N1*, in my population under precise viewing circumstances *C1*". There are other problems with Cohen's response. For instance, he doesn't address the "uniformity problem" mentioned in the text (see also Pautz 2010, 353).

20 For this problem, see Armstrong (1984, 170), Boghossian and Velleman (1989), and McGinn (1996). One response depends on the "neutrality thesis". For discussion, see McGinn (1999).

21 Recent proponents of irrealist representationalism, or something close to it, include Mackie (1976), Maund (1995), Wright (2003), Pautz (2006), and Chalmers (2010).

22 For a host of empirical and *a priori* reasons for denying that pain qualities and other sensible properties aren't instantiated in the extracranial world, see Pautz (2010) and Levine (2019). For instance, in the domain of speech perception, it often happens that a categorical change in the perceived sensible property (e.g. from /da/ to /ta/) corresponds to no categorical change in the objective stimulus. It is impossible to be a realist about audible qualities; they are projections of the brain.

23 For this objection, see Campbell (this volume), Papineau (2016, sect. 13), and Levine (2019).

24 A clarification: Even if irrealists must hold that the brain alone explains our ability to *perceptually represent* colours, they needn't say that it explains the *existence and character of the colours themselves*. Instead, they might accept a "transcendent" view of colour properties on which they exist necessarily and their character is entirely mind-independent (Russell 1912, chap. IX). Compare: the brain doesn't create numbers or the facts about numbers; it only grounds our capacity to represent numbers.

25 Indeed, on irrealist representationalism, the *central* puzzle about experience becomes: *how can we perceptually represent uninstantiated sensible properties?* To illustrate, consider Frank Jackson's knowledge argument. In her black and white room, Mary learns all the truths about the instantiation of fundamental physical properties in our world. On irrealist representationalism, when she is released, she learns certain truths about non-physical sensible colours, for instance, that there exist these specific qualities, with specific natures or quiddities. But since these properties are uninstantiated, they are not themselves a problem for the physicalist claim that all instantiated properties are grounded in physical properties (Jackson 2004, 431). (Compare: physicalists can believe that there exists the non-physical property *being a unicorn*, and that we are related to it in thought, as long as they say that it is uninstantiated.) So if we accept irrealist representationalism, then we should say that the "sensible properties question" is not the real problem for physicalism. Rather, it is the "representation relation question": how can the brain enable us to *perceptually represent* these peculiar, uninstantiated non-physical properties?

26 For discussion of the idea that relativity theory and quantum mechanics support irrealism about the spatio-temporal properties we perceptually represent (perceived simultaneity, perceived three-dimensional shape), see Boghossian (2011, 56), Chalmers (2012, 296–7, 333), and Ney (2013, 177–81).

27 Contemporary *naïve realism* is not as flexible as representationalism. While there are internalist versions of representationalism, naïve realism is essentially externalist and requires a response-independent theory of the sensible properties. So it faces versions of the structural-mismatch problem and the internal-dependence problem from section 2 above. For discussion of this issue, see Kalderon (2011, 250–6), Fish (2013, 58–9), Logue (2016), and Allen (2017, 68–73 and chap. 6).

28 I thank Keith Allen, Derek Brown, Brian Cutter, and Fiona Macpherson for very helpful comments on this chapter.

References

Allen, K. 2017. *A Naïve Realist Theory of Colour*. Oxford: Oxford University Press.

Armstrong, D.M. 1984. "Consciousness and Causality". In D.M. Armstrong and N. Malcolm (eds.), *Consciousness and Causality*. Oxford: Blackwell.

Armstrong, D.M. 1987. "Smart and the Secondary Qualities". In P. Pettit, R. Sylvan, and J. Norman (eds.), *Metaphysics and Morality: Essays in Honour of J. J. C. Smart*. Oxford: Blackwell. Reprinted in A. Byrne and D. Hilbert (eds.), *Readings on Color: Volume 1*. Cambridge, MA: MIT Press.

Bealer, G. 1982. *Quality and Concept*. Oxford: Clarendon Press.

Boghossian, P. 2011. "Three Kinds of Relativism". In S. Hales (ed.), *A Companion to Relativism*. Oxford: Blackwell.

Boghossian, P., and D. Velleman. 1989. "Colour as a Secondary Quality". *Mind* 98: 81–103.

Bohon, K., K. Hermann, T. Hansen, and B. Conway. 2016. "Representation of Perceptual Color Space in Macaque Posterior Inferior Temporal Cortex (the V4 Complex)". *eNeuro* preprint.

Brown, D. 2010. "Locating Projectivism in the Color Debates". *Philosophical Studies* 148: 69–78.

Brouwer, G., and D. Heeger. 2009. "Decoding and Reconstructing Color from Responses in Human Visual Cortex". *Journal of Neuroscience* 29: 13992–14003.

Byrne, A., and D. Hilbert. 1997. "Colors and Reflectances". In A. Byrne and D. Hilbert *Readings on Color: Volume 1*. Cambridge, MA: MIT Press.

Byrne, A. and D. Hilbert. 2003. "Color Realism and Color Science". *Behavioral and Brain Sciences* 26: 3–21.

Byrne, A. and D. Hilbert. Forthcoming. "Color Relationalism and Relativism". In K. Akins and B. Brogaard (eds.), *Topics in Cognitive Science*.

Byrne, A. and M. Tye. 2006. "Qualia Ain't in the Head". *Noûs* 4: 241–55.

Chalmers, D. 2010. *The Character of Consciousness*. Oxford: Oxford University Press.

Chalmers, D. 2012. *Constructing the World*. Oxford: Oxford University Press.

Chang, E.F., J.W. Rieger, K. Johnson, M.S. Berger, N.M. Barbaro *et al.* 2010. "Categorical Speech Representation in Human Superior Temporal Gyrus". *Nature Neuroscience* 13: 1428–32.

Coghill, R., C. Sang, J. Maisog, and M. Iadarola. 1999. "Pain Intensity Processing Within the Human Brain: A Bilateral, Distributed Mechanism". *Journal of Neurophysiology* 82(4): 1934–43.

Cohen, J. 2009. *The Red and the Real*. Oxford: Oxford University Press.

Conway, B.R. 2013. "Color Signals Through Dorsal and Ventral Visual Pathways". *Visual Neuroscience* 31: 197–209.

Corney, D., J. Haynes, G. Rees, and R. B. Lotto. 2009. "The Brightness of Colour". *PLoS ONE* 4, vol. e5091.

Cosmides, L., and Tooby, J. 1995. Foreword to S. Baron-Cohen, *Mindblindness*. Cambridge, MA: MIT Press, Bradford Books.

Crouzet, S.M., N.A. Busch, and K. Ohla. 2015. "Taste Quality Decoding Parallels Taste Sensations". *Current Biology* 25: 1–7.

Danilova, M. and J. Mollon. 2016. "Is Discrimination Enhanced at a Category Boundary? The Case of Unique Red". *Journal of the Optical Society of America* 33: 260–6.

Davies, W. 2014. "The Inscrutability of Color Similarity". *Philosophical Studies* 171: 289–311.

Dorr, C. 2008. "There are No Abstract Objects". In T. Sider, J. Hawthorne, and D. Zimmerman (eds.), *Contemporary Debates in Metaphysics*. Malden, MA: Blackwell, pp. 32–63.

Dretske, F. 1995. *Naturalizing the Mind*. Cambridge, MA: MIT Press.

Fish, W. 2013. "Perception, Hallucination, and Illusion: Reply to My Critics". *Philosophical Studies* 163: 57–66.

Forder, L., J. Bosten, X. He, and A. Franklin. 2017. "A Neural Signature of the Unique Hues". *Scientific Reports* 7: 42364.

Hardin, C.L. 1987. "Qualia and Materialism: Closing the Explanatory Gap". *Philosophy and Phenomenological Research* 48: 281–98.

Hardin, C.L. 1988. *Color for Philosophers: Unweaving the Rainbow*. Indianapolis: Hackett.

Harman, G. 1996. "Explaining Objective Color in Terms of Subjective Reactions". *Philosophical Issues* 7: 1–17.

Haynes, J. 2009. "Decoding Visual Consciousness from Human Brain Signals". *Trends in Cognitive Science* 13: 194–202.

Hill, C. 2009. *Consciousness*. Cambridge: Cambridge University Press.

Horgan, T. 2014. "Phenomenal Intentionality and Secondary Qualities: The Quixotic Case of Color". In B. Brogaard (ed.), *Does Perception Have Content?* Oxford: Oxford University Press.

Howard, J.D., J. Plailly, M. Grueschow, J.D. Haynes, and J.A. Gottfried. 2009. "Odor Quality Coding and Categorization in Human Posterior Piriform Cortex". *Nature Neuroscience* 12: 932–9.

Jackson, F. 1998. *From Metaphysics to Ethics*. Oxford: Oxford University Press.

Jackson, F. 2004. "Mind and Illusion". In P. Ludlow, D. Stoljar, and Y. Nagasawa (eds.), *There's Something about Mary*. Cambridge, MA: MIT Press, pp. 421–42.

Johnston, M. 1992. "How to Speak of the Colors". *Philosophical Studies* 68: 221–63.

Johnston, M. 2004. "The Obscure Object of Hallucination". *Philosophical Studies* 120: 113–83.

Johnston, M. 2011. "On a Neglected Epistemic Virtue". *Philosophical Issues* 21: 165–218.

Kalderon, M. 2011. "The Multiply Qualitative". *Mind* 120: 239–62.

Kriegel, U. 2009. *Subjective Consciousness*. Oxford: Oxford University Press.

Kriegeskorte, N., and R.A. Kievit. 2013. "Representational Geometry: Integrating Cognition, Computation, and the Brain". *Trends in Cognitive Sciences* 17: 401–12.

Levine, J. 2019. "On Phenomenal Access". In A. Pautz and D. Stoljar (eds.), *Blockheads! Essays on Ned Block's Philosophy of Mind and Consciousness*. Cambridge, MA: MIT Press, pp. 279–300.

Lewis, D. 1983. "New Work for a Theory of Universals". *Australasian Journal of Philosophy* 61: 343–77.

Lewis, D. 1993. "Many, but Almost One." In K. Cambell, J. Bacon, and L. Reinhardt (eds.), *Ontology, Causality, and Mind: Essays on the Philosophy of D. M. Armstrong.* Cambridge: Cambridge University Press, pp. 23–38.

Lewis, D. 1994. "Reduction of Mind." In Samuel Guttenplan (ed.), *A Companion to the Philosophy of Mind.* Oxford: Blackwell, pp. 412–31.

Locke, J. 1869. *An Essay Concerning Human Understanding.* www.earlymoderntexts.com.

Logue, H. 2016. "Are Experiences Just Representations?" In B. Nanay (ed.), *Current Controversies in Philosophy of Perception.* New York: Routledge, pp. 43–56.

Lycan, W. 2001. "The Case for Phenomenal Externalism". *Philosophical Perspectives* 15: 17–35.

MacAdam, D.L. 1985. "The Physical Basis of Color Specification". In his *Color Measurement: Theme and Variations.* New York: Springer-Verlag.

Mackie, J. 1976. *Problems from Locke.* Oxford: Oxford University Press.

Macpherson, F. 2003. "Novel Colors and the Content of Experience". *Pacific Philosophical Quarterly* 84: 43–66.

Margot, C. 2009. "A Noseful of Objects". *Nature Neuroscience* 12: 813–14.

Maund, J.B. 1995. *Colours: Their Nature and Representation.* New York: Cambridge University Press.

McGinn, C. 1996. "Another Look at Color". *Journal of Philosophy* 93: 537–53.

McGinn, Colin. 1999. "The Appearance of Colour." In his *Knowledge and Reality: Selected Essays.* Oxford: Clarendon Press.

Ney, A. 2013. "Ontological Reduction and the Wave Function Ontology". In A. Ney and D. Albert (eds.), *The Wave Function: Essays in the Metaphysics of Quantum Mechanics.* Oxford: Oxford University Press.

Papineau, D. 2016. "Against Representationalism (about Experience)". *International Journal of Philosophical Studies* 24: 324–47.

Pautz, A. 1998. "Representationalism and Phenomenal-Neural Dependence". *New England Undergraduate Philosophy Journal*: 73–89.

Pautz, A. 2003. "Have Byrne and Hilbert Answered Hardin's Challenge?" *Behavioral and Brain Sciences* 26: 44–5.

Pautz, A. 2006. "Can the Physicalist Explain Colour Structure in Terms of Colour Experience?" *Australasian Journal of Philosophy* 84: 535–65.

Pautz, A. 2010. "Do Theories of Consciousness Rest on a Mistake?" *Philosophical Issues* 20: 333–67.

Pautz, A. 2011. "Can Disjunctivists Explain our Access to the Sensible World?" *Philosophical Issues* 21: 384–433.

Robinson, H. 1994. *Perception.* New York: Routledge.

Rosen, G. 2010. "Metaphysical Dependence: Grounding and Reduction". In B. Hale and A. Hoffman (eds.), *Modality: Metaphysics, Logic and Epistemology.* Oxford: Oxford University Press.

Russell, B. 1912. *The Problems of Philosophy.* London: Williams and Norgate.

Schmidt, B., M. Neitz, and J. Neitz. 2014. "Neurobiological Hypothesis of Color Appearance and Hue Perception". *Journal of the Optical Society of America* 31: 195–207.

Shoemaker, S. 1994. "The Phenomenal Character of Experience". *Noûs* 28: 21–38.

Shoemaker, S. 2003. "Content, Character, and Color". *Philosophical Issues* 13: 253–78.

Sider, T. 2011. *Writing the Book of the World.* Oxford: Oxford University Press.

Stevens, S., J. Volkmann, and E. Newman. 1937. "A Scale for the Measurement of the Psychological Magnitude Pitch". *Journal of the Acoustical Society of America* 8: 185–90.

Thompson, E. 1995. *Color Vision.* London: Routledge.

Tye, M. 1995. *Ten Problems of Consciousness.* Cambridge, MA: MIT Press.

Tye, M. 2000. *Consciousness, Color and Content.* Cambridge, MA: MIT Press.

Tye, M. 2009. *Consciousness Revisited.* Cambridge, MA: MIT Press.

Tye, M. 2014. "Transparency, Qualia Realism and Representationalism". *Philosophical Studies* 170: 39–57.

Tye, M. and P. Bradley. 2001. "Of Colors, Kestrels, Caterpillars, and Leaves". *Journal of Philosophy* 98: 469–87.

Wright, W. 2003. "Projectivist Representationalism and Color". *Philosophical Psychology* 16: 515–29.

24

INDIRECT REALISM

Barry Maund

One of the central disputes in the philosophy of perception is that between Direct and Indirect Realists, and it is particularly here that questions about the nature of colour have arisen.

Indirect Realism is a theory of perception, most closely associated with Descartes and Locke, but is implicit in the thinking of many scientists. The theory, however, takes different forms, and some of its characterizations seem to have been introduced by its critics rather than its adherents (for a discussion, see, e.g., John Mackie 1976). Its major opponent is Direct Realism, but this theory, too, takes different forms: Naïve Realism, Cognitive Realism, Intentional Realism, Natural Realism, Representational Realism. Historically there have been other major opponents, for one, Berkeley's Idealism, but even that theory is, arguably, a form of Direct Realism: for Berkeley, the real items are ideas. (There would seem to be different senses of 'real' at stake: (1) real, i.e. mind-independent; (2) real, i.e. non-fictional, non-imaginary.) Another important opponent, in the twentieth century, has been Phenomenalism. Like Idealism, this theory is a form of direct perception (and like it, a different type of Realism from that implied by Indirect Realism).

1 Historical context

Indirect Realism is a theory of perception, commonly attributed to Descartes and Locke. It is also commonly known as "the Representative Theory of Perception". The theory is usually combined with a very distinctive view about colours, and about other "secondary qualities", one that seems contrary to our common sense view about colour. There is, however, a number of serious issues with this brief characterization. One is that there are different versions of Indirect Realism, and a second is that it is controversial whether historical figures such as Descartes and Locke held the theory, in any of its common versions. In addition, the view, on colours and secondary qualities, more generally, is complex, and precisely what the view is, is a matter of some controversy.

For one thing, there are modern forms of representationalism that are not indirect theories. It has indeed become quite common for contemporary philosophers to hold that perceptual experiences involves representations, in the sense that they involve representational states or intentional states, i.e. states that carry intentional content, but to deny that this commits them to a representative theory of perception. Colin McGinn illustrates the point very neatly when, after explicitly repudiating the classical representative theory, maintains that perception works through representations: "My view is that we see objects 'directly' by representing them in visual experience."[1] Other examples are Fred Dretske 1996, Michael Tye 2000, and A. Byrne 2001 (but the view is very common).

E.J. Lowe 1995 draws a useful distinction between 'representational theories' of perception and the representative theory of perception.[2] The contrast is between theories in which perceptual experiences are representational, or intentional, states, and theories which involve 'indirect realism': the view that we perceive a physical object and its properties, indirectly, in virtue of either perceiving, or being directly aware of, an intermediary: some sensory or mental item or state, which represents the physical objects and their properties.[3] It is interesting that while Lowe, in Lowe 1993, defended the representational theory, he defends the indirect version in Lowe 2008a.[4]

Indeed, it is quite common for historians of philosophy to argue that Descartes and Locke, who are usually thought of as indirect theorists, held the direct realist version of representationalism.[5] Lowe 1995, and Mackie 1976, 1985, hold this with respect to Locke, and John Yolton 1984 holds it with respect to both Descartes and Locke. There is a counter-argument which says that while some texts in Locke and Descartes suggest this kind of interpretation, there are other texts that go the other way. Indeed, as Mackie points out, part of the reason many historians had for not attributing the standard version of the Representative theory to Descartes and Locke, is the assumption that the theory is indefensible (and that Descartes and Locke could not have been so foolish as to accept it).[6] It is important to note that this assumption has been vigorously challenged by a number of recent philosophers: Mackie 1976, F. Jackson 1977, J. Harrison 1993, R. Oakes 1993, B. Maund 1993, and H.I. Brown 2008.

It was common for the classical Representationalists to make a distinction between two kinds of colour: colours as they are in physical bodies and colours as they are in sensation. On the standard view, the indirect representative theory, the latter kind of colour is a subjective quality; the former kind is a dispositional property: a power to produce sensations with the first kind of quality, under appropriate conditions. Descartes put it this way:

> It is clear then that when we say we perceive colors in objects, *it is really just the same as saying* that we perceived in objects something as to whose nature we are ignorant but which produces in us a very clear and vivid sensation, what we call the sensation of color.
>
> *(4)*

It should be noted that there are some texts in Descartes, which lead some commentators to deny that Descartes thinks of sensations of colours as subjective qualities (or as 'qualia'); on this alternative view, he is taken to mean by 'sensation of colour' something like 'sensory representation of colour'. (A similar view is held with respect to Locke's term 'idea of colour'.) However, it is clear enough that the former interpretation was widely accepted. David Hume, for example wrote:

> Sounds, colours, heat and cold, according to modern philosophy are not qualities in objects, but perceptions in the mind.[7]

Moreover, that Locke held a similar view would seem to be shown by his statement of the possibility of spectrum inversion: it is possible "that the idea that a violet produced in one man's mind by his eyes were the same that a marigold produced in another man's and vice versa".[8]

And later generations of scientists certainly held the view about the subjectivity of colour. Maxwell, for example, wrote: "It seems almost a truism to say that color is a sensation; and yet Young, by honestly recognizing this elementary truth, established the first consistent theory of color."[9] Some critics treat this sort of remark as absurd, but one can avoid the absurdity by treating Maxwell (and others) as saying that colour is not a quality of the sensation, but a subjective quality presented in the sensation.

This distinction between two kinds of colour is related to another distinction made by the classical Representationalists: the distinction between primary and secondary qualities. One important basis for the distinction is that, for primary qualities, the idea of the quality is said to resemble the quality in the physical body, whereas, for secondary qualities, it does not. For colours, that is to say, physical bodies do not have the qualities that are presented in experience (or, on the alternative interpretation, are represented as having). Instead the objects have characteristic dispositional properties: powers to induce in perceivers, sensations, or ideas, of colour (and they also have 'textures'—that ground the powers).

It would seem that, for colours and other secondary qualities, there is a crucial assumption being made about the qualities in (or represented in) the sensations or ideas—that they are features with a certain qualitative character: they are qualitative, not quantitative features. (And there is a further assumption: that the 'textures', that ground the dispositions in the physical bodies, do not have such a qualitative character.) The point might be expressed in modern terms as the following: the colours are features that have a certain qualitative character, one that enables them to be placed in a systematic, ordered array, one marked by a system of similarities and differences that hold between the features (see Chapter 5 on 'The Logic of Colour Concepts' in this volume).

It should also be noted that the classical Representationalists are sometimes described as denying that physical objects are coloured and, more often, as denying that physical objects have colours as we ordinarily suppose them to have, i.e. that they are denying our common sense view of objects as being coloured. The first part is not quite accurate, since they hold that objects do have colours: they have dispositions to cause sensations of colour (and, sometimes, Boyle and Descartes refer to colours-in-physical bodies as the textures grounding the dispositions).

Indeed, even the second part has been challenged: there are many philosophers who have claimed that the secondary quality view of colour is the common sense view. It is clear, however, that the classical theorists saw themselves as challenging our ordinary conceptions of colour. It was customary for these philosophers and scientists to make a distinction between a philosophical way of thinking and the common, everyday way of thinking of such qualities (which Newton describes as "such conceptions as vulgar people … would be apt to frame"[10]). As Descartes explains, the ordinary way of thinking involves the mistake of "judging that the feature of objects that we call 'color' is something 'just like the color in our sensation'", or of believing that "the self-same whiteness or greenness which I perceive through my senses is present in the body". (See also Locke II, XXXI, 2.) It would seem that the naïve perceiver conflates the two kinds of quality, that the philosopher distinguishes. If we fail to make this distinction, as we do in our ordinary, everyday thinking, we are liable to lapse into errors, although, as Descartes and Locke point out, such errors may well be beneficial, for our overall purposes.[11] As Locke says, it matters little at all, for our ordinary, everyday use of perception, whether the distinguishing mark in the violet (associated with the idea of *blue*) "be only a peculiar texture of parts or else that very colour, the idea whereof (which is in us) is the exact resemblance".[12]

2 Motivation for classical representationalism

There is an interesting question as to what is the motivation for the original introduction of the Representative theory. In classical authors, e.g. in Descartes and Locke, any argument for the thesis would seem to be implicit in their writings, rather than set out formally. And it has often been pointed out that Descartes and Locke take much for granted in exposition of their ideas. Accordingly, their argument for the thesis requires some reconstruction on our part. Taking this view, it is plausible to take the implicit argument, for Indirect Realism, to be that it helps explain how knowledge of the external world is possible—not so much a task in the Kantian sense, but more like the project of naturalistic epistemology. Indirect realism, together with the distinction between primary and secondary qualities, is part of an overall theoretical package.

This view would seem to fit Descartes' reasoning in the *Dioptrics* and *Principles of Philosophy*, as opposed to that in the *Meditations*. (See Nancy Maull 1980, for discussion.) In the *Meditations*, he is attempting to justify our claims to knowledge. In the *Dioptrics* and the *Principles*, the aim seems different: it is to explain the causal process, by virtue of which we acquire knowledge. Descartes has an extended discussion of the likely process underlying the perception of objects in the material world. By use of an analogy with the blind man who uses a stick to acquire knowledge, he tries to explain how we can acquire knowledge, by virtue of a causal process which involves mechanical impulses. (Putting it anachronistically, he is offering a theory of how information can be transmitted.) Descartes is both confronting naïve realism, and contributing to a tradition that is challenging the Aristotelian model of sense-perception.

More specifically, Descartes is aiming to do two things: (1) to show how we do get knowledge of qualities of external bodies; (2) to show that our experience of colours (and other secondary qualities) can be explained without assuming that there is in the external object a quality resembling the colour (and other secondary qualities), and without recourse to any kinds of properties, in the causal process, other than mechanical and mathematical properties. As a consequence, it would seem that if physical bodies did have such qualities, perceivers would have no reason to think that they did.

I take it that Descartes, with others such as Boyle and Locke, also accepts something stronger, namely that there are, in the external body, no such qualitative features—there are only primary qualities and dispositions/powers to cause experiences (and 'textures', i.e. arrangements of instances of primary qualities). He certainly doesn't prove that—as C.D. Broad, a more recent indirect realist, pointed out—but the weaker epistemic result would be significant enough. It is surely part of common sense, and of Aristotelian realism, that our experience does give us knowledge of such qualities. Moreover, the classical Representationalists might argue that if we have no good reason to think that material objects have such qualities, then we ought not postulate them (i.e. we might appeal to Occam's Razor considerations).

3 Two versions of indirect realism

There have been, more recently, more explicit defences of Indirect Realism. There are, however, different versions of the theory. One version is one that builds on a distinction between a direct and indirect objects of perception. It is just such a theory, for example, that Frank Jackson defends, in his *Perception*, 1977. On this theory, the subject perceives physical objects *mediately*, by perceiving, *immediately*, mental objects, i.e. sense data. The theory depends on a crucial distinction between two kinds of perceiving.

There is, however, another version that does not require two objects of *perception*. It holds that we perceive physical bodies but we do so by *being aware* of some intermediary entity: we do not *perceive* that entity. That is to say, in visual perception, the perceiver sees, say, a frog, by being aware of some sensory individual or state—which is related to the frog, but exists independently of it—but she does not see the item or state. We should note that such a theory might very well count as an instance of one form of Direct Realism, for it says that perception of an object is a process/activity that involves a certain kind of causal process in relation to that object, whereas this kind of process is not involved in the subject's being aware of the sensory item. We should also note that this terminological move does not remove the central philosophical issues that set adherents of the view apart from its opponents.

One colour theorist who adopted this version of the indirect theory was the philosopher C.D. Broad.[13] In *Scientific Thought*, Broad describes his theory of perception and of the role of sensa in that theory. He gives a theory of what is involved in perceiving material objects—bells, tables, etc. In this context, he writes of *seeing* material objects, but of *being aware of* sensa (and sometimes, of sensing a sensum). There are occasions on which he talks of seeing sensa, but he explains that 'see' here is used in a special sense, different from that sense in which we see material objects.[14]

Both versions of Indirect Realism should be contrasted with a third version, which might be called "Inferential Indirect Perception". On this account, perception of physical objects is interpreted as involving inferences—from perception or awareness of intermediaries, e.g. images, sense data. Actually it is not clear who actually held this doctrine (though see the last section which discusses the theories of the psychologists, Rock and Palmer). Many interpreters of Descartes and Locke, for example, reject this characterization as a true account of their Representational theories. Nor does the description fit the accounts of recent defenders of Indirect Realism—Broad, Jackson, Perkins, Brown, and Maund. Jackson's mediate/immediate distinction is an ontological one, not an epistemological one. Broad says that it is false psychologically that we infer the existence of physical objects and properties from our sensa, and false logically that we could so infer.[15] And he goes on to explain:

> The belief that our sensa are appearances of something more permanent and complex seems to be primitive and to arise inevitably in us with the sensing of the sensa.[16]
> *(For further discussion, see Maund 1993, Oakes 1993, J. Harrison 1993)*

4 Jackson non-epistemic seeing

One of the most important defences of Indirect Realism in recent times is the one that Jackson provides in his *Perception*, 1977. (It is important even though Jackson himself has come to repudiate it.[17]) It is the version that assumes a distinction between direct and indirect objects of perception. On Jackson's theory, the subject perceives physical objects *mediately*, by perceiving, *immediately*, mental objects, i.e. sense data.

Jackson explains the distinction between mediate perception and immediate perception, as being an ontological distinction, rather than an epistemic one, as in more traditional conceptions. Jackson follows Dretske in drawing a distinction between *seeing things* and *seeing that*, i.e. between *seeing A* and seeing that A is F, the former being non-epistemic. Both mediate and immediate seeings apply to the non-epistemic kind. The mediate/immediate distinction is explained as follows: one perceives x *mediately*, when one perceives x, *by virtue of* perceiving some other entity y; one perceives z *immediately*, when there is no other entity, in virtue of which, one perceives z. The relation of *in virtue of* is defined as follows:

An A is F in virtue of a B being F if the application of '—is F' to an A is definable in terms of its application to a B and a relation, R, between As and Bs, but not vice versa.

(19)

It is surprising that, while he takes for granted that there is such a thing as *seeing things, hearing things, smelling things,* etc., Jackson nowhere tells us, explicitly, what *seeing* is, mediate or immediate. However, we may take it that he is calling upon Fred Dretske's account of *non-epistemic seeing* ('simple seeing'), since Jackson modifies Dretske's account of epistemic seeing when he develops his own account of this notion, one that like Dretske's, presupposes the notion of *seeing things.*

This suggests that Jackson accepts that *seeing an X* consists in visually discriminating X from its background. To see a cabbage, in the non-epistemic sense, is to differentiate visually the cabbage but, holds Dretske, it does not require forming any judgements or beliefs about the cabbage. The phrase 'visual differentiation', so Dretske maintains, functions as a pre-intellectual, pre-discursive sort of capacity which a wide variety of beings possess:

> It is an endowment which is largely immune to the caprices of our intellectual life. Whatever judgements, interpretations, beliefs, inferences, anticipations, regrets, memories, or thoughts may be aroused by the visual differentiation of D, the visual differentiation of D is, itself, quite independent of these accompaniments.[18]

The notion of *seeing things* is central to Jackson's argument for the Representative theory. So too, is his account of colour—and in two ways. The argument has two crucial parts: (1) to show that all cases of seeing—veridical, illusory, and hallucinatory—involve sense data; (2) to argue that the sense data are mental objects. Claims about colour are central to both parts.

Step (2) is necessary since sense data are not mental or sensory items, by definition. Rather, sense data are (a) immediate objects of perception, and (b) objects which bear the relevant apparent properties that objects—mediate or immediate—appear to have.[19] The proof for (1), i.e. that there are sense data fitting this characterization, depends on the claims that (i) whenever seeing occurs, there is a coloured patch which is the immediate object of perception, and (ii) that this coloured patch bears the relevant apparent properties. Jackson devotes an entire chapter to establishing claim (ii). The controversial cases are cases of perceptual illusion, e.g. when I look at a white wall in circumstances in which it looks blue. Crucially, it is argued that:

> The fact that there is a material object that looks blue, to a subject S, implies that S sees (immediately) something that is blue.

This argument depends on his analysis of what it is for something to *look blue,* in the phenomenal sense of 'looks F' (a sense which applies to properties such as colour, shape, distance, number, etc.). For X to look blue to S, he argues, is for it to be the case that S sees something that is blue. This argument, we should note, would be resisted by many. One reason many have is based on the doubt that there is such a phenomenal use of 'looks F', or at least one that satisfies Jackson's requirements.

The argument in step (2), i.e. the argument that sense data are mental objects, goes as follows:

1   there is no good reason to believe that any material object is ever blue (nor any other colour);

therefore

2   the things that one sees, immediately, and are blue, are not material objects, but mental objects.

The argument for (1) depends on the claim that colour is not a "scientific property". A scientific property is held to be a property appealed to by current science in explaining the causal effect of one material thing on another material thing, or a logical consequence of such a property or properties.[20] Jackson then argues for an immediate conclusion: Either colour is a scientific property or we have no reason to believe that material things are coloured. He then argues that colour is not a scientific property. (In so doing, he rejects the colour physicalist's claim that colours can be identified with some physical property such as spectral reflectance.) We should note that Jackson's argument requires that Naïve Realism can be ruled out—on other grounds—since, on that theory, we could know that objects had the colours.

Jackson's argument raises a large set of issues. One is whether it proves too much: are there not many properties that we know about, but which are not "scientific properties"? There may be independent arguments for the claim that material objects are not coloured—or are not coloured in the way the immediate objects are coloured. Some of the issues on the ontological status of colours are taken up in Part IV on Colour Ontology, in this volume.

5 Seeing-of and seeing-that

Jackson makes an important amendment to the account Dretske gives of the distinction between *seeing* and *seeing-that*. He points out the following:

> A construction of the form 'S sees A is F' is ambiguous. It can be taken obliquely as 'S sees that A is F' or transparently as 'S sees of A that it is F'. (More precisely, it is 'S sees of—that it is F' which is a transparent mode of containment for singular terms ...)[21]

Jackson explains this distinction as reflecting a difference similar to a difference between *believing that* S is F and *believing of* X that it is F. The difference is reflected in the fact that descriptions of the former occur in what are called "opaque" contexts—cognitively opaque—and the latter, in contexts which are transparent. Having made this distinction, Jackson then makes an important admission:

> My arguments against analysing seeing things in terms of seeing-that apply only to the opaque seeing-that locution. I do not think that seeing A can be in any way analysed in terms of seeing that A is F, or in terms of seeing that B is F, where A = B; but it may be the case that seeing A can be analysed in terms of seeing of A that it is F. But if this is the case (*I do not know if it is*), it is not any kind of objection to the approach of this work. For 'S sees of A that it is F' may be taken to express a relation between A and S because 'A' in it is subject to substitutivity. Hence it accords with the approach of this work: the attempt to analyse seeing in terms of relations between persons and things.[22]

I have drawn attention to the clause, *I do not know if it is*, by putting it in emphasis. In making this admission, Jackson is allowing the possibility that Dretske's account ought to be seriously modified. For the possibility it allows is that the intended contrast between *non-epistemic seeing* and *seeing-that*, should be a contrast, rather, between two types of epistemic/conceptual *seeing*s. As a consequence, it allows that the second distinction is the crucial one to make.

In any case, there is reason to think that Dretske needs something like this distinction. It concerns the question of what exactly the phrase "visual differentiation" covers. He describes it as applying to "a pre-intellectual, pre-discursive sort of capacity which a wide variety of beings possess".[23] He also explains that S's visual differentiation of X consist in X's looking some way to S, and looking different from its immediate surroundings. But this raises the question of whether it involves something more than this. I assume that we are thinking of conscious perception. If so, we can ask: does visual differentiation imply being in a state that is a causal effect of X's presence, or does it require something extra on my part, e.g. that I am *aware of* X. At a minimum this involves an act of acquaintance with X, and would seem to imply awareness of X under some description.

After raising the possibility that we should construe Dretske's notion of *non-epistemic seeing* differently, i.e. read it as *seeing of A, that it has certain feature(s)*, Jackson then turns to the task of providing an analysis of *seeing-that* (henceforth understood *opaquely*) in terms of *seeing things*, and he does not explore the possibility that he has just raised. There are, however, other approaches that do take up this possibility.

In thinking about this notion, it is helpful to begin with the views, on the topic, of H.H. Price, one of the most important philosophers of perception in the first half of the twentieth century. He does not accept Indirect Realism, but much of his account of perceptual experience can be accepted by an Indirect Realist. Price predates Dretske, in drawing a distinction between *thing-awareness* and *fact-awareness*, but differs crucially from Dretske, in that his distinction draws on a distinction between different kinds of *fact-awareness* (consciousness), only one of which involves *thing-awareness (consciousness)*. Price writes:

> Perhaps we may say that there are two sorts of intuitive apprehension, one directed upon *facts*, e.g. the fact that I am puzzled or ... that 2 + 2 = 4, or that courage is good; another directed upon *particular existents*, e.g. this colour-patch or this noise or that visual image, or again upon this feeling of disgust and that act of wondering.[24]

Price adds that the first is *apprehension that*, the second, *apprehension of*. What is important, though, in Price's account, is that he acknowledges that it may well be true that one can never have the apprehension of something, without at the same time apprehending *that* it stands in certain relations or *that* it has certain qualities:

> In the language of Cambridge logicians what we apprehend is always a fact—something of the form 'that A is B' or 'the B-ness of A'. You cannot apprehend just A.

Price insists, however, that this point about the necessity of *fact-apprehension* does not eliminate the need for *thing-apprehension*; that is to say, it does not undermine the claim that the subject is acquainted with the sensory item. Russell makes a similar point:

> Knowledge by acquaintance is essentially simpler than any knowledge of truths, ... though it would be very rash to assume that human beings, in fact, have acquaintance with things without at the same time knowing some truths about them.[25]

Construing this idea of Price as an illustration of the modification that Jackson suggested, for Dretske's account of seeing an object (or event), we are in a position to see how there are versions of Indirect Realism that exploit the modification, the respective accounts of Moreland Perkins and Barry Maund (see the sections to follow). We might also use the idea to modify Jackson's account, so that it becomes: to see say a tomato mediately is to see of it as standing out from its background—which one does by seeing the sensory item as standing out from its background.

6 Perkins's version of Indirect Realism

One way of expanding on Price's view, in support of the Indirect theory, is that pursued by Moreland Perkins, in his *Sensing the World*. Here, he develops an interesting version of Indirect Realism.[26] Perkins sets out his theory as a response to the defences of direct realism that Dretske and Chisholm gave.[27] He has an extended discussion of what he refers to as the Dretske-Chisholm account of *simple seeing*, a discussion in which he brings out the tensions within that account.[28] Whereas these philosophers construe the kind of experience that constitutes *simple seeing*—seeing an object or event—as one that involves neither concepts, nor thought, nor the acquiring of knowledge, Perkins holds that the existence of such a kind of experience, contrary to the way Dretske and Chisholm argue, doesn't touch on the central dispute between direct and indirect realism.

> Both direct and indirect realism give accounts of the structure of that visual awareness of objects which is achieved in attentively looking at objects. They are accounts of consciously held, visual knowledge of objects. Indirect realism holds that when an object before our eyes holds our visual attention we are visually conscious of some feature of this object and that always this awareness of the object occurs in virtue of—and in part consists in—our (direct) awareness of something not before our eyes.
>
> *(207)*

Perkins's claim is that whatever value an account of *simple seeing* has (and perhaps it is valuable at the non-conscious level), the important dispute is at the level of conscious perception, and here, Dretske and Chisholm do not address the real issues. Perkins proposes an account of perceptual experience that does not have this shortcoming. On his rival account, a typical perceptual experience has an intentionalist structure—it carries representational content, and is, in that sense, Representationalist—but that content is complex. It contains two kinds of components: one that is sensuous and non-conceptual, and the other, conceptual. In an ordinary perceptual experience, say, hearing the loudness of a sound in the air, the perceiver is held to be directly aware of a *sensuous quality*—a sensuous 'loudness' internal to his consciousness. However, one is not simply aware of a sensuous quality that is presented in the experience. One's awareness of that quality is quite complex: it may be thought of as a kind of thought, one in which the perceiver attributes that very quality—the quality-instance—to an object in public space ("before one's sensory organs"). That is to say, the state of awareness contains a conceptualization of the external object and a sensory attribution of the quality to the object. One is said to "perceptually attribute" the sensuous quality to the object.

> Being directly aware of sensuous qualities interior to consciousness is closely analogous to being directly aware of a thought that corresponds to the predicate of a non-perceptual judgement—to being aware of what one predicates in making such a judgement about some particular. But here the what that is attributed is a purely sensuous content.
>
> *(Perkins 1983, p. 5)*

An important part of Perkins' account is the nature of the representation involved. The experience *represents* the external object as having the sensuous quality, the very quality-instance present in the experience. This type of representation is *representation-by-exemplification* (as when a blue colour in a photograph, say, represents the blue of the sky). Interestingly, the theory is perhaps best understood in Perkins's discussion of pain, especially a later paper on the subject.[29]

7 A hybrid version of Indirect Realism

There is another version of Indirect Realism, one that develops important points raised by Jackson and Perkins: that defended by Barry Maund (2003).[30] This version takes up the distinction that Jackson drew attention to, that between *seeing of A* that it is F, and *seeing that A* is F. There is an interesting parallel between this approach and that followed by Jackson. Just as Jackson drew upon the account of perception proposed by a direct realist, Fred Dretske, so Maund draws upon the views of perception held by two direct realists, Gareth Evans 1982 and John McDowell 1986.[31] The notion of someone's *seeing of something that it is F* depends on a notion of *knowledge-by-acquaintance*. Seeing of a certain man that he is approaching requires knowledge-by-acquaintance of that man. This notion is one that plays a central role in the accounts that Evans and McDowell have provided.

Maund seeks to align himself with these direct realists, since his version of the Indirect theory of perception trades upon, and emphasizes, the distinction between *seeing* material objects and *being aware of* sensory intermediaries. It is important to realize that—given the different ways the distinction *direct/indirect realism* can be drawn—such a theory can be properly thought of both as direct and indirect, in different senses of course. For this reason, Maund favours thinking of this form of the theory as a 'hybrid theory'.

This point is not a trivial one. The theory stresses the fact that perceiving a material object consist in being in a certain sort of causal contact with the material object, one involving the sensory organs; in the case of seeing, it means the use of the eyes, for hearing, the ears, and so on. Being aware of the intermediary is not like that. What seeing an object and being aware of the intermediary have in common is the acquiring of specific knowledge/beliefs, but the acquirings take different forms.

Accordingly, this theory is a form of *Indirect Realism*, while, at the same time, fitting one important characterization of *Direct Realism*. One advantage of this latter fact it that it enables the theorist to draw upon certain philosophical accounts of Direct Realism—specifically those of Evans and McDowell—while making room for the indirect component to perceiving.

Evans and McDowell are particularly helpful, since they develop theories of perception in which the notions of *knowledge-by-acquaintance*, and *perceptual-acquaintance* are central. Part of their project is to salvage these notions from the use Russell made of them. In Russell's framework, perceptual acquaintance is restricted to sense data, and to sense data of a very specific type, playing a very specific epistemological role. Evans and McDowell have no interest in this framework. They are not simply rejecting Russell, however. They think that he had an important insight that they wish to preserve: that there are certain kinds of thoughts (propositions) that are *object-dependent thoughts*—and among these, there is an important sub-class, one that involves *perceptual acquaintance*. The idea of object-dependency, in their accounts depends crucially on the central use of perceptual-demonstratives. (For discussion of an objection to this use, in this context, see section 9.)

Maund's strategy is to argue that their form of direct realism is compatible with the hybrid account that he defends, the account which implies that we can have a form of direct realism which incorporates an indirect component. The theory requires intermediaries that are sensa, or sensuous qualities, but these entities are not saddled with the Russellian legacy. Put briefly, and oversimplifying, the claim is that perceptual acquaintance of material object requires perceptual experience which, as Evans and McDowell argue, situates those objects in an egocentric space based on the perceiver's body, but this is compatible with the experience consisting in the awareness of sensory representations of the right sort. The experience situates material objects in the egocentric space by virtue of situating sensory representations in an egocentric space. By "situate in egocentric space", in this context, one means that the item is thought of as occupying a certain place in the space, where the spatial vocabulary for the thought is, according to Evans, "one whose terms derive their meaning partly from being linked with bodily actions".[32]

An important aspect to the theory is the claim that, as far as naïve perceivers are concerned— and as far as sophisticated perceivers in their frequent naïve moments are concerned—they don't distinguish between sensory representation and material object, they take them to be identical. Maund shares this idea with earlier writers, such as Price and Broad. In a section addressing the question of how sensa are related to physical objects, Broad says of 'the plain man' that he does not clearly distinguish between physical objects and sensa, and therefore feels no particular difficulty about their mutual relations.

> We first come to recognise sensa as distinct from physical objects by reflecting on the fact of sensible appearance, and the contrast between it and the supposed properties of physical reality.
>
> *(Broad 1923, p. 266)*

The form of Indirect Realism, as presented here, contains, as an ingredient, a conception of perceptual experience which fits a Projectivist account of experience. In holding that the ordinary perceiver conflates the representation with the object seen, the theorist holds that the experience effectively attributes to the material object—that one thinks of as in objective space— the having of properties that it presents the representation as having. Following Perkins, Maund explains this kind of representation as similar to *representation by exemplification*. (A number of philosophers have defended Projectivist theories of perception, e.g. Boghossian and Velleman 1997, Maund 2003, Maund 2011, Averill 2005.)

8 Indirect realism: the implications for colour

The indirect realist views outlined in the sections above exploit a Projectivist theory of perception. This theory, in turn, provides a distinctive understanding of colour.

In the case of our experiences of colour—let's say, a paradigmatic red sunset—the subject is presented, in the experience, with a sensory item with a qualitative feature, call it "colour*". The sensory item represents—by exemplification—the material object, in this case, the sun, as having that quality. However, the perceiver does not ordinarily distinguish between the sensory item and the material object. Accordingly, s/he takes the material objects to have a certain type of property: (a) ones with the sensuous, qualitative character distinctive of colours*; (b) ones that are qualities of material objects. It is these properties that we normally and naturally think of as colours of physical objects.

In actual fact, the material objects do not have such properties (or if they do, we do not know that they have them). The material objects are represented as having the features; they have dispositions to induce experiences that represent the objects as having the qualities; but they do not have the qualities. One of the important consequences of this kind of theory concerns our ordinary colour language. The colour terms that occur in ordinary language—'blue', 'orange', 'mauve', etc.—designate these fictional properties.

So far, this is an important part of our understanding of colour—but it is not the complete picture. Given the view of colours as fictional properties, there arises the important question of how we should proceed. There are two issues here that we need to keep distinct. One concerns what attitude we should take towards our ordinary conceptual and linguistic practices, concerning colour; the other concerns the question of what colour concepts and colour-language we should adopt, for purposes of doing science and metaphysics.

One approach, to the first concern, might be to attempt to remove the ordinary concepts of colour from our thinking, and to replace them with revised concepts; and to change the meaning of colour terms. Such an approach is by no means obligatory. We might adopt a fictionalist attitude to our ordinary concepts and terms: they designate fictional properties. Bodies do not have these properties but for many purposes it does not matter: the world is such that *it is as if* the bodies have the colours, i.e. they appear to have the colours.

As far as the second question is concerned, then, on the assumption that Indirect Realism is correct, there is room to introduce at least two new concepts of colour, designating two different, but related, kinds of property. (In so doing, we follow the model set out by Descartes and Locke.) One kind of property is that of colour★, the subjective quality presented in experience; another kind is the dispositional property, the power to induce experiences with colours★ instantiated in the experience. Moreover, there is no reason, in principle, why the range of colour concepts/terms should not be widened. For example, there may be space for a concept of colour that designates the property of physical bodies that grounds the relevant colour-disposition. This is the property which Locke and Boyle called "textures". In modern terms, the natural candidates for object surface colours, would be spectral reflectances.

That being said, there may be special reasons to rule out some of these candidate concepts. Jonathan Cohen, for example, defends a relational theory of colour, and C.L. Hardin, a subjectivist view of colour.[33] If their arguments are cogent, then there would not seem to be good reason to introduce the notions either of colour-as-a-physical-texture or of colour-as-a-disposition to cause types of experience (to normal perceivers in standard conditions). There is a host of issues here. For further discussion see Part IV on Colour Ontology in this volume.

We should also note that the requirements of science are complex. One purpose for retaining, for scientific purposes, the standard conventional concept—the 'folk concept'—is this: we need to understand how perception of material objects works and how in particular how colour perception works. The claim of the indirect realist is that the best theory is one that proposes that our experience works in a certain way—as outlined by the theory. Part of this story involves explaining, at least in outline, why and how ordinary perceivers acquire the folk concept of colour. Not only does experience work that way, but there is very good reason why it should. The Projectivist theories are error theories, but the errors serve a fruitful purpose. The way perception works, it is claimed, is that the naïve perceiver mistakes the sensory representation for the thing represented—but that mistake is a useful mistake. The perceiver can function just as well, or even better, by making that sort of systematic mistake.

9 Arguments for Indirect Realism and objections

Specific arguments for Indirect Realism are often presented by starting with a default theory of perception, say, some form of direct realism, and then showing how, in the light of its deficiencies, an indirect theory is superior. Historically, however, in different contexts there have been different default positions: sometimes it is Naïve Realism; sometimes it is one form or another of cognitive direct realism; in some cases it is Idealism or Phenomenalism. In the case of classical scientists, e.g. Descartes and Boyle, it is sometimes naïve realism, but sometimes what they are arguing against (even implicitly) is some form of Aristotelian direct realism, one that assumes his formal/material distinction. In the twentieth century, the major opposition has been, at one time, some form of Phenomenalism, at other times, some form of cognitive direct realism, and currently, both theories, as well as naïve realism.

Insofar as we are seeking an overall argument for Indirect Realism, the theory would seem to be best justified piecemeal, in a series of two-sided debates with different opponents, which may include other forms of indirect realism. Overall, the aim is to show how the theory gives the best account of the phenomenology of perceptual experience, which is consistent with what is known—both through science and common sense—of the causal mechanisms underlying the perception of things in the material world. In other words it appeals to a combination of the following: the phenomenology of perceptual experience; second, of the phenomena that (something like) the classical Argument from Illusion appeals to; and third, an appeal to what the best scientific theories say. Examples of specific individual arguments for Indirect realism can be found in Jackson 1977, Perkins 1983, Smythies 1994, 2008, Maund 2003, Lowe 2008a, Brown 2008.

Perhaps the dominant theme in defences of the theory is the following: the claim that in perceptual experience one is presented with a certain qualitative feature—a "sensuous", sensory, quality—together with the claim that, taking colour experience as paradigmatic, there is no reason to think that physical bodies have such qualities or anything resembling them. An important part of the argument for these claims will depend on considerations that lie at the heart of the classical Argument from Illusion, including appeal to the best scientific account of the causal mechanisms involved in perception. (I say 'considerations' since at least one prominent theorist, Jackson, rejects the Argument from Illusion.) Another theme is the emphasis that is placed on showing that the version defended escapes the standard objections that have been levelled at the theory.

One of the standard objections to the classical Representative theory was that introduced a 'veil of perception' between the subject and the world, making the external world unknowable. Different reasons for this claim have been advanced: if the theory were true, then either (1) the inference to external material objects could never be justified; (2) the material objects would be unperceivable and thus blocked off from our perceptual capacities; (3) we could not acquire the concept of a material object; or (4) it is possible that all of our experiences are the same and there is a different material world altogether (or even none). The standard reply to these objections is that the claim depends on either a misunderstanding of what the theory is committed to, or depends on faulty epistemological assumptions. (For examples of this reply, see Maund 1975, 1993, Mackie 1976, Jackson 1997, Oakes 1993, Wright 1993, Smythies 1994, Lowe 1995.) Another reply is that, with respect to some forms of the 'veil of perception', other theories are in the same position.

A stronger objection, which is a more sophisticated version of the objection above, can be found in the writings of Paul Snowdon and A.D. Smith.[34] Each claims that Indirect Realism is fatally flawed. The problem comes from explaining demonstrative expressions in perceptual contexts. The concern is with how to interpret expressions such as 'that __ is a violin', 'that __ is a horse-drawn carriage', etc., within the indirect realist framework. Both Smith and Snowdon argue that no satisfactory interpretation of such expressions is possible within this framework. The difficulty is especially important in the standard case in which the perceiver does not realize that she is perceiving material objects indirectly. Derek Brown has provided a detailed response to their arguments.[35] He argues that the objections depend on a range of assumptions that the indirect realist can plausibly resist.

Another objection is that the theory presupposes a faulty analogy/model: it presupposes an 'inner screen', and an 'inner man' looking at 'pictures' on the screen. It is said to commit the homunculus fallacy, which, among other things, involves a vicious infinite regress. Maund 1993 and Harrison 1993 have responded to this objection. First, it does not apply to those versions of the theory that make a distinction between seeing a material object/event and being aware of a sensum/sensory quality. Second, even for those versions that do not make this distinction, the accusation of a fallacy is itself a fallacy. To paraphrase Harrison, kicking a man requires kicking some part of him, e.g. his bottom, and even if kicking his bottom requires kicking some part of it, it does not follow—for each part in series—that kicking that part requires kicking a part of the part.

Yet another objection is one based on the claim that Indirect Realism involves the postulation of sensa or sense data. Many contemporary philosophers think that such theories have been discredited, by a weighty body of criticism, and hardly worthy of reconsideration. Against that, however, there has also been a revisionary body of thought, arguing that the strength of this criticism has been greatly over-estimated.

The strongest criticism against sensa/sense data would seem to be found in the writings of Sellars 1956, Austin 1962, Ryle 1966, and Cornman 1971, and before them, O. Bouwsma 1942/1965 and Martin Lean 1953. Tim Crane 2000, in an insightful historical essay, points out how much classical criticism of sense-data theories was flawed because of its misunderstandings, both of the intentions of the sense-data theories, and of the different ways the term "sense datum" was used by different authors. In the second place, many arguments for sensa/sense data have depended on the classical Argument from Illusion. This argument has been given short shrift in the latter half of the twentieth century, However, there are several philosophers, e.g. H. Robinson 1994 and A.D. Smith 2002, who have recently argued that much of this criticism has been based on serious misunderstanding, and that the argument, properly qualified, is much stronger than it is customarily described. It is worth noting that none of the authors—Crane, Smith, Robinson—are indirect realists. For arguments in similar vein, by indirect realists, see Harrison 1993, Maund 2003, Lowe 2008a.

It is worth pointing out, in this context, that as far as sense data/sensa are concerned, it is important, as Crane shows, to distinguish between epistemological motivations for such entities and metaphysical ones. One indicator of this importance is that while Wilfred Sellars is a scourge for sense data (epistemological entities), he argues for the importance of sensa (metaphysically motivated entities). One who is aware of the difference is W. Lycan, who, in his book, *Consciousness* (1987), has an extended discussion of Sellars' arguments (see his lengthy footnotes 33, 35 on p. 145).[36] A second comment is that while sensa/sensuous qualities are often thought of as non-physical, and this is thought by many to be a damaging consequence, not all Indirect theorists make this assumption. Smythies and Perkins, for example, state that their theories are materialist.[37] Price was very cautious about the nature of sense data.[38]

Many of these issues are the same as, or connected with, those surrounding *qualia*, and it is difficult to think that much could be said in this chapter to add to the vast literature on this topic.

Finally, it is important to note that, with the recent resurgence of interest in naïve realist theories of perception, and of disjunctivist theories of perceptual experience, the task of the indirect realist has become more complex. The issue at stake, here, is whether the disjunctivist and naïve realist accounts can cohere plausibly with the best scientific accounts of the causes of perceptual experience. (For a strong defence of Naïve Realism, combined with Disjunctivism, see Martin 2002.) Difficult cases for these theorists, so the indirect realist argues, are (a) those many experiences where, with respect to some features of the object, the experience is veridical, and with respect to others, non-veridical (see Smith 2010); (b) the phenomenon of seeing double, for which Lowe 2008b has a lengthy discussion. (For further discussion, see Haddock and Macpherson 2008.)

10 Indirect Realism in the context of psychology

There is a more narrow locus for the dispute between indirect and direct realisms, and that is within psychology itself, more narrowly defined. In 1997, the American psychologist, Irvin Rock, published (posthumously) a collection of essays, which he had edited, entitled *Indirect Perception*.[39] Stephen E. Palmer, in the foreword to the book, to which he contributes, sets out the terms of the debate, when he writes that this volume is based on a certain "big question":

> Is perception a "direct" process in which our experiences result simply from extracting information from retinal stimulation, as Gibson proposed, or is it an "indirect" process in which our experiences are derived by inference in a layered, hierarchical system of interpretation, as Helmholtz maintained?

In his book, *The Ecological Approach to Perception*, J.J. Gibson had offered a radical alternative to the approach taken by Rock, Palmer and others.[40] Furthermore, he describes his theory as a 'Direct Realist' theory.

Palmer's "big question", however, suggests that the proper terms of the dispute is not between Direct and Indirect Realisms, as we have been understanding them. It seems that the dispute is at the level of non-conscious processes. Certainly, the reference to Helmholtz, the great German physicist and physiologist/psychologist, suggests this. Helmholtz is a central figure in a tradition, which, in the words of Rock, holds the view that "perception is intelligent, in that it is based on operations similar to those that characterise thought".[41] (Against this, we should note, is the fact that Rock and Palmer both stress that what they are writing about is *conscious perception*.[42])

We need to be cautious here, however, for it may well be that Gibson's complaint was directed more at the constructivist element in the other tradition, and the implicit claim about the type of information available for the visual system. Indeed, this seems to be the force of the defence of Gibson, by Evan Thompson 1995 and Alva Noë 2004. They are certainly not uncritical of Gibson. Thompson accuses Gibson of not understanding his own approach well enough, that is, for expressing himself in opposition to representations, and not allowing that there may be *action-centred representations*. Noë thinks that some of Gibson's controversial claims are in need of rational reconstruction. However, they credit him with two insights that the traditional approach had been blind to. One is that the animal's data for visual perception are not as narrow as that tradition had supposed.[43] The second is that the role of perception is not the construction of "an internal representation of the external world". With respect to the second point, Noë defends an *enactive approach* to perception that holds that perception is not something that happens to us, or in us: it is something we do. Crucially, on this approach, perceptual experience acquires content thanks to our possession of bodily skills. "What we perceive is determined by what we do (or what we know how to do); it is determined by what we are ready to do."[44] In similar vein, Thompson defends the centrality of *action-centred representations*.

Thompson and Noë seem to accept Direct Realism but, given our earlier discussion, however, this leaves open the question of whether their theories might be compatible with the hybrid version of Indirect Realism, discussed above. There is reason to think that they are. Noë, for example, accepts the link between his ideas and those of Gareth Evans. Furthermore, in addressing the question of whether his theory is a form of direct realism, he discusses criticisms of sense-datum theories. He says that the criticisms, even if successful, "leave unscathed what is really the sense-datum theory's core idea: that perceiving is a way of finding out how things are from how they look or sound or, more generally, appear".[45]

There is a range of issues at stake here, which are not easily sorted out, let alone resolved. It is, perhaps, wise to conclude by saying that much more needs to be done on settling these issues.

Notes

1 C. McGinn 1983, p. 129.
2 E.J. Lowe 1995, p. 62.
3 It is possible that a theory might exemplify both types of theory.
4 E.J. Lowe 1993 defended a theory of perception "which is at once a causal theory, a representative theory and a direct realist theory". In this paper, the term, 'representative theory of perception', does not imply 'indirect theory'.
5 See for example, John Yolton 1984, and E.J. Lowe 1995, pp. 42–7; p. 59.
6 Mackie 1985, pp. 214–24.
7 D. Hume 1738/1911, Bk III, part I, Section I, 177; see also Bk I, IV, IV, p. 216.
8 Locke 1706/1961, Bk II, XXXII, 15.
9 Maxwell 1872/1970, p.75.
10 Descartes 1644/1988, p. 118; Locke 1706/1961, BkII, XXX.2; XXXII, 14–15.
11 Newton, 1704/1970, p. 23.
12 Locke 1706/1791, II, XXXII, 14.
13 Another is Barry Maund, see Maund 2003.
14 Broad 1923, p. 248.
15 Broad 1923, p. 267; see also p. 247.
16 Broad 1923, p. 268.
17 See Jackson 2004 and Jackson 2007.
18 Dretske 1969, p. 29.
19 See Jackson 1977, p. 88.
20 See Jackson 1977, p. 122.
21 Jackson 1977, p. 157.
22 Jackson 1977, p. 159.
23 Dretske 1969, p. 29.
24 Price 1932, p. 5.
25 Russell 1912, p. 46.
26 Perkins 1983.
27 See F. Dretske 1969, R. Chisholm 1957.
28 Perkins 1983, pp. 205–22.
29 Perkins 2005.
30 See Maund 2003, Chapters 2 and 4.
31 Evans 1982, esp. ch.6; McDowell 1986, esp. 138–43.
32 Evans, 1982, p. 157.
33 See Cohen 2009, and Hardin 2008.
34 Snowdon 1992, pp. 62–6; Smith 2002, pp. 15–17.
35 Brown 2009.
36 These occur in a chapter entitled, 'Color as a Paradigm Case of a Quale'.
37 M. Perkins, 1983, pp. 4–5; J.R. Smythies 1993, pp. 220–8.
38 Price 1932, pp. 18–19.
39 Irvin Rock 1997.
40 J.J. Gibson 1979.
41 Rock 1983, p. 1.
42 See Palmer 1997, Foreword, p. xi, p. xxi; Rock 1997, p. 3.
43 Noë 2004, p. 21.
45 Noë 2004, p. 1.
46 Noë 2004, p. 81.

References

Austin, J.L. 1962, *Sense and Sensibilia*, G. Warnock (ed.), Oxford: Oxford University Press.

Averill, E. 2005, 'Toward a Projectivist Account of Color', *The Journal of Philosophy*, 102: 217–34.

Aydede, M. 2005, *Pain: New Essays on its Nature and Methodology*, Cambridge, Mass.: MIT Press.

Boghossian, P.A. and Velleman, J.D. 1997, 'Physicalist Theories of Color', in *Readings on Color*, Vol. I, ed. A. Byrne and D. R. Hilbert, Cambridge, Mass.: MIT Press, pp. 105–36.

Bouwsma, O.K. 1942/1965, 'Moore's Theory of Sense Data', *Philosophical Essays*, Lincoln: University of Nebraska Press.

Broad, C.D. 1923, *Scientific Thought*, London: Kegan Paul.

Brown, Derek 2009, 'Indirect Perceptual Realism and Demonstratives'. *Philosophical Studies*, 145: 377–94.

Brown, H.I. 2008, 'The Case for Indirect Realism', in E. Wright 2008, pp. 45–58.

Byrne, A. 2001, 'Intentionalism Defended', *Philosophical Review*, 100: 199–240.

Chisholm, R. 1957, *Perceiving: A Philosophical Study*, Ithaca, NY: Cornell University Press.

Cohen, Jonathan 2009, *The Red and The Real*, Oxford: Oxford University Press.

Cornman, J.W. 1971, *Materialism and Sensation*, New Haven, CT: Yale University Press.

Crane, T. 2000, 'The Origins of Qualia', *History of the Mind-Body Problem*, T. Crane and S. Patterson (eds.), London: Routledge, pp. 169–94.

Descartes, Rene 1644/1988, *Principles of Philosophy*, in John Cottingham, Robert Stoothoff, and Dugald Murdoch (eds.), *Descartes: Selected Philosophical Writings*, Cambridge: Cambridge University Press.

Dretske, F. 1969, *Seeing and Knowing*, London: Routledge & Kegan Paul.

Dretske, F. 1996, *Naturalizing the Mind*, Cambridge, Mass.: MIT Press.

Evans, Gareth 1982, *The Varieties of Reference*, Oxford: Clarendon Press.

Gibson, J.J. 1979, *The Ecological Approach to Visual Perception*, Boston, MA: Houghton, Mifflin.

Haddock, A. and Macpherson, F. (eds.) 2008, *Disjunctivism: Perception, Action, Knowledge*, Oxford: Oxford University Press.

Hardin, C.L. 2008, 'Color Qualities and the Physical World', in E. Wright 2008, pp. 143–54.

Harrison, J. 1993, 'Science, Souls and Sense-Data', in E. Wright 1993, pp. 15–44.

Hume, David 1738/1911, *Treatise of Human Nature*, A. D. Lindsay (ed.), London: Dent.

Jackson, Frank 1977, *Perception: A Philosophical Study*, Cambridge: Cambridge University Press.

Jackson, Frank 2004, 'Representation and Experience', H. Clapin, P. Staines, and P. Slezak (eds.), *Representation in Mind*, Amsterdam: Elsevier, pp. 107–24.

Jackson, Frank 2007, 'Color for Representationalists', *Erkenntnis*, 66: 169–85.

Lean, Martin 1953, *Sense-Perception and Matter*, London: Routledge & Kegan Paul.

Locke, J., 1706/1961, John Yolton (ed.), *An Essay Concerning Human Understanding*, London: Dent.

Lowe, E.J. 1993, 'Perception: A Causal Representative Theory', in E. Wright 1993, pp. 136–52.

Lowe, E.J. 1995, *Locke on Human Understanding*, London: Routledge.

Lowe, E.J. 2008a, 'Illusions and Hallucinations as Evidence for Sense Data', in E. Wright 2008, pp. 59–72.

Lowe, E.J. 2008b, 'Against Disjunctivism', in Haddock and Macpherson 2008, pp. 95–111.

Lycan, W. 1987, *Consciousness*, Cambridge, Mass.: MIT Press.

Mackie, John 1976, *Problems in Locke*, Oxford: Clarendon Press.

Mackie, John 1985, 'Locke and Representative Perception', in J. Mackie and P. Mackie (eds.), *Logic and Knowledge*, Oxford: Clarendon Press, pp. 214–24.

Martin, M.G.F. 2002, 'The Transparency of Experience', *Mind and Language*, 17, 376–425.

Maull, Nancy 1980, 'Cartesian Optics and the Geometry of Nature', in S. Gaukroger, *Descartes: Philosophy of Mathematics and Physics*, Brighton: Harvester Press, pp. 23–40.

Maund, Barry 1975, 'The Representative Theory of Perception', *Canadian Journal of Philosophy*, 5: 41–55.

Maund, Barry 1993, 'Representation, Pictures and Resemblance', in Wright 1993, pp. 45–69.

Maund, Barry 2003, *Perception*, Chesham: Acumen.

Maund, Barry 2011, 'Colour Eliminativism', in L. Nolan 2011, pp. 362–85.

Maxwell, J.C. 1872/1970, 'On Color Vision', *Proc. of the Royal Institution of Great Britain*, repr. in David L. MacAdam 1970, *Sources of Color Science*, Cambridge, Mass.: MIT Press, pp. 75–83.

Newton, Isaac, 1704/1970, 'Optics' repr. in David L. MacAdam 1970, *Sources of Color Science*, Cambridge, Mass.: MIT Press, pp. 16–39.

McDowell, John 1986, 'Singular Thought and Inner Space', in P. Pettit and J. McDowell (eds.), pp. 137–68.

McGinn, Colin 1983, *The Subjective View: Secondary Qualities an Indexical Thoughts*, Oxford: Clarendon Press.

Noë, Alva 2004, *Action in Perception*, Cambridge, Mass.: MIT Press.

Nolan, L. (ed.), 2011, *Primary and Secondary Qualities*, Oxford: Oxford University Press.

Oakes, R. 1993, 'Representational Sensing: What's the Problem?', in E. Wright 1993, pp. 70–87.

Palmer, S.E.K. 1997, 'Foreword' to I. Rock (ed.), *Indirect Perception*, Cambridge, Mass.: MIT Press.

Perkins, M. 1983, *Sensing the World*, Indianapolis, Ind.: Hackett.

Perkins, M. 2005, 'An Indirectly Realistic, Representational Account of Pain(ed.) Perception', in M. Aydede 2005, pp. 199–218.

Pettit, P. and McDowell, J. (eds.), 1986, *Subject, Thought and Context*, Oxford: Clarendon Press.

Price, H.H. 1932, *Perception*, London: Methuen.

Robinson, H. 1994, *Perception*, London: Routledge.

Rock, Irvin 1983, *The Logic of Perception*, Cambridge, Mass.: MIT Press.

Rock, Irvin 1997 (ed.), *Indirect Perception*, Cambridge, Mass.: MIT Press.

Russell, B. 1912, *The Problems of Philosophy*, Oxford: Oxford University Press.

Ryle, G. 1966, *The Concept of Mind*, Harmondsworth: Penguin.

Sellars, W. 1956, 'Empiricism and the Philosophy of Mind', in *Minnesota Studies in the Philosophy of Science*, vol. I, H. Feigl and M. Scriven (eds.), Minneapolis, MN: University of Minnesota Press, pp. 253–329.

Smith, A.D. 2002, *The Problem of Perception*. Cambridge, Mass.: Harvard University Press.

Smith, A.D. 2010, 'Disjunctivism and Illusion', in *Philosophy and Phenomenological Research*, LXXX: 384–410.

Smythies, J.R. 1993, 'The Impact of Contemporary Neuroscience and Introspection Psychology on the Philosophy of Perception', in E. Wright 1993, pp. 205–32.

Smythies J.R. 1994, *The Walls of Plato's Cave*, Aldershot: Avebury.

Smythies, J.R. 2008, 'How Qualia Fit Into the Brain', in E. Wright 2008, pp. 191–9.

Snowdon, P. 1992, 'How to Interpret "Direct Perception"', in T. Crane (ed.), *The Contents of Experience*, New York: Cambridge University Press, pp. 48–78.

Thompson, Evan 1995, *Colour Vision*, London: Routledge.

Tye, M. 2000, *Color, Content and Consciousness*, Cambridge, Mass.: MIT Press.

Wright, Edmond 1993 (ed.), *New Representationalisms*, Aldershot: Avebury.

Wright, Edmond 2008 (ed.), *The Case for Qualia*, 45–58, Cambridge, Mass.: MIT Press.

Yolton, John 1984, *Perceptual Acquaintance from Descartes to Reid*, Minneapolis: University of Minnesota Press.

25

DOES THAT WHICH MAKES THE SENSATION OF BLUE A MENTAL FACT ESCAPE US?

John Campbell

1 The presence of redness in colour experience

So far as I know, the first clear statement of a broadly relationalist, primitivist view of colour experience is in G.E. Moore's 'Refutation of Idealism'. The picture is 'relationalist' in that visual experience is thought of as a relation between the perceiver and the environment. And it's 'primitivist' in that the qualitative colour, blueness or whatever, is taken at face value, as a characteristic of the external object, rather than being analysed as a tendency of the thing to produce sensations or any other aspect of experience, and without any presumption that the qualitative colour can be analysed in physicalistic terms. The Moore passage is famous, but its significance is not usually appreciated:

> that which makes the sensation of blue a mental fact seems to escape us: it seems, if I may use a metaphor, to be transparent—we look through it and see nothing but the blue.
>
> *(Moore 1903, 446)*

If the qualitative character of blueness were itself mentalistic—a *quale*—then 'that which makes the sensation of blue a mental fact' could hardly be said to 'escape us'. Moore's point here is that the qualitative blueness of the blue thing is not itself mentalistic; it is an external characteristic of the object out there. The experience itself is to be thought of as a matter of the perceiver standing in an experiential relation to that external blueness. This external blueness is what consequently constitutes the qualitative character of the experience.

This relational, primitivist picture of colour experience obviously captures the way in which the colour red itself is there in a visual experience of redness. The presence of the colour red in a visual experience of redness is hard to explain on any view that takes your colour experience to be a matter of you representing the colours in experience. Sometimes representationalists say that in visual experience, we have not representations but 'perceptual presentations' of the colours. I once heard someone say that in vision, we think about the colours, '*in colour*'.

It seems sometimes to be supposed that the representationalist can capture the sense in which redness is 'there' in the experience by acknowledging that visual experience is 'transparent', in Moore's term, in some sense that the representationalist can acknowledge. The idea is that when representing a situation, your attention is often focused not at all on the representation itself, but on the situation represented. If you and I are having a heated argument about whose turn it is to cook dinner, for example, our attention may be completely focused on the topic, and not at all on the words we're using. Vision, the representationalist suggests, is simply a particularly striking form of this general phenomenon. Try to attend to your visual experience, and you end up focusing on the scene before you. Perhaps, it's sometimes suggested, in vision it's simply impossible to attend to anything but the situation represented, you can't attend to the visual representation itself (cf., e.g., Tye 2013).

Whatever the representationalist should say about the modality here (is it really completely 'impossible', or just something we usually don't do, or what?), it should be evident that this kind of idea can't begin to explain the sense in which redness itself is 'there' in a visual experience of redness. Suppose that you and I are having an argument about the battle of Gallipoli. Our attention may be focused entirely on the situation represented; we are not thinking at all about the words we are using, or how we are talking about the people in question. In this case it's quite natural to say that the words are 'diaphanous', our attention falls through them and onto the things we are thinking about. But 'transparency' in this sense is not enough to make the situation at Gallipoli 'present' to us in the way in which colours are present in colour experience. The sense in which redness is 'there' in an experience of red can't be explained in terms merely of the transparency of visual representation.

Traditionally a natural reaction at this point has been to appeal to some non-representational aspect of visual experience, such as a 'sensation', in order to explain the sense in which redness is there in the experience. Representations merely tell you what is out there; sensations make the scene come alive, pump colour into it. One idea is that colour terms apply in the first instance to those sensations, and only derivatively, if at all, to physical objects. The sense in which redness is there in vision is that vision involves not only representations, but sensations which are, literally, red. Whether external objects can also be said to be 'red' is a further question, sometimes thought to have been decided negatively by science. The trouble with this idea is that our ordinary colour concepts quite obviously apply in the first instance to physical objects. To grasp colour concepts one has to have some at least implicit understanding of colour constancy—that objects typically aren't changing their colours just because the conditions of illumination change, for example—and this grasp of constancy makes no sense for the case of sensations, which don't have 'conditions of illumination' (for further discussion of colour constancy, see Smith 2002, Brown 2014, and 'Colour Constancy'—Chapter 16 by Brown in this volume).

You might therefore retreat to a more oblique use of sensations. You might say that redness is 'there' in ordinary visual experience in the sense that not only is redness represented, there is a suitable sensation accompanying that representation. But just having some sensation or other could not amount to redness itself being present in the visual experience, no matter how often that sensation accompanies the representation of redness.

Another line of thought for representationalism begins with the difficulty that the usual naturalistic accounts of perceptual representation have with colour experience. What is it for a cognitive system to represent redness? We need the system to be causally sensitive specifically to the presence or absence of redness, and for that to be the point of the system. But of course it's not only perceptual systems that could 'represent' redness in this sense. Any kind of linguistic system for talking about redness will represent redness in that sense. So the representation of redness, in this sense, doesn't bring with it the presence of redness itself.

You might then suggest that we need some further notion of 'phenomenal' representation, which will bring with the representation of redness the perceptual presence of redness. It's easy to see the pressure that leads the theorist to make this kind of claim. It's less easy to see how to make sense of the claim. How can the mere representation of a property demand the presence of the property itself?

One way of trying to make sense of this is to say that the perceptual representation of redness represents the *essence* of redness; that's the sense in which redness is 'present' in perception but not in other ways of representing redness. The trouble with this is to find an interpretation of 'essence' on which this kind of claim could be both true and a plausible description of perceptual presence. What is the essence of a colour? A natural thought is that this has something to do with the geometry of colour—the location of particular shades in the colour solid. So you might think that the essence of orange is that it's a binary colour located between red and yellow. But this description of the essences of the colours as having to do with their structural characteristics simply misses the key way in which redness is there in colour experience. It's not merely the *structure* of the colours that is present in colour experience. It's the absolute values of the colours themselves—the blueness of the blue thing, for example.

What you want to do is point to the qualitative character you're encountering in experience and say '*that*, that is what's essential to blueness'. So you might say: the sense in which blueness is present in experience is that the qualitative character that is essential to blueness is present in experience. But now we simply have arrived at the relational view. The relational view is that the experience itself is a relation to the blueness of the external object. That external blueness is the only thing you can be pointing to when you say, '*that*, that is what's essential to blueness'. It's the external qualitative character that matters.

2 The physical bases of colour and colour experience

I've been arguing that our only conception of 'the redness of a red experience', or 'phenomenal redness', is that the experience is a relation one stands in to that mind-independent property of redness. On a primitivist conception, colours are mind-independent characteristics of the objects and liquids and so on around us. Our understanding of one another's colour experiences depends on our knowledge of the colours, so conceived.

Colour, conceived in this way, is an indispensable element in our imaginative understanding of one another. Imaginative understanding has its own epistemic authority. We know of the existence and nature of one another's conscious lives on the basis of our imaginative understanding of each other. If we didn't have an imaginative understanding of one another, physical science couldn't provide us with knowledge of one another's conscious states. That was the point about Nagel's bat.

Even though imaginative understanding has its own epistemic authority, we can still ask whether the mind-independent colours we think about are grounded in the physical world. Here we hit problems. Given any candidate physical basis for colour, you can imagine the presence of the colour without the presence of that physical basis. You are more certain of the presence of the colour than you are of the presence of any physical basis. And the colour seems to have a certain unity and simplicity that the physical basis altogether lacks.

As Byrne (2006) notes, these arguments are counterparts of Descartes' arguments for the distinctness of mind and body. We do not seem to gain any traction in our understanding of the relation between the macroscopic world and the underlying physical reality by trying to explain colour in terms of some mentalistic construct and then explaining that in terms of the brain. Moreover, as we have seen, we do not seem to have a good way of explaining the required mentalistic construct—one that would acknowledge the sense in which colour is present in perceptual experience.

You might say, though, that the structure of the qualitative colours has a physical counterpart in the structure of the neural assemblies involved in colour vision, but has no physical counterpart in the structure of the physical environment of the observer. You might argue that it follows from this that to explain how the qualitative character of colour is grounded in physics, we need a two-stage procedure:

1 Explain the qualitative characters of the colours of objects in terms of the qualitative character of colour experience, and then,
2 Explain the qualitative character of colour experience in terms of the structure of neural processes involved in colour vision.

Is this argument any good? At the most abstract level we can see right away that it isn't. We can have a whole high-level explanatory structure in which there are mind-independent colours grounding our colour experiences, and yet the only physical systems that have a similar structure, identified now by its significance at the physical level, are neural, or defined by their relations to the neural. The whole high-level explanatory system could still be grounded in the physical, without our needing to postulate some notion of the 'qualitative character of colour experience', identifiable independently of the mind-independent colours themselves. But let's look further at the argument.

Let's accept for the moment that the colours of the objects and liquids and flames and so on do have a determinate structure, and that there is no corresponding structure in any of the physical characteristics of the objects and liquids and flames and so on. And let's also accept, for the moment, that there is a correspondence between the structure of the colours and the structures of neural assemblies.

On a primitivist view of colour, the colours of objects and so on supervene on the physical characteristics of the environment, but may not have any explanatory or reductive grounding in those physical characteristics. The argument that reduction may not be possible is the one already rehearsed: that we can readily conceive of colour and physical composition coming apart, and so on. The structure of colour is, therefore, the structure of a high-level set of absolute properties that cannot be reduced to the physical. There is, therefore, no *a priori* reason to suppose that this structure must be reducible to the physical.

There is, of course, nothing particularly remarkable about the idea that there may be high-level structures without any echo at the level of physics. Consider, for example, the dynamics of a credit squeeze. So far as the high-level economic properties go, there are quantitative models for what is happening: the failure of confidence, the liquidity crises for businesses, and so on. Now all this economic structure presumably supervenes on what is going at the level of gluons. But that's not to say that we should expect there to be quantum-mechanical structures, with independently identifiable quantum-mechanical significance, that correspond to the structure of a credit crunch.

Consider now what has to happen for there to be perceivers who can see those high-level properties, the colours. These perceivers must have perceptual systems that are causally responsive to those high-level structures. Now the scientific study of human perceptual systems generally assumes them to be describable at three levels. There is the level of computation, at which the task of the perceptual system is specified. There is the level of the algorithm, at which we characterize what strategies the system uses to that task. And there is the level of implementation, at which we say how these computations are implemented biologically (Marr 1982, cf. Griffiths *et al.* 2015). If, at the levels of computation and algorithm, we are describing representations that are sensitive to the high-level structure of the colours, then anything recognizable as a biological implementation of those representations will have to have a corresponding biological structure.

In other words, on the most straightforward reading of colour primitivism, the natural expectation would be that on this view, there may be no physical structures in the environment that correspond to the structure of the colours, but that we would expect there to be biological structures that echo the structure of the colours. Suppose now that a philosopher claims that this is exactly the situation that empirical science discovers (cf. Pautz 2014). It is difficult to see why this should be thought of as a threat to primitivism, rather than being a confirmation of it.

There is, however, a rather larger and vaguer way of interpreting this line of argument, one that does not claim that there is some direct contradiction between the empirical scenario envisaged and colour primitivism. Rather, the argument might be interpreted as an attempt to find considerations motivating one rather than another direction of research in attempting to ground colour phenomena in the physical. The idea would be that because of the difficulty of grounding the structures of the colours in the structures of the physical environment, the only path to take is to ground colours in colour experiences, and to ground colour experience neurally.

This argument limps at every step. The idea is that we should explain the structures of the colours of objects and so on in the structure of colour qualia, and then ground the colour qualia neurally. There are two problems with the proposed direction of research:

1   We have no idea what we are talking about when we talk about 'colour qualia'. I will amplify on this point in the next section, but we have already seen the basic problems. We can't explain colour qualia in representational terms, because doing so misses out the 'presence' of the colour itself in colour experience. When we try to add in the colour, saying that here we have a 'special type' of representation, we simply bring in the external colour itself. If we try to appeal to 'colour sensations', the basic problem we hit is that we have no way of saying what the various types of sensations are that we are talking about. We have no vocabulary to describe them.

2   The idea is that to find a physicalist reduction of colour, all we have to do is to abandon primitivism and make sense of colour qualia; then all that then stands in the way of a reduction of colour is resolution of the mind-body problem (framed in terms of 'qualia'). This may be part of a general programme, to reduce the relation between the medium-sized world generally and the world of physics to the mind-body problem. But this is not a promising programme; all we have done is make the mind-body problem insoluble.

To repeat, this is not to say that neural structure may not ultimately have a role to play in explaining the physical basis of the colours, but that the shuffle through an internalist construct, the 'colour qualia', merely leads to confusion: the construct cannot be properly explained.

3 Colour qualia

Let us look a little further at how people try to explain what they mean when they talk of 'colour sensations', or 'colour qualia'. In a recent article, Ned Block writes:

> Are phenomenological characters of perception—e.g. what it is like to experience redness or roundness—philosophically reducible to the redness or roundness of the objects one sees or to representation of redness or roundness? If there is no such reduction, then there can be said to be mental paint.
>
> *(Block 2010, 23–4)*

This seems to be his official explanation of what he means by 'mental paint'. Block is evidently struck by the thought that something more might be wanted, so he provides the following comment for the puzzled reader:

> I am not assuming that if there is mental paint, it is non-relational ("intrinsic") or has no representational aspect. Since I favor physicalism, I allow that mental paint may be a relational neural property. To avoid misunderstanding: I do not claim that there is anything red or round in the head when one veridically sees a red or round thing in the world as when red pigment in a painting represents a red barn.
>
> *(2010, 56, footnote 2)*

And that is it. So far as I can see, at any rate, that's all we get by the way of a positive description of what 'mental paint' is supposed to be. In all his voluminous writings on this topic, Block nowhere, so far as I know, provides any further substantial detail as to what mental paint is. There is, for example, no attempt to say what vocabulary you should use to specify particular types of mental paint.

I think that the most charitable reading here is that Block is using 'mental paint' as a term for a theoretical construct, whose further characterization has yet to be given. Block will introduce examples intended to show that no relational or representationalist theory can give a full description of colour perception. 'Mental paint' is simply his name for whatever it is that is missing. A parallel might be the use that physicists make of terms like 'dark energy' or 'dark matter'. When it's discovered that the rate of expansion of the universe is greater than current theories can explain, 'dark energy' is introduced as a name for whatever it is that is doing that. Someone using the term 'dark energy' typically isn't under any illusion that they have to hand a full characterization of the explanatory role that dark energy is playing. Still less are they under the illusion that they have an explicit characterization of what dark energy is. Still, the term 'dark energy' has some use, as pointing to some phenomenon that needs further explanation. Just so for Block's 'mental paint'. Block intends to point to phenomena of colour experience that current theories cannot explain; 'mental paint' is simply his name for whatever it is that is missing.

The trouble is that when we are talking about colour experience, it is hard to see how there can be any role for hidden aspects of the thing that can only be discovered by complicated thought-experiments or work in experimental psychology. Of course, students of the mind have always been fascinated by the idea of arcane levels of psychology not known to the ordinary person, from Kant's transcendental psychology through Freud's psychodynamics. Colour qualia do seem sometimes to be thought of as an arcane level of colour experience, unsuspected by the ordinary perceiver, who sees only the colours of objects. But the whole point about colour experience is that it has to do with what's on the surface; it can't be a home for arcana. The trouble is that 'mental paint' is supposed to figure in a characterization of what colour experience is like. How could that be consistent with taking mental paint to be a theoretical postulate like 'dark energy' whose characterization we have yet to discover?

In an influential discussion, Christopher Peacocke gave one of very few serious attempts to provide an explicit vocabulary for talking about colour sensations (and subsequently did more than any other philosopher to show how this kind of vocabulary might be put to work):

> It will help at this point if we introduce a simple piece of notation. If a particular experience *e* has the familiar sensational property which in normal circumstances is produced by a white object (such as a tilted plate) which would be precisely obscured

413

by an opaque elliptical region (*r*, say) of the imagined interposed plane, let us express this fact in the notation elliptical´ (*r*, *e*) and white´ (*r*, *e*)´.

(Peacocke 1983, 20)

I think the key phrase here is 'familiar sensational property'. Peacocke is taking it that we all already know perfectly well the phenomena he is talking about when he talks about 'red´ sensations'. That is why he does not think that the concepts need anything much in the way of explanation. But are we 'familiar' with sensational colour properties in vision? Recall Moore's remark 'that which makes the sensation of blue a mental fact seems to escape us'. All that experience gives us knowledge of, on Moore's view, is the blueness of the external object. How could you suppose that there is such a thing as the 'familiar sensational property' of being 'blue´', since what you encounter in experience is only the blueness of the external object? And in fact Moore is surely right about this: we don't encounter in experience any colour property other than the external property of things in the environment.

The dilemma you face in trying to explain the idea of 'colour qualia' is that you either (a) assume that in ordinary vision, when you see 'the blueness of the blue thing', you are merely encountering some aspect of your subjective life, not an aspect of your surroundings, in which case you deny the Moorean transparency of experience, and with it, the ability to recognize vision as giving you knowledge of what your surroundings are like, or (b) you take it that the very idea of 'colour qualia' is a theoretical construct, a posit to be characterized by describing its theoretical role. You might then try to give a fully explicit characterization of this theoretical role. This would then be comprehensible to Martian anthropologists who have no colour experience. But the whole idea of colour qualia was to describe 'what it is like' to have colour experience in terms of them, so how can we think that someone could have a full understanding of colour qualia without having any conception of what colour experience is like?

You might argue that in ordinary colour experience we are aware of two different phenomena, the redness out there and the 'red´-ness in the mind'. Thus Peacocke says, 'In the case of the sensational properties, the experienced properties are, in the visual case, properties and relations of the visual field and its parts' (Peacocke 2008). It is very hard to know how this idea is supposed to work. Does red´ness, as a characteristic of the visual field, exhibit colour constancy (that is, can something continue to be manifestly red´ through changes in the illuminant)? Does red´ness exhibit simultaneous colour contrast (that is, does the apparent red´ness or not of a region depend on the colours´ of neighbouring regions of space? If so, then 'red´' seems to be none other than the ordinary term 'red', with the prime indicating merely that it is being applied to some delimited region of space. Most of these ascriptions will then be false, since regions of space can't in general be said to have colours. The other possibility is that red´-ness does not exhibit colour constancy or simultaneous colour contrast, in which case I think we have as yet simply no idea what it means, although we're assured that it stands for a phenomenon that we're 'familiar' with. But ordinary visual experience seems to familiarize us only with the colours of the external objects.

The problems that we face in trying to interpret Block and Peacocke are exactly those that we should expect, if colour experience is in fact a relation between the perceiver and an external colour. Anyone trying to find some middle aspect of colour experience, 'the phenomenal colour', is then caught between regarding this thing as a purely theoretical postulate, like dark matter, or claiming that it's something we encounter in everyday experience, when in fact we encounter no such thing. A third option, of course, is to oscillate between these two positions.

I think the right reaction is to reflect on what materials we have for talking about colour and colour experience that clearly do make sense. And here there are two types of vocabulary:

1   The words we have in ordinary natural language for the colours of things—the redness of a red pepper, and so on.
2   The terms that vision scientists use for describing the information-processing that takes place when we see coloured things.

The relational, primitivist view of colour experience tries to characterize colour experience simply in terms of these vocabularies. It takes the relation 'X experiences colour Y' to be a generic relation that can hold between any perceiver and any colour in the environment. Or this austere position can be augmented: we can take it that what we have is a three-place relation, 'X experiences colour Y from standpoint Z', where the characterization of the standpoint might include, for example, specification of the conditions of illumination. Our understanding of colour experience is achieved by the exercise of the imagination, and in exercising imagination we take up the standpoint of the perceiver. The relation of experience is itself a theoretical construct; as Moore observed, it is this relation of experience that makes the sensation of blue a mental fact (not some 'blue' *quale*), and in ordinary experience this relation 'escapes us', it cannot be ostensively explained. Our grasp of this construct is implicit in the way we use imagination to understand how other people are experiencing the colours around them.

From the perspective of anyone who thinks that colour experience should be characterized as a three-place relation in this way, between the perceiver, the external colour, and the standpoint of the perceiver, the problem with thinking in terms of an 'inner' realm of qualitative colour qualia is that (a) the external, qualitative colour of the object has been regarded as an intrinsically mentalistic phenomenon, when in fact we have no way of identifying any such thing, and (b) the fact that we are dealing with a three-place relation has been misconstrued as implying that we are dealing with a two-place relation between the perceiver and the external phenomenon, mediated by the constituents of an inner realm of qualia. The problem here was already stated by Quine: 'immediate experience simply will not, of itself, cohere as an autonomous domain' (1960, 2).

As we saw earlier, people who think that visual experience is representational may hold that there is a concept of 'phenomenal intentionality' we can use to characterize colour experience. This will be like the ordinary notion of 'representing something as red', except that the 'phenomenal representation' requires the actual presence of redness itself.

The trouble is that there seems in principle to be no way of explaining the required conception of 'phenomenal intentionality'. 'Intentionality' itself is a fairly definite phenomenon. There are ordinary beliefs, which on the face of it illustrate intentionality, and goal-directed behaviours. But merely saying that colour experience is 'intentional' would leave out the striking difference between visual experience of the colours and having beliefs about colours. The difference is that in visually experiencing redness, redness itself is present, and that isn't so for having a belief about redness.

The 'rich' intentionalist tries to acknowledge this point by saying that we have here a particular variety of intentionality, 'phenomenal intentionality'. For a statement of this idea, consider Chalmers' approach:

> The phenomenal character of a perceptual experience is what it is like to have that experience …

> A representational content of a perceptual experience is a condition of satisfaction of that experience …

A *phenomenal content* of a perceptual experience is a representational content that is determined by the experience's phenomenal character.

(2006, 50)

The key term here is 'what it is like'. On one reading, perhaps not the intended reading, of this approach, 'what it is like' to have the experience is to be characterized in terms of qualia.

1   'What it is like' to have an experience is a matter of the qualia constituting that experience. The phenomenal character of an experience of yellow, for example, will be characterized by a yellow quale.

There will then be the question how this internal qualitative character determines a representional content, and a natural suggestion is this:

2   The representational content determined by that quale will be to the effect that some external object has an external property of yellowness. That external property of yellowness will be a resemblance of the qualitative character of yellowness possessed by qualia.

This idea that external objects might be represented as having properties that resemble the yellowness and so on of *qualia* then gives us a reading of what Chalmers means by 'Edenic' representational contents.

There are two problems with this conception of 'phenomenal intentionality'. One is that the talk of 'inner yellowness', yellowness as a characteristic of qualia, makes no sense. We can't explain it ostensively, because in ordinary visual experience we encounter only the yellowness of the external object. And we can't explain it as a theoretical construct, like 'dark matter', because we're trying to use it to characterize visual experience itself. So the talk of yellowness as a characteristic of qualia can't be sustained. The second problem is that the talk of 'resemblance' between the external objects and the qualia makes no sense. Even if we did have some conception of what it is for a purely mental item to be yellow, that would not of itself mean that we understand what it is for an ordinary physical object to resemble the mental item in point of colour.

An alternative reading is to set aside the talk of qualia, and interpret the talk of 'what it is like' not in terms of qualia, but in terms of our imaginative understanding of one another. Here we could use the idea of experience as a three-place relation between the perceiver, a standpoint, and the scene observed, as sketched about. On this reading, 'what it is like' to perceive a scene is specified by specifying the scene observed, the observer, and the point of view from which the observer is perceiving the scene. So you would specify a colour experience by saying which colours are there to be seen, who the observer is, and the standpoint from which the observer is seeing those colours. There is, of course, nothing representational about this way of saying what the experience is like for the observer. It would indeed, as Chalmers says, be possible to use that three-place relation to 'determine' any of a wide variety of representational contents, depending on which 'determination' relation is arbitrarily chosen by the theorist. But the specification of a representational content here will be idle in giving a description of the experience, it adds nothing to what is available at the level of imaginative understanding. We could eliminate all the talk about 'representation' and still have a full grasp of colour experience.

4 Imagining *de re*

There is a line of thought that can make the idea of a relational view of colour experience seem not just problematic but utterly incomprehensible. In a famous paper, Thomas Nagel wrote:

> At present we are completely unequipped to think about the subjective character of experience without relying on imagination—without taking up the point of view of the experiential subject.
>
> *(Nagel 2002, 224)*

I think it is fair to say that Nagel's comment here has not been effectively challenged in the voluminous subsequent literature. But if knowing about someone's experiences of colour requires imagining them 'from the inside', how can we so much as form the conception of experience as a relation between the experiencer and the qualitative environment? To address this, we have to look further at what it means to be imagining someone's experiences of colour.

Suppose you have committed a crime, let's say a murder. You have disposed of the body and are waiting to be interviewed by detectives. As they stand talking to you, you imagine how they are seeing the room. Can they see anything incriminating? Will they see the flashlight? What you are doing here is an exercise in imagining *de re*. That is, the exercise of the imagination constitutively depends on your perceptual knowledge of what is there in the room. You begin with your knowledge of the room, you can see quite well what's there and where it all is. You imagine *of that stuff* how it is seen by the detectives. Your imaginative understanding of their visual experiences constitutively depends on your knowledge of their surroundings. In contrast, what we might call 'imagining *de dicto*' is imagining someone's experiences in a way that does not constitutively depend on knowledge of their environment. It seems arguable that imagining *de dicto* depends on the ability to imagine *de re*. Imagining someone's visual experiences *de dicto* is a matter of imagining an environment for them; and then, within the context of that imaginative exercise, using one's capacity to imagine *de re* what the person is seeing. Imagining *de dicto* depends on imagining *de re* because imagining *de dicto* involves an exercise of the capacity to imagine *de re*.

To illustrate the point, recall Jackson's Mary, born in a black and white room, a brilliant scientist who knows all there is to know about the physics of colour and the science of colour vision (Jackson 2002). Jackson's question was, when Mary steps out into the world of colour, will she learn anything? His own answer was that she will: she'll learn what it's like to have the experience of colour. However, on the face of it, what Mary learns about in the first instance is not a psychological phenomenon at all. It's the surfaces of objects that she learns about: she learns what the colours of objects are. To see this, suppose we tweak the example a little. It's often said that people with autism have difficulty with mentalistic concepts. Whatever the merits of this as an approach to autism, suppose that this kind of analysis applies to Mary. Suppose that, though intelligent, she has no concept at all of visual experience. Then when she steps into the world of colour, she will not learn about any psychological phenomena. Will she then learn nothing at all? It seems evident that there is still a lot she will learn. She will learn about the colours of objects, even though she is learning nothing about visual experience.

This suggests that even when the original Mary is learning about visual experiences, she is able to do so only because she has first learned about a more basic phenomenon, the colours of the objects around her. She has first learned about the colours of the things around her. Now, *of* that phenomenon, she can imagine what it's like for people to see it. Her capacity to reflect on people's visual experiences of colour is provided by her capacity to imagine, *de re*, of the colours she knows about, what it is like to see *them*. Imagining people's experiences of colour requires first having knowledge of the colours themselves, and only then, in the context of that knowledge, imagining what it is like to see them. It is also true that you can imagine a group of coloured objects surrounding a person, and then, in the context of that imaginative exercise, imagine the person's experiences of those colours. But this is plainly a derivative exercise of imagination *de re*. The basic case is that in which your imaginative understanding depends on your knowledge of the shared environment.

It is, of course, possible to argue that physics has shown that colour, as a characteristic of the objects around us, simply does not exist. A full physical story about the objects around us does not involve ascribing colours to them. Nor does it involve ascribing to them any physical characteristics from which their colours might be derived. Right now, I remark only that the same line of argument would show that consciousness, as a characteristic of you or I, simply does not exist. A full physical story about ordinary humans does not involve ascribing consciousness to them. Nor does it involve ascribing to them any physical characteristics from which their conscious states must be derived. Since we are conscious, there must, therefore, be something wrong with this argument against the existence of colours, conceived as characteristics of the objects around us.

We can now reformulate the idea that colour experience should be thought of as a relation between the perceiver and the colours in the surroundings. If you think that all imagining is imagining *de dicto*, and the possibility of imagining *de re* does not even occur to you, then the idea of colour experience as a relation will seem absurd. Someone's colour experiences are what you can understand imaginatively; if imaginative understanding relates only to what is 'confined to the head', and can have no constitutive dependence on your knowledge of the surroundings of the other person, then colour experience itself must be confined to the head, and cannot be a relation to the perceiver's surroundings. The idea of colour experience as a relation to the surroundings is the idea of colour experience as something that has to be understood by imagination *de re*.

Recall the remark from Moore: 'that which makes the sensation of blue a mental fact seems to escape us: it seems, if I may use a metaphor, to be transparent—we look through it and see nothing but the blue' (Moore 1903, 446). As we saw, the key point here is that the blueness of the blue thing—that with which we are unmistakeably confronted in colour experience—is not, on this account, a mental phenomenon, it is not to be thought of as a *quale* produced by the external object, for example. The blueness is *out there*, on the object. The experience of blueness is a *relation* to that external phenomenon. We understand what this experience is by imagining *de re*. Nonetheless, the relation itself, the relation of *experiencing*, which is what makes it the case that we have a mental fact here, is not itself something that we confront, either in the initial perception or in having an imaginative understanding of it.

5 The inverted spectrum

The possibility of spectrum inversion is usually taken as a datum in discussions of colour and colour experience (for discussion, see 'Spectrum Inversion', Chapter 13 in this volume). What is certainly a datum is that you can imagine a world in which all the objects have different colours than they do in this one. You can imagine a world in which the fire engines are blue and the sky is red and so on. And you can imagine someone experiencing those colours.

What is meant by spectrum inversion, however, is usually the possibility that the colours in the environment are held constant, but that each of us experiences them differently. It is not at all obvious that this is possible. The use that's being made of the imagination here is relatively complex, and it's not at all obvious that this is a correct description of any imaginative exercise one is likely to carry out.

Why does it matter? Well, one way you might argue against colour primitivism is to say that (a) people's colour qualia might all be swapped around, and then (b) there would be no saying who was experiencing the colours correctly, but (c) colour primitivism implies that there would have to be just one correct way to experience the colours (cf., e.g., Chalmers 2006).

This line of argument does not give due weight to the point that imagining colour experience *de re* is more fundamental than is imagining colour experience *de dicto*. If you think that imagining other people's colour experiences is constitutively independent of your perceptual knowledge of their environment, then it makes perfect sense to think of varying everyone's colour experiences while holding constant the physics of the external environment. And you might well then face a difficult problem in saying which, if any, of these internalistic experiences resembles the external environment.

It is quite different if you are looking at the colours in your environment and imagining what other people are seeing when looking at *those colours*. Suppose you're a painter, working on a canvas. The colouration overall seems to you a bit heavy and flat, and you're working to lighten it a little and give it some more drama. You're imagining what other people will see when looking at *this*. Now if you've been reading about the inverted spectrum you might try to imagine what your canvas would be like with all the colours reversed, and then, within the compass of that imaginative project, you could imagine what it would be like to see it from various positions and distances. That imaginative exercise is providing you with information about what it would be like to be seeing all the colours round the other way from you. But it's not as if you can now sensibly ask the question, 'Does my colour experience provide knowledge of the colours of the canvas any better than my hypothetical subject's experiences provide knowledge of the colours of that same canvas?'.

Of course your own experiences are providing you with knowledge of the colours of the canvas before you. And of course this other subject, who you are imagining as seeing the colours on a quite different, colour-reversed, merely hypothetical canvas, is not getting knowledge of the colours on the canvas before you. That's just built into the description of the two imaginative exercises. Once we give due weight to the *de re* character of imaginative understanding, the idea of holding the external environment constant while varying the subjective experiences that people are having of it simply has to go.

References

Block, Ned. 2010. 'Attention and Mental Paint'. *Philosophical Issues* 20, 23–63.

Brown, Derek H. 2014. 'Colour Constancy and Colour Layering'. *Philosophers' Imprint* 14, 1–31.

Byrne, Alex. 2006. 'Color and the Mind-Body Problem'. *Dialectica* 60, 223–44.

Chalmers, David. 2006. 'Perception and the Fall From Eden'. In Tamar Gendler and John Hawthorne (eds.), *Perceptual Experience*. New York: Oxford University Press.

Griffiths, Thomas, Falk Lieder, and Noah Goodman. 2015. 'Rational Use of Cognitive Resources: Levels of Analysis Between the Computational and the Algorithmic'. *Topics in Cognitive Science* 7, 217–29.

Jackson, Frank. 2002. 'Epiphenomenal Qualia'. In David Chalmers (ed.), *Philosophy of Mind: Classical and Contemporary Readings*. New York: Oxford University Press.

Marr, David. 1982. *Vision*. San Francisco: W.H. Freeman.

Moore, G.E. 1903. 'The Refutation of Idealism'. *Mind* 48, 433–53.

Nagel, Thomas. 2002. 'What Is it Like to Be a Bat?'. In David Chalmers (ed.), *Philosophy of Mind: Classical and Contemporary Readings*. New York: Oxford University Press.

Pautz, Adam. 2014. In R. Brown (ed.), *Consciousness Inside and Out: Phenomenology, Neuroscience, and the Nature of Experience*, Studies in Brain and Mind 6. Dordrecht: Springer.

Peacocke, Christopher. 1983. *Sense and Content*. Oxford: Oxford University Press.

Peacocke, Christopher. 2008. 'Sensational Properties: Theses to Accept and Theses to Reject'. *Revue Internationale de Philosophie* 243.

Quine, W.V.O. 1960. *Word and Object*. Cambridge, Mass.: MIT Press.

Smith, A.D. 2002. *The Problem of Perception*. Cambridge, Mass.: Harvard University Press.

Tye, Michael. 2013. 'Transparency, Qualia Realism and Representationalism'. *Philosophical Studies* 170, 39–57.

26

COLOUR EXPERIENCES AND 'LOOK' SENTENCES

Wylie Breckenridge

Introduction

We have colour experiences. When you look at the patch below you have a colour experience of the patch (I will assume that grey is a colour). You also have a shape experience, and perhaps other kinds of experience, but in this chapter I am particularly interested in colour experiences.

We have ways of describing our colour experiences. One common way in English is to use a sentence whose main verb is 'look'. We might (correctly) describe your colour experience of the patch above, for example, using the following 'look' sentence:

> The patch looks grey to you

This description does not completely specify your colour experience, because 'grey' is too general a colour term, but it is still a true description.

There are other 'look' sentences that we might use. If it is understood that we are talking about your experience, rather than someone else's, then we might drop 'to you' and simply say:

> The patch looks grey

Care needs to be taken here—we might use this same sentence to talk about how the patch looks to people in general, not just to you on this occasion, so this use of the sentence might be misunderstood.

We might use a variety of other expressions in place of 'grey':

> The patch looks (to you) the way grey things do
> The patch looks (to you) like a grey thing
> The patch looks (to you) as if it is grey
> The patch looks (to you) to be grey

If we want to be non-committal about the presence of a patch, perhaps to allow that you are hallucinating, then we might use one of the following sentences (although each involves saying something slightly different from above):

> It looks (to you) as if you are seeing a grey patch
> There looks (to you) to be a grey patch in front of you

I'm interested in what we mean by these sentences. More generally, in what we mean by 'look' sentences when we use them to describe our colour experiences. Even more generally, in what we mean by 'look' sentences when we use them to describe our visual experiences. I will call these uses *visual experience* uses of 'look' sentences. Not all of our uses of 'look' sentences are visual experience uses. When I say, 'I looked out the window', I am using a 'look' sentence but it is not a visual experience use, because I am not describing a visual experience. We will see other examples later in the chapter.

My aim in this chapter is not to develop a theory of what we mean by our visual experience uses of 'look sentences—I've already done that, in Breckenridge (2018). Rather, my aim is to defend an assumption that the theory makes—that in our visual experience uses of 'look' sentences we do not use the word 'look', nor the sentences as a whole, with the variety of meanings that it might initially seem. But before getting to that I'll briefly illustrate that theory that I have developed.

What we mean by 'look' sentences

So what do we mean by our visual experience uses of 'look' sentences? I'll work through an example—our use of 'The patch looks grey to you' to describe your colour experience of the patch at the start of the chapter. I'll explain what we mean by the constituents of the sentence and how we combine them to give what we mean by the sentence as a whole. I will consider, as I go, how we might vary these constituents.

First, the verb 'look'. By this we mean a property of events—the property of being a looking event. So we can think of 'look' as being a predicate of events, one that is true of an event if and only if it is a looking event. We use the rest of the sentence to build up a more complex predicate, the meaning of which we build up by property conjunction (in a way that I will explain).

What is a looking event? I need to say some things about the nature of looking events, and introduce some labels for their features.

A looking event is an event in which things look some way to some one. Here I am using 'things' non-referentially, to allow that there is no thing that looks anyway (as might be the case during a hallucination).

A looking event has an *experiencer*—this is someone (or some thing) to whom things look some way. I suspect that a looking event must have at least one experiencer, although nothing that I say depends on this. I'm not sure whether it can have more than one. Suppose that you and I are looking at the patch above, both having a colour experience of it. Is that a looking event with two experiencers, or two looking events each with a single experiencer? I'm not sure.

A looking event might have a *stimulus*—this is a thing that looks some way. The event need not have a stimulus—some hallucinations are looking events that have no stimulus. It might have more than one stimulus, as when some *things* look some way to someone (here I am using 'things' referentially).

A looking event occurs in various *ways*. This is just like other kinds of events: walking events, swimming events, and so on—they all occur in various ways. What is it for a looking event to occur in a certain way? The kind *looking event* is a determinable kind—it has determinates. Each of these determinates is a way of looking. For a looking event to occur in a certain way is for it to be of one of these determinate kinds.

Now, back to 'The patch looks grey to you'. We have this: the verb 'look' is a predicate, by which we mean the property of being a looking event.

To the verb 'look' we add the present tense inflection '-s', to get the inflected verb 'looks'. By '-s' we mean the property of occurring now. What we mean by 'looks' is the conjunction of what we mean by 'look' and what we mean by '-s'; that is, the conjunction of the property of being a looking event and the property of occurring now; that is, the property of being a looking event and occurring now.

Next, to the tensed verb 'looks' we add the complement 'grey', to get the verb phrase 'looks grey'. By 'grey' we mean the property of occurring in a certain way. Which way? That's a bit complicated—I'll call it 'w' for now and come back to this. By 'looks grey' we mean the conjunction of the property that we mean by 'looks' and the property that we mean by 'grey'. That is, the conjunction of the property of being a looking event and occurring now and the property of occurring in way w. That is, the property of being a looking event and occurring now and occurring in way w.

Which way is w? In short, it is: the way that grey things look. That is, the way w such that grey things look w. Here I want 'grey things look w' to be understood *generically*. So, we might refer to it as: the way w such that it is generically true that grey things look w. Or, less ambiguously, as: the way w such that it is generically true that looking events whose stimulus is grey occur in way w. Actually, there are many such ways, varying in their degree of generality. By 'grey' we mean the *most specific* one of these. So, by 'grey' we mean: the *maximally specific* way w such that it is generically true that looking events whose stimulus is grey occur in way w.

When we use 'grey' in this way we use it *indirectly* to mean a way of looking—we use 'grey' to mean the property of being grey, and thereby mean a certain way of looking. Our use of 'grey' in this way is an application of a more general mechanism that we have for using adjectives to refer to ways of occurring. 'John walks proud', 'Brad talks American', etc. We have a mechanism for exploiting a certain function, f, which maps properties and kinds to ways of occurring. f(p, k) is the maximally specific way w such that it is generically true that events of kind k done by something with property p occur in way w.

We need not use this mechanism to mean w. We might, instead, mean it *directly*, by using a demonstrative such as 'this way', 'that way', or 'thus', or by using a definite description such as 'the way that grey things look'. Interestingly, we tend not to have names for ways of looking. But we can introduce them, as I did in the previous paragraph ('w').

Next, to 'looks grey' we add the modifier 'to you', to get the verb phrase 'looks grey to you'. By 'to you' we mean the property of having you as an experiencer. By 'looks grey to you' we mean the conjunction of the property that we mean by 'looks grey' and the property that we mean by 'to you'. That is, the conjunction of the property of being a looking event and occurring now and occurring in way w and the property of having you as an experiencer. That is, the property of being a looking event and occurring now and occurring in way w and having you as an experiencer. Adding such a modifier is optional. If it is understood that the experiencer is you then we might leave it off.

Next, to 'looks grey to you' we add 'The patch', to get the sentence 'The patch looks grey to you'. By 'The patch' we mean the property of having the patch as a stimulus. By 'The patch looks grey to you' we mean the conjunction of the property that we mean by 'looks grey to you' and the property that we mean by 'The patch'. That is, the property of being a looking event and occurring now and occurring in way w and having you as an experiencer and the property of having the patch as a stimulus. That is, the property of being a looking event and occurring now and occurring in way w and having you as an experiencer and having the patch as a stimulus.

It is a grammatical requirement of English that every sentence have a subject. If the looking event about which we are talking has no stimulus (e.g. it's a hallucination), or we'd like to leave the stimulus unspecified, then we can do so by using the semantically empty 'It' as the subject (as we do in 'It is windy outside'). 'It looks grey to you' is no good—we have to say something a bit different, such as 'It looks to you as if you are seeing a grey patch.' Alternatively, if the complement of 'look' is a clause that has a subject, then we can raise the subject of that clause into the subject position of the sentence. Semantically it is still interpreted as being the subject of the clause, so this makes no difference to what we mean by the sentence—it's just another way of satisfying the grammatical requirement that the sentence have a subject.

Finally, what we mean by the sentence when we assert it is that there is an event which has this property. So we mean:

> There is an event e such that e is a looking event, and is occurring now, and is occurring in the maximally specific way w such that it is generically true that looking events whose stimulus is grey occur in way w, and has you as an experiencer, and has the patch as a stimulus

More colloquially, we just say, 'The patch looks grey to you.'

Do we mean anything else by 'look'?

I have just briefly illustrated the account that I develop in Breckenridge (2018), of what we mean by our visual experience uses of 'look' sentences. On this account we use 'look' with the same meaning in every case. But is this right? It has been said that we have various uses of 'look', even when it comes to describing visual experiences. It is not always clear whether the claim is that we mean different things by 'look' itself or by 'look' sentences as a whole. I will consider both possibilities. In this section I consider the first possibility. I will look for evidence that we mean different things by 'look', and argue that there is no such evidence. In the next section I consider the second possibility.

Various categories of complements

In our visual experience uses of 'look' sentences we use, as the complement of 'look', expressions from a variety of syntactic categories. Here are some that we might use to describe your colour experience of the patch at the start of the chapter:

The patch looks grey
The patch looks a grey thing
The patch looks of a grey colour
The patch looks like a grey thing

> The patch looks greyer than the page
> The patch looks how grey things look
> The patch looks as if it is grey
> The patch looks to be grey

These examples include an adjective phrase ('grey'), a noun phrase ('a grey thing'), a preposition phrase ('of a grey colour'), a comparative phrase ('like a grey thing', 'greyer than the page'), a relative clause headed by 'how' ('how grey things look'), a phrase headed by 'as if' ('as if it is grey'), and a 'to'-infinitive ('to be grey').

Perhaps I should say that surface form *suggests* that we have expressions from a variety of syntactic categories. It could be that the complements above include one or more constituents that are not visible on the surface, possibly in such a way that the syntactic category of the complement is not what it appears to be. If that's so then the reason that I am about to consider, and reject, doesn't even get started.

But even if we do use expressions from a variety of syntactic categories this does not show that we use 'look' with more than one meaning in these uses. For consider the 'live'-sentences below:

> I live here
> I live in Wagga Wagga
> I live near Canberra
> I live where my parents live
> I live closer to Sydney than Melbourne

In these sentences we use complements from a variety of syntactic categories—a noun phrase ('here'), a preposition phrase ('in Wagga Wagga', 'near Canberra'), a relative clause headed by 'where' ('where my parents live'), and a comparative phrase ('closer to Sydney than Melbourne') (in these examples I am using 'live' in the sense of 'reside', rather than 'be alive'). But in these sentences we do not use 'live' with a variety of meanings—we use it with a single meaning (I take this to be clear). So the fact that we use a verb with complements from a variety of syntactic categories does not show that we use the verb with more than one meaning. (What's going on in the case of 'live', I suggest, is that we have various ways of specifying a location, more or less specifically. I would say the same of the 'look' case too.)

Paraphrasing

The verb 'pick' is ambiguous. What we (generally) mean by it in the first example below is different from what we (generally) mean by it in the second:

> John picked some strawberries for dinner
> John picked the door on the left

One way to see that what we mean is different in each case is to come up with a paraphrase of each and compare them. In the first example (but not the second) we mean something like 'pluck'—it is true of events which can (near enough) be described as 'plucking' events; in the second example (but not the first) we mean something like 'choose'—it is true of events which can (near enough) be described as 'choosing' events. Since plucking is not choosing, what we mean by 'pick' in each case is different. Call this *evidence from paraphrasing* that 'pick' is ambiguous.

Is there any evidence from paraphrasing that 'look' is ambiguous? There is, when we consider all uses of 'look' sentences. Consider the following two:

John looked embarrassed
John looked at his mum

In the first example above (but not the second), 'look' means something like 'visually appear', whereas in the second example (but not the first) it means something like 'visually observe', or 'gaze'.

But there is not, as far as I can tell, any evidence from paraphrasing when we confine our attention to visual experience uses of 'look' sentences. I cannot see any way to show, by coming up with different paraphrases, that we mean different things by 'look' when we use them to describe visual experiences. Consider the following sample:

The patch looks grey
He looks a character
Those women look in love
She looks like a duck
The top line looks longer than the bottom line
John's mum looks how she always looks
It looks as if these tomatoes are ripe
They look to be tired

When trying to paraphrase 'look' in each case I keep coming up with more or less the same thing, something like 'visually appears'.

It is important that the task in each case is to paraphrase just the word 'look', not the whole sentence. We would expect there to be differences between the meanings of these sentences as a whole, differences that we might be able to bring out by paraphrasing the sentences. But we are looking for differences in the meaning of the word 'look' in these sentences, and evidence for that must come from paraphrasing just the word 'look'.

Non-contradiction

Coming up with evidence from paraphrasing that a word is ambiguous might require us to be *explicitly* aware of any ambiguity, so perhaps the reason why there is no evidence from paraphrasing that 'look' is ambiguous in visual experiences uses of 'look' sentences is not that it's not ambiguous but that we are not explicitly aware of the ambiguity. The next kind of evidence does not require explicit awareness, just *implicit* awareness.

Another way to see that 'pick' is ambiguous is to see that there is a reading of the sentence below on which it expresses a non-contradictory proposition, a reading that is made more salient by emphasizing the second occurrence of 'pick'.

John picked the door on the left, but he didn't *pick* the door on the left

Call this *evidence from non-contradiction* that 'pick' is ambiguous.

It is important that the reading in question is made more salient by emphasizing the second occurrence of 'pick', rather than by emphasizing some other expression in the sentence. If there were a non-contradictory reading of the sentence that is made more salient by emphasizing the second occurrence of 'door' instead, then that might be evidence that 'door' is ambiguous, but it would not be evidence that 'pick' is ambiguous:

John picked the door on the left, but he didn't pick the *door* on the left

Is there evidence from non-contradiction that 'look' is ambiguous? There is, when we consider 'look' in all of its uses. Consider the sentence below:

John looked over the moon, but he didn't *look* over the moon

There is a reading of this sentence, one that is made more salient by emphasizing the second occurrence of 'look', on which it expresses a non-contradictory proposition (a proposition that is true if John visually appeared over the moon but did not direct his gaze over the moon).

But there is no evidence, as far as I can tell, when we just consider visual experience uses of 'look' sentences. None of the sentences below has a non-contradictory reading that is made more salient by emphasizing the second occurrence of 'look', and as far as I know the same is true for all visual experience uses of 'look' sentences.

The patch looks grey, but it doesn't *look* grey
He looks a character, but he doesn't *look* to be a character
Those women look in love, but they don't *look* to be in love
She looks like a duck, but she doesn't *look* like a duck
The top line looks longer than the bottom line, but it doesn't *look* longer than the bottom line
John's mum looks how she always looks, but she doesn't *look* how she always looks
It looks as if these tomatoes are ripe, but it doesn't *look* as if these tomatoes are ripe
They look to be tired, but they don't *look* to be tired

Conjunction reduction

Because 'pick' is ambiguous we have the following phenomenon. Suppose that John wants to give a flower to his girlfriend; he doesn't know much about flowers, so his mum chooses an appropriate one in the garden, which he then plucks; but he does know a lot about timing, so he chooses the best moment to give the flower. There is a reading of the first sentence below on which it expresses a proposition that is true in these circumstances. But any such reading of the conjunction-reduced second sentence requires a zeugmatic reading of 'pick'.

John picked a rose and John picked the ideal time to give it
John picked a rose and the ideal time to give it

We get the same phenomenon for 'look' when considered in all of its uses. If John appeared embarrassed while gazing out the window, then there is a true interpretation of the first sentence below, but any true interpretation of the second requires a zeugmatic reading of 'look'.

John looked out the window and John looked embarrassed
John looked out the window and embarrassed

427

But we do not get this phenomenon for 'look' in our visual experience uses of 'look' sentences. For any circumstances in which there is a true interpretation of the first sentences below, there is a true interpretation of the second sentence that does not require a zeugmatic interpretation of 'look'.

The patch looks grey and the patch looks a square thing
The patch looks grey and a square thing

John looks like a philosopher and John looks as if he thinks like one too
John looks like a philosopher and as if he thinks like one too

The sky looks how it usually looks but the sky looks slightly less cloudy
The sky looks how it usually looks but slightly less cloudy

Bill looks smarter than Ben but Bill looks to be less wise
Bill looks smarter than Ben but to be less wise

There may be pragmatic reasons why it is odd to use instances of some of these—it may, for example, be misleading to use 'and' rather than 'but'. But to be misleading in that kind of way is not to be zeugmatic.

Question formation

Because 'pick' is ambiguous there are contexts in which the conversation below would be perfectly felicitous (note the emphasis on 'pick' when A repeats her question):

A: What did John pick?
B: John picked a rose.
A: No, that's not what I meant. What did John *pick*?

If 'look' is ambiguous then there should be similarly felicitous conversations. And indeed there are, when we consider 'look' in all of its uses—there are contexts in which the conversation below is felicitous (take a context in which John looked through binoculars at the couple next door and what he saw made him look embarrassed).

A: How did John look?
B: John looked through binoculars.
A: No, that's not what I meant. How did John *look*?

If we use 'look' with more than one meaning in our visual experience uses of 'look' sentences then there should be similarly felicitous conversations. But as far as I can tell there are no such conversations. There is no context in which the conversation below, for example, is felicitous.

A: How does the patch look?
B: The patch looks as if it is grey.
A: No, that's not what I meant. How does the patch *look*?

428

The emphasis is important. There are felicitous conversations with different emphasis. For example, consider a context in which there are two patches. Then:

A: How does the patch look?
B: The patch looks as if it is grey.
A: No, that's not what I meant. How does *the patch* look?

A stronger conclusion

I have just argued that there is no evidence from syntactic variety, paraphrasing, non-contradiction, conjunction reduction, or question formation that we use 'look' with more than one meaning in our visual experience uses of 'look' sentences. Perhaps this can be made into an argument for a stronger conclusion, that we *don't* use 'look' with more than one meaning in our visual experience uses of 'look' sentences. The argument goes as follows: if we did then we would have evidence of at least one of these kinds; we don't have evidence of any of these kinds; therefore, we don't. I'm not sure whether the first premise is true, so I offer this argument only tentatively.

Do we mean anything else by 'look' sentences?

I have just considered whether we mean different things by 'look' in our visual experience uses of 'look' sentences, and I have argued that we have no reason to think so. What about the sentences themselves? Do we mean anything by them that is not accounted for by the theory that I have developed?

I will consider a fairly exhaustive list of our various purported uses of 'look' sentences, and argue in each case that either (a) if there is such a use then it is not a visual experience use, or (b) it is a visual experience use but one that is already accounted for by the theory that I have developed, or (c) it would be a visual experience use but we have no such use. If all of this is right then we have no reason to think that we mean anything by our visual experience uses of 'look' sentences that is not accounted for by the theory that I have developed.

I start by considering five purported uses that I think are of the first kind—if there are such uses then they are not visual experience uses.

Tentative assertion use

It has been claimed (e.g. by Price (1932, 1941, 1964), Quinton (1955, 1973), and Ayer (1940, 1956)) that we sometimes use 'look' sentences to make tentative assertions. For example, we might use 'The patch looks grey' to tentatively assert that the patch is grey. If we use 'The patch looks grey' to *tentatively* assert that the patch is grey then we use it to *assert* that the patch is grey, because tentative assertion is assertion, in which case we must mean by the sentence that the patch is grey. So the view can be put as follows:

There is a use of 'O looks F' on which we mean that O is F

Non-visual use

Price (1932, 1941, 1964), Leeds (1975, p. 199), and Jackson (1977, pp. 30–1) have all claimed that we have a non-visual use of 'look' sentences. They would say something like this:

There is a reading of 'It looks (to S) as if P' on which we mean that there is evidence (not necessarily visual) (for S) that P

Inclination-to-believe use

Price (1932, 1941, 1964), Chisholm (1957, 1965, 1966), and Travis (2004) all make something like the following claim:

> There is a use of 'O looks F to S' on which we mean that S is inclined to believe, on the basis of her visual experience of O, that O is F

Chisholm calls this the 'epistemic' use of 'look' sentences; I shall follow Price in calling it the *inclination-to-believe* use.

What-would-be-judged use

Vesey (1956, 1971a, 1971b) and Dretske (1995) each make what amounts to the following claim:

> There is a use of 'O looks F to S' on which we mean that if S were to judge, on the basis of how O looks to her, and with no reason to think otherwise, she would judge that O is F

Vesey calls this the 'epistemic' use of 'look'; Dretske calls it the 'doxastic' use. I will call it the *what-would-be-judged* use.

Visual evidence use

Jackson (1977) makes something like the following claim:

> There is a reading of 'It looks (to S) as if P' on which we mean that there is visually acquired evidence (for S) that P

He calls this the 'epistemic' use, but to avoid confusion with how others have used the 'epistemic' label I shall call this the *visual evidence* use.

I hope that it's clear enough that if there are these uses then none of them is a visual experience use, because none of them is a use on which we are describing a visual experience. We might be describing something that is somehow *connected* with a visual experience, but we are not describing the visual experience itself.

Comparative use

Various people (for example Vesey (1956, 1971a, 1971b), Chisholm (1957, pp. 45–6), Leeds (1975, p. 200), Jackson (1977, pp. 31–3), Dretske (1995, pp. 67–9), Pettit (2003), and Travis (2004)) have claimed something like the following:

> There is a use of 'O looks F (to S)' on which we mean that O looks (to S) the way F things look

Vesey calls this the 'resemblance' use of 'look' sentences; I will follow Chisholm and Jackson in calling it the *comparative* use.

None would agree that 'the way F things look' is the right definite description to use here—each would use a more qualified one. Chisholm would use 'the way F things ordinarily look', or 'the way F things might ordinarily be expected to look'. Jackson would use 'the way an F thing normally looks in C to S', for certain conditions C and observers S determined by the context of utterance. Leeds would prefer 'the way F things usually look in daylight', or 'the way F things usually look in standard conditions'. Dretske would add reference to an observer, and also his 'discriminatory clause': by 'O looks F to S' we mean that O looks to S the way F things normally look to S, and O looks different to S from certain other non-F things. Despite these differences, they all agree that once the definite description is suitably qualified, perhaps in a way that allows the meaning of 'O looks F (to S)' to vary across contexts of utterance, the claim above is true.

I agree that we do have such a use, and that it is a visual experience use. But it is already accounted for by the theory that I have developed. I would formulate the claim as follows:

> There is a use of 'O looks F (to S)' on which we mean that O looks (to S) the maximally specific way w such that it is generically true that F things look w

Phenomenal use

Price (1932, 1941, 1964), Quinton (1955, 1973), Vesey (1956, 1971a, 1971b), Chisholm (1957, 1965, 1966), and Jackson (1977) all claim that we sometimes use 'look' sentences to *directly describe* our visual experiences. I think we can understand the claim to be this:

> There is a use of 'O looks F to S' on which we mean that S's visual experience of O, or some feature of the experience, is F

Price calls this the 'basic' use, Vesey calls it the 'optical' use, and Chisholm calls it the 'non-comparative' use. I will follow Jackson in calling it the *phenomenal* use.

I take it that if we do have such a use then it is with a restricted class of complements of 'look'—colour adjectives such as 'grey', and perhaps also shape adjectives such as 'square'. It would be implausible to extend it to adjectives such as 'heavy'—it is implausible that there is a use of 'The patch looks heavy to you' on which we mean that your visual experience of the patch, or some feature of it, is heavy, since visual experiences and their features are not the kinds of things that can be heavy. Jackson explicitly acknowledges this restriction: "The phenomenal use is characterized by being explicitly tied to terms for colour, shape and/or distance ... That is, instead of terms like 'cow', 'house', 'happy', we have, in the phenomenal use, terms like 'red', 'square', and 'longer than'" (1977, p. 33).

If we do have such a use of 'look' sentences then it is clearly a visual experience use. But I don't see any reason to think that we have such a use. I will consider and reject the reasons that have been given for thinking that we do. Quinton and Vesey simply claim without argument that we have such a use. Chisholm, Price and Jackson each give arguments—I will consider their arguments in turn.

Chisholm

Chisholm (1965) talks about 'appear' rather than 'look'. I take it that he would be happy to say the same thinks about 'look', so I'll modify his discussion to match the rest of this chapter.

Chisholm argues that we have a phenomenal use (he calls it the 'noncomparative' use) by appealing to something like the sentence below:

> Things which are grey usually look grey in daylight

He claims that this sentence is ambiguous, between a reading on which it is 'analytic' and a reading on which it is 'synthetic'. On its analytic reading it can be paraphrased using the first sentence below, and on its synthetic reading it can be paraphrased using the second.

> Things which are grey usually look in daylight the way things which are grey usually look in daylight
> There is a certain way of looking, looking grey, such that things which are grey happen to usually appear that way in daylight

The reason why it has these two readings, Chisholm seems to think, is that 'look' itself has two readings—it can be read in the comparative sense, but also in a distinct phenomenal sense. When 'look' is read in its comparative sense, to look grey in daylight is to look the way things which are grey usually look in daylight, and this accounts for the analytic reading. When 'look' is read in its phenomenal sense, however, 'looks grey' is an unanalysable predicate, and it is this sense of 'look' that accounts for the synthetic reading.

Leeds (1975) argues that if there is such an ambiguity there is no need to think that it is due to an ambiguity in 'look'. I think that Leeds is right. Here I will present my own version of what is essentially Leeds' argument.

Leeds suggests, and I agree with him, that talk about the sentence being ambiguous between analytic and synthetic readings is unclear, and that the ambiguity Chisholm is pointing to is better brought out by embedding the sentence in a modal context. Thus, rather than the original sentence being ambiguous between analytic and synthetic readings, let's take the fact to be explained to be that the sentence below is ambiguous between true and false readings.

> Necessarily: things which are grey usually look grey in daylight

Chisholm's claim then translates as this: this sentence is ambiguous, between a true reading and a false reading, and this is because 'look' is ambiguous, between a comparative sense and a phenomenal sense.

The problem for Chisholm is that if there is a comparative reading of 'look' which is as Chisholm claims it is, then it alone can account for the true and false readings of this sentence. On the comparative reading of 'look', it can be paraphrased as follows:

> Necessarily: things which are grey usually look in daylight the way things which are grey usually look in daylight

This sentence is structurally ambiguous, between a reading on which the definite description 'the way things which are grey usually look in daylight' is within the scope of the operator 'necessarily', and a reading on which the operator 'necessarily' is within the scope of the definite description 'the way things which are grey usually look in daylight'. We can represent the two readings as follows:

> Necessarily: the way w such that grey things usually look w in daylight is such that: grey things usually look w in daylight
> The way w such that grey things usually look w in daylight is such that: necessarily: grey things usually look w in daylight

The first is true but the second is false (it might have been that grey things usually look w' in daylight, where w' is not the way grey things actually look in daylight). So the ambiguity here can be explained as a structural ambiguity in the sentence, rather than as a lexical ambiguity in the verb 'look'. There is, then, despite what Chisholm thinks, no good reason here to think that we have a use of 'look' sentences that is distinct from the comparative use.

Price

Here is an argument in the style of ones given by Price (1964, pp. 15–16):

> If the patch looks grey in the comparative sense, then the patch looks the way grey things look. Why does the patch look the way grey things look? Because the patch looks grey. This is an informative answer. Since it is an informative answer, we cannot be using 'the patch looks grey' comparatively, because then it would amount to saying that the patch looks the way grey things look because the patch looks the way grey things look, and that is not informative. Thus, there is a use of 'The patch looks grey' which is not the comparative use.

If this argument is sound it does not show that the extra use is the phenomenal use, but it does at least show that there is an extra use of 'The patch looks grey', in addition to the comparative use.

Nevertheless, I do not think that the argument is sound. The argument goes as follows. Consider the following two sentences:

> The patch looks the way grey things look, because the patch looks grey
> The patch looks the way grey things look, because the patch looks the way grey things look

There is a reading of the first sentence above on which it is informative; but there is no reading of the second sentence on which it is informative; so there is a reading of 'The patch looks grey' on which it does not mean 'The patch looks the way grey things look', for otherwise there would be no such difference between the two sentences; so there is a use of 'The patch looks grey' distinct from the comparative use.

But the second sentence *does* have a reading on which it is informative—at least one that is just as informative as any reading of the first. Consider the analogous sentence below:

> John loves the prettiest girl in class, because John loves the prettiest girl in class

This has a reading on which it is not informative. But it also has a reading on which it is informative. The informative reading can be given as follows:

John loves the prettiest girl in class, because John loves x, and x is the prettiest girl in class

In the same way, the second sentence above has a reading on which it is informative, a reading which can be given as follows:

The patch looks the way grey things look, because the patch looks w, and w is the way grey things look

This reading is at least as informative as any reading of the first sentence on which it is informative. For the first to be informative we need to understand it as meaning something like 'The patch looks the way grey things look, because the patch looks grey (and that's the way grey things look)'. This is no more informative than the informative reading of the second sentence.

Jackson

Jackson (1977, ch. 2) argues that we have a use of 'look' sentences which is neither the comparative use nor the inclination-to-believe use (which he calls the 'epistemic' use). His argument is this:

> We have a use of 'look' sentences on which what we mean by 'The patch looks grey' cannot be given by reference to the way grey things look to certain observers in certain conditions, nor by reference to beliefs; if this were the comparative use then what we mean by 'The patch looks grey' could be given by reference to the way grey things look to certain observers in certain conditions, so it is not the comparative use; if it were the inclination-to-believe use then what we mean by 'The patch looks grey' could be given by reference to beliefs, so it is not the inclination-to-believe use; thus, it is neither the comparative use nor the inclination-to-believe use.

He takes this additional use to be the phenomenal use.

I agree with Jackson that we have a use of 'look' sentences on which what we mean by 'The patch looks grey' cannot be given by reference to the way grey things look to certain observers in certain conditions, nor by reference to beliefs. But I disagree with Jackson that this use is not the comparative use, because, unlike Jackson, I think that what we mean by the comparative use cannot be given by reference to certain observers in certain conditions.

Jackson takes it that the comparative use of 'look' sentences is such that there is some expression, S, which refers to or quantifies over certain people, and some expression, C, which refers to or quantifies over certain conditions, such that the following is true:

By 'The patch looks grey to you' we mean that the patch looks to you the way grey things look to S in C

I believe, contrary to this, that by 'The patch looks grey to you' we just mean that the patch looks to you the way grey things look, where 'the way grey things look' is to be understood generically. Jackson's arguments do not work against this account of the comparative use. I will consider Jackson's argument that what we mean by 'The patch looks grey to you' cannot be given by reference to the way grey things look to certain observers in certain conditions, and briefly explain how it does not show that what we mean cannot be given in terms of the way grey things look, understood generically.

Jackson argues that there are no expressions S and C which make the sentence above true but non-trivial.

He starts by considering the following account:

> By 'The patch looks grey to you' we mean that the patch looks to you the way grey things look to *you* in *normal circumstances*

He points out that this cannot be right. Suppose that you see in shades of red, but with extremely good red vision—you can make amongst reds the same number of discriminations that a normal sighted person can make amongst colours in general. Then it might be true that the patch looks the way grey things look to you in normal circumstances, but false that the patch looks grey to you.

He next considers an account that refers to people other than you:

> By 'The patch looks grey to you' we mean that the patch looks to you the way grey things look to *most people* in *normal circumstances*

He points out that how things look to you does not depend on the existence of other people—things might look grey to you, even if no one else did, does, or will exist. So it will not do to make reference to other people.

He also points out that there is a problem explaining what 'normal circumstances' are in a way that does not make these accounts trivial. What are normal circumstances? Perhaps circumstances in daylight:

> By 'The patch looks grey to you' we mean that the patch looks to you the way grey things look to *you* in *daylight*

But your eyes might be dazzled in daylight in such a way that grey things do not look grey to you in daylight, but they do look grey to you under low intensity light instead.

He next considers explaining 'normal circumstances' as being circumstances which best facilitate colour discrimination. But, he points out, these are circumstances that exaggerate colour differences, so they are circumstances in which things look more different in colour than they really are, so do not look the colour they are.

The only way of correctly specifying what normal conditions are, he concludes, makes these accounts trivial: normal circumstances are those in which grey things look grey to you. But by 'The patch looks grey to you' we do not mean something trivial.

Jackson then argues that there is reason to think that the account cannot be right, for any actual observers or actual circumstances. There might be a shade of colour, call it c, such that the patch looks c to you even though no object actually is c. Then it would be true that the patch looks c to you but not true that the patch looks the way c things look to you (or anyone else) in normal circumstances (or any other circumstances)—since there are no c things there is no such way. This will be case for any value of S that is an actual observer and for any value of C that is an actual condition.

Jackson considers a counterfactual fix:

> By 'The patch looks grey to you' we mean that the patch looks to you the way grey things would look to you in normal circumstances if there were any

435

He argues (successfully, I think) that this cannot be right either.

Jackson concludes that by 'The patch looks grey to you' we do not mean that the patch looks to you the way grey things look to S in C, for any values of S and C.

I agree—we will not be able to find appropriate values for S and C. But I think that we don't need to in order to state what we mean by the comparative use. According to the account that I have developed, by 'The patch looks grey to you' we mean that the patch looks to you the way w such that grey things look w. Here, 'grey things look w' is to be understood generically; it expresses a relation between the property of being an event in which a grey thing looks some way to someone, and the property of being an event that occurs in way w. A generic like this can be true even if there are no actual events in which a grey thing looks some way to someone. In particular, it can be true even if there are no actual grey things.

References

Ayer, A. J. (1940), *The Foundations of Empirical Knowledge* (London: MacMillan Press).

Ayer, A. J. (1956), *The Problem of Knowledge* (London: MacMillan).

Breckenridge, W. (2018), *Visual Experience: A Semantic Approach* (Oxford: Oxford University Press).

Chisholm, R. M. (1957), *Perceiving: A Philosophical Study* (Ithaca, NY: Cornell University Press).

Chisholm, R. M. (1965), "'Appear', 'Take', and 'Evident'", in R. Swartz (ed.), *Perceiving, Sensing and Knowing* (New York: Anchor Books), pp. 473–85.

Chisholm, R. M. (1966), *Theory of Knowledge* (London: Prentice-Hall).

Dretske, F. (1995), *Naturalizing the Mind* (Cambridge, MA: MIT Press).

Jackson, F. (1977), *Perception: A Representative Theory* (Cambridge: Cambridge University Press).

Leeds, S. (1975), "Two Senses of 'Appears Red'", *Philosophical Studies* 28, pp. 199–205.

Pettit, P. (2003), 'Looks as Powers', *Philosophical Issues* 13, pp. 221–52.

Price, H. H. (1932), *Perception* (London: Methuen).

Price, H. H. (1941), 'Review of Ayer', *Mind* 50, pp. 280–93.

Price, H. H. (1964), 'Appearing and Appearances', *American Philosophical Quarterly* 1, pp. 3–19.

Quinton, A. M. (1955), 'The Problem of Perception', *Mind* 64, pp. 28–51.

Quinton, A. M. (1973), *The Nature of Things* (Boston: Routledge & Kegan Paul).

Travis, C. (2004), 'The Silence of the Senses', *Mind* 113, pp. 57–94.

Vesey, G. (1956), 'Seeing and Seeing As', *Proceedings of the Aristotelian Society* 56, pp. 109–24.

Vesey, G. (1971a), 'Analysing Seeing II', in F. N. Sibley (ed.), *Perception: A Philosophical Symposium* (London: Methuen), pp. 133–7.

Vesey, G. (1971b), *Perception* (London: MacMillan Press).

PART VI

Language, categories, and thought

27

COLOUR, COLOUR LANGUAGE, AND CULTURE

Don Dedrick

I Introduction

While philosophers are interested in the semantics of colour language—technical issues concerning the sense and reference of colour words—there has also been an interest in the relationship of colour words to both the colours they name and the cultures and languages in which such words are embedded. Sometimes this interest is in passing, when philosophers such as John Mackie use colour to illuminate questions about the reference of general terms, or Ludwig Wittgenstein discusses colour to help us understand his own views about language and ontology. On other occasions, the interest is focused on the relationship between colour words, colour, and culture for their own sake. Though this is somewhat of an artificial distinction the relationships between colour language, colour, and culture are the main concern here, though we shall draw some of the stage setting from those with a passing interest in colour, W.V. Quine, in particular. The reader will also come to appreciate, as with so much contemporary philosophical work on colour, the deep sense in which the issues discussed are empirically informed by the work of psychologists, anthropologists, linguists, and neuroscientists.

An assumption that many philosophers and others make: there is a colour continuum in nature that is not divided into discrete segments. Given that there is such a continuum and, then, given we do divide that continuum into some set of colours (more *determinate* colours such as red and blue of the *determinable* colour) where do the divisions originate? What is the basis for our classifications?

One view, exemplified by W.V. Quine, is that language and culture make for the divisions:

> Sameness of color, ordinarily so called, is not sameness of color in the sense in which red is a color. The very notion of a color, in the latter sense, is unnatural. Whether some arbitrary interval in the spectrum is a color, in this sense, depends on the causal matter of their being a word for it; and this matter of vocabulary varies from culture to culture. The notion of a color, in this sense, is less basic than the notion of a color word.
>
> *(Quine 1974, p. 71)*

Here are the moving parts in this account, more or less unanalysed. The order in which they appear has been changed for expository purposes.

1   A notion of a *colour1*, specified in relation to "sameness of color".
2   A notion of a *colour2* which is a colour in the way that "red is a color".
3   The claim that a *colour2* is unnatural.
4   The notion that a *colour2* corresponds to an "arbitrary interval in the spectrum".
5   The notion of a *colour2*, depends on the causal matter of their being a word for "it".
6   The notion that colour vocabulary–there being a word for a *colour2*—varies from culture to culture.
7   The notion of a *colour2* is "less basic" than the notion of a colour word.

Much that one wants to want to say about colour language and culture—not all of it in agreement with Quine—can be framed in terms of these seven "notions", as Quine typically refers to ideas, so that is the plan of action here. Some concluding remarks follow.

II Colour, colour language, and culture

1 Specifying a colour1 *in relation to sameness of colour. For example: "X is the same colour as Y"*

When we define a colour in relation to sameness of colour we need not suppose colour concepts or colour words. Sensory psychologists since Brindley (1960) distinguish Class A from Class B psychophysical observations. Class A observations, which are utilized in what the psychophysicist Davida Teller has called "identity experiments" (Teller and Palmer 2016) may ask a subject if two stimuli are identical, or ask the subject to manipulate one stimulus so that it matches another. Experiments that involve anything more than identity are, by Brindly's classic definition, Class B. Class A experiments are in general preferred by psychophysicists (psychologists that study the relationship between physical stimuli and their psychological effects) because they involve less judgement than, say, a task in which subjects are asked to order a series of colour samples. They are, we could say, less cognitively loaded.[1]

The claim that Quine's sameness of *colour1* does not require colour concepts or colour language does not demand that people lack such cognitive devices, but that their judgement need not recruit them. As a thought experiment, we might imagine that two individuals, with different sets of colour concepts and colour words could nonetheless agree on identity experiments. For those who prefer real experiments, non-human primates provide a model for colour identity and discrimination that is very similar to human colour judgement (essentially identical; see e.g. Stoughton *et al.* 2012). These animals—macaque monkeys are the classic example—have no colour words and, while their behaviour may not correspond to human behaviour for some tasks, there is no doubt they can discriminate between colours, and identify two colour samples as being the same/different, in the Class A sense.

2 *The sense in which "red is a color". For example: two shades of colour may not exhibit sameness of* colour1 *to an individual though each is the* colour2 *red for that person*

Here we are interested in a notion of a *colour2* which is a colour in the way that "red is a color". This is most likely what we are talking about when we speak of colour and are not talking about a particular shade of colour. This sense can be understood in relation to sameness of *colour1*. Red is a determinate of the determinable *colour* and a determinable itself that collects a variety of different shades of colour as coloured red. In relation to sameness *of colour1*, a range of colour shades that do not exhibit sameness of *colour1* will be classified as the colour red. This means that sameness of *colour1* is not exhaustive of sameness of *colour2*. One way to think about the difference between sameness of *colour1* and of *colour2*: all variable perceptual dimensions, and all values of those dimensions of colour experience (particular hue, saturation, and lightness values, say) matter in principle to sameness of *colour1*, only some dimensions and/or only some values of the dimensions matter to the notion of a *colour2*. For speakers of English, and indeed for most of the languages of the world, *hue* is the paramount dimension (the redness, greenness, yellowness, etc. of a shade), but the idea of a *colour2* is just the idea of a colour classification that collects shades together on the basis of something other than just identity.

Most of what Quine has to say, and much that is of philosophical, psychological, linguistic, and anthropological interest about colour language follows from this difference: If sameness of *colour1* can be captured by identity experiments, what is the basis for sameness of *colour2*? At the very least, some variable perceptual dimensions of colour will count for more than others. Or it may be that something non-perceptual is the determining factor (see the discussion of Wittgenstein, below, for an example). Whatever may be the case, no moderately strong (e.g. Class A) sense of identity is necessary for being a *colour2* just because the shades that are collected in a *colour2*, such as red, are often not identical shades: think about a light red and a dark red, for example.

3 A colour2 *is* "unnatural". *For example: the* colour2 *red is not found in nature*

Quine's use of the word "unnatural" is less than precise, but it is clear that he means it in the sense of "not-natural", i.e. not found in nature independent of humans, not, as Quine has said, "cosmic". The non-independence claim has been questioned by some philosophers (e.g. Byrne and Hilbert 2003), and it is not the purpose here to debate the metaphysics of colour. Nor need we do so. The real distinction for Quine is between [a] colour as a property or predicate in fundamental physics, and [b] colour as a property or predicate relevant to perceptual experience. In the first sense, [a], colour is not natural for Quine (though he might allow that there is a sense in which colour is *physical* without being *fundamental* (this is Byrne and Hilbert's claim). With respect to [b] we can employ our distinction between *colour1* and *colour2*. While *colour1* is natural in the perceptual sense, *colour2*, Quine claims, is not.

Humans with normal colour vision perceive the electromagnetic spectrum, visually, across a very narrow band from approximately 400nm to 700nm. Other animals have extended or restricted perceptual capabilities (Jacobs 1981, 2015; Thompson 1995). Within the range of normal human visual experience of colour, Quine has written that there is an "innate spacing of qualities" as well as a "natural sense of similarity" that is the prescientific foundation for our experience of colour (Quine 1969). While Quine is no authority on what is "innate" and what is natural we can accept his view if, by these things, we mean that sameness of *colour1* is both possible and actual, and prior to language. Humans and many other animals can distinguish between different shades of colour (qualities are "spaced"), and can make judgements about sameness and difference. As for this ability being grounded in "The brute irrationality of our sense of similarity" (Quine 1969, p. 125), Quine is again making a reasonable claim. Many psychological colour spaces are grounded in similarity, in what is called the "similarity colour space" (Westphal 1991; Clark 1993), whereby "space" we mean a geometric representation of the sum total of chromatic/achromatic discriminations a subject can make, ordered in terms of their similarities to one another, and organized along a number of axes. Such spaces can be used to represent the results of the Class A identity experiments discussed in I.1. One similarity space that is commonly referred to is the Munsell colour space or "system", but there are others. The Munsell system is a three-dimensional space organized in terms of hue (roughly, redness, greenness, yellowness, blueness ...), chroma (saturation of hue), and value (lightness).[2]

In what way is *colour2* different from *colour1* when it comes to sense [b] of "natural" (which, henceforth, will be the way in which the word "natural" is used here)? Is there a perceptual account of *colour2* that is similar (or similar enough) to the account we have given of spaced qualities and judgements of the Class A variety? Is *colour2* natural in this sense? The quotation from Quine, with its use of words such as "arbitrary", "language", and "culture" to describe and explain *colour2* makes it clear he believes "No" is the answer, but this is a bone of contention. Indeed, the great debate about colour language, over the past half-century can be construed in part as a debate over whether *colour2* is natural in some sense. We shall have more to say about this in the following sections. For the moment, let us simply note that Quine and many others accept the claim that while *colour1* is natural, *colour2* is not: colour in the sense which red is a colour is not natural, for the *colour2* red cannot be extracted from the similarity colour space without the help of language and culture.[3]

4 *The notion that a colour2 corresponds to an "arbitrary interval in the spectrum". For example: there is nothing about the spectrum that requires the colour2 red (as named by "red" in English) to have the range that English speakers identify it as having*

In saying that a *colour2* corresponds to an arbitrary interval in the spectrum Quine is not committed to the view that *colour2s* must be completely arbitrary in the sense that the shades collected in a *colour2* are randomly selected. The spacing of qualities and the similarity colour space that represents such qualities and their relations is crucial to Quine's view and may place constraints upon *colour2*.[4] There is also nothing in Quine's view that suggests *colour2* cannot be non-arbitrary relative to cultural or linguistic interests (as he goes on to say in the introductory quotation). His point is merely that, *relative to the spectrum itself* (more generally: a similarity colour space), separation of that continuum into *colour2s* is arbitrary. We shall soon consider views which suggest that *colour2* is not arbitrary in this way. Before doing so it is worth examining what is perhaps the strongest position on arbitrariness—that of Ludwig Wittgenstein (and of other Wittgensteinians who take up his position).

Wittgenstein wrote a great deal about colour and many of those writings are collected in his *Remarks on Colour* (1977). The *Remarks* exemplify a number of the philosopher's post-*Tractatus* themes: the correctness of description over theory, the idea of language games that play a role in socially embedded forms of life governed by "grammar", the relationship of language to ontology. The *Remarks on Colour* often articulate the idiosyncratic nature of the colours: why is there no light brown? No transparent white? No blackish yellow? Can there be a bluish green and not a reddish green? These and other observations (and Wittgenstein was keen at this) are designed to disabuse us of the idea that there can be a unified, unitary theory of the colours. Instead, we have our ways of talking about colours, evolved as social practices within forms of life—that is the reason why there is, for example, no transparent white: our "grammar" (our contingent rules for the use of language) does not permit it. For Wittgenstein, there is no way to disentangle colours from the forms of life in which they appear (including scientific forms): they are constituted by those forms and are not prior to them. A valuable example comes from Wittgenstein's *The Blue and Brown Books* (1958):

> Imagine the use of a language (a culture) in which there was a common name for green and red on the one hand and yellow and blue on the other. Suppose, e.g. that there were two castes, one the patrician caste, wearing red and green garments, the other the plebian, wearing blue and yellow garments ... Asked what a red patch and a green patch have in common, a man of our tribe would not hesitate to say that they were both patrician.
>
> *(1958, p. 134)*

In this remark Wittgenstein is implicitly distinguishing "our" ways of talking about colour, with its reds and yellows, greens and blues, from that of a hypothetical group. There is one game that we can play, focusing on perceptual similarities and differences which are used to direct our talk about and understanding of colour. In the context of this colour grammar, red and green are distinct colours or "hues", with nothing in common perceptually: they do not look similar to each other at all. But there is another sort of game, captured in Wittgenstein's remark, which views colour through the lens of a different cultural dimension. The red patch and the green patch fall under a colour classification that is driven not by perceptual properties but by other interests: the identification of social castes. The scenario described is not intended as a piece of amateur anthropology but as a thought experiment. Suppose one were to say that red and green do not look at all alike. Maybe so, but would that mean that the people sharing the language/culture described are mistaken? Wittgenstein's idea is that they are not, for the difference is at the level of different practices, different language games, which one can choose to engage in, possibly, but no one of which has epistemic or ontic priority. There is no fact of the matter as to which language game is correct because there are no facts about colour independent of one practice or another. Peter Hacker, a philosopher much influenced by Wittgenstein, makes the point this way:

> We are continually tempted to take our grammar as a projection of reality, instead of taking our conception of the structure of reality to be a projection of our grammar. For we are driven to justify our grammar by reference to putative facts about the world, e.g. 'But there really are four primary colours'. So we think of our concepts of colour as justified, for they characterize the world as it is ... It is against the conception of this sort of justification ... that the claim that grammar is arbitrary is directed. The relevant sense in which grammar is arbitrary is the doctrine of the autonomy of grammar.
>
> *(Hacker 1972, p. 160)*

There are different ways to understand the autonomy of linguistic conceptions and their "grammar" as Wittgenstein called it (e.g. Schwyzer 2001). For the purpose at hand, we can take Hacker's (and Wittgenstein's) claim to involve a denial of a certain kind of explanatory move which aims to justify, as Hacker says, a classification of colours in terms of the "colours themselves" when, in fact, there are no colours themselves. Our ways of talking about colours (and other things) are themselves constitutive of their objects of reference which are not prior to the classification but residue of it. Language games may collide, but there is no possibility of a third-party (read ontological) resolution. There is nothing but language games and their entwined ontologies.

Wittgenstein's views about colour, colour language, and culture are amongst the most radical. It is, for example, quite common to hold a Quinian view according to which *colour1* is natural, but *colour2* not natural, being determined by culture and language. This is the view described in II.3. Wittgenstein would reject that view, for *colour1* is claimed to be a conception of colour that can be understood independently of language, and that is off the table for Wittgenstein.[5]

Should we be Wittgensteinians about colour? It is a difficult view to hold since it entails that the basis for identity experiments and the colour spaces we can construct from them—what we have called *colour1*—is itself an artefact of language. Were we to take up this position it would be difficult to square it with our knowledge of animal and infant psychophysics. There is another sort of problem with Wittgenstein's view as well, most clearly articulated by Jonathan Westphal (1991) who argues that the puzzle questions (e.g. Why no transparent white?) have scientific answers. White objects are objects that reflect all light, while transparent objects are such that they transmit most of the light. That is why there is no transparent white. On Westphal's view, it is facts about objects and lights themselves that give us answers to the puzzle questions, and language is not autonomous and arbitrary in the extreme ways that Wittgenstein and Hacker imagined. It is one thing to think, as Quine does, that the divisions in a colour continuum are arbitrary relative to that continuum. It is another to think that all the structure of experience is a projection of our linguistic commitments.

5 The notion of a colour2, depends on the causal matter of their being a word for "it". For example: the colour2 red exists because a word (such as "red") for that colour exists

For Wittgenstein, being a colour of any sort depends upon linguistic practices and is not prior to them. But as we have said, this view makes it difficult to understand the behaviour of non-linguistic creatures that would appear to depend upon *colour1* in its natural sense: there is a spacing of qualities and it is prior to language, and that is why non-linguistic animals can engage in identity experiments from which we are able to develop models of their similarity colour spaces. There is also Westphal's argument to the effect that linguistic conventions that seem "grammatical" in Wittgenstein's sense may actually be grounded empirically in the nature (and science) of objects and lights.

Though we may find the Wittgensteinian approach wanting, we have no answer as to how it is that *colour2s* are formed and why there are the specific *colour2s* that we find in a language. Note that these are two different questions: [1] how are *colour2s* formed? [2] why a specific set of *colour2s*? Bernard Harrison is a philosopher who has addressed both of these questions in the context of a view that accepts that *colour1* is natural and views language as essential to the formation of *colour2* classifications. What follows is a precis of his central arguments.

Harrison's *Form and Content* (1973) was inspired by Wittgenstein, though when it comes to colour Harrison's view is less radical. Unlike Wittgenstein and Hacker, and like Quine, Harrison accepts *colour1* is natural, and he is, for colour, concerned to solve one central problem: how does colour language mark the boundaries in a colour space that is continuous? What, in our terms, are the resources necessary to establish colour classifications that are named; how does *colour2* work?

Philosophers are concerned with the nature of general terms. Are such classifications ("red" would be one) defined in terms of some property or properties all instances of the classification share, or is some weaker, less essentialist account of their classification correct? Nominalism is the most extreme alternative, according to which it is simply names that make for classifications. Almost no philosopher has held this extreme view, for it offers no explanation for the way people learn or apply their names. A less extreme view, resemblance nominalism, holds that similarities + names = classifications. J.L. Mackie, in a book discussing John Locke, opts for this view for colour classification and colour words. According to Mackie, "their use is determined not by the possession of a distinctive common property or cluster of properties—even functional or relational ones—but by a series of resemblances" (Mackie 1978, p. 137). This view recruits the resources of *colour1*, with its spacing of qualities and its judgements of sameness and difference, and Mackie is impressed by the fact that the colour continuum seems to offer nothing but resemblances. But even if this is the case, how do names + *colour1* generate *colour2s*? It is as if Mackie thinks that an account of *colour2* that merely adds colour names to *colour1* is sufficient to explain human colour naming and classification. Harrison argues that it is not.

The problem for this sort of resemblance nominalism, for Harrison (Quine 1969 recognized it as well), is that named colour classifications create demarcations in the colour continuum that are not in it—not a part of *colour1*. Mackie's view that resemblances make for colour names (for our ability to learn and apply them) is at a loss when it comes to explaining the boundaries between the *colour2* colours: if there is nothing but a "series of resemblances", as Mackie would have it, why is there more than one *colour2* in a colour space of continuously resembling but discriminable shades? Once we start the resemblance chain, what stops it so as to demarcate, say, blue from green—a notorious problem in the anthropological literature, since many languages have one word for blue and green shades (as named in English; see, e.g., MacLaury 1997). As a consequence of this problem, Harrison concludes that *colour2* is not a "natural nameable": there are no features of our colour experience that are themselves sufficient to divide experience into "separable elements prior to, and quite independently of, any linguistic capacities" (Harrison 1973, p. 19). Instead, *colour2* consists of "constructed nameables" where *colour2* individuation "is settled by some stipulated rule or convention to which all speakers of a language adhere " (1973, p. 24).[6] Harrison goes much further than simply articulating this conceptual point. His positive theory, roughly, is as follows. If there are no natural demarcations in the colour space, then we need an account of how *colour2* demarcations come about. Suppose one were to start with two colour terms, fixed in whatever way,[7] in two distinct regions of a similarity colour continuum. Let us say they are fixed on common examples of the English terms "red" and "green". For a language like this, all things named as *colour2* are called "red" or "green". Relative to the similarity colour space, this generates a decision problem. Some colours will clearly resemble red (orange, pink), and some green (blue), but others will be more problematical. What about yellow? Some shades of yellow are greenish, and some are reddish-orangish, yet *pure* yellow seems to best resemble examples of *neither* of our *colour2* terms "red" or "green" and thus poses a decision problem: is a pure yellow to be denominated "red" or "green", the terms which are exhaustive in the language described? Harrison argues that decision problems of the sort described here will motivate the introduction of new colour terms ("yellow" in this case), and that this introduction motivates a new set of decision problems (e.g. are orangish colours more like yellow than red?) We start, then, with two colour terms, somewhat far apart in the similarity colour space. For some shades of colour, it will be uncertain as to what term applies. Confusion as to term application motivates the introduction of a new colour term for the disputed cases. This introduction generates a new set of disputed cases, and so on. This is not an endless process. It is constrained by the nature of the similarity colour space (*colour1*), and by the psychologically and socially diminishing cognitive returns to ever finer segmentation into *colour2s*. Harrison's account is, we should say, primarily an account of how a linguistic *group* may come to have a set of referentially stable colour terms, where the process described is laid bare behaviourally at the group level: disagreement about boundaries between colours will drive a social process that aims to maximize (or at least increase) social agreement as to colour term application.

Harrison, like Wittgenstein, places emphasis on the role of the group (a language, a culture), and, like Wittgenstein, he does not view *colour2* to be a natural nameable. But Harrison does employ a version of *colour1* that he refers to as "The structure and content of the learner's prelinguistic (or extralinguistic) experience" (Harrison 1973, p. 56), and that version of *colour1* plays a significant (if not sufficient) role in his account of colour as constructed nameable, just as it enables Quine to get his discussion of *colour2* off the ground.

We have tried in the first part of this section to highlight the fact that merely saying a *colour2* depends on there being a word for a *colour2* is not very informative. We might, that is, believe that language is essential to the formation of *colour2* without having any idea how that might occur. The great virtue of Harrison's account is that it provides the basis for a psycholinguistics of colour, an answer to [1] discussed above: How are *colour2s* formed? The answer canvassed here is that they are formed in the context of a group seeking (not necessarily intentionally) a stable set of colour terms that can be used in a more or less reliable way across speakers. Such speakers are, in a way, constructing a language game (though not one Wittgenstein would like) that exploits prelinguistic or non-linguistic similarities and differences (*colour1*) to resolve decision problems via the introduction of fixed colour points which serve as constraints on judgements of similarity and difference. It is true that decision problems remain, and in strict numerical terms there will be *more* such decision sites: the more colour terms the more boundaries between terms, and boundaries are where uncertainty arises. That said, such decisions will be situated in the context of a set of *colour2s* that are relatively fixed, and in relation to which judgements about *colour2* membership can be made with confidence. The difficult cases will, in effect, be pushed into narrower and narrower ranges of potential disagreement such as we see, for example, at the blue-green boundary for English speakers.

What about question [2], above? That question was: why a specific set of *colour2s*?

We could treat Harrison's account as neutral with respect to the question: the particulars of a linguistic group will explain the colour names and *colour2s* found in their language and culture. This, again, is not very informative, for it merely transfers the answering of [2] to a vague and undefined appeal to linguistic-cultural value. On the other hand, why think there is more to it than that? If the names for *colour2s* vary across languages and cultures, and do so in unsystematic ways, then perhaps there is no interesting answer to why one set of colour words and corresponding *colour2s* are found in a given language. On this view, the answer to question [2] will be historical and anthropological in nature, specific to particular languages and groups.

One might view Harrison's account of colour terms, and with it *colour2* formation as speculative, an "inference to the best explanation" with all that type of inference's attendant risks. One can say, in defence of Harrison's account of *colour2* as a constructed nameable, that it is echoed in more recent and remarkably similar accounts of colour language and colour classification by the psychologists Kimberley Jameson (Jameson and Andrade 1997) and Terry Regier (Regier *et al.* 2007, 2009). This is an interesting case of interdisciplinary consilience (the psychologists had no knowledge of Harrison's work, which came first) that is in fact motivated by research we have yet to discuss. For Harrison was motivated, as was Jameson and as was Regier, by the work of the anthropologist Brent Berlin and the linguist Paul Kay, first published in their influential book *Basic Colour Terms: Their Universality and Evolution* (1969). It is their view which we turn to now.

6 There is the notion that colour vocabulary—there being a word for a colour2— varies from culture to culture. For example: English has a word for blue shades and a word for green shades, while other languages, Berinmo for instance, have one word for blue and green shades

The fact that colour vocabulary differs from language to language is not itself an interesting claim. French and English use the words "rouge" and "red" to denominate roughly the same *colour2*. The differences are superficial. When colour language researchers talk about differences in colour names they are interested in cases where not only the words differ, but the *colour2s* that are named differ as well. So, for example, English has the words "green" and "blue" and they denominate distinct *colour2s*. Berinmo, a language spoken by people from north-east Papua New Guinea, has the colour word "nol", and it denominates the shades included in English "blue" and "green". If we think of the colour space as a continuum (picture a visible electro-magnetic spectrum, 400 nm–700 nm—red to violet), then the range of Berinmo "nol" along that continuum includes both of English "blue" and "green".

Until 1969, contemporary anthropological literature on colour was relatively uniform in the view that colour words and the *colour2s* that they named were culturally specific and relative.[8] The anthropologist V. Ray wrote that "each culture has taken the spectral continuum and divided it upon a basis which is quite arbitrary except for pragmatic considerations" (Ray 1953, p. 102). This consensus view, based mainly on the observations of ethnographers—that colour nomenclature differed significantly and unpredictably across cultures—met a serious challenge from Berlin and Kay in their book *Basic Color Terms: Their Universality and Evolution* (Berlin and Kay 1969). It is fair to say that Ray's claim—and Quine's—to the cultural relativity of *colour2* is targeted by Berlin and Kay and much of the research tradition their work has generated.

Berlin and Kay (1969) claimed two striking discoveries in their original work: (1) There is a limited number of "basic color terms", as defined by stipulated criteria, in any language. These terms name basic colour classifications or "categories" (as psychologists call them), a species of *colour2*. In English, which possesses all 11 terms, the words are "red", "yellow", "green", "blue", "orange", "purple", "pink", "grey", "brown", "black", and "white". (2) Informants who share a basic term (within and across languages) are in *agreement* as to which shades of colour are the best examples of the basic colour categories that their basic colour terms name. Berlin and Kay called these exemplars "focal colours".

Let us put this work by Berlin and Kay into the context of our discussion of colour words and their relationship to *colour2*. On the Quinean view which is our touchstone, colour language brings with it *colour2s*. Colour language also varies between groups, and *colour2s* vary, correspondingly. The explanation for this variation is cultural, the "pragmatic" considerations mentioned by Ray. Berlin and Kay's work turned this story upside down. While they did not deny there was a great deal of variation in language related to colour, that variation was often superficial. If one looked to the colour related words that were used most often, that had shorter names, that elicited the highest degrees of agreement and confidence among speakers (these are some of the criteria for basicness, see Biggam (2012) for more detail), then one found not only that many colour related words were lacking with respect to these criteria, but that some—especially "red", "yellow", "green", and "blue" in their English gloss—stood out. And not only within a given language, but across all of the languages studied.[9] This is the basis for Berlin and Kay's claim to the "universality" of basic colour terms: any language will possess all or some subset of these basic terms.

The reader may wonder about this claim to universality. Consider our discussion of Berinmo and English. We said that Berinmo "nol" denominates the shades included in English "blue" and "green". The range of "nol" includes the range of "blue" and "green" shades and thus has a different range than either "blue" or "green". In what sense is there a common term between these two languages, a shared "universal"? It seems as if we are saying something analogous to this: Language A has a word for horses and cows and Language B has a word for horse and a word for cow. So A and B share a "universal" term for horses and cows! But this is a misreading of Berlin and Kay (though there are issues here; Dedrick (1998a)), and to understand why we need to consider the authors' second striking claim (2) about colour language, that there are shared and agreed upon "focal colours".

It is best to explain the notion of a focal colour in the context of the actual experiments used to uncover them. (Here we describe a specific experimental paradigm that is no longer in use but serves for illustrative purposes.[10]) Imagine that a two dimensional colour chart is placed in front of you. Its dimensions are hue (horizontal) and lightness (vertical). The chart is a subset of the Munsell colour space intended to represent the range of shades that one finds in an equal energy spectrum with some non-spectral shades such as brown and pink, and purple added. That means that, at the left side of the chart, there are shades of colour one would typically call "red" and, moving toward the right, one finds, in order, shades that an English speaker would typically call "orange", "brown", "yellow", "green", "blue", "violet", "pink". Not including the monochromatic colours (which are represented in a separate column) this chart has 240 individual shades of *chromatic colour* (colour that possesses some hue). Field ethnographers will have, in advance, determined the basic colour terms in your language, using the Berlin-Kay criteria (this can also be done *post facto*), and they ask you to select, for each of your basic colour terms, the *best example* of that colour term. Not only is this a request that makes sense to most participants in this kind of experiment, it is one which produces significant agreement: you are likely to choose a best example of your "red" that agrees with the choices of your fellow English speakers. Further, when the data gleaned from this sort of task (which the reader will note is Brindley's "Class B") is compared cross culturally, there is significant agreement as to best examples—"focal colors" as Berlin and Kay have it—for individuals speaking different languages. It is also possible to use a modified version of this task to explore boundary placement within basic colour categories: the ethnographer can ask you, the participant, to place a grain of rice on every shade of colour in the chart that you would name with a given basic term in your vocabulary. In this way, the range of your colour term can be specified. And unlike focal colours where there is great agreement, boundaries are more variable.

Let's return to the Berinmo, and the puzzle about basic term range discussed above. Berlin and Kay would say (as Kay does; Regier *et al.* 2005) that the Berinmo term is a universal term corresponding to an English universal term not because the range is the same for the two, but because there are two terms, one English and one Berinmo, that have one shared focal colour for both English and Berinmo experimental participants. In the case of "nol", the focal colour is located in what English speakers would call "green", though the range of the term extends across blue (for English) shades as well. It is focal colours and their uniformity across languages, not the range of the terms that is the basis for universality. More recently, this notion has come to be defined in terms of colour term "centeroids"—clusters of shades that constitute the statistically significant choices participants make when asked to select basic colour term focal colours (Regier *et al.* 2009; Abbot *et al.* 2016). Recent work has also claimed that colour category boundaries, cross culturally, are less variable than earlier research suggested (Kay and Regier 2007).

While there is much more to this story, we have enough for the task at hand. That task is to consider the idea of this section, that *colour2* varies from culture to culture. Berlin and Kay's work suggests this view is in an important sense incorrect. While *colour2* does vary from language to language and group to group, that variation is much more constrained than scholars prior to 1969 imagined, *if* we allow Berlin and Kay's conception of "basic colour term" to enter into play. One need not do this, and there is a substantial literature that is critical of this notion as well as other aspects of the Berlin and Kay research tradition.[11] The psychologist Terry Regier, in writing about disputes between "universalists" and "relativists" about colour classification, refers to "the battlefield of colour" (Regier *et al.* 2010, p. 166). The philosopher John Sutton, reviewing a philosophical book on colour language research, referred to the "colour wars" (Sutton 2001, p. 106). It is simply not possible, here, to describe the detailed and sometimes heated debate that has followed the publication of *Basic Color Terms*.[12]

That said, the dust has settled to some extent, at least as far as legitimacy of the basic colour term construct is concerned. It is true that much that is interesting about any culture and its ideas about colour are not fully captured in the study of basicness (think of the emotional connotations of *colour2s* such as red, yellow, green, and blue in English, for example). Yet the idea that some colour words are more basic than others has proved remarkably robust and "resistant to demolition", as the linguist Carole Biggam has said (Biggam 2012, p. 85). Contemporary debates as to the relativity or universality of colour words now tend to be debates about the extent to which colour vocabularies are similar across cultures—and the extent to which there is space for linguistic relativism.

In II.5 we asked two questions: [1] how are *colour2s* formed? And [2] why a specific set of *colour2s*? We offered one sort of answer to question [1], Harrison's theory of *colour2s* as constructed nameables. But we had no answer for [2], proposing only that this might be a contingent matter: you end up with the set of *colour2s* that you do because of the particularities of your culture. This is Quine's view, among others. The Berlin and Kay theory requires us to reconsider that proposal, though we need to reformulate question [2]. It is no longer "why a specific set"—that formulation is best suited to the cultural answer, since it allows us to consider sets that differ quite dramatically—but "why *the* specific set of basic colour terms, all or some subset of which are found in any language?" The Berlin-Kay theory, to the extent we have discussed it here, does not answer this question, telling us only that there is an interesting set of cross-cultural linguistic and classificatory regularities to be explained.

7 The notion of a colour2 is "less basic" than the notion of a colour word. For example: the colour word "red" is conceptually prior to the colour2 it names

Quine does not use the word "basic" in the same way that Berlin and Kay do. For Quine colour words are more basic than *colour2s* in the sense that they are conceptually prior to the colours they name (more on that, shortly). For Berlin and Kay, basicness is a linguistic-psychological construct that identifies a regularity that, they claim, occurs in all human languages. To focus on Quine first. Is a *colour2* less basic (in the sense of conceptually prior) than the word for a *colour2*?

If what one means by "conceptual priority" is that first there are words, and then there are *colour2s*, it is clear that colour words must be conceptually prior to *colour2s* for language users. It has long been known that children do not easily learn the correct (social) application of colour names. Recent work on this topic (Wagner *et al.* 2013) argues that children may learn colour term application for restricted cases (some shades) very quickly, but need to engage in a process of "slow mapping" whereby they use an inductive process to refine, over time, the boundaries of their colour terms. With adult competence used as the criterion for successful application of a colour term children are, essentially, engaging in a difficult process of cognitive social coordination. For these cases, there is a correct criterion for the application of colour names which is conceptually prior to colour name learning and against which competence is judged and achieved. This criterion will be messy, because *colour2* boundaries are messy—it is not a set of necessary and sufficient conditions—but it is functional and empirically evident. To modify a famous maxim of Quine's: colour language competence is a social art.[13]

This social sense of "conceptual priority" is, however, a *weak sense*. As the research on language learning suggests, it probably applies to all speakers of all languages, and is neutral with respect to the origins of both *colour2s* and colour names. A stronger sense of "conceptually prior" is, in fact, implicit in Quine's overall view. Suppose that *colour2* transcends our ability to simply discriminate colours: it is not exhausted by the resources of *colour1*. As such, it needs to be explained in some way that is distinct from the mere discrimination of sameness and difference. Such explanation cannot be in terms of the naturalness of *colour2s*. Though *colour1* may be natural in the perceptual sense, for humans, *colour2* is not: the divisions in the spectrum, or more generally a colour space, are arbitrary relative to the colour space itself. It does not come divided into *colour2s*. How do we know this? We see that, as Quine believes, words that denominate *colour2s* vary from "culture to culture". If they did not, then we would have a legitimate question as to conceptual priority. If everyone had the same *colour2s*, then perhaps something *natural* causes us to have the words for the *colour2s* that we have. This consequence is not logically required. It is possible, for example, that terms for *colour2s* have been spread by linguistic imperialism grounded in one language and culture and its choices (much the way television viewing has been spread; it's universal but hardly "natural" in the sense we have been using that word). That said, it is fair to say that the Quinean view, our touchstone, hinges on cultural difference. It is cultural difference that provides the surety for the non-natural, arbitrary character of *colour2s*. It is a surety that is challenged by Berlin and Kay because, following the research tradition their work initiated, we find a world in which there is greater unanimity in both *colour2s* and words for *colour2s* than any cultural relativist would expect to find. Berlin and Kay's theory suggests that the linguistic criteria that are in place for a language and its learners cannot ultimately be understood as culturally contingent. While Berlin and Kay's view does not require this interpretation, it has, and this has been a point of virtual unanimity, been taken to point toward explanations that are not primarily cultural. Let us consider one explanation for basicness, as an illustration.

The first and in many respects most attractive explanation for basicness was, in its origins, contemporaneous with Berlin and Kay's work. The psychologist Eleanor Rosch was a colleague of Berlin and Kay's at Berkeley in the 1960s. Rosch proposed, as a consequence of experimental, cross-cultural studies she conducted, that focal colours correlate positively to colour "prototypes" which provide a non-linguistic, non-cultural, "psychological salience" that is the basis for the formation of basic colour categories (Heider [Rosch] 1972; Rosch 1975). Imagine that some shades of colour (which are correlated positively with Berlin and Kay focal colours) stand out from others in that they are easier to recognize and remember than other shades (and that this is true cross-culturally, even for languages that possess a small number of basic terms). As such, they provide landmarks within colour experience from which *colour2s* could be formed by a process of generalization away from the prototype. This process would be constrained (thus solving the problem we described for Mackie) by the existence of other prototype colours which would function as boundaries or "foils" for the generalization process, much in the way that Harrison imagined the formation of *colour2s*. Indeed, Harrison's idea that you need to begin the *colour2* formation process with two shades of colour, relatively far apart in colour space, fits well with the prototype explanation. One's "extralinguistic experience", as Harrison called it— Quine's "brute irrationality of our sense of similarity"—will include brutely irrational colour prototypes to serve as landmarks. In relation to these one can judge an unnamed shade as more like prototype A (reddish, say) than prototype B (greenish, say). Both the Berlin and Kay regularities and Harrison's theory of *colour2* formation accord well with a third hypothesis formulated by Berlin and Kay: when you examine the distribution of basic colour words across different languages (synchronically) you can infer an *order* in which basic colour terms develop (diachronically). There is a major body of research dedicated to the diachronic claim, and we will not discuss it here (see Kay 2015 for a survey). We will note, only, that the diachronic scheme appears to privilege basic colour terms for red, yellow, green, and blue (along with the achromatics black and white), that the focal colours for English "red", "yellow", "green", and "blue" have corresponding prototypes, and that those prototypes have been claimed to correspond to the "unique hues" of opponent colour theory, the widely accepted psychophysical theory of primate colour vision. One can, perhaps, see the direction this explanatory strategy points: to a theory according to which linguistic basicness and its focal colours are underwritten by non-linguistic prototypes which, in turn, have their non-linguistic salience explained by features of the vision system itself. One may, in fact, be able to extend this reductive account even further than the psychophysical opponent theory, to its basis in actual mechanisms in retinal and post-retinal neural mechanisms, some of which are known to have an opponent structure (Abramov 1997).

This account can be described as "reductive" in the sense that it explains basicness in language in terms of lower-level psychological and physiological facts. The clearest statement of this reductive account has been articulated by the philosopher C.L. Hardin, who summarized it this way: "far from language carving out categories from a structureless color space, the basic linguistic categories themselves have been induced by perceptual saliencies common to the human race" (Hardin 1988, p. 168). This account has come to be called the "perceptual salience theory". As elegant as it may be, it is presently in disfavour.[14] Even Hardin, who remains attracted to this theory, discusses "alternative explanations" in a more recent publication. A contemporary, empirical version of Harrison's constructed namable theory is one of the alternatives. The different explanations may, Hardin notes, actually turn out to be compatible rather than truly alternative in the sense that they "focus on different aspects of color categorization" (Hardin 2013, p. 63; also Regier *et al.* 2005). One thing about these different views does seem clear: with allowance for some variation to occur both with respect to focal colour choices and the boundaries of *colour2*s named by basic terms, we are led away from the idea that colour words—basic colour terms at least—are derived from essentially cultural, contingent mechanisms. This is in keeping with an empirical research tradition that at present seems comfortable with the ideas that (1) the basic colour terms and focal colour centeroids constitute real cross-cultural regularities to be explained, and (2) there is presently no single explanation one can feel confident in accepting.

III Concluding remarks

We have followed a path sketched out by Quine not because that philosopher offers the right view of colour and its relationships to language and culture but because he identifies, in a very compact text, many of the issues that need to be addressed, and that form the conceptual backbone of philosophical as well as empirical investigations of colour, colour language, and culture. One thing that we have tried to do in this chapter is to balance the ideas of philosophers with empirical research, and it should be clear to the reader that it is very difficult to hold views on the topics under discussion that are not informed by empirical investigation. Indeed, it might seem that the question of whether *colour2*s are culturally relative or not, a theme of our discussion here, is likely to be decided by psychologists and anthropologists. Perhaps, but there is no sense in which such decision is forced upon us by "the data". While there are very good reasons for believing that the basic colour term construct identifies a real regularity in human thought and behaviour, that construct imposes a constraint on the way we think about colour that some will find, and do find, overly restrictive. Some anthropologists, for example, have pointed out that articulation of a language's basic colour terms which are then slotted into grander trans-cultural schemes does not, for many cases, capture the ways that colour matters to members of many cultures (Saunders 1992). Objections to the "eliminativist" nature of the basic colour term construct (eliminative of colour's cultural connotations) have fueled the "colour wars" as Sutton has described the general tenor of dispute, and such objections are unlikely to abate. As the psychologist Jules Davidoff, a "relativist" about colour categorization has said about a people and language we have discussed and that he has studied in depth:

> Take, for example, the color terms of the Berinmo ...: all five terms in that language have names that refer to objects in the world ... The distinction, in Berinmo, between leaves that are edible (green) and those that are inedible (yellow) makes up two of their terms. Their red term is the name of a berry which, like most berries, is a dark, saturated red when at its best to eat. The red term in other cultures is the word for blood (Rivers, 1905), which is a similar hue to the color of ripe berries. So a physiological explanation for the origin of color terms is not needed for any language, nor is it needed for the similarity of its terms to those in other languages for which there would be similar natural constraints.
>
> *(Davidoff 2015, pp. 272–3)*

This criticism of one kind of explanation for basicness is not new, as Davidoff notes in his article. Nor is it, as other comments by that author make clear, obviously incompatible with the sorts of explanation (physiological; constructed namable) we have discussed. So how are these alternative explanations—an overdetermination of explanation, one might say—to be dealt with, *assuming* that we grant explanatory status to all or some of them? These are questions going forward, questions the sciences have been largely silent on, and ones of some interest to philosophers.

Notes

1 See Teller and Palmer (2016) for a discussion of the relationships between Class A and Class B experiments; also Hardin (1988, p. 40) for comments appropriate to colour terms.
2 The Munsell colour space has figured into research on colour naming discussed later in this chapter. For a good introduction to the Munsell system and its importance see Long (2017). See Clark (1993) for an extended discussion of quality spaces with a philosophical orientation.
3 One part of the psychological colour categorization literature supports the idea that some colour categories, those that correspond to the main hue terms in English (and hence to *color2s*) *are* in fact natural in the sense that they possess a non-linguistic perceptual salience, specifically for infants (e.g. Franklin and Davies 2004). This phenomenon is referred to as "categorical perception" and it would seem to contradict Quine's view, and the view of many others as well. This research is not discussed here because it is problematical for a number of reasons. Here are some concerns: The "categorical perception" of colour has not been identified in other primates. If it were a function of the vision system's organization—a way in which groupings of qualities are spaced—one would expect this to be so (Davidoff and Fagot 2010). Colour categorical perception appears to be specific to a brain hemisphere, and to switch across hemispheres as a person learns linguistic classifications of colour. It is as if non-linguistic colour categories are "overwritten" in one hemisphere (the right hemisphere) through the normal course of cognitive development, appearing in the other hemisphere (the left) with language (Regier and Kay 2009)! This idea is compatible with research that shows categorical perception to be to some extent culturally relative: just as the range of colour terms may vary across cultures, so does the categorical perception of some *colour2s* (Roberson et al. 2004). In general, the relationships between language, perception, cognition, and colour categorization are poorly understood within this area of research, the experimental findings raising unresolved theoretical issues (Franklin 2015). That is not to disparage these results.
4 The idea that grouping shades of colour together on the basis of similarity constitutes the *only* non-cultural constraint upon human colour classifications (the formation of *colour2s*) has been advanced by the psychologist Debbi Roberson and colleagues. (Roberson et al. 2000). This view is not common in the psychological colour categorization literature.
5 A recent collection dealing with Wittgenstein's views on colour is Gierlinger and Riegelnik (2014). See also Dedrick (1998a, pp. 193–6), from which much of this discussion of Wittgenstein has been drawn.

6 Christopher Peacock has argued that colours are natural nameables on the ground that an organism without language "could manifest sensitivity to exactly the colour discriminations which are determined by Harrison's model of colour naming as applied to, say, English" (Peacock 1983, p. 44 fn. 15). This confuses *colour1* with *colour2*, for it imagines that *colour2* is determined by discrimination, which it is not. Non-human animals, macaques and other monkeys, do share discriminative capacities with humans (*colour1*), but there is little evidence that they share colour classifications (*colour2s*) such as those expressed in English or any other language. The evidence, such as it is, comes from work by the primatologist Tetsuro Matsuzawa (1985), who claimed that a chimpanzee classified colours (*colour2*) in much the same way as some humans. But Matsuzawa's chimp had been engaged in a language learning programme prior to the experiment, and it had been taught colour to symbol relationships (p. 283). This issue is discussed in the psychological literature on colour categorization, e.g. Davidoff and Fagot (2010).

7 Even a cursory glance at the ethnographic literature on colour naming (for non-Western, non-literate peoples in particular) reveals that many words which ethnographers treat as colour words have their linguistic origin in common nouns referring to things with a particular colour. Often, these nouns are duplicated to indicate their function as a colour word. Biggam discusses such "reduplicative" languages (Biggam 2012). See also the ethnographic data reported by Berlin and Kay (1969).

8 While this claim is a fair representation of the state of play within English speaking anthropology and ethnography circa 1969, it conceals a rich intellectual tradition concerned with the relationship between colour names and the colours they name. An excellent review of this history can be found in Biggam (2012); it is also discussed in the "Introduction" to Berlin and Kay (1969).

9 Berlin and Kay studied a small cross-cultural sample of language speakers experimentally in Berkeley, California, as a test of a basicness hypothesis. Subsequent to the experimental work, they applied their criteria for basicness to a larger body of ethnography concerning colour. Their methods in both instances have been criticized. See Dedrick (1998b) for a summary and discussion of this criticism; see also Kay (2015). The data set used in arguments for basicness has continued to expand since 1969. Much of it can be found online in the World Colour Survey (WCS Data Archives).

10 The anthropologist Robert MacLaury discusses the method described here as well as its limitations and related, improved methods in MacLaury (1997).

11 One often cited critical paper comes from the anthropologist Barbara Saunders and the philosopher Jaap van Brakel (Saunders and van Brakel 1997). See also Dedrick (1998b) for a review and critique of early criticism and, more recently, Kay (2015).

12 Research into colour classification and colour naming constitute a large research programme. To give the reader some idea of its scope, research from different disciplines that is about colour language and engages with the Berlin and Kay theory runs to, by this author's count, more than 1,000 published items. *Basic Color Terms: Their Universality and Evolution* (Berlin and Kay 1969) has been cited, according to Google Scholar, over 5,000 times.

13 "Language is a social art" is the epigraph to Quine's *Word and Object* (1960).

14 It may be that the perceptual salience theory is too ambitious. It requires mappings from focal colours, to colour prototypes, to psychophysical opponency, to neural opponent mechanisms. To get such an account to work, one needs robust correlations across these empirical domains. Such correlations have proved difficult to obtain (though their possibility is very tantalizing, especially to those with a reductive cast of mind). The interested reader is directed to the following as important primary sources critical of the perceptual salience theory: for issues relating to the relationship between focal colours and colour prototypes see Roberson *et al.* (2000); for issues related to the relationship between focal colours and opponent unique hues see Kuehni (2004); for issues related to psychophysical opponency and neural opponency see Abramov (1997). *The Handbook of Color Psychology*, Part IV, "Colour categorization" (2015) is also recommended. Dedrick (1998a) is an extended discussion and critique of the perceptual salience theory by a philosopher.

References

Abbott, J.T., Thomas L., Griffiths, T.L., and Regier, T. (2016) "Focal colors across languages are representative members of color categories". *PNAS*, 113, 11178–83.

Abramov, I. (1997) "Physiological mechanisms of color vision". *Color Categories in Thought and Language*. C.L Hardin and L. Maffi, Eds. (pp. 89–117). Cambridge University Press.

Berlin, B. and Kay, P. (1969) *Basic Color Terms: Their Universality and Evolution*. University of California Press.

453

Biggam, C. (2012) *The Semantics of Colour*. Cambridge University Press.

Brindley, G.S. (1960) *Physiology of the Retinal and Visual Pathways*. 1st ed. Edward Arnold.

Byrne, A. and Hilbert, D. (2003) "Color realism and color science". *Behavioral and Brain Sciences*, 26, 1–44.

Clark, A. (1993) *Sensory Qualities*. Clarendon Press.

Davidoff, J. (2015) "Color categorization across cultures". *Handbook of Color Psychology*. A.J. Elliot, M.D. Fairchild, and A. Franklin, Eds. (pp. 259–78). Cambridge University Press.

Davidoff, J.B. and Fagot, J. (2010) "Cross-species assessment of the linguistic origins of colour categories". *Comparative Cognition and Behavior Reviews*, 5: 100–16.

Dedrick, D. (1998a) *Naming the Rainbow: Colour Language, Colour Science and Culture*. Kluwer.

Dedrick, D. (1998b) "On the foundations of the universalist tradition in colour naming research (and their supposed refutation)". *Philosophy of the Social Sciences*, 28(2): 179–204.

Elliot, A.J., Fairchild, M.D., and Franklin, A. (2015) *Handbook of Color Psychology*. Cambridge University Press.

Franklin, A. (2015) "Development of color categorization". *Handbook of Color Psychology*. A.J. Elliot, M.D. Fairchild, and A. Franklin, Eds. (pp. 279–94). Cambridge University Press.

Franklin, A. and Davies, I.R.L. (2004) "New evidence for infant colour categories". *British Journal of Developmental Child Psychology*, 22, 349–77.

Gierlinger, F.A. and Riegelnik, S., Eds. (2014) *Wittgenstein on Colour*. De Gruyter.

Hacker, P.M.S. (1972) *Insight and Illusion*. Oxford University Press.

Hardin, C.L. (1988) *Color for Philosophers: Unweaving the Rainbow*. Hackett Publishers.

Hardin, C.L. (2013) "Berlin and Kay Theory". *Encyclopedia of Color Science and Technology*. Springer Science + Business Media.

Harrison, B. (1973) *Form and Content*. Blackwell.

Heider, E.R. [Rosch] (1972) "Universals in color naming and memory". *Journal of Experimental Psychology*, 93: 10–20.

Jacobs, G.H. (1981) *Comparative Color Vision*. Academic Press.

Jacobs, G.H. (2015) "Evolution of color vision and its reflections in contemporary mammals". *Handbook of Color Psychology*. A.J. Elliot, M.D. Fairchild, and A. Franklin, Eds. (pp. 110–30). Cambridge University Press.

Jameson, K. and D'Andrade, R.G. (1997) "It's not really red, yellow, green, and blue: an inquiry into perceptual color space". *Color Categories in Thought and Language*. C.L. Hardin and L. Maffi, Eds. (pp. 295–319). Cambridge University Press.

Kay, P. (2015) "Universality of colour categorization". *Handbook of Color Psychology*. A.J. Elliot, M.D. Fairchild, and A. Franklin, Eds. (pp. 245–58). Cambridge University Press.

Kay, P., and Regier, T. (2007) "Color naming universals: the case of Berinmo". *Cognition*, 102, 289–98.

Kuehni, R.G. (2004) "Variability in unique hue selection: a surprising phenomenon". *Color Research and Application*, 29: 158–62.

Long, J. (2017) *The New Munsell Student Color Set*. Bloomsbury Academic Publishers.

Mackie, J.L. (1978) *Problems from Locke*. Oxford University Press.

MacLaury, R.E. (1997) *Color and Cognition in Mesoamerica: Constructing Color Categories as Vantages*. University of Texas.

Matsuzawa, T. (1985) "Color naming and classification in a chimpanzee (Pan troglodytes)". *Journal of Human Evolution*, 14: 283–91.

Peacock, C. (1983) *Sense and Content*. Oxford University Press.

Quine, W.V. (1960) *Word and Object*. MIT Press.

Quine, W.V. (1969) *Ontological Relativity and Other Essays*. Columbia University Press.

Quine, W.V. (1974) *The Roots of Reference*. Open Court Publishers.

Ray, V.F. (1953) "Human color perception and behavioral response". *Transactions of the New York Academy of Sciences*, 2(16): 98–105.

Regier, T., and Kay, P. (2009) "Language, thought and culture: Whorf was half-right". *Trends in Cognitive Science*, 13(10): 440–6.

Regier, T., Kay, P., and Cook, R. (2005) "Focal colors are universal after all". *Proceedings of the National Academy of Sciences*, 102, 8386–91.

Regier, T., Kay, P., and Khetarpal, N. (2007) "Color naming reflects optimal partitions of color space". *Proceedings of the National Academy of Sciences*, 104, 1436–41.

Regier, T., Kay, P., and Khetarpal, N. (2009) "Color naming and the shape of color space". *Language*, 85, 884–92.

Regier, T., Kay, P., Gilbert, A., and Ivry, R. (2010) "Language and thought: which side are you on, anyway?" *Words and the Mind: How Words Capture Human Experience*. B. Malt and P. Wolff, Eds. (pp. 165–82). Oxford University Press.

Roberson, D., Davies, I., & Davidoff, J. (2000) "Color categories are not universal: replications and new evidence from a stone-age culture". *Journal of Experimental Psychology: General*, 129(3), 369–98.

Roberson, D., Davidoff, J., Davies, I. R. L., and Shapiro, L.R. (2004) "The development of colour categories in two languages: a longitudinal study". *Journal of Experimental Psychology: General*, 129, 369–98.

Rosch, E. (1975) "Universals and cultural specifics in human categorization". *Cross Cultural Perspectives on Learning*. S. Bochner, W.J. Lonner, and R.W. Brislin, Eds. Halstead Press.

Saunders, B.A.C. (1992) *The Invention of Basic Colour Terms*. ISOR.

Saunders, B.A.C., and van Brakel, J. (1997) "Are there non-trivial constraints on colour categorization?" *Behavioral and Brain Sciences*, 20(2): 167–79.

Schwyzer, H. (2001) "Autonomy". *Wittgenstein: A Critical Reader*. Hans-Johann Glock, Ed. Wiley.

Stoughton, C.M., Lafer-Sousa, R., Gagin, G., and Conway, B.R. (2012) "Psychophysical chromatic mechanisms in macaque monkey". *The Journal of Neuroscience*, 32(43): 15216–26.

Sutton, John. (2001) "Review of Don Dedrick, *Naming the Rainbow: Colour Language, Colour Science, and Culture*". *Philosophy in Review*, XXI: 106–9.

Teller, D., and Palmer, J. (2016) *Vision and the Visual System*. (Manuscript unpublished and incomplete at the author's death). The text is available at http://faculty.washington.edu/jpalmer/files/Teller/Teller-Book2016/tellerbookChapters1to7.pdf.

Thompson, E. (1995) *Colour Vision: A Study in Cognitive Science and the Philosophy of Perception*. Routledge.

Wagner, K., Dobkins, K., and Barner, D. (2013) "Slow mapping: color word learning as a gradual inductive process". *Cognition*, 127(3): 307–17.

Westphal, J. (1991) *Colour: A Philosophical Introduction*. 2nd ed. Blackwell Publishers.

Wittgenstein, L. (1958) *Blue and Brown Books*. Basil Blackwell.

Wittgenstein, L. (1977) *Remarks on Colour*. G.E.M. Anscombe, Ed. Linda L. McAlister and Margarete Schatte, Trans. University of California Press.

World Color Survey (WCS). The WCS Data Archives: www1.icsi.berkeley.edu/wcs/data.html.

28

COLOUR CATEGORIZATION AND CATEGORICAL PERCEPTION

Robert Briscoe

Introduction

Human beings with normal, trichromatic vision have the capacity to discriminate approximately 2 million different shades of colour (Pointer and Attridge 1998; Linhares *et al.* 2008; Kuehni 2013).[1] Despite the fine-grained specificity with which we perceive colour, we tend to think and speak about colour in terms of a comparatively much small number of coarse-grained categories. English, for example, contains only 11 basic colour terms (BCTs)—'black', 'white', 'red', 'yellow', 'green', 'blue', 'brown', 'orange', 'pink', 'purple', and 'grey'—while the unwritten languages of many non-industrialized societies contain as few as two or three BCTs.[2]

A long-standing debate in cognitive science, linguistics, anthropology, and philosophy concerns the basis of human colour categorization and naming practices. Are there psychologically or culturally universal constraints on how speakers of different languages sort fine-grained shades of colour into compact sets of coarse-grained categories? Or is it rather the case that 'each culture has taken the spectral continuum and divided it on a basis which is quite arbitrary except for pragmatic considerations' (Ray 1953: 102)? One aim of this chapter is to survey some of the recently more influential ways of answering these questions.

Another related question concerns the relationship between colour naming practices and colour perception. Do linguistic representations of colour categories influence the way human beings visually experience colour? In particular, can learning to use a set of colour terms cause shades that straddle a category boundary to appear phenomenally less similar (and, hence, easier to discriminate) or cause shades that fall within the boundaries of a named category to appear phenomenally more similar (and, hence, harder to discriminate)? If so, then visually perceiving colour, like phoneme discrimination in language (Liberman and Mattingly 1985; Harnad 1987; Kuhl 2004), may be described as 'categorical'. Alternatively, linguistic representations of colour categories might influence the speed or accuracy with which fine-grained shades colours are discriminated or remembered without having any effects on their appearance.

The colour categorization debate has been traditionally framed as a conflict between 'universalist' and 'relativist' conceptions of the relation between language, thought, and perception (for helpful overviews, see Dedrick 1998, 2014a; Hardin 2005; Jameson 2005b; Regier and Kay 2009; Roberson and Hanley 2009; Regier *et al.* 2010; Roberson 2012; Winawer and Witthoft

2012; and Lindsey and Brown 2014).[3] To simplify greatly, *strong universalism* maintains (1) that coarse-grained colour concepts corresponding to BCTs are unlearned, psychological universals that recur across maximally different cultures; (2) that the psychological universality of these colour concepts is due to the perceptual salience of their best examples or 'foci'; and, finally, (3) that the representation of colour categories in language has no influence on the way colours are represented at the level of either thought or perception. *Strong linguistic relativism*, in contrast, denies claim (1): basic colour concepts aren't psychological universals, but vary instead with cultural and communicative needs. Hence, there are no cross-cultural patterns in colour categorization and colour-naming practices that demand scientific explanation, as assumed by claim (2). Strong linguistic relativists also deny claim (3), maintaining instead that colour terms are the primary vehicles of colour category representation and, strikingly, that an object's apparent colour can vary as a function of the colour terms present in the perceiver's language. In denying claim (3), strong linguistic relativism has an affinity with the writings of Benjamin Lee Whorf (1956).

As will be shown below, this stark way of framing the colour categorization debate has probably outlived its usefulness. On the one hand, prominent universalists no longer maintain that considerations of perceptual salience are what best account for the cross-cultural recurrence of certain basic colour concepts. They also accept that colour language can have experimentally measurable effects on colour memory and colour discrimination tasks. In other words, they have distanced themselves from claims (2) and (3) above. On the other hand, prominent linguistic relativists now deny that so-called colour 'categorical perception' effects are properly interpreted as effects of language on the way colours visually appear. Speakers of different languages do not experience the colours present in their environment in different ways. Both sides of the debate, in short, have moved closer toward the moderate centre of the theoretical spectrum between strong universalism and strong linguistic relativism.

In the next two sections of this chapter, I critically examine two of the main approaches to colour categorization in cognitive science: the *perceptual salience theory* and *linguistic relativism*. I then turn to reviewing several decades of psychological research on colour categorical perception (CP). A careful assessment of relevant findings suggests that most of the experimental effects that have been understood in terms of CP actually fall on the cognition side of the perception-cognition divide: they are effects of colour language, for example, on memory or decision-making.

The perceptual salience theory

Theories of colour categorization can be distinguished by the constraints that they respectively impose on the colour concept formation process. Two constraints, however, appear to be common ground across different theories. The first is *grouping by similarity* (or *grouping* for short). Debi Roberson and co-authors write:

> There are, indeed, constraints on color categorization linked to the properties of the visual system. The most important constraint would be that similar items (as defined by perceptual discrimination) are universally grouped together. Thus, no language would exhibit categories that include two areas of color space but excludes an area between them. … Grouping by similarity can explain, for example, why there is no composite category that includes yellow and blue but excludes green. There is no associative chain of similarity that could connect yellow to blue without passing through green.
>
> *(2000: 395)*

A second shared constraint is that colour categorization systems are constructed so as maximize perceptual similarity within categories, while minimizing perceptual similarity between different categories (Garner 1974). Since systems that comport with this constraint, other things being equal, are more informative, i.e. communicatively efficient, than those that don't (Jameson and D'Andrade 1997; Jameson 2005a, 2005b; Regier *et al.* 2007; Regier *et al.* 2015), I shall here refer to it as the *informativeness* constraint.

Proponents of the *perceptual salience theory* (Rosch 1973; Kay and McDaniel 1978; Hardin 1988, 2005; Kay *et al.* 1997; Kay and Maffi 1999; Kuehni 2005a; Kay and Regier 2007) maintain that a third universal constraint on colour categorization and naming comes from the way in which human beings experience colour. The 'basic linguistic categories themselves', C.L Hardin writes, 'have been induced by perceptual saliencies common to the human race' (1988: 168).

According to the theory, certain shades of colour, in particular, the 'Hering primaries' black, white, unique red (**UR**), unique yellow (**UY**), unique green (**UG**), and unique blue (**UB**) (Hering 1878/1964), are especially salient in visual experience prior to their representation in either language or thought. (I shall follow Byrne and Hilbert 2003 in referring to these chromatic shades collectively as the **4UH**.) The perceptual salience or 'attention-grabbingness' of these shades is often said to arise from their distinctively pure or non-mixed appearance. As Justin Broackes puts it, 'There are no purples that do not look to have some red and some blue in them, no turquoises that do not in some way seem bluish and also greenish; but there are reds that don't look in any way bluish or yellowish and yellows that seem to contain no hint of either red or green' (Broackes 2011: 602). It has also been argued that terms for the 4UH are both necessary and sufficient for linguistically describing all of the other colours (Sternheim and Boynton 1966; Hardin 1981, chap. 5). This fact, Hardin says, 'justifies singling them out as perceptually elementary' and as having 'psychological primacy' (2005: 74). Byrne and Hilbert (2003) go beyond Hardin in arguing that colours are actually represented in visual experience itself in terms of the proportions of the primary hue-magnitudes that they contain. For example, a surface will look purple to a perceiver just in case it is represented in her experience as having roughly equal proportions of UR and UB, but relatively low proportions of UG and UY (Byrne and Hilbert 2003: 14).[4]

According to the best known version of the salience theory, the Hering primaries function as 'natural prototypes' in colour concept formation (Rosch 1973): whether a shade belongs in the category red, for example, is based on its perceived similarity to UR; whether a shade is in the category blue is based on its perceived similarity to UB; and so on. The Hering primaries, as Paul Kay and Luisa Maffi put it, thus function as 'perceptual landmarks [that] individually or in combination form the basis of the denotation most of the major color terms of most of the languages of the world' (1999: 774).

The perceptual salience theory is an expression of universalism about the relationship between language and thought in the colour domain. '[F]ar from being a domain well suited to the study of the effects of language on thought', Eleanor Rosch concluded at the end of her influential 'Universals in color naming and memory' (Rosch Heider 1972), 'the color space would seem to be a prime example of the influence of underlying perceptual-cognitive factors on the formation and reference of linguistic categories' (20). Unlike the relativist views considered below, universalism maintains that, in representing colour, 'languages make semantic distinctions drawn from a palette of universally available options' (Regier *et al.* 2010: 165).

Early sources of empirical support for the salience theory came from Rosch's pioneering studies of colour naming and colour memory among the Dugum Dani, a hunter-gatherer tribe living in the highlands of western New Guinea (Rosch Heider 1972; Rosch Heider and Olivier 1972;

Rosch 1973). One of Rosch's goals was to test the linguistic relativistic hypothesis that 'verbal color coding acts on memory imagery such that the "structure" of colors in memory comes to resemble the "structure" of color names in a given language' (Rosch Heider and Olivier 1972: 338). The Dani have only two BCTs, which divide colour space into warm-light and cool-dark regions. Hence, linguistic relativism predicts that the Dani performance on colour memory tasks should significantly differ from that of English speakers, who use many more BCTs.

At odds with what the linguistic relativist would predict, Rosch and Olivier found 'no indication that the differences between the naming structures for the two languages carried over in parallel fashion to the two memory structures' (1972: 350). On the contrary, the Dani and English speakers exhibited similar confusions in memory. For instance, good examples of colour categories named in English such as red, blue, and green were better remembered by Dani participants than colours less easily named by English speakers. These findings were taken to furnish strong support for the view that certain perceptually salient colours are 'the cognitive underpinning for cross-language naming universals' (Kay and Regier 2007: 290).

This account was subsequently challenged two decades later by the work of Jules Davidoff, Debi Roberson, and others on the Berinmo of Papua New Guinea and the Himba of Northern Namibia (Davidoff *et al.* 1999; Roberson *et al.* 2000; Roberson *et al.* 2002; Roberson *et al.* 2005a). Davidoff and Roberson found no evidence in their studies of short-term memory and long-term category learning indicating that Berinmo and Himba speakers find it easier to recall basic colour categories named in English than those named in their own languages. Further, in similarity and forced-choice recognition memory judgement tasks, Berinmo and Himba speakers exhibited categorical perception (CP) effects for colour boundaries that were marked in their own languages, but not for the supposedly universal boundary between green and blue marked in English and other written languages (Roberson *et al.* 2005b). (These studies and the proper interpretation of putative colour CP effects will be addressed later in this chapter.)

A second, more important source of evidence for the salience theory is linguistic. To date there have been two large-scale investigations of cross-cultural colour-naming practices, the landmark study of 20 different written languages conducted by Brent Berlin and Paul Kay (1969) and the more recent World Color Survey (WCS), which identified BCTs in an additional 110 unwritten languages (Kay *et al.* 2009). On the basis of their findings, Berlin and Kay advanced two hypotheses. First, 'although different languages encode in their vocabularies different *numbers* of basic color categories, a total inventory of exactly eleven basic color categories exists from which the eleven or fewer basic color categories of any given language are always drawn' (Berlin and Kay 1969: 2). In the lexicon of American and British English, the 11 basic categories are picked out by the terms 'black', 'white', 'red', 'yellow', 'green', 'blue', 'brown', 'orange', 'pink', 'purple', and 'grey'. Second, BCT inventories evolve through time by incorporating these categories in a highly constrained sequence, starting with just two BCTs referring to the composite categories *warm/light* and *dark/cool*.

The World Color Survey (WCS) collected colour naming data from 110 unwritten languages spoken in small, non-industrialized societies (Kay *et al.* 2009). Speakers were asked to name each of 320 maximally saturated Munsell colours and 10 grey-scale colours, presented in random order, from the array reproduced in Figure 28.1(A). They were also asked to demonstrate the best examples or foci of each of their named colours.

Regier *et al.* (2005) calculated how many best-example 'hits' fell on each chip of the array for all speakers interviewed in the WCS. The contour plot in Figure 28.1(B) shows the number of WCS best-example hits that fell on each chip in the chromatic portion of the stimulus array (with a contour interval of 100 hits). The black dots correspond to the foci of the English colour terms 'red', 'yellow', 'green', and 'blue' provided by one American speaker (Berlin and Kay

(A)

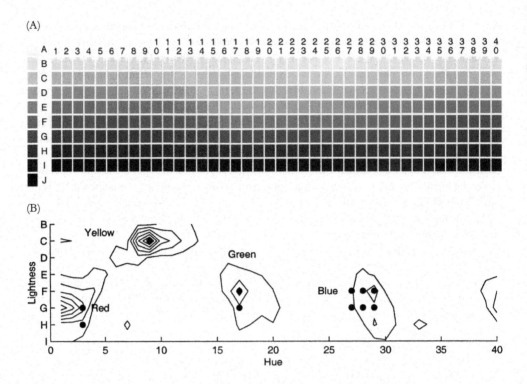

(B)

Figure 28.1 (A) Munsell colour palette and (B) contour plot of WCS best-example choices compared with best examples of English colour terms for the chromatic Hering primaries.

1969). As indicated by the contour plot, the best examples of named chromatic colour categories across the 110 languages of the WCS cluster around the best examples of four English terms: G1 (focal red), C9 (focal yellow), F17 (focal green), and F29 (focal blue). Regier *et al.* (2005) also found that best examples of BCTs are more tightly clustered across the languages of the WCS than are the centroids of category extensions. 'This pattern', they write,

> would be expected if best examples reflect universal foci against a background of cross-linguistically varying category extensions. However, it would not be predicted if best examples are abstracted instead as the centers of categories defined at their boundaries by linguistic convention, because on this latter view, best examples are category centers and will cluster only as tightly as those centers.
>
> *(2005: 8389)*

Critics have posed a number of challenges to the methodology used to collect cross-cultural naming data for the WCS. Use of highly saturated colour stimuli, Roberson and Hanley (2009) argue, may have led researchers to overestimate the similarity of colour categorization systems across different languages. Others have questioned the foundational assumption that every language contains a set of BCTs in the sense of Berlin and Kay (1969) (Levinson 1997).

These methodological criticisms notwithstanding, there appears to be converging linguistic evidence for the existence of cross-cultural tendencies in colour-naming practices. Lindsey and

Brown (2006) performed a cluster analysis on the individual colour-naming systems of the 2,367 informants in the WCS. At the level of eight clusters, they found a close correspondence between clusters in the WCS naming data and familiar English chromatic colour categories. Two exceptions were a composite yellow-or-orange category, and, a composite green-or-blue category (grue). A second cluster analysis by Lindsey and Brown (2009) found that WCS colour-naming systems can be divided into approximately four recurrent patterns or 'motifs'.

Despite evidence for the existence of cross-cultural tendencies in colour naming-practices, the perceptual salience theory has been recently abandoned as an account of how lexicalized colour categories are formed. Three main objections recur in the literature. First, even if the best examples of colour categories across many languages in the WCS cluster around the Hering primaries (4UH plus black and white), the perceptual salience theory is only a name for this fact, not explanation of it (Byrne and Hilbert 1997; Dedrick 1997; Jameson 2005a, 2005b). Regier and co-authors (2005) appear to concede this point:

> The degree to which ... universally favored regions [of color space] are based on color appearance, universal statistical tendencies in the distribution of reflective surfaces in the environment, universal properties of ambient light sources, the topography of perceptual color space, or sociolinguistic negotiation among speakers cannot be assessed with any degree of certainty at this time. It is possible that all these factors, and perhaps others, play a role.
>
> *(Regier et al. 2005: 8390)*

A second objection has to do with the variation in unique hue settings across observers with normal, trichromatic colour vision. Figure 28.2 presents the Munsell hue diagram with angular ranges in unique hue selections for approximately 300 normal, trichromat subjects (Kuehni 2005b). The broadness of the ranges of stimuli selected for the 4UH hues is large, with variation in settings for UG alone spanning nearly 30 per cent of the complete hue circle. One surprising consequence of this variability is that some observers will select as their best example of orange a stimulus that other observers respectively choose as their best example of UY or UR (Malkoc et al. 2005: 2156). Such dramatic variability in the way human beings perceive colour speaks

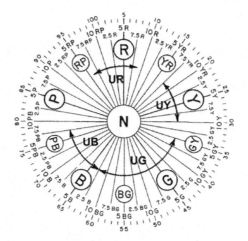

Figure 28.2 Munsell hue diagram with ranges of colour chip stimuli selected for the four unique hues.
Source: reproduced with permission from Kuehni (2005a).

against the view that the 4UH function as pan-human 'perceptual landmarks' that stabilize colour naming practices within and across linguistic communities (Jameson 2005b).

A final set of criticisms pose empirical objections to the assumption that the 4UH are perceptually more salient than other shades. Boynton (1997) found that when criteria of intra-subjective consistency in naming, consensus in naming, and short response times are applied, 'there are no differences between primary and derived basic colors [like pink and brown] except for the compound sensory aspect of the latter, which really does not seem to matter' (148). Similarly, Smallman and Boynton (1990, 1993) report that when embedded in visual information displays, best examples of English BCTs are not detected faster than other shades that are as widely separated in colour space. More recent studies have also failed to find greater intersubjective consistency in stimuli selection for the 4UH than for binary hues. Malkoc *et al.* (2002), in fact, report more consistency in subjects' choices for 'focal' blue-green than for UB and UG: in other words, there was less variability in selecting the boundary between blue and green than in selecting the best example of either category. Relatedly, Bosten and Lawrance-Owen (2014) found that subjects do not select examples of the 4UH in a display containing a complete hue circle more reliably than they select best examples of binary hues. According to Hardin, names for the 4UH are necessary and sufficient for naming all of the other colours, 'a fact that justifies singling them out as perceptually elementary' (2005: 74). A recent study by Bosten and Boehm (2014) challenges this assessment. Subjects were assigned to one of two experimental conditions in a hue-scaling experiment. In the 'unique' condition, they rated the proportions of UR, UY, UB, and UG that they perceived in each of a series of test stimuli. In the 'intermediate' condition, they rated the proportions of the binary colours teal, purple, orange, and lime. Results from the two conditions were found to be broadly the same. English speakers, Bosten and Boehm conclude, don't need to use names for the 4UH in order adequately to describe colour appearances.

In the last decade, erstwhile proponents of the perceptual salience theory have gravitated toward the view that cross-cultural patterns in colour naming may result from application of the informativeness constraint together with the irregular shape of colour space, as originally proposed by Kimberly Jameson and Roy D'Andrade (1997). Jameson and D'Andrade point out that the colour solid isn't a smooth globe, but an irregular blob with several large 'bumps'. For example, the regions around UR and UY achieve more saturation and, hence, protrude more from the solid than do the regions around UB and UG. The bumpy shape of perceptual colour space, they argue, means that certain ways of partitioning colour space into a small number of categories will be more informative than others (Jameson and D'Andrade 1997: 313; see also Jameson 2005a).

Building on this interpoint-distance model (IDM), Terry Regier and co-authors have recently proposed a 'shape-based' account of colour categorization, according to which naming systems across languages partition colour space in different, but close to optimally informative ways (Regier *et al.* 2007; Regier *et al.* 2015): 'The hypothesis is that … irregularities in [colour] space, interacting with general principles of categorization, cause natural clusters to form that correspond to observed color-naming universals' (Regier *et al.* 2007: 1437). Regier *et al.* (2007) introduce the notion of *well-formedness* as a measure of the extent to which a lexical colour categorization system maximizes perceptual similarity of colours within a category and minimizes it across categories, where the perceptual similarity of two shades is inversely related to the distance between them in the CIELAB colour space. Colour-naming systems documented in the WCS, they argue, tend to have higher well-formedness than do systematic variants with the same number of categories, and attested divergences in the location of category boundaries tend to have only a minor impact on relative well-formedness. On this approach, cross-cultural patterns in colour naming practices aren't explained by any privileged set of focal colours. Instead, they result from the structure of perceptual colour space, the pragmatic need to communicate efficiently about colour, and cognitively universal categorization principles.

The IDM is perhaps the most prominent of recent attempts to explain recurrent patterns in colour-naming practices without appealing to the perceptual salience of the 4UH. Other approaches have also attracted attention. Yendrikhovskij (2001), building on Shepard (1992), links the structure of human colour categorization systems to the statistical distribution of colours in the natural environment. Steels and Belpaeme (2005) employ theoretical models and computer simulations of artificial agents to investigate the different ways in which the physiology of the human visual system, the colour statistics of natural scenes, and communicative needs respectively constrain the acquisition of a shared set of colour categories. Jameson and Komarova (2009a, 2009b) use agent-based, evolutionary game theory to explore the consequences of empirically observed heterogeneity in human colour-processing mechanisms, e.g. the absence of either long- or short-wavelength cones in dichromat observers, for the development colour categorization systems. They argue that evolved colour categorization systems tend to optimize communication among all members of the population, rather than only among members of the majority trichromat subset.

Linguistic relativism

Moderate linguistic relativism, as I shall call it, comprises three distinct claims:

(LR1) There are no psychologically universal constraints on colour categorization beyond *perceptual grouping* and *informativeness* and the structure of perceptual colour space (Roberson *et al.* 2000; Jameson 2005a, 2005b; Roberson *et al.* 2005b). Other non-universal constraints come from cultural or pragmatic needs, e.g. the need to distinguish in communication between edible and non-edible fruits, as well as from the distribution of shades in the natural and social environment.

(LR2) The process of colour category formation begins with boundary demarcation, and best examples or foci are extracted only at secondary stage of conceptual development (Roberson *et al.* 2000).

(LR3) Colour terms are the primary vehicles of colour category representation (Quine 1973; Roberson *et al.* 2000; Davidoff 2001; Roberson *et al.* 2005b): 'the results of recent experimental research would suggest that there are no cognitive color categories that are independent of the terms used to describe them' (Roberson 2005: 66). This claim reflects a robustly 'cognitive' conception of colour language.[5]

Strong linguistic relativism endorses a fourth, additional claim concerning the influence of colour terminology on the content and phenomenal character of colour experience.

(LR4) Learning to use a set of BCTs can cause shades that fall within the boundaries of a named category to appear phenomenally more similar to one another in appearance and shades that fall on opposite sides of a category boundary to appear phenomenally less alike. The 'structure of linguistic categories', as Davidoff puts it, 'distorts perception by stretching perceptual distances at category boundaries'.

(2001: 386)

In maintaining LR1, linguistic relativists deny that certain perceptually salient shades constrain processes of colour concept formation (Roberson *et al.* 2000). The perceptual grouping and informativeness constraints by themselves, however, place only loose restrictions on the construction of colour categorization systems. Among other things, they leave open how the different, independently variable dimensions of colour appearance, that is, hue, saturation, and lightness, are to be respectively weighted in perceptual grouping, as attested by the significant amount of variability in weightings across empirically observed categorization systems (Jameson 2005a, 2005b). Further, application of the grouping constraint, as Dedrick has pointed out, presupposes prior identification of certain 'chromatic landmarks':

> ... there is no principled way to delimit the range of a linguistic color category that is constructed on the basis of generalization from a single sample. No way, that is, to know when to stop the process of associating color samples to one another. This problem is solved if judgement involves relative similarity: sample *x* is more like *A* than like *B*. With *A* and *B* (or whatever number of landmark colors) fixed, there is a cognitive constraint upon attribution of category membership.
>
> *(Dedrick 1998: 156)*

The informativeness constraint also leaves a lot of wiggle room in the construction of colour categorization systems. It ensures that systems will be communicatively efficient, but it does not specify how *many* categories a system should contain.

On analogy with Chomsky's 'principles-and-parameters' approach to linguistic syntax (Chomsky 1995), we can think of grouping and informativeness as universal cognitive rules that govern the production of colour categorization systems. The selection of chromatic landmarks, dimensional weightings, and number of categories, in turn, can be thought of as setting parameters on application of these universal rules. It is a core tenet of linguistic relativism that the values of these parameters are determined locally by culture and language. This means that considerable variation across colour naming systems is, in principle, possible.[6]

According to the perceptual salience theory, basic colour concepts are formed by setting up boundaries around regions in three-dimensional colour space centred on the Hering primaries. In this respect, the representation of category foci or best examples is psychologically prior to the representation of category boundaries. Linguistic relativism, by contrast, maintains that the process of colour category formation begins with the demarcation of boundaries in colour space that are significant to observers for perhaps culturally quite local reasons (LR2).

An illustrative example is the *wor-nol* category boundary in Berinmo (Roberson *et al.* 2000). The term 'wor' applies to leaves that are ready to fall from a tree, covering shades of yellow, orange, khaki, and brown. The term 'nol' covers shades of chartreuse, green, blue, and purple This *wor-nol* boundary, Roberson and her co-authors emphasize, is far from arbitrary: 'tulip leaves, a favorite vegetable, are bright green when freshly picked and good to eat, but quickly yellow if kept. Agreement over the [wor-nol] boundary coincides with agreement over when they are no longer good to eat and is highly salient in a community that talks little about color' (Roberson *et al.* 2000: 395). By contrast, the ability to identify certain shades as the best examples or foci of the categories *wor* and *nol* is pragmatically much less important to the Berinmo and is argued to emerge only during a second phase of conceptual development: 'Once a category has been delineated at the boundaries, exposure to exemplars may lead to the abstraction of a central tendency so that observers behave as if their categories have prototypes' (Roberson *et al.* 2000: 395).

The view that colour terms shape the way human beings think about colour is supported by empirical findings adduced on behalf of LR3, that is, the claim that colour terms are the *primary vehicles* of colour category representation. On this view, internalized colour language is the medium in which human beings think thoughts involving coarse-grained colour categories.

Support for LR3 comes from neuropsychological studies of subjects with colour naming deficits (but otherwise normal vision) who also exhibit impairments in the performance of seemingly non-linguistic colour categorization tasks. Roberson *et al.* (1999) report that a neuropsychological patient with severe impairments in colour naming is unable to sort coloured stimuli into groups except by pair-wise similarity. The same patient is also unable to judge which of three objects differs from the other two in an odd-colour-out task (Davidoff and Roberson 2004). Similar findings have been reported by the Lupyan lab at the University of Wisconsin. Lupyan and Mirman (2013) asked aphasic subjects to select objects from a group of 20 pictured objects using either a high-dimensional, 'thematic' category criterion (e.g. FRUIT, TOOLS, or FARM ANIMALS) or a low-dimensional, 'taxonomic' category criterion (e.g. BLUE, SMALL, or ROUND). They found that aphasics do not perform well on trials that require selection on the basis of a low-dimensional criterion and that the degree of impairment was predicted by their previously assessed naming performance. Categories 'held together by one or a small number of dimensions', Lupyan and Mirman write,

> may require more on-line support from language. For example, the ability to selectively attend to objects having a particular color—classifying objects into a category of RED THINGS—may be facilitated by naming insofar as words such as 'red' help to group together objects that do not have pre-existing semantic associations and which differ substantially in surface appearance (e.g., a cherry and a brick).
>
> *(2013: 1191)*

Consistent with this view, there is evidence that verbal interference selectively impairs normal subjects' ability to focus on particular perceptual dimensions such as size or colour. In fact, under verbal interference conditions, normal subjects have been reported to perform much like aphasic patients in odd-colour-out tasks (Lupyan 2009).

Additional support for LR3 come from studies of colour term acquisition and colour memory. Roberson and co-authors studied colour name learning and colour memory patterns in Berinmo and Himba speakers (Roberson *et al.* 2000; Roberson *et al.* 2005a; Roberson *et al.* 2005b). Contrary to findings garnered by Eleanor Rosch (Rosch Heider 1972, Rosch Heider and Olivier 1972), they found no evidence that the supposedly universal or 'prototypical' colour categories named in English are either learned or remembered more easily than the best examples of the participants' own linguistic categories. A three-year, longitudinal study of colour term acquisition among young children learning to speak either English or Himba also found no learning advantage for English BCTs (Roberson *et al.* 2004). While these results don't conclusively establish that colour categorization is generally language-dependent, they do pose a challenge to the view that the process of BCT acquisition is guided by a pre-linguistic system that groups fine-grained shades into a universal set of coarse-grained categories.

Critics of linguistic relativism have put forward two main objections. The first has to do with patterns in colour-naming across different languages. Linguistic relativism is frequently taken to imply that colour naming is 'largely a matter of arbitrary linguistic convention' (Kay and Regier 2006: 52). But, if so, then lexical colour categorization systems could be expected to vary freely from one language to another. This prediction, however, is at odds with evidence for recurrent motifs in colour-naming practices discussed in the last section (Regier *et al.* 2005; Lindsey and Brown 2006, 2009).

Linguistic relativists have two ways of responding to this objection. The first is that the objection targets a straw man: colour-naming practices, according to the version of linguistic relativism advanced by Roberson and her colleagues, aren't arbitrary:

> Even if there are genuine similarities between certain color systems, there are obvious cultural factors that could explain at least some of these similarities. Similar cultural needs, such as evolutionary pressure for successful frugivory, could also cause some category divisions to be more likely than others. Cultural contact between speakers of different languages has also clearly increased the similarity of the color categorization systems that these languages employ; for example, the term *burou* can be traced from German to Herero and subsequently to Himba.
>
> *(Robertson 2012: 42)*

In addition to appealing to common cultural and environmental factors, linguistic relativists can also appeal to common categorization principles. Indeed, as pointed out at the end of the last section, recent universalist models have explored the hypothesis that cross-cultural patterns in colour categorization result from application of the informativeness constraint to an irregularly shaped colour space. Systems containing the same number of categories that conform to the informativeness constraint will partition colour space in similar, 'well-formed' ways (Regier *et al.* 2015).

Whereas the first objection had to do with evidence for convergence in colour-naming across different languages, the second objection has to do with evidence for intersubjective divergence in colour-naming within languages. Webster and Kay (2005) write:

> [A] prominent property of actual color-naming data is the pronounced variation among speakers of the same language. ... For example, the wavelengths that individuals select for unique green within a linguistically homogeneous group span a range of more than 80 nm; these variations are in fact so large that the same wavelength might be chosen as unique green by one observer and unique yellow or blue by another (Kuehni 2004). ... Mean foci across languages vary much less than individual foci within languages. This suggests that a common language imposes only a weak constraint, and a difference in language produces relatively little divergence.
>
> *(512; for a similar assessment, see Lindsey and Brown 2014: 524)*

Two lines of response are open to the linguistic relativist. First, the surprising amount of within-language variability in colour-naming is a problem for *all* theories of colour categorization and not just for linguistic relativism. (And, as pointed out in the last section, intersubjective differences in colour perception present a special challenge to theories that base colour-naming practices on panhuman universals of colour experience.) Second, intersubjective variation in colour processing may be smoothed over by *linguistic charity*: minor differences in colour naming may often be disregarded as irrelevant to speakers' communicative purposes (Jameson 2005b: 315). In this connection, it is important to investigate just how much intersubjective agreement in the use of a set of BCTs is actually required for effective communication within a group of speakers and, so, for the diachronic stabilization of a colour lexicon (Levinson 1997). To answer this question, it is necessary to know, among other things, how often fine-grained variations in colour appearance need to be communicated to ensure successful performance of individual and multi-agent tasks. Objects belonging to a certain artifactual or natural kind, for example, may vary quite a bit in colour appearance across subjects, but much of that variation may not affect how agents interact with or communicate about the kind.

Strong linguistic relativism goes beyond moderate linguistic relativism in maintaining that colour perception is categorical: learning to use a set of BCTs causes shades that fall within the boundaries of a named category to appear phenomenally more similar to one another in appearance and shades that fall on opposite sides of a category boundary to appear phenomenally less similar (LR4). In the next section, we will see that there is a substantial amount of evidence against this claim.

Is colour perception categorical?

A *categorical perception* (CP) effect occurs

> when (1) a set of stimuli ranging along a physical continuum is given one label on one side of a category boundary and another label on the other side and (2) the subject can discriminate smaller physical differences between pairs of stimuli that straddle that boundary than between pairs that are entirely within one category or the other.
>
> *(Harnad 1987: 3)*

The paradigm of CP is phoneme discrimination in language: sounds straddling a phonemic category boundary, e.g. the boundary /ra/ and /la/ in English, are more discriminable to speakers of a language in which those phonemes occur than are sounds separated by equal acoustic step sizes, but from within the same phonemic category (Liberman and Mattingly 1985; Kuhl 2004). If colour perception is similarly categorical (LR4), then acquiring a set of colour terms could cause shades that straddle a named colour category boundary to appear phenomenally less similar (and, thus, easier to discriminate) and cause shades that fall within the boundaries of a named category to appear phenomenally more similar.

Tarahumara is an indigenous language of northern Mexico in which a single BCT ('siyd-name') is used to name both blue and green. In a classic study conducted by Paul Kay and Willett Kempton (1984), Tarahumara and English speakers were shown triads of Munsell colour chips in which only two of the chips fell on the same side of the blue-green boundary (whether blue or green). They were then asked to select the chip least similar in appearance to the other two. They found that English speakers were much more likely to choose the chip that fell on the other side of the blue-green boundary, even when within-category discrimination distances, as measure by justice noticeable difference (JND) steps, were greater than cross-category discrimination distances. Judgements made by Tarahumara speakers, by contrast, did not show any distorting effect of language and reflected objective discrimination distances.

What is the proper explanation of this effect? In a recent discussion, Jesse Prinz suggests that the 'presence of a linguistic color boundary between blue and green makes it impossible for English-speakers to perceive color distances objectively' (2012: 187). In other words, an object's apparent fine-grained shade of colour can vary as a function of the meanings of the colour terms present in a speaker's language, as maintained by strong linguistic relativism (LR4). Kay and Kempton, however, explicitly rejected this conclusion: 'it cannot be the case', they write, 'that the vision of English speakers is distorted in some way by the language they speak, because the discrimination distances that the Tarahumara faithfully reproduce on the subjective triads task were established on speakers of English' (1984: 72). Instead, they proposed that English speakers were relying on an unconscious, post-perceptual 'name strategy', when making their selections:

> ... faced with this situation the English-speaking subject reasons unconsciously as follows: 'It's hard to decide here which one looks the most different. Are there any other kinds of clues I might use? Aha! *A* and *B* are both CALLED green while *C* is CALLED blue. That solves my problem; I'll pick *C* as most different.' Of course this cognitive strategy, which we will call the 'name strategy', is not available to the Tarahumara speaker precisely because he or she doesn't have ready lexical labels for the concepts green and blue.
>
> *(Kay and Kempton 1984: 72)*

To test the name strategy theory, Kay and Kempton conducted a second experiment using the same colour triads. In each trial, three chips were presented in a box with a sliding top that enabled subjects to compare only two chips at a time. The three chips were always arranged by hue, so that the middle chip was intermediate in hue between its flankers. Here is a description of their method:

> Experimenter exposes pair (*A*, *B*). 'You can see that this chip (points to *A*) is greener than this chip (points to *B*).' (All subjects readily agreed.) Experimenter slides cover so that *A* is covered and *C* exposed along with *B*; that is, the pair (*B*, *C*) is now exposed, 'You can see that this chip (points to *C*) is bluer than this chip (points to *B*).' (Again all subjects agreed without problems.) 'Now', experimenter hands stimuli to subject, 'you may slide the cover back and forth as often as you like. I'd like you to tell me which is bigger: the difference in greenness between the two chips on the left or the difference in blueness between the two chips on the right.'
>
> ... The subject cannot reasonably ask himself (herself) whether chip *B* is called *green* or *blue* because he (she) has already in effect both called it *green* and called it *blue* in agreeing to compare *B* in *greenness* to A and in *blueness* to C. It is thus irrelevant to this task whether chip *B* would be called *green* or *blue* in another, neutral context.
>
> *(Kay and Kempton 1984: 73)*

Under these conditions, English and Tarahumara speakers discriminated colours identically: 'Subjective similarity judgments follow discrimination distance and reflect no influence from lexical category boundaries' (1984: 73). This result suggests, contrary to strong linguistic relativism, that colour categories in language can exert a distorting influence on colour similarity judgements without having any effect on the way the colours themselves phenomenally appear. In other words, it suggests that colour CP effects are effects of colour language on post-perceptual decision-making or other cognitive processes and do not result from a 'distortion' of colour appearances near category boundaries. If this is right, then so-called colour categorical perception, as Roberson *et al.* (2009) put it, 'is categorical but not perceptual, and *should rather be referred to simply as a category effect*' (487, emphasis added). In the remainder of this section, I adopt this terminological recommendation.

Three additional sources of empirical evidence furnish support for the name strategy theory. First, subsequent studies have confirmed that language-relative colour category effects (CCEs) disappear with verbal interference (Roberson and Davidoff 2000; Gilbert *et al.* 2006; Winawer *et al.* 2007). Winawer and co-authors (2007), for example, looked for CCEs in speakers of Russian, who, unlike speakers of English, use distinct terms for dark blue (*siniy*) and light blue (*goluboy*). Subjects were shown three coloured squares arranged in a triad and were asked to judge which of the two squares on the bottom was identical in colour to the square on top. Winawer and co-authors found that Russian speakers' judgements were faster when the shades of the squares on the bottom straddled the *siniy-goluboy* boundary, than when they were from within the same category. English speakers did not show the same cross-category advantage. Consistent with Kempton and Kay's name strategy theory, CCEs in Russian speakers' discrimination performance disappeared when they performed a simultaneous verbal interference task.

This finding supports a 'dual code' model of the involvement of language in colour discrimination tasks (Roberson *et al.* 2008; Winawer and Witthoft 2012). Jon Winawer and Nathan Witthoft (2012) write in a passage worth quoting at length:

> If a category effect goes away when labels become unavailable or not useful, then it is unlikely that the effect is due to color terms affecting early perceptual processes. While such an account is logically possible, it would require color appearance to be altered only during those moments when one is accessing the labels. A more parsimonious explanation is that the decision process is affected by language. Verbal labels may be used to help keep track of the various stimuli in an experiment, either over a memory delay or when comparing stimuli spread over space. If, on a particular trial, all the stimuli come from the same verbal category (e.g., they are all blue), then labels are unlikely to help accomplish the task (and might even hinder performance). In contrast, if stimuli in a trial can easily be assigned different labels (e.g., one blue and one green), then access to the labels may facilitate memory or the comparison process. If a verbal dual task interferes with the ability to label stimuli, even implicitly, then this may eliminate one strategy or source of information for accomplishing the task, and hence may change performance. Thus, verbal interference effects are more likely to reflect a role of color terms on decisions, strategy, and memory, rather than perception.
>
> *(4)*

A second source of evidence for the name strategy explanation comes from studies that have found CCEs to be significantly stronger on the right side of the visual field (RVF) than on the left (LVF) (Gilbert *et al.* 2006; Roberson *et al.* 2008; Roberson and Pak 2009; for a review, see Regier and Kay 2009). This is relevant because stimuli presented in the RVF project to the left hemisphere of the brain, which is typically dominant for language.[7]

A final source of evidence for the name strategy theory comes from experiments that have investigated JND thresholds among speakers of languages with different lexicalized colour categories. If language 'stretches' perceptual distances at boundaries between colour categories (LR4), then discrimination thresholds should be lower at category boundaries, that is, shades near category boundaries should be more finely discriminated, than near category centres.[8] Contrary to predictions based on LR4, Roberson *et al.* (2009) found that colour discrimination is neither enhanced for English speakers at the boundary between blue and green boundary, nor for Korean speakers at the boundaries between categories that are named in Korean, but not in English. 'In the case of color', they suggest, 'humans may already have hyper-acuity (Churchland & Sejnowski 1994), so that no further "tuning" occurs with category learning' (486).[9]

Conclusion

In concluding this chapter, it may be helpful to review some main points of convergence between universalists and linguistic relativists about colour categorization. To begin with, there is general agreement on the existence of interesting patterns in colour-naming across speakers of different languages. Moreover, it is now widely accepted that these patterns are not supported by the distinctive appearance or perceptual salience of the Hering primaries (4UH plus black and white). Second, prominent universalists now accept that colour category effects (CCEs) are language relative. Kay and Regier (2007), for example, agree that 'there is ample evidence that differences in color category boundaries between languages may influence color memory, learning or discrimination' (294). In other words, CCEs don't indicate the existence of pre-linguistic colour concepts that constrain the construction of colour categorization systems across speakers of different languages. Finally, contemporary linguistic relativists have distanced themselves from the Whorfian view that colour language can modulate the phenomenology of colour experience: CCEs reflect the influence of colour terms on memory and decision-making rather than on the way fine-grained shades of colour visually appear.

Notes

1 The number of perceptually distinct surface colours actually present in natural scenes, however, is probably much smaller (Marín-Franch and Foster 2010).
2 A colour term is said to be *basic*, when among other things it is monolexemic, e.g. 'blue' vs. 'sky blue' or 'dark blue', applied to different types of objects, and used by most speakers of the language in which it occurs (Berlin and Kay 1969). For discussion, see the chapter by Dedrick in this volume.
3 Also see the target articles by Saunders and van Brakel (1997) and Steels and Belpaeme (2005) in *Behavioral and Brain Sciences* and their invited commentaries for valuable discussions.
4 It should be emphasized, however, that Byrne and Hilbert (1997) reject the claim that the perceptual salience of the Hering primaries is by itself explanatory of colour-naming practices.
5 For discussions of cognitive or 'extracommunicative' theories of language, see Clark (1998) and Carruthers (2002).
6 The perceptual salience theory, by contrast, maintains that colour categorization systems in all languages are based on a universal set of chromatic landmarks—black, white, UR, UY, UG, and UB—and, accordingly, that hue is universally the most heavily weighted dimension of variation in colour appearance.
7 It should be emphasized that the existence of CCEs in the RVF is not uncontroversial. Brown *et al.* (2011) found no CCE on visual search reaction times involving stimuli at the blue-green boundary presented in either visual field. 'Taken as a whole', they write, 'the results and analyses suggested that the overall shape of the [reaction time] data sets was controlled entirely by visual signals that arise in the cones and are combined in a color-opponent fashion in the earliest stages of visual processing' (2).
8 Winawer and Witthoft (2012: 6) write:

> Threshold discrimination experiments are among the least ambiguous experiments in psychology. If an observer can discriminate two stimuli, then we can be certain that the observer's perceptual system has encoded the two stimuli differently. If the stimuli are indistinguishable (below threshold), then information distinguishing the stimuli was either not encoded or was lost in subsequent processing. If discrimination thresholds were altered by the color terms in one's language, this would provide the most direct evidence that color terms affect perception of colors.

9 Regier and Kay (2009) review evidence that prior to language acquisition colour categories may be represented in the right hemisphere and cause CCEs in the LVF of young infants (Bornstein *et al.* 1976; Franklin *et al.* 2005; Franklin *et al.* 2008). For present purposes, it is important to emphasize that even if pre-linguistic infants do exhibit CCEs (but for a sceptical assessment, see Roberson and Hanley (2009)), the relevant effects don't appear to facilitate colour term acquisition or have any other effects on later colour cognition. The psychologist Marc Bornstein observes: 'An otherwise reasonable surmise from the fact that hue characterization precedes color naming developmentally would be that, in this one realm at least, linguistic identification simply overlays perceptual cognitive organization and thereby facilitates semantic development. Paradoxically, it does not' (1985: 74). After language is learned, right hemisphere categories appear to be 'permanently erased' (Regier and Kay 2009: 441). For critical discussion of 'Bornstein's paradox', see Dedrick (2014b).

References

Berlin, B., and Kay, P. (1969). *Basic Color Terms: Their Universality and Evolution*. Berkeley, CA: University of California Press.

Bornstein, M. H. (1985). On the development of color naming in young children: Data and theory. *Brain and Language, 26*, 72–93.

Bornstein, M. H., Kessen, W., and Weiskopf, S. (1976). Color vision and hue categorization in young human infants. *Journal of Experimental Psychology: Human Perception and Performance, 2*, 115–29.

Bosten, J. M., and Boehm, A. E. (2014). Empirical evidence for unique hues? *Journal of the Optical Society of America, 31(4)*, A385–93.

Bosten, J. M., and Lawrance-Owen, A. J. (2014). No difference in variability of unique hue selections and binary hue selections. *Journal of the Optical Society of America, 31*, A357–64.

Boynton, R. (1997). Insights gained from naming the OSA colors. In C. L. Hardin (Ed.), *Color Categories in Thought and Language*. Cambridge: Cambridge University Press, pp. 135–50.

Broackes, J. (2011). Where do the unique hues come from? *Review of Philosophy and Psychology, 2*, 601–8.

Brown, A. M., Lindsey, D. T., and Guckes, K. M. (2011). Color names, color categories, and color-cued visual search: Sometimes, color perception is not categorical. *Journal of Vision, 11*, 2–21.

Byrne, A., and Hilbert, D. R. (2003). Color realism and color science. *Behavioral and Brain Sciences, 26*(1), 3–21.

Carruthers, P. (2002). The cognitive functions of language. *Behavioral and Brain Sciences, 25*, 657–726.

Churchland, P. S., and Sejnowski, T. J. (1994). *The Computational Brain*. Cambridge, MA: MIT Press.

Chomsky, Noam. (1995). *The Minimalist Program*. Cambridge, MA: MIT Press.

Clark, A. (1998). Magic words. In P. Carruthers and J. Boucher (Eds.), *Language and Thought: Interdisciplinary Themes*. Cambridge: Cambridge University Press, pp. 162–83.

Davidoff, J. (2001). Language and perceptual categorisation. *Trends in Cognitive Sciences, 5*(9), 382–7.

Davidoff, J., and Roberson, D. (2004). Preserved thematic and impaired taxonomic categorisation: A case study. *Language and Cognitive Processes, 19*(1), 137–74.

Davidoff, J., Davies, I., and Roberson, D. (1999). Colour categories of a stone-age tribe. *Nature, 398*, 203–4.

Dedrick, D. (1997). Colour categorization and the space between perception and language. *Behavioral and Brain Sciences, 20*, 187–8.

Dedrick, D. (1998). *Naming the Rainbow: Colour Language, Colour Science, and Culture*. Dordrecht: Kluwer.

Dedrick, D. (2014a). Colour language, thought, and culture. In F. Sharifiian (Ed.), *Routledge Handbook to Mind, Language and Culture*. New York: Routledge, pp. 270–93.

Dedrick, D. (2014b). Bornstein's paradox (redux). In W. Anderson, C. P. Biggam, C. Hough, and C. Kay (Eds.), *Colour Studies: A Broad Spectrum*. Amsterdam: John Benjamins, pp. 181–99.

Franklin, A., Clifford, A., Williamson, E., and Davies, I. R. L. (2005). Color term knowledge does not affect categorical perception of color in toddlers. *Journal of Experimental Child Psychology, 90*, 114–41.

Franklin, A., Drivonikou, G. V., Bevis, L., Davies, I. R. L., Kay, P., and Regier, T. (2008). Categorical perception of color is lateralized to the right hemisphere in infants, but to the left hemisphere in adults. *Proceedings of the National Academy of Sciences of the United States of America, 105*, 3221–5.

Garner, W. R. (1974). *The Processing of Information and Structure*. Hillsdale, NJ: Erlbaum.

Gilbert, A. L., Regier, T., Kay, P., and Ivry, R. B. (2006). Whorf hypothesis is supported in the right visual field but not the left. *Proceedings of the National Academy of Sciences of the United States of America, 103*, 489–94.

Hardin, C. L. (1988). *Color for Philosophers: Unweaving the Rainbow*. Indianapolis, IN: Hackett.

Hardin, C. L. (2005). Explaining basic color categories. *Cross-Cultural Research: The Journal of Comparative Social Science, 39*, 72–87.

Harnad, S. (1987). Psychophysical and cognitive aspects of categorical perception: A critical overview. In S. Harnad (Ed.), *Categorical Perception: The Groundwork of Cognition*. Cambridge: Cambridge University Press, pp. 1–28.

Hering, E. (1878/1964). *Grundzüge der Lehre vom Lichtsinn (Outlines of a Theory of the Light Sense)*. L. M. Hurvich and D. Jameson (trans.). Cambridge, MA: Harvard University Press.

Jameson, K. A. (2005a). Why GRUE? An interpoint distance model analysis of composite color categories. *Cross-Cultural Research, 39*, 159–204.

Jameson, K. A. (2005b). Culture and cognition: What is universal about the representation of color experience? *The Journal of Cognition & Culture, 5*(3–4), 293–347.

471

Jameson, K. A., and D'Andrade, R. G. (1997). It's not really red, green, yellow, blue: An inquiry into cognitive color space. In C. L. Hardin and L. Maffi (Eds.), *Color Categories in Thought and Language.* Cambridge: Cambridge University Press, pp. 295–319.

Jameson, K. A., and Komarova, N. L. (2009a). Evolutionary models of color categorization. I. *Journal of the Optical Society of America, A, 26,* 1414–23.

Jameson, K. A., and Komarova, N. L. (2009b). Evolutionary models of categorization. II. *Journal of the Optical Society of America, A, 26,* 1424–36.

Kay, P., and Kempton, W. (1984). What is the Sapir-Whorf hypothesis? *American Anthropologist, 86,* 65–78.

Kay, P., and Maffi, L. (1999). Color appearance and the emergence and evolution of basic color lexicons. *American Anthropologist, 101,* 743–60.

Kay, P., and McDaniel, C. (1978). The linguistic significance of the meanings of basic color terms. *Language, 54,* 610–46.

Kay, P., amd Regier, T. (2006). Language, thought and color: Recent developments. *Trends in Cognitive Sciences, 10*(2), 51–4.

Kay, P., and Regier, T. (2007). Color naming universals: The case of Berinmo. *Cognition, 102,* 289–98.

Kay, P., Berlin, B., Maffi, L., Merrifeld, W. R., and Cook, R. (2009). *The World Color Survey.* Stanford, CA: Center for the Study of Language and Information.

Kuehni, R. G. (2004). Variability in unique hue selection: A surprising phenomenon. *Color Research and Application, 29,* 158–62.

Kuehni, R. G. (2005a). Unique hue stimulus choice: A constraint on hue category formation. *Journal of Cognition and Culture, 5*(3–4), 387–408.

Kuehni, R. G. (2005b). Focal color variability and unique hue stimulus variability. *Journal of Cognition and Culture, 5*(3–4), 409–26.

Kuehni, R. G. (2013). *Color: An Introduction to Practice and Principles,* 3rd ed. Hoboken, NJ: John Wiley & Sons.

Kuhl, P. K. (2004). Early language acquisition: Cracking the speech code. *Nature Reviews Neuroscience, 5*(11), 831–43.

Levinson, S. C. (1997). *Yélî dyne and the theory of basic color terms.* Paper presented in a seminar at the Max Plank Institute for Psycholinguistics, June 1997.

Liberman, A. M., and Mattingly, I. G. (1985). The motor theory of speech perception revised. *Cognition, 2,* 1–36.

Lindsey, D. T., and Brown, A. M. (2006). Universality of color names. *Proceedings of the National Academy of Sciences of the United States of America, 103,* 16608–13.

Lindsey, D. T., and Brown, A. M. (2009). World Color Survey color naming reveals universal motifs and their within-language diversity. *Proceedings of the National Academy of Sciences of the United States of America, 106,* 19785–90.

Lindsey, D. T., and Brown, A. M. (2014). Color appearance, language, and neural coding. In J. S. Werner and L. M. Chalupa (Eds.), *The New Visual Neurosciences.* Cambridge, MA: MIT Press, pp. 511–31.

Linhares, J. M. M., Pinto, P. D., and Nascimento, S. M. C. (2008). The number of discernible colors in natural scenes. *Journal of the Optical Society of America A, Optics, Image Science, and Vision, 25,* 2918–24.

Lupyan, G. (2009). Extracommunicative functions of language: Verbal interference causes selective categorization impairments. *Psychonomic Bulletin & Review, 16*(4), 711–18.

Lupyan, G., and Mirman, D. (2013). Linking language and categorization: Evidence from aphasia. *Cortex, 49*(5), 1187–94.

Malkoc, G., Kay, P., and Webster, M. A. (2002). Individual differences in unique and binary hues. *Journal of Vision, 2*: 32a.

Malkoc, G., Kay, P., and Webster, M. A. (2005). Variations in normal color vision. IV. Binary hues and hue scaling. *Journal of the Optical Society of America A, 22,* 2154–68.

Marín-Franch, I., and Foster, D. (2010). Number of perceptually distinct surface colors in natural scenes. *Journal of Vision, 10*(9), 1–7.

Pointer, M. R., and Attridge, G. G. (1998). The number of discernible colours. *Color Research & Application, 23*(1), 52–4.

Prinz, J. (2012). *Beyond Human Nature.* New York: W. W. Norton & Company.

Quine, W. V. O (1973). *The Roots of Reference.* La Salle: Open Court.

Ray, V. (1953). Human color perception and behavioral response. *Transactions of the New York Academy of Sciences, 2*(16), 98–105.

Regier, T., and Kay, P. (2009). Language, thought, and color: Whorf was half right. *Trends in Cognitive Sciences, 13*, 439–46.

Regier, T., Kay, P., and Cook, R. S. (2005). Focal colors are universal after all. *PNAS, 102*, 8386–91.

Regier, T., Kay, P., and Khetarpal, N. (2007). Color naming reflects optimal partitions of color space. *Proceedings of the National Academy of Sciences of the United States of America, 104*, 1436–41.

Regier, T., Kay, P., Gilbert, A., and Ivry, R. (2010). Language and thought: Which side are you on, anyway? In B. Malt and P. Wolff (Eds.), *Words and the Mind: How Words Capture Human Experience*. New York: Oxford University Press, pp. 165–82.

Regier, T., Kemp, C., and Kay, P. (2015). Word meanings across languages support efficient communication. In B. MacWhinney and W. O'Grady (Eds.), *The Handbook of Language Emergence*. Hoboken, NJ: Wiley-Blackwell, pp. 237–63.

Roberson, D. (2005). Color categories are culturally diverse in cognition as well as in language. *Cross-Cultural Research, 39*(1), 56–71.

Roberson, D. (2012). Culture, categories and color—Do we see the world through t(a)inted lenses? In M. Gelfand, C. Chiu, and Y. Hong (Eds.), *Advances in Culture and Psychology* (Vol. 2). New York: Oxford University Press, pp. 3–52.

Roberson, D., and Davidoff, J. (2000). The categorical perception of colors and facial expressions: The effect of verbal interference. *Memory and Cognition, 28*, 977–86.

Roberson, D., and Hanley, J. R. (2009). Relatively speaking: What is the relationship between language and thought in the color domain? *Glimpse, 2*(3), 68–77.

Roberson, D., and Pak, H. S. (2009). Categorical perception of color is restricted to the right visual field in Korean speakers who maintain central fixation. *Journal of Cognitive Science, 10*, 41–51.

Roberson, D., Davidoff, J., and Braisby, N. (1999). Similarity and categorization: Neuropsychological evidence for a dissociation in explicit categorization tasks. *Cognition, 71*, 1–42.

Roberson, D., Davies, I. R. L., and Davidoff, J. (2000). Colour categories are not universal: Replications and new evidence from a stone-age culture. *Journal of Experimental Psychology: General, 129*, 369–98.

Roberson, D., Davidoff, J., Davies, I. R. L., and Shapiro, L. R. (2004). The development of color categories in two languages: A longitudinal study. *Journal of Experimental Psychology: General, 133*, 554–71.

Roberson, D., Davidoff, J., Davies, I. R. L., and Shapiro, L. (2005a). Colour categories in Himba: Evidence for the cultural relativity hypothesis. *Cognitive Psychology, 50*, 378–411.

Roberson, D., Davies, I. R. L., Corbett, G., and Vandervyver, M. (2005b). Free-sorting of colors across cultures: Are there universal grounds for grouping? *Journal of Cognition and Culture, 5*, 349–86.

Roberson, D., Hanley, J. R., and Pak, H. (2009). Thresholds for color discrimination in English and Korean speakers. *Cognition, 112*, 482–7.

Roberson, D., Pak, H. S., and Hanley, J. R. (2008). Categorical perception of colour in the left and right visual field is verbally mediated: Evidence from Korea. *Cognition, 107*, 752–62.

Rosch, E. (1973). Natural categories. *Cognitive Psychology, 4*, 328–50.

Rosch Heider, E. (1972). Universals in color naming and memory. *Journal of Experimental Psychology, 93*, 10–20.

Rosch Heider, E., and Olivier, D. (1972). Universals in color naming and memory. *Journal of Experimental Psychology, 93*, 10–20.

Saunders, B. A. C., and van Brakel, J. (1997). Are there non-trivial constraints on color categorization? *Behavioral and Brain Sciences, 20*, 167–78.

Shepard, R. N. (1992). The perceptual organization of colors: An adaptation to regularities of the terrestrial world? In J. H. Barkow, L. Cosmides, and J. Tooby (Eds.), *The Adapted Mind: Evolutionary Psychology and the Generation of Culture*. New York: Oxford University Press, pp. 495–532.

Smallman, H., and Boynton, R. (1990). Segregation of basic colours in an information display. *Journal of the Optical Society of America A, 7*(10), 1985–94.

Smallman, H., and Boynton, R. (1993). On the usefulness of color coding in an information display. *Displays, 14*, 158–65.

Steels, L., and Belpaeme, T. (2005). Coordinating perceptually grounded categories through language: A case study for colour. *Behavioral and Brain Sciences, 28*, 469–89.

Sternheim, C. E., and Boynton, R. M. (1966). Uniqueness of perceived hues investigated with a continuous judgmental technique. *Journal of Experimental Psychology, 72*(5), 770–6.

Webster, M. A., and Kay, P. (2005). Variations in color naming within and across populations. *Behavioral and Brain Sciences, 28*, 512–13.

Whorf, B. L. (1956). *Language, Thought, and Reality: Selected Writings of Benjamin Lee Whorf.* Cambridge, MA: Technology Press of Massachusetts Institute of Technology.

Winawer, J., and Witthoft, N. (2012). Effects of color terms on color perception and cognition. In *Encyclopedia of Color Science and Technology.* Springer: New York, pp. 1–8. doi:10.1007/SpringerReference_300496.

Winawer, J., Witthoft, N., Frank, M. C., Wu, L., Wade, A. R., and Boroditsky, L. (2007). Russian blues reveal effects of language on color discrimination. *Proceedings of the National Academy of Sciences of the United States of America, 104,* 7780–5.

Yendrikhovskij, S. N. (2001). Computing color categories from statistics of natural images. *Journal of Imaging Science and Technology, 45,* 409–17.

29

COGNITIVE PENETRATION AND THE PERCEPTION OF COLOUR

Dustin Stokes

Consider two observations. First, we see—visually experience—colours. Second, our thoughts influence how we perceive the world. At face value, it may seem that there is little to resist here; both observations seem to capture intuitive features of human mental life. But face value has little purchase in all but a few quarters of philosophical theorizing. The first observation, once disambiguated and made precise, engages more or less immediately, controversy concerning the reality of colours, the (non-)relational nature of perceptual experience, and perceptual phenomenology, among many other topics discussed in this very volume. And if 'perceive' in the second observation is disambiguated so as to concern conscious perceptual experience (in this case, visual appearances), then once again, controversy abounds. Indeed, one standard line in cognitive scientific and philosophical theorizing has it that one's beliefs, desires, intentions and so on are certainly influenced by visual experience, but they do not influence visual experience itself. At the very least, there is a live debate concerning this possible phenomenon or phenomena. That debate concerns whether visual experience, and perceptual experience more generally, is *cognitively penetrable*. This chapter focuses on this possible phenomenon, with an emphasis on visual experience of colour, thus offering an analysis that brings together the two observations above.

§I offers a brief introduction to the notion of cognitive penetrability. §II focuses on relevant empirical research and its interpretation. §III further identifies the special importance of alleged cases of the cognitive penetration of colour vision.

I Cognitive penetration and its general importance

The term 'cognitively penetrable' originated with the work of Zenon Pylyshyn (1980, 1984, 1999). Pylyshyn works from within a computationalist framework of the mind, and so was motivated to distinguish parts of mental life that require, for their explanation, the attribution of rules and representation from those that do not. Pylyshyn argues that things like beliefs and inferences fall in the former category, and perceptual processes in the latter. Much debate has ensued, however, on how 'cognitive penetrability' should be defined so as to secure the distinction Pylyshyn and other computationalists have sought. Pylyshyn ultimately settled on the characterization found in the now often-cited passage, "[I]f a system is cognitively penetrable, then the function it computes is sensitive, in a semantically coherent way, to the organism's goals and beliefs, that is, it can be altered in a way that bears some logical relation to what the person knows" (Pylyshyn 1999: 343). Although this falls short of a definition (providing only a necessary condition for a state or process being cognitively penetrable), one can glean from it important lessons.

First, the importance of a 'semantic criterion' is that it ensures that cognitive penetration is no mere causal relation running from, say, a belief to perception. Instead, it is a causal relation where, on one interpretation, the content of the penetrating cognitive state stands in an inference-supporting relation with the content of the resultant perceptual state. Compare: if we simply said that cognitive penetration is any instance where one's cognitive states causally influence one's perceptual states, then any time my beliefs, say, direct where I look, or what I listen to or touch, then my visual or auditory or tactile experiences are thereby cognitively penetrated. This would render cognitive penetration a trivially common phenomenon.[1]

Others have attempted to capture the non-trivial nature of the possible phenomenon, but without any commitment to a semantic or inference-supporting relation. For example, Siegel (2012) characterizes the phenomenon in terms of contrasting perceivers:

> Cognitive Penetrability (second pass): If visual experience is cognitively penetrable, then it is nomologically possible for two subjects (or for one subject in different counterfactual circumstances, or at different times) to have visual experiences with different contents while seeing *and attending to* the same distal stimuli under the same external conditions, as a result of differences in other cognitive (including affective) states.
>
> *(Siegel 2012: 205–6)*

This shares the motivation for the semantic criterion but without commitment to that very criterion: cognitive penetration of vision is a phenomenon where, as Macpherson (2012) puts it, holding fixed the viewing conditions, attentional focus, and sensory organs, two subjects have distinct perceptual experiences. Another similarly motivated definition maintains that[2] instances of cognitively penetrated experience are ones where the causal link between background cognitive state and resultant experience is "internal and mental" (Stokes 2013; see also 2012). All of these characterizations share the motivation that cognitive penetration is a non-trivial phenomenon, and not one that results (in any straightforward way) from change in environmental circumstances, or simple bodily actions, or shifts in attention (looking or listening in the ways that one wants, believes relevant, and so on). So while Pylyshyn is right to distinguish cognitive penetrability as a non-trivial cognitive-perceptual relation, the need for the semantic criterion remains a point of debate.

Another clarification is gleaned from comparing Pylyshyn's characterization from those offered just above. Pylyshyn's emphasis is, usually explicitly, on whether goals, beliefs, and other cognitive processes can influence perceptual *processing*. This comports with the research agenda of other computationalists like Jerry Fodor, who maintain that some parts of mental architecture are *modular*, operating independently of beliefs, goals, and so on (Fodor 1983). Modularists of this strength maintain that modular systems—Fodor takes visual "input systems" to be of this sort—are therefore *informationally encapsulated* with respect to cognitive processes. By contrast, one might note that all the theorists in the previous paragraph emphasize cognitive effects on perceptual *experience*. There are good reason for this. First, a philosophy of perception concerns, first and foremost, person-level conscious perceptual experiences, not the mere computational mechanisms that cause or subvene those experiences. Second, and related, a central area of concern for philosophers of perception is epistemological, most basically, whether and how perception provides knowledge about one's environment. And, by the standards of just about any epistemological theory, the perceptual *things* that do (or do not) provide knowledge or epistemic warrant or reason for belief, are person-level experiences: what the subject sees, hears, and otherwise experiences in a first-person accessible way.[3]

It is worth noting that although the modularists focus on processing, they too are interested in person-level experiences, and for the reasons just given. Part of Fodor's motivation for positing informationally encapsulated (and thus cognitively *im*penetrable) visual input systems is that those systems should (and apparently do) provide fast and objective information about the creature's environment, such that the creature "can detect what is right here, right now—what is available, for example, for eating or being eaten by" (Fodor 1985: 4). Now of course for some very simple creatures, this kind of detection could be entirely automatic and dumb, with nothing answering to "personal" or "conscious". But Fodor is perfectly clear that at least for creatures like us, perception must function less like a true reflex and more like a filter. This is due to the remarkable variability in proximal stimuli—in vision, the array of light wave reception on the retina—by contrast to the largely stable distal stimuli—the object/s or event/s reflecting those light waves. And what an organism needs so that it doesn't get eaten, as Fodor is fond of putting it, is to know what of the variability in proximal stimulus accurately corresponds to variation (or stability) in the distal environment. After all, tigers can eat you, rod and cone stimulation cannot. Thus "the function of perception ... is to propose to thought a representation of the world from which such irrelevant variability has been effectively filtered" (4). Accordingly, perception here is understood at the level of experience: the kinds of states that are "proposed" to higher level-thought for consideration and further decision making. Accordingly, 'perception' will be assumed to denote perceptual experience in the remainder of this chapter.

It should by now be clear that much of the cognitive penetration debate concerns just what such a phenomenon is or would be. Accordingly, there are reasons to be cautious about committing to any extant definition here. Instead, the following rough characterization will do. Cognitive penetration of perception involves, at least, a cognitive effect on conscious perceptual experience, where this effect is non-trivially direct, and the effect on perception involves a phenomenal difference (put in Siegel's counterfactual terms, a difference that would not be there absent the relevant background cognitive state). This (relevant) effect is not one on postperceptual judgement or memory, and is not the result of active bodily movements or acts of attention.[4]

Finally, it should be emphasized that the question about cognitive penetration of perception is an empirical one. Theorists are asking whether, in human beings, cognition penetrates perceptual experience and, if so, with what frequency. The consequences that would follow are then theoretical-scientific and epistemological. There is little interesting metaphysics to be done here. There are possible worlds where creatures much like us engage in rampant wishful seeing, or regularly perceive in ways infected by their theories. Put another way, there seems to be nothing in the concept of sense perception that precludes its compatibility with cognitive penetration. Accordingly, the discussion that follows concerns relevant empirical research on colour perception (§II), followed by an emphasis on the epistemic importance of this research (§III).

II Alleged cases of cognitive penetration of colour perception

Like many other organisms, human visual systems acquire information about the light reflectance wavelengths given by their environments. Processing of this information gives rise to (or just is) conscious colour experience (this is true whether one is a colour realist or sceptic). And further, we abstract information on the basis of that and related experience. We learn that certain kinds of natural and artefactual things are typically coloured in one way or another. So, we acquire colour *concepts*, and explanation of this acquisition may take many forms. Perhaps we first learn to group a kind of thing—say tomatoes—and then abstract a feature that they all share—being red. Or perhaps we first learn to distinguish red things from non-red things by simple identification of sameness and difference relations, and then identify the distinctive kinds among them—*this* red thing is a tomato, *this* red thing is a stop sign, and so on. In any case, at some point we learn what redness is and this learning has a perceptual basis. We also form *beliefs*, a type of thought of which concepts are constituents (or so many theorists think anyway). So we have beliefs—evidenced by dispositions to act in certain ways and make particular verbal reports about what is true—that tomatoes and stop signs are red, bananas are yellow, and so on. Thus we have (constituents of) cognitive states concerning visibly perceptible features of the world. A number of experiments, both old and recent, exploit the relation between colour-related cognitive representations and colour experience.

II.1 *Some cases*

A case recently revived in philosophical discussion is Delk and Fillenbaum's 1965 study involving (in the experimental condition) items of characteristic colours and (in the control condition) items of a kind that have no characteristic colour. In both conditions, the task was an online matching task (this term is clarified below), where subjects were instructed to colour-match cutouts of various shapes, all of them cut from a uniformly orange piece of paper (e.g. a love-heart shape, which is characteristically red, or an oval which has no characteristic colour), to a background that could be adjusted from various shades from yellow to orange to red. In the experimental conditions, subjects matched the cutout shape (when of a characteristically red item like a loveheart) to a significantly more red background than in the control condition (where the control condition cutouts, again, were of kinds not characteristically one colour or other). On the face of it, and so Macpherson (2012) argues, this is an instance where beliefs about red-coloured kinds (loveheart shapes, apples, human lip shapes) influence visual experience such that the relevant perceptual stimuli are experienced as more red than they in fact are. It is a plausible case where beliefs about kinds or kind-concepts influence, in a non-trivial and relatively direct way, phenomenal colour experience. If this is its proper explanation, it would be a case of cognitively penetrated colour perception. But as Macpherson notes, the results of this experiment underdetermine the choice of explanation: it *may* be cognitive penetration, or it may be a case where repeated exposure to a kind results in heightened visual sensitivity, that is, a case of perceptual learning.[5]

In a much more recent series of studies, experimenters again explored the way that cognitive representations of objects with "high colour diagnosticity" may influence current perceptual colour experience. In Hansen *et al.* (2006), subjects were presented, on a computer monitor, with digital images of fruits/vegetables, in their typical colour. The task was to adjust the image, in real-time, to (subject-specific) achromatic grey.[6] For these images, by contrast with the control task involving uniformly coloured discs, subjects adjust the image past achromatic grey and into the opponent hue range while reporting that it is grey (e.g. adjusting a banana image into the opponent blue range). By hypothesis, the subjects must then make a typically yellow object more blue (objectively) in order to see it as achromatic grey. As the researchers quantify it, this "memory colour effect" ranges from three to five times the threshold for discrimination. In the first follow-up study, Olkkonen *et al.* (2008) found the effect more pronounced for images natural in appearance (with texture, appearance of depth, etc.) and statistically weak for mere fruit/vegetable outlines (more on the importance of this difference below). In the most recent follow-up study, Witzel *et al.* (2011) performed roughly the same set of procedures, but this time with images of human-made objects of high colour diagnosticity. The results were similar: they found memory colour effects for images of the Red Coca-Cola icon, the blue Smurf, green ping-pong table, and several others. In controls, no effects were found for images of colour-variant kinds (e.g. socks) or typically achromatic kinds (e.g. golf balls).[7] In each of these experiments, the subjects made online adjustments, attempting to make a match between the target object and background. So, although there are reasons for doubt, these effects are plausibly explained as instances of cognitive penetration: background cognitive states (say beliefs about the colours of natural and artefactual kinds) influence perceptual experience such that, in these cases, subjects are making errors.

One final study that has received philosophical discussion is Levin and Banaji (2006). In this study, researchers explored the way that race categories (or, if one likes, beliefs about features of race) might influence perception. Here again there are numerous iterations and complexities of the research, but the basic thrust can be captured by a brief description of what Levin and Banaji call Experiment 2. All conditions involve presentation of realistic, 2D male human face images, presented in precisely the same shade of grey. Here researchers first create a racially ambiguous face by morphing the image of a prototypical black male face with an image of a prototypical white male face; they then confirm the racial ambiguity with a preliminary controlled experiment. Subjects are then presented with an instruction screen involving both the racially ambiguous face and an unambiguously black face or an unambiguously white face, where the latter would be labelled accurately as 'BLACK' or 'WHITE' respectively, and the former labelled oppositely (thus for example: the ambiguous face would be labelled 'BLACK' and an unambiguous face white face would be labelled 'WHITE'). A subject is then then presented with one of the same instruction phase faces adjacent to an adjustable greyscale rectangle. The task is to adjust the rectangle to match the target face in luminance. In all conditions, the reports co-vary significantly with the semantic label given on the instruction screen. Perhaps the most striking result is this: the very same ambiguous face results in an adjustment that is 0.465 levels darker (than the objective luminance of the face) when labelled 'BLACK' and 15.95 levels lighter when labelled 'WHITE'.[8] A change in label appears to affect racial classification (a cognitive process) which in turn affects basic lightness perception. This looks like a plausible instance where higher-level mental states (beliefs or concepts about race) directly influence visual experience. And in this case, there could be consequences for moral philosophy and psychology.[9]

Differences aside, there are important features common to all of these studies. First, the task performance is "online", where subjects are asked to make a report on the basis of current perceptual experience (by contrast to post-perceptual memory reports). Second, the report method is non-verbal, typically involving some kind of matching task. Finally, colour is a basic phenomenal feature of visual perception if any feature is (by contrast to the high-level contents that some argue are admissible contents of experience). These features prove important for the theorist of cognitive penetration in defending against the critical, alternative explanations discussed below.

II.2 *Critics and discussion*

Because cognitive penetration is supposed to be a two-part relation between cognition and perception, challenges to any alleged case may take three basic forms: one for each *relatum* and one for the relation itself. First, one may argue that the penetrating state or process is not in fact cognitive (or that there is no relevant antecedent relatum). Second, one may argue that the apparent effect is not in fact one on perceptual experience. Finally, one may argue that the relation between cognition and perception is mediated such that the phenomenon is not of the type of interest. All forms of challenge to alleged cases have been made in extant literature but have a harder time sticking to cases involving colour perception.

The most common example of the third type of challenge is what has been dubbed the *attention-shift interpretation* (see Macpherson 2012; Stokes 2012). Fodor articulates this reply to alleged cases in a number of places. In reply to theorists like Hanson (1958, 1969) and Church-land (1979, 1988), Fodor argues that some perceptual stimuli can be changed, so to speak, by the subject depending upon her beliefs and goals. So for example, once one "knows the trick", one can shift one's focus of attention from certain parts of the ambiguous duck-rabbit image to other parts and thereby "flip" from seeing the image as a duck to seeing it as a rabbit.[10] This flipping may well be a change in visual phenomenology, and one dependent upon knowledge and goals concerning the duck-rabbit image, but it is mediated by an agent-driven act of attention. Accordingly, Fodor suggests, if this is supposed to be cognitive penetration, then the phenomenon is relevantly trivial.[11]

Suppose Fodor is right about this kind of case. Notice, however, that it involves not just basic shape perception, but visually perceiving an image as falling under one category or other.[12] The colour cases discussed in II.1 are importantly different, involving more basic colour perception. In these cases, there is no obvious place where active shifts in attention would affect changes in colour perception, and for at least two reasons. Looking harder or more carefully at some sub-section of the visual field (say at the right side of Delk and Fillenbaum's loveheart cutout) will not yield the result that that portion (or the entire field) looks differently coloured, say more red. Second, and related, there is no compelling reason to think that the experimental procedures would encourage this shift in attention. Here the contrast with the duck-rabbit is apt: one way to teach a newcomer to "see" the rabbit and then "see" the duck is to direct her attention to specific parts of the image. Likewise for the Necker Cube and other familiar ambiguous figures. By contrast, what cognitive state would drive a subject to attend differently to some part of a heart-shape cutout or a greyscale racially ambiguous face? At bottom, then, application of the attention-shift interpretation to these colour cases simply looks unprincipled.[13]

A memory interpretation alleges of a case that an apparent effect is one on memory rather than perceptual experience. This kind of explanation is most plausible when the target stimulus is removed from view and the subject then must make some kind of report based on the now past perceptual experience. For example, food deprived experimental subjects might be shown ambiguous inkblot images and then asked, once the images are removed, whether they perceived images of food or not. The memory interpretation has very little plausibility, however, for any of the above experiments since, as stressed above, each experiment is online, involving a report simultaneous with perceptual experience of the target stimulus.

Similarly, a judgement interpretation claims that an alleged effect is only one on post-perceptual judgement, maintaining that perceptual experience is not penetrated. Here the interpretation is applied by simply maintaining that colour experiences are veridical (and thus invariant across experimental manipulations where the target stimulus is unchanged, as in Experiment 2 of Levin and Banaji 2006). The reports of experimental subjects (that the extra-red background matches the orange loveheart cutout, that the greyscale 'WHITE' labelled face matches an objectively much lighter grey rectangle, and so on) are then explained by errors in judgement, not perception. So, subjects enjoy veridical visual perception, on the basis of which they make errors in judgement.

One might resist this interpretation as follows. In many of these experiments, there is some kind of error made as evidenced by the report data. Thus subjects report a match between cutout and background when the second is objectively more red than the first; they report that a banana image is perfect grey when in fact it is noticeably tinged with blue; they match a grey-scale face to a noticeably lighter or darker shade. An explanation must then account for the error. The judgement interpretation makes this a person-level error, where subjects enjoy veridical experience but then make judgements that are inconsistent with that experience even while on the basis of that experience. The "on the basis" of qualification here is key: these experiments all involve online methodologies, where subjects are encouraged to use what they see to make a report. This requires consistent mistakes about what one is seeing: somehow, while seeing the target accurately, the experimental subject makes a judgement and accordant report that mischaracterizes that very seen target. Introspection is notoriously fallible, but it may seem implausible that subjects could be so badly mistaken in judgements about their own current experience. Subjects are not being asked to perform any complex judgement or report; they are only asked to make colour matches or simple colour adjustments. In this light, the judgement interpretation may look even less plausible.[14] Alternatively, a cognitive penetration interpretation explains the error as a perceptual one: subjects make the reports they do because they are *not* enjoying veridical colour experience, where this is a consequence of background cognitive states.

Here it is worth saying a bit more about the basic-ness of colour perception, and how this figures into possible interpretations of the relevant experimental data. There is a long philosophical tradition of taking colour perception to be a basic form of visual experience. Aristotle took colour to be the proper sensible of vision; colour is represented only by vision, by contrast to shape, a sensible feature common to vision and touch. Berkeley took colour to be an essential feature of visual experience, and indeed famously used this observation to argue against Locke's primary/secondary quality distinction. Early sense datum theorists maintained that colours are among the features given by experience, either as bound with other features like shape and size (as in, plausibly, Price 1932) or as unbound features out of which objects are constructed by cognition (as in Russell 1910). The same is true today: theorists of varied commitments maintain that as far as conscious visual experience goes, colour is foundational or "bedrock". Accordingly, enjoying visual experience of colour requires much less cognitive sophistication than, by contrast, seeing something as being of a kind (supposing for the moment that the latter is a possible kind of visual experience). One way to articulate a relevant point here is in terms of Fred Dretske's distinction between non-epistemic seeing vs. epistemic seeing.[15] As Dretske illustrates:

> The first time I became aware of an armadillo (I saw it on a Texas road), I did not know what it was. I did not even know what armadillos were, much less what they looked like. My ignorance did not impair my eyesight, of course. I saw the animal. I was aware of it ahead of me on the road. That is why I swerved. Ignorance of what armadillos are or how they look can prevent someone from being conscious of certain facts (that the object crossing the road is an armadillo) without impairing in the slightest one's awareness of the things the armadillos crossing roads-that (so to speak) constitute these facts.
>
> *(Dretske 1993: 266)*

Dretske saw, as in visually identified and then avoided, a moving object with armadillo-like features, but without identifying *that* they were armadillo-like features, or seeing *that* the object with those features was an armadillo. Achieving the latter requires the deployment of the concept ARMADILLO which, as the story goes, Dretske lacks at the time. As he suggests, one can be aware of, can have a conscious visual experience of, complex *things* like armadillos without being aware of the *fact* that the thing seen is an armadillo. To do the latter, one must apply the concept to what is seen (see Dretske 1993: 265).

A couple of points to note: first, theorists debate whether the second kind of seeing—epistemic seeing—is really a kind of seeing at all. Indeed, most of what Dretske says characterizes epistemic seeing as a kind of belief, where the basic contents of the relevant perceptual experience (say, as of an armadillo) are the same for the case when one just sees an F and the case when one sees that x is an F. What's different is that only in the second case has one formed a belief about a fact involving Fs. Epistemic seeing is then, on this line, really perceptually based belief or judgement, where seeing only provides access to basic features like colour and shape.[16] The second point follows from here. Focus just on non-epistemic seeing for a moment. Note how seeing a thing—an armadillo crossing the road—is already a fairly complex visual achievement. It requires seeing colours, shapes with varying size, all bound together and in motion. Even if one lacks the concept ARMADILLO, any reports made on the basis of this visual experience may be rather sophisticated. One could make errors about a variety of features in addition to colour: size, shape, texture, speed, how the creature moves, and so on. So it is an experience that encourages a variety of judgements, it encourages the formation of numerous beliefs). So even if one lacks the concept ARMADILLO, one probably has a variety of other relevant concepts and so may judge that (see that) there is an animal crossing the road, or that the thing crossing the road is low to the ground or oddly shaped or frightened. Contrast that with the kinds of visual experience had by subjects in the above experiments. In those experiments, the stimuli are dramatically simpler, lacking motion and presented only on a computer monitor or paper. And importantly the experimental tasks only require attention to the most basic feature of the scene, namely, colour. To perform these colour matching tasks, one need no sophisticated concepts (of colours or otherwise); one only need to understand basic sameness and difference relations. It is in this light that the experiments on colour perception look well interpreted as involving cognitive penetration and, comparatively, much less plausibly interpreted as errors in post-perceptual judgement. Making a colour match is not like seeing an armadillo (let alone seeing that there is an armadillo). It lacks substantial complexity, requires no sophisticated concepts, and does not encourage a variety of perceptual beliefs in the way that seeing an animal scurrying across the road would. So it is plausible that the subjects' errors are explained not by post-perceptual deployment of concepts but instead by pre-perceptual cognitive effects on perceptual processing (concepts or beliefs about natural and artefactual kinds, for instance). This again highlights why colour cases are especially important for the cognitive penetrability debate.

A fourth alternative interpretation claims of a case that there is no relevant cognitive relatum and instead that the apparent effects are instead some kind of intra-perceptual adjustment, where sensory systems become more sensitive to patterns, in a way that is partially hardwired while partially plastic. One way to describe this is in terms of perceptual learning, on many models of which sensory changes are not ones brought by higher-level or semantic learning, and are not under the control of the agent. Fodor invokes this kind of interpretation in his debate with Churchland (1988), arguing that adaptation to inverting goggles does not involve cognitive penetration. Instead, he claims

> For there are, after all, good ecological reasons why you might expect plasticity of this sort ... what needs to be kept open for re-calibration is whatever mechanisms compute the appropriate motor commands for getting to (or pointing to, or grasping) a visible object on the basis of its perceived location. Adaptation to inverted (and otherwise spatially distorting) lenses is plausibly an extreme case of this sort of recalibration.
>
> *(Fodor 1988: 193)*

One might think that this kind of interpretation similarly applies to some of the colour cases discussed above. So, for example, the initial Hansen *et al.* (2006) studies were performed with realistic, textured images of fruits and vegetables, while the Olkkonen *et al.* (2008) studies suggested that the relevant memory colour effects were pronounced only for those realistic images but not for mere outline shapes of fruits and 15 vegetables. One possible explanation is that creatures like us are naturally cued to quickly distinguish food that is safe to eat (ripe yellow bananas for example), and that this sensitivity is enhanced as we mature but not in a way influenced by thoughts or high-level concepts about food. Accordingly, this sensitivity is triggered by realistic looking fruit images (in such a way that perhaps we experience their relevant colours in more pronounced ways, enjoying a kind of pop-out effect), but not for mere outline shapes of those same fruits. Deroy (2013) suggests this kind of explanation, where the results in these particular studies may involve purely perceptual changes that co-vary with other available sensory features, in this case, shape, volume, and texture.

For all that has been said here, the intra-perceptual interpretation may be the most plausible alternative explanation of apparent cases of cognitive penetration of colour. Again, these cases all involve fairly simple colour matching tasks, and so an explanation involving a genuine perceptual effect (by contrast to mere post-perceptual judgement) and little special activity on the part of the subjects (by contrast to agent driven shifts in attention) seems most attractive. The Witzel *et al.* (2011) studies do seem to provide additional leverage for the cognitive penetration interpretation, since here the images used are human-made (smurfs; ping-pong tables; the Pink Panther) and culturally sensitive (the experimental subjects were German, and so for them items like the UHU glue tube and Nivea tin are highly colour-diagnostic; these same images would not be highly colour diagnostic for most American subjects). Subjects in these studies reported the same memory colour effects, and by the same method of report (though, it is worth noting, with some possibly confounding differences between colours). It is much harder to make the case that there are "good ecological reasons" for this kind of (culturally sensitive) plasticity. And the same might be said for the cutout shapes of artificial images (lovehearts) in the Delk and Fillenbaum studies, and for semantically primed faces in the Levin and Banaji studies. In any case, colour perception cases provide an especially interesting testbed for comparing cognitive penetration explanations with intra-perceptual types of explanations. This is a fruitful area for future research.[17]

III The importance of colour perception research and the cognitive penetrability debate

The above cases and their interpretation may have implications for standard metaphysical questions in philosophy of colour and perception—say about the objectivity of colour or debates concerning phenomenal character versus representational content—but the central emphasis in this final section, like much of the literature concerning cognitive penetration, is on epistemological concerns. The general implication involves concerns about the epistemic status of perception; if perception is cognitively penetrable, does this somehow threaten, or at least force revised epistemologies about, the supposed rational and knowledge providing roles of perception?

As discussed in II.2 above, colour is among the basic features represented by vision, the others are typically supposed to be shape, size, depth, and motion. Recently, some philosophers have argued that in addition to these *low-level* properties, visual experience may represent *high-level* properties. Typically included among the latter are emotional properties, causal properties, kind/ categorical properties, and agential properties. Siegel (2006, 2010) argues for high-level

483

admissible contents by appeal to phenomenology. Plausibly, overall experience had in the presence of pine trees or Cyrillic text is different before versus after acquiring a capacity to recognize pine trees or Cyrillic text as such. This contrast, Siegel argues, is best explained as a difference in perceptual content, where after acquiring the recognitional capacity one perceptually represents as instantiated the property of being a pine tree or being a word in Cyrillic text.[18] This explanation, however, is highly contested. A plausible reply, and one that Siegel attempts to rebut, is that the phenomenal sensory experience of, say, pine trees is the same before and after. What's different is that in the after-case one judges that the object is a pine tree, where this may come with a feeling of familiarity that explains the phenomenal contrast. This position has tradition on its side, according to which perception represents basic properties of colour, shape, size, and motion. Being of a kind or being a cause or being an instance of someone trying to perform an action are recognized but at the level of cognition. *We* make judgements that such properties are instantiated, but this is not something that *perception* "picks up".

Notice how this debate connects nicely with the above discussion of the judgement interpretation of alleged cases of cognitive penetration. In that context, like Siegel's pine tree and comparable cases, it is natural to claim that the apparent change (in perceptual report or introspected phenomenology) is one in how the subject makes judgements about the perceived scene. This is plausible if the task involves, for example, identifying objects of a kind. But as suggested above, it is much less plausible for the cases involving mere colour matching. As Macpherson puts the point,

> [C]olour is a low-level property—it is a property that all people agree is represented by visual experience—as opposed to a high-level property, like a natural kind property. Therefore a common strategy that is employed by low-level theorists to maintain that two experiences are the same and that they represent the same properties cannot be employed here. The strategy is to claim that any evidence that the experiences are different is really evidence that the contents of judgments formed on the basis of those experiences are different, for it is claimed that experiences cannot represent the properties in question, as they are high-level properties. But this strategy can't be applied to this case for the properties at issue—colour properties—are low-level properties.
>
> *(Macpherson 2012: 42)*

So the judgement interpretation seems less apt in two related ways. First, one cannot deploy, as Macpherson notes, a high-level property judgement interpretation since colour is, by all theorists' lights, a low-level property. And second, and for that very reason, these cases less plausibly involve a judgement, let alone one that deviates from current experience. (Recall from II.2 that this is what the judgement interpretation would require: repeated erroneous judgement on the basis of current colour experience). So while alleged cases of cognitive penetration of high-level perceptual content may be live only for certain theorists, apparent cases of cognitive penetration of colour perception are live for low-level and high-level theorists alike.

In some respects, this renders the epistemological consequences of cognitive penetration (supposing it occurs) more striking. The relevant consequences all concern the normativity of perception, should it be cognitively penetrable. And they all start with the assumption that in an important, foundational sense, experience is first. Experience is what we first ... experience. And it is the feature of mental life that receives final appeal when justifying one's beliefs, theories, and decisions. We can then distinguish three questions, each of them prefixed with the antecedent condition: If perception is cognitively penetrated—What does this imply for perception's role in providing justified belief? What does this imply for perception's role in providing true belief or knowledge? Is there some special set of worries that attach to cases involving vision?

The first possible consequence concerns the rational role of perception, should it be penetrated by background cognitive states. The structure of the challenge is one familiar in contemporary philosophy of science. If one's perceptual observations are already infected with one's theoretical beliefs, then the former observations cannot provide a neutral arbiter for theory choice or support.[19] Siegel (2012) puts this general epistemic worry in terms of circularity. If I believe, before meeting her, that my friend is angry, and then upon meeting and because of that background belief I have a visual experience as of my friend being angry, the penetrated experience seems undermined as support for the consequent belief that my friend is angry. Lyons (2011) rejects the suggestion that the relevant epistemic consequence concerns circularity, arguing instead that the issue is reliability. He suggests further that it shouldn't be assumed without argument that the consequence is epistemically pernicious (see also Vance 2015). Instead, it depends upon the particular process of belief formation, rather than the penetrating state. In some cases the process will be of an unreliable type and, accordingly, the resultant belief unjustified; other instances will involve a boost of reliability (where beliefs formed via a process of that type are more likely to be true) and the belief is accordingly justified. So if my beliefs regarding morel mushrooms prime my visual system such that I form more true beliefs about the presence of morel mushrooms (more than I would absent that background belief) then this is arguably a good example of penetration. Finally, Siegel (2013a, 2013b) argues that some cases of cognitive penetration are such that when beliefs are formed on their basis, experience is "downgraded" in its justificatory role. Her argument is that when the structure of the etiologies of experience mirrors an epistemically problematic etiology of belief (for example, where one "jumps to conclusions"), then in neither case are the resultant beliefs epistemically justified; in neither case does experience or belief rationally serve what she calls the "endorsement role" (where one rationally endorses the content of the mental state). Siegel attempts to show that this downgrade principle applies widely to epistemologies ranging from process reliabilism to dogmatism to mentalistic internalism.[20] Some of the latter theorists will naturally resist this claim, arguing instead that endorsing the content of the (unknowingly) penetrated experience, absent defeating evidence, is precisely the rational thing to do. As one commentator puts it, "What am I supposed to think?" (McGrath 2013; see also Huemer 2013; Fumerton 2013).

So it is very much debated whether this challenge takes such broad scope, and the points of debate pivot around independent commitments regarding epistemic justification. What's important to note is that, here again, the colour cases could prove extremely important. Colour perception is taken by all of these epistemologists to be basic, in at least two senses. Colours are an admissible content of visual experience; all parties agree that we have colour experiences while all parties do not agree that we have visual experiences as of, say, pine trees. And a perceptual belief about the colour of an object is an uncontroversial candidate for a non-inferential belief. Put in Fodorian terms of modularity, colour processing is part of the visual "input system" that is supposed to be informationally encapsulated and, thus, impenetrable by higher-level cognition, and with important stakes for the objectivity of perception (Fodor 1983). So if the colour cases are best interpreted as bona fide cases of cognitive penetration, then each of these epistemologies will have to wrestle with their respective consequences, good or bad.

The second consequence is related, concerning not whether penetrated experience can provide a rational or justified basis for belief, but instead whether these cases are such that they undermine knowledge. This point requires marking the difference between a truth condition for knowledge and a non-redundant justification or warrant condition. The latter is the relevant condition for the first consequence discussed above. But one can imagine some of these cases described in the following ways. According to the seemings internalist, absent any knowledge about the problematic etiology, one should take one's colour experience at face value and relevant beliefs formed on that basis will be (prima facie) justified. Generally, the view claims that how things seem to the subject—thus a state internal and cognitively accessible to the subject—provide the subject with defeasible evidence about how things are. But in the alleged examples of cognitive penetration discussed above, it often seems that the etiology undermines the accuracy of the colour experience (the experience is non-veridical) and the resultant belief is thereby false (for example, one believes that the image is perfect grey when in fact it is bluish). This is still a rationally held belief, but it is not knowledge.

For an externalism like process reliabilism, a belief is justified just in case it results from a type of belief-forming process that produces true beliefs with sufficiently high frequency.[21] A traditionally important question for this epistemology is how belief-forming processes should be *typed*, that is, by what criteria and to what specificity should the distinct types of processes that cause beliefs be distinguished. Thus from coarse to more fine, one might think that perception is a belief-forming process type, or that vision is, or that colour vision is, and so on. Now if belief-forming processes are typed coarsely enough, the etiology involved in alleged cases of cognitive penetration of colour perception might be generally reliable and the resultant belief thereby justified. But here again, the etiology may be problematic vis-a-vis knowledge insofar as it undermines the truth-tracking role of experience and, accordingly, resultant belief.

So the second lesson is one familiar in contemporary epistemology, beliefs may be justified but false. Most recent attention has been paid to the question concerning justification, but this simple exercise concerning colour cases reveals another simple way that cognitive penetration may be problematic: it may simply undermine our capacity to access the truth about our immediate environments.

The third and final consequence focuses on the epistemic importance of vision by contrast to other sense modalities. It is common to describe humans as "visual creatures", and vision has most certainly dominated the psychological and philosophical research on perception. One might ask why vision is dominant in this way. One plausible answer points to the kind of information that vision provides, and arguably more efficiently than all other sense modalities. Healthy human vision provides, all-at-once, *rich spatial information*, enabling recognition of allocentric, macrospatial properties like shape, size, and orientation (Stokes and Biggs 2014). Upon entering a room, say a movie theatre, vision will rapidly provide a perceiver with information about the broad spatial layout of the room, how certain objects are organized into rows (chairs), and set at distinctive distances from a much larger rectangular object (the screen), differences in illumination and colour in various locations in the room, objects (movie goers) moving in between the rows, and so on. For most perceivers, vision will also enable identification of objects at the level of kind: chairs, a screen, lights, people. No other modality can provide this richness of spatial information. For humans, only touch is relevant, but it would require, by contrast, laboriously extensive haptic exploration (and even then one could not acquire, by touch alone, all of the same information, say about lighting conditions or colour).

Stokes and Biggs argue that the distinctively rich spatial nature of the visual explains why visual perception (and visual imagery) dominates human perception in all sense modalities. And, they argue further, this is epistemically virtuous: insofar as one is performing perceptual tasks where rich spatial information is needed, it is good that vision will dominate the *judgements* made on the basis of sensory experience and, as evidenced in a variety of recent empirical studies, sometimes dominate *experience* in those modalities.[22] The lesson here is that the platitude that we are visual creatures is tracking something: vision is the most important means by which humans acquire rich spatial information about the immediate environmental space. The rich spatial information vision provides includes experience of edges and shapes, depth, motion, and of course, colour.

All of this further highlights the epistemic importance of the (possible) cognitive penetrability of colour perception. Visual perception, including visual perception of colour, is generally (which is not to say always) the epistemically best source we have for information about the immediate environmental space, what's "here and now". The cases discussed in §II suggest that, in some instances, visual processing and thus visual experience may be sensitive to more (or less) than the colours (or light reflectance properties) that are here and now. In these cases perception is plausibly causally dependent on what has been learned or cognized independent of the current environmental space, for example the characteristic colours of natural and artificial categories of object, or the lightness/darkness of faces of distinct racial categories. If some theorists are correct, this could be of double (or at least exacerbated) epistemic consequence: since not only does vision dominantly affect the vision-based judgements one makes about rich spatial features, it also appears to dominate (for rich spatial tasks) judgements made on the basis of the *non-visual* sense modalities. Therefore if basic colour perception is cognitively penetrated, then non-visual perception (or belief) may thereby be cognitively penetrated.

Conclusion

Here is a prediction by way of conclusion. The prediction is ambitious in scope, but safely supported by the above discussions. Possible cases of the cognitive penetration of colour perception will continue to be an important testbed for a variety of empirical, epistemological, and metaphysical questions. These questions concern cognitive architecture and how colour perception fits in the best model of the mind, the epistemic role of vision and perception, and even the reality of colours. How one thinks about colour may influence how one sees colour, and this may properly influence our best theories of colour.

Notes

1 Macpherson (2012) makes clear this virtue of Pylyshyn's semantic criterion.
2 Distinct in some type: in content, in qualitative character, or both. And to be clear, Macpherson (2012) does seem to endorse Pylyshyn's semantic criterion, in spite of being presented here alongside theorists who do not.
3 There are of course tricky cases, like those involving agnosic patients who can successfully manipulate objects in the visual environment, but who appear unable to report visually detectable features of those same objects (their shapes, colours, or kind). Such patients act upon these objects reliably and so, some epistemic externalists might say, know that the object is in such-and-such position, or in motion, and so on. Other theorists, for example mentalistic internalists, might deny the knowledge attribution since the agnosic cannot report on those features (even if some of those features are clearly represented somewhere in the sub-personal cognitive system). But this case is non-standard.
4 Stokes (2016) argues that securing a definition for a (single) phenomenon called 'cognitive penetration' is less important, theoretically, than its supposed consequences. An alternative methodological approach is then to characterize the phenomenon in terms of the consequences that were and are of interest to parties on both sides of the debate. The three standard consequences concern: modularity theories of mind, the theory-ladenness of scientific observation, and the knowledge-providing role of perception. These are discussed in §III. For similar emphasis on epistemic consequences, see Raftopoulos (2001).
5 Macpherson goes on to argue that the Levin and Banaji (2006) studies, discussed below, provide better candidate evidence for genuine cognitive penetration.
6 There are individual differences in how people see (or judge) perfectly achromatic grey. Accordingly, in a preliminary norming study, experimenters determine the "perfect grey" for each participating subject.

7 This is only a rough summary, skirting over the many complexities of details of each of these experiments. For detailed analysis of the Delk and Fillenbaum, see Macpherson (2012) and Zeimbekis (2013). For detailed discussion of the Hansen *et al.* (2006) and the Witzel *et al.* (2011), see Stokes and Bergeron (2015). And for discussion of Olkkenen *et al.* (2008), see Deroy (2013).

8 Levin and Banaji used a computer monitor with 265 greyscale measures

9 See Macpherson (2012); Siegel (2012); Stokes and Bergeron (2015) for discussion. See Firestone and Scholl (2016) for criticism. See Payne (2001) and Payne *et al.* (2005) for related work on race and shape perception and kind-identification.

10 See www.illusionsindex.org/i/duck-rabbit

11 Trivial how? Well, for example, these common phenomena would not impugn the modularity *of perception* nor its role in providing knowledge. The attention-shift interpretation has been recently challenged by Mole (2016); Wu (2017); Stokes (forthcoming).

12 As discussed below, philosophers debate whether this kind of *seeing as* (or, related but distinct, *seeing that*) is after all a perceptual phenomenon rather than a post-perceptual judgement or belief. Put in related terms, philosophers debate whether perception can represent a high-level property like 'being a rabbit' at all. But ignore this complication for the present discussion.

13 Of course there may be other colour perception phenomena where attentional shifts are relevant. For example, one can wilfully undo colour constancy effects by attending more carefully to, for example, a patch of green in the shade and then comparing it to a patch of green in direct sunlight (where both patches are in the same visual field). But there is no reason to think that the above experiments involve constancy mechanisms. And one might worry, with respect to the Levin and Banaji (2006) studies specifically, that contours of typical black faces versus typical white faces are different in such a way that attention is drawn differently to more/less luminant parts of the face. However, Levin and Banaji devised an additional study that used either white line or black line drawings, with no additional shading or contour, and the same results are obtained. This discounts the contour/attention-shift interpretation.

14 See Macpherson (2012) for a defence of this sort against the judgement interpretation. See Stokes (2012) for a similar defence against the judgement interpretation when applied to experiments on the visual perception of size.

15 Dretske uses a number of pairs of terms, in a number of places, to mark the same distinction: seeing vs. seeing that; thing-perception vs. fact-perception; awareness of things vs. awareness of facts. See Dretske (1969, 1979, 1993). Hanson (1969) marks a very similar distinction.

16 The related topic of the admissible contents of experience is taken up in III.1 below.

17 For related philosophical discussion, see Connolly (2014). For the psychology of perceptual learning, see Gibson (1963) and Goldstone (1998).

18 For a cross-section of papers on the topic, see Hawley and Macpherson (2011).

19 For the now classic discussions of theory-ladenness of observation, see Hanson (1958, 1969); Kuhn (1962).

20 The details of some of these theories are discussed below. See also Tucker (2014); Vance (2014).

21 Goldman (1979) is the classic source.

22 For visual perceptual dominance over touch, see Rock and Victor (1964), Power and Graham (1976), Power (1980), Ernst and Banks (2002). For visual imagery dominance over touch, see Sathian *et al.* (1997), Zangaladze *et al.* (1999), Zhang *et al.* (2004). For visual dominance over audition, see McGurk and MacDonald (1976) and Rosenblum *et al.* (1997). For visual dominance over proprioception, see Botnivick and Cohen (1998). For visual dominance over olfaction, see Royet *et al.* (1999), Sakai *et al.* (2005). For visual dominance over flavour experience, see Johnson and Clydesdale (1982); Morrot *et al.* (2001); Spence (2010).

References

Botvinick, M. and Cohen, J. 'Rubber Hands "Feel" Touch That Eyes See'. *Nature* 391 (1998): 756.

Churchland, P. M. *Scientific Realism and the Plasticity of Mind*. Cambridge: Cambridge University Press, 1979.

Churchland, P. M. 'Perceptual Plasticity and Theoretical Neutrality: A Reply to Jerry Fodor'. *Philosophy of Science* 55 (1988): 167–87.

Connolly, K. 'Perceptual Learning and the Contents of Perception'. *Erkenntnis* 79 (2014): 1407–18.

Delk, J. L. and Fillenbaum, S. 'Differences in Perceived Colour as a Function of Characteristic Color'. *The American Journal of Psychology* 78 (1965): 290–3.

Deroy, O. 'Object-Sensitivity or Cognitive Penetration of Perception'. *Philosophical Studies* 162 (2013): 87–107.

Dretske, F. *Seeing and Knowing*. Chicago: University of Chicago Press, 1969.

Dretske, F. 'Simple Seeing'. In *Body, Mind and Method: Essays in Honor of Virgil Aldrich*. Ed. D. F. Gustafson and B. L. Tapscott. Dordrecht: Reidel, 1979.

Dretske, F. 'Conscious Experience'. *Mind* 102 (1993): 263–83.

Ernst, M. O. and Banks, M. S. 'Humans Integrate Visual and Haptic Information in a Statistically Optimal Fashion'. *Nature* 415 (2002): 429–33.

Firestone, C. and Scholl, B. 'Cognition Does Not Affect Perception: Evaluating the Evidence for "Topdown" Effects'. *Behavioral and Brain Sciences* 39 (2016): 1–72.

Fodor, J. *Modularity of Mind*. Cambridge, MA: MIT Press, 1983.

Fodor, J. 'Observation Reconsidered'. *Philosophy of Science* 51(1984): 23–43.

Fodor, J. 'Precis of *The Modularity of Mind*', *The Behavioural and Brain Sciences* 8 (1985): 1–5.

Fodor, J. 'A Reply to Churchland's "Perceptual Plasticity and Theoretical Neutrality"'. *Philosophy of Science* 55 (1988): 188–98.

Fumerton, R. 'Siegel on the Epistemic Impact of "Checkered" Experience'. *Philosophical Studies* 162 (2013): 733–9.

Gibson, E. J. 'Perceptual Learning'. *Annual Review of Psychology* 14 (1963): 29–56.

Goldman, A. (1979). 'What Is Justified Belief?' In *Justification and Knowledge*. Ed. G. Pappas. Dordrecht: D. Reidel, 1–23.

Goldstone, R. L. 'Perceptual Learning'. *Annual Review of Psychology* 49 (1998): 585–612.

Hansen, T., Olkkonen, M., Walter, S., and Gegenfurtner, K. R. 'Memory Modulates Color Appearance'. *Nature Neuroscience* 9 (2006) 1367–8.

Hanson, N. R. *Patterns of Discovery*. Cambridge: Cambridge University Press, 1958.

Hanson, N. R. *Perception and Discovery: An Introduction to Scientific Inquiry*. San Francisco: Freeman and Cooper, 1969.

Hawley, K. and Macpherson, F. *The Admissible Contents of Experience*. London: Wiley-Blackwell, 2011.

Huemer, M. 'Epistemological Asymmetries Between Belief and Experience'. *Philosophical Studies* 162 (2013): 741–8.

Johnson, J. and Clydesdale, F. M. 'Perceived Sweetness and Redness in Colored Sucrose Solutions'. *Journal of Food Science* 47 (1982): 747–52.

Kuhn, T. *The Structure of Scientific Revolutions*. Chicago: University of Chicago Press, 1962.

Levin, D. and Banaji, M. 'Distortions in the Perceived Lightness of Faces: The Role of Race Categories'. *Journal of Experimental Psychology: General* 135 (2006): 501–12.

Lyons, J. 'Circularity, Reliability, and Cognitive Penetrability of Perception'. *Philosophical Issues* 21 (2011): 283–311.

Macpherson, F. 'Cognitive Penetration of Colour Experience: Rethinking the Issue in Light of an Indirect Mechanism'. *Philosophy and Phenomenological Research* 84 (2012): 24–62.

McGrath, M. 'Siegel and the Impact for Epistemological Internalism'. *Philosophical Studies* 162 (2013): 723–32.

McGurk, H. and MacDonald, J. 'Hearing Lips and Seeing Voices'. *Nature* 264 (1976): 746–8.

Mole, C. 'Attention and Cognitive Penetration'. *Cognitive Penetrability*. Ed. A. Raftopoulos and J. Ziembekis. Oxford: Oxford University Press, 2016.

Morrot, G., Brochet, F., and Dubourdieu, D. 'The Color of Odors'. *Brain and Language* 79 (2001): 309–20.

Olkkonen, M., Hansen, T., and Gegenfurtner, K. R. 'Colour Appearance of Familiar Objects: Effects of Object Shape, Texture and Illumination Changes'. *Journal of Vision* 8 (2008): 1–16.

Payne, K. 'Prejudice and Perception: The Role of Automatic and Controlled Processes in Misperceiving a Weapon'. *Journal of Personality and Social Psychology* 81 (2001): 181–92.

Payne, K., Shimizu, Y., and Jacoby, L. 'Mental Control and Visual Illusions: Toward Explaining Race-Biased Weapon Misidentifications'. *Journal of Experimental Social Psychology* 41 (2005): 36–47.

Power, R. 'The Dominance of Touch by Vision: Sometimes Incomplete'. *Perception* 9 (1980): 457–66.

Power, R. and Graham, A. 'Dominance of Touch by Vision: Generalization of the Hypothesis to a Tactually Experienced Population'. *Perception* 5 (1976): 161–6.

Price, H. H. *Perception*. London: Methuen, 1932.

Pylyshyn, Z. 'Computation and Cognition: Issues in the Foundations of Cognitive Science'. *Behavioral and Brain Sciences* 3 (1980): 111–32.

Pylyshyn, Z. *Computation and Cognition*. Cambridge, MA: MIT Press, 1984.

Pylyshyn, Z. 'Is Vision Continuous with Cognition? The Case for Cognitive Impenetrability of Visual Perception'. *Behavioral and Brain Sciences* 22 (1999): 341–65.

Raftopoulos, A. 'Reentrant Pathways and the Theory-Ladenness of Perception'. *Philosophy of Science* (Proceedings) 68 (2001): 187–99.

Rock, I., and Victor, J. 'An Experimentally Created Conflict between the Two Senses'. *Science* 143 (1964): 594–6.

Rosenblum, L., Schmuckler, M., and Johnson, J. 'The McGurk Effect in Infants'. *Perception and Psychophysics* 59 (1997): 347–57.

Royet, J.-P., Koenig, O., Gregoire, M.-C., Vigouroux, M., and Mauguière, F. 'Functional Anatomy of Perceptual and Semantic Processing for Odors'. *Journal of Cognitive Neuroscience* 11 (1999): 94–109.

Russell, B. 'Knowledge by Acquaintance and Knowledge by Description'. *Proceedings of the Aristotelian Society* 11 (1910): 108–28.

Sakai, N., Imada, S., Saito, S., Kobayakawa, T., and Deguchi, Y. 'The Effect of Visual Images on Perception of Odors'. *Chemical Senses* 30 (2005): i244–5.

Sathian, K., Zangaladze, A., Hoffman, J., and Grafton, S. 'Feeling with the Mind's Eye'. *Neuroreport* 8 (1997): 3877–81.

Siegel, S. 'Which Properties Are Represented in Perception?' *Perceptual Experience*. Ed. T. Szabo Gendler and J. Hawthorne. Oxford: Oxford University Press, 2006, 481–503.

Siegel, S. *The Contents of Visual Experience*. Oxford: Oxford University Press, 2010.

Siegel, S. 'Cognitive Penetrability and Perceptual Justification'. *Nous* 46 (2012): 201–22.

Siegel, S. 'The Epistemic Impact of the Etiology of Belief'. *Philosophical Studies* 162 (2013a): 697–722.

Siegel, S. 'Reply to Fumerton, Huemer, and McGrath'. *Philosophical Studies* 162 (2013b): 749–57.

Spence, C. 'Does Food Color Influence Taste and Flavor Perception in Humans?' *Chmosensory Perception* 3 (2010): 68–84.

Stokes, D. 'Perceiving and Desiring: A New Look at the Cognitive Penetrability of Experience'. *Philosophical Studies* 158 (2012): 479–92.

Stokes, D. 'Cognitive Penetrability of Perception'. *Philosophy Compass* 8 (2013): 646–63.

Stokes, D. 'Towards a Consequentialist Understanding of Cognitive Penetration'. *Cognitive Penetrability*. Ed. A. Raftopoulos and J. Ziembekis. Oxford: Oxford University Press, 2016.

Stokes, D. 'Attention and the Cognitive Penetrability of Perception'. *Australasian Journal of Philosophy*, forthcoming.

Stokes, D. and Bergeron, V. 'Modular Architectures and Informational Encapsulation: A Dilemma'. *European Journal for Philosophy of Science* 5 (2015): 315–38.

Stokes, D. and Biggs, S. 'The Dominance of the Visual'. *Perception and its Modalities*. Ed. D. Stokes, M. Matthen, and S. Biggs. New York: Oxford University Press, 2014.

Tucker, C. 'If Dogmatists Have a Problem with Cognitive Penetration, You Do Too'. *Dialectica* 68 (2014): 35–62.

Vance, J. 'Emotion and the New Epistemic Challenge from Cognitive Penetrability'. *Philosophical Studies* 169 (2014): 257–83.

Vance, J. 'Cognitive Penetration and the Tribunal of Experience'. *Review of Philosophy and Psychology* 6 (2015): 641–63.

Witzel, C., Valkova, H., Hansen, T., and Gegenfurtner, K. 'Object Knowledge Modulates Colour Appearance'. *i-Perception* 2 (2011): 13–49.

Wu, W. 'Shaking up the Mind's Ground Floor: The Cognitive Penetration of Visual Attention'. *Journal of Philosophy* 114 (2017): 5–32.

Zangaladze. A., Epstein, C., Grafton, S., and Sathian, K. 'Involvement of Visual Cortex in Tactile Discrimination of Orientation'. *Nature* 401 (1999): 587–90.

Zeimbekis, J. 'Color and Cognitive Penetrability'. *Philosophical Studies* 165 (2013): 167–75.

Zhang, M., Weisser, V. D., Stilla, R., Prather, S. C., and Sathian, K. 'Multisensory Cortical Processing of Object Shape and its Relation to Mental Imagery'. *Cognitive Affective Behavioral Neuroscience* 4 (2004): 251–9.

INDEX